DATE DUE

DEMCO 38-296

The Philosophy of Legal Reasoning

*A Collection of Essays by Philosophers
and Legal Scholars*

Series Editor

Scott Brewer
Harvard Law School

A GARLAND SERIES

READINGS IN PHILOSOPHY
ROBERT NOZICK, *ADVISOR*
HARVARD UNIVERSITY

Contents of the Series

Evolution and Revolution in Theories of Legal Reasoning

Nineteenth Century Through the Present

Edited with an introduction by

Scott Brewer
Harvard University

GARLAND PUBLISHING, INC.
A MEMBER OF THE TAYLOR & FRANCIS GROUP
New York & London
1998

Library of Congress Cataloging-in-Publication Data

Evolution and revolution in theories of legal reasoning : nineteenth
 century through the present / edited with an introduction by Scott
 Brewer.
     p. cm. — (The philosophy of legal reasoning ; 4)
     Includes bibliographical references.
     ISBN 0-8153-2658-0 (v. 4 : alk. paper). — ISBN 0-8153-2654-8
(set : alk. paper)
     1. Law—Methodology. 2. Law—Interpretation and construction.
3. Law—Philosophy. 4. Reasoning. I. Brewer, Scott. II. Series.
K213.P494 1998
340'.1 s—dc21   98-5167
[340'.1]   CIP

Printed on acid-free, 250-year-life paper
Manufactured in the United States of America

Contents

Introduction

This five-volume set contains some of this century's most influential or thought-provoking articles on the subject of legal argument that have appeared in Anglo-American philosophy journals and law reviews. Legal decisions have long been a deeply significant part of the history and life of societies that aspire to satisfy some version of the "rule of law" ideal. These decisions—at least those rendered by a jurisdiction's most prominent courts—are also often accompanied by detailed publicly available statements of the arguments supporting those decisions. For these reasons, among many others, understanding the dynamics of legal argument is of vital interest not only to legal academics, judges, lawyers, and law students, but also to citizens who are subject to law and who vote, directly or indirectly, for the legislators, regulators, and judges who write and interpret laws.

Because of the importance to civil societies of legal decisons and the legal arguments offered to justify them, the subject of legal argument has long been closely studied by scholars and other analysts. These theorists have explicated and criticized the dynamics of legal argument from vastly different perspectives. It is thus not surprising that these theorists have reached strikingly different conclusions, with equally distinct concerns and emphases. Theorists of legal argument have, for example, maintained that legal argument is principally driven by *a priori* legal-cum-moral truths applied to individual cases by formal logical inferences, or that the driving force of legal argument is a more or less thinly veiled imposition of a judge's preferred social or economic policy, or that legal argument is or should be (theorists sometimes blur the line between the descriptive and the prescriptive in their analyses) the incessantly self-critical and self-correcting reasoned elaboration of legal rules and standards that transcend immediate partisan results, or that legal arguments offered by judges are little more than a mystificatory and would-be legitimating veneer covering such darker motives as race, class, or gender bias, or that legal argument is the interpretive effort by judges in the forum of principle to make the law the best it can be from a moral point of view, or is the decision of those legal officials who hold authoritative power by virtue of socially adopted rules.

This set of volumes represents all of the theories just encapsulated, and others as well. As the brief, and certainly incomplete, list in the foregoing paragraph suggests, theorists of legal argument produce what can seem a whelming welter of diverse explanations. Even so, the vast majority of theories of legal argument revolve around two central focal points—rather, perhaps, like the oval-shaped ellipse, which orbits around two fixed foci.

One focus is the role of different *modes of logical inference* in legal argument. There are four basic logical structures that operate in legal argument (indeed, it can be argued plausibly that these are the four that organize all arguments, in all intellectual domains): *deduction, induction, abduction,* and *analogy.* It may help the reader to have a few basic definitions of these terms at the outset—even though by no means all the theorists whose articles are included will use these terms in their analyses. First, the basic term 'argument.' The defining characteristic of *argument*, including legal argument, is the inference of a conclusion from one or more premises. As just noted, all arguments, including legal argument, deploy one or more of four principal and irreducible (though analogical inference is tricky in this regard) modes of logical inference: (i) *deductive inference*, in which the truth of the premises guarantees the truth of the conclusion as long as the conclusion is arrived at by an acceptable deductive inference rule; (ii) *inductive inference*, in which the truth of the premises cannot guarantee the truth of the conclusion, but when the premises are carefully chosen, their truth can warrant belief in the truth of the conclusion to greater or lesser degrees of probability; (iii) *abductive inference*, in which an explanatory hypothesis is inferred as the conclusion of an argument with two distinct types of premise: first, a proposition that describes some event or phenomenon that the abductive reasoner believes stands in need of *explanation*, and second, a proposition to the effect that, *if* the explanatory hypothesis that is inferred ("abducted") were in fact *true* or otherwise warranted, then the explanandum would be sufficiently explained for the reasoner's purposes; and (iv) *analogical inference*, in which a reasoner relies on particular examples to discover (indeed, to "abduce") a rule that states what are the relevant similarities or differences between a less well-known item (the "target" of the analogical inference) and a better known item (the "source" of the analogical inference). The other focal point of theories of legal argument is the role of various types of *norms* in legal argument, including *legal norms* (norms issued by proper legal authorities or endorsed by other social norms—the proper account of legal norms divides "legal positivists" and "natural law" theorists), *moral norms* (norms concerned with right and wrong), *epistemic norms* (norms concerned with true or otherwise warranted beliefs), *linguistic norms* (norms concerned with understanding the meaning of texts), and "instrumental" or "prudential" norms (those nonmoral norms that are "instrumental" to helping a reasoner achieve a goal he or she has chosen to pursue).

Even when they do not explicitly use this exact terminology of "logical inference," "deduction," "induction," "norm," and the like, in one way or another all of the articles in these volumes are within the intellectual gravitational orbit of these two focal points. One hastens to add that, far from being dry and remote "academic" exercises, the inquiries pursued by these articles touch on many of the most pressing and contentious issues in contemporary legal, moral, and political debate—as the list of conclusions of various theories of legal argument in the second paragraph of this introduction clearly indicates.

Several criteria have guided the selection of articles in this set. The broad impact of an article among scholars, judges, and lawyers was certainly a leading criterion, and a great many of the articles satisfy it. But that criterion was by no means the only one. Some of the articles in these volumes are fairly recent, and more time will be needed to assess their enduring impact on the worlds of legal thought and practice. It can be said fairly that even these more recent articles present fresh and thought-provoking claims and insights, worthy of being considered even if only to be ultimately rejected. The criterion of intellectually fertile provocation guided the selection of some of the older articles in the volumes (for example, some of those in volume one), which were chosen neither for fame nor influence but rather because they present an important perspective on an issue that—in this editor's opinion—has received far too little attention in twentieth-century American jurisprudence and legal education: the role of *deductive* inference in legal argument. Even though the role of one or more of the four basic logical inferences is a focus of theories of legal argument, generations of legal academics, judges, and lawyers have tended to ignore or understate the role of deductive inference, largely without understanding enough about what deductive inference is or the many very important ways in which it does guide legal argument. They have been led to this point largely because of the influentially expressed and often parroted sentiment of Justice Oliver Wendell Holmes Jr. and several of his followers, that "[t]he life of the law has not been logic: it has been experience."[1] By 'logic' Holmes meant deductive logic, and his maxim-al hyperbole has done much to encumber the proper understanding of the rational dynamics of legal argument. Several of the articles in these volumes were chosen to help readers rediscover and revivify this important issue and to see its importance for broader political and moral questions.

All in all, I am confident that the articles in these volumes will well repay the attentiveness of readers who wish to think seriously about the nature of significance of legal argument as a vital part of broader legal and political processes, as long as they bring reading minds that are fairly "braced with labor and invention."

Notes

[1] Oliver W. Holmes, *The Common Law*, ed. Mark DeWolfe Howe (Boston: Little, Brown, 1963) p.5.

[1] Oliver W. Holmes, *The Common Law* 1 ed. Mark DeWolfe Howe (?: ?, 1963).

Deconstructive Practice and Legal Theory

J. M. Balkin†

*The stone that the builders rejected has become
the chief cornerstone.*

—*Psalms* 118:22

The purpose of this Article is to introduce legal readers to the ideas of
the French philosopher Jacques Derrida, and to his philosophical practices regarding the interpretation of texts, sometimes known as deconstruction.[1] The term "deconstruction" is much used in legal writings these
days,[2] and in this Article I propose to explain its philosophical underpinnings. Many persons who use the word "deconstruction" regard it as no
more than another expression for "trashing," that is, showing why legal

---

† Assistant Professor of Law, University of Missouri-Kansas City. Harvard University A.B.,
1978, J.D. 1981. I would like to thank my research assistants, Linda Talley, Suzanne Bardgett, and
Jan Dodd, for their help in the preparation of this Article, and my colleagues, Joan Mahoney and
James Kushner, for their comments on a previous draft.

1. Derrida has developed his ideas in several books and essays dating from 1967, some of which
have only recently been translated into English. J. DERRIDA, DISSEMINATION (B. Johnson trans.
1981) [hereinafter DISSEMINATION]; J. DERRIDA, MARGINS OF PHILOSOPHY (1982) [hereinafter
MARGINS OF PHILOSOPHY]; J. DERRIDA, OF GRAMMATOLOGY (1976) [hereinafter OF GRAM-
MATOLOGY]; J. DERRIDA, POSITIONS (1981) [hereinafter POSITIONS]; J. DERRIDA, SPURS (1979)
[hereinafter SPURS]; J. DERRIDA, SPEECH AND PHENOMENA (1973) [hereinafter SPEECH AND PHE-
NOMENA]; J. DERRIDA, WRITING AND DIFFERENCE (1978) [hereinafter WRITING AND DIFFER-
ENCE]; Derrida, *The Law of Genre*, 7 GLYPH 202 (1980); Derrida, *Limited Inc abc* . . ., 2 GLYPH
162 (1977) [hereinafter *Limited Inc abc*].
   The best general introduction to Derrida's thought is J. CULLER, ON DECONSTRUCTION (1982).
Other good sources are H. STATEN, WITTGENSTEIN AND DERRIDA (1984) (suggesting Anglo-
American philosophical approach to deconstruction); Johnson, *Translator's Introduction* to DISSEMI-
NATION, supra, at vii; Rorty, *Philosophy as a Kind of Writing: An Essay on Derrida*, 10 NEW
LITERARY HIST. 141 (1978); Spivak, *Translator's Preface* to OF GRAMMATOLOGY, supra, at ix
(essay requires familiarity with continental philosophers and Freud). None of these has considered the
relevance of Derrida's thought to legal theory.
2. *See, e.g.*, Dalton, *An Essay in the Deconstruction of Contract Doctrine*, 94 YALE L.J. 997
(1985); Frug, *The Ideology of Bureaucracy in American Law*, 97 HARV. L. REV. 1276, 1288-99
(1984) (citing Derrida's notions of "dangerous supplement"); Hegland, *Goodbye to Deconstruction*,
58 S. CAL. L. REV. 1203 (1985); Spann, *Deconstructing the Legislative Veto*, 68 MINN. L. REV. 473
(1984); Tushnet, *Critical Legal Studies and Constitutional Law: An Essay in Deconstruction*, 36
STAN. L. REV. 623 (1984); Note, *Overshooting the Target: A Feminist Deconstruction of Legal Education*, 34 AM. U.L. REV. 1141 (1985); Hutchinson, *From Cultural Construction to Historical
Deconstruction* (Book Review), 94 YALE L.J. 209, 229-35 (1984).

743

doctrines are self-contradictory, ideologically biased, or indeterminate.[3] By the term "deconstruction," however, I do not have in mind merely stinging criticism, but specific techniques and philosophical ideas that Derrida and his followers have applied to various texts. These techniques often do involve teasing out the hidden antinomies in our language and thought, and that is primarily how I came to be interested in them.[4] However, I hope to demonstrate that "deconstruction," as I use the term, is not simply a fancy way of sticking out your tongue, but a practice that raises important philosophical issues for legal thinkers.

Lawyers should be interested in deconstructive techniques for at least three reasons. First, deconstruction provides a method for critiquing existing legal doctrines; in particular, a deconstructive reading can show how arguments offered to support a particular rule undermine themselves, and instead, support an opposite rule. Second, deconstructive techniques can show how doctrinal arguments are informed by and disguise ideological thinking. This can be of value not only to the lawyer who seeks to reform existing institutions, but also to the legal philosopher and the legal historian. Third, deconstructive techniques offer both a new kind of interpretive strategy and a critique of conventional interpretations of legal texts.

Although Derrida is a philosopher, his work has been applied mainly to problems of literary criticism; as a result much of the literature on deconstruction is written by literary critics and scholars.[5] Adapting the work of Derrida and other literary critics to the problems of legal and political thought is not, however, as difficult as might first appear. Derrida is above all interested in the connection (and misconnection) between what we want to say and the signs we use to express our meaning. In short, he is interested in the interpretation of texts, and that is hardly strange territory for lawyers, who spend most of their time trying to understand what other lawyers have said in legal texts. On the other hand, explaining deconstructive practice is no small undertaking. Like many French intellectuals of his day, Derrida was schooled in the continental

---

3. For example, Spann associates deconstruction with a critique of formalism in legal reasoning, or with the more general project of demonstrating that legal reasoning is indeterminate. Spann, *supra* note 2, at 536–43. *But see* Hegland, *supra* note 2, at 1203–05 (uses term "deconstruction" in same way, but argues that premise of deconstruction is wrong; principles can be determined).

4. I have argued that legal and moral thought in general is antinomal though not irrational. Balkin, *The Crystalline Structure of Legal Thought*, 39 RUTGERS L. REV. 1 (1987); Balkin, *Taking Ideology Seriously: Ronald Dworkin and the CLS Critique*, 55 U.M.K.C. L. REV. (forthcoming).

5. *E.g.*, H. BLOOM, P. DE MAN, J. DERRIDA, G. HARTMAN & J. MILLER, DECONSTRUCTION AND CRITICISM (1979); J. CULLER, *supra* note 1; B. JOHNSON, THE CRITICAL DIFFERENCE (1980); V. LEITCH, DECONSTRUCTIVE CRITICISM (1983); P. DE MAN, ALLEGORIES OF READING: FIGURAL LANGUAGE IN ROUSSEAU, NIETZSCHE, RILKE, AND PROUST (1979); P. DE MAN, BLINDNESS AND INSIGHT (1983).

tradition of philosophy, whose major influences are Hegel, Husserl, and Heidegger. None of these philosophers is known for clarity of exposition, and Derrida often does little better than his intellectual predecessors.[6] For this reason, I will attempt to translate his ideas into a form that can be more easily understood by those familiar with the Anglo-American schools of philosophy.

The use of the term "translation" is quite deliberate. It is now commonplace to suggest that a translation can never fully capture the sense of the original. However, this point is especially significant in discussing Derrida's work. Derrida has chosen a self-consciously obscure and self-referential style, overflowing with concealed allusions and counterallusions. As I will discuss more fully later, his style may reflect his critique of Western thought's emphasis on unambiguous and foundational concepts.[7] I am thus put in an especially precarious position because my goal is to represent clearly and simply the ideas of a philosopher who eschews clarity and simplicity in his own work. My explanation must involve a kind of alteration—I must simplify, interpret, and reinterpret Derrida as much as I explain him.[8]

I also engage in translation in the sense that Derrida does not write about legal, but rather about philosophical and literary, texts. In explaining Derrida's practices to a legal audience, I will focus on those areas of his work that have the most relevance to legal writing and thought. This too, requires selection, editorial judgment, and reinterpretation. What interests me most about Derrida's work is the possibility that deconstruction can shed light on theories of ideological thinking: how people form and use ideologies, consciously or unconsciously, in legal discourse. Derrida's work is not primarily about epistemology or the sociology of knowledge, but his work has relevance to these disciplines. For that reason, I emphasize some points in Derrida's writings that others (including Derrida) might not choose to emphasize.

A final obstacle to explaining deconstruction comes from the nature of Derrida's project. Because Derrida and his followers insist that decon-

---

6. At least one writer believes that structuralist and post-structuralist thinkers, most of whom were French, deliberately adopted an obfuscatory style in reaction to the bourgeois French preference for *la clarité*: a simple, clear, and elegant style in accordance with the "narrower stylistic bounds of orthodox academic discourse" expected of French intellectuals. Sturrock, *Introduction* to STRUCTURALISM AND SINCE 16–17 (J. Sturrock ed. 1979). The style of modern French philosophical writers, such as Jacques Lacan, Roland Barthes, Michel Foucault, and Derrida, was designed to challenge that paradigm of "proper" philosophical expression. *Id.* If this were in fact the goal of these writers, it bears noting that one can always have too much of a good thing.

7. *See infra* text accompanying notes 12–16.

8. Indeed, a deconstructionist might argue that the process of repetition alters as it repeats, so that any explanation involves alteration of some sort. *See infra* note 53. This point takes on a special urgency with a writer as elusive as Derrida, whose very work celebrates the gap between that which represents and that which is represented.

struction is not a philosophical position but rather a practice,[9] it is neither possible nor desirable to state a deconstructionist creed. Thus, my goal in this Article is to offer ways of bringing the concerns and methods of deconstructionists to the study of legal issues. Instead of describing what a deconstructionist believes, I will explain what a deconstructionist does and will attempt to show how one does "it" to legal texts. Not surprisingly, underlying deconstructive activities are philosophical presuppositions about language, thought, and the world. Such presuppositions are implicated in Derrida's work, even if he himself would not admit to them as a statement of a "position." I will try to make clear these hidden assumptions as the need arises.[10]

The two deconstructive practices that this Article will address are the inversion of hierarchies and the liberation of the text from the author. I believe these issues have the most relevance to what legal thinkers do when they analyze legal texts. They also have the most relevance to the study of ideology and the social and political theories underlying our legal system.

I. THE INVERSION OF HIERARCHIES

A. *The Metaphysics of Presence*

Described in its simplest form, the deconstructionist project involves the identification of hierarchical oppositions, followed by a temporary reversal of the hierarchy. Thus, to use Derrida's favorite example, if the history of Western civilization has been marked by a bias in favor of speech over writing we should investigate what it would be like if writing were more important than speech. We should attempt to see speech as a kind of writing, as ultimately parasitic upon writing, as a special case of writing, rather than the other way around. In so doing, we reverse the privileged position of speech over writing, and temporarily substitute a new priority. This new priority is not meant to be permanent, for it may in turn be reversed using identical techniques. The point is not to establish a new conceptual bedrock, but rather to investigate what happens when the

---

9. *E.g.*, J. CULLER, *supra* note 1, at 95 (deconstruction as philosophical strategy); C. NORRIS, DECONSTRUCTION: THEORY AND PRACTICE 31 (1982) ("Deconstruction is . . . an activity of reading which remains closely tied to the texts it interrogates, and which can never set up independently as a self-enclosed system of operative concepts."); C. NORRIS, THE DECONSTRUCTIVE TURN: ESSAYS IN THE RHETORIC OF PHILOSOPHY 6 (1983) ("It has become almost a ritual gesture among writers on deconstruction to insist that what they are doing is in no sense a species of conceptual exegesis or analysis. Deconstruction is first and last a textual *activity*.").

10. In doing so, my descriptions may well be seen by literary theorists, for example, as untrue to their understanding of deconstruction. However, just as deconstructive theorists take pride in the inability of others to systematize their work, I take comfort in the fact that an "orthodox deconstruction" is a contradiction in terms.

given, "common sense" arrangement is reversed. Derrida believes that we derive new insights when the privileging in a text is turned on its head.

For Derrida, hierarchies of thought are everywhere. They can be found in the following assertions: A is the rule and B is the exception; A is the general case and B is the special case; A is simple and B is complex; A is normal and B is abnormal; A is self-supporting and B is parasitic upon it; A is present and B is absent; A is immediately perceived and B is inferred; A is central and B is peripheral; A is true and B is false; A is natural and B is artificial. Indeed, my labelling of these ideas as A and B involves a hierarchical move because the letter A *precedes* B in the alphabet.

For Derrida, any hierarchical statements about a set of ideas A and B is an invitation for a deconstructive reversal—to show that the property we ascribe to A is true of B and the property we ascribe to B is true of A. Our deconstruction will show that A's privileged status is an illusion, for A depends upon B as much as B depends upon A. We will discover, then, that B stands in relation to A much like we thought A stood in relation to B. Indeed, it is possible to find in the very reasons that A is privileged over B the reasons that B is privileged over A. Having reversed the hierarchy, we are able to see things about both A and B that we had never noticed before.[11]

Any hierarchical opposition of ideas, no matter how trivial, can be deconstructed in this way. For Derrida, however, deconstruction is more than a clever intellectual parlor game. It is a means of intellectual discovery, which operates by wrenching us from our accustomed modes of thought. In fact, Derrida was led to this practice of deconstruction by his dissatisfaction with Western philosophical practice from Plato's time to our own.[12]

Derrida sees his major project as exposing the bias in Western philosophy he calls the "metaphysics of presence."[13] Each of the above oppositions privileges a kind of "presence" over a corresponding kind of "absence." To Derrida, Western conceptions of philosophy proceed from the hidden premise that what is most apparent to our consciousness—what is

---

11. The word "hierarchy" probably has political connotations to many legal readers. These connotations are unfortunate, for they may lead to a misunderstanding and oversimplification of Derrida's critique. Derrida's work is not concerned with the privileging of certain social groups over others (although it can be so applied), but with the privileging of certain *ideas* over others. We may, in fact, discover as we deconstruct legal texts that the privileging of ideas (as occurs in an ideology) has a connection to the privileged place that certain social groups enjoy. However, this connection is not a direct one. Our first task is to investigate the connections among ideas.

12. *See* J. CULLER, *supra* note 1, at 92-94, 100; OF GRAMMATOLOGY, *supra* note 1, at 3, 10-18, 46; *see also* Rorty, *supra* note 1, at 145.

13. *See* OF GRAMMATOLOGY, *supra* note 1, at 49 (metaphysics of presence is irrepressible desire for transcendental signified presence, the thing itself, or truth); *see also* J. CULLER, *supra* note 1, at 92 ("Philosophy has been a 'metaphysics of presence,' the only metaphysics we know.").

747

5

most simple, basic, or immediate—is most real, true, foundational, or important.

For example, the philosophical positions of an empiricist like Hume indicate a bias in favor of immediately perceived sense data.[14] This is a privileging of "presence" in Derrida's sense of the word. However, what Derrida means by "presence" need not be the presence of sense data to the mind, for a philosopher like Plato would argue that it is a Form or Essence which the mind grasps most immediately[15] and which is therefore most "present." Rather, Derrida sees the theories of Western philosophers as expressing, at various times, a series of different metaphysical valuations: subject over object, normal over abnormal, good over evil, positive over negative, identity over difference, being over non-being, ideal over non-ideal. Western philosophy has used the preferred concept as a ground for theorizing and has explained the other concept in terms of it. In each case, the preferred concept constitutes a belief in "presence," a self-sufficient, immediately cognizable existence.[16]

Three examples may help to demonstrate how Derrida hopes to reverse these oppositional hierarchies. I will begin with perhaps the most fundamental concept in Western thought—the notion of identity. Philosophers have regarded identity as a basic ground for metaphysical thought: Anything that exists is identical to itself. Difference is a derivative concept based upon identity: Two things are different if they are not identical. The deconstructionist wants to show that the notion of identity, which seems so basic, so "present," actually depends upon the notion of difference. Self-identity depends upon difference because a thing cannot be identical to something unless it can be different from something else. Identity is only comprehensible in terms of difference, just as difference can only be understood in terms of identity. We have just deconstructed the opposition identity/difference by showing the mutual dependence these ideas have upon each other. In doing so, we show that what was thought to be foundational (identity) is itself dependent upon the concept it was privileged over (difference).

It is true that having reversed this hierarchy, we could then show that difference cannot be a foundational term for metaphysics; difference depends upon identity as much as identity depends upon difference. This outcome is not a refutation of our previous deconstructive reading. The conclusion that neither term is foundational, but that both are mutually

---

14. See generally D. HUME, A TREATISE OF HUMAN NATURE (L. Selby-Bigge 2d ed. 1888) (all knowledge derived from sense data).

15. See PLATO, THE COLLECTED DIALOGUES OF PLATO 40, 575 (E. Hamilton & H. Cairns eds. 1961) (theory of Forms in *Phaedo* and *Republic*).

16. See WRITING AND DIFFERENCE, supra note 1, at 278-79; *Limited Inc abc, supra* note 1, at 236.

dependent upon each other, is precisely the conclusion that Derrida wants us to reach.

Next consider the opposition between serious discourse and non-serious discourse.[17] This opposition also involves the metaphysics of presence, although at first glance the connection is not quite as obvious. When I am speaking seriously, I mean what I say to you, so that my true intentions are immediately present in the meaning of what I say. On the other hand, when I am not being serious, for example, when I am joking, lying, or reciting lines in a play, I do not really intend what I say. There is a divergence between my true thoughts and intentions and what you hear me saying. Now philosophers naturally are more concerned with serious discourse than non-serious, for serious discourse is, obviously, to be taken seriously. A philosopher would use the paradigm of serious communication as the foundation either for a theory of meaning or for a theory of performative speech acts like promising, warning, or marrying. Non-serious discourse, such as jokes, lies, or dramatic readings, is an aberration, an additional feature of discourse that one would explain in terms of serious discourse after one has worked out the basic theory of serious communication.

The opposition between the serious and the non-serious can be deconstructed in the same manner as the opposition between identity and difference. Once again, the goal is to subvert the notion that serious discourse is a self-contained, self-supporting ground upon which we can base a philosophical theory of meaning or promising.

To deconstruct this opposition, we must introduce the notion of iterability. Iterability is a property of signs. If one makes a sign, one can make the sign again at another time, in another place, in another context. In a simple sense, words are like signs. We are able to communicate because we can use words and combinations of words over and over again. If we had to create new signs to express our thoughts every time we attempted to communicate, we would never be able to communicate with anyone. Thus, iterability, or the property of being able to be repeated in many different contexts, is essential to any form of communication.

When I say "It is raining outside" or "I promise to pay you thirty dollars for that coat," the statements I make are iterable. They can be repeated many different times, in many different places, and in many different contexts. I can say them when in fact I believe it is raining, or when I do intend to make a promise. But the feature of iterability means that I can also say them when I am merely joking or reciting lines in a

---

17. The discussion that follows is loosely based on Derrida's deconstruction of J.L. Austin's work in MARGINS OF PHILOSOPHY, *supra* note 1, at 307, 321–29, and in *Limited Inc abc*, *supra* note 1, at 162.

play. Indeed, we are brought to the surprising conclusion that we could not use words to express ourselves seriously unless we could use the same words non-seriously. The same property of words that allows us to express what we mean requires that we also be able to express what we do not mean.

Serious discourse thus depends on the ability to make statements whether or not they conform with our true intentions. That is to say, the serious ultimately depends upon the prior existence of the non-serious. Indeed, we can go further. If we now reconceptualize "non-serious" statements as those statements in which there is no necessary connection between the statement and real intention, we may describe serious statements as merely a special case of iterable non-serious statements in which what we say happens to coincide with what we really intend.[18]

The work of the Swiss linguist Ferdinand de Saussure presents a third example of deconstruction. Saussure distinguished between *langue*, the background system of linguistic rules, and *parole*, the set of speech acts made by members of a linguistic community.[19] Saussure argued that *langue* was the more important element in the understanding of language because the system of relations among various signs is what constitutes a language. Specific examples of *parole*, that is specific speech acts by speakers in a linguistic community, are only possible because of the preexisting *langue* that speakers unconsciously rely upon to understand each other. Thus, the word "cat" is possible in English because English speakers can distinguish it from "mat," "cot," and "cad." In this sense, languages are systems of differences; when an English speaker uses English words, those words carry with them the system of differences that makes them intelligible to other English speakers. In Derrida's terminology, English words carry the "traces" of other words from which they are distinguished and in opposition to which they possess intelligibility.[20]

However, Saussure's privileging of *langue* over *parole* as the basis of language leads to an historical paradox: How did language begin at a time in which there was no established system of differences that constituted a language? As Jonathan Culler explains, "If a cave man is successfully to inaugurate language by making a special grunt signifying 'food,'

---

18. In this last statement, I have used the word "non-serious" in a new sense. Originally, I used it to mean "not serious." By the end of the deconstruction, however, it has taken on a new meaning, namely, "stated without regard to whether the statement conforms to real intention." In reversing the serious/non-serious opposition, I have created a broader notion of non-serious speech upon which both the serious and the non-serious (in the former sense of the word) depend. This is a common practice in a deconstructive reversal and involves the creation of a paleonym, a new concept with an old name that recalls the previously subordinated concept. *See infra* text accompanying notes 42-44.

19. F. DE SAUSSURE, COURSE IN GENERAL LINGUISTICS 9, 13-15, 17-20, 77 (3d ed. 1959).

20. *See infra* note 25 and accompanying text.

we must suppose that the grunt is already distinguished from other grunts and that the world has already been divided into the categories 'food' and 'non-food.' "[21]

Language must have begun with speech acts, and through history the collection of past speech acts (*parole*) was consolidated to create a linguistic system (*langue*). On the other hand, speech acts could not have been understood without some pre-existing structure that made others understand that certain primordial grunts signified "This is a rock," rather than "I am in pain." No matter how far back we go in history, each speech act seems to require a pre-existing linguistic and semantic structure in order to be intelligible, but any such structure could not come into being without a history of pre-existing speech acts by past speakers. Neither *langue* nor *parole* could be a foundational concept in a theory of language because each is mutually dependent upon the existence of the other.[22]

B. Différance *and Trace*

The three examples of privileging that I have given all have a single feature in common. Once the hierarchy of the more basic term over the less basic term is deconstructed, we see that the more basic term depends upon the less basic. Because we already know that the less basic term depends upon the more basic, we end up asking the proverbial question: "Which came first, the chicken or the egg?" This question neatly summarizes what Derrida is trying to show in deconstructing hierarchical oppositions. He is not attempting to show that we were wrong in thinking that difference is dependent upon identity, that the non-serious is dependent upon the serious, or that *parole* is dependent upon *langue*. Rather, he wants to expose what we have forgotten: that identity is also dependent upon difference, the serious is also dependent upon the non-serious, and *langue* is also dependent upon *parole*. In other words, neither term of the opposition can be originary and fundamental because both are related to each other in a system of mutual dependences and differences. Each is continually calling upon the other for its foundation, even as it is constantly differentiating itself from the other.

---

21. *See* J. CULLER, *supra* note 1, at 96.

22. *See* J. DERRIDA, *Semiology and Grammatology*, in POSITIONS, *supra* note 1, at 15, 17, 28 [hereinafter *Semiology and Grammatology*]. Culler refers to this as the paradox of structure and event. J. CULLER, *supra* note 1, at 94–96. The same problem arises for theorists who explain obligations in terms of the existence of "practices." *See* Rawls, *Two Concepts of Rules*, 64 PHIL. REV. 3 (1955). Promissory obligations, for example, are explained by the practice of promising. *See* H.L.A. HART, THE CONCEPT OF LAW 42–43 (1961). By arguing that acts of promising could not come into being before the creation of a practice of promising, these thinkers face the problem of showing how a practice of promising could have arisen before there were any specific acts of promising.

751

9

Derrida has a special term for the chicken-and-egg quality of mutual dependence and difference that the terms of hierarchical oppositions have for each other: *différance*. *Différance* is a pun based upon the French word *différer*, which means both to differ and to defer. Derrida replaces an "e" with "a" in *différence* to make it *différance*; the two words sound exactly the same in French.[23] *Différance* simultaneously indicates that (1) the terms of an oppositional hierarchy are differentiated from each other (which is what determines them); (2) each term in the hierarchy defers the other (in the sense of making the other term wait for the first term), and (3) each term in the hierarchy defers *to* the other (in the sense of being fundamentally dependent upon the other).

From *différance*, we can understand the idea of "trace." Both of the terms in a hierarchical opposition rely for their coherence on the differentiation between them. The relation between identity and difference, serious and non-serious, *langue* and *parole*, is one of mutual dependence and difference, or *différance*. However, Derrida would also say that in each case the first concept bears the traces of the second concept, just as the second concept bears the traces of the first.

The word "trace" is a metaphor for the effect of the opposite concept, which is no longer present but has left its mark on the concept we are now considering.[24] The trace is what makes deconstruction possible; by identifying the traces of the concepts in each other, we identify their mutual conceptual dependence.[25]

One might ask whether the ideas of *différance* and trace between two opposed concepts could form a new ground for explaining both. However, *différance* and trace are not stable conceptions; they simply represent the play of differences and dependences between two mutually opposed concepts. Neither *différance* nor trace could serve as a foundational concept.[26]

---

23. *See* MARGINS OF PHILOSOPHY, *supra* note 1, at 3; J. DERRIDA, *Positions*, in POSITIONS, *supra* note 1, at 39–40 [hereinafter *Positions*]; *Semiology and Grammatology, supra* note 22, at 26–28.

24. *See* OF GRAMMATOLOGY, *supra* note 1, at 46–47.

25. *See id.* at 62–63. The phoneme /b/ is a sound in English because of its differentiation from the set of other available sounds in that language. The idea of "trace" may be compared to the way in which speakers are able to distinguish /b/ from other phonemes, while simultaneously being able to identify the /b/ spoken by one person with the /b/ spoken by another. In a similar way, the concepts in hierarchical oppositions create the possibility for each other's existence; they form, shape, or identify each other by their absence. This necessary conceptual support is the "trace" of the absent concept.

26. *See Positions, supra* note 23, at 39–40. Note that this statement is itself deconstructible. The concept of *différance* is essential (hence foundational?) to Derrida's own thought, at least as I present it here.

Two points follow from this deconstruction. First, if we attempted to give concepts like "*différance*" and "trace" a special status, whether as foundations for deconstruction or as ineffable concepts that escape analysis, we would fall into the very trap that Derrida seeks to avoid. Rorty, *supra* note 1, at 151–53. Thus, trace cannot be "divinized," as Rorty says, *id.* at 153, and neither can *différance*. These conceptions must simply describe the situation of foundationlessness, provisionality, or revers-

Having seen one originary concept after another fall under the deconstructionist sword, the reader might be tempted to ask whether Derrida means to deny that there is any self-sufficient, originary foundation for a system of thought. This is precisely the point of the deconstructionist critique of Western philosophy. Proposed foundational terms all depend ultimately upon the subordinate concepts we would like to depend upon those foundational terms. Derrida is denying the validity of the Cartesian project of discovering an unquestionable, self-sufficient ground for philosophy.[27]

The notions of *différance* and trace suggest a revolutionary theory of how people grasp abstract ideas. Our commonsense view is that one holds an idea in one's mind, and that idea is immediately present as one conceives it. Thus, when I think about the idea of identity, I am thinking about it, and not about another idea (difference). When I think about speech, I am thinking about speech and not about writing. But we can read Derrida's work as challenging this commonsense conception. When we hold an idea in our minds, we hold both the idea *and its opposite*; we think not of speech but of "speech as opposed to writing," or speech with the traces of the idea of writing, from which speech differs and upon which it depends.[28] The history of ideas, then, is not the history of individual conceptions, but of favored conceptions held in opposition to disfavored conceptions.[29]

---

ibility. The second point is that this lack of foundational concepts puts any expositor of Derrida's thought in an unfortunate situation. These concepts are important to understanding Derrida, and one cannot do justice to his work without discussing them. I therefore present them as essential, although Derrida would not approve. This dilemma merely demonstrates the impossibility of giving a fully deconstructionist account of deconstruction. *See infra* note 54.

27. *See* Rorty, *supra* note 1, at 159. I use the term "Cartesian" because in many ways Descartes is the high priest of the metaphysics of presence: Descartes believed that one could ultimately base a philosophical system upon the indubitable truth that one's existence is *immediately present* to one's own consciousness. R. DESCARTES, *Meditations on First Philosophy*, in THE PHILOSOPHICAL WORKS OF DESCARTES 131 (E. Haldane & G. Ross trans. 1911).

The *cogito* of Descartes attempted to ground philosophy on a metaphysics of presence. Derrida did not need to deconstruct the assertion because David Hume had already performed the task. Hume argued that one's sense of identity is dependent upon the continuous flow of thoughts that one experiences. Thus, instead of thought being dependent upon the self's identity, identity is dependent upon the experience of thought. When Descartes said, "I think, therefore I am," he believed that he had demonstrated the privileged nature of existence over thought (I must be, in order to be thinking at all). Instead, Hume showed that Descartes' conclusion made knowledge of identity only an inference from the continuous experience of thought (I know that I exist because there is a continuous stream of thoughts). D. HUME, *supra* note 14, at 6. A deconstructive reading of Descartes' *cogito*, then, demonstrates that identity and thought are mutually dependent upon each other in a relation of *différance*.

28. *See Semiology and Grammatology, supra* note 22, at 26. What speech is opposed to, of course, depends upon the context.

29. This is an epistemological interpretation of Derrida. Derrida does not purport to offer a theory specifically about epistemology, metaphysics, or any traditional field of philosophy. Indeed, Derrida would probably resist the idea that his theories were "about" anything in particular, although it is my belief that they have many applications in such fields as literary criticism, philosophy, psychology, and law. I offer my interpretation because of the connection I am about to make between

753

It might seem at first that deconstructive practice is less important to lawyers than to philosophers. Derrida's critique of foundational thinking might be of great concern to philosophers searching for ultimate truth. Philosophy usually involves a search for ultimate groundings, and so the power of Derrida's critique is troubling. On the other hand, we do not expect that all or even most legal doctrines can be proven to have a basis in objective moral truth. Law is a much more pragmatic enterprise than philosophy. However, Derrida's critique is not simply directed at metaphysics. Derrida's point is that the privileging of presence may be found in everyday thought as much as in abstract philosophy. *Any* system of thought that proceeds by marking out the fundamental, the essential, the normal, or the most important—in short, virtually any rational system—can be analyzed from the standpoint of deconstructive practice.

Our understanding of legal ideas may indeed involve, as Derrida says of speech and writing, the simultaneous privileging of ideas over their opposites. Legal doctrines are based upon a group of foundational concepts and principles. Thus, in tort law, one learns the basic concepts of fault, intent, or causation, and more recently, the notions of cost-benefit analysis and economic efficiency. Such concepts are building blocks for further development. Using Derrida's methods, we discover that each legal concept is actually a privileging, in disguise, of one concept over another. By revealing the opposition, and deconstructing it, we are brought to an entirely different vision of moral and legal obligation.

One example of legal doctrines' reliance on privileging is the Supreme Court's doctrine of standing. By holding that the Constitution requires a plaintiff to show "actual" injury in order to sue,[30] the Court has created a privileging of plaintiffs who have actual injury over plaintiffs whom the Court classifies as purely "ideological."[31] One way to deconstruct this opposition would be to show how arguments in favor of the actual injury requirement "undo" themselves. The goal would be to examine the standard arguments for the actual injury requirement: Plaintiffs with actual injury are more reliable, more adversarial, and more likely to present a concrete record for decision. We could then use these arguments against themselves to demonstrate that ideological plaintiffs also possess these de-

---

privileging and ideological thinking. If we apply Derrida's work to the way people formulate and use legal concepts, we are making a point about human psychology and the sociology of knowledge. An epistemological interpretation is consistent with the work of Derrida's structuralist predecessors, such as Saussure and Levi-Strauss. These thinkers argue that human consciousness is structured in terms of mutually defined oppositions. *See generally* T. HAWKES, STRUCTURALISM AND SEMIOTICS 19-58 (1977).

30. *See, e.g.*, Warth v. Seldin, 422 U.S. 490 (1975).

31. *See, e.g.*, Schlesinger v. Reservists Comm. to Stop the War, 418 U.S. 208 (1974); Sierra Club v. Morton, 405 U.S. 727 (1972).

sired traits. Conversely, we could show how plaintiffs who possess actual injury, but who lack ideological zeal, are less dependable, less adversarial, and less likely to produce a concrete record for decisionmaking than their ideological counterparts.[32]

This example suggests that law provides a fertile field of discourse for deconstructive readings. Lawyers are continually involved in establishing principles of regulatory behavior, whether in contract law, constitutional law, or other areas, and this project necessitates the privileging of concepts. Deconstruction can serve another purpose. The law reflects social visions that involve privilegings of particular conceptions of human nature. As we deconstruct legal principles, we deconstruct the ideology or world view that informs them. Although we can use deconstruction to show that doctrines are incomplete, or that the arguments for a given doctrine "undo" themselves, we can also use deconstruction as a tool for ideological and historical analysis.

C. *Arguments that Undo Themselves*

Deconstructive reversals show that the reasons given for privileging one side of an opposition over the other often turn out to be reasons for privileging the other side. The virtues of the first term are seen to be the virtues of the second; the vices of the second are revealed to be true of the first as well. This undoing of justifications for privileging is part of the deconstructionist aim of "ungrounding" preferred conceptions by showing that they cannot act as self-sufficient or self-explanatory grounds or foundations.

The most famous example of this "ungrounding" is Derrida's treatment of speech and writing in *Of Grammatology*.[33] Derrida finds in the texts of several writers, including Rousseau, Saussure, and Levi-Strauss, a consistent valuing of speech over writing as a form of communication.[34] Derrida argues that this preference is not accidental; it relates to the general "logocentric" bias of Western thought.[35] By "logocentric," Derrida means centered on the concept of *logos*, which he often equates with the idea of presence. Derrida believes that a privileging of speech over writing is a symptom of a more general bias in favor of presence as a foundational term in Western philosophical thought.[36]

---

32. For examples of deconstruction of this doctrine, see Tushnet, *The Sociology of Article III: A Response to Professor Brilmayer*, 93 HARV. L. REV. 1698 (1980); J. Balkin, Deconstructing Article III (Sept. 27, 1986) (unpublished manuscript on file at Yale Law School Library).

33. OF GRAMMATOLOGY, *supra* note 1, at 34-43, 166-67.

34. *Id.* at 29-44 (discussing Saussure); *id.* at 101-268 (discussing Levi-Strauss and Rousseau).

35. *Id.* at 3; *see infra* text accompanying notes 53-55.

36. Derrida also speaks of "phonocentrism," or the privileging of voice. *See, e.g.,* OF GRAMMATOLOGY, *supra* note 1, at 11-12. Phonocentrism normally appears in discussions of the privileging

One might ask why speech is more "present" than writing, and why it is more highly valued. Derrida considers several plausible arguments to explain the privileging. First, writing is only a method of representing speech. It was invented as a means of recording what people said.[37] Writing consists of a series of signs that stand for spoken words. Thus, writing is only a substitute for speech, and an imperfect substitute at that. For example, written language often uses non-phonetic spellings. People who have encountered certain words in writing but not in speech often mispronounce them, and written language occasionally leads to corruptions and alterations in natural forms of speech.

Second, speech is connected more closely to the immediate thoughts of the communicator than is writing. When one hears a person talk, that person's intention is immediately communicated by her speech.[38] Our understanding is derived not only from words, but also from inflections and tone of voice. Sarcasm, enthusiasm, and a hundred other nuances are immediately apparent when we listen to a person; they are less discernible when the text of a speech has been transcribed.[39] Thus, the preference for speech over writing is a privileging of presence: The immediacy of meaning in speech is privileged over the mediation of thought that occurs in writing.[40] Speech is immediate, unambiguous, and sincere; writing is distant, ambiguous, and potentially misleading.[41]

---

of speech over writing.

37. Speech is prior to writing both culturally and historically. J. GREENBERG, ANTHROPOLOGICAL LINGUISTICS 22-23 (1968). Spoken language arrives in a culture before written language, and to this day there are primitive cultures that have no written language. *Id.* at 22; *see also* S. MULLER, THE WORLD'S LIVING LANGUAGES 107, 119 (1964) (most languages in Africa, Indonesia, and New Guinea still unwritten). Thus, speech is a prior, and therefore more fundamental, development in the creation of cultures and civilizations than writing.

38. Derrida argues that the direct temporal connection between speech and thought leads us to this conclusion. He points out that in French, the expression *s'entendre parler* means both to hear oneself and to understand oneself. OF GRAMMATOLOGY, *supra* note 1, at 98.

39. An old joke illustrates this point. A man walks past a laundry which bears a sign reading: "My name is Fink /and what do you think /I'll do your wash for free." Thinking he has spotted a bargain, the man takes his laundry there. The next day, when he returns to pick up his laundry, the proprietor, Mr. Fink, asks for a payment of five dollars.

"Five dollars?" asks the man. "What about your sign?"

"Can't you read?" replies Fink. "The sign says: " 'My name is Fink, and what do you think, I'll do your wash for *free*?' "

The joke seems to demonstrate the capacity of writing to mislead and the superior expressive abilities of speech. However, this joke also undermines the very point that the phonocentrist (the privileger of speech) wants to make, because it *was* possible, in writing, to express inflection and avoid misunderstanding by using the correct punctuation. Indeed, were it otherwise, no one would understand the joke in its written form. Conversely, if Mr. Fink had spoken his lines in a monotone, he still might have been misunderstood.

40. Indeed, many people prefer to receive information from a lecture rather than by reading because they find it easier to comprehend and assimilate meaning from what a person is saying than from what she has written. The belief that speech is a privileged way of understanding the "true meaning" of communication is connected to Derrida's notion of logocentrism, or the privileging of presence.

41. Barbara Johnson sums up the privileging of speech over writing:

14

There are additional connections between speech and presence. Normally, a speaker is physically present when she talks to you; in contrast, you may be reading the words written by a person who is far away and perhaps no longer even alive. A person who is speaking to you can be interrupted and asked to clarify what she means. The same cannot be done with the author of a text one is reading. The author is not present, and only the representations of her past thoughts remain on the page.

After identifying all of the characteristics that define writing, and after arguing how they make writing inferior to speech, one can deconstruct the opposition of speech to writing by showing how the arguments "undo themselves." One can demonstrate that each identified characteristic of writing is true of speech as well; in other words, speech is a kind of "writing" that suffers from the same inadequacies attributed to writing.

First, speech itself is only a sign of what is present in a person's mind; it too is only a signifier of thought. A person's true thoughts and real meanings must be mediated through the use of speech. Furthermore, speech can be as unclear and ambiguous as writing, as most persons who have attended a law school lecture can testify.

Second, for speech to function as a signifier, as a sign, speech must be iterable. It must be possible to speak when one does not mean what one says. Speech also can be separated from the speaker and the moment of intention, in both space and time. One can listen to a politician speak over a radio or television, with no chance to stop the speaker and ask for clarification. One can play a recording of a speech by Martin Luther King over and over again; the sounds one hears are no longer connected to the thoughts of a living person. The emotional impact of recorded speech does not come from the presence of living thought in the speech, but only from its efficacy as a signifier of past thoughts, which have long ago faded away.

Derrida thus shows that speech, as a signifier of thought, shares all of the properties that we had associated with writing. Speech is merely a special case of a generalized idea of writing. This "arche-writing"[42] is the iterable representation of a signified by a signifier. Speech and writing (in the normal sense of the word) are both varieties of this more generalized form of "writing."

Derrida uses the word "writing" in this broader sense to stand for three

---

The spoken word is given a higher value because the speaker and listener are both present to the utterance simultaneously. There is no temporal or spatial distance between speaker, speech, and listener, since the speaker hears himself speak at the same moment the listener does. This immediacy seems to guarantee the notion that in the spoken word we know what we mean, mean what we say, say what we mean, and know what we have said.
Johnson, *supra* note 1, at viii.

42. *See* OF GRAMMATOLOGY, *supra* note 1, at 56–57.

basic properties of signification: (1) the substitution of the signifier for what it signifies; (2) the mediation of the experience of the signified by the signifier, and (3) the iterability of the signifier at different times and in different contexts.[43] "Writing," as used by Derrida, is a *paleonym*[44]—a word with an old meaning which has had a new meaning grafted on to it. "Writing" in Derrida's general sense recalls the reversal of the hierarchy of speech over writing from which the broader conception arises. Derrida's project, at least in its initial incarnation, was a call for a science of "writing," or a Grammatology, which would investigate and expose the hidden logocentric biases of Western thought.[45]

D. *The Logic of the Supplement*

Derrida also deconstructs the hierarchy of speech over writing through the "logic of the supplement." The term "supplement" comes from Rousseau, who describes writing as a "supplement" to speech.[46] Writing is a supplement to speech in that it represents speech. The "natural" condition of language is spoken; writing is merely added later:

> [S]peech being natural or at least the natural expression of thought, . . . writing is added to it, is adjoined, as an image or representation. In that sense, it is not natural. It diverts the immediate presence of thought to speech into representation and the imagination. This recourse is not only "bizarre," but dangerous. It is the addition of a technique, a sort of artificial and artful ruse to make speech present when it is actually absent. It is a violence done to the natural destiny of the language . . . .[47]

However, the word "supplement" has many meanings. First, it can mean something added to an already complete or self-sufficient thing. For example, I teach out of the latest edition of a constitutional law casebook. The book is finished, complete in itself, but every year the publisher distributes a supplement adding cases decided by the Supreme Court after the date of the casebook's publication. However, the fact that the publisher provides a supplement to my casebook indicates that the casebook is incomplete as a teaching aid—it needs supplementation to make it com-

---

43. *See id.* at 44-45, 55-57; H. STATEN, *supra* note 1, at 60-61, 121; *Limited Inc abc, supra* note 1, at 189-90.

44. *See supra* note 18.

45. *See Semiology and Grammatology, supra* note 22, at 35-36.

46. *See* OF GRAMMATOLOGY, *supra* note 1, at 144. Similarly, Rousseau speaks of culture as a supplement to nature and masturbation as a supplement to normal sexual relations. The latter supplement Rousseau refers to as a "dangerous supplement," a phrase Derrida seizes upon as characteristic of all supplementation. *See infra* text accompanying notes 47-48.

47. OF GRAMMATOLOGY, *supra* note 1, at 144.

plete. This is the second meaning of "supplement"—something added to something lacking in order to complete it, as one takes vitamin supplements to achieve a healthy diet.

If writing is a supplement to speech, in the sense that it is added to speech, it may well be dangerous. Writing may infect the naturalness of speech, alter speech, or even supplant it. Some people may begin to speak in the same stylized way in which they write. Writing may lead to mistakes in pronunciation. For example, uneducated French people occasionally pronounce the silent consonants in their language. As time passes, writing may become so important that all official acts are recorded, certain types of oral promises are no longer enforced, and storytellers and town criers are replaced by authors and journalists. Rousseau's life provides an example of the displacement of speech by writing. Rousseau, who exalted the naturalness of speech, was a writer by profession; he is now best remembered not for what he said, but for what he wrote.[48]

Yet, Derrida would argue, writing can only supplement speech in the first sense (representation of speech) if speech can be supplemented in the second sense (having a lack that could be fulfilled). By now we know what that lack is: Speech is not thought made present to the listener, but aural symbols that represent thoughts. Speech only appears to possess "presence," or a direct connection to the mind of the speaker because of the fortuity that people speak and think simultaneously. In reality, however, speech-as-thought is a sham; like writing, speech is a mediation of thought, a delaying through representation. It is for that reason that writing can supplement, or take the place of, speech.

Thus, we see a new meaning of the term "dangerous supplement." Writing is indeed a dangerous supplement, not because, as Rousseau feared, it might infect the purity of speech, but because the supplementary capacity of writing demonstrates that speech already possesses that which we dislike about writing. It is as if one met a lover's relatives and saw for the first time unpleasant qualities common to the whole family.

From this Derrida wants to make a larger claim: If we thought that speech was present and writing a mere representation of speech, we now see that speech, too, is only a mediation of something more present. Speech, like writing, is a supplement. (Note the crucial move in Derrida's argument: A signifier supplements that which it signifies.) But if speech is a supplement, that which it supplements must also be lacking, for otherwise speech could not represent it. That new thing must, in turn, be a

---

48. Writing may be dangerous in still another way. Derrida argues that both Rousseau and Levi-Strauss identified speech with nature and writing with culture. The invention of writing and its introduction to primitive peoples brought a moral and spiritual decline that is closely associated with the corrupting influence of culture upon nature. *See id*. at 101–40.

supplement (signifier), which represents something further, and so on. The result is a chain of supplements, reaching towards an unmediated, complete, self-sufficient presence.[49] To speak the language of signs, the result is a chain of signifiers, each pointing to the next, each reaching towards a pure, unmediated signified.[50]

But now comes the great irony of this logic. The Real Thing, Presence Itself, must, by definition, be something that could not be supplemented or represented by a sign, for it is self-sufficient, and could not serve as a signifier or supplement. The world as we know it is only a world of representations, and representations of representations, ad infinitum. Every signified is actually a signifier in disguise. Derrida describes the ultimate deconstruction òf presence:

> *There is nothing outside of the text* . . . . What we have tried to show by following the guiding line of the "dangerous supplement," is that in what one calls . . . real life . . . there has never been anything but writing; there have never been anything but supplements; substitutive significations which could only come forth in a chain of differential references. . . . [T]he absolute present, Nature, . . . ha[s] always already escaped, ha[s] never existed . . . .[51]

"Writing" is all there is. This conclusion follows from Derrida's argument that a sign can only represent still another sign. Derrida's famous aphorism *il n'y a pas de hors-texte* (there is nothing outside of the text) is a metaphor which proclaims that all understanding is metaphorical.[52] The "text" of which Derrida speaks is not merely words, but life itself: "[O]ur very relation to 'reality'. . . functions like a text."[53]

Derrida's critique can be viewed as nihilistic because it appears to deny the existence of objective truth. On the other hand, Derrida's own arguments subtly rely on the notion of truth. The basic claim is that a signifier only *imperfectly represents* the thing it signifies. This is not a mistake of logic, or an oversight on Derrida's part. We speak in logocentric terms, so that our critique of logocentrism must rely on suspect categories of thought. This is the case with all deconstructions; each uses the conceptual apparatus of the very thing that it wishes to subvert.[54]

---

49. *Cf. id.* at 152–57 (describing chain of supplements involved in Rousseau's love object).
50. *Id.* at 49–50.
51. *Id.* at 158–59.
52. *Id.* at 158.
53. Johnson, *supra* note 1, at xiv.
54. Derrida demonstrates the precarious position of the deconstructionist by placing certain concepts *sous rature* ("under erasure"). For example, he uses the word "is" with a line through it to show that the word is logocentrically biased ("being" is the ultimate expression of presence) yet necessary for expression. OF GRAMMATOLOGY, *supra* note 1, at 19.
It should now become clear why explanations of deconstruction necessarily involve a modification of

Derrida's seemingly nihilistic conclusion must be understood in the context of his method of reaching it. Derrida does not deny the existence of objective truth as much as he affirms the interpretative character of our attempts to comprehend truth. Our "truth"—the conceptual apparatus we create to explain the world to ourselves—is only a sign or metaphor for an endless succession of still other signs and metaphors, and we have forgotten that it is only that. Thus, the Real Truth seems always beyond our grasp, outside the dominant conceptual apparatus, because that apparatus is necessarily always incomplete and capable of further supplementation.

Our frustation in our attempts to experience the Real Thing, whether we call it "truth" or "presence," stems from the desire in Western philosophy to foundationalize. Here is the agenda of traditional Western philosophy: One can only seek truth if one discovers fundamental principles and builds upon them.[55] We should recognize this "agenda" by now as privileging. The act of privileging requires the privileged term to be foundational, complete, self-sufficient; however, it is none of these things. It is related to the non-privileged term in a system of mutual differentiation and dependence, or *différance*.

The privileged concept is incomplete; it is only a supplement, a signifier, a metaphor. For that reason, we are able to use it against itself, to deconstruct it. The act of privileging, of asserting that one of two mutually dependent concepts is really foundational, is like drinking from the springs of the mythical river Lethe, after which we forget our past. Once we have accepted the privileging, we forget that the foundational concept was only a metaphor, a supplement. Deconstruction awakes us from our dogmatic slumber, and reminds us that our "truth" is only an interpretation.

E. *Deconstruction and Ideology*

Although these issues seem metaphysical, we can translate Derrida's concerns into a legal setting.[56] Legal doctrines both reflect and regulate

---

it. My attempt at explanation is a logocentric project. I seek to present the foundations of Derrida's thought in a clear, easily comprehensible, logical progression, beginning with simple ideas and then working to more complicated results. Obviously, there is something paradoxical about using logocentric methods to develop a critique of logocentrism. However, to argue that a logocentric presentation of deconstruction is suspect because it misstates the "true" content of Derridean thought is simply to engage in another logocentric move, that is, that there is a privileged reading of Derrida, a true unmediated presence, of which all interpretations are inferior copies.

55. OF GRAMMATOLOGY, *supra* note 1, at 97 (history of metaphysics is history of logocentrism); J. CULLER, *supra* note 1, at 92–93 (logocentric practice in Western philosophy moves from fundamental ideas to elaboration of ideas); *Limited Inc abc, supra* note 1, at 236 (single recurrent gesture in Western metaphysics is move from good, positive, pure, simple, and essential to evil, negative, impure, complex, and accidental).

56. Note that I am presenting my interpretation of Derrida, which is my own "dangerous supplement" to his work and my own metaphor.

761

social life. The choice of protected rights and of enforcement techniques reflect views, whether obvious or obscure, about social relations. Law tells a story about what people are and should be.[57]

To give an obvious example, laws that permit (or enforce) discrimination on the basis of race or sex tell a different story about people than laws that prohibit such discrimination. The principles of a social theory like Liberalism tell a story about human nature, which some accept and others criticize.[58] Even the seemingly most insignificant or neutral doctrines and rules, taken as a whole, have a story to tell, if we are willing to listen to them.[59]

We can think of a system of law as a community's attempt to realize human ends. This presupposes a description of the good and bad in human nature: what people want from their lives and what their limitations are. This description necessarily involves privilegings of certain aspects of human nature over others. Later, we justify our system by claiming that it is the best, given the natural constraints of the human condition. For example, an advocate of laissez-faire might argue that, given the natural self-interestedness of people, unregulated market transactions are the best way to realize human goals. But the deconstructive critique reminds us that our social vision and system of laws are not based upon human nature as it really is, but rather upon an interpretation of human nature, a metaphor, a privileging. We do not experience the "presence" of human nature; we experience different versions of it in the stories we tell about what we are "really like." These stories are incomplete; they are metaphors and can be deconstructed. Too often we forget that our systems of law are based upon metaphor and interpretation; we mistake the dominant or privileged vision of people and society for real "present" human nature, as Rousseau confused speech with the presence of thought.

---

57. Clare Dalton uses this metaphor in her deconstruction of contract doctrine. Dalton, *supra* note 2, at 999.

58. For example, it is often asserted that Liberalism's emphasis upon individual autonomy ignores other aspects of human nature, such as the need for communal sharing of values. The vision of human personality and responsibility that Liberalism poses is disputed both by the right and the left. Libertarians argue that Liberals violate principles of self-determination and autonomy by asking people to contribute to a common good, while Marxists argue that Liberal capitalism hides the real nature of relations between worker and capitalist under a veneer of free exchange. Of course, one also can criticize each of these alternatives to Liberalism as portraying a fundamentally false picture of human nature.

59. In her deconstruction, Dalton argues that the ideology of contract law, which privileges the view of contracts as the "neutral facilitator of private volition," and is "concerned at the periphery with the imposition of social duties," Dalton, *supra* note 2, at 1014, is also present in the doctrines of implied contracts, parol evidence, and consideration. *Id.* at 1014-24, 1048-52, 1066-95. She concludes that although these doctrines in contract law may seem less overtly political in nature than others, such as duress and unconscionability, the same tensions are at work: "[In] contract doctrine . . . a comparatively few mediating devices are constantly deployed to displace and defer the otherwise inevitable revelation that public cannot be separated from private, or form from substance, or objective manifestation from subjective intent." *Id.* at 1113.

At that point, the metaphor becomes mistaken for what it describes. But latent within the metaphor is a countervision that can be located and brought to the surface through deconstruction. It exists within the privileged conception because the latter ultimately depends upon it in a relation of *différance*.

The argument of the laissez-faire advocate presupposes a vision of what is most important about people, and necessarily relegates other aspects of the human condition, such as altruism and community, to marginal status. We could deconstruct this vision of humanity by showing how economic individualism ultimately depends upon social cooperation and the sharing of values. We could show the incompleteness of this vision of human nature, its poverty in describing what people are like and the nature of their relations to each other. A part of humanity will always escape this vision because it is only a metaphor, a signifier. The vision suffers from a lack that needs to be supplemented, and the supplement is a countervision that has been relegated to the periphery. This supplement is indeed "dangerous," for it threatens to subvert the picture of human nature posed by the dominant conception.[60]

The deconstruction of legal concepts, or of the social vision that informs them, is not nihilistic. Deconstruction is not a call for us to forget about moral certainty, but to remember aspects of human life that were pushed into the background by the necessities of the dominant legal conception we call into question. Deconstruction is not a denial of the legitimacy of rules and principles; it is an affirmation of human possibilities that have been overlooked or forgotten in the privileging of particular legal ideas.

Any social theory must emphasize some human values over others. Such categorizing necessarily involves a privileging, which in turn can be deconstructed. But the goal of deconstruction is not the destruction of all possible social visions. By recalling the elements of human life relegated to the margin in a given social theory, deconstructive readings challenge us to remake the dominant conceptions of our society. We can choose to accept the challenge or not, but we will no longer cling to our social vision blindly. Nor can we assume that this vision is the "real essence" of human

---

60. *See supra* notes 46–48 and accompanying text (discussing danger in supplementation). The deconstruction of the philosophy of economic individualism is a favorite topic of the Critical Legal Studies movement. For a classic discussion of the *différance* between individualism and altruism, see Kennedy, *Form and Substance in Private Law Adjudication*, 89 HARV. L. REV. 1685 (1976). Kennedy's famous statement of the "fundamental contradiction" of social life is a more general expression of *différance*. Kennedy, *The Structure of Blackstone's Commentaries*, 28 BUFFALO L. REV. 209, 211–13 (1979) ("[T]he goal of individual freedom is at the same time dependent on and incompatible with the communal coercive action that is necessary to achieve it. . . . [R]elations with others are both necessary to and incompatible with our freedom.").

nature because that would be a claim to have experienced presence, an experience that Derrida denies that we can ever have.

As Robert Gordon has observed, people "build structures, then act as if (and genuinely come to believe that) the structures they have built are determined by history, human nature, economic law."[61] Deconstruction allows us to see that ideologies are signs or metaphors that describe social life. They are privileged conceptions of social reality; they are supplements, which can in turn be supplemented. Like Derrida's signs, they are not self-sufficient, but ultimately depend upon the very aspects of human life that they deny and from which they differentiate themselves. Every ideology suffers from an elementary lack: its dependence on what it denies, on what it is exalted over. This lack, this *différance*, is what we seize upon and exploit in a deconstructive reading.

We now see that the legal deconstructor deconstructs *ideologies*, which are manifested in particular legal doctrines. By challenging what is "given," deconstruction affirms the infinite possibilities of human existence. By contesting "necessity," deconstruction dissolves the ideological encrustations of our thought.

F. *Deconstruction as a Critical Theory*

One might object that a deconstructive reassessment of our legal and social institutions offers us no logical stopping point. If the results of a deconstructive reading can themselves be deconstructed, deconstruction threatens to become an endless series of reversals and counter-reversals. Once again, nihilism seems an unavoidable consequence.

To answer this charge, I would like to compare deconstructive practice (or at least my interpretation of it) to psychoanalysis. Such an analogy is not at all farfetched. The psychoanalyst engages in a process similar in many ways to deconstruction. The psychoanalyst reverses the privileging of the conscious over the unconscious as the explanation of human behavior.[62] The psychoanalyst also performs a deconstructive reversal by focusing on seemingly marginal or unimportant elements of the patient's experience, such as everyday events, free associations of ideas, and dream material, to understand the deeper connections that are the key to unconscious motivation.[63]

---

61. Gordon, *New Developments in Legal Theory*, in THE POLITICS OF LAW 289 (D. Kairys ed. 1982).

62. Michels, *The Basic Propositions of Psychoanalytic Theory*, in INTRODUCING PSYCHOANALYTIC THEORY 12 (S. Gillman ed. 1982) (psychoanalysis reverses emphasis on outer world as determinant of human behavior and concerns itself with inner dispositions of individual).

63. *See* L. KOLB & H. BRODIE, MODERN CLINICAL PSYCHIATRY 750–55 (10th ed. 1982); *see also* F. REDLICH & D. FREEDMAN, THE THEORY AND PRACTICE OF PSYCHIATRY 276 (1966) ("*Free association* [involves] full and unedited reporting of mental events, including seemingly trivial

Furthermore, both deconstruction and psychoanalysis offer critical theories.[64] A critical theory may be distinguished by three characteristics. First, the goal of a critical theory is not to develop a series of true factual propositions, but to achieve enlightenment and emancipation.[65] Second, a critical theory is self-referential; it may be applied to itself or to the process of its application.[66] Third, a critical theory is confirmed not by a process of experimentation and empirical verification, but through a more complicated process of self-reflection. The critical theorist determines whether she has achieved enlightenment and emancipation in terms of knowledge and beliefs she has developed in the course of applying the critical theory.[67]

Psychoanalysis possesses all of the characteristics of a critical theory. Its goal is emancipation of the patient from unfulfilling behavior patterns caused by unconscious repressed material.[68] This emancipation is achieved by a process of progressive enlightenment: The patient learns how her behavior patterns have been caused by unconscious forces and this, in turn, alters her behavior.[69] Psychoanalysis is potentially self-referential because the process of analysis itself can be understood and criticized in terms of hidden motivations and desires of the analyst.[70] Finally, the success of analysis often can only be judged through a process of self-reflection by the patient, aided by the therapist.[71]

Like psychoanalysis, deconstructive readings of texts offer the possibility of emancipation from customary ways of thinking. Deconstruction operates by a momentary reversal of privileging. This reversal alters our

---

or obnoxious details.").

64. In this discussion of critical theory, I follow the ideas developed in R. GEUSS, THE IDEA OF A CRITICAL THEORY 55-95 (1981).

65. *Id.* at 55.

66. This distinguishes critical theories from other types of theories. For example, Newton's theory about particles in motion is not itself a particle in motion, and therefore, does not refer to or explain itself. *Id.* By contrast, Marxism as a social theory is potentially self-referential. *Id.* at 56. It tries to explain not only the connections between a person's beliefs and her relation to various economic classes in society, but also why a Marxist holds the beliefs that she does.

67. *Id.* at 55-56, 85-86.

68. L. KOLB & H. BRODIE, *supra* note 63, at 748-49.

69. *Id.* at 749, 755.

70. For example, psychoanalytic psychotherapy applies the techniques of analysis to the analyst herself when it addresses mistakes and failures in therapy due to countertransference:
[C]ountertransference reactions arise in the therapist as a result of the patient's influence on the physician's unconscious feelings and have their origin in the latter's irrational projections and identifications. The therapist must not permit his own unconscious feelings and attitudes, aroused during phases of treatment, to intrude in his relations with the patient.
Id. at 752; *see also* S. LORAND, TECHNIQUE OF PSYCHOANALYTIC THERAPY 209-22 (1946) (discussing countertransference); Peters, *Transference,* in INTRODUCING PSYCHOANALYTIC THEORY, *supra* note 62, at 99-101 (same).

71. *See* M. BASCH, DOING PSYCHOTHERAPY 36-37, 52, 178 (1980).

view of the privileging, just as the act of uncovering repressed material liberates the psychoanalytic patient.

As a critical theory, deconstruction can also be a self-referential activity because it can be performed on previous deconstructive readings indefinitely. It is this very property that leads to the charge of nihilism. However, the analogy to psychoanalysis shows us why this charge is illfounded. We do not think that psychoanalysis is futile because a patient can be psychoanalyzed indefinitely or because the act of psychoanalysis can itself be investigated psychoanalytically. Rather, we believe that the psychoanalyst is performing a meaningful function even though her own work is potentially subject to further psychoanalysis. More importantly, the psychoanalyst and patient may properly decide that the patient has progressed sufficiently to end analysis. Similarly, deconstruction need not continue indefinitely if it has achieved the goals of emancipation and enlightenment.

On the other hand, how is one to tell when these goals have been achieved? There is no foolproof answer to this question for deconstruction, but the same may be said for psychoanalysis. There is simply no mechanical method for the analyst and patient to identify when analysis should end. The decision is an act of self-reflection on the part of both that the patient has been sufficiently enlightened and emancipated from the burdens of repressed material.[72] Of course, this decision may be questioned on the grounds that it is subjective, that one person's "enlightenment" may be another's neurosis. However, the analyst and patient are entitled to employ a personal judgment based upon a vision of normalcy and good mental health developed in the course of the analysis.[73]

In the same fashion, the deconstructionist must engage in a process of self-reflection to determine when the insights provided by deconstruction have produced sufficient enlightenment with respect to a view of law, legal doctrine, or human society previously accepted as privileged, natural, or complete. This decision is, of course, a political and moral choice, but it is one informed by insights gained through the activity of deconstruction itself. At the moment the choice is made, the critical theorist is, strictly speaking, no longer a deconstructionist. However, the purposes of engaging in the deconstruction have been served. In both psychoanalysis and deconstruction, the justification of when one should cease analysis may

---

72. *Id.*
73. *Cf.* F. REDLICH & D. FREEDMAN, *supra* note 63, at 277 ("Analysis is essentially an educational process. . . . After a successful analysis, the patient will take with him the ability to introspect . . . with candor and to apply such insights . . . to life problems.").

appear self-supporting, and so it is. But such justification is a characteristic of any critical theory.[74]

G. An Example of a Legal Deconstruction

At this point it might be useful to give an example of a deconstructive argument in a legal context. I will use an argument by the noted British legal scholar P.S. Atiyah, who is not generally known as a deconstructionist. There is nothing unusual about the appearance of deconstructive arguments in the texts of non-deconstructionists; recall Hume's deconstruction of Descartes' *cogito*.[75]

In his *Promises, Morals, and Law*,[76] Atiyah argues against a theory of contract that bases obligation upon individual will or intention. Atiyah notes that the commonsense view of promissory obligation is that promises are binding because of the intent of the party and its objective manifestation by the act of promising. He suggests that the explicit promise, with its deliberate manifestation of intent, is usually viewed as the paradigmatic case of contractual obligation. The law then attempts to explain the binding nature of implied promises in terms of the standard case of promising:

> In law and, I think, with most contemporary writers on philosophy, the traditional explanation of an implied promise assumes that the explicit promise is the paradigm case. The implied promise is then treated as a case where no explicit promise is made in so many words, but where, from his words and conduct, it is plain that the party intends to bind himself. Simple examples . . . concern contracts made by boarding a bus . . . or ordering a meal in a restaurant. . . . The lawyer explains these obligations by saying that there are implied promises.[77]

We can already see the hierarchical relationship at work. The paradigmatic case of promissory obligation concerns explicit promises, in which intention is manifested by specific promissory words. Implicit promises are parasitic upon explicit promises: The intention to be bound is mani-

---

74. *See* R. GEUSS, *supra* note 64, at 85–88. *Compare* Unger, *The Critical Legal Studies Movement*, 96 HARV. L. REV. 561, 580 (1983) ("Legal doctrine rightly understood and practiced is the conduct of internal development through legal materials.") *with* J. RAWLS, A THEORY OF JUSTICE 48–51 (1971) (sense of justice comes from matching initial convictions with proposed reconceptions in attempt to achieve reflective equilibrium). Note that the establishment of a "reflective equilibrium" creates a new privileging. The defense of the new privileging is a constructive, and not a deconstructive, activity.

75. *See supra* note 27.

76. P. ATIYAH, PROMISES, MORALS, AND LAW (1981) [hereinafter PROMISES, MORALS, AND LAW].

77. *Id.* at 173 (footnote omitted).

fested (and thus implied) not by the defendant's words of promise, but by her conduct. Thus, one explains the legal obligation of ordering a meal in a restaurant in terms of previous cases in which people have intended to purchase a meal and have said: "If you serve me food, I will pay you the price listed on the menu," or words to that effect. But basing the obligatory nature of implied promises upon explicit promises opens the way for a deconstructive reversal of the hierarchy, a reversal that may tell us something new about why promises are binding:

> [T]here are difficulties with this traditional explanation. What of the person who does not intend to pay his fare on boarding the bus, or pay for the meal supplied to him in the restaurant? The lawyer brushes aside this difficulty, appealing to what he calls the "objective test" of promise or assent. There is the appearance of a promise and that is enough. But this explanation is not very satisfying. For it dismisses what is—on the traditional view—the very central requirement of a promise. If a person who intends to steal a ride on a bus is liable to pay his fare in exactly the same way as the person who intends to pay his fare, it seems odd to say that it is the intention which creates the liability in both cases.[78]

Atiyah's argument calls into question whether it is really the intention that creates the obligation. Indeed, even in the case of explicit promises, we may wonder whether intention creates obligation. Imagine the person who walks into the restaurant and says "I promise to pay for the food I consume," when he has no intention of paying. Will his intention not to be bound shield him from moral culpability or legal liability? Indeed, it is precisely because he lacks the intention that he should be made to pay. Atiyah notes that there is something strange about a theory of contractual liability based upon intent:

> [T]o imply a promise suggests that it is because of the promise that the relevant party is bound by an obligation. He is obliged to pay for the meal or pay the bus fare *because* he has promised. However, it seems quite plausible to suggest that the truth is the other way round. It is because he is bound by an obligation that we generally feel impelled to imply a promise. Naturally, if that is right, the source of the obligation cannot lie in the implied promise itself, but must be sought elsewhere. . . . [I]t is often, perhaps always, the case that the conduct itself justifies the creation of the obligation. . . . In the great majority of cases of this nature . . . the intention to pay will exist, and so will the intention to assume or accept the legal obligation. But we must never forget the defaulter.

---

78. *Id.*

Occasionally people do order meals in restaurants without any intention of paying. Nobody doubts—least of all the lawyer—that this makes not the slightest difference to the obligation to pay.[79]

We may translate this argument into Derrida's terminology. The classical theory of contract involves a privileging of explicit promises over implicit promises because in explicit promises the thing that makes the contract binding—the intention of the actor to enter into an agreement and be bound by it—is in some sense more "present." The speaker's explicit promise gives evidence of her "real" intentions. In the case of an implied promise, these intentions are hidden, and can only be inferred from the circumstances. A theory of implied promises supplements the will theory, which explains the binding nature of explicit promises. The supplementary theory explains why there is a binding obligation when the promisor's present intent is not immediately known to the promisee.

Following the logic of the supplement, however, we can argue that a theory of explicit promises can only be supplemented if explicit promises also defer presence (the present intention of the promisor at the moment of promising). Explicit promises are binding because they manifest intent, but the objective manifestation of intent in an explicit promise is only binding because it acts as a signifier for presence (the promisor's actual will or intent). However, as a sign, the explicit promise must be iterable. Thus, an explicit promise could only bind a promisor if it could bind regardless of the promisor's intent, that is to say, only if the dishonest promisor also could be bound.

Atiyah has argued that this is how the law treats the dishonest promisor.[80] Promises are binding even if there is no connection between the objective manifestation and the presence of subjective intention. The "presence" of the promisor's intent at the moment of promising does not create the moral obligation. Rather, we explain the obligation of explicit promises in terms of the reasons implicit promises are binding: They confer a benefit on the promisor that it would be unjust not to repay, or they induce justified reliance on the part of the promisee.

This argument leads to a broader generalization. The privileging of a will theory of contract over a theory based upon effect (unjust enrichment or reliance) involves a relation of *différance*—of mutual differentiation and dependence. A theory that postulates the will of the promisor as binding must explain the moral obligation involved in cases in which the promisor does not will herself to be bound, but accepts a benefit or creates

---

79. *Id.* at 173-74.
80. *Id.*

detrimental reliance to the promisee. Thus, a will theory ultimately depends upon the theory over which it is privileged.

Of course, the relation between privileging of ideas and construction of ideologies gives Atiyah's deconstruction additional importance. Atiyah is an historian as well as a legal theorist, and he recognizes the connection between the will theory and the ideology of the nineteenth century.[81] Indeed, he argues that a consequence of the privileging of the will theory of contract was the emphasis on purely executory contracts as the paradigmatic case of moral and legal obligation (in contrast to cases of detrimental reliance or unjust enrichment) and the emphasis on the expectation interest as the paradigm of what the law of contracts was designed to protect (as opposed to the reliance or restitution interest).[82]

Needless to say, the law has moved a considerable distance from the nineteenth century model in both respects. What is important for our purposes is that the deconstruction of a privileging in a limited area of contract doctrine exposes a more pervasive underlying ideology, which gave rise to the privileging. Ironically, it also gives us the chance to investigate the unquestioned ideological assumptions in our current doctrines. Thus, the techniques of deconstruction, as a tool for the analysis of past and present ideological thinking, are especially valuable to the legal philosopher or historian.

Atiyah has used the tools of deconstructive practice to criticize the classical will theory of contract. A deconstruction of an opposition, however, cannot by itself establish a new hierarchy in place of an old one, because the new hierarchy also could be deconstructed. This is a point Atiyah neglects, for he wants to argue that reliance and benefit are the "real" sources of promissory obligation.[83] In so doing, he wants to establish a new hierarchy. However, a theory of contract based wholly upon benefit or reliance must explain why promises are binding immediately after the parties enter into them, before detrimental effects have developed. Atiyah has great difficulty explaining the binding nature of these promises, and concludes that if they are binding (which he doubts they should be), there are only weak grounds for enforcing them.[84] His conclusion is not surprising, because the best explanation for the binding nature

---

81. *Id.* at 4–5, 7, 33. *See generally* P. ATIYAH, THE RISE AND FALL OF FREEDOM OF CONTRACT (1979) [hereinafter THE RISE AND FALL OF FREEDOM OF CONTRACT] (historical treatment of nature of contractual and promissory liability).

82. *See* THE RISE AND FALL OF FREEDOM OF CONTRACT, *supra* note 81, at 424–29, 441–43, 456; PROMISES, MORALS AND LAW, *supra* note 76, at 33.

83. More specifically, he argues that the social group has determined that reliance and benefit are the conditions for promissory obligation. PROMISES, MORALS, AND LAW, *supra* note 76, at 129, 166–67, 193–94.

84. *Id.* at 208–12.

of these promises is the intent of the two parties to bind themselves, an explanation Atiyah has already rejected. In essence, Atiyah's benefit/reliance theory of promissory obligation must admit its own "dangerous supplement" to explain mutually unrelied upon executory promises. This "dangerous supplement," of course, is a disguised version of the will theory.

Note the irony: In the classical theory, the purely executory promise was the paradigm case; the implied promise was the exception, and the classical theory had to be supplemented with a theory explaining the binding nature of implied obligations. However, this supplement was a dangerous one, as Atiyah has shown. One might view explicit promises as merely a special case of implied promises; that is, promises whose binding nature lies in socially imposed norms and not in the assumption of individual will. On the other hand, under Atiyah's benefit/reliance theory, the acceptance of benefits or the creation of reliance becomes the paradigmatic case of promissory obligation and the purely executory unrelied upon promise becomes the exception, which must be explained by the use of a supplementary theory of obligation.

Similarly, even Atiyah's basic premise, that promises are binding if there is a pre-existing obligation in the form of a benefit received or detrimental reliance incurred, must smuggle in the will theory through the back door:

> Suppose, for example, that A and B "agree" on the sale of B's house to A for £ 20,000. A promises to pay the price, and B promises to convey the house. . . . The promises do not simply create obligations, on their own as it were. A's obligation to pay the price will not arise just because he has promised: it will arise if and when he receives a conveyance of the house. B's obligation to convey does not arise just from his promise: it arises if and when he receives the price. . . . If [A] gets the house, he surely has an obligation to pay, irrespective of the promise: *it is not A's house, and B has no intention of making a gift* . . . .[85]

Atiyah argues that A is obligated because B has conferred a benefit on him (and therefore A would be unjustly enriched if he did not perform). This raises the question of how we know that A would be unjustly enriched. Atiyah responds that B did not *intend* to make a gift of the house. Thus, Atiyah's benefit/reliance theory of obligation turns upon the intent of B, and we are back to a version of the will theory.

I have not refuted Atiyah's skeptical arguments regarding the will the-

---

ory of contract. On the contrary, Atiyah's deconstruction of the will theory of contract is quite successful. Atiyah is wrong, however, in thinking that he has shown that a new ground of explanation will succeed where the old one has failed. Rather, he has demonstrated that the will theory and the benefit/reliance theory of promissory obligation exist in a relation of *différance*, that is, of mutual differentiation and dependence. This conclusion is unsatisfying to someone who seeks an ultimate ground for contractual obligation, but Derrida's work suggests that this is the best that can be done.

II. THE LIBERATION OF TEXT FROM AUTHOR

A. *Readings and Misreadings*

Derrida's conclusion that there is only "writing," that there are only signs and metaphors for still other signs and metaphors, has interesting consequences for a theory of interpretation. These consequences are important to lawyers, who are greatly concerned with the interpretation of texts.

I want to introduce these ideas with a simple paradigm of textual interpretation. According to this simple paradigm, a text is a representation of an author's intent. Thus, a novel represents a story (and artistic ideas) that a novelist wishes to express. A philosophical treatise represents ideas that a philosopher wishes to convey. A judicial opinion stands for the principles of decision that are used to decide a case. The goal of interpretation is understanding the meaning of the text, that is, the author's intent. If we interpret correctly, we grasp the author's intent; if we interpret incorrectly, we miss the author's intent.

This simple paradigm of interpretation is not a popular theory of interpretation among literary critics these days.[86] However, the simple paradigm of interpretation continues to be well-respected among legal thinkers as a preferred method of interpreting legal texts. Indeed, if most lawyers or judges were asked how statutes or judicial decisions should be interpreted, they would probably respond that the author's intent is the most

---

86. Indeed, the reader-response movement in literary criticism has championed the role of the reader in constructing the meaning of texts. *See generally* S. FISH, IS THERE A TEXT IN THIS CLASS? (1980); S. MAILLOUX, INTERPRETIVE CONVENTIONS: THE READER IN THE STUDY OF AMERICAN FICTION (1982); THE READER IN THE TEXT (S. Suleiman & I. Crosman eds. 1980); READER-RESPONSE CRITICISM (J. Tompkins ed. 1980). Only a few literary critics, such as E.D. Hirsch, still hold to the view that the author's intent is the primary source of interpretation. *See, e.g.*, E.D. HIRSCH, THE AIMS OF INTERPRETATION (1976); E.D. HIRSCH, VALIDITY IN INTERPRETATION (1967).

Of course, the argument that the primary source of meaning lies in the reader's response rather than in the author's intention involves a privileging as much as the reverse claim, and therefore, is equally subject to deconstruction. The relation between author and reader is one of *différance*.

important factor.[87] As I shall argue later, the strong hold that the theory of authorial intent has upon legal thinkers probably arises from its association with the principle of the Rule of Law.[88]

I would now like to give a particular example of how the simple paradigm of interpretation operates in a legal setting. Suppose that *Brown v. Board of Education*[89] had just been decided. A black janitor files suit in a federal district court in Mississippi, contesting a "coloreds only" seating section in a cafeteria at a municipal office building. The district court must decide whether *Brown* (and the text of the Fourteenth Amendment that it interprets) outlaws the maintenance of "separate but equal" dining facilities in an establishment operated by a municipal government. According to the simple paradigm of interpretation, if the court holds one way, it has read *Brown* correctly, while if it holds another way, it has misinterpreted or misapplied *Brown*.[90]

It is possible to distinguish *Brown* on the ground that it applies only to schools, where impressionable children will be greatly affected by the perception of separate treatment. This is a possible interpretation of *Brown*, and I mention it because it is important to understand that distinguishing a case is as much an interpretation as following it. On the other hand, following the simple paradigm of interpretation, this reading may misinterpret *Brown* because the authors of *Brown* intended that all separate but

---

87. "Although there have been occasional heretics, it is an article of faith among American lawyers that the function of a court when dealing with a statute is to ascertain and effectuate the intent of the legislature." Murphy, *Old Maxims Never Die: The "Plain-Meaning Rule" and Statutory Interpretation in the "Modern" Federal Courts*, 75 COLUM. L. REV. 1299, 1299 (1975) (footnote omitted); *see also* R. DICKERSON, THE INTERPRETATION AND APPLICATION OF STATUTES 36 (1975) (same); J. HURST, DEALING WITH STATUTES 32–40 (1982) (fundamental principle of statutory construction is inquiry into legislative intent); 2A N. SINGER, STATUTES AND STATUTORY CONSTRUCTION § 45.05, at 20–22 (Sands 4th ed. 1984) ("An overwhelming majority of judicial opinions considering statutory issues are written in the context of legislative intent."). Although Professor Murphy expresses the prevailing view, the number of "heretics" is greater than his quotation suggests. *See, e.g.*, Radin, *Statutory Interpretation*, 43 HARV. L. REV. 863 (1930) (legislative intent fictional and irrelevant concept); H. Hart & A. Sacks, The Legal Process 1410 (tent. ed. 1958) (unpublished manuscript) (legislative purpose created by courts and not identical with intent).

In constitutional law, where there is perhaps the greatest controversy about proper methods of textual interpretation, the simple paradigm remains surprisingly strong. *E.g.*, R. BERGER, GOVERNMENT BY JUDICIARY (1977); Bork, *Neutral Principles and Some First Amendment Problems*, 47 IND. L.J. 1 (1971); Monaghan, *Our Perfect Constitution*, 56 N.Y.U. L. REV. 353 (1981). Even more liberal authors often pay lip service to the principle of authorial intent. Ronald Dworkin, who argues that the Framers' intent is not a psychological fact to be discovered but something to be invented, still makes an obeisance to the simple paradigm when he proposes that one should look to the Framers' general abstract concepts of "due process" and "equal protection," rather than to specific concrete conceptions of these ideas in practice. Dworkin, *The Forum of Principle*, 56 N.Y.U. L. REV. 469, 477, 488–91, 497 (1981).

88. *See infra* text accompanying notes 108–09.

89. 347 U.S. 483 (1954).

90. This statement is true not only of the simple paradigm. Many other theories of interpretation label readings as proper or improper, although they might reach different results in individual cases.

equal public facilities for blacks and whites should be considered presumptively unconstitutional.

The simple paradigm of interpretation involves a privileging. There are many possible readings of *Brown v. Board of Education*, and these readings can take place in a multitude of different factual and legal contexts. However, some of these readings are correct, and others are incorrect. Incorrect readings are mistakes of legal reasoning, which should be eliminated from a legal system to the greatest extent possible. The commonsense understanding of legal reasoning, then, is premised upon a distinction between readings and misreadings of legal materials. Therefore, the goal of good legal interpretation is to separate the correct readings from the incorrect readings.[91]

Now this privileging of readings over misreadings can be deconstructed. Culler's treatment of the subject, although it does not specifically concern legal texts, is excellent:

> When one attempts to formulate the distinction between reading and misreading, one inevitably relies on some notion of identity and difference. Reading and understanding preserve or reproduce a content or meaning, maintain its identity, while misunderstanding and misreading distort it; they produce or introduce a difference. But one can argue that in fact the transformation or modification of meaning that characterizes misunderstanding is also at work in what we call understanding. If a text can be understood, it can in principle be understood repeatedly, by different readers in different circumstances. These acts of reading or understanding are not, of course, identical. They involve modifications and differences, but differences which are deemed not to matter. We can thus say, in a formulation more valid than its converse, that understanding is a special case of misunderstanding, a particular deviation or determination of misunderstanding. It is misunderstanding whose misses do not matter. The interpretive operations at work in a generalized misunderstanding or misreading give rise both to what we call understanding and to what we call misunderstanding.
>
> The claim that all readings are misreadings can also be justified by the most familiar aspects of critical and interpretive practice. Given the complexities of texts, the reversibility of tropes, the extendability of context, and the necessity for a reading to select and organize, every reading can be shown to be partial. Interpreters are able to discover features and implications of a text that previous interpreters neglected or distorted. They can use the text to show that previous readings are in fact misreadings, but their own readings

---

91. Again, even if one did not subscribe to the simple paradigm of interpretation, it still might make sense to speak of correct and incorrect interpretations of legal texts. One would not even have to claim that there was only one correct interpretation to speak in this way.

will be found wanting by later interpreters, who may astutely identify the dubious presuppositions or particular forms of blindness to which they testify. The history of readings is a history of misreadings, though under certain circumstances these misreadings can be and may have been accepted as readings.[92]

Lawyers' readings of cases are partial in two senses of the word. First, they are partial in Culler's sense, in that they represent only some aspects of the meaning of texts. They are also partial in a second sense, in that they are interpretations that benefit (and thus are partial *to*) the position they advocate. Certainly, the second kind of partiality is likely to lead to the first. The interpretations of judges are no less partial in either sense of the word. The materials of the law—cases, constitutions, and statutes—take on new meanings as legal contexts change. Throughout history, interpretations are constantly offered, some of which are later labelled misreadings. The history of the law is iteration; the development of law is the development of legal materials, which are subjected to new interpretations as we read them over and over again in different factual, historical, and political contexts.

The deconstruction of the opposition of readings and misreadings is at first troubling to lawyers because our legal system seems to depend upon the ability to distinguish readings from misreadings. If all readings of legal materials are actually misreadings, then law cannot be a rational enterprise and the Rule of Law is impossible to achieve. Before reaching this conclusion, however, we should consider exactly what the deconstruction of the understanding/misunderstanding privileging has accomplished. Once again, Culler's thoughts on the matter prove instructive:

Attacks on deconstructionists . . . frequently emphasize that if all reading is misreading, then the notions of meaning, value, and authority promoted by our institutions are threatened. Each reader's reading would be as valid or legitimate as another, and neither teachers nor texts could preserve their wonted authority. What such inversions do, though, is displace the question, leading one to consider what are the processes of legitimation, validation, or authorization that produce differences among readings and enable one reading to expose another as a misreading. In the same way, identification of the normal as a special case of the deviant helps one to question the

---

92. J. CULLER, *supra* note 1, at 176. The same arguments may be applied to my interpretation of Derrida in this Article. By interpreting Derrida, I present his ideas in a necessarily selective and ordered fashion. My reading of Derrida is partial, and therefore, may be classified as a "misreading" in the more general sense Culler describes. However, to use Culler's phrase, I would argue that it is a misreading whose misses do not matter much.

775

institutional forces and practices that institute the normal by marking or excluding the deviant.

In general, inversions of hierarchical oppositions expose to debate the institutional arrangements that rely on the hierarchies and thus open possibilities of change—possibilities which may well come to little but which may also at some point prove critical.[93]

Put another way, the deconstructive reversal has not demonstrated that all readings of *Brown v. Board of Education* are equally legitimate, but rather has called into question the ways in which we decide that a given interpretation of *Brown* is illegitimate. This issue is important for two reasons. First, our justifications of what are "proper" interpretations of a text are not always consistent.[94] Second, our method of privileging interpretations as appropriate or inappropriate is often tantamount to deciding a legal issue. It becomes the process by which we formulate legal doctrine, and will serve to foster or foreclose later doctrinal developments.

We may make a comparison here with the use of deconstruction to privilege legal concepts informed by ideological thinking. Just as deconstruction does not prove the bankruptcy of all social visions but rather affirms the many possible characterizations of social life, so too the decon-

---

93. *Id.* at 179.

94. For example, there are clauses of the Constitution we would probably read quite literally, confining our interpretations to the plain meaning of the words. *E.g.*, U.S. CONST. art. II, § 1, cl. 5 (president must be at least 35 years old). Other clauses, like the equal protection clause, are more ambiguous and require a fuller theory of interpretation, which would no doubt be more controversial. In still other cases, we read the Constitution in ways clearly at odds with the ordinary meaning of its language. The Eleventh Amendment, for example, literally bans all suits, in law or equity, against a state by citizens of another state. U.S. CONST. amend. XI. Yet the amendment is most often invoked to bar suits by citizens against their own state, *e.g.*, Edelman v. Jordan, 415 U.S. 651 (1974). Suits in equity against a state are permitted through the fiction of suing a state officer in her official capacity, *e.g.*, Ex Parte Young, 209 U.S. 123 (1908); suits for monetary damages are permitted if the relief sought is prospective rather than retrospective, *e.g.*, *Edelman*, 415 U.S. at 664, 668. Even suits for retrospective relief in the form of damages are permitted, if the state is held to waive its immunity. *Id.* at 671-74.

Ironically, the rule for determining waiver is that a state will be deemed to have waived its immunity "only where stated 'by the most express language or by such overwhelming implications from the text as [will] leave no room for any other reasonable construction.'" *Id.* at 673 (quoting Murray v. Wilson Distilling Co., 213 U.S. 151, 171 (1909)). This interpretive principle is quite at odds with the principles used to interpret the Eleventh Amendment itself.

Our use of different methods of reading constitutional and statutory texts does not necessarily mean that we are contradicting ourselves. We could defend different hermeneutical principles for interpreting waiver under the Eleventh Amendment and for interpreting the amendment itself on the grounds that the rules for statutory interpretation must be different from those for divining the meaning of the Constitution. A similar explanation could be developed to show why the Eleventh Amendment should be interpreted differently than other clauses of the Constitution. Rather, deconstruction calls these interpretive practices into question and requires us to articulate a political and legal theory to explain the differences. This process also may cause us to reevaluate our hermeneutical practices. *Compare* Atascadero State Hosp. v. Scanlon, 105 S. Ct. 3142 (1985) (defending current Eleventh Amendment doctrines on general grounds of preserving federalism) *with Edelman*, 415 U.S. at 687-88 (Brennan, J., dissenting) (Eleventh Amendment immunity should be restricted to cases falling within its literal meaning: suits against a state brought by citizens of another state).

struction involved here is designed to create possibilities for interpretation rather than to foreclose them. In introducing deconstructive strategies to texts it cannot be stressed too much that freedom and nihilism are not the same thing.

The deconstructive critique of the privileging of readings over misreadings does have a further consequence, which may at first prove unsettling to lawyers: The simple (or intent-based) theory of interpretation of legal texts is necessarily incomplete. However, as I will now show, this consequence is actually necessary for the Rule of Law to operate in the manner we think it should.

B. *The Free Play of Text and the Rule of Law*

Someone says to me:

> "Shew the children a game." I teach them gaming with dice, and the other says "I didn't mean that sort of game." Must the exclusion of the game with dice have come before his mind when he gave me the order?[95]

One of the most important ideas that Derrida's work demonstrates is that if (as everyone thinks) we mean more than we say, we also say more than we mean. Our words seem to perform tricks that we had not intended, establish connections that we had not considered, lead to conclusions that were not present to our minds when we spoke or wrote. Students of statutory construction and the law of contracts are no doubt familiar with many examples of this phenomenon. This curious habit of our words to burst the seams of our intentions and to produce their own kind of logic is what Derrida labels the free "play" of text.[96]

For Derrida, what we did not intend to say is as interesting as what we did intend. That is why so much of his work makes use of puns, or investigates how what a text says refers to itself or what it does. Much of deconstructive criticism involves the discovery of unintended connections between words. One reason for looking for such connections is that they may condense or crystallize important ideas that are already present in a text. (This is one reason we find slogans and aphorisms so effective in conveying ideas.) But there is a more important reason to investigate the unintended connections between the words in our texts. It is simply a

---

95. L. WITTGENSTEIN, PHILOSOPHICAL INVESTIGATIONS § 70 (1953).

96. *See, e.g.,* WRITING AND DIFFERENCE, *supra* note 1, at 292 ("Play is the disruption of presence."). A more trivial, yet classic, example of unexpected connections between words is the common pun. Derrida's work often relies on puns to emphasize connections among ideas in a text. *See, e.g.,* DISSEMINATION, *supra* note 1, at 65–171, 173–285 ("Plato's Pharmacy" and "The Double Session").

777

logocentric bias on our part to think that the most important meanings in a text are those the author intended to put there.

In literature, the critic does not think less of her interpretation of *Moby Dick* because Melville did not see the same connections as he composed his work. A philosopher does not think less of her critique of the *Phaedo* when she discovers a connection between ideas that Plato did not recognize in his text. Indeed, there is generally great critical importance in discovering that a text says more than the author meant it to say, or that the logic of a text leads to an unexpected difficulty or contradiction. Often, hidden flaws or strengths in a work of literature or philosophical treatise only become apparent over time. Legal texts, like other texts, often present later readers with new meanings, connections, and difficulties that their creators did not contemplate. These meanings are uncovered by the interpretations of successive readers in different historical and cultural contexts.

There are two different reasons that one might be concerned with unintended connections. The first is not Derrida's purpose, although the second is. One might use unintended meanings in a legal text to criticize the reasoning of the author. In her dissent in *City of Akron v. Akron Center for Reproductive Health*,[97] Justice O'Connor argued that the viability-based doctrine of *Roe v. Wade*[98] would self-destruct as the point of the fetus' viability came earlier and earlier during pregnancy while technology assured that the time at which abortions were virtually risk free to the mother came later and later.[99] This consequence of the *Roe* decision was not envisioned by its author, Justice Blackmun, and Justice O'Connor believed that this unintended consequence was an important criticism of the logic of Justice Blackmun's opinion.

On the other hand, the discovery of unintended connections and difficulties may not involve any criticism of the author at all. A good example is our current understanding of the equal protection clause. The drafters of the equal protection clause probably did not contemplate that one day its words would strike constitutional scholars and judges as requiring equality between men and women. However, when we read the equal protection clause today, with an expansive notion of equality that would have greatly upset the framers of that amendment, we do not mean to

---

97. 462 U.S. 416, 458 (1983) (O'Connor, J., dissenting).
98. 410 U.S. 113 (1973).
99. The *Roe* framework . . . is clearly on a collision course with itself. As the medical risks of various abortion procedures decrease, the point at which the State may regulate for reasons of maternal health is moved further forward to actual childbirth. As medical science becomes better able to provide for the separate existence of the fetus, the point of viability is moved further back toward conception.
462 U.S. at 458.

criticize their choice of words. Indeed, we demonstrate how their linguistic commitment to equality has brought us to a deeper political commitment to equality. We celebrate the manner in which the authors' words have worked themselves pure in spite of the authors' intentions.

When Derrida hunts for unseen connections in a text, he is usually not attempting to discover errors in the thought of the author. His is not the sort of task that Justice O'Connor undertook in the *Akron* case. Instead, he is looking for the type of connections that no author can avoid because no author intends them. Derrida seeks to understand the gap between what the author commands by her language and what the language performs—the uncontrollable incongruity in human language and thought. As Barbara Johnson explains, "the deconstructive reading does not point out the flaws or weaknesses or stupidities of an author, but the *necessity* with which what he *does* see is systematically related to what he does *not* see."[100]

There is an important connection between the principle of the "free play" of text and Derrida's theory of the sign. For Derrida, a sign can only signify to the extent that it can signify repeatedly, in a number of different contexts. The essential property of the sign is its iterability. It follows from Derrida's theory of the sign that we can use signs if and only if they are separable from our intent—if and only if they "mean" whether or not they mean what we intend. Thus, if I write a heartfelt love letter to my girlfriend, in order to communicate my most deeply felt sentiments through language, it must also be possible for the same words to be written insincerely, in jest, or even through random creation by a computer program. Language can signify only if it can escape the actual present meaning it had to the person who used it.[101]

This surprising conclusion stems from the fact that signs can only be used for communication if they are public. They must be capable of repetition and manipulation by any possible user.[102] But the public nature of communication necessitates that signs signify repeatedly, regardless of the presence or absence of a present meaning that informs them. A piece of graffiti continues to signify as long as it remains on the wall. Thus, to the extent that B can understand A, it is A's (iterable) signs, and not A's intention, which permits this understanding.

Moreover, the essence of the sign, iterability, carries with it the notion of a repetition of the same in a different context. Language can only operate to the extent that it is repeatable, but language is repeatable only to

---

100. Johnson, *supra* note 1, at xv.
101. *See* MARGINS OF PHILOSOPHY, *supra* note 1, at 317.
102. *Id.* at 315.

the extent that what A says means something, albeit not identical to what A meant, to another person B. According to Derrida:

> [I]t belongs to the sign to be legible, even if the moment of its production is irremediably lost, and even if I do not know what its alleged author-scriptor meant consciously and intentionally at the moment he wrote it, that is[,] abandoned it to its essential drifting . . . . [B]y virtue of its essential iterability[,] one can always lift a written syntagma from the interlocking chain in which it is caught or given without making it lose every possibility of functioning, if not every possibility of "communicating," precisely.[103]

The structural precondition of the sign is its ability to break free from the author, and to mean other than what the author meant. The very act of "meaning" something creates a chasm between the sign and the producer's intention. This detachability makes iterability, and thus intersubjective meaning, possible. The repetition of the sign in the new context is simultaneously a relation of identity and difference; the repeated sign is syntactically identical, yet semantically different. The result is that the text, as it is repeatedly understood, takes on a life of its own in a relation of *différance* with the person who "meant" it:

> [A]t the very moment when someone would like to say or to write, "On the twentieth . . . etc.," the very factor that will permit the mark (be it psychic, oral, graphic) to function beyond this moment—namely the possibility of its being repeated *another* time—breaches, divides, expropriates the "ideal" plenitude or self-presence of intention, of meaning (to say) and, *a fortiori*, of all adequation between meaning and saying. Iterability alters, contaminating parasitically what it identifies and enables to repeat "itself"; it leaves us no choice but to mean (to say) something that is (already, always, also) other than what we mean (to say) . . . .[104]

Derrida's aphorism, "iterability alters,"[105] is a shorthand way of saying that once the signifier leaves the author's creation and is let loose upon the world, it takes on a life of its own in the other contexts in which it can be repeated.[106] The liberation of the text from the author at the moment of creation results in the free play of the text.

---

103. *Id.* at 317.
104. *Limited Inc abc, supra* note 1, at 200.
105. *Id.* Derrida also makes a pun on the two possible origins of the word "iterable": "iter-," or "again," comes from the Sanskrit "itera," or "other." The philological ploy suggests that repetition differentiates even as it imitates. *Id.*
106. Under the simple theory of interpretation, we might still insist that the text has a meaning independent from its context: a clearly definable "core" of meaning that cannot be varied by context. According to this theory, context affects only the "peripheral" meanings of the text while preserving

Moreover, if the meaning of a signifier is context bound, context is boundless—that is, there are always new contexts that will serve to increase the different meanings of a signifier.[107] This should come as no surprise to a legal thinker: The words in a statute or in a case used as precedent take on new meanings in new factual contexts, and cannot be confined to a limited number of meanings. There are an indefinite number of possible contexts in which a given legal text could be read. For this reason, a text is always threatening to overflow into an indefinite number of different significations.[108]

Most of us assume that the Rule of Law requires that legal materials will be essentially determinate in meaning; that there will be a privileged interpretation of a legal text. If a text had many meanings, and no one "authentic" or privileged meaning, it would be impossible to treat like cases alike according to general and knowable universal principles equally applicable to all citizens. Moreover, if a text had many equally valid interpretations, no interpretation could have an exclusive claim to legitimacy and command the respect of all citizens.

The simple theory of interpretation seems to offer us just such a privileged interpretation. It provides that the privileged interpretation of a legal text is the one consistent with the intention of the author who created it. The simple theory has two advantages. First, it avoids the uncertainty and arbitrariness that would follow if all interpretations were equally valid. It creates the possibility of a single, knowable interpretation of legal materials, which can be applied in a non-arbitrary fashion to all citizens.

---

the "core." Thus, context is only supplementary to the basic, unchanging meaning of the text.

The "core/periphery" distinction can be deconstructed by noting that the "core" depends as much on the context as the "periphery" does. Both the core and the periphery are context dependent. The core meaning of the word "cow" provides a simple example. If two parties have adopted a code for contracts involving livestock where "cow" means "horse," the core meaning of "cow" will shift radically. This may look like a trick, but it is the "normal" context in which we use the word "cow" that gives us its "core" meaning.

In Derrida's terminology, context is a dangerous supplement to the meaning of a text. "Context" indicates both that which accompanies the text (con- as in convocation) and that which is posed against the text, or which the text is read against (con- as in contra). Both readings are important, for the text is both dependent upon and differentiated from its context. Text and context thus exist in a relation of *différance*. There is no text without a context.

107. *See* J. CULLER, *supra* note 1, at 123–28.

108. I use the word "indefinite" and not "infinite." What is important is not the number of possible new contexts, but their unexpectedness. Theoretically, it always should be possible to derive an infinite number of meanings from a text if we are willing to acknowledge all sorts of bizarre ways of reading the text. However, some of these contexts are probably irrelevant in the further context of our legal institutions. (For example, one might look for meanings in a legal text by searching for hidden anagrams that stated a rule.) Although we can be sure that some contexts will be irrelevant, we cannot predict which contexts *will* be relevant in the future. The number of such contexts may not be infinite, but it is indefinite. We cannot create an all-inclusive list in advance. To use an earlier example, what makes the equal protection clause uncanny in its moral force is the unexpected nature of classifications we may come to see in time as requiring equal treatment or permitting differential treatment.

781

39

Second, the simple theory establishes the legitimacy of the interpretation, for it adopts the meaning of the author (judge, framer, or legislator) who had the authority to create the legal text in the first place. Thus, at first glance, the Rule of Law appears to reject the idea of the free play of text and to embrace instead the simple theory of interpretation: The meaning of a legal text is the meaning of its author, which does not change as the text is introduced into new factual situations or contexts.

However, the grounding of the Rule of Law on the privileging of the author's intent can be deconstructed, and then we see that the relation of the Rule of Law to the author's intent is not so unambiguous. We discover that the Rule of Law must also depend upon the free play of legal texts, an idea which bears a relationship of *différance* to the simple theory of interpretation.

Let us consider, as an example, a published opinion of a judge appearing in a case reporter. What is the legal effect of this opinion on subsequent cases? The simple theory of interpretation would suggest that (if the precedent is binding) what the judge/author intended is the principle that controls succeeding cases. However, this will not do. The intent of the author does not control, but rather the interpretation of the author's intent as derived by subsequent readers of the text controls. It is the text as read, and not the text as written, that becomes the law.

The principle of iterability explains this result. The Rule of Law cannot operate unless legal materials (which in theory, are what bind persons) are iterable. The Rule of Law presupposes that the same corpus of legal materials will be applied to case A as to case B. If a different rule were applied in each case we would not have the Rule of Law.[109] However, the author's present intent when she creates legal materials is not iterable; it is forever lost at the moment of creation. All that remains is the sign, the existence of which makes intersubjective communication possible. The iterability of the sign of the author's intent, and not the intent itself, is essential to the operation of the Rule of Law.

In addition, the Rule of Law is based upon the premise that it is not the individual wills of people that control, but laws passed by elected representatives or case law construed and developed by judges. Rule by the arbitrary will of persons would violate the Liberal principle of autonomy;[110] social coercion is not achieved according to arbitrary will, but ac-

---

109. I pass over the obvious difficulty that the corpus of laws is constantly changing, so that if case B appears later in time than case A, different legal rules may apply to it. This is a problem for the theory of the Rule of Law, not for my deconstruction.

110. The principle of autonomy holds that persons should be free from coercion by the arbitrary will of another. *See* F. HAYEK, THE CONSTITUTION OF LIBERTY 139–40 (1960). Recognition of legal rights according to the Rule of Law preserves this principle by preventing inconsistent and arbitrary treatment of persons. *Id.*.

cording to general, equally applicable rules. Once the rules are established by the governing authority, the rules constitute the authority for deciding cases. Thus, the Rule of Law presupposes that texts rule, and not the persons who created them.

Of course, in deciding the proper application of the rule, we look to the purpose of the governing body that created it. However, that body may not have had a single purpose or it may not have explicitly considered the factual situation at issue. Indeed, many of the legislators may not have read the measure thoroughly before voting on it.

The "purpose" used by a legal interpreter or decisionmaker is not the pure present purpose of the creator of the legal text. Instead, it is a constructed purpose: a reading of the text (a statute or decision) and of other texts (legislative history) in a particular context. The "purpose" that we discover and use in the application of a legal rule comes from texts, and not from the author.

Moreover, the Rule of Law *requires* that a legal text be separated from the purpose present in the mind of the creator of the text. As an example, suppose that airlines lobby for the passage of a law that sets minimum prices for airfares. Assume that legislator A voted for the bill in return for a favor from legislator B. This is not the kind of purpose that a judge can use to construe a statute's operation in a particular context. Nor could A's intent to receive a bribe in exchange for a vote be properly considered. The Rule of Law ultimately relies upon a distinction between proper and improper interpretive purposes. This distinction, in turn, can be deconstructed, but my point here is that the decisionmaker who seeks a purpose must reconstitute, reconstruct, or interpret a purpose from still other interpretations or signs. She must separate those purposes which are "appropriate" from those which are inappropriate. This act of discovery is an interpretation and deferral of "presence," i.e., the purpose "present" to the mind of the creator of the legal text at the time of its creation, and indeed, may even be a rejection of it.

Another example may prove instructive. Assume that the sole purpose of price control regulation is to benefit the airline industry. After intense lobbying, the legislators are convinced that they need to outlaw "cutthroat competition" among the airlines. Suppose that economic conditions then change, and the airlines will lose revenue unless they can increase volume by dropping their prices below the minimum price levels. We would not read the statute to mean that minimum prices no longer control, even though that would achieve the authors' purpose of benefiting the airline industry. Rather, we must admit that the text of the statute has taken on a life of its own, apart from the original purpose of the legislators who created it.

783

41

The statute's claim to legal authority is derived not from the intent of its framers, but from its present signification. The institutional rules that give binding authority to acts of government recognize the sign (the text) and not the signified (the purpose). The Rule of Law presupposes that the only legitimate solution to the change in economic conditions is to pass a new statute repealing the old price support legislation.[111]

The simple theory of interpretation is a logocentric theory, relying upon the "presence" of the author's intent at the moment of textual creation. By deconstructing, or "ungrounding" it, we see that the Rule of Law depends upon the free play of text, as much as it depends upon the author's intent. From this deconstruction emerge two mutually differentiated and dependent visions of interpretative practice:

> The one seeks to decipher, dreams of deciphering a truth or an origin which escapes play and the order of the sign, and which lives the necessity of interpretation as an exile. The other, which is no longer turned toward the origin, affirms play and tries to pass beyond [the] man . . . who . . . [—]throughout his entire history—has dreamed of full presence, the reassuring foundation, the origin and the end of play . . . .
>
> There are more than enough indications today to suggest we might perceive that these two interpretations of interpretation—which are absolutely irreconcilable even if we live them simultaneously and reconcile them in an obscure economy—together share the field which we call, in such a problematic fashion, the social sciences.
>
> For my part, although these two interpretations must acknowledge and accentuate their difference and define their irreducibility, I do not believe that today there is any question of *choosing*—in the first place because here we are in a region (let us say, provisionally, a region of historicity) where the category of choice seems particularly

---

111. The same arguments apply to the interpretation of judicial opinions. If the simple theory of interpretation were required by the Rule of Law, we might be tempted to try to solve today's difficult problems of constitutional law by communicating with the spirit of Chief Justice Marshall, and by asking him what exactly he meant in Marbury v. Madison, 5 U.S. (1 Cranch) 137 (1803). However, I hope that the reader will find something odd about this solution, aside from the idea that judges should be performing seances or raising the dead. Like the Constitution itself, *Marbury* as text has meanings that live on independently of the meanings of its creator. Therefore, even the author of the text, were he here to communicate with us, would not have a monopoly on the "real" meaning of *Marbury.* Rather, we understand intuitively that the author has already had his "bite at the apple." Once he has expressed himself, it is the opinion that binds future judges. This, too, is a necessary consequence of the Rule of Law.

Of course, if a Supreme Court Justice writes an opinion, she does, in a sense, have a "second bite at the apple" because she will be able to vote for subsequent applications of the original opinion. But her interpretation of her own writing will not be conclusive; she will have to convince four other Justices. The point is easier to understand if one considers a Justice who retires after writing a given opinion. In subsequent cases, it would be inappropriate to ask her what she meant in her opinion and to accept her views as binding.

trivial; and in the second, because we must first try to conceive of the common ground, and the *différance* of this irreducible difference.[112]

The purpose of the deconstruction is not to establish that any interpretation of a text is acceptable, but that the yearning for originary meaning in the simple theory of interpretation is incomplete and cannot serve as a foundation for interpretation. We must, to some degree, acknowledge the free play of the text. However, as Derrida notes above, there can be no question of choosing the free play of legal texts as a new ground for interpretative practice, a fact that critics of original intent theory may too easily forget. The intent theory and a theory of free play must coexist in an uneasy alliance in which neither can be master nor servant. The relation of *différance* between them prevents either from serving as an originary ground of interpretative practice.

Of course, I have only considered two possible approaches to interpretation: one that looks to the intent of the author, and one that acknowledges the free play of the text. Derrida's critique, however, extends much further. As soon as the author's original intent is displaced as the foundation of interpretative practice, the critic finds that she must substitute a new ground for her interpretative theory, and this theory too, must depend upon and define itself in terms of that which it excludes. Thus, the critic who replaces "original intent" by "intersubjective meaning," "historical development," or "shared consensus of values," must reinstitute a new form of presence, which is subject to further deconstruction.[113]

---

112. WRITING AND DIFFERENCE, *supra* note 1, at 292-93.

113. Consider, for example, theorists who advocate using tradition, moral consensus, or conventional morality as the basis of constitutional interpretation. *See, e.g.*, Lupu, *Untangling the Strands of the Fourteenth Amendment*, 77 MICH. L. REV. 981, 985, 1040-41 (1979); Perry, *Substantive Due Process Revisited: Reflections on (and Beyond) Recent Cases*, 71 Nw. U.L. REV. 417, 425 (1976); Wellington, *Common Law Rules and Constitutional Double Standards: Some Notes on Adjudication*, 83 YALE L.J. 221, 284 (1973). Such a proposal involves a privileging of traditional over nontraditional values, of non-controversial over controversial attitudes, and of conventional over nonconventional morality. Dean Ely deconstructs this privileging by showing that arguments for this interpretative theory undo themselves: "[P]art of the point of the Constitution is to check today's majority . . . . 'If the Constitution protects only interests which comport with traditional values, the persons most likely to be penalized for their way of life will be those least likely to receive judicial protection.'" J. ELY, DEMOCRACY AND DISTRUST 62 (1980) (quoting Karst, *The Supreme Court, 1976 Term Foreword: Equal Citizenship Under the Fourteenth Amendment*, 91 HARV. L. REV. 70, 136 (1977)). Thus, the argument for enforcing the privileged concept, traditional values, becomes an argument for enforcing the excluded concept, non-traditional values. Similarly, one can show that the argument for enforcing values agreed upon by a majority of the public deconstructs itself. As Ely notes, "it makes no sense to employ the value judgments of the majority as the vehicle for protecting minorities from the value judgments of the majority." *Id.* at 69.

785

III. CONCLUSION

Deconstruction by its very nature is an analytic tool and not a synthetic one. It can displace a hierarchy momentarily, it can shed light on otherwise hidden dependences of concepts, but it cannot propose new hierarchies of thought or substitute new foundations. These are by definition logocentric projects, which deconstruction defines itself against. Deconstruction is thus revelatory, and what the legal theorist does with the revelation is not dictated by the deconstruction itself, nor could it be.

In theory then, deconstructive readings of legal texts can be a tool of analysis for the right as well as for the left. In practice, left legal scholars will probably make more use of deconstructive techniques for two reasons: first, because of the historical connection between continental philosophy and left political thought, and second, because the left usually has more to gain from showing the ideological character of the *status quo* than does the right.[114]

Deconstructive readings, at least in the sense used in this Article, do not demonstrate that legal thought is incoherent any more than they demonstrate that all forms of logocentric practice are incoherent. Similarly, deconstructive readings do not demonstrate that legal thought is any more irrational than any other form of logocentric thought. Rather, what deconstruction demonstrates is the *différance* between what is privileged and what is excluded in legal thought. Deconstruction thus reveals the antinomal character of legal thought, a characterization which is at first disturbing, but in the end is the best description of our actual experience in using legal concepts.

---

114. On the other hand, an economic libertarian might well use deconstructive techniques to criticize the modern welfare state on the grounds that it rests upon a false privileging of certain aspects of human nature.

FEMINIST LEGAL METHODS

Katharine T. Bartlett*

Legal methods are the basic tools that lawyers and legal scholars use. Critics of law have sought to challenge and develop alternatives to traditional methodologies. In this Article, Professor Bartlett identifies and critically examines a set of feminist legal methods. These techniques, grounded in women's experiences of exclusion, include "asking the woman question," feminist practical reasoning, and consciousness-raising. Each of these methods is both critical and constructive, and helps to reveal features of a legal issue that more traditional methods tend to overlook or suppress. Professor Bartlett then addresses the epistemological implications of feminist legal methods by examining the nature of the claims to truth that they generate. After analyzing three theories of knowledge reflected in feminist legal writing — rational empiricism, standpoint epistemology, and postmodernism — Professor Bartlett offers a fourth approach, positionality, which she believes provides for feminists the best explanation of what it means to be "right" in law. Positionality retains a concept of nonarbitrary truth based upon experience, yet because it deems truth situated and provisional rather than

* Professor of Law, Duke University School of Law. Many people helped me with this Article. Among these, Paul Carrington, Peter Gabel, Rosanne Kennedy, Toni Massaro, Martha Minow, Judith Resnik, Deborah Rhode, Tom Rowe, Joseph Singer, and William Van Alstyne took the time to review a draft and to give me useful comments and suggestions. I leaned especially heavily on Chris Schroeder and Jeff Powell, who on numerous occasions put aside their own work to help me figure out mine. Twenty-seven Duke law students enrolled in my seminar in Feminist Legal Theory in the fall 1989 semester helped me to think through many of the issues I raise in this Article, primarily by pressing me to show how my own theories did not contain the same weaknesses I found in the writings of others. Finally, although they claim not to be able to understand my work, my mother Elizabeth Clark Bartlett and my grandmother Katharine Tiffany Clark passed on to me the optimism about human goodness and the human capacity for mutual understanding that grounds this work. I thank all of these people.

I had wanted to humanize and particularize the authors whose ideas I used in this Article by giving their first as well as last names. Unfortunately, the editors of the *Harvard Law Review*, who otherwise have been most cooperative, insisted upon adhering to the "time-honored" Bluebook convention of using last names only, *see* A UNIFORM SYSTEM OF CITATION 91 (14th ed. 1986), except when the writing is a "book," in which case the first initial is given, *id.* at 83, and except when the writing is by a student, in which case no name whatsoever is given (unless the student has a name like "Bruce Ackerman," in which case "it may be indicated parenthetically," *id.* at 91), *see id.* In these rules, I see hierarchy, rigidity, and depersonalization, of the not altogether neutral variety. First names have been one dignified way in which women could distinguish themselves from their fathers and their husbands. I apologize to the authors whose identities have been obscured in the apparently higher goals of Bluebook orthodoxy.

external or final, it obligates feminists to use their methods to continue to extend and transform this truth.

I. INTRODUCTION

A. "Doing" and "Knowing" in Law

IN what sense can legal methods be "feminist"? Are there specific methods that feminist lawyers share? If so, what are these methods, why are they used, and what significance do they have to feminist practice? Put another way, what do feminists mean when they say they are doing law,[1] and what do they mean when, having done law, they claim to be "right"?

Feminists have developed extensive critiques of law[2] and proposals for legal reform.[3] Feminists have had much less to say, however, about what the "doing" of law should entail and what truth status to give to the legal claims that follow. These methodological issues matter because methods shape one's view of the possibilities for legal practice and reform. Method "organizes the apprehension of truth; it determines what counts as evidence and defines what is taken as verification."[4] Feminists cannot ignore method, because if they seek to challenge existing structures of power with the same methods that

---

[1] Although many individuals participate in doing and making law, *see* Dalton, *Where We Stand: Observations on the Situation of Feminist Legal Thought*, 3 BERKELEY WOMEN'S L.J. 1, 2 & n.2 (1987–1988), this Article is primarily about "doing law" in the limited sense encompassed by the professional activities of practicing lawyers, lawmakers, law professors, and judges.

[2] These critiques have ranged from attacks on specific legal rulings to deconstructions of fundamental concepts of modern law. Among the major feminist critiques of the last decade are Freedman, *Sex Equality, Sex Differences, and the Supreme Court*, 92 YALE L.J. 913 (1983); Harris, *Race and Essentialism in Feminist Legal Theory*, 42 STAN. L. REV. (forthcoming 1990); Kay, *Models of Equality*, 1985 U. ILL. L. REV. 39; Law, *Rethinking Sex and the Constitution*, 132 U. PA. L. REV. 955 (1984); Littleton, *Reconstructing Sexual Equality*, 75 CALIF. L. REV. 1279 (1987); MacKinnon, *Feminism, Marxism, Method, and the State: An Agenda for Theory*, 7 SIGNS 515 (1982) [hereinafter MacKinnon, *Agenda for Theory*]; MacKinnon, *Feminism, Marxism, Method, and the State: Toward Feminist Jurisprudence*, 8 SIGNS 635 (1983) [hereinafter MacKinnon, *Toward Feminist Jurisprudence*]; Minow, *The Supreme Court, 1986 Term — Foreword: Justice Engendered*, 101 HARV. L. REV. 10 (1987); Olsen, *Statutory Rape: A Feminist Critique of Rights*, 63 TEX. L. REV. 387 (1984); Scales, *The Emergence of Feminist Jurisprudence: An Essay*, 95 YALE L.J. 1373 (1986); Schneider, *The Dialectic of Rights and Politics: Perspectives from the Women's Movement*, 61 N.Y.U. L. REV. 589 (1986); Taub & Schneider, *Perspectives on Women's Subordination and the Role of Law*, in THE POLITICS OF LAW: A PROGRESSIVE CRITIQUE 117 (D. Kairys ed. 1982); West, *Jurisprudence and Gender*, 55 U. CHI. L. REV. 1 (1988); and W. Williams, *The Equality Crisis: Some Reflections on Culture, Courts and Feminism*, 7 WOMEN'S RTS. L. REP. 175 (1982).

[3] These proposals cover a broad range of subject matters and political agendas. In addition to the literature cited above in note 2, see sources cited below in notes 164–70.

[4] MacKinnon, *Agenda for Theory*, *supra* note 2, at 527.

have defined what counts within those structures, they may instead "recreate the illegitimate power structures [that they are] trying to identify and undermine."[5]

Method matters also because without an understanding of feminist methods, feminist claims in the law will not be perceived as legitimate or "correct." I suspect that many who dismiss feminism as trivial or inconsequential misunderstand it. Feminists have tended to focus on defending their various substantive positions or political agendas, even among themselves. Greater attention to issues of method may help to anchor these defenses, to explain why feminist agendas often appear so radical (or not radical enough), and even to establish some common ground among feminists.

As feminists articulate their methods, they can become more aware of the nature of what they do, and thus do it better. Thinking about method is empowering. When I require myself to explain what I do, I am likely to discover how to improve what I earlier may have taken for granted. In the process, I am likely to become more committed to what it is that I have improved. This likelihood, at least, is a central premise of this Article and its primary motivation.

I begin this Article by addressing the meaning of the label "feminist," and the difficulties and the necessity of using that label. I then set forth in Part II a set of legal methods that I claim are feminist. All of these methods reflect the status of women as "outsiders," who need ways of challenging and undermining dominant legal conventions and of developing alternative conventions which take better account of women's experiences and needs. The methods analyzed in this Article include (1) identifying and challenging those elements of existing legal doctrine that leave out or disadvantage women and members of other excluded groups (asking the "woman question"); (2) reasoning from an ideal in which legal resolutions are pragmatic responses to concrete dilemmas rather than static choices between opposing, often mismatched perspectives (feminist practical reasoning); and (3) seeking insights and enhanced perspectives through collaborative or interactive engagements with others based upon personal experience and narrative (consciousness-raising).

As I develop these methods, I consider a number of methodological issues that feminists have not fully confronted and that are crucial to the potential growth of feminist legal theory and practice. I examine, for example, the relationship between feminist methods and substantive legal rules. Feminist methods emerged from feminist politics and find their justification, at least in part, in their ability to advance substantive feminist goals. Thus, one might argue that the methods

---

[5] Singer, *Should Lawyers Care About Philosophy?* (Book Review), 1989 DUKE L.J. (forthcoming).

I describe are not really methods at all, but rather substantive, partisan rules in the not-very-well-disguised shape of method. I argue, however, that the defense of any particular set of methods must rest not on whether it is nonsubstantive — an impossibility — but whether its relationship to substantive law is defensible. I defend the substantive elements of feminist methods and argue that these methods provide an appropriate constraint upon the application of substantive rules.

Throughout my analysis of feminist legal methods, I also critically examine the place of feminist methods within the general context of legal method. I reject the sharp dichotomy between abstract, deductive ("male") reasoning, and concrete, contextualized ("female") reasoning because it misdescribes both conventional understandings of legal method and feminist methods themselves. The differences between the two methodologies, I argue, relate less to differences in principles of logic than to differences in emphasis and in underlying ideals about rules. Traditional legal methods place a high premium on the predictability, certainty, and fixity of rules. In contrast, feminist legal methods, which have emerged from the critique that existing rules overrepresent existing power structures, value rule-flexibility and the ability to identify missing points of view.

After describing and analyzing feminist legal methods, I examine in Part III the nature of the claims to truth that those who use these methods can make. This examination is important because the status given to assertions of knowledge or truth establishes the significance of the methods that produce those assertions. A theory of knowledge that assumes the existence of objective truth accessible through rational or empirical inquiry, for example, has different methodological implications than a theory that treats knowledge as a question of special privilege, or one that denies its existence altogether. In Part III, I explore four theories of knowledge reflected in feminist legal writings: rational empiricism, standpoint epistemology, postmodernism, and positionality. I then describe the implications of each of these theories for feminist methods and politics. I conclude that the theory of positionality offers the best explanatory grounding for feminist knowledge. Positionality rejects both the objectivism of whole, fixed, impartial truth and the relativism of different-but-equal truths. It posits instead that being "correct" in law is a function of being situated in particular, partial perspectives upon which the individual is obligated to attempt to improve. This stance, I argue, identifies experience as a foundation for knowledge and shapes an openness to points of view that otherwise would seem natural to exclude. I close the Article by explaining that feminist methods are not only useful means to reach feminist goals, but also fundamental ends in themselves.

B. "Feminist" As a Descriptive Label

Although this Article necessarily represents a particular version of feminism, I refer to positions as feminist in a broad sense that encompasses a self-consciously critical stance toward the existing order with respect to the various ways it affects different women "as women."[6] Being feminist is a political choice about one's positions on a variety of contestable social issues. As Linda Gordon writes, "feminism . . . is not a 'natural' excretion of [woman's] experience but a controversial political interpretation and struggle, by no means universal to women."[7] Further, being feminist means owning up to the part one plays in a sexist society; it means taking responsibility — for the existence and for the transformation of "our gendered identity, our politics, and our choices."[8]

Use of the label "feminist" has substantial problems. First, it can create an expectation of feminist originality or invention that feminists do not intend and cannot fulfill. This expectation itself demonstrates a preoccupation with individual achievement and ownership at odds with the feminist emphasis on collective, relational discovery.[9] Fem-

---

[6] As I argue later, feminist method reaches other categories of exclusion as well. *See infra* pp. 847–49.

[7] Gordon, *What's New in Women's History*, in FEMINIST STUDIES/CRITICAL STUDIES 20, 30 (T. de Lauretis ed. 1986). I favor a definition of "feminist" that allows men, as well as women, to make this choice. Some feminists disagree. *See, e.g.*, Littleton, *supra* note 2, at 1294 n.91 (claiming that women's experiences are a necessary prerequisite to being feminist); *see also* C. MACKINNON, FEMINISM UNMODIFIED 55–57 (1987) (noting that men can be feminized by experiences such as rape, but that such identifications with women are temporary and unusual).

[8] Alcoff, *Cultural Feminism Versus Post-Structuralism: The Identity Crisis in Feminist Theory*, 13 SIGNS 405, 432 (1988).

Rosalind Delmar's definition of feminist is, for my purposes, one of the most useful: "at the very least a feminist is someone who holds that women suffer discrimination because of their sex, that they have specific needs which remain negated and unsatisfied, and that the satisfaction of these needs would require a radical change . . . in the social, economic and political order." Delmar, *What Is Feminism?*, in WHAT IS FEMINISM 8, 8 (J. Mitchell & A. Oakley eds. 1986). Deborah Rhode uses a similar definition in setting forth the three core assumptions of feminist critical theories: that gender is a central category for analysis; that equality between women and men is a crucial social objective; and that such equality for all women cannot be achieved without fundamental social transformation. *See* Rhode, *Feminist Critical Theories*, 42 STAN. L. REV. (forthcoming 1990).

[9] Martha Minow makes this point in a powerful way:

Why is it so important for feminism to be distinctive, as that notion has been understood? The preoccupation with distinctiveness shows a preoccupation with pinning things down: with knowing by categorizing and dividing, claiming, naming, and blaming, and with tracking ownership of things and ideas. Some would characterize these preoccupations as male. They also fit a description of Western cultural conceptions of knowledge, in contrast to Eastern and African conceptions. Fascination with tracing distinctive ownership of things and ideas risks distracting feminists from challenging the patterns of

inists acknowledge that some important aspects of their methods and theory have roots in other legal traditions. Although permeated by bias, these traditions nonetheless have elements that should be taken seriously.[10] Still, labeling methods or practices or attitudes as feminist identifies them as a chosen part of a larger, critical agenda originating in the experiences of gender subordination. Although not every component of feminist practice and reform is unique, these components together address a set of concerns not reached by existing traditions.

Second, use of the label "feminist" has contributed to a tendency within feminism to assume a definition of "woman" or a standard for "women's experiences" that is fixed, exclusionary, homogenizing, and oppositional, a tendency that feminists have criticized in others.[11] The tendency to treat woman as a single analytic category has a number of dangers. For one thing, it obscures — even denies — important differences among women and among feminists, especially differences in race, class, and sexual orientation, that ought to be taken into account.[12] If feminism addresses only oppressive practices that operate against white, privileged women, it may readjust the allocation of privilege, but fail either to reconstruct the social and legal significance of gender or to prove that its insights have the power to illuminate other categories of exclusion. Assuming a unified concept of "woman" also adopts a view of the subject that has been rendered highly problematic. Poststructural feminists have claimed that woman has no core identity but rather comprises multiple, overlapping social

thought that historically excluded women and risks forcing us to fight over the few, if any, remaining plots of ground left.

Minow, *Beyond Universality*, 1989 U. CHI. LEGAL F. 115, 131.

I discuss the feminist emphasis on collective discovery at pp. 863–65 below.

[10] In this belief, I am more generous than some other feminists have been to mainstream legal traditions. Although existing legal tools limit the scope of possible change, *see* A. LORDE, *The Master's Tools Will Never Dismantle the Master's House*, in SISTER OUTSIDER 110 (1984), I think it important not only to critique our traditions, but to acknowledge their useful — and in some respects subversive — features. *Cf.* Z. EISENSTEIN, THE RADICAL FUTURE OF LIBERAL FEMINISM 5 (1986) (arguing both that "the liberal underpinnings of feminist theory are essential to feminism [and that] the patriarchal underpinnings of liberal theory are also indispensable to liberalism").

[11] *See* J. GRIMSHAW, PHILOSOPHY AND FEMINIST THINKING 75–103 (1986); E. SPELMAN, INESSENTIAL WOMAN: PROBLEMS OF EXCLUSION IN FEMINIST THOUGHT (1988); Flax, *Postmodernism and Gender Relations in Feminist Theory*, 12 SIGNS 621, 633–34, 637–43 (1987); Harding, *The Instability of the Analytical Categories of Feminist Theory*, 11 SIGNS 645, 646–47 (1986); Minow, *Feminist Reason: Getting It and Losing It*, 38 J. LEGAL EDUC. 47 (1988).

[12] *See* M. FRYE, THE POLITICS OF REALITY: ESSAYS IN FEMINIST THEORY (1983); B. HOOKS, FEMINIST THEORY FROM MARGIN TO CENTER 17–65 (1984); Harris, *supra* note 2; Kline, *Race, Racism, and Feminist Legal Theory*, 12 HARV. WOMEN'S L.J. 115 (1989); Omolade, *Black Women and Feminism*, in THE FUTURE OF DIFFERENCE 247 (H. Eisenstein & A. Jardine eds. 1980); Rich, *Compulsory Heterosexuality and Lesbian Existence*, 5 SIGNS 631 (1980); Scales-Trent, *Black Women and the Constitution: Finding Our Place, Asserting Our Rights*, 24 HARV. C.R.-C.L. L. REV. 9 (1989). For a fuller discussion of this point, see pp. 847–49 below.

structures and discourses.[13] Using woman as a category of analysis implies a rejection of these claims, for it suggests that members of the category share a set of common, essential, ahistorical characteristics that constitute a coherent identity.[14]

Perhaps the most difficult problem of all with use of the terms "feminist" and "woman" is its tendency to reinstate what most feminists seek to abolish: the isolation and stigmatization of women.[15] All efforts to take account of difference face this central dilemma. Although ignoring difference means continued inequality and oppression based upon difference, using difference as a category of analysis can reinforce stereotyped thinking and thus the marginalized status of those within it.[16] Thus, in maintaining the category of woman or its corresponding political label "feminist" to define those who are degraded on account of their sex, feminists themselves strengthen the identification of a group that thereby becomes more easily degraded.

Despite these difficulties, these labels remain useful. Although feminists have been guilty of ethnocentrism and all too often fail to recognize that women's lives are heterogeneous, that women who have had similar experiences may disagree about political agendas, and that women's gender is only one of many sources of identity, gender remains a category that can help to analyze and improve our world.[17] To sustain feminism, feminists must use presently understandable categories, even while maintaining a critical posture toward their use. In this Article, I retain feminist as a label, and woman as an analytical category, while trying to be sensitive to the misleading or dangerous tendencies of this practice.[18] I try to acknowledge the extent to which

---

[13] See infra pp. 877–78.

[14] See Fraser & Nicholson, Social Criticism Without Philosophy: An Encounter Between Feminism and Postmodernism, in UNIVERSAL ABANDON? THE POLITICS OF POSTMODERNISM 96, 101 (A. Ross ed. 1988).

[15] See D. RILEY, AM I THAT NAME?: FEMINISM AND THE CATEGORY OF "WOMEN" IN HISTORY (1988). In reviewing Denise Riley's book, Ann Snitow puts the problem as follows: "How to use the category 'women' to take the category apart; how to be a woman, and make claims for women, without having that identity overdetermine one's fate." Snitow, What's in a Name?: Denise Riley's Categorical Imperatives, VOICE LITERARY SUPPLEMENT, Jan.–Feb. 1989, at 36.

[16] See Minow, Learning To Live with the Dilemma of Difference: Bilingual and Special Education, LAW & CONTEMP. PROBS., Spring 1985, at 157–58.

[17] As Susan Bordo writes, "dominance does not require homogeneity in order to function as dominant." Bordo, Feminist Skepticism and the "Maleness" of Philosophy, 85 J. PHIL. 619, 623 (1988).

[18] On this point, Clare Dalton writes:

[I]t may not be possible, ultimately, to 'transcend' the kinds of categories our current ways of thinking and imagining condemn us to use in order to make sense of our experience. But being self-conscious about the particular set of categories inhering in particular doctrine may at least enable us to expand our repertoire, and enlarge the

feminist methods and theory derive from, or are related to, familiar legal traditions. I also try to avoid — to the extent one can — the ever-present risks of ethnocentrism and of unitary and homogenizing overgeneralizations.[19] Where I fail, I hope I will be corrected, and that no failures, or corrections, will ever be deemed final.

II. FEMINIST DOING IN LAW

When feminists "do law," they do what other lawyers do: they examine the facts of a legal issue or dispute, they identify the essential features of those facts, they determine what legal principles should guide the resolution of the dispute, and they apply those principles to the facts. This process unfolds not in a linear, sequential, or strictly logical manner, but rather in a pragmatic, interactive manner. Facts determine which rules are appropriate, and rules determine which facts are relevant.[20] In doing law, feminists like other lawyers use a full range of methods of legal reasoning[21] — deduction, induction, analogy, and use of hypotheticals, policy, and other general principles.[22]

In addition to these conventional methods of doing law, however, feminists use other methods. These methods, though not all unique to feminists, attempt to reveal features of a legal issue which more traditional methods tend to overlook or suppress. One method, asking the woman question, is designed to expose how the substance of law may silently and without justification submerge the perspectives of women and other excluded groups. Another method, feminist practical reasoning, expands traditional notions of legal relevance to make legal decisionmaking more sensitive to the features of a case not

---

number of concrete alternatives available to use . . ., even while recognizing the limits of our culture.

Dalton, *An Essay in the Deconstruction of Contract Doctrine*, 94 YALE L.J. 997, 1113 n.507 (1985) (emphasis in original); *see also infra* note 159.

[19] *See infra* pp. 847–49.

[20] *See* K. SCHEPPELE, LEGAL SECRETS 95 (1988).

The mutual construction of facts and rules is an iterative process in which the facts of the case determine the legal categories that will be invoked which in turn determine how the facts will be sorted into those that are relevant and those that are irrelevant, which in turn determines which rules are to be invoked.

Id.

[21] *See* Littleton, *Feminist Jurisprudence: The Difference Method Makes* (Book Review), 41 STAN. L. REV. 751, 763–71 & 763 n.60 (1989).

[22] The literature about these and other conventional legal methods is legion. A few of the important works include S. BURTON, AN INTRODUCTION TO LAW AND LEGAL REASONING (1985); M. EISENBERG, THE NATURE OF THE COMMON LAW (1988); M. GOLDING, LEGAL REASONING (1984); E. LEVI, AN INTRODUCTION TO LEGAL REASONING (1949); N. MAC-CORMICK, LEGAL REASONING AND LEGAL THEORY (1978); Gordley, *Legal Reasoning: An Introduction*, 72 CALIF. L. REV. 138 (1984); and Wellman, *Practical Reasoning and Judicial Justification: Toward an Adequate Theory*, 57 U. COLO. L. REV. 45 (1985).

already reflected in legal doctrine. A third method, consciousness-raising, offers a means of testing the validity of accepted legal principles through the lens of the personal experience of those directly affected by those principles. In this Part, I describe and explore the implications of each of these feminist methods.

A. Asking the Woman Question

A question becomes a method when it is regularly asked. Feminists across many disciplines regularly ask a question — a set of questions, really — known as "the woman question,"[23] which is designed to identify the gender implications of rules and practices which might otherwise appear to be neutral or objective. In this section, I describe the method of asking the woman question in law as a primary method of feminist critique, and discuss the relationship between this method and the substance of feminist goals and practice. I also show how this method reaches beyond questions of gender to exclusions based upon other characteristics as well.

1. The Method. — The woman question asks about the gender implications of a social practice or rule: have women been left out of consideration? If so, in what way; how might that omission be corrected? What difference would it make to do so? In law, asking the woman question means examining how the law fails to take into account the experiences and values that seem more typical of women than of men, for whatever reason, or how existing legal standards and concepts might disadvantage women. The question assumes that some features of the law may be not only nonneutral in a general sense, but also "male" in a specific sense. The purpose of the woman question is to expose those features and how they operate, and to suggest how they might be corrected.[24]

---

[23] *See, e.g.,* Gould, *The Woman Question: Philosophy of Liberation and the Liberation of Philosophy,* in WOMEN AND PHILOSOPHY: TOWARD A THEORY OF LIBERATION 5 (C. Gould & M. Wartofsky eds. 1976) (discussing the woman question in philosophy); Hawkesworth, *Feminist Rhetoric: Discourses on the Male Monopoly of Thought,* 16 POL. THEORY 444, 452–56 (1988) (examining the treatment of the woman question in political theory). The first use of the term "woman question" of which I am aware is in S. DE BEAUVOIR, THE SECOND SEX at xxvi (1957).

[24] In her thoughtful article on feminist jurisprudence, Heather Wishik suggests a series of questions that could all be characterized as "asking the woman question." *See* Wishik, *To Question Everything: The Inquiries of Feminist Jurisprudence,* 1 BERKELEY WOMEN'S L.J. 64, 72–77 (1985). Wishik proposes that feminists ask:

(1) What have been and what are now all women's experiences of the 'Life Situation' addressed by the doctrine, process, or area of law under examination? (2) What assumptions, descriptions, assertions and/or definitions of experience — male, female, or ostensibly gender neutral — does the law make in this area? . . . (3) What is the area of mismatch, distortion, or denial created by the differences between women's life experiences and the law's assumptions or imposed structures? . . . (4) What patriarchal interests are served by the mismatch? . . . (5) What reforms have been proposed in this

Women have long been asking the woman question in law. The legal impediments associated with being a woman were, early on, so blatant that the question was not so much whether women were left out, but whether the omission was justified by women's different roles and characteristics. American women such as Elizabeth Cady Stanton and Abigail Adams may seem today all too modest and tentative in their demands for improvements in women's legal status.[25] Yet while social stereotypes and limited expectations for women may have blinded women activists in the eighteenth and nineteenth centuries, their demands for the vote, for the right of married women to make contracts and own property, for other marriage reforms, and for birth control[26] challenged legal rules and social practices that, to others in their day, constituted the God-given plan for the human race.

Within the judicial system, Myra Bradwell was one of the first to ask the woman question when she asked why the privileges and immunities of citizenship did not include, for married women in Illinois, eligibility for a state license to practice law.[27] The opinion of the United States Supreme Court in Bradwell's case evaded the gender

---

area of law or women's life situation? How will these reform proposals, if adopted, affect women both practically and ideologically? . . . (6) In an ideal world, what would this woman's life situation look like, and what relationship, if any, would the law have to this future life situation? . . . and (7) How do we get there from here? *Id.* at 72–75.

[25] *See* C. DEGLER, AT ODDS: WOMEN AND THE FAMILY IN AMERICA FROM THE REVOLUTION TO THE PRESENT 189–90 (1980) (describing eighteenth- and nineteenth-century conceptions of individualism for women as partial and tentative, as illustrated by arguments of Mary Wollstonecraft and Abigail Adams); *see also* Minow, *Rights of One's Own* (Book Review), 98 HARV. L. REV. 1084 (1985) (analyzing Elizabeth Cady Stanton's use of an "old scheme of ideas" which could not adequately capture her own more radical, if somewhat inconsistent, views). Some early reform efforts, of course, were quite radical in scope. The Seneca Falls Convention of 1848, generally considered the "official" beginning of the first women's rights movement, adopted a bold declaration which demanded for women full equality with men. *See* J. LINDGREN & N. TAUB, THE LAW OF SEX DISCRIMINATION 14–16 (1988).

[26] For historical treatments of these activities, see B. BERG, THE REMEMBERED GATE: ORIGINS OF AMERICAN FEMINISM (1978); W. CHAFE, THE AMERICAN WOMAN (1972); N. COTT, THE BONDS OF WOMANHOOD: "WOMAN'S SPHERE" IN NEW ENGLAND 1780–1835 (1977); A HERITAGE OF HER OWN: TOWARD A NEW SOCIAL HISTORY OF AMERICAN WOMEN (N. Cott & E. Pleck eds. 1979); C. DEGLER, *supra* note 25; E. DUBOIS, FEMINISM AND SUFFRAGE: THE EMERGENCE OF AN INDEPENDENT WOMEN'S MOVEMENT IN AMERICA, 1848–1869 (1978); S. EVANS, BORN FOR LIBERTY: A HISTORY OF WOMEN IN AMERICA (1989); E. FLEXNER, CENTURY OF STRUGGLE (1959); G. LERNER, THE MAJORITY FINDS ITS PAST: PLACING WOMEN IN HISTORY (1979); L. NICHOLSON, GENDER AND HISTORY: THE LIMITS OF SOCIAL THEORY IN THE AGE OF THE FAMILY 43–66 (1986); W. O'NEILL, EVERYONE WAS BRAVE: THE RISE AND FALL OF FEMINISM IN AMERICA (1969); and M. RYAN, WOMANHOOD IN AMERICA: FROM COLONIAL TIMES TO THE PRESENT (2d ed. 1979).

[27] *See* Bradwell v. Illinois, 83 U.S. (16 Wall.) 130 (1873). For a detailed historical analysis of the *Bradwell* case, see Olsen, *From False Paternalism to False Equality: Judicial Assaults on Feminist Community, Illinois 1869–1895*, 84 MICH. L. REV. 1518 (1986).

issue,[28] but Justice Bradley in his concurring opinion set forth the "separate spheres" legal ideology underlying the Illinois law:

> [T]he civil law, as well as nature herself, has always recognized a wide difference in the respective spheres and destinies of man and woman. Man is, or should be, woman's protector and defender. The natural and proper timidity and delicacy which belongs to the female sex evidently unfits it for many of the occupations of civil life. The constitution of the family organization . . . indicates the domestic sphere as that which properly belongs to the domain and functions of womanhood.[29]

Women, and sometimes employers, continued to press the woman question in challenges to sex-based maximum work-hour legislation,[30] other occupation restrictions,[31] voting limitations,[32] and jury-exemption rules.[33] The ideology, however, proved extremely resilient.

Not until the 1970's did the woman question begin to yield different answers about the appropriateness of the role of women assumed by law. The shift began in 1971 with the Supreme Court's ruling on a challenge by Sally Reed to an Idaho statute that gave males pref-

---

[28] The Court declared, simply, that the privileges and immunities clause did not apply to her claim, and that the fourteenth amendment did not transfer protection of the right to practice law to the federal government. *See Bradwell*, 83 U.S. (16 Wall.) at 138–39.

[29] *Id.* at 141 (Bradley, J., concurring in the judgment).

[30] *See* Muller v. Oregon, 208 U.S. 412 (1908) (upholding against an employer challenge an Oregon statute prohibiting employment of women in certain establishments for more than ten hours per day). "That woman's physical structure and the performance of maternal functions place her at a disadvantage in the struggle for subsistence is obvious," the *Muller* court declared. *Id.* at 421.

> [H]istory discloses the fact that woman has always been dependent upon man. . . . [S]he is so constituted that she will rest upon and look to him for protection; that her physical structure and a proper discharge of her maternal functions . . . justify legislation to protect her from the greed as well as the passion of man.

Id. at 421–22.

[31] *See* Goesaert v. Cleary, 335 U.S. 464 (1948) (upholding a Michigan statute distinguishing between wives and daughters of owners of liquor establishments and all other women, and prohibiting the latter from serving as bartenders).

[32] *See, e.g.*, Minor v. Happersett, 88 U.S. (21 Wall.) 162, 178 (1874) (holding that the right to vote was not among the privileges and immunities of United States citizenship and thus states could limit "that important trust to men alone"); *In re* Lockwood, 154 U.S. 116 (1894) (upholding Virginia's reading of its statute providing that any "person" admitted to practice in any state could also practice in Virginia to mean any "male" person).

[33] Gwendolyn Hoyt challenged Florida's automatic exemption of women from juries. *See* Hoyt v. Florida, 368 U.S. 57 (1961). Although women in Florida had a right to serve on juries, the automatic exemption meant that they did not have the same duty to serve as men; consequently, the jury of "peers" made available to women defendants systematically underrepresented women. In denying Hoyt's challenge to a jury that had no women, the Supreme Court reiterated Justice Bradley's reasoning in *Bradwell* focusing on the special role and responsibilities of woman: "Woman is still regarded as the center of home and family life." *Id.* at 62.

erence over females in appointments as estate administrators.[34] Although the Court in *Reed* did not address the separate spheres ideology directly, it rejected arguments of the state that "men [are] as a rule more conversant with business affairs than . . . women,"[35] to find the statutory preference arbitrary and thus in violation of the equal protection clause.[36] This decision was followed by a series of other successful challenges by women arguing that beneath the protective umbrella of the separate spheres ideology lay assumptions that disadvantage women in material, significant ways.[37]

Although the United States Supreme Court has come to condemn explicitly the separate spheres ideology when revealed by gross, stereotypical distinctions, the Court majority has been less sensitive to the effects of more subtle sex-based classifications that affect opportunities for and social views about women. The Court ignored, for example, the implications for women of a male-only draft registration system in reserving combat as a male-only activity.[38] Similarly, in upholding a statutory rape law that made underage sex a crime of males and not of females, the Court overlooked the way in which

---

[34] *See* Reed v. Reed, 404 U.S. 71 (1971).

[35] Brief for Appellee at 12, *Reed* (No. 70-4). The Idaho court's opinion, which the Supreme Court reversed, had suggested that the Idaho legislature might reasonably have concluded that "in general men are better qualified to act as an administrator than are women." Reed v. Reed, 93 Idaho 511, 514, 465 P.2d 635, 638 (1970).

[36] *See Reed*, 404 U.S. 71.

[37] *See, e.g.*, Stanton v. Stanton, 421 U.S. 7 (1975) (holding that a sex-based difference in age of majority for purposes of child support obligations by parents is not justified by the assumption that girls tend to mature and marry earlier than boys and have less need to continue their education); Frontiero v. Richardson, 411 U.S. 677 (1973) (plurality opinion) (rejecting a rule requiring a female member of the armed services to prove her spouse's dependency while automatically assuming the dependency of the spouse of a male member as not justified by a conclusion that a husband in our society is generally the breadwinner).

Many of the successful challenges to sex-based discrimination have been brought by men challenging the stereotypes underlying statutes that, on their surface, at least, favored women. *See, e.g.*, Mississippi Univ. for Women v. Hogan, 458 U.S. 718 (1982) (finding that the single-sex admissions policy of a state nursing school is not justified by the stereotyped view of nursing as an exclusively women's job); Caban v. Mohammed, 441 U.S. 380 (1979) (finding that a law allowing adoption of out-of-wedlock children without their father's, but not without their mother's, consent is not justified by the assumption that mothers, but not fathers, have a significant parental interest in their children); Orr v. Orr, 440 U.S. 268 (1979) (holding that a statute requiring husbands, but not wives, to pay alimony is not justified by the assumption that wives are always the dependent spouses); Craig v. Boren, 429 U.S. 190 (1976) (holding that different drinking ages for females and males are not justified by higher incidence of traffic arrests and accidents involving liquor by males); Weinberger v. Wiesenfeld, 420 U.S. 636 (1975) (concluding that the availability of social security survivor's benefits to mothers but not fathers is not justified by the notion that men are more likely than women to be the primary supporters of their spouses and children).

[38] *See* W. Williams, *supra* note 2, at 181-90 (criticizing Rostker v. Goldberg, 453 U.S. 57 (1981), which upheld a male-only draft registration requirement on the ground that only men were eligible for combat).

assumptions about male sexual aggression and female sexual passivity construct sexuality in limiting and dangerous ways.[39]

Pregnancy has been a special problem for the Court. In 1974, Carolyn Aiello and other women asked the woman question by challenging California's singling-out of pregnancy as virtually the only medical condition excluded from its state employee disability plan.[40] Revealing a telling blindness, the Supreme Court's answer to the question defined the relevant groups to compare in a way that severed the connection between gender and pregnancy. "The program divides potential recipients into two groups — pregnant women and nonpregnant persons."[41] Although only women are in the first group, "the second includes members of both sexes."[42] Because women as well as men are in the group who could receive benefits under the plan, the Court concluded that the exclusion of "pregnant persons" could not be discrimination based on sex.[43]

Dissatisfied, feminists continued to refine the woman question about pregnancy, and increasingly supplied their own clear answers to the questions they posed: Do exclusions based on pregnancy disadvantage women? (Of course, because only women can become pregnant.) What are the reasons for singling out pregnancy for exclusion? (Because the inclusion of pregnancy is costly; usually it is also a voluntary condition.) Are other disabilities costly? (Yes.) Are other covered disabilities voluntary? (Yes, some are, like cosmetic surgery and sterilization.)[44] Are there other reasons for treating pregnancy differently? (Well, now that you mention it, pregnant women should be home, nesting.)[45]

Feminists' persistent questioning led to an Act of Congress in 1978, The Pregnancy Discrimination Act,[46] which established the legal con-

---

[39] See id. (criticizing Michael M. v. Superior Ct., 450 U.S. 464 (1981), which upheld a statute criminalizing male, but not female, involvement in underage sex on the grounds that the state had a legitimate interest in preventing illegitimate teenage pregnancies, which only males can cause); Olsen, supra note 2 (same).

[40] See Geduldig v. Aiello, 417 U.S. 484 (1974).

[41] Id. at 497 n.20.

[42] Id.

[43] See id. at 496–97 ("There is no risk from which men are protected and women are not."). The Court adopted this same conclusion in reviewing a challenge to the exclusion of pregnancy from a private employer's disability plan under title VII. See General Elec. Co. v. Gilbert, 429 U.S. 125 (1976).

[44] See Geduldig, 417 U.S. at 499–500 (Brennan, J., dissenting).

[45] See Bartlett, Pregnancy and the Constitution: The Uniqueness Trap, 62 CALIF. L. REV. 1532 (1974); Comment, Geduldig v. Aiello: Pregnancy Classifications and the Definition of Sex Discrimination, 75 COLUM. L. REV. 441 (1975); see also W. Williams, supra note 2, at 190–200 (reviewing the Supreme Court's stereotyped notions of women).

[46] The Pregnancy Discrimination Act became § 701(k) of title VII.

The terms "because of sex" or "on the basis of sex" include, but are not limited to, because of or on the basis of pregnancy, childbirth, or related medical conditions; and women

nection between gender and pregnancy. The nature of that connection remains contested. Do rules granting pregnant women job security not available to other workers violate the equality principle that has been broadened to encompass pregnancy? The Supreme Court has said "no."[47] Although feminists have split over whether women have more to lose than to gain from singling out pregnancy for different, some would say "favored," treatment,[48] they agree on the critical question: what are the consequences for women of specific rules or practices?

Feminists today ask the woman question in many areas of law. They ask the woman question in rape cases when they ask why the defense of consent focuses on the perspective of the defendant and what he "reasonably" thought the woman wanted, rather than the perspective of the woman and the intentions she "reasonably" thought she conveyed to the defendant.[49] Women ask the woman question when they ask why they are not entitled to be prison guards on the same terms as men;[50] why the conflict between work and family responsibilities in women's lives is seen as a private matter for women to resolve within the family rather than a public matter involving restructuring of the workplace;[51] or why the right to "make and

---

affected by pregnancy, childbirth, or related medical conditions shall be treated the same for all employment-related purposes, including receipt of benefits under fringe benefit programs, as other persons not so affected but similar in their ability or inability to work . . . .

42 U.S.C. § 2000e (1982).

[47] See California Fed. Sav. & Loan Ass'n v. Guerra, 479 U.S. 272 (1987).

[48] Compare W. Williams, Equality's Riddle: Pregnancy and the Equal Treatment/Special Treatment Debate, 13 N.Y.U. REV. L. & SOC. CHANGE 325, 370–74 (1984–1985) [hereinafter W. Williams, Equality's Riddle] (noting, with qualifications, the advantages of an equal-treatment approach) with Krieger & Cooney, The Miller-Wohl Controversy: Equal Treatment, Positive Action and the Meaning of Women's Equality, 13 GOLDEN GATE U.L. REV. 513 (1983) (arguing that women have more to gain from the special-treatment approach). Chris Littleton has recast this debate in terms of "symmetrical" vs. "asymmetrical" models of equality. See Littleton, supra note 2, at 1291–301. The line-up of feminist groups on each side of California Federal Savings & Loan Association v. Guerra, 479 U.S. 272 (1987), demonstrates the breadth of the division on the equal-treatment/special-treatment issue. See Strimling, The Constitutionality of State Laws Providing Employment Leave for Pregnancy: Rethinking Geduldig After Cal Fed, 77 CALIF. L. REV. 171, 194 n.108 (1989).

A number of scholars recently have attempted to combine aspects of the equal-treatment and special-treatment approaches. See, e.g., J. Williams, Deconstructing Gender, 87 MICH. L. REV. 797 (1989) [hereinafter J. Williams, Deconstructing Gender] (urging a combination of equal-treatment and special-treatment approaches, in order to deinstitutionalize the gendered structure of society); Kay, Equality and Difference: The Case of Pregnancy, 1 BERKELEY WOMEN'S L.J. 1 (1985) (urging "episodic analysis" whereby women receive treatment different from men only during episodes of reproductive activity when their needs differ); Strimling, supra, at 205 (advocating "nonstigmatizing distinctions based on actual, biologically created needs").

[49] See S. ESTRICH, REAL RAPE 92–104 (1987).

[50] See W. Williams, supra note 2, at 188 n.75 (criticizing Dothard v. Rawlinson, 433 U.S. 321 (1977)).

[51] See Dowd, Work and Family: The Gender Paradox and the Limitations of Discrimination

enforce contracts" protected by section 1981 forbids discrimination in the *formation* of a contract but not discrimination in its *interpretation.*[52] Asking the woman question reveals the ways in which political choice and institutional arrangement contribute to women's subordination. Without the woman question, differences associated with women are taken for granted and, unexamined, may serve as a justification for laws that disadvantage women. The woman question reveals how the position of women reflects the organization of society rather than the inherent characteristics of women. As many feminists have pointed out, difference is located in relationships and social institutions — the workplace, the family, clubs, sports, childrearing patterns, and so on — not in women themselves.[53] In exposing the hidden effects of laws that do not explicitly discriminate on the basis of sex, the woman question helps to demonstrate how social structures embody norms that implicitly render women different and thereby subordinate.

Once adopted as a method, asking the woman question is a method of critique as integral to legal analysis as determining the precedential value of a case, stating the facts, or applying law to facts. "Doing law" as a feminist means looking beneath the surface of law to identify the gender implications of rules and the assumptions underlying them and insisting upon applications of rules that do not perpetuate women's subordination. It means recognizing that the woman question always has potential relevance and that "tight" legal analysis never assumes gender neutrality.

2. *The Woman Question: Method or Politics.* — Is asking the woman question really a method at all, or is it a mask for something else, such as legal substance, or politics? The American legal system has assumed that method and substance have different functions, and that method cannot serve its purpose unless it remains separate from, and independent of, substantive "bias." Rules of legal method, like rules of legal procedure, are supposed to insulate substantive rules from arbitrary application. Substantive rules define the rights and obligations of individuals and legal entities (what the law is); rules of method and procedure define the steps taken in order to ascertain and

---

Analysis in Restructuring the Workplace, 24 HARV. C.R.-C.L. L. REV. 79 (1989); Olsen, *The Family and the Market: A Study of Ideology and Legal Reform,* 96 HARV. L. REV. 1497 (1983); Taub, *From Parental Leaves to Nurturing Leaves,* 13 N.Y.U. REV. L. & SOC. CHANGE 381 (1985); J. Williams, *Deconstructing Gender, supra* note 48; W. Williams, *Equality's Riddle, supra* note 2, at 374–80.

[52] *Cf. The Supreme Court, 1988 Term — Leading Cases,* 103 HARV. L. REV. 137, 330 (1989) (criticizing Patterson v. McLean Credit Union, 109 S. Ct. 2363 (1989), which held that § 1981 does not reach cases of sexual harassment in the workplace because it protects only formation, not interpretation, of the employment contract).

[53] *See, e.g.,* S. DE BEAUVOIR, *supra* note 23; Harris, *supra* note 2, at 32; Littleton, *supra* note 2, at 1306–07; Minow, *supra* note 2, at 34–37.

apply that substance (how to invoke the law and to make it work).[54]
Separating rules of method and procedure from substantive rules,
under this view, helps to ensure the regular, predictable application
of those substantive rules. Thus, conventional and reliable ways of
working with substantive rules permit one to specify in advance the
consequences of particular activities. Method and process should not
themselves have substantive content, the conventional wisdom insists,
because method and process are supposed to protect us from substance
which comes, "arbitrarily," from outside the rule. Within this conventional view, it might be charged that the method of asking the
woman question fails to respect the necessary separation between
method and substance. Indeed, asking the woman question seems to
be a "loaded," overtly political activity, which reaches far beyond the
"neutral" tasks of ascertaining law and facts and applying one to the
other.

Of course, not only feminist legal methods but *all* legal methods
shape substance;[55] the difference is that feminists have been called on
it. Methods shape substance, first, in the leeway they allow for reach-

---

[54] *See* S. BURTON, *supra* note 22, at 2–3. Although rules of legal method and procedural
rules are similar in the way I describe here, they refer to somewhat different activities in the
law. Legal methods identify and interpret rules of substance and process. Procedural rules
govern the manner in which legal claims are asserted and processed. For a discussion of the
purposes of the procedure/substance distinction in constraining authority and imposing regularity,
see Cover, *For James Wm. Moore: Some Reflections on a Reading of the Rules*, 84 YALE L.J.
718, 726–28 (1975).

The substance/procedure distinction in law has been examined in many different contexts.
See, e.g., Cook, *"Substance" and "Procedure" in the Conflict of Laws*, 42 YALE L.J. 333 (1933)
(discussing the substance/procedure distinction in the conflict of laws); Cover, *supra* (discussing
the relationship between rules of procedure and substantive law); Dan-Cohen, *Decision Rules
and Conduct Rules: On Acoustic Separation in Criminal Law*, 97 HARV. L. REV. 625 (1984)
(advocating the separation of "decision rules" and "conduct rules" in criminal law); Ely, *The
Irrepressible Myth of* Erie, 87 HARV. L. REV. 693 (1974) (discussing the substance/procedure
distinction in the context of *Erie* problems); Hazard, *The Effect of the Class Action Device upon
the Substantive Law*, 58 F.R.D. 307 (1973) (discussing the substantive effects of class action
law); Simon, *The Ideology of Advocacy: Procedural Justice and Professional Ethics*, 1978 WIS.
L. REV. 29, 44–52 (discussing lawyers' use of litigation strategy to affect substantive results of
cases).

In the case of both legal method and legal process, as Jeff Powell has pointed out in
conversations with me, an infinite number of levels of meta-rules might be added on to further
protect us from the "arbitrary" application of those rules — process as well as substantive rules
— that already exist. I am not concerned here with the question of how many such levels of
rules might be desirable, but only whether *some* rules of application might be desirable to ensure
some level of regularization in the application of other rules.

[55] *See* Mossman, *Feminism and Legal Method: The Difference It Makes*, 3 WIS. WOMEN'S
L.J. 147, 163–65 (1987). Sir Henry Maine offered the classic view of the substantive content
of methods. *See* H. MAINE, DISSERTATIONS ON EARLY LAW AND CUSTOM 389 (1886) (noting
that "substantive law has . . . the look of being gradually secreted in the interstices of procedure"); *see also* Kennedy, *Form and Substance in Private Law Adjudication*, 89 HARV. L. REV.
1685 (1976) (exploring the various substantive implications of the different forms of legal rules).

ing different substantive results. Deciding which facts are relevant, or which legal precedents apply, or how the applicable precedents should be applied, for example, leaves a decisionmaker with a wide range of acceptable substantive results from which to choose. The greater the indeterminacy, the more the decisionmaker's substantive preferences, without meaningful methodological constraints, may determine a particular outcome.[56] Not surprisingly, these preferences may follow certain patterns[57] reflecting the dominant cultural norms.

Methods shape substance also through the hidden biases they contain. A strong view of precedent in legal method, for example, protects the status quo over the interests of those seeking recognition of new rights.[58] The method of distinguishing law from considerations of policy, likewise, reinforces existing power structures and masks exclusions or perspectives ignored by that law.[59] The endless academic debates over originalism, interpretivism, and other theories of constitutional interpretation[60] demonstrate further that methodological principles convey substantive views of law and make a difference to legal results.

Does recognition of the substantive consequences of method make the distinction between method and substance incoherent and pointless? If methods mask substance, why not dispose with method altogether and analyze every legal problem as one of substance alone? There is both a practical and a normative reason to treat legal methods as at least *somewhat* distinct from the substance of law. The practical reason is the virtual impossibility of thinking directly from substance to result in law, except in the most superficial of senses, without methods. Consider, for example, whether a rule against discrimination in the workplace against women with children applies only to hiring policies, or whether it requires particular employee benefits, such as on-the-job childcare or liberal parenting-leave policies? In resolving this question, how relevant are such factors as the previous application of other antidiscrimination rules, the childrearing respon-

---

[56] *See* Mossman, *supra* note 55, at 158.

[57] Judith Resnik, for example, has shown how distinguishing a question of law from a question of fact may have systematic effects on which kinds of litigants win or lose lawsuits at the appellate level. *See* Resnik, *Tiers*, 57 S. CAL. L. REV. 837, 998–1005, 1013–14 (1984).

[58] A well-known exception is *Ex parte* Young, 209 U.S. 123 (1908). For a historical analysis of the range of views on the role of precedent within legal method, see Collier, *Precedent and Legal Authority: A Critical History*, 1988 WIS. L. REV. 771.

[59] *See* Mossman, *supra* note 55, at 157–58; Singer, *The Player and the Cards: Nihilism and Legal Theory*, 94 YALE L.J. 1, 30–33 (1984).

[60] For a review of the most significant works in this debate, and one of the most coherent statements of the "originalist" position, see Kay, *Adherence to the Original Intentions in Constitutional Adjudication: Three Objections and Responses*, 82 NW. U.L. REV. 226 (1988). The basic statement of the "non-originalist" position remains Brest, *The Misconceived Quest for the Original Understanding*, 60 B.U.L. REV. 204 (1980).

sibilities actually born by a claimant, or by mothers in general, the cost of particular benefits to employers, or the possible ramifications of the rule as applied for the free market system? Further substantive rules will help to resolve these issues, but even their application assumes some set of background principles about which facts matter and which sources of interpretation are available to decisionmakers.

Such background principles, or methods, are not only inevitable, but desirable, because they can help to preserve the integrity of the substantive rules which the legal system produces. Feminists, as well as nonfeminists, have a stake in this integrity. As Toni Massaro points out, not all substantive rules are bad rules,[61] and feminists will want to ensure faithful application of the good ones. Whether all decisionmakers can be entirely faithful to the methodological constraints imposed upon them, the existence of these constraints can make a difference.[62]

The real question is neither whether there is such a thing as method — method is inevitable — nor whether methods have substantive consequences — also inevitable — but whether the relationship between method and substance is "proper."[63] Some relationships are improper. A purely result-oriented method in which decisionmakers may decide every case in order to reach the result they think most desirable, for example, improperly exerts no meaningful constraints on the decisionmaker. Also improper is a method that imposes arbitrary or unjustified constraints, such as one that requires a decisionmaker to decide in favor of all female claimants or against all employers.

In contrast, the method of asking the woman question establishes a justifiable relationship to legal substance. This method helps to expose a certain kind of bias in substantive rules. Asking the woman question does not require decision in favor of a woman. Rather, the method requires the decisionmaker to search for gender bias and to reach a decision in the case that is defensible in light of that bias. It demands, in other words, special attention to a set of interests and concerns that otherwise may be, and historically have been, overlooked. The substance of asking the woman question lies in *what* it seeks to uncover: disadvantage based upon gender. The political

---

[61] See Massaro, *Empathy, Legal Storytelling, and the Rule of Law: New Words, Old Wounds?*, 87 MICH. L. REV. 2099, 2120 (1989) ("Discretion may license a decisionmaker to ignore the rules we think are worthy of support, in favor of her private agenda or personal experiential understanding.").

[62] Newman, *Between Legal Realism and Neutral Principles: The Legitimacy of Institutional Values*, 72 CALIF. L. REV. 200 (1984) (arguing that despite the existence of some indeterminacy in law, many conscientious judges reach results contrary to their personal predilections out of respect for the orderly development of law).

[63] In his discussion of procedural rules, Robert Cover makes the distinction between "proper" and "improper" ways of relating substance and process. *See* Cover, *supra* note 54, at 721.

nature of this method arises only because it seeks information that is not supposed to exist. The claim that this information may exist — and that the woman question is therefore necessary — is political, but only to the extent that the stated or implied claim that it does not exist is *also* political.

Asking the woman question confronts the assumption of legal neutrality, and has substantive consequences only if the law is not gender-neutral. The bias of the method is the bias toward uncovering a certain kind of bias. The bias disadvantages those who are otherwise benefited by law and legal methods whose gender implications are *not* revealed. If this is "bias," feminists must insist that it is "good" (or "proper") bias, not "bad."[64]

3. Converting the Woman Question into the Question of the Excluded. — The woman question asks about exclusion. Standing alone, and as usually posed in feminist legal method, it asks about the exclusion of women. Feminists have begun to observe, however, that any analysis using the general category of woman is itself exclusionary, because it treats as universal to women the interests and experiences of a particular group of women — namely white, and otherwise privileged women.[65] Adrienne Rich calls this problem "white solipsism."[66]

It is not surprising that white women, identifying the oppression they experience primarily as gender-based, have come to describe their feminism as a politics of "women." It is also not surprising that in a movement which grounds its claims to truth in experience, white women would develop a feminism that closely corresponds to their own experiences as white women. Like the male world that feminists seek to expose as partial, the world of feminism betrays the partiality of its makers.

The problem is how to correct this failing while maintaining feminism's ability to analyze the social significance of gender. Elizabeth Spelman argues that one cannot do so merely by adding an analysis of the race issue to an analysis of the gender issue because race changes how women experience gender.[67] Not simply an additional basis for

---

[64] *See* Cain, *Good and Bad Bias: A Comment on Feminist Theory and Judging*, 61 S. CAL. L. REV. 1945 (1988).

[65] *See* E. SPELMAN, *supra* note 11; Harris, *supra* note 2; Minow, *supra* note 2; *see also* Fraser & Nicholson, *supra* note 14, at 97–98 (arguing that use of categories like sexuality, mothering, and reproduction as cross-cultural phenomena risks projecting socially dominant features by some onto others).

[66] A. RICH, *Disloyal to Civilization: Feminism, Racism, Gynephobia*, in ON LIES, SECRETS, AND SILENCES 299 (1979); *see also* E. SPELMAN, *supra* note 11, at 116, 128.

[67] A common example of the additive approach is the reference to "women and blacks." The unstated but powerful implications of such a reference, Spelman argues, is that black women belong to only one category (women) or the other (blacks), usually the latter. *See* E. SPELMAN, *supra* note 11, at 114–15.

oppression, race is a *different* basis for oppression that entails different kinds of subordination and requires different forms of liberation.[68] For this reason, analysis of gender must occur not apart from but within the contexts of multiple identities.

To correct feminism's exclusionary failing, Spelman suggests that in speaking of "women," the speaker should name explicitly which women she means.[69] This suggestion deserves intensive efforts, though the job is anything but easy. The category of women includes innumerable other categories, and the mention of any of these categories will leave unmentioned many others. One cannot talk about "black women" (as Spelman often does), for example, without implying that one is talking about *heterosexual* black women. One cannot talk about heterosexual black women without implying that one is talking about heterosexual *able-bodied* women. Any category, no matter how narrowly defined, makes assumptions about the remaining characteristics of the group that fail to take account of members of the group who do not have those characteristics.[70] Spelman's suggestion, therefore, requires distinctions between those categories that should be separately recognized, and those that need not be. The speaker can make such distinctions based upon her understanding about which characteristics are most important to recognize given current social realities. But this is tricky business that requires great sensitivity to multiple, invisible forms of exclusion that many people face. The privileged who attempt this business must recognize the ever-present risks of solipsism without succumbing to a paralyzing paranoia about those risks.[71]

Using the "woman" question as a model for deeper inquiry into the consequences of overlapping forms of oppression could also help to correct the problem Spelman identifies. This inquiry would require a general and far-reaching set of questions that go beyond issues of gender bias to seek out other bases of exclusion: what assumptions are made by law (or practice or analysis) about those whom it affects? Whose point of view do these assumptions reflect? Whose interests are invisible or peripheral? How might excluded viewpoints be identified and taken into account?

Extended beyond efforts to identify oppression based only upon gender, the woman question can reach forms of oppression made invisible not only by the dominant structures of power but also by the efforts to discover bias on behalf of women alone. These forms

---

[68] *See id.* at 125.

[69] *See id.* at 186.

[70] *See* Minow, *supra* note 11, at 51.

[71] *See* D. FUSS, ESSENTIALLY SPEAKING: FEMINISM NATURE & DIFFERENCE 1 (1989) (arguing that the "perceived threat of essentialism" fosters paranoia that "foreclose[s] more ambitious investigations of specificity and difference").

of oppression differ from gender subordination in kind as well as in degree, and those who have not experienced them are likely to find them difficult to recognize. The difficulty in recognizing oppression one has not experienced, however, makes the necessity of a "method" all the more apparent. As I indicated earlier, a method neither guarantees a particular result nor even the right result. It does, however, provide some discipline when one seeks something that does not correspond to one's own interests.

Will this expanded inquiry dilute the coherence of gender critique? Far from it. As Spelman writes, fine-tuning feminism to encompass the breadth and specificity of oppressions actually experienced by different women — and even some men — can only make feminism clearer and stronger.[72] Coherence, or unity,[73] is possible only when feminism's underlying assumptions speak the truth for many, not a privileged few.

B. Feminist Practical Reasoning

Some feminists have claimed that women approach the reasoning process differently than men do.[74] In particular, they say that women are more sensitive to situation and context, that they resist universal principles and generalizations, especially those that do not fit their own experiences, and that they believe that "the practicalities of everyday life" should not be neglected for the sake of abstract justice.[75] Whether these claims can be empirically sustained,[76] this reasoning process has taken on normative significance for feminists, many of whom have argued that individualized factfinding is often superior to the application of bright-line rules,[77] and that reasoning from context allows a greater respect for difference[78] and for the perspectives of the powerless. In this section, I explore these themes through a discussion of a feminist version of practical reasoning.

---

[72] *See* E. SPELMAN, *supra* note 11, at 175–77.

[73] *See infra* p. 886.

[74] *See* C. GILLIGAN, IN A DIFFERENT VOICE: PSYCHOLOGICAL THEORY AND WOMEN'S DEVELOPMENT (1982); M. BELENKY, B. CLINCHY, N. GOLDBERGER & J. TARULE, WOMEN'S WAYS OF KNOWING: THE DEVELOPMENT OF SELF, VOICE, AND MIND (1986); Menkel-Meadow, *Portia in a Different Voice: Speculations on a Women's Lawyering Process*, 1 BERKELEY WOMEN'S L.J. 39 (1985); Sherry, *Civic Virtue and the Feminine Voice in Constitutional Adjudication*, 72 VA. L. REV. 543 (1986).

[75] M. BELENKY, B. CLINCHY, N. GOLDBERGER & J. TARULE, *supra* note 74, at 149.

[76] Some of the literature challenging the claims that women reason differently from men is cited in note 174 below.

[77] Bartlett, *Re-Expressing Parenthood*, 98 YALE L.J. 293, 321–26 (1988); Sherry, *supra* note 74, at 604–13.

[78] *See* Minow & Spelman, *Passion for Justice*, 10 CARDOZO L. REV. 37, 53 (1988); Scales, *supra* note 2, at 1388.

1. The Method. — As a form of legal reasoning, practical reasoning has many meanings invoked in many contexts for many different purposes.[79] I present a version of practical reasoning in this section that I call "feminist practical reasoning." This version combines some aspects of a classic Aristotelian model of practical deliberation with a feminist focus on identifying and taking into account the perspectives of the excluded. Although this form of reasoning may not always provide clear decision methods for resolving every legal dispute, it builds upon the "practical" in its focus on the specific, real-life dilemmas posed by human conflict — dilemmas that more abstract forms of legal reasoning often tend to gloss over. In focusing on the "real" rather than the abstract, practical reasoning has some kinship to legal realism and critical legal studies, but there are important differences which I will explore in this section.

(a) Practical Reasoning. — According to Amélie Rorty, the Aristotelian model of practical reasoning holistically considers ends, means, and actions in order to "recognize and actualize whatever is best in the most complex, various, and ambiguous situations."[80] Prac-

---

[79] *See, e.g.*, Burton, *Symposium: The Works of Joseph Raz: Law as Practical Reason*, 62 S. CAL. L. REV. 747 (1989) (arguing in favor of "practical reason" in law, as an alternative to Holmes' view of law as predictions of what courts will do); Farber, *Brilliance Revisited*, 72 MINN. L. REV. 367 (1987) (using the concept of "common sense" to argue against counterintuitive or "brilliant" legal scholarship); Farber & Frickey, *Practical Reason and the First Amendment*, 34 UCLA L. REV. 1615, 1649–50 (1987) (advocating practical reasoning as a reform-promoting alternative to foundationalism in first amendment scholarship); Grey, *Holmes and Legal Pragmatism*, 41 STAN. L. REV. 787 (1989) (applauding Holmes' "pragmatism"); Hawthorn, *Practical Reason and Social Democracy: Reflections on Unger's Passion and Politics*, 81 NW. U.L. REV. 766, 766 (1987) (arguing that more modest conclusions similar to those of Unger might be reached more realistically by "pragmatic" means, without "drastic reconstructive proposals"); Kronman, *Alexander Bickel's Philosophy of Prudence*, 94 YALE L.J. 1567 (1985) (describing "prudentialism," with approval, as the political philosophy of Alexander Bickel); Kronman, *Practical Wisdom and Professional Character*, in PHILOSOPHY AND LAW 203, 223 (J. Coleman & E. Paul eds. 1987) (using the concept of "practical wisdom" to argue for a particular view of the professional character of lawyers which combines visualization and detachment); Michelman, *The Supreme Court, 1985 Term — Foreword: Traces of Self-Government*, 100 HARV. L. REV. 4, 24 (1986) (urging "practical reason" as the path to understanding the republican tradition of civic dialogue); Posner, *The Jurisprudence of Skepticism*, 86 MICH. L. REV. 827, 838 (1988) (arguing that practical reasoning, which encompasses a set of methods for finding "beliefs about matters that cannot be verified by logic or exact observation," is not a distinctively *legal* form of reasoning, but it yields determinative outcomes in many legal problems); Sunstein, *Interest Groups in American Public Law*, 38 STAN. L. REV. 29, 31–32 (1985) (endorsing "practical reason" as the model of public discussion through which people can rise above private interest in pursuit of the public good); Wellman, *supra* note 22 (arguing that practical reasoning provides the most valid basis for a theory of judicial justification). For a critique of "practical legal studies" as a "liberal/moderate/conservative response to the radicalism of Critical Legal Studies," see Feinman, *Practical Legal Studies and Critical Legal Studies*, 87 MICH. L. REV. 724, 731 (1988). *See also* Tushnet, *Anti-Formalism in Recent Constitutional Theory*, 83 MICH. L. REV. 1502, 1534–36 (1985) (arguing that the social conditions necessary for the sound exercise of "practical reason" do not exist).

[80] A. RORTY, MIND IN ACTION 272 (1988). According to Rorty, an essential component of

tical reasoning recognizes few, if any, givens. What must be done, and why and how it should be done, are all open questions, considered on the basis of the intricacies of each specific factual context.[81] Not only the resolution of the problem, but even what counts as a problem emerges from the specifics of the situation itself, rather than from some foreordained definition or prescription.

Practical reasoning approaches problems not as dichotomized conflicts, but as dilemmas with multiple perspectives, contradictions, and inconsistencies. These dilemmas, ideally, do not call for the choice of one principle over another, but rather "imaginative integrations and reconciliations,"[82] which require attention to particular context. Practical reasoning sees particular details not as annoying inconsistencies or irrelevant nuisances which impede the smooth logical application of fixed rules. Nor does it see particular facts as the *objects* of legal analysis, the inert material to which to apply the living law. Instead, new facts present opportunities for improved understandings and "integrations." Situations are unique, not anticipated in their detail, not generalizable in advance. Themselves generative, new situations give rise to "practical" perceptions and inform decisionmakers about the desired ends of law.[83]

---

the Aristotelian form of practical reasoning is its deliberation about appropriate ends. *See id.* So understood, practical reasoning in law requires not only determining how to best meet certain specified goals, but also constantly reevaluating, with the aid of new information and experience, which ends to pursue.

[81] John Dewey's conception of the continuum of ends and means conveys a similar notion. According to Dewey, human activity is not directed toward the achievement of distinct, fixed ends. Instead, it represents an integration of ends and means, whereby goals are provisional, and the means toward achieving them are intrinsically as well as extrinsically significant. My reading of Dewey comes from Grey, cited above in note 79, at 854–55.

This view of the means-ends continuum contrasts with the utilitarian dichotomy between the two. According to Amélie Rorty, Aristotelian practical reasoning or *phronesis* became transformed, through the work of Hobbes, Hume, Mandeville, and Kant, into a utilitarian, ends-means instrumentalism. *See* A. RORTY, *supra* note 80, at 271–82. The work of a number of prominent legal theorists on practical reasoning epitomizes the transformation that Rorty describes. *See, e.g.,* A. KENNY, WILL, FREEDOM AND POWER 70–71 (1975); J. RAZ, PRACTICAL REASON AND NORMS 12 (1975); Wellman, *supra* note 22, at 88–115.

[82] A. RORTY, *supra* note 80, at 274. Rorty writes:

When we are conflicted, we are not torn by the large dichotomized conflicts between altruism and egoism, or between principles of morality and the psychology of desire and interest. Our conflicts are those between particular thoughtful desires or thoughtful habits that cannot all be simultaneously realized or enacted, because they eventually undermine each other. The resolutions of such conflicts rarely involve denying or suppressing one side, for both sides of intrapsychic conflicts, like both sides of political conflicts, represent functional contributions to thriving. Such conflicts are at least sometimes best resolved by imaginative integrations and reconciliations . . . rather than by abstract selection and denial.

Id. Rorty speaks of moral rather than legal decisionmaking, but her descriptions of the dilemmas that occur apply to both.

[83] *See* M. NUSSBAUM, THE FRAGILITY OF GOODNESS: LUCK AND ETHICS IN GREEK TRAGEDY AND PHILOSOPHY 301–05 (1986). Nussbaum writes that ethical choice must be "seized in

The issue of minors' access to abortion exemplifies the generative, educative potential of specific facts. The abstract principle of family autonomy seems logically to justify a state law requiring minors to obtain their parents' consent before obtaining an abortion. Minors are immature and parents are the individuals generally best situated to help them make a decision as difficult as whether to have an abortion. The actual accounts of the wrenching circumstances under which a minor might seek to avoid notifying her parent of her decision to seek an abortion, however, demonstrate the practical difficulties of the matter. These actual accounts reveal that many minors face severe physical and emotional abuse as a result of their parents' knowledge of their pregnancy. Parents force many minors to carry to term a child that the minor cannot possibly raise responsibly; and only the most determined minor will be able to relinquish her child for adoption, in the face of parental rejection and manipulation.[84] Actual circumstances, in other words, yield insights into the difficult problems of state and family decisionmaking that the abstract concept of parental autonomy alone does not reveal.

Practical reasoning in the law does not, and could not, reject rules. Along the specificity-generality continuum of rules, it tends to favor less specific rules or "standards," because of the greater leeway for individualized analysis that standards allow.[85] But practical reasoning in the context of law necessarily works from rules. Rules represent accumulated past wisdom, which must be reconciled with the contingencies and practicalities presented by fresh facts. Rules provide signposts for the appropriate purposes and ends to achieve through law.[86] Rules check the inclination to be arbitrary and "give constancy and stability in situations in which bias and passion might distort

---

a confrontation with the situation itself, by a faculty that is suited to confront it as a complex whole." *Id.* at 300–01.

[84] *See* Brief for Petitioners at 6-25, Hodgson v. Minnesota, 110 S. Ct. 400 (1989) (Nos. 88-1125 & 88-1309).

[85] Some of the most basic literature on the distinctions and tradeoffs between "rules" and "standards" includes Diver, *The Optimal Precision of Administrative Rules*, 93 YALE L.J. 65 (1983); Kennedy, *supra* note 55; and Rawls, *Two Concepts of Rules*, 64 PHIL. REV. 3 (1955).

Those feminists and critical scholars most concerned about unchecked prejudice and power reject loose standards and forms of reasoning like practical reasoning in favor of specific formal rules. *See* Held, *Feminism and Moral Theory*, in WOMEN AND MORAL THEORY 119 (E. Kittay & D. Meyers eds. 1987); Matsuda, *Public Responses to Racist Speech: Considering the Victims' Story*, 87 MICH. L. REV. 2320, 2325 (1989); P. Williams, *Alchemical Notes: Reconstructing Ideals from Deconstructed Rights*, 22 HARV. C.R.-C.L. L. REV. 401, 406–08 (1987); *see also* Fineman, *The Politics of Custody and the Transformation of American Custody Decision Making*, 22 U.C. DAVIS L. REV. 829 (1989) (arguing that the "best interests of the child" standard has led to greater concentration of power in hands of child "advocates" and child welfare professionals); *see also* Delgado, Dunn, Brown, Lee & Hubbert, *Fairness and Formality: Minimizing the Risk of Prejudice in Alternative Dispute Resolution*, 1985 WIS. L. REV. 1359.

[86] *See* M. NUSSBAUM, *supra* note 83, at 305.

judgment. . . . Rules are necessities because we are not always good judges."[87]

Ideally, however, rules leave room for the new insights and perspectives generated by new contexts. As noted above, the practical reasoner believes that the specific circumstances of a new case may dictate novel readings and applications of rules, readings and applications that not only *were not*, but *could not* or *should not* have been determined in advance.[88] In this respect, practical reasoning differs from the view of law characteristic of the legal realists, who saw rules as open-ended by necessity, not by choice.[89] The legal realist highly valued predictability and determinacy, but assumed that facts were too various and unpredictable for lawmakers to frame determinate rules.[90] The practical reasoner, on the other hand, finds undesirable as well as impractical the reduction of contingencies to rules by which all disputes can be decided in advance.[91]

---

[87] *Id.* at 304.

[88] *See* M. NUSSBAUM, *supra* note 83, at 298–306. One critique of the practical reasoning I describe is that even if flexibility in the application of rules is desirable in some cases, as a general matter fixed rules are necessary to let individuals know what the law is and predict the consequences of their actions. Insofar as practical reasoning permits law to be made *as it is applied* rather than before the facts arise to which law is applied, the argument goes, law ceases to be a rule-bound activity; and where rules do not constrain decisionmaking their very reason for being disappears. *See* Schauer, *Is the Common Law Law?* (Book Review), 77 CALIF. L. REV. 455, 455–56 (1989).

This critique misapprehends both the rule-boundedness of our legal system and the rule-openness of practical reasoning. As to our legal system, Professor Melvin Eisenberg has demonstrated that the model of common law pervasive in American jurisprudence has incorporated a practice of rule "enrichment" that goes well beyond those instances that require filling a gap in the law. *See* M. EISENBERG, *supra* note 22, at 6–7. This practice also extends, Eisenberg shows, to the process of statutory and constitutional interpretation. *See id.* at 196 n.35; *see also* Grey, *supra* note 79, at 819 (noting that Holmes considered law to be "guidelines, rules of thumb, instruments of inquiry designed as practical aids to making sound decisions" rather than "mathematical axioms"). Actors often cannot accurately predict the consequences of their actions, not only because clarity does not exist, but because of the richness of interpretative possibilities within our rule-based system. We can, and do, live in a system that is less rule-bound than we may commonly suppose.

As to practical reasoning, I emphasize that neither the ideal nor the expected practice approaches the state of being rule-free. As I have stated, rules are critical to practical reasoning, which attempts to reconcile accumulated past wisdom, represented by rules, with the contingencies and practicalities of fresh facts.

[89] Perhaps the clearest statement of this view of law comes from Justice Cardozo:

No doubt the ideal system, if it were attainable, would be a code at once so flexible and so minute, as to supply in advance for every conceivable situation the just and fitting rule. But life is too complex to bring the attainment of this ideal within the compass of human powers.

B. CARDOZO, THE NATURE OF THE JUDICIAL PROCESS 143 (1921).

[90] *See* Singer, *Legal Realism Now*, 76 CALIF. L. REV. 465, 471 (1988). Legal realist scholars did not find this desired predictability in abstract rules and legal concepts, and therefore attempted "to develop new kinds of general rules that would be useful in predicting legal outcomes." *Id.*

[91] Chris Schroeder and Lawrence Baxter first suggested to me the distinction between the

Another important feature of practical reasoning is what counts as justification. The legal realist view is that rules allow a certain range of manipulation; judges may select on the basis of unstated, external considerations those interpretations that best serve those considerations. Thus, the "real reason" for a decision — the social goals the decisionmaker chooses to advance — and the reasons offered in a legal decision may differ.[92] Practical reasoning, on the other hand, demands more than *some reasonable* basis for a particular legal decision. Decisionmakers must offer their *actual* reasons — the same reasons "that form its effective intentional description."[93] This requirement reflects the inseparability of the determinations of means and ends; reasoning is itself part of the "end," and the end cannot be reasonable apart from the reasoning that underlies it. It reflects, further, the commitment of practical reasoning to the decisionmaker's acceptance of responsibility for decisions made. Rules do not absolve the decisionmaker from responsibility for decisions. There are choices to be made and the agent who makes them must admit to those choices and defend them.[94]

(b) *Feminist practical reasoning.* — Feminist practical reasoning builds upon the traditional mode of practical reasoning by bringing to it the critical concerns and values reflected in other feminist meth-

---

impracticability and the undesirability of a completely comprehensive system of rules. Professor Eisenberg makes a similar distinction between the by-product and the enrichment model of common law decisionmaking. *See* M. EISENBERG, *supra* note 22, at 6. Under the by-product model, courts are justified in filling in law not already specified in previous cases, but "only insofar as is necessary to resolve the dispute before it, and no further." *Id.* Under the enrichment model, on the other hand, "the establishment of legal rules to govern social conduct is treated as desirable in itself — although subordinated in a variety of important ways to the function of dispute-resolution -- so that the courts consciously take on the function of developing certain bodies of law . . . ." *Id.*

[92] *See* Singer, *supra* note 90, at 472.

[93] A. RORTY, *supra* note 80, at 283; *see also* Michelman, *supra* note 79, at 31 (linking having one's own reasons for action with the positive or ethical notion of freedom); Singer, *supra* note 59, at 32 (arguing that judges should "feel free honestly to express what they really were thinking about when they decided the case" in order to "clarify the moral and political views at stake in legal controversies"). For a general discussion of the problem of judicial candor, which also collects the standard scholarly positions on this subject, see Shapiro, *In Defense of Judicial Candor*, 100 HARV. L. REV. 731 (1987).

[94] On the desirability of accepting this kind of responsibility, see Singer, cited above in note 90, at 533. *See also* Michelman, *supra* note 79, at 15, 35 (criticizing objective legal standards for absolving decisionmakers of responsibility for the fates of individual parties); Mossman, *supra* note 55, at 157–58 (criticizing neutral principles of interpretation for carrying with them the "absence of responsibility on the part of the male judges for any negative outcome"); Sunstein, *supra* note 79, at 69–72 (proposing that rationality review should consider only the real, not the hypothetical, reasons for legislation). On the unavoidability of taking responsibility, see B. SMITH, CONTINGENCIES OF VALUE: ALTERNATIVE PERSPECTIVES FOR CRITICAL THEORY 159–60 (1988), which argues that "since the contingency of all value cannot be evaded, whoever does the *urging* cannot ultimately suppress, or ultimately evade taking responsibility for, the *particularity* of the perspective from which he does so." *Id.* (emphasis in original).

ods, including the woman question. The classical exposition of practical reasoning takes for granted the legitimacy of the community whose norms it expresses, and for that reason tends to be fundamentally conservative.[95] Feminist practical reasoning challenges the legitimacy of the norms of those who claim to speak, through rules, for the community. No form of legal reasoning can be free, of course, from the past or from community norms, because law is always situated in a context of practices and values.[96] Feminist practical reasoning differs from other forms of legal reasoning, however, in the strength of its commitment to the notion that there is not one, but many overlapping communities to which one might look for "reason." Feminists consider the concept of community problematic,[97] because they have demonstrated that law has tended to reflect existing structures of power. Carrying over their concern for inclusionism from the method of asking the woman question, feminists insist that no one community is legitimately privileged to speak for all others. Thus, feminist methods reject the monolithic community often assumed in male accounts of practical reasoning,[98] and seek to identify perspectives not represented in the dominant culture from which reason should proceed.[99]

Feminist practical reasoning, however, is not the polar opposite of a "male" deductive model of legal reasoning. The deductive model

---

[95] *See* Singer, *supra* note 90, at 540 (arguing that modern theorists who separate law from politics and seek community consensus through existing community practices are conservative); *see also* Singer, *supra* note 5, at 731 (describing "Practical Legal Studies" as a "liberal/moderate/conservative response to the radicalism of Critical Legal Studies").

[96] An excellent discussion of this point, along with an analysis of the law as an instrumental means to achieve socially useful goals, appears in Grey, cited above in note 79, at 805–15.

[97] *See* Abrams, *Law's Republicanism*, 97 YALE L.J. 1591, 1606–07 (1988) (noting that "localities have a disturbing history of intolerance toward non-conforming groups"); Sullivan, *Rainbow Republicanism*, 97 YALE L.J. 1713, 1721 (1988) (criticizing the failure of "republicanism" to nurture private associations through which "deviance, diversity, and dissent" are possible).

[98] *See* Letter from Joseph W. Singer to Katharine Bartlett (Sept. 12, 1989) (on file at the Harvard Law School Library).

[99] Martha Minow has explored how judges do, and do not, attempt to consider nondominant perspectives in deciding cases. *See* Minow, *supra* note 2. A remarkable statement recognizing the necessity of this search appears in a dissenting opinion by Judge Cudahy in a case upholding the validity of an employer's fetal protection policy which affected fertile women but not fertile men. *See* UAW v. Johnson Controls, Inc., 886 F.2d 871, 902 (7th Cir. 1989) (en banc) (Cudahy, J., dissenting). This statement reads:

> It is a matter of some interest that, of the twelve federal judges to have considered this case to date, none has been female. This may be quite significant because this case, like other controversies of great potential consequence, demands, in addition to command of the disembodied rules, some insight into social reality. What is the situation of the pregnant woman, unemployed or working for the minimum wage and unprotected by health insurance, in relation to her pregnant sister, exposed to an indeterminate lead risk but well-fed, housed and doctored? Whose fetus is at greater risk? Whose decision is this to make?

Id.

assumes that for any set of facts, fixed, pre-existing legal rules compel a single, correct result. Many commentators have noted that virtually no one, male or female, now defends the strictly deductive approach to legal reasoning.[100] Contextualized reasoning is also not, as some commentators suggest,[101] the polar opposite of a "male" model of abstract thinking. All major forms of legal reasoning encompass processes of both contextualization and abstraction. Even the most conventional legal methods require that one look carefully at the factual context of a case in order to identify similarities and differences between that case and others.[102] The identification of a legal problem, selection of precedent, and application of that precedent, all require an understanding of the details of a case and how they relate to one another. When the details change, the rule and its application are likely to change as well.

By the same token, feminist methods require the process of abstraction, that is, the separation of the significant from the insignificant.[103] Concrete facts have significance only if they represent some generalizable aspect of the case. Generalizations identify what matters and draw connections to other cases. I abstract whenever I fail to identify every fact about a situation, which, of course, I do always.[104] For feminists, practical reasoning and asking the woman question may make more facts relevant or "essential" to the resolution of a legal case than would more nonfeminist legal analysis. For example, feminist practical reasoning deems relevant facts related to the woman question — facts about whose interests particular rules or legal reso-

---

[100] *See, e.g.*, Bennett, *Objectivity in Constitutional Law*, 132 U. PA. L. REV. 445, 495 (1984) ("'Mechanical' jurisprudence has no visible contemporary adherents."); Stick, *Can Nihilism Be Pragmatic?*, 100 HARV. L. REV. 332, 363–65 (1986) (asserting that outside a "core area," in which the application of legal rules is certain, "only the most unreconstructed logical positivist" accepts a strict deductive model of legal reasoning); *see also* Soper, *Legal Theory and the Obligation of a Judge: The Hart/Dworkin Dispute*, 75 MICH. L. REV. 473, 476 (1977) ("Not since Blackstone has the view that judges only 'find' and do not 'make' the law been preached with any fervor from academic pulpits . . . .").

[101] *See, e.g.*, Matsuda, *Liberal Jurisprudence and Abstracted Visions of Human Nature: A Feminist Critique of Rawls' Theory of Justice*, 16 N.M.L. REV. 613, 618–24 (1986); Menkel-Meadow, *supra* note 74, at 45–46; Scales, *supra* note 2, at 1376–78.

[102] *See* S. BURTON, *supra* note 22, at 59–60; M. GOLDING, *supra* note 21, at 44–46.

[103] *Cf.* K. LLEWELLYN, THE BRAMBLE BUSH: ON OUR LAW AND ITS STUDY 48 (1960) (arguing that a concrete fact is significant because it is *"representative"* of a wider abstract *category* of facts" (emphasis in original)).

[104] Martha Nussbaum addresses the need for generalizations based upon past experience as well as new detail; she states that practical wisdom would be "arbitrary and empty" if every situation were truly "new and nonrepeatable." M. NUSSBAUM, *supra* note 83, at 306. Nussbaum views the relationship between the universal and the particular as one of "two-way illumination": "Although . . . the particular takes priority, they are partners in commitment and share between them the honors given to the flexibility and responsiveness of the good judge." *Id.*; *see also* Gould, *supra* note 23, at 25–31 (developing a concept of "concrete universality" requiring appreciation of and generalizations about both similarities and differences among concrete situations).

lutions reflect and whose interests require more deliberate attention. Feminists do not and cannot reject, however, the process of abstraction. Thus, though I might determine in a marital rape case that it is relevant that the wife did not want sexual intercourse on the day in question, it will probably not be relevant that the defendant gave a box of candy to his mother on St. Valentine's Day or that he plays bridge well.[105] No matter how detailed the level of particularity, practical reasoning like all other forms of legal analysis requires selecting and giving meaning to *certain* particularities. Feminist practical reasoning assumes that no a priori reasons prevent one from being persuaded that a fact that seems insignificant *is* significant, but it does not require that every fact be relevant. Likewise, although generalizations that render detail irrelevant require examination, they are not a priori unacceptable.

Similarly, the feminist method of practical reasoning is not the polar opposite of "male" rationality. The process of finding commonalities, differences, and connections in practical reasoning is a rational process. To be sure, feminist practical reasoning gives rationality new meanings. Feminist rationality acknowledges greater diversity in human experiences[106] and the value of taking into account competing or inconsistent claims.[107] It openly reveals its positional partiality by stating explicitly which moral and political choices underlie that partiality,[108] and recognizes its own implications for the distribution and exercise of power.[109] Feminist rationality also strives to integrate emotive and intellectual elements[110] and to open up the possibilities of new situations rather than limit them with prescribed categories of

---

[105] See infra pp. 858–62.

[106] See Minow, supra note 2, at 60–61; see also J. Williams, Deconstructing Gender, supra note 48, at 805 (arguing on behalf of "a new kind of rationality, one not so closely tied to abstract, transcendental truths, one that does not exclude so much of human experience as Western rationality traditionally has done").

[107] See Minow, supra note 2, at 61–62; see also Wiggins, Deliberation and Practical Reason, in PRACTICAL REASONING 144, 145 (J. Raz ed. 1978) (arguing that practical reasoning must account for competing claims).

[108] See Haraway, Situated Knowledges: The Science Question in Feminism and the Privilege of Partial Perspective, 14 FEMINIST STUD. 575, 590 (1988); supra p. 854.

[109] See Haraway, supra note 108, at 590; Minow, supra note 2, at 65–66; see also Flax, supra note 11, at 633 (describing the need to be sensitive to interconnections between knowledge and power); Minow & Spelman, supra note 78, at 57–60 (calling for "a direct human gaze between those exercising power and those governed by it"); Gabel & Harris, Building Power and Breaking Images: Critical Theory and the Practice of Law, 11 N.Y.U. REV. L. & SOC. CHANGE 369, 375 (1982–1983) (suggesting a focus on "counter-hegemonic" law practice that draws attention to issues of power distribution).

[110] See M. BELENKY, B. CLINCHY, N. GOLDBERGER & J. TARULE, supra note 74, at 134, 176–82; see also Brennan, Reason, Passion, and "The Progress of the Law," 10 CARDOZO L. REV. 3 (1988) (noting that rational judicial decisionmaking requires passion); M. NUSSBAUM, supra note 83, at 307–09.

analysis.[111] Within these revised meanings, however, feminist method is and must be understandable. It strives to make more sense of human experience, not less, and is to be judged upon its capacity to do so.

2. *Applying the Method.* — Although feminist practical reasoning could apply to a wide range of legal problems, it has its clearest implications where it reveals insights about gender exclusion within existing legal rules and principles. In this subsection, I show how one appellate court has dealt with the validity of the common law marital exemption to rape, in order to illustrate the tradition of contextual reasoning in the common law, which practical reasoning extends, and to point out what additional features a feminist practical reasoning approach might add to this tradition.

The example is the 1981 New Jersey Supreme Court case, *State v. Smith*.[112] In rejecting the defendant's marital-exemption defense in a criminal prosecution for rape, the court engaged in a multi-layered process of reasoning; it examined the history of the exemption, the strength and evolution of the common law authority, the various justifications offered by the state for the exemption, the surrounding social and legal context in which the defendant asserted the defense, and the particular actions of the defendant in this case that gave rise to the prosecution. This process of reasoning deserves close analysis because it differs markedly from the abstract, formalistic reasoning used by other courts considering related issues.[113]

In his opinion for a unanimous court, Justice Pashman began with an examination of the source of the common law marital exemption to rape. It found the basis for the exemption "in a bare, extra-judicial declaration made some 300 years ago"[114] by Sir Matthew Hale: "'But the husband cannot be guilty of a rape committed by himself upon his lawful wife, for by their mutual matrimonial consent and contract

---

[111] *Cf.* Johann, *An Ethics of Emergent Order*, in JAMES M. GUSTAFSON'S THEOCENTRIC ETHICS 103, 109 (H. Beckley & C. Swezey eds. 1988).

[112] 85 N.J. 193, 426 A.2d 38 (1981).

[113] The courts that have faced issues relating to the marital rape exemption in recent years have used very formalistic styles of reasoning to avoid application of the exemption. *See, e.g.*, State v. Rider, 449 So. 2d 903, 904 (Fla. Dist. Ct. App. 1984) (finding no common law "interspousal exception," and stating that even if it had existed, legislative abolition of codified common law crime of rape abolished the exemption); Commonwealth v. Chretien, 383 Mass. 123, 131–32, 417 N.E.2d 1203, 1209 (1981) (holding that the state Domestic Violence Act, by implication, eliminated the marital rape exemption); People v. Liberta, 64 N.Y.2d 152, 152–53, 474 N.E.2d 567, 570–71, 485 N.Y.S.2d 207, 210–11 (1984) (applying a statutory exception to the marital rape exemption). Also following formalistic styles of reasoning, other courts have upheld the marital rape exemption. *See, e.g.*, People v. Hawkins, 157 Mich. App. 767, 404 N.W.2d 662 (1987) (holding a statute abrogating common law spousal exemption where one party has filed for divorce not applicable, because although the wife had filed for divorce, the court lacked subject matter jurisdiction due to the wife's failure to satisfy the state's residency requirements).

[114] 85 N.J. at 200, 426 A.2d at 41.

the wife hath given up herself in this kind unto her husband, which she cannot retract.'"[115] From this authority, the court determined that the common law exemption to rape "derived from the nature of marriage at a particular time in history."[116] At that time, marriages were "effectively permanent, ending only by death or an act of Parliament."[117] The court reasoned that the rule was stated "in absolute terms, as if it were applicable without exception to all marriage relationships,"[118] because marriage itself was not retractable at the time of Lord Hale. But things have changed. "In the years since Hale's formulation of the rule," the court observed, "attitudes towards the permanency of marriage have changed and divorce has become far easier to obtain."[119] Moreover, even during Lord Hale's time, the court surmised, the rule may not have applied in all situations, as when a judicial separation was granted. The court drew from its historical analysis a tentative conclusion, but reserved the ultimate question in the case for fuller analysis: "The rule, formulated under vastly different conditions, need not prevail when those conditions have changed."[120]

The court then explored the major justifications "which might have constituted the common law principles adopted in this State,"[121] including the notion that the woman was the property of her husband or father, the concept that a husband and wife were one person, and the justification that a wife consents to sexual intercourse with her husband.[122] The court engaged in a detailed analysis of each justification. The property notion, it concluded, was never valid in this country in that rape statutes "have always aimed to protect the safety and personal liberty of women."[123] The marital unity concept could not now be valid, the court decided, given the other crimes against a wife, such as assault and battery, of which a husband could be convicted, and because in many other areas of the law the "'principle' of marital unity was discarded in this State long before the commission of defendant's alleged crime."[124] The implied-consent justification, the court reasoned, is not only "offensive to our valued ideals of personal liberty," but is "not sound where the marriage itself is not

---

[115] *Id.* (quoting 1 M. HALE, HISTORY OF THE PLEAS OF THE CROWN *629).

[116] *Id.* at 201, 426 A.2d at 42.

[117] *Id.* (citing H. CLARK, LAW OF DOMESTIC RELATIONS 280–82 (1968)).

[118] *Id.*

[119] *Id.*

[120] *Id.*

[121] *Id.* at 204, 426 A.2d at 43 (footnote omitted).

[122] *See id.* at 205, 426 A.2d at 44.

[123] *Id.* at 204, 426 A.2d at 44.

[124] *Id.* at 205, 426 A.2d at 44 (citing as examples the Married Women's Acts, abolition of spousal tort immunity, alienability of a wife's interest in property held in tenancy by the entirety, the rule allowing wife to use her own surname, and indictment of husband and wife for conspiracy).

irrevocable."[125] The court noted that under the facts of this case — a year before the attack, a judge allegedly had ordered defendant to leave the marital home following another violent incident, the parties lived apart in different cities, the defendant broke into his wife's apartment at about 2:30 a.m., "over a period of a few hours, repeatedly beat her, forced her to have sexual intercourse and committed various other atrocities against her person," and caused her to require medical care at a hospital[126] — the husband could not claim that consent was implied.[127]

The *Smith* court's analysis is typical of many judicial opinions which "interpret" the common law and statutes by delving deeply into historical and policy considerations.[128] Thus, its use of practical reasoning has deep roots in American jurisprudence. I use it as an example because it demonstrates a conventional model upon which feminist practical reasoning can usefully build.

The *Smith* case helps to show, for example, how the particular facts of a case do not just present the problem to be solved, but also instruct the decisionmaker about what the ends and means of law ought to be. The circumstances of the estrangement, the middle-of-the-night break-in (two doors were broken to get inside), and defendant's repeated attacks and "atrocities" illustrate a kind of broken relationship that puts into perspective the interests a state might have in spousal reconciliation, in preventing false recriminations, or in marital privacy. Faced with the abstract question whether the marital exemption to rape should be available to husbands who have separated from their wives, more serene images come to the minds of most judges, even those who have experienced unhappy marriages. The concrete facts of *Smith* present one picture that might not readily surface to inform decisionmakers about what legal rules are practical and wise.

The *Smith* case also illustrates how practical reasoning respects, but does not blindly adhere to, legal precedent. In contrast to courts that have followed more formalistic approaches,[129] the *Smith* court saw itself as an active participant in the formulation of legal authority.

---

[125] *Id.*

[126] *Id.* at 197, 426 A.2d at 40.

[127] *See id.* at 207, 426 A.2d at 45. The Virginia Supreme Court used similar reasoning to reach the same result. *See* Weishaupt v. Commonwealth, 227 Va. 389, 405, 315 S.E.2d 847, 855 (1984) (holding that a wife had manifested her intent to end the marriage, thereby revoking her implied consent). *But see* Kizer v. Commonwealth, 228 Va. 256, 260–62, 321 S.E.2d 291, 293–94 (1984) (holding that although the spouses had separated, the marital exemption constituted a defense to the charge of rape because the wife did not manifest an objective intent to terminate the marriage).

[128] *See* M. EISENBERG, *supra* note 22, at 196 n.35.

[129] *See supra* note 113.

Without ignoring the importance to law of consistency and tradition, the Court took an approach sensitive to the human factors that a more mechanical application of precedent might ignore.

Although the *Smith* case illustrates some of the attributes of a highly contextual, pragmatic approach to decisionmaking, feminist practical reasoning would pursue some elements further than the court did. For example, feminist practical reasoning would more explicitly identify the perspective of the woman whose interest a marital rape exemption entirely subordinates to that of her estranged husband. This recognition would help to demonstrate how a rule may ratify gender-based structures of power, and thus provide the court stronger grounds for finding the exemption inapplicable to the *Smith* facts. On the other hand, feminist practical reasoning would also require more explicit recognition of the interests that supported the exemption and that the court too summarily dismissed. For example, the court rejected without discussion the state's interest in the reconciliation of separated spouses that the marital rape exemption was intended in part to serve. It also failed to address the state's concern about the evidentiary problems raised in marital rape cases.[130] The facts of the *Smith* case illustrate the weakness of these state interests. A more forthright analysis of them would have given a fuller picture of the issues, as well as guidance for other courts to which these factors may seem more significant.[131]

A fuller, practical-reasoning approach would also have given greater attention to the "due process" notice interests of the defendant who, when he acted, may have thought his actions were legal. Despite the heinous nature of the defendant's actions in this case, practical reasoning requires the examination of all perspectives, including those that a court might ultimately reject. The *Smith* court examined some relevant factors in its due process analysis, such as whether the court's ruling would be unexpected, the relationship between the exemption and the rule to which the exemption applied, and the type of crime.[132] It failed, however, to examine the role social conditioning plays in acculturating men to expect, and demand, sex. Such an examination,

---

[130] The *Smith* court mentioned this and other purposes, but did not analyze them. *See* 85 N.J. at 204 n.4, 426 A.2d at 43 n.4 (citing Note, *The Marital Rape Exemption*, 52 N.Y.U. L. REV. 306, 313–16 (1977)).

[131] In upholding the distinction between marital and nonmarital sexual assault, for example, the Colorado Supreme Court in People v. Brown, 632 P.2d 1025 (Colo. 1981), accepted without critical examination the view that the distinction encourages the preservation of family relationships, as well as "averts difficult emotional issues and problems of proof inherent in this sensitive area." *Id.* at 1027.

[132] *See* 85 N.J. 208–10, 426 A.2d at 45–47. For a discussion of the inevitable hardships resulting from the "postponement" of rules until action is complete, see B. CARDOZO, cited above in note 89, at 142–49. Justice Cardozo concludes that "cases are few in which ignorance has determined conduct." *Id.* at 145.

repeated in other cases, may help to identify the real problems society has to face in rape reform, and to challenge more deeply both male and female expectations about sex.

3. *Feminist Practical Reasoning: Method or Substance?* — The *Smith* case raises further questions about the relationship between feminist method and substance. Do feminists reason contextually in order to avoid the application of rules — like the marital rape exemption — to which they substantively object? Or can the substantive consequences of feminist practical reasoning be justified as a proper means of moving from rules to results in specific cases?

Whether the relationship between feminist practical reasoning and legal substance is a "proper" one[133] depends upon some crucial assumptions about legal decisionmaking. If one assumes that methods can and should screen out political and moral factors from legal decisionmaking, practical reasoning is not an appropriate mode of legal analysis. To the contrary, its open-endedness would seem to provide the kind of opportunity for deciding cases on the basis of political or moral interests that method, operating independently from substance, is supposed to eliminate.

On the other hand, if one assumes that one neither can nor should eliminate political and moral factors from legal decisionmaking, then one would hope to make these factors more visible. If political and moral factors are necessarily tied into any form of legal reasoning, then bringing those factors out into the open would require decision-makers to think self-consciously about them and to justify their decisions in the light of the factors at play in the particular case.

Feminists, not surprisingly, favor the second set of assumptions over the first. Feminists' substantive analyses of legal decisionmaking have revealed to them that so-called neutral means of deciding cases tend to mask, not eliminate, political and social considerations from legal decisionmaking.[134] Feminists have found that neutral rules and procedures tend to drive underground the ideologies of the decision-maker, and that these ideologies do not serve women's interests well. Disadvantaged by hidden bias, feminists see the value of modes of legal reasoning that expose and open up debate concerning the un-

---

[133] See supra p. 846.

[134] See, e.g., Minow, supra note 2, at 34–45 (describing how unstated norms and assumptions about differences affect substantive legal decisionmaking); Mossman, supra note 55, at 156–63 (arguing that traditional methods of characterizing the legal issue, choosing legal precedent and interpreting statutes mask political choices); see also Kairys, *Legal Reasoning*, in THE POLITICS OF LAW: A PROGRESSIVE CRITIQUE, supra note 2, at 11, 11–17 (arguing that the stare decisis principle serves primarily an ideological rather than a functional role); Gabel & Harris, supra note 109, at 373 (arguing that legal reasoning is an "ideological form of thought" that "*presupposes* both the existence of and the legitimacy of existing hierarchical institutions" (emphasis in original)); Singer, supra note 59, at 6, 30–39, 43–47 (arguing that legal reasoning obscures political and moral commitment and fails to transcend contradictory value choices).

derlying political and moral considerations. By forcing articulation and understanding of those considerations, practical reasoning forces justification of results based upon what interests are actually at stake. The "substance" of feminist practical reasoning consists of an alertness to certain forms of injustice that otherwise go unnoticed and unaddressed. Feminists turn to contextualized methods of reasoning to allow greater understanding and exposure of that injustice. Reasoning from context can change perceptions about the world, which may then further expand the contexts within which such reasoning seems appropriate, which in turn may lead to still further changes in perceptions. The expansion of existing boundaries of relevance based upon changed perceptions of the world is familiar to the process of legal reform. The shift from *Plessy v. Ferguson*[135] to *Brown v. Board of Education*,[136] for example, rested upon the expansion of the "legally relevant" in race discrimination cases to include the actual experiences of black Americans and the inferiority implicit in segregation.[137] Much of the judicial reform that has been beneficial to women, as well, has come about through expanding the lens of legal relevance to encompass the missing perspectives of women and to accommodate perceptions about the nature and role of women.[138] Feminist practical reasoning compels continued expansion of such perceptions.

C. Consciousness-Raising

Another feminist method for expanding perceptions is consciousness-raising.[139] Consciousness-raising is an interactive and collaborative process of articulating one's experiences and making meaning

---

[135] 163 U.S. 537 (1896).

[136] 347 U.S. 483 (1954).

[137] Professor Paul Mishkin provided me with this example.

[138] *See, e.g.*, Stanton v. Stanton, 421 U.S. 7, 14–15 (1975) (invalidating sex-based differences in the age of majority for child support purposes because the assumption that the female is destined for the home and that the male is destined for the marketplace has become outmoded); Frontiero v. Richardson, 411 U.S. 677 (1973) (plurality opinion) (invalidating a sex-based dependency presumption on grounds that gross, stereotypical distinctions between the sexes relegate females to an inferior legal status without regard to their actual capabilities); Reed v. Reed, 404 U.S. 71 (1971) (invalidating a sex-based presumption in favor of men in the appointment of estate administrators, based upon change in perceptions about the appropriate role of women).

[139] Catharine MacKinnon sees consciousness-raising as *the* method of feminism. "Consciousness-raising is the major technique of analysis, structure of organization, method of practice, the theory of social change of the women's movement." MacKinnon, *Agenda for Theory, supra* note 2, at 519. Many feminist legal thinkers have emphasized the importance of consciousness-raising to feminist practice and method. *See, e.g.*, Law, *Equality: The Power and Limits of the Law* (Book Review), 95 YALE L.J. 1769, 1784 (1986); Matsuda, *supra* note 101, at 618–22; Scales, *supra* note 2, at 1401–02; Schneider, *supra* note 2, at 602–04. For historical perspectives on consciousness-raising in the American women's movement, see C. HYMOWITZ & M. WEISSMAN, A HISTORY OF WOMEN IN AMERICA 351–55 (1978); and G. LERNER, cited above in note 26, at 42–44.

of them with others who also articulate their experiences. As Leslie Bender writes, "Feminist consciousness-raising creates knowledge by exploring common experiences and patterns that emerge from shared tellings of life events. What were experienced as personal hurts individually suffered reveal themselves as a collective experience of oppression."[140]

Consciousness-raising is a method of trial and error. When revealing an experience to others, a participant in consciousness-raising does not know whether others will recognize it. The process values risk-taking and vulnerability over caution and detachment. Honesty is valued above consistency, teamwork over self-sufficiency, and personal narrative over abstract analysis. The goal is individual and collective empowerment, not personal attack or conquest.

Elizabeth Schneider emphasizes the centrality of consciousness-raising to the dialectical relationship of theory and practice. "Consciousness-raising groups start with personal and concrete experience, integrate this experience into theory, and then, in effect, reshape theory based upon experience and experience based upon theory. Theory expresses and grows out of experience but it also relates back to that experience for further refinement, validation, or modification."[141] The interplay between experience and theory "reveals the social dimension of individual experience and the individual dimension of social experience"[142] and hence the political nature of personal experience.[143]

Consciousness-raising operates as feminist method not only in small personal growth groups, but also on a more public, institutional level, through "bearing witness to evidences of patriarchy as they occur, through unremitting dialogues with and challenges to the patriarchs, and through the popular media, the arts, politics, lobbying, and even

---

[140] Bender, *A Lawyer's Primer on Feminist Theory and Tort*, 38 J. LEGAL EDUC. 3, 9 (1988) (citations omitted); *see also* Z. EISENSTEIN, FEMINISM AND SEXUAL EQUALITY: CRISIS IN LIBERAL AMERICA 150–57 (1984) (stressing the importance of building feminist consciousness out of sex-class consciousness); T. DE LAURETIS, ALICE DOESN'T: FEMINISM, SEMIOTICS, CINEMA 185 (1984) (describing consciousness-raising as "the collective articulation of one's experience of sexuality and gender — which has produced, and continues to elaborate, a radically new mode of understanding the subject's relation to social-historical reality"); J. MITCHELL, WOMAN'S ESTATE 61 (1971) (maintaining that through consciousness-raising, women proclaim the painful and transform it into the political).

[141] Schneider, *supra* note 2, at 602 (footnote omitted).

[142] *Id.* at 603.

[143] *See id.* at 602–04. Hence the feminist phrase: "The personal is the political." MacKinnon's explanation of this phrase is perhaps the best: "It means that women's distinctive experience as women occurs within that sphere that has been socially lived as the personal — private, emotional, interiorized, particular, individuated, intimate — so that what it is to *know* the *politics* of woman's situation is to know women's personal lives." MacKinnon, *Agenda for Theory, supra* note 2, at 535.

litigation."[144]   Women use consciousness-raising when they publicly share their experiences as victims of marital rape,[145] pornography,[146] sexual harassment on the job,[147] street hassling,[148] and other forms of oppression and exclusion, in order to help change public perceptions about the meaning to women of events widely thought to be harmless or flattering.

Consciousness-raising has consequences, further, for laws and institutional decisionmaking more generally. Several feminists have translated the insights of feminist consciousness-raising into their normative accounts of legal process and legal decisionmaking. Carrie Menkel-Meadow, for example, has speculated that as the number of women lawyers increases, women's more interactive approaches to decisionmaking will improve legal process.[149] Similarly, Judith Resnik has argued that feminist judging will involve more collaborative decisionmaking among judges.[150] Such changes would have important implications for the possibilities for lawyering and judging as matters of collective engagement rather than the individual exercise of judgment and power.

---

[144] Bender, *supra* note 140, at 9–10. In a recent example of litigation as consciousness-raising, three women filed a lawsuit against *Hustler Magazine* for "libel, invasion of privacy, intentional infliction of emotional injury, 'outrage,'" and various civil rights claims, following publication of a pornographic cartoon and photographs. Some of this material referred specifically to anti-pornography activist Andrea Dworkin, who was one of the plaintiffs. *See* Dworkin v. Hustler Magazine, Inc., 867 F.2d 1188 (9th Cir. 1989). The lawsuit, which was dismissed on motion for summary judgment, sought $150 million in damages for both direct harm caused to the women who are the subjects of such pornographic material, and the indirect harm of the material to other women "who are afraid to exercise [political freedoms on behalf of women] for fear of an ugly, pornographic representation of them appearing in such a magazine." *Id.* at 1191. The plaintiffs in this case probably did not expect to prevail on their claims, or to be awarded damages on the scale they sought. Such a lawsuit, however, can contribute to public education and dialogue on the issues it raises. Parties, of course, are subject to sanctions for pursuing "frivolous" litigation. In *Dworkin*, the Ninth Circuit denied a request for double costs and attorneys' fees pursuant to rule 38 of the *Federal Rules of Appellate Procedure* and 28 U.S.C. § 1912, but suggested that if the plaintiffs raise similar contentions in subsequent cases, sanctions may be appropriate. *See* 867 F.2d at 1200–01.

[145] *See, e.g.*, L. WALKER, THE BATTERED WOMAN 1–9 (1979); E. PIZZEY, SCREAM QUIETLY OR THE NEIGHBORS WILL HEAR (1977).

[146] *See, e.g.*, L. LOVELACE & M. McGRADY, ORDEAL (1980), *discussed in* C. MACKINNON, *supra* note 7, at 10–14, 234–35.

[147] *See, e.g.*, C. MACKINNON, SEXUAL HARASSMENT OF WORKING WOMEN 25–55 (1979).

[148] *See, e.g.*, West, *The Difference in Women's Hedonic Lives: A Phenomenological Critique of Feminist Legal Theory*, 3 WIS. WOMEN'S L.J. 81, 106–08 (1987).

[149] *See* Menkel-Meadow, *supra* note 74, at 55–58.

[150] *See* Resnik, *On the Bias: Feminist Reconsiderations of the Aspirations for Our Judges*, 61 S. CAL. L. REV. 1877, 1942–43 (1988); *see also* Sherwin, *Philosophical Methodology and Feminist Methodology: Are They Compatible?*, in FEMINIST PERSPECTIVES: PHILOSOPHICAL ESSAYS ON METHOD AND MORALS 13, 19 (L. Code, S. Mullett & C. Overall eds. 1988) (linking consciousness-raising with interactive processes of thought).

The primary significance of consciousness-raising, however, is as meta-method. Consciousness-raising provides a substructure for other feminist methods — including the woman question and feminist practical reasoning — by enabling feminists to draw insights and perceptions from their own experiences and those of other women and to use these insights to challenge dominant versions of social reality.

Consciousness-raising has done more than help feminists develop and affirm counter-hegemonic perceptions of their experiences. As consciousness-raising has matured as method, disagreements among feminists about the meaning of certain experiences have proliferated. Feminists disagree, for example, about whether women can voluntarily choose heterosexuality,[151] or motherhood;[152] or about whether feminists have more to gain or lose from restrictions against pornography,[153] surrogate motherhood,[154] or about whether women should be

---

[151] *Compare, e.g.,* Rich, *Compulsory Heterosexuality and Lesbian Existence,* SIGNS, Summer 1980, at 4 (arguing that compulsory heterosexuality is the central social structure perpetuating male domination) *and* A. DWORKIN, INTERCOURSE (1987) (arguing that heterosexual intercourse oppresses women) *and* C. MACKINNON, *supra* note 7, at 7 (arguing that heterosexuality "organizes women's pleasure so as to give us a stake in our own subordination") *with* Colker, *Feminism, Sexuality and Self: A Preliminary Inquiry into the Politics of Authenticity* (Book Review), 68 B.U.L. REV. 217, 259–60 (1988) (arguing that either exclusive lesbianism or heterosexuality may prevent women from coming closer to their "authentic sexuality").

[152] *Compare* S. FIRESTONE, THE DIALECTIC OF SEX: THE CASE FOR FEMINIST REVOLUTION (1970) (arguing that motherhood is a primary source of oppression for women) *and* Macintyre, *"Who Wants Babies?" The Social Construction of "Instincts,"* in SEXUAL DIVISIONS AND SOCIETY: PROCESS AND CHANGE 150 (D. Barker & S. Allen eds. 1976) (exploring how the concept of maternal instincts fulfills societal norms of reproduction) *with* A. RICH, OF WOMAN BORN: MOTHERHOOD AS EXPERIENCE AND INSTITUTION (1976) (arguing that although motherhood is oppressive under patriarchy, it is also the source of creativity and joy) *and* Rossi, *A Biosocial Perspective on Parenting,* DAEDALUS, Spring 1977, at 1 (defending motherhood within a dialectical view that takes both biology and social behavior into account) *and* B. SICHTERMANN, FEMINITY: THE POLITICS OF THE PERSONAL 17–31 (1986) (arguing that women's desire to have children derives from physical need).

[153] *Compare* C. MACKINNON, *supra* note 7, at 163–97 (defending the civil rights ordinance against pornography because of the harm to women caused by defining sex in terms of male dominance and female submission) *and* A. DWORKIN, PORNOGRAPHY: MEN POSSESSING WOMEN (1981) (describing ways in which pornography harms women) *with* Dunlap, *Sexual Speech and the State: Putting Pornography in Its Place,* 17 GOLDEN GATE U.L. REV. 359 (1987) (arguing that restrictions on pornography are undesirable because they would prevent necessary public debate on sexual issues) *and* WOMEN AGAINST CENSORSHIP (V. Burstyn ed. 1985) (collecting essays opposing censorship of pornography) *and* Hollibaugh, *Desire for the Future: Radical Hope in Passion and Pleasure,* in PLEASURE AND DANGER: EXPLORING FEMALE SEXUALITY 401 (C. Vance ed. 1984) (arguing that some pornography can improve healthy sexual expression for women).

[154] *Compare* B. ROTHMAN, RECREATING MOTHERHOOD: IDEOLOGY AND TECHNOLOGY IN A PATRIARCHAL SOCIETY 229–45 (1989) (arguing against surrogate motherhood) *with* M. FIELD, SURROGATE MOTHERHOOD (1988) (arguing that surrogate parent contracts should be neither criminalized nor legally enforceable) *and* L. ANDREWS, BETWEEN STRANGERS: SURROGATE MOTHERS, EXPECTANT FATHERS, & BRAVE NEW BABIES 252–72 (1989) (disputing claims of feminists who oppose surrogacy).

subject to a military draft.[155] They disagree about each other's roles in an oppressive society: some feminists accuse others of complicity in the oppression of women.[156] Feminists disagree even about the method of consciousness-raising; some women worry that it sometimes operates to pressure women into translating their experiences into positions that are politically, rather than experientially, correct.[157]

These disagreements raise questions beyond those of which specific methods are appropriate to feminist practice. Like the woman question and practical reasoning, consciousness-raising challenges the concept of knowledge. It presupposes that what I thought I knew may not, in fact, be "right." How, then, will we know when we *have* got it "right"? Or, backing up one step, what does it mean to *be* right? And what attitude should I have about that which I claim to know? The next Part will focus on these questions.

III. FEMINIST KNOWING IN LAW

A point — perhaps *the* point — of legal methods is to reach answers that are legally defensible or in some sense "right." Methods themselves imply a stance toward rightness. If being right means having discovered some final, objective truth based in a fixed physical or moral reality, for example, verification is possible and leaves no room for further perspectives or for doubt. On the other hand, if being right means that one has expressed one's personal tastes or interests which have no greater claim to validity than those of anyone else, being right is a rhetorical device used to assert one's own point of view, and verification is both impossible and pointless.

In this section, I explore several feminist explanations for what it means to be "right" in law.[158] I look first at a range of positions that have emerged from within feminist theory. These include the three positions customarily included in feminist epistemological discussions:

---

[155] *Compare* W. Williams, *supra* note 2, at 189 (reporting her opposition to single-sex draft) *with* Scales, *Militarism, Male Dominance and Law: Feminist Jurisprudence As Oxymoron*, 12 HARV. WOMEN'S L.J. 25, 42 (1989) (arguing that "militarism *normalizes* the oppression of women" (emphasis in original)).

[156] *See* C. MACKINNON, *supra* note 7, at 198–205 (accusing women who defend first amendment values against restrictions on pornography of collaboration).

[157] *See* Colker, *supra* note 151, at 253–54 (noting that consciousness-raising may influence women to adopt "inauthentic" expressions of themselves).

[158] Separating attitude about knowledge from the knowledge itself might appear a hopeless task. My attitude toward knowing is, in a sense, a claim about what I know. Moreover, my attitude about knowing, like other claims, may itself be strategic. *Cf.* C. WEEDON, FEMINIST PRACTICE AND POSTSTRUCTURALIST THEORY 131–35 (1987) (offering a strategic rationale for a radical feminist critique); W. Williams, *Equality's Riddle, supra* note 48, at 351–52 (justifying equal-treatment over special-treatment theory for tactical reasons). Despite the analytical overlap, the separation of issues of attitude from other knowledge claims enables greater focus on these issues.

the rational/empirical position, standpoint epistemology, and postmodernism.[159] In addition I examine a fourth stance called positionality,[160] which synthesizes some aspects of the first three into a new, and I think more satisfactory, whole. I evaluate each position from the same pragmatic viewpoint reflected in the feminist methods I have described: how can that position help feminists, using feminist methods, to generate the kind of insights, values, and self-knowledge that feminism needs to maintain its critical challenge to existing structures of power and to reconstruct new, and better, structures in their place? These criteria are admittedly circular: I evaluate theories of knowledge by how well they make sense in light of that which feminists claim as knowledge and in light of the methods used to obtain knowledge. This circularity, however, is consistent with one of the central features of the version of feminism I advocate. Any set of values and truths, including those of feminists, must make sense within the terms of the social realities that have generated them. Any explanation of that verification must also operate in the context in which verifications take place — in practice.

A. The Rational/Empirical Position

Feminists across many disciplines have engaged in considerable efforts to show how, by the standards of their own disciplines, to improve accepted methodologies. These efforts have led to the unraveling of descriptions of women as morally inferior, psychologically unstable, and historically insignificant — descriptions these disciplines long accepted as authoritative and unquestionable.[161]

Similarly, feminists in law attempt to use the tools of law, on its own terms, to improve law. Using the methods discussed in Part II

---

[159] Sandra Harding, Mary Hawkesworth, and others use these categories. *See* S. HARDING, THE SCIENCE QUESTION IN FEMINISM 24–28 (1986); Hawkesworth, *Knowers, Knowing, Known: Feminist Theory and Claims of Truth*, 14 SIGNS 533, 535–37 (1989). I define these categories somewhat differently than either Harding or Hawkesworth to reflect the categories into which feminists doing law have seemed to fall.

In using these categories, I am mindful of Leslie Bender's observation that labels and categorizations are divisive and cause ideas to "become fixed instead of remaining fluid and growing." Bender, *supra* note 140, at 5 n.5. Regretfully, I find the labels necessary to order, describe and clarify differences in ways of thinking. *See supra* note 18.

[160] This term I have adapted from Linda Alcoff's description of the appropriate feminist view toward the concept of "woman." *See* Alcoff, *supra* note 8, at 428–36.

[161] *See, e.g.*, R. BLEIER, SCIENCE AND GENDER: A CRITIQUE OF BIOLOGY AND ITS THEORIES ON WOMEN (1984) (analyzing the androcentric bias of biology); N. CHODOROW, THE REPRODUCTION OF MOTHERING: PSYCHOANALYSIS AND THE SOCIOLOGY OF GENDER (1978) (reinterpreting, within psychoanalytic theory, the Freudian account of mothering); C. GILLIGAN, *supra* note 74 (demonstrating that conventional stages of moral development underlying psychological theory are invalid because drawn from study groups that did not include women); G. LERNER, *supra* note 26 (reformulating objects of historical inquiry to include women's experiences).

of this Article, feminists often challenge assumptions about women that underlie numerous laws and demonstrate how laws based upon these assumptions are not rational and neutral, but rather irrational and discriminatory. When engaged in these challenges, feminists operate from a rational/empirical position that assumes that the law is not objective, but that identifying and correcting its mistaken assumptions can make it more objective.

When feminists challenged employment rules that denied disability benefits to pregnant women, for example, they used empirical and rational arguments about the similarity between pregnancy and other disabilities.[162] Faced with state laws designed to address the disadvantages experienced by pregnant women in the workplace, some feminists argued that such "special treatment" for pregnant women reinforces stereotypes about women and should be rejected under the equality principle. Other feminists argued that pregnancy affects only women and that lack of accommodation for it will prevent women from achieving equality in the workplace.[163] Each side of the debate defended a different concept of equality, but the underlying argument focused upon which is the most rational, empirically sound and legally supportable interpretation of equality.

In other areas of the law, feminists have also operated from within this rational/empirical stance. Susan Estrich, for example, argues that the correction of certain factual inaccuracies can better achieve the purposes of rape law — to prevent rape, to protect women, and to punish rapists. Estrich contends, for example, that the assumption that women mean "yes" when they say "no" is false and that a rational rape law would define consent so that "no means no."[164]

Feminists also argue that particular reforms in child custody law would more rationally meet the law's express purpose of protecting the best interests of the child. Some feminists favor the tender-years doctrine or the maternal-preference rule, on the ground that women are likely to be the actual caretakers of children,[165] and that the bias against women of the white, male judges who decide custody cases makes such a rule necessary to give women a fair shot at custody.[166]

---

[162] See supra pp. 841–42; see also W. Williams, Equality's Riddle, supra note 48, at 335–58 (arguing that although pregnancy is unique for some purposes, it resembles other disabilities for the purposes of disability benefit plans).

[163] See supra note 48.

[164] S. ESTRICH, supra note 49, at 102. Estrich argues also that rape law would be more rational if a negligence standard were applied to the defendant's intent. See id. at 92–104.

[165] See, e.g., Klaff, The Tender Years Doctrine: A Defense, 70 CALIF. L. REV. 335 (1982).

[166] See, e.g., P. CHESLER, MOTHERS ON TRIAL: THE BATTLE FOR CHILDREN AND CUSTODY 239–68 (1986); Sheppard, Unspoken Premises in Custody Litigation, 7 WOMEN'S RTS. L. REP. 229, 233 (1982); Uviller, Fathers' Rights and Feminism: The Maternal Presumption Revisited, 1 HARV. WOMEN'S L.J. 107, 121–23 (1978); see also Polikoff, Why Are Mothers Losing: A Brief Analysis of Criteria Used in Child Custody Determinations, 7 WOMEN'S RTS. L. REP. 235, 237–

Other feminists argue that applying the best-interests-of-the-child test on a case-by-case basis will produce the fairest and most neutral child-custody decisions.[167] Still other feminists advocate a primary care-taker presumption on the empirical ground that a child's primary caretaker is most likely to be the parent in whose custody the child's best interests lies,[168] and that this standard minimizes the potential intimidation that can be exercised against a risk-averse parent who has invested the most in the child's care.[169] Finally, some feminists favor rules that promote joint custody, based upon empirical claims about which rules best serve the interests of children and women.[170]

All of these arguments from the rational/empirical stance share the premise that knowledge is accessible and, when obtained, can make law more rational. The relevant empirical questions are often very difficult ones: if parents, usually men, who fall behind in their child support obligations face almost certain jail sentences, will they be more likely to make their child support payments on time?[171] If state law singles out pregnancy as the only condition for which job security is mandated, how much additional resistance to hiring women, if any, is likely to be created, and what impact on the stereotyping of women, if any, is likely to result?[172] The rational/empirical position presumes, however, that answers to such questions can be improved — that there is a "right" answer to get — and that once gotten, that answer can improve the law.

Some feminists charge that improving the empirical basis of law or its rationality is mere "reformism" that cannot reach the deeper

---

39 (1982) (discussing male bias in decisionmaking, but favoring a primary-caretaker presumption).

[167] See, e.g., Schulman & Pitt, *Second Thoughts on Joint Child Custody: Analysis of Legislation and Its Implications for Women and Children*, 12 GOLDEN GATE U.L. REV. 539, 552 (1982); Scott & Derdeyn, *Rethinking Joint Custody*, 45 OHIO ST. L.J. 455, 484–95 (1984).

[168] See, e.g., Chambers, *Rethinking the Substantive Rules for Custody Disputes in Divorce*, 83 MICH. L. REV. 477, 560–65 (1984) (advocating a preference for primary caretakers in cases involving young children); Fineman, *Dominant Discourse, Professional Language, and Legal Change in Child Custody Decisionmaking*, 101 HARV. L. REV. 727, 770–74 (1988) (advocating the use of the primary-caretaker rule in all custody cases); Polikoff, *supra* note 166, at 237–39.

The question of a child's "best interests" is, of course, as much a normative as an empirical question. See Bartlett & Stack, *Joint Custody, Feminism and the Dependency Dilemma*, 2 BERKELEY WOMEN'S L.J. 9, 11 (1986); Mnookin, *Child-Custody Adjudication: Judicial Functions in the Face of Indeterminacy*, LAW & CONTEMP. PROBS., Summer 1975, at 226, 258–61.

[169] See Olsen, *The Politics of Family Law*, 2 J.L. & INEQUALITY 1, 19 (1984); see also Mnookin & Kornhauser, *Bargaining in the Shadow of the Law*, 88 YALE L.J. 950, 979 (1979) (arguing that the best-interests standard disadvantages the more risk-averse parent); Fineman, *supra* note 168, at 772 (arguing that the best-interests test disadvantages the lower-income parent because of need to hire experts).

[170] See, e.g., Bartlett & Stack, *supra* note 168.

[171] This was one of the principal research questions in D. CHAMBERS, MAKING FATHERS PAY: THE ENFORCEMENT OF CHILD SUPPORT (1979).

[172] See W. Williams, *Equality's Riddle*, *supra* note 48, at 355.

gendered nature of law.[173] This charge unfortunately undervalues the enormous transformation in thinking about women that the empirical challenge to law, in which all feminists have participated, has brought about. Feminist rational/empiricism has begun to expose the deeply flawed factual assumptions about women that have pervaded many disciplines, and has changed, in profound ways, the perception of women in this society.[174] Few, if any, feminists, however, operate entirely within the rational/empirical stance, because it tends to limit attention to matters of factual rather than normative accuracy, and thus fails to take account of the social construction of reality through which factual or rational propositions mask normative constructions.[175] Empirical and rational arguments challenge existing assumptions about reality and, in particular, the inaccurate reality conveyed by stereotypes about women. But if reality is not representational or objective and not above politics, the method of correcting inaccuracies ultimately cannot provide a basis for under-

---

[173] Christine Littleton and Catharine MacKinnon, for example, associate rational/empirical efforts to open up more opportunities for women with "assimilationism" or "liberal feminism," which, in retaining its focus on individualism, provides no basis from which to challenge the way in which women's individuality has been determined by men rather than freely chosen, or to validate any of the choices that individuals make. See Littleton, *supra* note 21, at 754–63; C. MacKinnon, *supra* note 7, at 137.

[174] The most well-known example outside of law is Carol Gilligan's challenge to Lawrence Kohlberg's paradigm of moral reasoning. In showing that Kohlberg had erred in drawing his study sample too narrowly by excluding women, Gilligan uncovered a source of systematic bias that ran throughout the discipline of psychology. See C. Gilligan, *supra* note 74, at 18–21. Confronted with a more inclusive and thus representative study group, psychologists could recognize the error within the terms of their own discipline. Disputes persist about the significance and validity of Gilligan's findings, which have kept alive the empirical debate. *Compare* Auerbach, Blum, Smith & Williams, *Commentary on Gilligan's* In a Different Voice, 11 Feminist Stud. 149 (1985) (criticizing Gilligan's developmental stages theory for ignoring social factors and arguing that Gilligan's interview material does not support her generalizations) *and* Broughton, *Women's Rationality and Men's Virtues: A Critique of Gender Dualism in Gilligan's Theory of Moral Development*, 50 Soc. Res. 597 (1983) (arguing that Gilligan exaggerates the duality in moral development) *and* Nails, *Social-Scientific Sexism: Gilligan's Mismeasure of Man*, 50 Soc. Res. 643 (1983) (questioning social-scientific research that leads to the oppression of disadvantaged groups) *with* Flanagan & Adler, *Impartiality and Particularity*, 50 Soc. Res. 576 (1983) (suggesting that the flaws and limitations of the Kohlberg thesis also constrain Gilligan). *See also* Kerber, Greeno, Maccoby, Luria, Stack & Gilligan, *On* In a Different Voice: *An Interdisciplinary Forum*, 11 Signs 304 (1986). Despite these disputes, Gilligan's work has moved the discipline in more rational, empirically correct directions, with revolutionary implications for many other disciplines. *See generally* Women and Moral Theory, *supra* note 85 (exploring in a collection of essays the potential of feminist research, especially that begun by Gilligan, to redirect and enhance moral theory).

[175] Feminists have made significant contributions to understandings about the social construction of reality. *See generally* S. de Beauvoir, *supra* note 23 (describing how men have defined women as other and created a myth of woman); S. Harding, *supra* note 159 (arguing that science is gendered); MacKinnon, *Agenda for Theory, supra* note 2 (arguing that gender is a social construct that embodies male sexual dominance).

standing and reconstructing that reality. The rational/empirical assumption that principles such as objectivity and neutrality can question empirical assumptions within law fails to recognize that knowability is itself a debatable issue. I explore positions that challenge, rather than presuppose, knowability in the following sections.

B. Standpoint Epistemology

The problem of knowability in feminist thought arises from the observation that what women know has been determined — perhaps overdetermined[176] — by male culture. Some of the feminists most concerned about the problem of overdetermination have adopted a "standpoint epistemology"[177] to provide the grounding upon which feminists can claim that their own legal methods, legal reasoning, and proposals for substantive legal reform are "right."

Feminist standpoint epistemology identifies woman's status as that of victim, and then privileges that status by claiming that it gives access to understanding about oppression that others cannot have. It grounds this privilege in the contention that pain and subordination provide the oppressed "with a motivation for finding out what is wrong, for criticizing accepted interpretations of reality and for developing new and less distorted ways of understanding the world."[178] The experience of being a victim therefore reveals truths about reality that non-victims do not see.

> Women know the world is out there. Women know the world is out there because it hits us in the face. Literally. We are raped, battered, pornographed, defined by force, by a world that begins, at least, entirely outside us. No matter what we think about it, how we try to think it out of existence or into a different shape for us to inhabit, the world remains real. Try some time. It exists independent of our

---

[176] Cf. Alcoff, supra note 8, at 416 (describing Derrida's and Foucault's view that "we are overdetermined . . . by a social discourse and/or cultural practice"); J. MITCHELL, supra note 140, at 99–122. Juliet Mitchell defines overdetermination as "a complex notion of 'multiple causation' in which the numerous factors can reinforce, overlap, cancel each other out, or contradict one another." J. MITCHELL, PSYCHOANALYSIS AND FEMINISM 309 n.12 (1974). The concept of overdetermination appears to have originated with Freud, see id., who used it to explain the causes of hysterical symptoms and the content of dreams. See S. FREUD, The Aetiology of Hysteria, in 1 SIGMUND FREUD: COLLECTED PAPERS 183, 213 (1959); S. FREUD, The Interpretation of Dreams, in THE BASIC WRITINGS OF SIGMUND FREUD 181, 338 (A. Brill trans. & ed. 1938).

[177] Sandra Harding finds the roots of the standpoint approach in Hegel's analysis of the relationship between master and slave, which was elaborated by Engels, Marx, and Lukacs, and extended to feminist theory by Jane Flax, Hilary Rose, Nancy Hartsock, and Dorothy Smith. See S. HARDING, supra note 159, at 26.

[178] A. JAGGAR, FEMINIST POLITICS AND HUMAN NATURE 370 (1983).

will. We can tell that it is there, because no matter what we do, we can't get out of it.[179]

Feminists have located the foundation of women's subordination in different aspects of women's experiences. Feminist post-Marxists find this foundation in women's activities in production, both domestic and in the marketplace;[180] others emphasize women's positions in the sexual hierarchy,[181] in women's bodies,[182] or in women's responses to the pain and fear of male violence.[183] Whatever the source, however, these feminists claim that the material deprivation of the oppressed gives them a perspective — an access to knowledge — that the oppressors cannot possibly have.[184]

Standpoint epistemology has contributed a great deal to feminist understandings of the importance of our respective positioning within society to the "knowledge" we have. Feminist standpoint epistemologies question "the assumption that the social identity of the observer is irrelevant to the 'goodness' of the results of research," and reverse the priority of a distanced, "objective" standpoint in favor of one of experience and engagement.[185]

Despite the valuable insights offered by feminist standpoint epistemology, however, it does not offer an adequate account of feminist knowing. First, in isolating gender as a source of oppression, feminist legal thinkers tend to concentrate on the identification of woman's true identity beneath the oppression and thereby essentialize her characteristics. Catharine MacKinnon, for example, in exposing what she finds to be the total system of male hegemony, repeatedly speaks of "women's point of view,"[186] of "woman's voice,"[187] of empowering women "on our own terms,"[188] of what women "really want,"[189] and of standards that are "not ours."[190] Ruth Colker sees the discovery of women's "authentic self"[191] as a difficult job given the social con-

---

[179] C. MacKinnon, supra note 7, at 57.

[180] See Hartsock, The Feminist Standpoint: Developing the Ground for a Specifically Feminist Historical Materialism, in Discovering Reality: Feminist Perspectives on Epistemology, Metaphysics, Methodology, and Philosophy of Science 283 (S. Harding & M. Hintikka eds. 1983).

[181] See MacKinnon, Agenda for Theory, supra note 2.

[182] See generally Z. Eisenstein, The Female Body and the Law (1988); West, supra note 2.

[183] See West, supra note 148, at 94.

[184] See MacKinnon, Agenda for Theory, supra note 2, at 534–38.

[185] S. Harding, supra note 159, at 162.

[186] See C. MacKinnon, supra note 7, at 88, 91, 160.

[187] See id. at 195.

[188] See id. at 22.

[189] See id. at 83.

[190] See id. at 76.

[191] See Colker, supra note 151, at 218.

structions imposed upon women, but nonetheless, like MacKinnon, insists upon it as a central goal of feminism. Robin West, too, assumes that woman has a "true nature" upon which to base a feminist jurisprudence.[192]

Although the essentialist positions taken by these feminists often have strategic or rhetorical value,[193] these positions obscure the importance of differences among women and the fact that factors other than gender victimize women. A theory that purports to isolate gender as a basis for oppression obscures these factors and even reinforces other forms of oppression.[194] This error duplicates the error of other legal theories that project the meaning speakers give to their own experiences onto the experiences of others.[195]

In addition to imposing too broad a view of gender, standpoint epistemologists also tend to presuppose too narrow a view of privilege.

---

[192] See West, *supra* note 2, at 4. West devoted an earlier article to the need for a "phenomenological critique" of women's subjective experiences, which West suggested could be accomplished by women "speaking the truth about the quality of our internal lives." West, *supra* note 148, at 144. In *Jurisprudence and Gender*, West seems to have partially resolved the ambiguities she earlier saw in women's nature to find women's experience to be one of connection in contrast to the experience of separation presupposed in all modern legal theory. See West, *supra* note 2, at 1–3; *see also* West, *Feminism, Critical Social Theory and Law*, 1989 U. CHI. LEGAL F. 59, 96 (rejecting the anti-essentialism of critical social theory).

Other feminists also assume that women have an essential, discoverable identity, but do not seem to claim a privileged knowledge based on this identity. See, e.g., Finley, *Transcending Equality Theory: A Way out of the Maternity and the Workplace Debate*, 86 COLUM. L. REV. 1118, 1139–40 (1986) (attributing certain unique, "mystical" qualities to pregnancy); Sherry, *supra* note 74, at 584–85 (defining the "'basic feminine sense of self,'" which is "'connected to the world'" in a way the male self is not (quoting N. CHODOROW, *supra* note 161, at 169)).

[193] See D. FUSS, *supra* note 71, at 20 (distinguishing between "deploying" essentialism for strategic purposes and "lapsing into" essentialism by mistake).

[194] Angela Harris and Patricia Cain, from different perspectives, each make this point specifically about MacKinnon and West. See Harris, *supra* note 2 (criticizing West and MacKinnon for "essentialism," which brackets race and results in black women's voices being ignored); Cain, *Feminist Jurisprudence: Grounding the Theories*, 4 BERKELEY WOMEN'S L.J. (forthcoming 1990) (challenging the exclusion of lesbian experience from feminist legal theory). Elizabeth Spelman and Martha Minow make the point more generally about feminist theory. See E. SPELMAN, *supra* note 11; Minow, *supra* note 11; *supra* pp. 847–49.

[195] The minority critique of critical legal studies (CLS) has given this theme particular prominence. See, e.g., Dalton, *The Clouded Prism*, 22 HARV. C.R.-C.L. L. REV. 435 (1987) (highlighting the differences in background between critical legal scholars and minority scholars); Delgado, *The Ethereal Scholar: Does Critical Legal Studies Have What Minorities Want?*, 22 HARV. C.R.-C.L. L. REV. 301 (1987) (arguing that the CLS critique of legal rules and rights and its championing of informal decisionmaking offer little hope of curbing racism); Matsuda, *Looking to the Bottom: Critical Legal Studies and Reparations*, 22 HARV. C.R.-C.L. L. REV. 323 (1987) (suggesting that critical scholars attend to the "distinct normative insights" of victims of social oppression); Williams, *supra* note 85 (criticizing the CLS rejection of rights and ignoring the importance of rights in the lives of blacks); *see also* D. BELL, AND WE ARE NOT SAVED 51–74 (1987) (arguing that whites have gained more than blacks from the civil rights movement). For a counter-critique, see Kennedy, *Racial Critiques of Legal Academia*, 102 HARV. L. REV. 1745 (1989), which challenges the "racial distinctiveness thesis."

I doubt that being a victim is the only experience that gives special access to truth. Although victims know something about victimization that non-victims do not, victims do not have exclusive access to truth about oppression. The positions of others — co-victims, passive by-standers, even the victimizers — yield perspectives of special knowledge that those who seek to end oppression must understand.

Standpoint epistemology's claim that women have special access to knowledge also does not account for why all women, including those who are similarly situated, do not share the same interpretations of those situations — "a special explanation of non-perception."[196] One account argues that the hold of patriarchal ideology, which "intervenes successfully to limit feminist consciousness,"[197] causes "false consciousness." Although feminist legal theorists rarely offer this explanation explicitly, it is implicit in theories that associate with women certain essential characteristics, variance from which connotes a distortion of who women really are or what they really want.[198]

False consciousness surely does not satisfactorily explain women's different perceptions of their experiences. Such an explanation negates the standpoint claim that experience itself, not some external or objective standard, is the source of knowledge. In addition, to suggest that one's consciousness is "false," and thus another's "true," is at odds with the assumption of MacKinnon and others that male patriarchy has totally constructed women's perceptions for its own purposes.[199] If male patriarchy is as successful as MacKinnon claims, on what basis can some women pretend to escape it?

MacKinnon herself recognizes the unfeasibility of false consciousness as an explanation for women's different perceptions;[200] yet throughout her writings, her branding of women with whom she does not agree as collaborators[201] and rejection of the suggestion that feminism is either subjective or partial implies this explanation.[202] Colker

---

[196] Charles Taylor uses this phrase in describing the general phenomenon of false consciousness. *See* C. TAYLOR, PHILOSOPHY AND THE HUMAN SCIENCES 95 (1985).

[197] Z. EISENSTEIN, *supra* note 140, at 153.

[198] *See* Colker, *supra* note 151, at 217–22, 217 n.2 (declaring that feminists aspire to discover their authentic selves). West labels mistakes in describing women's realities as "false," *see* West, *supra* note 148, at 114, or as "lies," *see id.* at 126, 127, 144.

[199] *See, e.g.,* MacKinnon, *Toward Feminist Jurisprudence, supra* note 2, at 638 (describing male domination as "metaphysically nearly perfect").

[200] *See id.* at 637–38 n.5. MacKinnon also rejects the explanation that women's different perceptions are based upon different subjective experiences; as constructions of men, she argues, women cannot be subjects. *See id.* Having rejected both of these explanations, MacKinnon concludes that women's different perceptions are proof of women's contradictory situation: "Feminism affirms women's point of view by revealing, criticizing, and explaining its impossibility." *Id.* at 637. I accept this conclusion, but do not think it is consistent with MacKinnon's other work which reflects the false-consciousness view.

[201] *See* C. MACKINNON, *supra* note 7, at 198–205, 216–28.

[202] *See* C. MACKINNON, TOWARD A FEMINIST THEORY OF THE STATE 116 (1989).

is sensitive to the problem of selecting one version of women's experience as politically correct, but she also remains trapped in the contradiction between the claim that women have "authentic selves" and the claim that they are victims of someone else's fantasy.[203]

A final difficulty with standpoint epistemology is the adversarial we/they politics it engenders. Identification from the standpoint of victims seems to require enemies, wrongdoers, victimizers.[204] Those identified as victims ("we") stand in stark contrast to others ("they"), whose claim to superior knowledge becomes not only false but suspect in some deeper sense: conspiratorial, evil-minded, criminal. You (everyone) must be either with us or against us. Men are actors — not innocent actors, but evil, corrupt, irredeemable. They conspire to protect male advantage and to perpetuate the subordination of women.[205] Even women must choose sides, and those who chose badly are condemned.[206]

This adversarial position hinders feminist practice. It impedes understanding by would-be friends of feminism and paralyzes potential sympathizers.[207] Even more seriously, it misstates the problem that women face, which is not that men act "freely" and women do not, but that both men and women, in different but interrelated ways, are confined by gender.[208] The mystifying ideologies of gender construction control men, too, however much they may also benefit from them. As Jane Flax writes, "Unless we see gender as a social relation, rather than as an opposition of inherently different beings, we will not be able to identify the varieties and limitations of different wom-

---

[203] See Colker, *supra* note 151, at 255–60.

[204] Mary Hawkesworth associates this linkage with the "rhetoric of oppression." See Hawkesworth, *supra* note 23, at 445–48. In another article, Hawkesworth describes a related phenomenon whereby feminist treatments of knowledge shift "from a recognition of misinformation about women to a suspicion concerning the dissemination of disinformation about women." Hawkesworth, *supra* note 159, at 538–39.

[205] Thus, MacKinnon writes, "men author scripts to their own advantage" and "set conditions" which maintain their own power and the subordination of women. See MacKinnon, *Sexuality, Pornography and Method: "Pleasure Under Patriarchy,"* 99 ETHICS 314, 316 (1989). Although sometimes careful to distinguish male power as a system from the power individual men have, or do not have, see Littleton, *supra* note 2, at 1318, Chris Littleton also frequently slips into the conspiratorial mode. See *id.* at 1302 ("[T]he terms of social discourse have been set by men who, actively or passively, have ignored women's voices . . . ."); *id.* at 1333 (suggesting that men have "[taken] the best for themselves and assign[ed] the rest to women"); see also C. MACKINNON, *supra* note 7, at 198–205, 216–28.

[206] See *supra* note 201. For an example of how bitter exchanges between feminists carried on in this framework can become, see *The 1984 James McCormick Mitchell Lecture: Feminist Discourse, Moral Values, and the Law — A Conversation,* 34 BUFFALO L. REV. 11, 68–76 (1985). MacKinnon extends her side of the argument in C. MACKINNON, *supra* note 7, at 305 n.6. For an insightful feminist commentary on this exchange, see Colker, cited above in note 151, at 249–50.

[207] See Hawkesworth, *supra* note 23, at 447.

[208] See Flax, *supra* note 11, at 629.

en's (or men's) powers and oppressions within particular societies."[209] In short, gender reform must entail not so much the conquest of the now-all-powerful enemy male, as the transformation of those ideologies that maintain the current relationships of subordination and oppression.

C. Postmodernism

The postmodern or poststructural critique of foundationalism resolves the problem of knowability in a quite different way.[210] While standpoint epistemology relocates the source of knowledge from the oppressor to the oppressed, the postmodern critique of foundationalism questions the possibility of knowledge, including knowledge about categories of people such as women. This critique rejects essentialist thinking as it insists that the subject, including the female subject, has no core identity but rather is constituted through multiple structures and discourses that in various ways overlap, intersect, and contradict each other.[211] Although these structures and discourses "overdetermine" woman and thereby produce "the subject's experience of differentiated identity and . . . autonomy,"[212] the postmodern view posits that the realities experienced by the subject are not in any way transcendent or representational, but rather particular and fluctuating,

---

[209] *Id.* at 641. As Flax also writes, women cannot be "free of determination from their own participation in relations of domination such as those rooted in the social relations of race, class, or homophobia," while men are not. *Id.* at 642.

[210] Postmodernism and poststructuralism are often used interchangeably, although each term has a somewhat unique genealogy. Postmodernism, originally used to describe a movement in art and architecture, has been used by Jean-Francois Lyotard and Fredric Jameson to describe the general character of the present age. For Lyotard, whose concern is primarily epistemological, the postmodern condition has resulted from the collapse of faith in the traditional "Grand Narratives" that have legitimated knowledge since the Enlightenment. *See* J. LYOTARD, THE POSTMODERN CONDITION: A REPORT ON KNOWLEDGE 37–41, 51, 60 (G. Bennington & B. Massumi trans. 1984). For Jameson, who focuses mainly on changes in the cultural realm, postmodernism characterizes the "cultural dominant" of the "logic of late capitalism." Jameson, *Postmodernism, or the Cultural Logic of Late Capitalism*, 146 NEW LEFT REV. 53, 55 (1984).

Poststructuralism refers to a series of regional analyses that have undermined notions of foundationalism and of a unified self-transparent subject. As a movement that has undermined the ideals and the project of the Enlightenment, poststructuralism has contributed to the general condition of postmodernism. I am grateful to Rosanne Kennedy for clarifying these distinctions for me.

In this Article, I use the terms postmodernism and poststructuralism more or less interchangeably, and I am concerned primarily with the critique of foundationalism that both postmodernism and poststructuralism have produced. For the most concise, comprehensive statement of the Enlightenment beliefs which postmodernism and poststructuralism reject that I have found, see Flax, cited above in note 11, at 624–25.

[211] *See* Alcoff, *supra* note 8, at 415–16; Schultz, *Room To Maneuver (f)or a Room of One's Own? Practice Theory and Feminist Practice*, 14 LAW & SOC. INQUIRY 123, 132 (1989).

[212] Coombe, *Room For Manoeuver: Toward a Theory of Practice in Critical Legal Studies*, 14 LAW & SOC. INQUIRY 69, 85 (1989).

constituted within a complex set of social contexts. Within this position, being human, or female, is strictly a matter of social, historical, and cultural construction.[213]

Postmodern critiques have challenged the binary oppositions in language, law, and other socially-constituting systems, oppositions which privilege one presence — male, rationality, objectivity — and marginalize its opposite — female, irrationality, subjectivity.[214] Postmodernism removes the grounding from these oppositions and from all other systems of power or truth that claim legitimacy on the basis of external foundations or authorities. In so doing, it removes external grounding from any particular agenda for social reform. In the words of Nancy Fraser and Linda Nicholson, postmodern social criticism "floats free of any universalist theoretical ground. No longer anchored philosophically, the very shape or character of social criticism changes; it becomes more pragmatic, ad hoc, contextual, and local."[215] There are no external, overarching systems of legitimation; "[t]here are no special tribunals set apart from the sites where inquiry is practiced." Instead, practices develop their own constitutive norms, which are "plural, local, and immanent."[216]

The postmodern critique of foundationalism has made its way into legal discourse through the critical legal studies movement. The feminists associated with this movement have stressed both the indeterminacy of law and the extent to which law, despite its claim to neutrality and objectivity, masks particular hierarchies and distributions of power. These feminists have engaged in deconstructive projects that have revealed the hidden gender bias of a wide range of laws and legal assumptions.[217] Basic to these projects has been the critical insight that not only law itself, but also the criteria for legal validity and legitimacy, are social constructs rather than universal givens.[218]

---

[213] *See* Fraser & Nicholson, *supra* note 14, at 83–91; Rabine, *A Feminist Politics of Non-Identity*, 14 FEMINIST STUD. 11, 25–26 (1988); Gould, *supra* note 23, at 7.

[214] *See* Z. EISENSTEIN, *supra* note 140, at 20; Poovey, *Feminism and Deconstruction*, 14 FEMINIST STUD. 51 (1988).

[215] Fraser & Nicholson, *supra* note 14, at 85.

[216] *Id.* at 87.

[217] *See, e.g.*, Dalton, *supra* note 18; Olsen, *supra* note 51; Bender, *supra* note 140.

[218] Although feminist legal theory has taken seriously the postmodern critique of foundationalism, it has yet to make much sense or use of the postmodern critique of the subject. Marie Ashe has argued that the poststructural subject, defined as "a being that is maintained only through interactive exchanges within a social order," Ashe, *Mind's Opportunity: Birthing a Poststructuralist Feminist Jurisprudence*, 38 SYRACUSE L. REV. 1129, 1165 (1987), "appears utterly at odds with the notions of individual autonomy and personhood valued as fundamental in the liberal legal tradition." *Id.* at 1151. The direction in which Ashe urges feminist jurisprudence should move, however, appears to turn on the existence of certain "real" experiences on the part of women who are pregnant and bear children, which are at odds, she suggests, with the reality assumed by law. In universalizing these experiences and speaking of the "inner

Although the postmodern critique of foundationalism has had considerable influence on feminist legal theory, some feminists have cautioned that this critique poses a threat not only to existing power structures, but to feminist politics as well.[219] To the extent that feminist politics turns on a particular story of woman's oppression, a theory of knowledge that denies that an independent, determinate reality exists would seem to deny the basis of that politics. Without a notion of objectivity, feminists have difficulty claiming that their emergence from male hegemony is less artificial and constructed than that which they have cast off, or that their truths are more firmly grounded than those whose accounts of being women vary widely from their own.[220] Thus, as Deborah Rhode observes, feminists influenced by postmodernism are "left in the awkward position of maintaining that gender oppression exists while challenging [their] capacity to document it."[221]

Feminists need a stance toward knowledge that takes into account the contingency of knowledge claims while allowing for a concept of truth or objectivity that can sustain an agenda for meaningful reform. The postmodern critique of foundationalism is persuasive to many feminists, whose experiences affirm that rules and principles asserted as universal truths reflect particular, contingent realities that reinforce their subordination. At the same time, however, feminists must be able to insist that they have identified unacceptable forms of oppression and that they have a better account of the world free from such

---

discourses of mothers," Ashe seems to abandon the poststructural view. *See* Ashe, *Law-Language of Maternity: Discourse Holding Nature in Contempt,* 22 NEW ENG. L. REV. 521, 527 (1988).

Drucilla Cornell has hinted at a concept of gender differentiation drawn from poststructural theory that might prove fruitful for feminist legal practice. Building on the importance of the excluded "Other" in the construction of woman, she suggests that "what we are as subjects [can never be] fully captured by gender categories," that an interrelational intersubjectivity is more than the sum of its parts, and that immanent in the gender system is a "more than this" which has the potential for freeing us from the false choice between universality and absolute difference. *See* Cornell & Thurschwell, *Feminism, Negativity, Intersubjectivity,* in FEMINISM AS CRITIQUE 143, 161–62 (S. Benhabib & D. Cornell eds. 1987). Cornell makes the same basic point with respect to law generally, not connected with feminist themes, in Cornell, *Post-Structuralism, the Ethical Relation, and the Law,* 9 CARDOZO L. REV. 1587, 1627 (1988) ("[D]isjuncture between the ethical and the real preserves the ideal as a redemptive perspective which can maintain its critical force precisely because it is not actually identified with what is . . . ."). Cornell, however, has yet to explain the significance of her highly theoretical analysis for feminist practice.

[219] *See, e.g.,* Bordo, *Feminism, Postmodernism, and Gender-Scepticism,* in FEMINISM/POSTMODERNISM 133 (L. Nicholson ed. 1990); Fraser & Nicholson, *supra* note 14, at 83; Poovey, *supra* note 214, at 51. Robin West attacks postmodern social theorists on the different ground that their concepts of power, knowledge, morality, and the self ignore the types of nondiscursive, violent silencing experienced by women and also women's different experiences of selfhood. *See* West, *supra* note 192.

[220] As Linda Alcoff asks, "Why is a right-wing woman's consciousness constructed via social discourse but a feminist's consciousness not?" Alcoff, *supra* note 8, at 419.

[221] D. RHODE, *supra* note 8.

oppression. Feminists, according to Linda Alcoff, "need to have their accusations of misogyny validated rather than rendered 'undecidable.'"[222] In addition, they must build from the postmodern critique about "how meanings and bodies get made," Donna Haraway writes, "not in order to deny meanings and bodies, but in order to build meanings and bodies that have a chance for life."[223]

To focus attention on this project of rebuilding, feminists need a theory of knowledge that affirms and directs the construction of new meanings. Feminists must be able to both deconstruct *and construct* knowledge. In the next section, I develop positionality as a stance toward knowledge from which feminists may trust and act upon their knowledges, but still must acknowledge and seek to improve their social groundings.

D. Positionality

Positionality is a stance from which a number of apparently inconsistent feminist "truths" make sense. The positional stance acknowledges the existence of empirical truths, values and knowledge, and also their contingency. It thereby provides a basis for feminist commitment and political action, but views these commitments as provisional and subject to further critical evaluation and revision.

Like standpoint epistemology, positionality retains a concept of knowledge based upon experience. Experience interacts with an individual's current perceptions to reveal new understandings and to help that individual, with others, make sense of those perceptions. Thus, from women's position of exclusion, women have come to "know" certain things about exclusion: its subtlety; its masking by "objective" rules and constructs; its pervasiveness; its pain; and the need to change it. These understandings make difficult issues decidable and answers non-arbitrary.[224]

Like the postmodern position, however, positionality rejects the perfectibility, externality, or objectivity of truth. Instead, the positional knower conceives of truth as situated and partial. Truth is situated in that it emerges from particular involvements and relationships. These relationships, not some essential or innate characteristics of the individual, define the individual's perspective and provide the location for meaning, identity, and political commitment.[225] Thus, as discussed above,[226] the meaning of pregnancy derives not just from its biological characteristics, but from the social place it occupies —

---

[222] Alcoff, *supra* note 8, at 419.
[223] Haraway, *supra* note 108, at 580.
[224] *See id.* at 585.
[225] *See* Alcoff, *supra* note 8, at 435.
[226] *See supra* p. 843.

how workplace structures, domestic arrangements, tort systems, high schools, prisons, and other societal institutions construct its meaning.[227]

Truth is partial in that the individual perspectives that yield and judge truth are necessarily incomplete. No individual can understand except from some limited perspective. Thus, for example, a man experiences pornography as a man with a particular upbringing, set of relationships, race, social class, and sexual preference, and so on, which affect what "truths" he perceives about pornography. A woman experiences pregnancy as a woman with a particular upbringing, race, social class, set of relationships, sexual preference, and so on, which affect what "truths" she perceives about pregnancy. As a result, there will always be "knowers" who have access to knowledge that other individuals do not have, and no one's truth can be deemed total or final.[228]

Because knowledge arises within social contexts and in multiple forms, the key to increasing knowledge lies in the effort to extend one's limited perspective. Self-discipline is crucial.[229] My perspective gives me a source of special knowledge, but a limited knowledge that I can improve by the effort to step beyond it, to understand other

---

[227] *See* Finley, *supra* note 192 (exploring different ways in which legal doctrines and social institutions construct the meaning of pregnancy); Littleton, *supra* note 2, at 1306–07 (arguing that "difference . . . is created by the relationship of women to particular and contingent social structures" (emphasis omitted)).

[228] In Iris Murdoch's Platonic dialogue *Art and Eros*, Socrates expresses a view of truth that, in simultaneously denying and affirming truth, comes close to the concept of positional knowledge:

> Any high thinking of which we are capable is faulty. . . . We are not gods. What you call the whole truth is only for them. So our truth must include, must *embrace* the idea of the second best, that all our thought will be incomplete and all our art tainted by selfishness.

I. MURDOCH, *Art and Eros: A Dialogue About Art*, in ACASTOS: TWO PLATONIC DIALOGUES 62 (1986) (emphasis in original).

Chris Schroeder observes that the notion of "unknowable yet indispensable truths is central to many religions." Schroeder, *Foreword, A Decade of Change in Regulating the Chemical Industry*, LAW & CONTEMP. PROBS., Summer 1983, at 13 n.45 (citing R. NEIBUHR, CHRIST AND CULTURE 233–41 (1951)).

[229] A number of legal writers in other theoretical contexts have sought to incorporate the notion of effort as a component of truth-seeking. *See, e.g.,* B. JACKSON, LAW, FACT AND NARRATIVE COHERENCE 5 (1988) (emphasizing "integrity in relation to one's own subjectivity"); Cornell, *supra* note 218, at 1625 (describing "a self that constantly seeks to divest itself of sovereign subjectivity"); Minow, *supra* note 2, at 95 (advocating "deliberate attention to our own partiality"); Schultz, *supra* note 211, at 137 (describing "the practice of 'self-consciousness'"); Sherwin, *supra* note 150 (urging "suspicion" of examinations limited to one's own perspective); *see also* Donovan, *Beyond the Net: Feminist Criticism As a Moral Criticism*, DENVER Q., Winter 1983, at 56 (describing Iris Murdoch's orientation toward increasing one's sense of realities beyond the self); Lewis, *From This Day Forward: A Feminine Moral Discourse of Homosexual Marriage*, 97 YALE L.J. 1783, 1792 (1988) ("Stretching the moral imagination is a question of willpower . . . .").

perspectives, and to expand my sources of identity.[230] To be sure, I cannot transcend my perspective; by definition, whatever perspective I currently have limits my view. But I can improve my perspective by stretching my imagination to identify and understand the perspectives of others.[231]

Positionality's requirement that other perspectives be sought out and examined checks the characteristic tendency of all individuals — including feminists — to want to stamp their own point of view upon the world.[232] This requirement does not allow certain feminist positions to be set aside as immune from critical examination.[233] When feminists oppose restrictive abortion laws, for example, positionality compels the effort to understand those whose views about the sanctity of potential human life are offended by assertion of women's unlimited right to choose abortion. When feminists debate the legal alternative of joint custody at divorce, positionality compels appreciation of the desire by some fathers to be responsible, co-equal parents. And (can it get worse?) when feminists urge drastic reform of rape laws, positionality compels consideration of the position of men whose social conditioning leads them to interpret the actions of some women as "inviting" rather than discouraging sexual encounter.

---

[230] Neither postmodernism nor standpoint epistemology fosters or even makes possible this attitude. The privilege that standpoint epistemology grants to a particular perspective leaves little reason to look beyond that perspective for further truth. Postmodernism, by denying any meaningful basis for making qualitative judgments between perspectives, leaves no reason to stretch beyond one's current perspective in order to improve it.

[231] One might question, as does Barbara Herrnstein Smith, whether, given one's dependence on one's perspective, it is possible to will one's choices about perspective. See B. SMITH, *supra* note 94, at 176. I argue here, however, that the will to transcend one's perspective helps to enlarge or transform that perspective, even though at any point in the never-ending transformation one is configured by a single, limiting perspective.

[232] I have already discussed how many feminists remain unaware of all of the subtle ways in which they marginalize the perspectives of those who are not white, middle-class, heterosexual, temporarily able-bodied and so on. See *supra* pp. 847–49. I believe that most feminists want to improve their sensitivities on this score. Positionality, however, requires more than to improve one's understanding of those points with which one sympathizes. Positionality requires self-criticism also on those points that one does not wish to concede, such as those I discuss in this section.

[233] The absence of a self-critical account is the principal difficulty I have with Christine Littleton's presentation of feminist method (interpreting Catherine MacKinnon) as that of believing women's accounts of sexual use and abuse by men. See Littleton, *supra* note 21, at 764–65. Neither Littleton nor MacKinnon bring into their discussions of feminist method the necessity for feminists to be critical of themselves or of other women. See *id.* at 764–65; MacKinnon, *Agenda for Theory, supra* note 2, at 510. Self-criticism does not even enter into their respective discussions of consciousness-raising, where it could play an enormously valuable role. See Schneider, *supra* note 2, at 602. Although feminists want to give full voice to women whose accounts of their experiences have for so long been ignored or devalued, feminists cannot assume that women's accounts will always be truthful or valid, or for that matter that men's accounts will always be untruthful or invalid.

Although I must consider other points of view from the positional stance, I need not accept their truths as my own. Positionality is not a strategy of process and compromise that seeks to reconcile all competing interests. Rather, it imposes a twin obligation to make commitments based on the current truths and values that have emerged from methods of feminism, and to be open to previously unseen perspectives that might come to alter these commitments. As a practical matter, of course, I cannot do both simultaneously, evenly, and perpetually.[234] Positionality, however, sets an ideal of self-critical commitment whereby I act, but consider the truths upon which I act subject to further refinement, amendment, and correction.

Some "truths" will emerge from the ongoing process of critical reexamination in a form that seems increasingly fixed or final. Propositions such as that I should love my children, that I should not murder others for sport, or that democracy is as a general matter better than authoritarianism seem so "essential" to my identity and my social world that I experience them as values that can never be overridden, even as standards by which I may judge others.[235] These truths, indeed, seem to confirm the view that truth does exist (it must; these things are true) if only I could find it. For feminists, the commitment to ending gender-based oppression has become one of these "permanent truths." The problem is the human inclination to

---

[234] This ideal seems beyond human capacity, because people must act upon judgments as if those judgments are correct, and the need for stability seems to require that they deem some judgments true, at least for a time. As Chris Schroeder told me, "Continual reappraisal is impossible, except for God, who has no need for it."

[235] One of the most well-known, and most powerful, of lists of such propositions was invented by Arthur Leff, who concluded both that truth is humanly constructed, and that some standards could be known:

> All I can say is this: it looks as if we are all we have. Given what we know about ourselves, and each other, this is an extraordinarily unappetizing prospect; looking around the world, it appears that if all men are brothers, the ruling model is Cain and Abel. Neither reason, nor love, nor even terror, seems to have worked to make us "good," and worse than that, there is no reason why anything should. Only if ethics were something unspeakable by us, could law be unnatural and therefore unchallengeable. As things now stand, everything is up for grabs.
> Nevertheless:
> Napalming babies is bad.
> Starving the poor is wicked.
> Buying and selling each other is depraved.
> Those who stood up to and died resisting Hitler, Stalin, Amin, and Pol Pot — and General Custer too — have earned salvation.
> Those who acquiesced deserve to be damned.
> There is in the world such a thing as evil.
> [All together now:] Sez who?
> God help us.

Leff, *Unspeakable Ethics, Unnatural Law*, 1979 DUKE L.J. 1229, 1249. Charles Taylor refers to values that are incomparably more important than others — those that define my identity and give "me a sense of wholeness, of fulness of being as a person or self" — as "hypergoods." C. TAYLOR, SOURCES OF THE SELF: THE MAKING OF THE MODERN IDENTITY 63 (1989).

make this list of "truths" too long, to be too uncritical of its contents, and to defend it too harshly and dogmatically.

Positionality reconciles the existence of reliable, experience-based grounds for assertions of truth upon which politics should be based, with the need to question and improve these grounds. The understanding of truth as "real," in the sense of produced by the actual experiences of individuals in their concrete social relationships, permits the appreciation of plural truths. By the same token, if truth is understood as partial and contingent, each individual or group can approach its own truths with a more honest, self-critical attitude about the value and potential relevance of other truths.

The ideal presented by the positionality stance makes clear that current disagreements within society at large and among feminists — disagreements about abortion, child custody, pornography, the military, pregnancy, and motherhood, and the like — reflect value conflicts basic to the terms of social existence. If resolvable at all, these conflicts will not be settled by reference to external or pre-social standards of truth. From the positional stance, any resolutions that emerge are the products of human struggles about what social realities are better than others. Realities are deemed better not by comparison to some external, "discovered" moral truths or "essential" human characteristics, but by internal truths that make the most sense of experienced, social existence. Thus, social truths will emerge from social relationships and what, after critical examination, they tell social beings about what they want themselves, and their social world, to be.[236] As Charles Taylor writes, "What better measure of reality do we have in human affairs than those terms which on critical reflection and after correction of the errors we can detect make the best sense of our lives?"[237]

In this way, feminist positionality resists attempts at classification either as essentialist on the one hand, or relativistic on the other.[238] Donna Haraway sees relativism and essentialism, or what she calls totalization, as mirror images, each of which makes seeing well dif-

---

[236] Charles Taylor describes this concept as the "best account" we have of ourselves. *See* C. TAYLOR, *supra* note 235, at 58. Nel Noddings calls it "the best picture I have of myself." *See* N. NODDINGS, CARING: A FEMININE APPROACH TO ETHICS AND MORAL EDUCATION 5 (1984); *see also* Johann, *supra* note 111, at 109 (arguing that reasoned ethical values are those which "fulfill our quest for good order"); Kay, *Preconstitutional Rules*, 42 OHIO ST. L.J. 187, 207 (1981) (arguing that principles of constitutional interpretation should "attempt to shape the unruly facts of the world and of our natures into such forms as will best serve our own purposes"); Leff, *supra* note 235, at 1249 (arguing that by speaking ethics, we can challenge law, and make ourselves better).

[237] C. TAYLOR, *supra* note 235, at 57.

[238] *Cf.* H. ARENDT, BETWEEN PAST AND FUTURE (1961); R. BERNSTEIN, BEYOND OBJECTIVISM AND RELATIVISM (1985); R. RORTY, THE CONSEQUENCES OF PRAGMATISM 167 (1982); B. SMITH, *supra* note 94.

ficult: "Relativism and totalization are both 'god tricks' promising vision from everywhere and nowhere equally and fully . . . ."[239] Positionality is both nonrelative and nonarbitrary. It assumes some means of distinguishing between better and worse understanding; truth claims are significant or "valid" for those who experience that validity.[240] But positionality puts no stock in fixed, discoverable foundations. If there is any such thing as ultimate or objective truth, I can never, in my own lifetime, be absolutely sure that I have discovered it. I can know important and non-arbitrary truths, but these are necessarily mediated through human experiences and relationships. There can be no universal, final, or objective truth; there can be only "partial, locatable, critical knowledges";[241] no aperspectivity — only improved perspectives.

Because provisional truth is partial and provisional, the nature of positional truth-seeking differs from that assumed under either a relativist or an essentialist stance. Positional meanings are what Moira Gatens calls meanings in "*becoming* rather than being, [in] *possibilities* rather than certainty and [in] meaning or *significance* rather than truth."[242] The attitude of positional understanding assumes that arrival is not possible; indeed, there is no place at which we *could* finally arrive. Truth-seeking demands "ceaseless critical engagement"; as Gatens writes, "there cannot be an unadulterated feminist theory which would announce our arrival at a place where we could say we are 'beyond' patriarchal theory and patriarchal experience."[243] Not only is truth unfixed, but the human capacity to attain it is limited. Iris Murdoch's Socrates captures the point dynamically: "We put the truth into a conceptual picture because we feel it can't be expressed in any other way; and then truth itself forces us to criticize the picture."[244]

A stance of positionality can reconcile the apparent contradiction within feminist thought between the need to recognize the diversity of people's lives and the value in trying to transcend that diversity. Feminists, like those associated with the critical legal studies movement, understand that when those with power pretend that their

---

[239] Haraway, *supra* note 108, at 584.

[240] *Cf.* C. TAYLOR, *supra* note 235, at 111 (arguing that social theory can be validated through the "changed quality of the practice it enables").

[241] Haraway, *supra* note 108, at 584.

[242] Gatens, *Feminism, Philosophy and Riddles Without Answers*, in FEMINIST CHALLENGES 13, 26 (C. Pateman & E. Gross eds. 1986) (emphasis in original).

[243] *Id.* at 29.

[244] I. MURDOCH, *Above the Gods: A Dialogue About Religion*, in ACASTOS: TWO PLATONIC DIALOGUES, *supra* note 228, at 85; *see also* B. SMITH, *supra* note 94, at 179 ("'[T]he best' is always both heterogeneous and variable: . . . it can never be better than a state of affairs that remained more or less than good *for some people*, or got considerably better for many of them *in some respects*, or became, *for a while*, rather better on the whole." (emphasis in original)).

interests are natural, objective and inevitable, they suppress and ignore other diverse perspectives. This understanding compels feminists
to make constant efforts to test the extent to which they, also, unwit-
tingly project their experiences upon others. To understand human
diversity, however, is also to understand human commonality. From
the positional stance, I can attain self-knowledge through the effort
to identify not only what is different, but also what I have in common
with those who have other perspectives. This effort, indeed, becomes
a "foundation" for further knowledge.[245] I achieve meaning in my
own life when I come to know myself in knowing others.[246] In fact,
it is when I cease to recognize my mutual relatedness with others that
I inevitably project my own experiences upon them to make "identification with them impossible."[247]

Because of its linkage between knowledge and seeking out other
perspectives, positionality provides the best foothold from which feminists may insist upon both the diversity of others' experiences, and
their mutual relatedness and common humanity with others. This
dual focus seeks knowledge of individual and community, apart and
as necessarily interdependent. As others have noted, much of the
recent scholarship that attempts to revive ideals of republicanism and
the public virtue has given inadequate attention to the problem of
whose interests are represented and whose are excluded by expressions
of the "common" or "public" interest.[248] Positionality locates the
source of community in its diversity and affirms Frank Michelman's
conclusions about human commonality: "The human universal becomes difference itself. Difference is what we most fundamentally
have in common."[249]

All three of the methods discussed in this Article affirm, and are
enhanced by, the stance of positionality. In asking the woman ques-

---

[245] *See, e.g.*, Cornell, *Toward a Modern/Postmodern Reconstruction of Ethics*, 133 U. PA.
L. REV. 291, 360–68 (1986); Holler, *Is There a Thou "Within" Nature? A Dialogue with H.
Richard Niebuhr*, 17 J. RELIGIOUS ETHICS 81, 83 (1989); Minow, *supra* note 16, at 206; *see
also* Gabel, *Creationism and the Spirit of Nature*, TIKKUN, Sept.–Oct. 1987, at 62 (arguing that
we can know "with certainty" from "our own fundamental need for the confirmation and love
of others," that "this need fundamentally motivates all living things").

[246] *See* Gabel, *supra* note 245, at 59–60 (stating that we can only understand, and correct,
ourselves, by approaching others as "differentiated presences like ourselves and putting ourselves
in their place in order to comprehend them").

[247] Holler, *supra* note 245, at 82. Holler writes: "insofar as we are severed from the community of diverse beings, we are unaware of our own being, and, like Narcissus, we will see
that community only in our own image." *Id.* at 83.

[248] *See, e.g.*, Bell & Bansal, *The Republican Revival and Racial Politics*, 97 YALE L.J. 1609
(1988); Young, *Impartiality and the Civic Public: Some Implications of Feminist Critiques of
Moral and Political Theory*, in FEMINISM AS CRITIQUE, *supra* note 218, at 66.

[249] Michelman, *supra* note 79, at 32. Michelman incorporates points made by Drucilla
Cornell and Martha Minow. *See* Cornell, *supra* note 245, at 368–69; Minow, *supra* note 16, at
206.

tion, feminists situate themselves in the perspectives of women affected in various ways and to various extents by legal rules and ideologies that purport to be neutral and objective. The process of challenging these rules and ideologies, deliberately, from particular, self-conscious perspectives, assumes that the process of revealing and correcting various forms of oppression is never-ending. Feminist practical reasoning, likewise, exposes and helps to limit the damage that universalizing rules and assumptions can do; universalizations will always be present, but contextualized reasoning will help to identify those currently useful and eliminate the others. Consciousness-raising links that process of reasoning to the concrete experiences associated with growth from one set of moral and political insights to another. Positional understanding enhances alertness to the special problems of oppressive orthodoxies in consciousness-raising, and the insights developed through collaborative interaction should remain open to challenge, and not be held hostage to the unfortunate tendency in all social structures to assume that some insights are too politically "correct" to question.[250]

Positional understanding requires efforts both to establish good law and to keep in place, and renew, the means for deconstructing and improving that law. In addition to focusing on existing conditions, feminist methods must be elastic enough to open up and make visible new forms of oppression and bias. Reasoning from context and consciousness-raising are self-renewing methods that may enable continual new discoveries. Through critical practice, new methods should also evolve that will lead to new questions, improved partial insights, better law, and still further critical methods.

IV. CONCLUSION: FEMINIST METHODS AS ENDS

I have argued that feminist methods are means to feminist ends: that asking the woman question, feminist practical reasoning, and consciousness-raising are methods that arise from and sustain feminist practice. Having established the feminist stance of positionality, I now want to expand my claim to argue that feminist methods are also ends in themselves. Central to the concept of positionality is the assumption that although partial objectivity is possible, it is transitional, and therefore must be continually subject to the effort to reappraise, deconstruct, and transform. That effort, and the hope that must underlie it, constitute the optimistic version of feminism to

---

[250] See Dimen, Politically Correct? Politically Incorrect?, in PLEASURE AND DANGER: EXPLORING FEMALE SEXUALITY 139 (C. Vance ed. 1984) ("The appearance of political correctness in feminism creates a contradiction."); Bottomley, Gibson & Meteyard, Dworkin; Which Dworkin? Taking Feminism Seriously, 14 J.L. & SOC'Y 47, 56 (1987); Colker, supra note 151, at 253–54.

which I adhere. Under this version, human flourishing means being engaged in the world through the kinds of critical yet constructive feminist methods I have described. These methods can give feminists a way of doing law that expresses who they are and who they wish to become.

This is, I contend, a goal central to feminism: to be engaged, with others, in a critical, transformative process of seeking further partial knowledges from one's admittedly limited habitat. This goal is the grounding of feminism, a grounding that combines the search for further understandings and sustained criticism toward those understandings. Feminist doing is, in this sense, feminist knowing. And vice versa.

PRAGMATISM, OPPRESSION, AND THE FLIGHT TO SUBSTANCE

Scott Brewer*

This Comment will discuss what appears to be a tension between two intuitively compelling moral norms. The articulation of both norms plays a central role in Professor Radin's paper for this Symposium,[1] as well as in the work of many of the other Symposium scholars, such as Cornel West, Martha Minow, Frank Michelman, and Mari Matsuda. After identifying the two norms, I shall explain why I believe they are in tension. Next, I shall argue that the intuitions of many who are sympathetic to both norms ultimately lead them to allow one of the norms to trump the other when they clash. In conclusion, I shall briefly indicate why in my view that "trumping" is the morally correct outcome.

THE TWO VALUES

Many of us, perhaps not enough of us, adhere to a value that we may for the sake of simplicity label "value 1"; that value is to look to what Professor Radin calls the "perspective of the oppressed" when trying to reach a decision on some matter of substantive value (that is, some matter of policy or principle, such as, to use Professor Radin's examples, the desirability of an affirmative action scheme or a pregnancy leave policy[2]) that affects us.

Looking to the perspective of the oppressed is a value central to Professor Radin's analysis of feminism's contribution to pragmatism. For example, she tells us that "rootedness in the experiences of oppression [is] the distinctive critical contribution that feminism can make to

---

* Assistant Professor of Law, Harvard University (on leave 1989-1991).
1. Radin, *The Pragmatist and the Feminist*, 63 S. CAL. L. REV. 1699 (1990).
2. *See id.* at 1701-02.

105

pragmatism,"[3] and that "[t]he perspective of domination, and the critical ramifications it must produce once it is taken seriously, seem to be feminism's contribution to pragmatism."[4] Of course, many other scholars have articulated the importance of value 1. Martha Minow, for example, has adduced materials from philosophy, psychology, feminist theory, and American constitutional law to argue for the value of looking to the perspective of those who are different.[5]

In an interesting and significant way, value 1 is a *formal* value, a value of *deference* based on the supposed *authority* of the person or group to whom one defers.[6] The formal nature of the value is revealed, for example, in Professor Minow's assertion that "[g]iven the relationship between knowledge and power, those with less privilege may well see better than those with more."[7] Similarly, Professor Matsuda has not only argued that "victims of racial oppression have distinct normative insights," but she has also suggested that they have "distinct claims to normative *authority*."[8] In addition, she has defended this claim to authority on the ground that it is an instance of "affirmative action epistemology."[9] As Professor Minow's and Professor Matsuda's arguments illustrate, one might describe the formal nature of this kind of deference by saying that it is the willingness to withhold, to some extent, one's own

---

3. *Id.* at 1708.

4. *Id.* at 1711; *see also id.* at 1720 ("[T]he commitment to perspectivism finds its concrete payoff in the perspective of feminism and in the perspectives of oppressed people generally.").

5. *See* Minow, *Justice Engendered*, 101 HARV. L. REV. 10. At an important point in her paper Professor Radin incorporates Minow's analysis into her own argument. *See* Radin, *supra* note 1, at 1723.

6. For an extensive and illuminating discussion of the concept of formality in legal reasoning, see P. ATIYAH & R. SUMMERS, FORM AND SUBSTANCE IN ANGLO-AMERICAN LAW (1986). The type of formality I have in mind here is a version of what Atiyah and Summers call "authoritative formality" and "rank formality." *See id.* at 12 (describing "purely formal," "wholly source-oriented" standard for legal validity, which "requires inquiry not into substance, but solely into the mode of origin to determine validity."). I am of course not saying that value 1 as it appears in Professor Radin's analysis is a legal formalistic value, which is what Atiyah and Summers describe. Rather, value 1 is a moral value whose role in a system of moral reasons is structurally analogous to the role occupied by formal values in legal analysis.

7. Minow, *supra* note 5, at 86; *see also id.* at 83 (questioning value of deference as tool of legal reasoning in Constitutional law). This is analogous to what Atiyah and Summers call "rank formality," part of "authoritative formality." *See* P. ATIYAH & R. SUMMERS, *supra* note 6, at 12 (stating, in discussion of example of rank formality, that "in Anglo-American law, constitutional provision displaces contrary statute, statute displaces contrary contract, contract displaces contrary custom, and so on").

8. Matsuda, *Looking to the Bottom: Critical Legal Studies and Reparations*, 22 HARV. C.R.-C.L. L. REV. 323, 326 & n.14 (1987) (emphasis added).

9. *See Afterword*, 63 S. CAL. L. REV. 1911, 1913 (1990).

judgment on a matter of substantive value, and to defer to the judgment of another.[10]

I turn next to what we may for the sake of simplicity call "value 2," a value to which many proponents of value 1 also adhere. Value 2 is the value of *not* withholding one's judgment on a matter of substantive value *when one concludes that the would-be deferees do not have a proper understanding of their situation.*

Like value 1, value 2 plays an important role in Professor Radin's analysis, especially when she describes the problem of what she calls "bad conceptual coherence." Her example of bad conceptual coherence is one in which in the ancient world it might have been "unthinkable" for anyone to believe that all people were equal and that slavery was wrong—unthinkable even for the slaves themselves. Thus, if asked about the acceptability of their own condition, they might well have expressed some kind of moral acceptance for it.[11]

Value 2 is familiar to some traditions of political theory under the heading of "false consciousness,"[12] an epistemic state in which, to put it roughly, some persons (or groups) do not know what is good for them. One of the most succinct expressions of value 2 is found in Professor Putnam's discussion, in his paper for this Symposium, of Dewey's idea of the impermissibility of "blocking the path of inquiry," i.e., of failing to give a person access to important information about her circumstances. As Professor Putnam puts it:

---

10.   Justice Holmes expressed the value to American judges of this kind of formal deference when he quipped, "If my fellow citizens want to go to Hell I will help them. It's my job." 1 HOLMES-LASKI LETTERS 249 (M. Howe ed. 1953). (This is an expression of legal formalism if Holmes' use of the term "Hell" expresses his own substantive judgment.) In the relevant literature, this formal value—deferring to the judgment of a person who is in a putatively better position to decide questions of substantive value—is known as "standpoint epistemology." *See, e.g.,* Bartlett, *Feminist Legal Methods,* 103 HARV. L. REV. 829, 872-77 (1990). In the discussion that followed Professor Radin's presentation of her paper, it was unclear to me whether she accepted my reading of her argument as a defense of value 1. *See Afterword,* 63 S. CAL. L. REV. 1911, 1922-24 (1990). Even if I have misunderstood her argument as a defense of value 1, however, this Comment still addresses much of the "standpoint epistemology" literature, which, it seems to me, quite clearly defends value 1. For a discussion of some of the compelling reasons to reject the claims of standpoint epistemology, see Minow, *supra* note 5, at 62-65. *See also infra* note 14. Minow, however, appears to be divided in her view of the value of this method. *See supra* note 7 and accompanying text.

11.   *See* Radin, *supra* note 1, at 1720.

12.   *See, e.g.,* G. LUKACS, HISTORY AND CLASS CONSCIOUSNESS 256-59 (R. Livingstone trans. 1971); MacKinnon, *Feminism, Marxism, Method, and the State: Toward Feminist Jurisprudence,* 8 SIGNS 635, 636 & n.4 (1983); Minow, *supra* note 5, at 73 & n.290 (discussing "familiar and troubled concept of false consciousness").

The fact that someone feels satisfied with a situation means little if the person has no information or false information concerning either her own capacities or the existence of available alternatives to her present way of life. The real test is not what women who have never heard about feminism say about their situation . . . .[13]

THE TENSION BETWEEN VALUES 1 AND 2

One might reconstruct values 1 and 2 in an inferential scheme of rule and exception, that is, as a defeasible rule, as follows: Defer to the "perspective of the oppressed" *unless* that perspective is the product of "false consciousness."

However, although both are perhaps initially intuitively appealing, values 1 and 2 are not so harmonious as this construction of them as a single defeasible rule would suggest. Rather, they are in a tension deep enough that the exception threatens to swallow the rule. Indeed, I shall argue that the tension appears to be so great as to call into question whether we are capable of *identifying* a "perspective of the oppressed" worthy of the deference that value 1 counsels.[14]

Let us assume that we accept value 1, that of giving some deference to the perspective of the oppressed when considering certain issues of substantive value.[15] How do we go about doing that?

---

13. Putnam, *A Reconsideration of Deweyian Democracy*, 63 S. CAL. L. REV. 1671, 1676 (1990).

14. What I am inclined to call the "conceptual" questioning I pursue here seems to me to be different from Minow's empirical questioning, the latter of which is exemplified by the following:

> Yet by urging the corrective of women's perspective, or even a feminist standpoint, feminists have jeopardized our own challenge to simplification, essentialism, and stereotyping. Women fall into every category of race, religion, class and ethnicity, and vary in sexual orientation, handicapping conditions, and other sources of assigned difference. Claims to speak from women's point of view, or to use women as a reference point, threaten to obscure this multiplicity and install a particular view to stand for the views of all.

Minow, *supra* note 5, at 62-63 (citations omitted); *see also id.* at 76 (" 'Standpoint theories' may also deny the multiple experiences of members of the denigrated group and create a new class of essentialism.' "); Kennedy, *Racial Critiques in Legal Academia*, 102 HARV. L. REV. 1745, 1802-03 (1989) (discussing difficulty of locating criterion of "blackness" to give substantive content to concept of "black perspective").

15. It is not clear regarding which issues of substantive value scholars like Professor Radin would have us defer to the perspective of the oppressed. Her examples—affirmative action and pregnancy leave, *see* Radin, *supra* note 1, at 1701-02—suggest that we should defer regarding those substantive value decisions that affect oppressed persons disproportionately. But then one would like to have some idea of how one measures the relative "proportion" of impact on an oppressed, as opposed to non-oppressed, group. An affirmative action plan for a fire department, for example, obviously substantially affects both blacks (or women) and whites (or men). *Cf. id.* at 1707 ("It is not just the fact that these are women's issues that makes these writings feminist—they are after all human issues . . . ."). Professor Radin does not address this difficult point in her paper.

To begin executing that step, we must heed the instruction of the tidy philosophical dictum: there is no entity without identity.[16] We cannot look to the oppressed for their perspective until we have some method of *identifying* them. That is, we need identity criteria for them. What might those criteria be?

Obviously we do have some initial idea of what those criteria might be. In their paper for this Symposium, for example, Professors Minow and Spelman mention what I shall call the "macrocriteria" of race, gender, and class;[17] these might seem to be good starting points for identifying those persons to whose oppressed perspectives we ought to give some deference regarding matters of substantive value.

We know from value 2, however, that macrocriteria like race, gender, and class are not *sufficient* conditions for identifying those whose perspective we ought to seek pursuant to the instruction of value 1; for, by the hypothesis of value 2, a woman, a black person, or a poor person might, by the hypothesis of value 2 itself, not have a true appreciation of his or her situation, and in such a case we are inclined *not* to defer. Given the strong moral intuition supporting value 2, i.e., of not deferring to a person who in our view does not properly understand her situation, we cannot rely on such macrocriteria as gender, class, and race to determine who is in the group of oppressed people to whose perspective we should defer. When added to value 1 as a defeasing condition, value 2 tells us that it is not just *any* oppressed perspective to which we ought to defer, but rather only a *worthy, suitably situated* oppressed perspective. Without some additional criterion to tell us which oppressed perspective is *worthy* of our deference regarding a matter of substantive value, we cannot proceed to satisfy value 1.

Indeed, as suggested above, the logic of the interaction of these values goes further: value 2 seems always to *undermine* value 1, for every time we are called upon to defer, we must first decide whether the person has a proper appreciation of her circumstance. But when *we* make that assessment of whether the person properly appreciates her circumstance, we are necessarily *not* deferring.

One might try to resolve the tension between values 1 and 2 by adding to the macrocriteria of race, gender, and class an additional criterion: *representativeness.* This method of identifying those oppressed persons to whose perspectives we ought to defer regarding matters of

---

16.   *See* W. QUINE, *On What there Is,* in FROM A LOGICAL POINT OF VIEW 4 (1957).
17.   Minow & Spelman, *In Context,* 63 S. CAL. L. REV. 1597, 1632-33 (1990).

substantive value takes seriously the idea that the perspective of the oppressed is the perspective that is *representative* of the ideas of members of that group. This additional criterion may seem a promising way to undo the tension between values 1 and 2 in that it might allow us to get rid of the oddball at either end of the bell curve and to defer to the substantive views that *most* members of the group would offer. This means of identifying the worthy oppressed perspective has the additional attraction of capturing an intuition that is repeatedly confirmed by survey data: that members of oppressed groups sometimes, perhaps often, do have a majority or supermajority view on certain substantive matters.[18]

This response to the tension between values 1 and 2 fails, however, to resolve the tension. Professor Radin shows us why. Value 2 leads us to want to feel convinced that a representative *majority* of group members properly understands their situation in just the same way it leads us to need to feel convinced that a given *individual* properly understands hers. That is the point of Professor Radin's example of slaves in ancient Greece who might have "bad conceptual coherence."

To see how the slave example illustrates this point, assume regarding these slaves that we had some means by which accurately to ascertain their beliefs about the value of slavery, and assume also that, as in Professor Radin's example, a majority of them did not disapprove of slavery. Would we under those circumstances be willing to defer, pursuant to value 1, to the perspective of that majority of oppressed persons? I think not.[19] And the reason we would not is that we have some independent sense that the substantive value at issue—slavery—is wrong, no matter what its victims think about it.

At this stage in the argument it may be useful to pause to consider one of the principal justifications offered in defense of value 1. Virtually all defenses of value 1 proceed from the belief that because a person has

---

18. *See, e.g.*, Kennedy, *supra* note 14, at 1816 & nn.299-300.

19. Note that moral intuitions similar to those at work here make us uncomfortable with normative moral relativism—the view that an action is morally good for a person (or group) when, and because, she (or the group) sincerely believes that the action is good. Dworkin presses this point in his debate with Stanley Fish. *See* R. DWORKIN, A MATTER OF PRINCIPLE 171-77 (1985); *see also* P. ATIYAH & R. SUMMERS, *supra* note 6, at 10 ("[F]ormal reasoning is nearly always subject to limitations. At some point in determining the bearing of even the most formal reason, it may become appropriate to examine substantive reasons and even to allow substantive reasons to outweigh formal reasons.").

experienced oppression, she therefore has a "distinct claim[] to normative authority."[20] Insofar as this defense of value 1 infers from the experience of oppression the merit of the substantive views of the person possessed of that experience, the defense seems to fail to justify value 1 for precisely the reasons offered above. It is crucial to distinguish experience from substantive expertise, only the latter of which is relevant to the question of the legitimacy of deference. Value 2 instructs us that experience does not always yield substantively correct insight. That is, value 2 teaches us not to assume that a person's substantive views regarding the best methods of correcting oppression deserve credence simply because he has the experience of oppression.

Of course, for many substantive issues a substantive-decisionmaker will want to take testimony, as it were, from those who have had certain experiences of oppression. The kind and amount of testimony the decisionmaker seeks, the reasons for which she seeks it and the uses to which she puts it, will all differ from one substantive-decision setting to the next. It is also clear that a given person who has experienced oppression may also have compelling normative insights regarding a given substantive-value issue related to his oppression. Value 2 denies neither of these important propositions. Value 2 does insist, however, that when evaluating a substantive recommendation by anyone—whether oppressed or not—the substantive-decisionmaker must satisfy herself that to experience (whether it be the experience of being oppressed, not being oppressed, or even of oppressing) has been added compelling substantive insight. And the only way to satisfy that epistemic obligation is to evaluate a given substantive judgment independently of the experiential identity of the judge.[21]

THE FLIGHT TO SUBSTANCE

We might characterize the force of value 2 as a "flight to substance." This powerful component of our moral intuitions compels us to be paternalistic at least to the extent that as moral judges we want to "reach the merits" of a substantive value issue even when the supposedly authoritative source—here, according to value 1, those possessed of the "perspective of the oppressed"—might well "rule" on the issue differently.

---

20. *See* Matsuda, *supra* note 8, at 326 & n.14.

21. For a similar and more extended argument about the relation of experience to substantive judgment, see Kennedy, *supra* note 14, at 1788-1807.

Recall that we were on a quest for an additional criterion to add to the macrocriteria of race, class, and gender, to *identify* those who have an oppressed perspective that deserves our deference. We have seen that one prospective additional criterion—representativeness—fails to resolve the tension between values 1 and 2. Perhaps there are other additional criteria capable of eliminating the tension that have evaded me, but for now this is as far as I have come in my thinking. We threaten to become impaled on the horns of a dilemma: either we must abandon the idea that there is such a thing as the worthy perspective of the oppressed to which we ought to defer in some questions of substantive value,[22] or we must be prepared to abandon our moral instinct to subject every would-be act of deference regarding matters of substantive value to the court of appeal of our own nondeferring judgment. That is, either we must give up value 1—the value so central to Professor Radin's paper—or give up the limited paternalistic intuition that underlies value 2.

I think that, on reflection, most of us would sooner give up value 1 than value 2, for the same reason that we are so uncomfortable with normative moral relativism:[23] we feel compelled to fly to substance. I may be wrong in this descriptive claim about how most of us would resolve the tension (assuming that it cannot be dissolved, as it might be in the now-fashionable self-styled "Wittgensteinian" or "pragmatic" criticism). However, even if I am wrong about that *descriptive* claim about our moral intuitions, I believe that allowing value 2 to trump value 1 is the *morally superior* result as well.

Professor Putnam quotes an exuberantly threatening passage from William James, who is himself quoting, which likens us to those who are "stand[ing] on a mountain pass in the midst of whirling snow and blinding mist, through which we get glimpses now and then of paths which may be deceptive."[24] If indeed we stand in such a mist, all of us are standing in it together, oppressed and (both well- and ill-intentioned) oppressor alike. Perhaps our circumstance is that much more tragic precisely because we cannot be confident that even those who are most harmed by oppressive substantive judgments are in the best, or even in a superior, position to know what to do to repair the injury. We cannot escape that tragic circumstance by looking for answers automatically from a black skin, an empty pocket, or an XX-chromosome.

---

22. In my view, we lack criteria both for identifying those issues of substantive value on which we should defer, *see supra* note 15, and for identifying to whose oppressed perspective we should defer.

23. *See supra* note 19.

24. Putnam, *supra* note 13, at 1693-94 (quoting W. JAMES, THE WILL TO BELIEVE 33 (1897)).

We do—and we ought to—feel compelled to exercise, not to flee from, substantive judgment, no matter who we are, no matter who else shares the podium of debate. That, it seems to me, is one very important way in which we express our commitment to treat one another with the deep respect our common humanity demands. Even those who are oppressed have their full measure of blindnesses and insights; to think otherwise is to treat them with less than their full measure of respect. To indulge in the fiction of a superior oppressed perspective or vantage point or situated embodiment is to deny victims of oppression their right to be wrong as well as to be right.

I hasten to add two points in conclusion. First, I am not recommending that we "exclude voices." In solving problems regarding matters of substantive value, it is invaluable to have many different perspectives, ideas, and insights. Professor Grey's excerpt from Mill,[25] and chapter II of Mill's *On Liberty*,[26] canvass some of the familiar and compelling reasons for not excluding voices. When faced with questions of substantive value, we should credit any idea that is persuasive on the basis of its substantive merits. For reasons offered above, I think that many of us both should, and do in fact, choose *not* to treat any view as meritorious simply because it is the view of a person who belongs to an oppressed group. (By the same token, we should not credit the view of anyone simply because he or she belongs to an *oppressor* group either— and, as Professors Radin, Minow, West, and many others have pointed out, we have rather more work to do to correct the latter than the former error.)

Second, and finally, when I speak of value 2 superseding or "trumping" value 1, of our felt and in my view proper need to "fly to substance" rather than deferring on the basis of status, I do not assume that there is anything like a "neutral" position from which to assess substantive values. For some purposes, we ought indeed to "shift the focus of our vision from a stage in which social and professional prejudices wear the terrible armor of pure reason to an arena in which human hopes and expectations wrestle naked for supremacy."[27] The position expressed in this

---

25. *See* Grey, *Hear the Other Side: Wallace Stevens and Pragmatist Legal Theory*, 63 S. CAL. L. REV. 1569, 1591-92 (quoting J.S. MILL, *Coleridge*, in UTILITARIANISM AND OTHER ESSAYS 177, 181 (1987)).

26. J.S. MILL, ON LIBERTY ch. II (1975).

27. Cohen, *The Ethical Basis of Legal Criticism*, 41 YALE L.J. 201 (1931). Some of those purposes are discussed in W. JAMES, *The Present Dilemma in Philosophy*, in THE WRITINGS OF WILLIAM JAMES 362 (J. McDermott ed. 1968), and in B. RUSSELL, *Philosophy's Ulterior Motives*, in UNPOPULAR ESSAYS 45 (1950).

Comment does not lapse into some kind of objectivism; it is fully consonant with the suasive perspectivist argument that Professor Putnam offers when he expresses the (Nietzschean) insight that "[t]here is no God's eye point of view that we can know or usefully imagine; there are only various points of view of actual persons reflecting various interests and purposes that their descriptions and theories subserve."[28]

Indeed, the argument I offer above actually presses perspectivism further than would anyone who treats the "perspective of the oppressed" as a kind of moral-epistemological monolith. Value 2 is compelling to us precisely because we realize that even within an oppressed group there will be many competing perspectives.[29] Again, one ought not to rule out any of these perspectives simply because it belongs to an oppressed group member, and again I note that Professors Radin and Minow, among many others, do an immense service by laying bare the unjust exclusion of some of these perspectives. But one should not argue for the inclusion of the perspectives of oppressed group members on the assumption that they have some special insight; rather, the proper argument for inclusion is that every person deserves to have the opportunity for his or her perspective to enter the fray of debate.

---

28. H. PUTNAM, REASON, TRUTH AND HISTORY 50 (1981); *see also* F. NIETZSCHE, *On Truth and Lie in an Extra-Moral Sense*, in THE PORTABLE NIETZSCHE 42-47 (W. Kaufmann tran. 1954).
29. Minow's discussion of this point is especially cogent. *See supra* note 14.

114

LANGDELL'S ORTHODOXY*

*Thomas C. Grey***†

It seems natural to begin the history of modern American legal thought in 1870. In that year, Oliver Wendell Holmes, Jr., in the first words of his first major essay, wrote "It is the merit of the common law that it decides the case first, and determines the principle afterwards."[1] In the same year, Christopher Columbus Langdell joined the faculty and became the first Dean of the Harvard Law School. Teaching his first class in Contracts, he began not with the customary introductory lecture, but by asking "Mr. Fox, will you state the facts in the case of *Payne v. Cave?*"[2]

Holmes' words broke with orthodoxy and anticipated legal realism by finding merit in intuitive case-by-case adjudication. But what did Langdell's twin debut as Dean and teacher have to do with the beginning of modern legal thought? Two connections are fairly obvious. First, the method of teaching that Langdell launched in his first Contracts class, by shifting the focus of legal instruction from abstract principles to cases, ended up promoting the same modern

---

* Copyright 1983, Thomas C. Grey and University of Pittsburgh Law Review.

** Professor of Law, Stanford University. This is a much-expanded version of the Mellon Lecture delivered at the University of Pittsburgh School of Law on October 28, 1982. Financial support for the research was provided by the Stanford Legal Research Fund, made possible by a bequest from the Estate of Ira S. Lillick and by gifts from Roderick M. and Carla A. Hills and other friends of the Stanford Law School. I am grateful for the research assistance of Carl Ruggiero and Walter Johnson and for the typing and retyping of Ann Babb. My thanks to the colleagues and friends—too many to name—who made helpful comments on earlier drafts, and extra thanks to those whose criticisms got me to make substantial changes: Barbara Babcock, John Ely and Bob Gordon.

† Due to the specialized nature of the sources used, the author has certified to the University of Pittsburgh Law Review the accuracy of a substantial amount of the bibliographical information.

1. Holmes, *Codes, and the Arrangement of the Law*, 5 AM. L. REV. 1, *reprinted in* 44 HARV. L. REV. 725 (1931).

2. Langdell was named Dane Professor in January, 1870, and taught courses in Negotiable Paper and Partnerships in the spring of that year, apparently by the traditional lecture method. 2 C. WARREN, HISTORY OF THE HARVARD LAW SCHOOL 359, 363 (1908). He was named first Dean in September, *id.* at 370-71; and gave the first case-method class that fall, *id.* at 372-73.

case-centered view of adjudication that Holmes had stated.[3] Second, during his Deanship, Langdell created at Harvard the model for the standard American three-year graduate law school staffed by a career faculty committed to research that has since been the institutional basis for the development of modern legal thought.[4]

The third connection between Langdell's debut and the beginning of the modern era is more obscure. As Langdell taught his course in Contracts, and later as he and his many colleagues and disciples carried on all their teaching and writing,[5] they promulgated a distinctive system of legal thought that I call classical orthodoxy.[6] But what is modern about this classical orthodox system? Is

---

3. This was a common observation of later critics who traced the Legal Realist "jurisprudence of the hunch" back to the pedagogy of the case. *See, e.g.*, Dickinson, *Legal Rules: Their Function in the Process of Decision*, 79 U. PA. L. REV. 833, 846 (1931); Lucey, *Natural Law and American Legal Realism*, 30 GEO. L.J. 493, 526 n.67 (1942). Marcia Speziale has imaginatively expanded on the point while reversing the perspective, treating Langdell as a proto-Realist hero, in Speziale, *Langdell's Concept of Law as Science: The Beginnings of Anti-Formalism in American Legal Theory*, 5 VT. L. REV. 1 (1980). One must avoid identifying Langdell's pedagogic innovations with his jurisprudence; the two were independent, in the sense that articulate critics of the latter were at the same time defenders and practitioners of the former. *See* O. HOLMES, COLLECTED LEGAL PAPERS 42-43 (1920) [hereinafter cited as HOLMES, COLLECTED PAPERS]; Gray, *Methods of Legal Education*, 1 YALE L.J. 159 (1891); and *see infra* text accompanying note 83.

4. On the establishment of Langdell's model at Harvard, see 2 C. WARREN, *supra* note 2, at 354-418, 428-53. Chase, *The Birth of the Modern Law School*, 23 AM. J. LEGAL HIST. 329 (1979) stresses the large role that Langdell's patron, Harvard president Charles Eliot, played in the process. For Eliot's own account, see Eliot, *Langdell and the Law School*, 33 HARV. L. REV. 518 (1920).

On the spread of the Langdellian model of the law school beyond Harvard, see, for a general account, Stevens, *Two Cheers for 1870: The American Law School*, in 5 PERSPECTIVES IN AMERICAN HISTORY 405, 426-35 (D. Fleming & B. Bailyn eds. 1971); and for case-studies, J. GOEBEL, FOUNDATION FOR RESEARCH IN LEGAL HISTORY, A HISTORY OF THE SCHOOL OF LAW, COLUMBIA UNIVERSITY 131-58 (1955), and W. JOHNSON, SCHOOLED LAWYERS (1978).

5. James Barr Ames, Joseph Beale and Samuel Williston, junior colleagues of Langdell at Harvard, were the most important of his disciples in classical orthodoxy.

6. "Orthodoxy" refers loosely to the view, held more or less and in different forms by lawyers at all times, that legal judgments are made by applying pre-existing law to facts. I take the term "classical" (and much more than the term, *see infra* note 176) from D. Kennedy, The Rise and Fall of Classical Legal Thought, 1850-1940 (1975) (unpublished). *See also* Kennedy, *Toward an Historical Understanding of Legal Consciousness: The Case of Classical Legal Thought in America, 1850-1940*, 3 RESEARCH IN LAW AND SOCIOLOGY 3 (1980); and Kennedy, *Form and Substance in Private Law Adjudication*, 89 HARV. L. REV. 1685, 1728-31 (1976). Kennedy's line between "classical" and "pre-classical" legal thought roughly corresponds to Llewellyn's familiar distinction between the "Formal" and the "Grand" Style, *see* K. LLEWELLYN, THE COMMON LAW TRADITION—DECIDING APPEALS 35-45 (1960); I reserve the term "formal" to describe one of the traits of classical legal thought, *see infra* text accompanying note 26.

A particularly helpful treatment of classical thought is Gordon, *Legal Thought and Legal Practice in the Age of American Enterprise, 1870-1920* in PROFESSIONS AND PROFESSIONAL IDEOLOGIES IN AMERICA, 1730-1940 (L. Stone & G. Geison eds. 1983). Other useful discussions are W.

it not the very antithesis of modernity in legal thought? Rather, classical orthodoxy is the thesis to which modern American legal thought has been the antithesis. This relation between them was manifested very early. Just a decade after the year of their common debut, Langdell's most Langdellian book provoked Holmes, who was reviewing it, to formulate the central slogan of legal modernism: "The life of the law has not been logic; it has been experience."[7] Thereafter, as Langdell's book stood to Holmes' aphorism, so stood classical orthodoxy to modern legal thought generally: the indispensable foil, the parental dogma that shapes the heretical growth of a rebellious offspring.

Langdell was mainly a doctrinal writer rather than a philosopher, and to get a sense of his legal theory it is best to begin by looking at his treatment of a doctrinal problem. When someone accepts a contractual offer by mail, does the contract become binding when the acceptance is mailed or when it is received? There are practical arguments on both sides of the question, but most modern writers have agreed that the balance of convenience favors making the acceptance binding when mailed—the so-called "mailbox rule." And modern writers, thinking it more important to have the question settled than to worry endlessly over whether it is settled right, have agreed to treat the mailbox rule as established law.[8]

When Langdell confronted it, the question had not yet been settled. The courts of England and New York had adopted the mailbox rule, but those of Massachusetts had rejected it.[9] Accord-

---

TWINING, KARL LLEWELLYN AND THE REALIST MOVEMENT 10-25 (1973); and White, *The Impact of Legal Science on Tort Law, 1880-1910*, 78 COLUM. L. REV. 213, 214-32 (1978).

7. Holmes, Book Review, 14 AM. L. REV. 233, 234 (1880). Langdell's book was his SUMMARY OF THE LAW OF CONTRACTS (1880) [hereinafter SUMMARY]. An earlier version of this work was appended to the second edition of Langdell's contracts casebook in 1879; it was itself the descendant of a much shorter doctrinal summary appended to the first edition, C. LANGDELL, CASES ON CONTRACTS (1st ed. 1871; 2d ed. 1879). [Hereinafter citations to the casebook are to the second edition.]

Holmes repeated the line about logic and experience in the first lecture of his series on the common law given at the Lowell Institute in late 1880, possibly in Langdell's presence. M. HOWE, JUSTICE OLIVER WENDELL HOLMES: THE PROVING YEARS, 1870-1882 157 (1963). It then appeared as the third sentence of the book derived from those lectures, O. HOLMES, THE COMMON LAW 5 (M. Howe ed. 1963; orig. 1881) [hereinafter THE COMMON LAW] and has since passed into the common idiom of English-speaking lawyers.

8. 1 CORBIN ON CONTRACTS § 78 (1963). For more extensive discussion of the practicalities, see Llewellyn, *On Our Case-Law of Contract: Offer and Acceptance, II*, 48 YALE L.J. 779 (1939).

9. Adams v. Lindsell, 1 B. and Ald. 681 (England, 1818); Mactier's Admin. v. Frith, 6 Wend. 101 (New York, 1830); McCulloch v. Eagle Ins. Co., 18 Mass. (1 Pick.) 278 (1822).

ing to Langdell, the issue between the alternatives was not merely a practical one. In his view, fundamental principles dictated that the acceptance must be received before the contract could be formed. This followed from the doctrine that a promise could not be binding unless it was supported by consideration. The consideration for the offer was the offeree's return promise. But a promise by its nature is not complete until communicated; a "promise" into the air is no promise at all. Since there was no promise, there was no consideration and could be no contract, until the letter of acceptance was received and read. The mailbox rule could not be good law.[10]

Langdell took note of the argument that the mailbox rule would best serve "the purposes of substantial justice, and the interests of the contracting parties, as understood by themselves," and responded that this was "irrelevant"[11]—a claim that has ever since been taken to express the wretched essence of his kind of legal thinking. It was in dismay at these very words that Holmes called Langdell a "legal theologian" and wrote that law is not logic but experience.[12]

For all his rejection of the idea, Holmes himself well understood what it meant to conceive of law chiefly as "logic." The first great critic of classical orthodoxy, he thoroughly grasped its premises, many of which he shared.[13] By contrast, our view of the old

---

10. SUMMARY, *supra* note 7, at 1-2, 12-15. It is worth noting from the first cited passage that Langdell's argument is based squarely on the doctrine of consideration, not on "the nature of an acceptance." He thought acceptance of a gift, for example, could become effective as soon as there was any manifestation of consent to the gift by the donee, whether or not communicated to the donor. But an acceptance could not become a return promise until it was communicated.

11. *Id.* at 20-21. The statement was an intentional jurisprudential flourish; Langdell went on to say "but, assuming it to be relevant . . ." and supplied some perfunctory practical and policy arguments for his position.

12. *See* Holmes, *supra* note 7.

13. There has been a recent scholarly tendency to find contradictions between the formalist elements in Holmes' doctrinal writing and his famous realist jurisprudential aphorisms. *See* Gordon, *Holmes' Common Law as Legal and Social Science*, 10 HOFSTRA L. REV. 719, 727 n.60 (1982). For my view on this subject, see *infra* notes 162-63 and accompanying text.

Holmes' ambivalence toward Langdell's work appears in his review of the SUMMARY, *supra* note 7. Holmes did say that law was not logic but experience, and called Langdell "the greatest living legal theologian," *id.* at 234, but at the same time praised his talents: "There cannot be found in the legal literature of this country, such a *tour de force* of patient and profound intellect working out original theory though a mass of detail . . . ." *Id.* at 233-34. Holmes' later comment on the SUMMARY in a letter to Pollock expressed the same ambivalence:

A more misspent piece of marvelous ingenuity I never read, yet it is most suggestive and instructive. I have referred to Langdell several times in dealing with contracts because to my mind he represents the powers of darkness. He is all for logic and hates any reference to anything outside of it, and his explanations and reconciliations of the cases

system is less clear, obscured by nearly a century of polemics against "mechanical jurisprudence," "Bealism," "transcendental nonsense" and similar targets set up for summary demolition.[14] But as we should guess from the very persistence and intensity of the polemical assault on classical orthodoxy, when taken as a whole, it was a powerful and appealing legal theory, not the feeble dogma portrayed in the critics' parodies.

The heart of the theory was the view that law is a science. Langdell believed that through scientific methods lawyers could derive correct legal judgments from a few fundamental principles and concepts, which it was the task of the scholar-scientist like himself to discover.[15] The view had considerable continuity with aspirations toward legal science that Anglo-American lawyers had stated in the past.[16] But Langdell and his followers took the view of law as science seriously and carried it out programmatically in a way that had no precedent in the common law world,[17] erecting a vast discursive structure that came to dominate legal education and to greatly influence the practical work of lawyers and judges. It is my purpose to reconstruct the premises of this classical orthodox system of thought;

---

would have astonished the judges who decided them. But he is a noble old swell whose knowledge, ability and idealist devotion to his work I revere and love. 1 HOLMES-POLLOCK LETTERS 17 (M. Howe ed. 1941) (letter of April 10, 1881) [hereinafter cited as HOLMES-POLLOCK LETTERS]. Cf. Holmes' later letter, id. at 140.

14. J. FRANK, LAW AND THE MODERN MIND 53-61 (2d ed. 1949); Cohen, *Transcendental Nonsense and the Functional Approach*, 35 COLUM. L. REV. 809 (1935); Pound, *Mechanical Jurisprudence*, 8 COLUM. L. REV. 605 (1908).

15. *See infra* text accompanying note 42. By way of contrast, *see* Holmes, *supra* note 1, at 728: "Law is not a science, but is essentially empirical. Hence, although the general arrangement should be philosophical, even at the expense of disturbing prejudices, compromises with practical convenience are highly proper."

16. For earlier Anglo-American expressions of the ideal of legal science, see the inaugural lectures of Blackstone and Story as, respectively, Vinerian Professor at Oxford in 1758, and Dane Professor at Harvard in 1829. 1 W. BLACKSTONE, COMMENTARIES *3-37; J. STORY, MISCELLANEOUS WRITINGS 440-76 (1835). For discussions of ante-bellum American ideas of legal science, see M. HORWITZ, THE TRANSFORMATION OF AMERICAN LAW 1780-1860, 253-66 (1977); P. MILLER, THE LIFE OF THE MIND IN AMERICA 117-85 (1965). For still earlier antecedents, see Shapiro, *Law and Science in Seventeenth Century England*, 21 STAN. L. REV. 727 (1969).

17. "Legal Science" of a type closely related to Anglo-American classical orthodoxy has been the dominant enterprise of legal writers in Europe since the beginning of the nineteenth century, and remains so to this day. The prototype is F. VON SAVIGNY, POSSESSION (E. Perry trans. 1st ed. 1848; German orig., 1806); a methodological exposition is K. GAREIS, THE SCIENCE OF LAW (A. Kocourek trans. 1911). For accounts aimed at the Anglo-American reader, see M. CAPPELLETTI, J. MERRYMAN, J. PERILLO, THE ITALIAN LEGAL SYSTEM 164-96 (1967); Schmidt, *The German Abstract Approach to Law* 1965 SCANDINAVIAN STUDIES IN LAW 131. Historical accounts are A. WATSON, THE MAKING OF THE CIVIL LAW (1981) and J. DAWSON, THE ORACLES OF THE LAW (1968).

to explain its central concept, legal science, and to account for its rise and fall as a dominant legal ideology.

I.

Classical orthodoxy was a particular kind of legal theory—a set of ideas to be put to work from *inside* by those who operate legal institutions, not a set of ideas about those institutions reflecting an *outside* perspective, whether a sociological, historical or economic explanation of legal phenomena. This inside-outside distinction is not quite the same as the familiar distinction between normative and descriptive theories. Inside as well as outside theories purport to represent legal institutions accurately, and many outside theories have normative as well as descriptive force.

An ideal inside theory would contain an accurate account of legal institutions, a method for operating them, a creed for legal professionals, and a justification of the institutions for outsiders, all combined in a single comprehensive and coherent formulation. An inside theory is thus an *ideology* in the sense of that term that excludes the pejorative connotation of a mystifying apologetic for bad institutions.[18] Even the best imaginable set of legal institutions needs an ideology, and a good ideology does not falsely represent its sponsoring institutions.

The following analytic scheme is meant to allow a somewhat more precise description of Langdell's classical orthodoxy than has been usual, and one that permits us to compare it with other legal theories. According to this scheme, legal theories are defined by the relations they establish among five possible goals of legal systems: comprehensiveness, completeness, formality, conceptual order and acceptability.[19]

Comprehensiveness. A legal system is fully *comprehensive* if it provides an institutional mechanism for the unique resolution of every case within its jurisdiction. A system can fail to be comprehensive through procedural gaps or procedural overlaps. There

---

18. For the different senses of "ideology," see R. GEUSS, THE IDEA OF A CRITICAL THEORY 1-26 (1981); G. LICHTHEIM, THE CONCEPT OF IDEOLOGY 3-46 (1967).

19. Sources I have drawn on in formulating this scheme include C. ALCHOURRON & E. BULYGIN, NORMATIVE SYSTEMS 61-64 and *passim* (1971); A. KRONMAN, MAX WEBER 72-95 (1983); R. UNGER, LAW IN MODERN SOCIETY 48-58 (1976); M. WEBER, ON LAW IN ECONOMY AND SOCIETY 61-64 (M. Rheinstein ed., E. Shils & M. Rheinstein trans. 1969); Friedman, *On Legalistic Reasoning—A Footnote to Weber*, 1966 WIS. L. REV. 148; and Kennedy, *Form and Substance in Private Law Adjudication*, *supra* note 6, at 1687-1701.

would be a procedural *gap* if courts could decline to decide a case because they found that substantive law provided no clear right answer.[20] There would be a procedural *overlap* if two courts had jurisdiction of the same dispute, and power to issue conflicting relief, without any institutional mechanism for resolving the conflict.[21] Almost all legal systems purport to be fully comprehensive, and legal theory generally takes this requirement as a given—itself an important fact, which highlights the centrality of the dispute-resolving role of the law.[22]

Completeness. A legal system is *complete* if its substantive norms provide a uniquely correct solution—a "right answer"—for every case that can arise under it. A system can be incomplete by containing either substantive *gaps*—factual situations to which no existing norms apply—or *inconsistencies* between overlapping norms.[23] Most modern legal theorists believe that completeness cannot be achieved, though comprehensiveness can; if every case must be decided, there will inevitably be some for which the norms of the system provide no answer, or provide inconsistent answers. In these cases, modern theory says the judge must exercise discretion, either to create a new norm or to choose between the conflicting norms.[24] Recently a number of theorists, headed by Ronald

---

20. As with the celebrated (because exotic in legal history) *référé* established by the French revolutionary organic act of 16 August 1790, allowing courts to refer cases to the legislature where existing law was unclear; the procedure was rejected and comprehensiveness restored to French law by Article 4 of the Napoleonic Code, which provides: "A judge who refuses to decide a case, under pretext of the silence, obscurity or insufficiency of the law, may be prosecuted as being guilty of a denial of justice." See the discussion in F. GENY, METHOD OF INTERPRETATION AND SOURCES IN POSITIVE PRIVATE LAW 49-59 (J. Mayda trans. 1954).

21. For example, conflicting judgments were issued by common law and equity courts in the dispute between Coke and Ellesmere, until James I resolved the dispute in favor of equity. 1 W. HOLDSWORTH, HISTORY OF ENGLISH LAW 248-51 (1903).

22. On my formulation, a legal system is complete if there is a procedurally unique resolution of every *case*. A stronger formulation would require unique resolution of every *dispute*, defining a case as a dispute over which the law takes jurisdiction. The two versions can be partly harmonized by treating disputes over which the law does not take jurisdiction as resolved in favor of the *status quo*, though the equivalence does not hold to the extent it is unclear what the *status quo* is.

23. Alchourron and Bulygin analyze and further subcategorize gaps and inconsistences. AL-CHOURRON & BULYGIN, *supra* note 19, at 31-34, 61-64, 145-48, and 170-75. They treat a distinction between "consistency" (no contradictions) and "completeness" (no gaps) as of major significance. I believe the distinction is not as important in law as it is in more theoretical domains, which unlike the law work under no requirement of comprehensiveness. Any legal inconsistency can be treated as a gap—that is, a gap in the system of meta-norms that are provided to settle clashes between inconsistent lower level norms.

24. Many post-classical civil law codes give general instructions on how such decisions are to

Dworkin, have disagreed with this; Dworkin, for example, asserts, in his claim that even hard cases have "right answers," the orthodox view that our legal system is complete.[25]

Formality. A legal system is *formal* to the extent that its outcomes are dictated by demonstrative (rationally compelling) reasoning. The universal formality of a system is a *sufficient* condition to guarantee its completeness; necessarily, if every case can be decided by uncontroversial reasoning then every case has a right answer. It was a central goal of classical orthodoxy to achieve completeness through formality. But universal formality is not a *necessary* condition for completeness; Dworkin, for example, claims completeness for our legal system without universal formality. In his view, there is a right answer for every case, but no demonstrative reasoning to the answers in hard cases.[26]

Conceptual Order. A legal system is conceptually ordered to the extent that its substantive bottom-level rules can be derived from a small number of relatively abstract principles and concepts, which themselves form a coherent system. The conceptual ordering is formal where the derivation of the decisive rules of the system from its more general principles and concepts is demonstrative; the derivation can also take some less rigorous form, producing an informal but ordered system.[27] Among the concepts of an ordered le-

---

be made, the best-known of which is Article 1 of the Swiss Civil Code: "In the absence of an applicable legal provision, the judge pronounces in accordance with customary law and, in the absence of a custom, according to the rules that he would establish if he had to act as legislator." A. WATSON, *supra* note 17, at 169. *See* J. MAYDA, FRANCOIS GENY AND MODERN JURISPRUDENCE 31-64 (1978) for an analysis of the Swiss courts' experience under Article 1. Geny's notice of "free objective search" *(libre recherche scientifique)*, expounded in F. GENY, *supra* note 20, at 352-431, has been particularly influential in modern civil law treatment of the "gap" problem.

25. R. DWORKIN, TAKING RIGHTS SERIOUSLY (paperback ed. 1978) [hereinafter cited as TAKING RIGHTS SERIOUSLY]; *see also* R. SARTORIUS, INDIVIDUAL CONDUCT AND SOCIAL NORMS 181-210 (1975). Alchourron and Bulygin distinguish between the Ideal and the Postulate of Completeness: the former takes completeness as a goal, while the latter states that it has been achieved within a legal system. The confusion of Ideal and Postulate, which they attribute to Dworkin, they call the "rationalist illusion." C. ALCHOURRON & E. BULYGIN, *supra* note 19, at 175-80.

26. R. DWORKIN, *supra* note 25; *see also* R. SARTORIUS, *supra* note 25. Both Dworkin and Sartorius believe that the "right answers" in hard cases derive from the applications of decisional standards that have "weight" and hence lend themselves to being "balanced." For criticism of the use of the metaphor of weighing or balancing when there exists no procedure by which people can either measure the attributes in question or serially order actions or states of affairs with respect to them, see A. DONAGAN, THE THEORY OF MORALITY 23-24 (1977). For an interesting formalization of "balancing" see Nozick, *Moral Complications and Moral Structures*, 13 NAT. L. FOR. 1 (1968).

27. Thus, a legal theory may pursue conceptual order, without any assumption that general principles can lead by formal reasoning to decisions. Such an approach was characteristic of

gal system, one can distinguish the classificatory *categories* that demarcate bodies of law (e.g., tort, contract, crime) from the operative *concepts* used in the principles from which decisive rules are derived (e.g., consideration, proximate cause, malice).[28]

The notions of completeness, formality and conceptual order—which we may group together as the values of legality—allow us to give a relatively clear meaning to otherwise vague terms commonly used in debates about legal theory. Thus, a "discovery" or "declaratory" theory of adjudication asserts the goal (or claims the achievement) of completeness for a legal system; right answers are *there*, to be discovered and declared. "Formalism" describes legal theories that stress the importance of rationally uncontroversial reasoning in legal decision, whether from highly particular rules or quite abstract principles.[29] "Conceptualism" describes legal theories that place a

---

American judges before the Civil War, working in what Llewellyn called "the Grand Style," *see* K. LLEWELLYN, *supra* note 6, at 38; they sought guidance, but not dictation, from general principles. A classic statement was Chief Justice Shaw's:

> It is one of the great merits and advantages of the common law, that, instead of a series of detailed practical rules, established by positive provisions, and adapted to the precise circumstances of particular cases, which would become obsolete and fail, when the practice and course of business, to which they apply, should cease or change, the common law consists of a few broad and comprehensive principles founded on reason, natural justice, and enlightened public policy *modified and adapted to the circumstances of all the particular cases which fall within it*.

Norway Plains Co. v. Boston & Maine R.R. Co., 67 Mass. 263, 267 (1854) (emphasis added).

For a contemporary natural law philosopher's statement of the notion of informal (nondemonstrative) reasoning from the most general moral principles down to intermediate moral rules *see*, A. DONAGAN, *supra* note 26, at 66-74. Ronald Dworkin likewise illustrates informal conceptualism in his treatment of reasoning from "concepts" to more concrete "conceptions," *see* R. DWORKIN, *supra* note 25, at 101-05, 134-37. However, Dworkin disparages what I here call "conceptual ordering." *Id.* at 44, 344. He apparently believes principles and general concepts play a large role in legal reasoning, but thinks their arrangement and systematization not worthwhile. Finally, Holmes was a master and devotee of legal conceptual ordering, but believed it could not greatly contribute to the formality of the law (a goal he also pursued, but through different means); *see infra* notes 162-63 and accompanying text.

28. The distinction, though not a sharp one, is useful. The operative concepts will be seen by modern lawyers as result-determining in most instances; typically it affects the result whether there was "acceptance," or "assumption of the risk," or "possession" (to add three examples to those in the text). By contrast, except in rare cases (such as those turning on which statute of limitations applies) the classification of a case as one of tort, contract, property, business regulation or the like will not directly affect how the case comes out.

The indirect effect of category-assignments and the ideological importance of legal categorical schemes have been neglected both by advocates and by legal scholars. For a rare full-scale study, see Kennedy, *The Structure of Blackstone's Categories*, 28 BUFFALO L. REV. 205 (1979) and for an application of the approach, see Rabin, *The Historical Development of the Fault Principle: A Reinterpretation*, 15 GA. L. REV. 925, 948-54 (1981).

29. Non-conceptualist formalism is a common attitude among lawyers; they want clear rules,

high value on the creation (or discovery) of a few fundamental principles and concepts at the heart of a system, whether reasoning from them is formal or informal.[30] One could give a purely descriptive sense to the term "mechanical jurisprudence" by applying it to a system which achieved comprehensive completeness through a defined decision procedure guaranteed to produce a correct judgment in every case.[31]

Acceptability. A legal system is *acceptable* to the extent that it fulfills the ideals and desires of those under its jurisdiction.[32] Putting the point another way: we aspire that our legal systems fulfill extra-legal values. But this latter way of speaking begs controversial questions in legal philosophy; there is an old debate between those who think the values encompassed under "acceptability" are to be viewed as extra-legal considerations, and those who regard these values as themselves part of the law.[33]

A further point must be made about the goal of acceptability. Social values are already implicit in the internal goals of the legal system, the goals of legality. In particular, the aspiration toward completeness through formality rests in part on the practical social demand that official action be reasonably predictable, so that people

---

but place little importance on more abstract doctrinal formulations. Holmes detached his formalism from his conceptualism; *see infra* notes 162-63 and accompanying text.

30. *See supra* note 27.

31. To expand on this somewhat cryptic formulation: A system is comprehensive if there is a definite institutional sequence for deciding every case; it is complete if there is a substantive correct answer for every case. Obviously, the established procedure might not achieve the correct answer. (Suppose it takes great moral sensitivity to reach the right answer in many cases, but the judges given jurisdiction over these cases are a bunch of clods.) This incongruence can be escaped if the correct answers are such that they can be reached by applying an essentially mechanical decision procedure to the case. Then, by analogy to the theory of formal systems, the system would be not only consistent and complete but also, in the logicians' term, "decidable." In such a system, all cases (once properly coded) could be decided by a computer, which would make the term "mechanical jurisprudence" quite apt.

32. In speaking of ideals and desires, I mean to distinguish between "ideal interests" and "material interests," both of which are distinct from ideas. ("Not ideas, but material and ideal interests, directly govern men's conduct." M. WEBER, *The Social Psychology of the World Religions*, FROM MAX WEBER: ESSAYS IN SOCIOLOGY 267, 280 (H. GERTH & C. MILLS eds. 1946)). The distinction appears in social theory in various guises; for example, Habermas distinguishes between "value" (the material) and "meaning" (the ideal) as the chief alternative sources of legitimation. J. HABERMAS, LEGITIMATION CRISIS 93 (T. McCarthy trans. 1973).

33. *Compare* H.L.A. Hart, *Positivism and the Separation of Law and Morals*, 71 HARV. L. REV. 593, 627-29 (1958) *with* Fuller, *Positivism and Fidelity to Law: A Reply to Professor Hart*, 71 HARV. L. REV. 630 (1958), *and both with* B. CARDOZO, THE NATURE OF THE JUDICIAL PROCESS 133 (1921) (debates between treating considerations of policy as part of the law or as a legitimate source of judge-made law are mere "verbal disputations" which "do not greatly interest me").

may plan their lives. At the same time formality is often linked to the ideal goal of personal liberty by the slogan "a government of laws and not of men." Legality may also intrinsically involve values additional to these. When I speak of acceptability, as distinguished from other goals of legal systems, I thus refer to values apart from those already implicit in the goals of legality.[34]

II.

In the terms of the analytic scheme just sketched, the heart of classical theory was its aspiration that the legal system be made complete through universal formality, and universally formal through conceptual order. A few basic top-level categories and principles formed a conceptually ordered system above a large number of bottom-level rules. The rules themselves were, ideally, the holdings of established precedents, which upon analysis could be seen to be derivable from the principles.[35] When a new case arose to which no existing rule applied, it could be categorized and the correct rule for it could be inferred by use of the general concepts and principles; the rule could then be applied to the facts to dictate the unique correct decision in the case.

The system was doubly formal. First, the specific rules were framed in such terms that decisions followed from them uncontroversially when they were applied to readily ascertainable facts. Thus, classical orthodoxy sought objective tests, and avoided vague standards, or rules that required determinations of state of mind.[36]

---

34. Lon Fuller's notion of an "inner morality of law" might correspond to those aspects of acceptability implicit in the goals of legality. L. FULLER, THE MORALITY OF LAW 33-94 (1964).

35. The lack of correspondence between the explicit holdings of judicial decisions and the "real rules" that in his view justified the results in those cases was one of the most remarkable features of Langdell's doctrinal writing. A good example of his style is the passage at SUMMARY, *supra* note 7, at 16-18, in which he manages to reduce all judicial affirmations of the mailbox rule, but one, to dicta, and then condemns the sole survivor of the massacre on the ground that it had rested on the authority of a slain predecessor. See Holmes' comment on this practice in his letter to Pollock, HOLMES-POLLOCK LETTERS *supra* note 13, at 140, and J.C. Gray's criticism, quoted *infra* note 70. A more moderate classical approach to case law is lucidly described in E. WAMBAUGH, THE STUDY OF CASES 8-29 and *passim* (1894). In a curious way, Langdell's practice anticipated the theory later adopted by the Legal Realists, according to which the only authoritative parts of a judicial opinion were the facts (the stimulus) and the result (the response). Oliphant, *A Return to Stare Decisis*, 6 AM. L. SCH. REV. 215 (1927).

36. This aspect of classical theory is best illustrated in the work of Williston; *see* G. GILMORE, THE DEATH OF CONTRACT 35-44 (1974). Holmes was the strongest advocate of objective and formal tests, but in my view he was not proceeding from classical premises. *See infra* note 163. Among the classical writers, Ames was least insistent on objectivity and formality; *see infra*

Second, at the next level up one could derive the rules themselves analytically from the principles.[37]

For example, reconstructing Langdell's argument against the mailbox rule, we start with the top-level principle, based on authority,[38] that a contract cannot be formed until there is bargained-for consideration, which is either promise or performance (definition). In a bilateral contract case, there is no performance, and the only promise is contained in the offeree's acceptance (definition). But a promise requires communication of its content to its promisee (analytic truth). And when the promise is by letter, the content is not communicated until the letter is received and read (analytic truth). Therefore, the contract is not formed until the letter is received and read. The reasoning has been formal down to the bottom-level rule, which is itself framed in such terms as to be formally applicable to objectively ascertainable facts. Thus, if the bottom-level rule were, for example, that the acceptance letter had to be received, read *and understood*, the requirement of rule-formality would not be met.

It was crucial to the completeness of the system that it be conceptually ordered, and that its fundamental principles and their constitutive concepts be sufficiently abstract to cover the whole range of possible cases. Bottom-level rules, specific as they were, could not be available in advance to deal with all new fact situations; if the law were only a collection of specific rules it would not be complete.[39] But though the concepts should be abstract, they could not be vague or ambiguous. Unless they were precise as well as ab-

---

note 102. Langdell fell between Williston and Ames on this score; he retained vestiges of the pre-classical "meeting of the minds" view of contract formation, but would invariably substitute objective tests by way of presumption whenever state of mind could not be clearly shown. *See* SUMMARY, *supra* note 7, at 193-94, 243-44.

37. "Analytically" is a better term than "deductively" here, as it avoids the latter term's connotations of purely formal inference. A more specific rule follows "analytically" from a more general principle, if its content can be derived from the principle by "conceptual analysis" or "from the meaning" of the terms used in the principle. (Philosophy of language buffs will recognize the difficulties raised by the scarce-quoted terms; *see* Moore, *The Semantics of Judging*, 54 S. CAL. L. REV. 151, 180-246 (1981).)

38. For Landgell's view on the basis of the consideration doctrine, see *infra* notes 81-87 and accompanying text.

39. This view is implicit in Langdell's famous description of legal science, *infra* text accompanying note 42. Williston made it explicit and articulately defended it late in his life, after the Legal Realists had made it part of their program to break law into "narrower categories," *infra* note 177. *See also* S. WILLISTON, LIFE AND LAW 208-09, 213-14 (1940). *See also* the discussion of "generality" in Kennedy, *Form and Substance in Private Law Adjudication*, *supra* note 6, at 1689-90.

stract, the derivations of the rules from them could not be formal, and judges would have arbitrary power. Can norms be both abstract and precise? Consider the axioms and postulates of geometry.

All this was aspiration; the actual state of the common law was such as to leave the legal scientists a great deal to do. Judges often did not accurately state the rules on which they decided cases.[40] Further, the basic principles had not been properly formulated and arranged. The law consisted of a mass of haphazardly arranged cases: a "chaos with a full index."[41] Langdell himself concisely stated the project of classical legal science in a poignantly optimistic passage:

> Law, considered as a science, consists of certain principles or doctrines. To have such mastery of these as to be able to apply them with constant facility and certainty to the ever-tangled skein of human affairs, is what constitutes a true lawyer . . . . The number of fundamental legal doctrines is much less than is commonly supposed; the many different guises in which the same doctrine is constantly making its appearance, and the great extent to which legal treatises are a repetition of each other, being the cause of much misapprehension. If these doctrines could be so classified and arranged that each should be found in its proper place, and nowhere else, they would cease to be formidable in their number.[42]

Now we come to the omitted factor: what was the role of acceptability in the classical orthodox system? One can easily be misled by Langdell's notorious claim that substantial justice and the interests of the parties were *irrelevant* to the validity of the mailbox rule.[43] Did this mean that considerations of acceptability played no role in doctrinal reasoning? Examination of Langdell's work shows that he held no such view.

Throughout his work, Langdell appealed to considerations of justice or policy.[44] Thus, he wrote that equitable defenses are im-

---

40. *See supra* note 35.

41. T.E. Holland wrote that "the old-fashioned English lawyer's idea of a satisfactory body of law was a chaos with a full index." Quoted in Holmes, *Book Review*, 5 AM. L. REV. 114 (1870).

42. C. LANGDELL, *supra* note 7, at viii-ix.

43. *See supra* text accompanying note 11.

44. In one of his rare jurisprudential essays, Langdell distinguished between "obligations" and "duties." The former were created by the acts of individuals and enforced by the State, whose only object in merely enforcing them was "to see that all persons within its jurisdiction act justly towards others." By contrast, duties "originate in commands of the State," commands based on "motives of policy." Abstractly, then, justice and policy were the whole basis of law for him. C. LANGDELL, A BRIEF SURVEY OF EQUITY JURISDICTION 224 (1908) [hereinafter cited as SURVEY].

posed where "the substantive law . . . is inadequate to the purposes of justice."[45] He said that the law adopts fictions "only . . . to promote justice, i.e., in order to prevent some injustice or some inconvenience which would otherwise arise."[46] Where contractual covenants are to be performed on the same day, the law "does perfect justice" by "raising a presumption . . . that they are to be performed at the same moment, and concurrently." This constructive dependency "is founded upon equality, which is justice" and so "is regarded by the law with favor."[47] The law presumes mental consent from the physical act of promising; but this presumption is "only for purposes of justice and convenience;" thus, the presumption is not made and the offer lapses when actual consent would be impossible, as in the case of the offeror's death or insanity.[48] The common law gives an inventor no property right to his invention, because the consequences would be "intolerable," but does protect an author's work, because such a right "clashes with the interest of only one class of persons, namely, those who desire to reap where others have sown."[49]

It is fair to say that these arguments of justice and policy do not bulk large in the Langdellian corpus.[50] Langdell's most common form of doctrinal discourse was simple dogmatic pronouncement, and when he went beyond that, his more usual appeal was to authority or to "principle" (that is, doctrinal coherence). But he clearly regarded the appeal to "justice or convenience" (acceptability) as legitimate in at least some circumstances. Why then did Langdell insist that such an appeal was "irrelevant" to the validity of the mailbox rule, an issue on which authority was divided?

The answer will emerge more clearly after we look at what Langdell said when he rejected concerns of acceptability in sponsoring another famously unattractive doctrinal position. In unilateral

---

45. SURVEY, *id.* at 253.

46. SUMMARY, *supra* note 7, at 8.

47. *Id.* at 170.

48. *Id.* at 224.

49. Langdell, *Patent Rights and Copy Rights*, 12 HARV. L. REV. 553, 554 (1899).

50. For other examples of appeal to justice or policy, see SUMMARY, *supra* note 7, at 11, 177, 202-03, 209-10; SURVEY, *supra* note 44, at 16, 46, 101. Langdell was much more apt to explain and justify rules of pleading and procedure on instrumental grounds than doctrines of substantive law, as illustrated throughout C. LANGDELL, SUMMARY OF EQUITY PLEADING (2d ed. 1883). As a classical legal scientist he regarded procedure as instrumental to the enforcement of substantive, scientifically ascertained rights; procedure was thus a kind of technology in the service of legal science. *Cf. infra* text accompanying note 173.

contract cases, where the offeror promises something in exchange for performance by the offeree rather than for a return promise (offers of rewards are an example), Langdell argued that there was no consideration and hence could be no contract until the performance was actually completed. Offers were always revocable until the contract was formed.[51] Thus in a hypothetical case familiar to generations of law students, A offers B one hundred dollars if he will touch the top of the flagpole; B then laboriously climbs the pole, and just as he is about to touch the top, A shouts, "I revoke." On Langdellian doctrine, A owes B nothing.

As Langdell freely admitted, this doctrine "may cause great hardship and practical injustice," and as a result, "ingenious attempts have been made to show that the offer becomes irrevocable as soon as performance of the consideration begins."[52] But in his view, well-intentioned as such arguments were, they could not prevail because they "have no principle to rest upon."[53]

This argument captures the essence of Langdell's view of the place of acceptability in legal doctrine. Considerations of justice and convenience were relevant, but only insofar as they were embodied in *principles*—abstract yet precise norms that were consistent with the other fundamental principles of the system. To let considerations of acceptability directly justify a bottom-level rule or individual decision would violate the requirement of conceptual order, on which the universal formality and completeness of the system depended. In classical orthodox thought, acceptability was to influence decision only subject to the constraint of universally formal conceptual order.[54]

What explains the strict primacy of formal conceptual order in classical theory? The short answer is that it was necessary to justify the claim that law was a science. To grasp what this meant, we must understand the conception of science that was involved. Then we can see better why the classical theorists thought it so important that the law be a science of that kind.

---

51. SUMMARY, *supra* note 7, at 3. For the same reason, an offer for a bilateral contract that by its terms stipulated that it would remain open for a time (a "firm offer") was nevertheless revocable at the will of the offeror. *Id.* at 240.

52. *Id.* at 4.

53. *Id.*

54. *See supra* note 39 and accompanying text.

III.

On first encounter, the very idea of "legal science" held by Langdell and his followers is baffling. Everyone understands the idea of empirical scientific study of legal institutions. There are also two recognized normative approaches to law that are thought scientific in some sense: a Benthamite legal policy science on the one hand, or a deductive natural law system based on self-evident moral axioms on the other. But Langdell's kind of theory fits none of these patterns. It claims to be empirical and yet its practice is highly conceptual; it delivers normative judgments, yet proclaims the positivist autonomy of law from morals. This seems to be an incomprehensible jumble of induction with deduction and of norm with fact.[55]

Behind the apparent jumble is a theory that can be made intelligible, if not ultimately satisfying. The core notion of classical legal science can be grasped through the analogy to geometry, as that subject was understood in the late nineteenth century. The geometric analogy can then be twice qualified in an attempt to make it more applicable to law, once to take account of the role of legal precedent, and a second time to allow for the historical and progressive claims of classical legal thought. Let me first develop the primary analogy, and then introduce the qualifications.

Geometry

The aspiration of classical orthodoxy toward a conceptually ordered and universally formal legal system readily suggests a structural analogy with Euclidean geometry. The axioms and postulates of Euclid stand to his theorems as the principles of classical law stood to its rules. The application of legal rules to individual fact situations in the decision of cases was then like the application of geometric theorems to solve practical problems of measurement.

Of course, I have not invented the analogy between legal science and geometry. The geometric ideal pervades the literature of the whole rationalist movement to create exact sciences of ethics, politics and law that dominated European thought from Grotius to Kant, and that still remains strong in European legal scholarship today.[56] In England, more than on the Continent, that movement

---

55. For a lucid statement of the standard critique, see Dickinson, *The Law Behind Law, I & II*, 29 COLUM. L. REV. 113, 141-46; 285-96 (1929).

56. Characteristic exponents of the geometric method were Spinoza, Leibniz, Pufendorf and Wolff; for a summary account of their application of the method to law see C. FRIEDRICH, THE

struggled against a politically potent pre-Enlightenment common law tradition. Blackstone's *Commentaries*, with their blend of rationalist principle and Gothic tradition—"science" and "mystery" in Daniel Boorstin's words—illustrate the characteristic English compromise.[57] But major English figures also spoke for pure Enlightenment and science, proclaiming the undiluted geometric ideal. Thus, Locke spoke of replacing the rhetorician and the common lawyer with the moral geometer,[58] and later John Austin, founder of legal science in England, urged his followers to "imitate the methods so successfully pursued by geometers."[59] That the geometric ideal is still alive today in moral and political theory, though much chastened in the immediacy of its ambitions, is evident when John Rawls writes: "We should strive for a kind of moral geometry with all the rigor which this name connotes. Unhappily the reasoning I shall give will fall short of this . . . . Yet it is essential to have in mind the ideal one would like to achieve."[60]

To capture the parallel between classical legal science and geometry, we must lay aside the modern school-taught view that Euclidean geometry, like other mathematical theories, is simply an uninterpreted formal system of terms and inference rules. We must go back to the view people held for over two thousand years, and which all of us who are not specialists in relativity theory or philosophers of mathematics still intuitively accept. We believe that Euclid's axioms are not merely human constructs, but rather obvious and indubitable physical truths about the structure of space, from which nonobvious truths (like the Pythagorean theorem) can be proved by sequences of indubitable deductive steps.[61] It is the

---

Philosophy of Law in Historical Perspective 110-21 (1958). The passage from Descartes, quoted *infra* note 62, is a classic statement of the rationalist faith that the method of geometry could conquer the whole field of human knowledge. *See supra* note 17 on European legal science.

57. *See* D. Boorstin, The Mysterious Science of the Law 11-30 (1941).

58. "[I]f Men would in the same method, and with the same indifferency, search after moral, as they do mathematical Truths, they would find them to have a stronger Connection one with another, and a more necessary Consequence from our clear and distinct Ideas, and to come nearer perfect Demonstration, than is commonly imagined." J. Locke, An Essay Concerning Human Understanding 552 (P. Nidditch ed. 1975).

59. J. Austin, The Province of Jurisprudence Determined 77-78 (H.L.A. Hart, ed. 1954; orig. 1832).

60. J. Rawls, A Theory of Justice 121 (1971).

61. The traditional and modern views, respectively, are summarized in P. Davis & R. Hersh, The Mathematical Experience 322-30, 339-44 (1981). Relativity theory has joined with mathematical formalism in our century to dethrone Euclidean geometry by showing that "space is Riemannian."

breathtaking nature of this movement from truisms to new knowledge about the world through pure thought that has made Euclidean geometry the great paradigm of the power of reason throughout the history of the West.[62]

But how can the geometric analogy capture the claim of classical legal science to be experimental and inductive? To understand this, we must make a further assumption about geometry that departs from both traditional rationalism and modern conventionalism. We must see the geometric axioms neither as rationally self-evident intuitions, nor as stipulated formal definitions, but rather as especially well-confirmed inductive generalizations about the physical world. This was a standard view of geometry in the late nineteenth century, reflecting the treatment of the subject in the bible of Victorian philosophy of science, J.S. Mill's *System of Logic*.[63]

---

62. The magic of geometric demonstration has its classic illustration in Socrates' dialogue with the slave in Plato's *Meno*, THE DIALOGUES OF PLATO 82b-85b. A wonderful example of the seductive power of Euclid's method of proof appears in John Aubrey's life of Hobbes:

> He was 40 yeares old before he looked on Geometry; which happened accidentally. Being in a Gentleman's Library, Euclid's Elements lay open, and 'twas the 47 *El. libri* 1 [Euclid's proof of the Pythagorean theorem]. He read the proposition. By G—, sayd he (he would now and then sweare an emphaticall Oath by way of emphasis) *this is impossible*— So he reads the Demonstration of it, which referred him back to such a Proposition; which proposition he read. That referred him back to another, which he also read. *Et sic deincips* [and so on] that at last he was demonstratively convinced of that trueth. This made him in love with Geometry.

1 J. AUBREY, BRIEF LIVES 332 (A. Clark, 1898).

Compare Descartes' formulation of the geometric ideal in the *Discourse on Method*:

> Those long chains of perfectly simple and easy reasonings by means of which geometers are accustomed to carry out their most difficult demonstrations had led me to fancy that everything that can fall under human knowledge forms a similar sequence; and that so long as we avoid accepting as true what is not so, and always preserve the right order for deduction of one thing from another, there can be nothing too remote to be reached in the end, or too well hidden to be discovered.

R. DESCARTES, PHILOSOPHICAL WRITINGS 21 (E. Anscombe & P. Geach ed. and trans., 1964).

63. "It remains to inquire, what is the ground of our belief in axioms—what is the evidence on which they rest? I answer, they are experimental truths; generalizations from observation. The proposition, two straight lines cannot enclose a space . . . is an induction from the evidence of our senses." J. MILL, A SYSTEM OF LOGIC 151-52 (People's Edition 1889) [hereinafter SYSTEM OF LOGIC]. *See generally* Mill's discussion of mathematical knowledge, *id.* at 141-64, and his preceding discussion of deductive reasoning, *id.* at 119-41. The other view of geometry current among educated Anglo-Americans during the classical orthodox period was the Kantian position—that geometric axioms are synthetic *a priori* truths constituting the necessary forms of human experience of space—particularly as expounded in 1 W. WHEWELL, PHILOSOPHY OF THE INDUCTIVE SCIENCES 19-21, 91-111 (London 1840).

The modern idea of Euclidean geometry as conventional or purely formal was not generally current in the late 19th century, though the non-Euclidean geometries had been discovered earlier in the century. Thus, the leading British geometer Arthur Cayley could still assert in 1883 that

In Mill's view, we learn the geometric axioms by observing over and over again that, for instance, two straight lines never enclose a space.[64] If we observed an apparent violation of this general law, we would know that our senses or our measurement techniques were deceiving us. Though not a truth of logic, the axiom is so well-confirmed by prior experience that no inconsistent observation could rationally overthrow it, just as, according to Hume, no miraculous claim could rationally be accepted.[65]

Mill, the great empiricist, himself strongly urged the importance of deductive systematization of theory in natural science. As he pointed out, observations inductively supporting a generalization transfer their confirming power undiminished to any proposition that logically follows from that generalization. At the same time, the derived proposition transfers its own independent inductive support back to the generalization, since the logical derivation has shown it to be within that generalization's scope. The arrangement of inductively derived generalizations into a deductive system thus vastly extends our use of the resources of experience, by spreading the confirming force of observations undiminished even through long and difficult chains of deductive inference. Geometry provides the clearest example of this method, but it was exemplified in classical physics as well.[66]

When this structure—induction of axioms, deduction of theorems—is applied to law, it helps clarify the otherwise baffling talk of observation, experiment and the like that appeared in Langdellian literature, while the legal scientists so extensively devoted themselves to pure conceptual reasoning in their doctrinal work.[67] For them, the fundamental principles of the common law were discerned by induction from cases; rules of law were then derived from principles conceptually; and finally, cases were decided, also conceptually, from rules.

Euclid's parallel axiom (which the non-Euclidean geometries dispense with) "does not need demonstration, but is part of our notion of space." *Quoted in* M. KLINE, MATHEMATICS: THE LOSS OF CERTAINTY 95 (1980).

    64. SYSTEM OF LOGIC, *supra* note 63, at 151-52.

    65. *See id.* at 153-55 for Mill's explanation of the illusion of the self-evidence of geometric truth, and *see id.* at 407-18 for his discussion of Hume's argument. Mill's view of mathematical knowledge as at base empirical, long wholly rejected, has staged a contemporary comeback. *See* Lakatos, *A Renaissance of Empiricism in the Recent Philosophy of Mathematics?*, in PROBLEMS IN THE PHILOSOPHY OF MATHEMATICS 199 (I. Lakatos ed. 1967).

    66. SYSTEM OF LOGIC, *supra* note 63, at 141-43, 209-11.

    67. *See infra* note 104.

For legal science, the universe of data was not the totality of sense experience of the physical world, but rather the restricted set of reported common law decisions—hence Langdell's often-reviled remark that all the materials of legal science were to be found in printed books.[68] The legal scientist inductively generalized legal principles from the cases. As with Mill's treatment of inductive evidence, the better existing case-law confirmed a principle, the more proper it was to disregard as a mistake any single judicial decision inconsistent with the principle.[69]

To illustrate: in geometry, the Pythagorean theorem, for which we have no direct inductive confirmation, draws to itself the great mass of experience supporting the Euclidean axioms as soon as it is shown to follow from them as a matter of logic. Similarly, in legal science, the rule that an acceptance by mail must be received to be effective—a doctrine for which there was little common law authority—took on all the precedential support underlying the principle of consideration once Langdell "demonstrated" that the rule followed logically from the general principle. Once the logic of Langdell's substantive derivation was granted, there was then nothing unscientific about his dismissal of the New York and English decisions endorsing the mailbox rule, any more than there would be in treating as clearly mistaken a recorded observation that the sides of a right triangle were of lengths 3, 4 and 6.[70]

Circularity

The analogy between legal science and Mill's conception of geometry seems to fail at an important point. Our observations, which (in Mill's view) support the geometric axioms, themselves draw their force from our general trust in the direct evidence of our senses. They thus have an authority independent of the theory they support.

---

68. Langdell, Speech (Nov. 5, 1886), 3 Law Q. Rev. 123, 124 (1887).

69. Sir Frederick Pollock made explicit the analogy between the deviant precedent and the wayward observation in his unusually sophisticated statement of classical legal-scientific method, Pollock, *The Science of Case Law*, Essays in Jurisprudence and Ethics 237, 246-49 (1882).

70. For the criticism of Langdell as unscientific on this account, note his colleague John Chipman Gray's letter to President Eliot:

> In law the opinions of judges and lawyers as to what the law is, *are* the law, and it is in any true sense of the word as unscientific to turn from them, as Mr. Langdell does, with contempt because they are 'low and unscientific,' as for a scientific man to decline to take cognizance of oxygen or gravitation because it was low or unscientific.

Letter from John Chipman Gray to President Eliot (January 8, 1883), *quoted in* M. Howe, Justice Oliver Wendell Holmes: The Proving Years, 1870-1882, at 158 (1963).

In orthodox legal science, by contrast, there is no obvious analog to sense-perception as a validating basis for judicial decisions. Decisions are thought authoritative in orthodox legal theory because they follow from the rules and principles that constitute the law; but in the classical conception of legal science, the rules and principles constituting the common law are themselves inductively derived from the cases.[71] The enterprise thus seems to be circular in a way Mill's conception of geometry is not.

There are two general lines of response the legal scientist might make to this point. One would be to admit that legal science is circular, while insisting that natural science is circular in the same way and none the worse for it. The other would be to break out of the circle by finding a source of validity for judicial decisions that was independent of the rules and principles.

Though the first or "confession and avoidance" approach was not historically available to the classical legal scientists, we can, in the spirit of rational reconstruction, sketch the argument. Writers in contemporary philosophy of science and epistemology argue that science cannot rest firmly, as positivist theory insists it should, on the evidence of the senses; natural science itself is in important respects circular. Thus, Kuhn and others have shown that every successful scientific theory coexists with significant counter-instances and anomalies. An established theory is not killed by observations or even by a "crucial experiment" alone, but only by a rival theory that the scientific community of the day finds more attractive and illuminating.[72] Further, the old clarity has been taken from the very distinction between observed fact and theory on which traditional empiricism rests. Not only philosophy of science but experimental psychology now teaches us that there is no pure and pre-theoretical sense experience, no innocent eye; all our data are "theory laden."[73]

---

71. It would be wrong to reconstruct classical orthodoxy as requiring that the cases must determine a *unique* set of principles. To say that would deny any role for considerations of acceptability in the discovery of principles, but as shown, *supra* notes 43-54 and accompanying text, even Langdell conceded acceptability a place in doctrine as long as it was brought to play only at the level of principle.

72. T. KUHN, THE STRUCTURE OF SCIENTIFIC REVOLUTIONS 77-91 and *passim* (2d ed. 1970). *See also* N. HANSON, PATTERNS OF DISCOVERY (1958); T. KUHN, THE ESSENTIAL TENSION 266-92, 320-39 (1977); L. LAUDAN, PROGRESS AND ITS PROBLEMS (1977); M. POLANYI, PERSONAL KNOWLEDGE 18-48 (1958). *Compare* Lakatos, *Falsification and the Methodology of Scientific Research Programmes*, CRITICISM AND THE GROWTH OF KNOWLEDGE 91-196 (I. Lakatos & A. Musgrave eds. 1970).

73. *See* E. GOMBRICH, ART AND ILLUSION, 291-329; N. HANSON, *supra* note 72, Chapter 1;

As Einstein said, "It is the theory which decides that we can observe";[74] the philosopher Nelson Goodman has said more recently that "facts are small theories, and true theories are big facts."[75] Quine tells us that our belief-system faces "the tribunal of experience" as "a corporate body," and does not naturally divide into discrete propositions that can be tested for their correspondence to discrete facts.[76] Taken together and pushed hard, these ideas can make the relation between data and theory in natural science seem almost as circular as the relation between cases and principles in classical legal theory. Contemporary "neo-orthodox" legal theorists have seen and exploited the point.[77]

But these modern ideas would have been alien to the world of the classical legal scientists. Their natural response to a charge of circularity would not be to concede then justify it, but to deny the circle by identifying an extra-theoretical source of validation for judicial decisions, comparable to sense-perception in the case of natural science.[78] Two candidates suggest themselves to serve as such an alternative source of validity: intuition and the doctrine of precedent.

Take intuition first. Just as the data of natural science are validated by sense-perception, so individual judicial decisions might be thought validated by a "sixth sense" that permits direct decision of cases from the facts, without the mediation of general norms. We can distinguish three separate versions of such a sixth sense: first, there might be a "moral sense," a supposed universal human faculty

---

J. HOCHBERG, PERCEPTION 105-57 (2d ed. 1977); T. KUHN, THE STRUCTURE OF SCIENTIFIC REVOLUTIONS, *supra* note 72, at 111-35.

74. Or so Heisenberg reported him to have said, in a book of reminiscences written many years after the event. W. HEISENBERG, PHYSICS AND BEYOND 63 (1971). Heisenberg recalls that it was rumination on this remark of Einstein's that led him to his Uncertainty Principle. *Id.* at 77-78.

75. N. GOODMAN, WAYS OF WORLDMAKING 97 (1978). *See also* N. GOODMAN, LANGUAGES OF ART 68 (2d ed. 1976) ("Is a metaphor, then, simply a juvenile fact, and a fact a senile metaphor?").

76. W. QUINE, *Two Dogmas of Empiricism*, FROM A LOGICAL POINT OF VIEW 20, 41 (2d ed. 1961).

77. *See, e.g.*, Fried, *The Laws of Change: The Cunning of Reason in Moral and Legal History*, 9 J. LEGAL STUD. 335, 343-44 (1980). Compare this to Ronald Dworkin's more complex discussion, distinguishing legal from natural scientific reasoning, while claiming close resemblance between the two, in TAKING RIGHTS SERIOUSLY, *supra* note 25, at 159-68.

78. The Victorian positivist-empiricist account of science received its classic statement in Mill's SYSTEM OF LOGIC, *supra* note 63; a view nearer the modern one appeared in W. WHEWELL, *supra* note 63.

for the direct intuition of right and wrong in concrete situations; second, there might be a "common sense," or generally shared tacit knowledge of the conventional morality of a particular society; and finally, there might be a "trained intuition," a specialized professional skill developed by lawyers in the course of their apprenticeship and practice, which allows them to make legal judgments peculiar to their own system.[79]

Some version of a sixth sense theory is presupposed by the common legal argumentative technique of *reductio ad absurdum*, under which a putative legal principle is refuted by deriving from it a judgment in a particular case, real or hypothetical, that is intuitively seen to be unacceptable. Reliance on such intuitions in formal legal argument necessarily grants that they have legally authoritative force. Similarly, the "Socratic" method of pedagogy uses the *reductio*. The student's offer of a putative rule is tested by the teacher's statement of a hypothetical case in which the rule would produce an unacceptable result, as all can see—and here the shared intuitions of even novice students are taken as decisive. Since beginning students cannot have developed any peculiarly legal "trained intuition," reliance on the *reductio* in elementary teaching seems to presuppose a latent legal "common sense" in the lay mind, the content of which can be elicited by supplying appropriate cases for judgment.[80]

But the classical scientists, proponents of the pedagogic case-

---

79. The notions of "moral sense" and "moral sentiment" dominated eighteenth century British moral philosophy; see the summary in A. MACINTYRE, A SHORT HISTORY OF ETHICS 157-77 (1966), and the detailed analytic treatment in Broad, *Some Reflections on Moral Sense Theories in Ethics*, READINGS IN ETHICAL THEORY 363 (W. Sellars & J. Hospers eds. 1952).

The idea of "common sense" as I use it here stresses the origin of the common law in shared community morality. For an expression of this view, see J. REDLICH, THE COMMON LAW AND THE CASE METHOD 37 (1914):

In the common law country, the law appears in the national thought as a quality which to a certain extent comes of itself to men and to the relations which bind men together; as something that is always there and for that reason is known and understood by every one of the people themselves.

The notion that experienced judges have an often inarticulate "trained intuition" that leads them to right decisions is commonplace among case-law theorists; *see, e.g.*, R. POUND, INTRODUCTION TO THE PHILOSOPHY OF LAW 54 (1922).

A "sixth sense" theory could of course combine the three kinds of intuition in various mixtures to justify case decisions, apart from their consistency with doctrine. No actual "sixth sense" theory proclaims intuition, trained or otherwise, to be infallible; even the strongest intuitionistic legal theories retain some notion that individual judgments should be checked against rules and principles. *See, e.g.*, J. FRANK, LAW AND THE MODERN MIND 140-141 (2d ed. 1949).

80. As the linguist elicits judgments of "grammaticality" by appealing to the tacit knowledge

method though they were, stated no "sixth sense" view of case-decision, and for good reason. Any such approach accepts intuitions of the acceptability of particular results in individual cases as legitimate building blocks for legal doctrine. But such "khadi justice" intuitionism would violate the cardinal classical tenet that correct legal judgments must be principled—that is, formally derivable from general principles.[81] In the classical synthesis, as I have argued, considerations of acceptability could properly be taken into account only at the level of general principle.[82] The case-method was thus in contradiction with classical orthodox theory—a contradiction manifested in practice by the historical paradox that Langdell's own educational innovations did help to undermine his approach to legal doctrine.[83]

Apart from a theoretically unacceptable "sixth sense," the other independent source of authority for case-decisions—and the one reluctantly adopted by classical legal theory to break out of its logical circle—was the doctrine of *stare decisis*. Recall the vicious circle again: the source of common law principles was the cases, the standard for correct case decision was consistency with the principles. Breaking out required a source for the legal validity of decisions independent of the principles—an analog to the fallible but independent authority of sense-perception in supporting the observation-statements that supply the data of natural science.

Precedent

Let me approach the use of *stare decisis* as an independent source of legal validity in a somewhat roundabout way. The classical scientist accepted that a legal system must be comprehensive, as well as having the logical virtues of completeness, formality and conceptual order. To recall what this means, consider that to the classical scientist, a judicial decision, unlike the hypothetical legal judgment of a lawyer or a scholar, could be evaluated along two separate dimensions. First, one could ask if the decision was substantively correct, derived logically from the right legal rules and principles. Second, one could ask of a judicial decision whether it

---

of the grammar of his language possessed by every native speaker. For a development of the linguistics analogy, see *infra* note 98.

81. *See supra* text accompanying notes 36-37.
82. *See supra* text accompanying note 54.
83. *See supra* note 3 and accompanying text.

was jurisdictionally and procedurally correct; that is, did it issue from the designated court, and according to the prescribed forms. The legal system would achieve comprehensiveness if every decision satisfied this second dimension of evaluation.[84]

In the practice of natural science, there is no analog to the requirement of comprehensiveness for a legal system. Scientists, unlike judges, have no professional obligation to decide every "case" within their "jurisdiction." Quite consistently with the premises of their enterprise, they can admit that there are things science cannot explain. Thus, science sets its own jurisdiction, which it defines by the scope of its substantive theories.[85] Indeed, the pronouncement of a "scientific solution" that is not backed by the theoretical scientific wherewithal constitutes pseudo-science, one of the chief sins against the scientific ethic.

By contrast, a judge must decide a case over which he has jurisdiction, whether or not he is satisfied that his decision is scientifically correct.[86] Where the procedurally final court decides "incorrectly", it has still produced a judgment terminating the case. The legal system gives such a judgment binding authority over the parties by the principle of *res judicata*; as to them, it is the law's last word.

Further—coming finally to the main point—the common law doctrine of *stare decisis* gives a decided case authoritative force with respect to future decisions in other cases, whether or not the case is later thought to have been decided correctly in the light of principle. This precedential force is traditionally justified mainly on the ground that people will rely on even "scientifically incorrect" official precedents in ordering their affairs.[87] Under the classical view of precedent, a decision or two that is out of whack with "principle" might be set aside as "not good authority," though never entirely dismissed from consideration until overruled. But an established line of precedent, however inconsistent with "principle" in its incep-

---

84. *See supra* notes 20-22 and accompanying text, and note 31.

85. Scientists commonly hold the article of faith (or working rule of method) that all events are "in principle" subject to scientific explanation. This is very different from being subject to a professional obligation to give scientific explanations for events defined by "jurisdictional" rules that are separate from substantive scientific theories.

86. *See supra* notes 20-22, *infra* note 153 and accompanying text.

87. Other justifications are given for *stare decisis*—the convenience of relying on the wisdom of the past, the unfairness of not treating like cases alike (apart from considerations of notice)—but it is the reliance argument that supports giving precedential force to "wrong" past decisions.

tion, becomes binding law, and the seamless web of doctrine must somehow be rearranged to accommodate it.[88]

Stare decisis thus provided the outside source of validity for decided cases that was necessary to save the classical science of law from vicious circularity. But it could do so only at the price of compromising the classical orthodox aspiration toward universally formal conceptual order. The partial authority of even "incorrect" decisions meant that *stare decisis* jostled against what Williston called *stare principiis*, without any formal higher level principle to decide between them.[89] In law, unlike science, error, if persisted in, at some point became truth; and where that point lay could only be determined according to considerations of acceptability that were never satisfactorily formalized.[90]

Langdell himself reluctantly accepted this unformalizable tension among principle, precedent and acceptability; it is well illustrated in his discussion of the doctrine of consideration. Langdell did not regard that doctrine as essential to a rational system of contract law. He recognized, for example, that European civil law enforced promises lacking consideration, and that the common law itself required no consideration for promises under seal.[91] He also recognized the unhappy results that flowed from the consideration doctrine; it was the villain of the piece of the flagpole problem, where Langdell conceded that it produced "hardship and injustice."[92] Further, he believed that the original adoption of the doc-

---

88. *See* Pollock, *supra* note 69. *Compare* Langdell's treatment of the mailbox rule precedents, *supra* note 9 and accompanying text, *with* his treatment of the doctrine of consideration itself, *infra* notes 91-97 and accompanying text.

89. S. WILLISTON, *supra* note 39, at 205. *"Stare decisis*, or follow the precedents, was the old legal maxim. In effect for this Langdell's followers substituted *stare principiis*, follow the principles, even if they overthrow some decisions." *Id.* Some—but classical theory had no formal way to decide how many.

A difference, greater in theory than in practice, between legal science in England and the United States during the classical period, was that English judges purported to be absolutely bound by precedent; the distinction was blurred by manipulation of the distinction between holding and dictum. And see the assessment of American doctrine in E. WAMBAUGH, *supra* note 35, at 108: "We live under a system of *stare decisis*, tempered slightly by a power to overrule."

90. Considerations of acceptability as used at the level of principle, *see supra* notes 43-54 and accompanying text, were presumably themselves not formal; but one of the points of allowing them to be invoked only at the level of principle was to insulate the normal workings of the system from their effect, thus preserving its general formality. *Stare decisis* meant that whenever there was a clash between "principle" and "authority," formality was lost; hence the frantic efforts of classical scientists to reconcile apparently inconsistent cases, *see supra* note 35.

91. SUMMARY, *supra* note 7, at 58, 100.

92. *See supra* note 52.

trine had not been logically required by pre-existing law—indeed, going the other way might have been "the more rational course."[93] "But," Langdell went on, "whatever may have been the merits of the question originally, it was long since conclusively settled" in favor of the consideration doctrine.[94] That being so, the courts could not, consistent with their proper role, abandon the doctrine; and it must be enforced with full rigor within its logical scope, as in the flagpole situation.

On the other hand, Langdell argued, some courts had carried the doctrine beyond its logically proper area by applying it to various contracts governed by mercantile law; that certain merchant promisors should not properly be held to the requirement of consideration was in his view "very clear upon principle."[95] However, "it must be confessed . . . that the generally received opinion among lawyers is otherwise."[96] What does the legal scientist do with a line of existing decisions that follow received opinion, but are contrary to principle, and extend a doctrine better never adopted in the first place? Langdell's response to this conflict of precedent with principle and acceptability was to say, with uncharacteristic equivocation, that these decisions, "if they cannot be pronounced erroneous, must at least be deemed anomalous."[97] Thus was the geometric structure of law's universally formal conceptual order caught in the ever-tangled skein of human affairs.[98]

---

93. SUMMARY, *supra* note 7 at 60-61.

94. *Id.* at 61.

95. *Id.* at 63.

96. *Id.*

97. *Id.* Langdell's more philosophical colleague Beale later stated, "The law of a given time must be taken to be the *body of principles* which is accepted by the legal profession, whatever that profession may be . . . ." J. BEALE, TREATISE ON THE CONFLICT OF LAWS 150 (1916) (emphasis added). This did not resolve the Langdellian dilemma; only those received professional opinions that fitted into a "body of principles" constituted the law for Beale. *Cf. infra* note 109.

Langdell's view of the relative importance of principle and precedent is perhaps best expressed in his discussion of Lord Mansfield's view that a promise to do what the promisor was under a pre-existing moral obligation to do was binding. He noted two theories that might be given for such a view; 1) that the moral obligation was sufficient consideration, and 2) that in such cases, no consideration was required. As between these theories, the second

would have been less untenable, and less mischievous in its tendency. It would indeed have been liable to the serious objection of involving judicial legislation, but the theory of moral consideration was liable to the much greater objection, at least from the scientific point of view, that it could only succeed at the expense of involving a fundamental legal doctrine in infinite confusion.

SUMMARY, *supra* note 7, at 89.

98. Langdell's dilemma was comparable to that of the prescriptive grammarian trying to

Progress

Viewed on a larger scale, the problem of the place of precedent in classical orthodoxy became the problem of the place to be given to history and change in legal theory. Did the fundamental principles of the law change, and if so how? Under the geometric analogy, legal principles should be universal and eternal; history would be simply the record of their gradual discovery. This was indeed the view held by natural law theorists.[99] But it was a position the classical legal scientists firmly rejected. They accepted the nineteenth-century evolutionary idea that law, even in its fundamentals, was not unchanging but progressively evolving; as Sir Henry Maine had

---

establish when "bad but common" usage has become "correct," while necessarily conceding that the grammar of a language has its only source in the usage of its native speakers. The analogy between a people's law and its language is an old one; indeed it was the foundation metaphor of the historical school of jurisprudence, see F. VON SAVIGNY, THE VOCATION OF OUR AGE FOR LEGISLATION AND JURISPRUDENCE 24-31 (1st ed. London, A. Hayward trans. 1831. German orig. 1814). But the analogy has not been exploited since the rise of modern scientific linguistics. It seems an extraordinarily illuminating one, both where it holds and where it does not; perhaps a full development of the analogy would count as a "structuralist" legal theory, in the one fairly clear sense of that term. For example, Saussure's distinctions between *langue* (language, treated as an abstract object) and *parole* (its application); and between diachronic (historical) and synchronic (present time-slice) study of language both cast useful light on "legal science." *See* F. DE SAUSSURE, COURSE IN GENERAL LINGUISTICS 13-14, 80-85 (W. Baskin trans. 1974). Chomsky's distinction between "competence" and "performance," and the use he makes of intuitions of "grammatically" are suggestive in thinking about intuitionistic theories of case law of the sort sketched in *supra* text accompanying notes 79-80. N. CHOMSKY, ASPECTS OF THE THEORY OF SYNTAX, Chapter 1 (1965). Finally, both law and language have aspects of the "conventional" in the rigorous sense of that term developed in D. LEWIS, CONVENTION (1969), following T. SCHELLING, THE STRATEGY OF CONFLICT (1960); for some exploration of the connections, see Johnson, *On Deciding and Setting Precedent for the Reasonable Man*, 62 ARCHIV FUR RECHTS-UND-SOZIALPHILOSOPHIE 161 (1976).

99. And given contemporary exposition by Charles Fried, *supra* note 77 at 349-50, where Fried amusingly, and *almost* dead-pan, analogizes the history of legal thought to the history of logic or mathematics. Fried has more recently, and with apparent solemnity, announced "doubts" about his earlier view on the ground that "a priori moral reflection on rights seems inadequate to yield the necessary richness of our legal system" so that after all perhaps law cannot be fully reduced to "a branch of moral philosophy." Fried, *The Artificial Reason of the Law or: What Lawyers Know*, 60 TEX. L. REV. 35, 37 (1981).

The classical legal scientists unanimously rejected natural law jurisprudence—some of them in a mild tone, as in the case of Langdell, *see supra* note 49, or in the case of Beale, *see infra* note 108 and accompanying text. On the other hand there was Sir Frederick Pollock, who wrote thus after reading an exposition of natural law theory:

> I had long known of *Naturrecht* as a thing existing in German books, but it had never come in my way to any serious extent . . . . We have to thank Professor Lorimer for revealing the mystery in as good English as the nature of the subject admits. As I came to the last page I said to myself with a mental gasp and shiver 'Ugh— Ugh— now I know what *Naturrecht* is.' "

F. POLLOCK, *The Nature of Jurisprudence*, *supra* note 68, at 1, 20.

argued, the legal order grew from the primitive to the advanced, from a regime based on status to one based on contract.[100]

Thus, Langdell wrote in the Preface to his *Cases on Contracts* that each basic legal doctrine "has arrived at its present state by slow degrees; in other words, it is a growth, extending in many cases through centuries."[101] His disciple, Ames, wrote of the gradual evolution of legal norms from the formal and amoral rules of primitive law toward a closer coincidence of the principles of law and morals.[102] And Beale, the most self-consciously philosophical exponent of classical orthodoxy, wrote that "the common law changes . . . . The law of today must of course be better than that of seven centuries ago, more in accordance with the general principles of justice, more in accordance with the needs of the present age, more humane, more flexible and more complex."[103]

Langdell's reference to legal doctrine as a "growth extending through centuries" also suggests an analogy between classical legal science and evolutionary biology—one thinks of legal categories as species and genera, and of cases as specimens.[104] To the extent that biological taxonomy involves the development of an ordered conceptual hierarchy, the biological and geometrical analogies were not in conflict. And insofar as biology suggests a changing rather than a

---

100. H. MAINE, ANCIENT LAW 170 (9th ed. 1883); P. STEIN, LEGAL EVOLUTION (1980).

101. C. LANGDELL, *supra* note 42, at viii.

102. J. AMES, *Law and Morals*, in LECTURES ON LEGAL HISTORY (1913). Ames was much more the practicing historian than the other classical orthodox scholars; he tended to find doctrines evolving, through a kind of inner logic, in a progressive direction. He was also much more given to moralism and a spirit of reform than was Langdell. For example, against the spirit of formalism, he answered the question raised by the title of his essay *How Far an Act May Be a Tort Because of the Wrongful Motive of the Actor?*, *id.* at 399, by saying: quite far. On other occasions, his work reflected the purest formalist spirit, as illustrated by his essays *The Nature of Ownership*, *id.* at 192, and *Can a Murderer Acquire Title by his Crime and Keep It?*, *id.* at 310.

103. J. BEALE, *supra* note 97, at 149. Beale was the philosopher of classical orthodoxy; the cited work (an early-published fragment of his full TREATISE ON THE CONFLICT OF LAWS (1935)) at 114-89, contained the fullest published expression of his jurisprudential views. *See also*, *Notes by Robert Lee Hale from Jurisprudence Lectures given by Joseph Henry Beale, Harvard Law School, 1909*, 29 U. MIAMI L. REV. 281-333 (1975) (hereinafter *Jurisprudence Lectures*).

104. Cf. Langdell, *supra* note 67, at 124: "We have also constantly inculcated the idea that the library is the proper workshop of professors and students alike; that it is to us all that the laboratories of the university are to the chemists and physicists, the museum of natural history to the zoologists, the botanical garden to the botanists." In fact, like Langdell in this passage, when classical orthodox writers drew their frequent analogies between legal and experimental science, they seem to have referred quite at random to the various natural sciences. *See, e.g.*, Keener, *The Inductive Study of Law*, 28 AM. L. REV. 713 (1894) (physics); W. KEENER, CASES ON QUASI-CONTRACT, Preface (1888) (geology); LIEBER'S HERMENEUTICS 329 (W. Hammond ed. 1880) (astronomy).

static subject matter, with the scientist seen as the rational classifier of slowly evolving categories of natural phenomena, it actually does come closer than geometry to the classical orthodox conception of legal science. But the biological metaphor cannot supplant the geometric, because law, like geometry, but unlike taxonomic biology, uses its ordered intellectual system not only to classify specimens but to solve problems.[105]

Langdell's evolutionary language likewise suggests the connection between classical legal science and the historical school of jurisprudence, whose central thesis was that a nation's law is necessarily rooted in the contingent and evolving traditions and customary practices of its people.[106] But it would be a mistake to identify classical orthodoxy too closely with the historical school, which was represented in America particularly by Langdell's contemporary, James Coolidge Carter.[107] Langdell and his followers placed more emphasis than did Carter on principle and reason as against precedent and custom; the classical view thus straddled the natural law and historical schools.

According to classical legal science, history did provide the necessary raw material—the cases—on which reason operated in extracting legal principles. The classical writers thus viewed traditional natural law theories that lacked this positive basis as philosophical speculation rather than legal science.[108] But classical scientists did not identify legal principles with customs; thus Beale wrote, "the common law from its inception has been based upon principles, not upon custom."[109]

If law was not a body of eternal truths but rather a set of evolving principles, and yet these principles were not identified with cus-

---

105. That is, biological taxonomies are systems of categories; legal systems, like geometry, combine categories with operative concepts. See supra note 28.

106. See, e.g., F. VON SAVIGNY, supra note 98.

107. J. CARTER, THE PROVINCES OF THE WRITTEN AND THE UNWRITTEN LAW (1889); J. CARTER, LAW, ITS ORIGIN, GROWTH AND FUNCTION (1907).

108. J. BEALE, supra note 97, at 143. He pressed the same charge, with more acerbity, against the project of Benthamite codification in Beale, The Development of Jurisprudence During the Past Century, 18 HARV. L. REV. 271, 282-83 (1905). In the latter piece, Beale praised Savigny and the other scholars of the historical school for their "great work" in correcting the abstract errors both of Benthamism, and of what he oddly called "the subjective and deductive philosophy of the middle ages." Id. at 283.

109. Beale, Book Review, 20 HARV. L. REV. 164 (1906) (signed "J.H.B."); and see Jurisprudence Lectures, supra note 103, at 291-92. Elsewhere, Beale insisted that "the one most important feature of law" is "that it is not a mere collection of arbitrary rules, but a body of scientific principle." J. BEALE, supra note 97, at 135.

tom, what was the vehicle for legal change in classical theory? Of course, there was legislation, but the classical writers saw statutes as haphazard and anomalous incursions into the body of common law, not fit for scientific study.[110] Precedent too could bring change in the law; a decision not originally supported by existing principles could, if adhered to, eventually establish itself as authoritative doctrine.[111] But such a decision was in the first instance an error, from the classical perspective. If error that managed to entrench itself was the only mechanism of change, how did the law progress?

Recalling the biological metaphor, one can imagine a Darwinian explanation.[112] But classical orthodoxy instead provided an idealist account of the progress of the common law, one that gave a central role to the legal scientist.[113] Progress occurred when the scholar (or the great judge or lawyer) discovered a previously unrecognized principle, one that provided a simple and satisfying explanation for existing decisions, and that at the same time reflected the slowly changing needs and conditions of society. Such a principle, because immanent in decided cases, was already the law, so that its articulation was an act of discovery, not one of illegitimate legislation. On the other hand, once discovered it would produce different, better decisions than had the older, less scientific formulation of doctrine and hence would contribute to the progress of the law.

A famous example of this sort of classical law reform was Brandeis' and Warren's extraction of a right to privacy from a scattering of older cases previously regarded as unrelated.[114] Brandeis, a master of Langdellian technique, artfully argued that these cases were better explained by a general principle of protection of privacy than by the grounds given by the judges who had decided them.[115]

---

110. *See infra* note 171 and accompanying text.

111. *See, e.g.*, Langdell's discussion of the consideration doctrine, *supra* notes 91-97, and accompanying text.

112. That is, there could be a process of essentially random judicial deviation from established law, and those judicial "errors" that turned out to be socially useful would survive while the rest were forgotten. For such an argument see Priest, *The Common Law and the Selection of Efficient Rules*, 6 J. LEGAL STUD. 65 (1977).

113. This view of the role of the legal scientist may be implicit in Langdell's reference to the scientific law teacher as analogous to "the Roman jurisconsult," LANGDELL, *supra* note 67, at 124. It becomes explicit in Ames, *The Vocation of the Law Professor*, *supra* note 92, 354, 364-67. Beale *supra* note 97, at 150, positively trumpets it where he speaks of the influence of law teachers on the growth of the law "comparable in degree" to that of judges and "likely to increase in the future more rapidly than that of judges."

114. Brandeis & Warren, *The Right to Privacy*, 4 HARV. L. REV. 193 (1890).

115. *Id.* at 198-214.

But at the same time as he rooted it in a principle that elegantly reconciled the cases, Brandeis explicitly justified the new right on forward-looking grounds of policy, arguing that it was required by changed social conditions such as mass literacy, the rise of a popular press, the crowded conditions of modern life, and the increased personal sensitivity that supposedly accompanied higher general standards of education.[116]

Because Brandeis' attention to these considerations of policy supported his doctrine at the level of general principle, it was consistent with the tenets of classical orthodoxy.[117] But in the stress he gave to policy as against logic in carrying the burden of his argument, he was straining the spirit of orthodoxy and anticipating the direction of post-classical legal theory. Brandeis' argument showed that Langdellian techniques could serve the cause of conscious law reform. But the classical system could not in the end make too much of a virtue of its flexibility without undermining its promise of determinate geometric order.

IV.

What was the special appeal of classical orthodoxy in late nineteenth century America? The natural place to start is with its promise of universal formality—"every case an easy case." The legal system was to be so arranged that it resolved hard disputes by indubitable (even if complex) reasoning, as Euclidean geometry resolves intuitively problematic spatial questions. The system would be predictable; people could know in which circumstances they would get the aid and in which they would face the opposition of state power. Further, people would be free from public force exerted for the arbitrary personal ends of its guardians. Other things being equal, these would be gains for everyone. But businessmen, the ascendant group in late nineteenth century America, had special needs for legal predictability, and were particularly drawn to the associated "rule of law" conception of freedom.[118]

Though legal realists were later to question it, the classical link between conceptual order and formality seemed clear in 1900.[119] So

---

116. *Id.* at 195-96.

117. *See supra* text accompanying note 54.

118. *See* Trubek, *Max Weber on Law and the Rise of Capitalism*, 1972 Wis. L. Rev. 720, 739-46.

119. On the Realist challenge, see *infra* notes 162-69 and accompanying text.

modern-minded an observer as Max Weber believed that classical legal science—he focused on its German Pandectist rather than its American Langdellian version—enhanced the kind of practical legal predictability that businessmen care about.[120] He even carried this acceptance of classical assumptions to the point of being puzzled at how capitalism could have developed and flourished in England, which with its common law writ system and absence of university legal scholarship lacked a proper conceptually formal system.[121]

Beyond its promise of predictability, a more directly political explanation of the appeal of classical legal science was the ideological support it provided for business through its treatment of economic power relations as neutral, scientifically derived private law rights. The progressive proponents of social legislation certainly saw this ideological connection; all the early critiques of legal classicism linked it with political conservatism.[122]

Nor was the point confined to critics of legal science. John Austin had earlier made an unusually candid pitch for the geometric method in law and ethics on the ground that its impersonal certainty could fortify existing institutions against popular unrest.[123] And nearly a century after Austin, the sponsors of the American Law Institute and its Restatement project were still promising that sound legal science could quell popular discontent by convincing people that judicial protection of the private law status quo was neutrally scientific rather than political.[124]

It is more doubtful whether classical legal science actually influenced the course of judicial decision in a pro-business direction. During the period from 1870 to 1940, the most important political issues in the legal system were questions of public law: how the Populist-Progressive-New Deal legislative program was to be received by legal professionals.[125] The conservative position was that

---

120. For Weber's association of "formal legal rationality" with Pandectist legal science, see M. WEBER, ON LAW IN ECONOMY AND SOCIETY, *supra* note 19, at 64.

121. *See, e.g., id.* at 353; Weber's various and contradictory remarks on "the England Problem" are collected in Trubek, *supra* note 118, at 746-48.

122. *See, e.g.,* HOLMES, COLLECTED PAPERS, *supra* note 3; R. Pound, *supra* note 14.

123. J. AUSTIN, *supra* note 59, at 79; *cf. id.* at 67-70.

124. 1 A.L.I. PROC. 8 (1923) (uncertainty and complexity of law create disrespect for law and consequent unrest); *id.* at 10 ("lack of agreement among lawyers concerning the fundamental principles of the common law is the most potent cause of uncertainty").

125. As compared with the ante-bellum period, where a good case can be made for the greater importance of private law; this is a central thesis of M. HORWITZ, *supra* note 16.

the important common law private rights were constitutionally protected against collective interference unless the legislation could be shown to be closely related to the accepted police power goals of health, safety or morals.[126] For conservative judges, legislation that passed the constitutional hurdle still faced the canon that statutes in derogation of the common law were to be strictly construed.[127]

Neither of these conservative doctrines was particularly congenial to classical orthodoxy. The classicists did not regard public law, including constitutional law, as amenable to scientific study at all. Thus, Langdell's Harvard colleagues and disciples Beale and Ames threatened to withdraw their offer to help the new University of Chicago Law School get started, because its organizers proposed to teach a substantial number of public law courses, thus violating the Harvard curricular dogma that students must be exposed only to scientific "pure law" courses.[128] Constitutional law was unscientific, because hopelessly vague, as typified by the police power doctrine; the question whether a statute was "reasonably related to safety, health or morals" could not be treated formally. To the legal science mentality such open-ended questions were political, not legal, and the courts abandoned any scientific role in trying to answer them. On the rare occasions when the classicists discussed constitutional questions, they thus tended to follow the line laid down by James Bradley Thayer (himself not a classicist)[129]—deference to the legislature unless there was clear violation of a positive constitutional command.[130]

The legal scientists were likewise not much attracted to the problems of statutory interpretation; they believed that the haphazard law laid down in the statute books did not lend itself to conceptual ordering.[131] When they did confront statutory problems they

---

126. C. TIEDEMAN, LIMITATIONS OF POLICE POWER (1886).

127. Pound, *Common Law and Legislation*, 21 HARV. L. REV. 383 (1908).

128. F. ELLSWORTH, LAW ON THE MIDWAY 67 (1977).

129. Thayer, *The Origin and Scope of the American Doctrine of Constitutional Law*, 7 HARV. L. REV. 129 (1893). For Thayer's generally pragmatic and unclassical approach to law, see his essay *The Present and Future of the Law of Evidence*, 12 HARV. L. REV. 71 (1898).

130. *See, e.g.*, Langdell, *The Status of Our New Territories*, 12 HARV. L. REV. 365 (1898) (the Constitution places no restraint on administration of territories annexed from Spain); Williston, *Freedom of Contract*, 6 CORNELL L. REV. 365, 375-80 (1921) (constitutional decisions enforcing "liberty of contract" disapproved).

131. *See Jurisprudence Lectures, supra* note 103, at 297-301. Beale distinguishes between the rare successful statute, which is "capable of having its corners rubbed off, and of being assimilated by the common law," *id.* at 298 (there are only "a very narrow range" of such statutes, *id.* at 300); and the typical statute which is "done by haphazard legislation by a legislature chosen not primar-

did not tend to rely on the canon about statutes in derogation of the common law. Their formalism rather pointed them toward literal readings that avoided both narrowing and expansive purposive interpretation.[132]

It would have been surprising if the classical scientists had been enthusiastic supporters of late nineteenth century big business. They were men of a scholastic bent, generally drawn from an old commercial and professional class that was being pushed from its place in the hierarchy of power by the new industrial and transportation tycoons. The natural political orientation for people of their type was to the Mugwumps, and later to the right wing of the Progressive movement. They were believers in science, traditional virtue and apolitical expertise, who favored sound currency, free trade, civil service reform and clean municipal government.[133]

Classical legal thought thus took only a moderately conservative stance in the political struggles of its time. On the one hand, the classical scientists drew a sharp line between neutral law and partisan politics, placing the fundamentals and many of the details of the market and private property system on the legal rather than the political side of the line. On the other hand, they accepted, however reluctantly, the legitimate power of the legislative majority to step across that line in pursuit of goals too vague for legal-scientific definition.[134]

---

ily for wisdom," often at the insistence of a lawyer who has lost a case and drafts a statute to correct the injustice but who "is not wise enough to foresee its effects other than the particular injustice in mind." *Id.* at 300-01.

Reviewing Dicey's LAW AND PUBLIC OPINION IN ENGLAND, Langdell complained that the title was misleading; Dicey used the word "law" but wrote about "legislation." Clearly in Langdell's mind the two were separate. Langdell, *Dominant Opinions in England During the Nineteenth Century in Relation to Legislation as Illustrated by English Legislation, or the Absence of It, During that Period*, 19 HARV. L. REV. 151 (1906).

132. A good example is Ames' discussion of the famous case of *Riggs v. Palmer* in *Can a Murderer Acquire Title by his Crime and Keep It?*, *supra* note 102, at 310. The New York statute of wills made no provision for the case where the devisee murdered the testator in order to acquire his property. The court interpreted the statute to deprive the murderer of his ill-gotten gains, a view Ames found "impossible to justify" because of its conflict with the literal terms of the statute. *Id.* at 312. *See also* Langdell, *The Northern Securities Case and the Sherman Anti-trust Act*, 16 HARV. L. REV. 538, 551 (1903).

133. *See generally* G. BLODGETT, THE GENTLE REFORMERS 19-47 (1966); R. HOFSTADTER, THE AGE OF REFORM 131-73 (especially 157-58) (1955).

134. In this respect, I disagree with Duncan Kennedy's claim that decisions such as *Lochner v. New York*, 198 U.S. 45 (1905), were representative of the classical mode. Kennedy, *Toward an Historical Understanding of Legal Consciousness: The Case of Classical Legal Thought in America, 1850-1940*, *supra* note 6. *Lochner* represented rather the pre-classical and relatively "political"

Such was the relation of classical orthodoxy to Americans' material interests; how did it appeal to their ideal interests, their urge to find meaning in life? During the post-Civil War period, many Americans experienced at once the complication and the disenchantment of their world. The security of living in a coherent and cognizable life-world—the "island community" of Robert Wiebe's phrase—was destroyed for many by a communications and transportation revolution that left people experiencing their lives as newly controlled by distant and invisible forces.[135] At the same time, the consolations of both traditional religion and liberal humanist self-esteem were assaulted by Darwinism, with its implication that human as well as physical nature could be fully explained in terms of blind and purposeless mechanism.[136]

Against this background, the dry geometry of classical legal orthodoxy had a certain paradoxical quasi-religious appeal to the educated elite. Legal science promised a complete and universally formal system of norms, and so offered determinate answers in an increasingly incomprehensible world. As traditional religion lost its capacity to supply an underlying order to moral and political life (for portions of the elite), legal orthodoxy promised just such an order in the form of the "few fundamental principles" of the common law. In these few simple principles, the individual could comprehend the fundamentals of the whole law, and the society that had come to seem inconceivably vast, unmanageably complex and mechanistically amoral could be seen as having a set of established norms at its center.[137]

More concretely, the legal science movement supplied an ideo-

---

constitutionalism that received its most striking exposition in the famous preface to C. TIEDEMAN, *supra* note 126, at vi-viii. *See also* the thunderous rhetoric of J. DILLON, THE LAWS OF ENGLAND AND AMERICA 203-15 (1894). For the authentic classical approach, see *supra* note 130 and accompanying text. Dillon and Tiedeman looked back to Story, Webster, Rufus Choate and the spirit of Whig constitutionalism, under which the judges were seen as guardians of order, virtue and property against the passions of the mob.

135. *See* T. HASKELL, THE EMERGENCE OF PROFESSIONAL SOCIAL SCIENCE 24-47 (1977); R. WIEBE, THE SEARCH FOR ORDER, 1877-1920 11-75 (1967).

136. P. BOLLER, AMERICAN THOUGHT IN TRANSITION: THE IMPACT OF EVOLUTIONARY NATURALISM, 1865-1900 22-46 (1969); Meyer, *American Intellectuals and the Victorian Crisis of Faith*, VICTORIAN AMERICA 59-77 (D. Howe ed. 1976).

137. The religious dimension of the quest for legal certainty is evoked in Cardozo's words:

I was much troubled in spirit, in my first years upon the bench, to find how trackless was the ocean on which I had embarked. I sought for certainty. I was oppressed and disheartened when I found that the quest for it was futile. I was trying to reach land, the solid land of fixed and settled rules, the paradise of a justice that would declare itself by

logical background for the emerging national bar. The bar, despite all its growth and new wealth, passed through a crisis of institutional self-doubt during the last third of the nineteenth century, even as it was first organizing into a cohesive nationwide professional group. It is hardly possible to read a speech given at a bar association meeting during that period without finding either lamentation for the lost independence of the American lawyer, newly in servitude to business, or defensive bluster against charges that the profession had been commercialized and degraded.[138]

During the same period, secular science and the new major universities where science was practiced were in the ascendancy of their prestige, replacing the church in the minds of the social and intellectual vanguard as the locus of higher, spiritual value in otherwise materialist America.[139] Lawyers who saw themselves in that vanguard were happy to hear Holmes, for example, say that law is "an enterprise for the thinker" in which "a man may live greatly."[140] Holmes, the first great critic of classical orthodoxy, was also drawn by his own philosophic ambitions to the classical enterprise of conceptual ordering.[141] While he recognized that "general principles do not decide concrete cases,"[142] he practiced and revered conceptual jurisprudence, which for him raised law above mere commerce, as he celebrated in words that have adorned many law school graduation speeches since:

> Happiness . . . cannot be won simply by being counsel to great corporations and having an income of fifty thousand dollars . . . . The remoter and more general aspects of the law are those which give it universal interest. It is through them that you not only become a great master in your calling, but connect your subject with the universe and catch an echo of the infinite, a glimpse of its unfathomable process, a hint of the universal law.[143]

At a still more concrete level, legal science built a bridge between lawyers' urge to feel that they practiced a learned profession,

---

tokens plainer and more commanding than its pale and glimmering reflections in my own vacillating mind and conscience.
B. CARDOZO, *supra* note 33, at 166.
138. *See* R. HOFSTADTER, *supra* note 133, at 158-61 and sources by him.
139. L. VEYSEY, THE EMERGENCE OF THE AMERICAN UNIVERSITY 121-79 (1965).
140. HOLMES, COLLECTED PAPERS, *supra* note 3, at 29-30.
141. *See infra* notes 162-63.
142. Lochner v. New York, 198 U.S. 45, 76 (1905).
143. HOLMES, COLLECTED PAPERS, *supra* note 3, at 202.

and the need of the new universities for an alliance with the rich and influential bar. The university's pretensions to be the seat of pure learning stood in the way of this alliance as long as the study of law was seen as the mere craft-training that Veblen, for instance, said it was.[144] The idea of legal science met this difficulty, as Langdell spelled out:

> If law be not a science, a university will consult its own dignity in declining to teach it. If law be not a science, it is a species of handicraft, and may best be learned by serving an apprenticeship to one who practices it. If it be a science, it will scarcely be disputed that it is one of the greatest and most difficult of sciences, and that it needs all the light that the most enlightened seat of learning can throw upon it.[145]

It is impossible to believe that Langdell was cynical or manipulative in what he said, or that there was not genuine passion behind Holmes' eloquence. For them, and for a handful of their contemporaries, legal scholarship was an end in itself.[146]

Apart from disinterested love of scholarship, the classical scientists in their work as law teachers necessarily had to carry out the organization and simplification of the mass of legal materials that is prerequisite to successful teaching. Earlier, Blackstone, Kent and Story had found their vocation as legal system-builders when they agreed to teach law to beginners.[147] So, in their time, Langdell's followers—the first full-time American legal professoriate—faced with the need to make outlines and summaries of their subjects for pedagogic purposes, perhaps were especially inclined to confer a high value on the task of conceptual ordering, thus making a virtue out of necessity.

Pulling these strands together, we can see a converging network

---

144. T. VEBLEN, THE HIGHER LEARNING IN AMERICA 211 (1918). ("the law school belongs in the modern university no more than a school of fencing or dancing.")

145. Langdell, *supra* note 67, at 124.

146. On Langdell's idealism (and Holmes' own), see Holmes' letter to Pollock quoted in *supra* note 13.

147. The connection between university law teaching and conceptual, systematic legal thought was one of Weber's central themes; M. WEBER, *supra* note 19, at 216-17, 274-78. It is significant that German legal science was intimately linked to university legal education from its origins early in the nineteenth century. Similarly, the English legal science movement, closely related to American classical orthodoxy, arose with the development of serious university-based law study at Oxford during the 1870's and 1880's. *See* F. LAWSON, THE OXFORD LAW SCHOOL, 1850-1965 69-85 (1968). On the other hand, not all university-based law teachers were classical in their approach; there were also Whig throwbacks, like Tiedeman and Baldwin, and precursors of modernity, like Gray and Thayer.

of demands—political, spiritual, professional and educational—that defined the situation of late nineteenth century American legal thinkers. It would be an exercise in the old historical game of hindsight determinism to say that this situation necessarily produced classical orthodoxy. What can fairly be said is that Langdell's system did nicely meet this particular group of demands, at least for a brief moment in time.

V.

Though classical orthodoxy haunts us still, it did fall from its position of explicit dominance, for reasons that are worth recalling. One reason was certainly political; Progressive and later New Deal lawyers saw classical orthodoxy as a form of conservative ideology. In part this was a confusion of Langdellian legal science with the laissez-faire constitutional doctrines epitomized by the *Lochner* decision. But it was also in part a realistic assessment. Classical orthodoxy did claim to discover politically neutral private law principles by rigorous scientific methods, and thus reinforced the view of the common law contract and property system as a "brooding omnipresence in the sky" rather than as a contingent allocation of power and resources.[148]

Apart from its perceived political bias, classical theory, with its vision of the law as determined by a few relatively fixed and fundamental principles, was not readily adapted to a period of rapid social change. The very factors that made classicism reassuring to people frightened by change—its suggestion that there were stable fundamentals under a chaotic surface—made it seem hopelessly unrealistic to those who felt the need to confront the turmoil. In this sense, the turn against classical orthodoxy was part of that "revolt against formalism" that characterized much American social thought during the early years of the twentieth century.[149] The

---

148. For Holmes' famous "brooding omnipresence" phrase *see* Southern Pacific Co. v. Jensen, 244 U.S. 205, 222 (1917). The notion captured by the familiar phrase that there was a general law of private rights, common to the Anglo-American world, toward which the actual decisional law of the various common law jurisdictions should ideally converge was a central doctrine of classicism. It is most clearly articulated and defended in J. BEALE, *supra* note 97, at 138-39, 144-50. Beale proved the existence of such a body of law by a kind of transcendental deduction, thus: "To say that the Common Law in the broader sense is not truly law would logically lead to the abolition of every law school of more than local importance and the transfer of its students to the faculty of philosophy." *Id.* at 139. The general common law was a "condition of possibility" for the existence of the Harvard Law School.

149. M. WHITE, SOCIAL THOUGHT IN AMERICA: THE REVOLT AGAINST FORMALISM (1947).

point is related to the prior one; most of the rebels against formalism were political reformers, too. But the tendencies are separable; Holmes, for example, no reformer, was a leader of the anti-formalist revolt, whose spirit he captured when he denigrated the "human longing for certainty and repose" that is flattered by "logical method and form" while hiding from the reality that "certainty generally is illusion and repose is not the destiny of man."[150]

As these familiar explanations of the fall of classical orthodoxy suggest, it was, like any significant ideology, not a closed system of ideas, but rather continuous with the life around it. But for purposes of study, I have abstracted the ideas of classical orthodoxy into an intellectual system. Thus abstracted, its fall is best represented, though with some artificiality, not by recounting the interests or motives of its critics but by stating the content of their critique.[151] Let me now translate that critique into the terms that I originally used to describe the classical system itself.

First, recall the outlines of classical orthodoxy. The uniquely correct judgments required so that the legal system could be *complete* were supplied by an array of bottom-level rules, stated in precise and objective *(formal)* terms, only one of which would properly apply to any fact situation. The rules were deducible from the top-level fundamental principles, themselves inductively extracted according to scientific canons from the mass of prior decisions. The principles had to be relatively few and consistent among themselves *(conceptually ordered)*, independently appealing *(acceptable)* and had to reconcile most decided cases *(stare decisis)*. Where a situation occurred for which no existing rule was available, the appropriate rule had to be derivable from the existing principles, which by their abstract formulation provided gapless and unambiguous coverage of all potential cases. Direct appeal to acceptability in deciding a new case by itself, or in formulating a bottom-level rule to cover it, was precluded by the requirement of conceptual ordering, which in turn was necessary to guarantee completeness. Ideally, every decision was correct "in principle"; that is, its decisive rule

---

150. HOLMES, COLLECTED PAPERS, *supra* note 3, at 181.

151. Thus, I remain in the domain of systematic description (or "interpretation," which sounds fancier), and duck what to many is the crucial question: the relative causal significance of the interests and the ideas. I do think causal questions in social theory meaningful and potentially answerable, even if we will never have scientific laws in this area. But I do not know enough to answer this one—except to point back to my text, and to say that I would not be so interested in the ideas if I did not think they had some significant causal force.

followed by analytical reasoning from abstract norms that were themselves immanent in the existing case law of the system.

Holmes, Pound and others attacked this classical structure with a two-part critique. They began by pressing the question *why* considerations of acceptability should not be considered in formulating bottom-level rules and in deciding individual cases. The classical response was that to allow *ad hoc* practical judgment meant abandoning legal science, which meant abandoning the certainty, predictability and accountability of legal decision generally. The critics then mounted their decisive denial of the success and indeed the possibility of the central classical project of formal conceptual ordering.

Let me spell out these points in more detail; the presentation takes the form of a rational reconstruction, not purporting to fit exactly the argument of any one critic, but trying to capture the essence of their common position. The critique begins by stressing the practical function of the courts. Adjudication is first of all an instrument for the peaceful and orderly resolution of disputes.[152] This point draws support from the requirement of comprehensiveness to which all legal systems adhere. Judges must decide cases within their jurisdiction; they cannot refuse to decide because no clear answer is supplied by the law. There is a live dispute that must be resolved whether or not it is covered by a rule. The requirement of comprehensiveness is not suspended to achieve completeness, or conceptual order, as might be expected if the primary goal of the legal system were to develop or maintain a harmonious body of substantive law.[153]

Further, once disputes are settled in a procedurally final way, they generally are left alone by the law, even if later shown to have been decided incorrectly. This is the force of the familiar legal principle of *res judicata*, which has no counterpart in science. In addition, unresolved jurisdictional conflicts—threats to comprehensiveness—within the legal system are perceived as serious crises.[154]

---

152. It would be an interesting bit of intellectual history to trace the idea of adjudication as primarily "dispute resolution." The notion is implicit in Holmes' early remark that it is the merit of the common law to decide the case first. *See supra* note 1. It is given the first explicit statement I have found by Gray: "The function of a judge is not mainly to declare the law, but to maintain the peace by deciding controversies." J. GRAY, THE NATURE AND SOURCES OF THE LAW 100 (1921).

153. *See supra* notes 20-21 and accompanying text.

154. As with the Coke-Ellesmere dispute, *supra* note 21; or as with President Nixon's equiv-

Perceived substantive anomalies in legal doctrine arise constantly and create no similar sense of crisis.

Our views of courts primarily as dispute-settlers rather than scientific authorities likewise appears in our tendency to discourage them from ruling on hypothetical or abstract questions of law. Where there is a dispute, the court must rule; where there is no dispute the court should not.

Given the essentially practical *function* revealed by these features of the courts, is it not natural to judge their work by the practical *standard*, the standard of acceptability?[155] Of course, we do not simply direct courts to decide every dispute in the most acceptable way, but that is because to do so would vest in these powerful institutions a degree of discretion that would itself be unacceptable. The values of legality—completeness, formality and conceptual ordering—have their place, but each invocation of these values must be subject to the ultimate test of acceptability. Why should unacceptable results be imposed—as in the flagpole case—when there is available a rule that produces more satisfactory and fairer resolutions of real disputes?

The classical response to this was that rigorous adherence to principle both allowed the law as a whole to be understood[156] and allowed courts, by derivation of correct rules from established principles, to decide new and previously unanticipated cases.[157] It was at this point that the critics mounted their second and decisive assault—their challenge to the scientific pretensions of classical theory.

The classical scientists had been bold enough to set out a concrete test for the success of their enterprise, implying that failure to achieve it would amount to a refutation of their claims. The test was stated in Langdell's statement quoted earlier: "The number of fundamental legal doctrines is much less than is commonly sup-

---

ocation over whether he would consider himself bound by a Supreme Court ruling that he must surrender his tapes to the Watergate prosecutor.

155. A point is typically made by saying that case-decisions inevitably *are* influenced by considerations of acceptability, whether this is officially admitted or not; thus Holmes: "Behind the logical form lies a judgment as to the relative worth and importance of competing legislative grounds, often an inarticulate and unconscious judgment, it is true, and yet the very root and nerve of the whole proceeding." HOLMES, COLLECTED PAPERS, *supra* note 3, at 181.

156. S. WILLISTON, *supra* note 39, at 213-14.

157. Hence Langdell's reference to mastery of "the ever-tangled skein of human affairs," *supra* text accompanying note 42.

posed . . . . If these doctrines could be so classified and arranged that each should be found in its proper place, and nowhere else, they would cease to be formidable in their number."[158]

Langdell and his followers set out to realize this program with impressive ability and energy. They wrote articles, organized cases into structured case-books, and composed huge treatises.[159] Finally, they inspired the Restatement project whose purpose was to establish a grand consensus, enlightened by legal science, on the fundamental principles of the common law.[160] As the Restatements appeared toward the end of the '20s, the failure of the great classical project to attain Langdell's goal of discovering the few simple principles that underlie the mass of cases became wholly obvious. Thurman Arnold wittily summarized the situation:

> [T]he Restatement . . . has become another book which must be consulted, while the cases and tests pour out as before. No sooner is the Restatement of Trusts completed than Bogert produces seven volumes on trusts in place of his own volume work, backed by 22,000 cases . . . . No sooner is the Restatement of Contracts off the press than lawyers find a new edition of Williston, increased in size from four volumes to eight. . . . Are students relieved of their labors? The answer is found in any great law office . . . . [M]emoranda are carefully preserved . . . but their indexing is so difficult and their quantity so formidable that it is easier to start afresh with the digests . . . . Are the professors' labors relieved? The answer is found in the fact that the number of legal articles written by members of his craft which the brethren are supposed to read . . . are increasing daily . . . . All this has advanced the art of advocacy since the time of Daniel Webster in the same manner as the inflation of the German mark advanced business in Germany.[161]

Thus were the boldest claims of classical orthodoxy empirically undermined. But its critics had been convinced long before on analytical grounds that the enterprise was unsound. The basic flaw was the failure of the link between conceptual order and formality. Practical predictability of judicial decision can often be obtained by the framing of formal and objective bottom-level rules to govern

---

158. *See supra* note 42.
159. G. GILMORE, *supra* note 36, at 57-60.
160. "The restatement here described, if adequately done, will do more to improve the law than anything the legal profession can undertake. It will operate to produce agreement on the fundamental principles of the common law, give precision to use of legal terms, and make the law more uniform throughout the country." 1 A.L.I. PROC., *supra* note 124, at 18.
161. Arnold, *Institute Priests and Yale Observers—A Reply to Dean Goodrich*, 84 U. PA. L. REV. 811, 820 (1936).

decision. A will, for example, is valid if it is attested by two witnesses, not if it is "adequately" or "reasonably" attested. But rules of this sort have to be manufactured by arbitrary acts of human will; they cannot be deduced from the kind of high-level abstract principles classical science sought to discover.

Holmes, who himself valued both conceptual order and formality, insisted on the disjunction between them when he observed that "general principles do not decide concrete cases."[162] Easy cases were those settled by unambiguously applicable specific rules. In hard cases, where no single clear rule was applicable, plausible deductions from general principles could always be constructed on both sides. The actual decision of such cases required drawing a line, arbitrarily, on a continuum between competing concepts.

Holmes believed that judges could establish rules in such situations by observing the clustering of decided cases and then imposing artificially sharp boundaries around the fuzzy clusters formed. These rules, arbitrary as they were, could provide useful predictability if imposed uniformly by judges in later cases. But rules of this kind could not be logically derived from the principles, whose abstract character guaranteed that they would be indeterminate at the edges.

For the more moderate critics of classical orthodoxy like Holmes, the formulation and conceptual ordering of the legal principles was far from useless to the decision process; that principles did not by themselves decide concrete cases was not to say that the cases could be as well decided without them. The principles focused attention on the competing considerations relevant to the decision, providing guidance by confining the range of argument. But in hard cases this guidance ran out before the decision was reached.[163]

---

162. Lochner v. New York, 198 U.S. 45, 76 (1905). The "general principle" that Holmes referred to was his own: "a constitution is not intended to embody a particular economic theory." Having said that the principle could not by itself decide the case he went on "But I think that the proposition just stated, if it is accepted, will carry us far toward the end." As always with Holmes, the correct general principle was useful in directing the mind toward the appropriate considerations for decision, though it could not dictate decision by itself. See generally infra note 163.

163. Throughout his career, Holmes consistently adhered to the view of the relation between general principles and specific rules stated in the text. He believed, early and late, that it was important to arrange and conceptually arrange the law "philosophically"—that is, according to an appropriate set of abstract and legally autonomous concepts. See supra note 15; HOLMES, THE COMMON LAW, supra note 7, at 104 (doctrine should be reduced to "a philosophically continuous series"); HOLMES, COLLECTED PAPERS, supra note 3 at 195-97 (jurisprudence as a valuable study; law should be analyzed into "philosophical" categories like contract and tort, rather than "empiri-

Other Realists showed that formality itself did not always produce predictability, the virtue it was supposed to serve, giving as evidence some of Holmes' own unsuccessful efforts to impose clear rules on intrinsically variable situations.[164] Judges and juries would respond to direct considerations of acceptability whether they should or not. When clear and objective rules produced injustice or inconvenience in application, some courts would continue to apply them according to their terms while others would find ways to wriggle out and reach the sensible result. Thereby was predictability, the reason for imposing the rule in the first place, lost. In many situations decisions would be both more predictable and more acceptable if the ruling norm were a vague standard that allowed judges or juries to apply their intuitive sense of fairness case-by-case, rather than a clear rule that was sporadically and covertly evaded.[165]

Similar difficulties inevitably arose from the effort actually to stick to more abstract principles. Sometimes accepted principles *did* point strongly to one result rather than another, but the indicated result conflicted with established practice, or with widely shared views of acceptability. In these situations some courts would evade the implications of principle and reach the results suggested by policy or custom, while others would conscientiously and woodenly fol-

---

cal" ones like shipping and telegraphs). He believed that such abstractions did not decide hard cases; it was a fallacy to suppose that "a given system, ours for instance, can be worked out like mathematics from some general axioms of conduct." *Id.* at 180. But a sound conceptual scheme and accurately stated general principles could guide and aid decision; *supra* note 162.

At the fuzzy periphery of even the best general concepts and principles indeterminate cases would arise, and for this, the remedy was the imposition of arbitrary rules in the interest of legal predictability. *See* Baltimore and Ohio R.R. v. Goodman, 275 U.S. 66 (1927); HOLMES, THE COMMON LAW, *supra* note 7, at 88-103; HOLMES, COLLECTED PAPERS, *supra* note 3, at 232-38. Holmes stated this view of the relation between principles and rules in a way he was never to improve on or significantly alter in his essay *The Theory of Torts*, 7 AM. L. REV. 652 (1873), *reprinted in* 44 HARV. L. REV. 773, 775 (1931):

> The growth of law is apt to take place in this way: Two widely different cases suggest a general distinction which is a clear one when stated broadly. But as new cases cluster around the opposite poles, and begin to approach each other, the distinction becomes more difficult to trace; the determinations are made one way or the other on a very slight preponderance of feeling, rather than articulate reason; and at last a mathematical line is arrived at by the contact of contrary decisions, which is so far arbitrary that it might equally well have been drawn a little further the one side or the other. The distinction between the groups, however, is philosophical, and it is better to have a line drawn somewhere in the penumbra between darkness and light, than to remain in uncertainty.

164. *See, e.g.*, Pokora v. Wabash Railway Co., 292 U.S. 98 (1934) (Cardozo, J.).

165. Fuller, *American Legal Realism*, 82 U. PA. L. REV. 429, 432-38 (1934).

low principle. A lawyer could not tell a client in advance how a court would come out.

Several elements of the Realists' critique of classical orthodoxy are drawn together in their treatment of an aspect of the doctrinal problem we started with: when does contract acceptance by mail become effective? Even though Langdell had demonstrated the unprincipled nature of the mailbox rule, it had become uniformly accepted by doctrinal writers. Williston, the orthodox scientist of contract law, pronounced the rule to be binding, though with some regret given its lack of sound basis in "principle."[166] It did not occur to him that the actual decisions might reveal a still more particularized (hence unprincipled) pattern. But Realist contract scholars noticed that courts were frequently holding certain contracts to have been formed even *before* the acceptance was mailed. In cases involving life insurance policies, where applicants (offerors) submitted applications subject to approval by the central office of the company, and then died after the central office approved the application but before the signed policy (the acceptance) was mailed, courts often held that the policy had gone into effect and the benefits must be paid.[167]

Here was a special rule for life insurance cases, not announced by the courts because it conflicted with orthodox "established law," but based on a sensible bias toward compensating survivors and a feeling that no injustice was done once the insurer had decided to issue the policy. Williston did not so much disapprove this pattern of decisions as fail even to notice it. He cited some of these cases in a footnote to his treatise, identifying them only as anomalous departures from the general doctrine;[168] he could not even conceive that there might be rules governing acceptance still more particularized than what he saw as the already too *ad hoc* mailbox rule. Thus the pursuit of generality of principle that was the hallmark of the classical scientists led them to miss altogether lines of doctrine that were acceptable and that could produce predictable results once recognized, but that, to recall Langdell's words, "had no principle to support them."[169]

---

166. 1 S. WILLISTON & G. THOMPSON, CONTRACTS 234 (1936).

167. Patterson, *The Delivery of a Life Insurance Policy*, 33 HARV. L. REV. 198, 203-05 (1919).

168. 1 S. WILLISTON & G. THOMPSON, *supra* note 166, at 204 n.4.

169. The lesson just summarized was drawn in Cook, *Williston on Contracts*, 33 ILL. L. REV. 497, 511-14 (1939).

For the critics, conceptual ordering was not, as in classical orthodoxy, a form of scientific discovery, but rather a pragmatic enterprise, to be judged by its success in achieving its practical ends. High-level generalization of legal doctrine in the form of principles might give some rough guidance in the process of judicial decision and can serve as a kind of information storage and retrieval indexing system for lawyers. Its main importance, however, is pedagogic: a newcomer to the law needs an overview of its main doctrines, stated in oversimplified but readily comprehensible form.[170]

But in the eyes of sophisticated modern lawyers, using the general formulas devised for these pedagogic and indexing purposes to deduce legal judgments is the mark of a tyro, a black letter lawyer. The real law is seen as an intricate filigree formed by the interaction of social policies with the specific, detailed fact-patterns of worldly practice. The exemplars of legal craft in post-classical doctrinal technique are thus the scholar Corbin and the judge Cardozo, both renowned for their refusal to accept dictation from general principles and for their masterfully attentive use of the facts of particular cases.[171]

VI.

The modern critics' denigration of conceptual ordering meant that even in its fall classical orthodoxy achieved a secret triumph. The classical scientists had purported to do no more than make precise and scientific what had always been implicit in the substance of the common law and the methods of common lawyers. But in their pursuit of logical order Langdell and his colleagues had actually created a largely new conceptual structure that effectively replaced the older Blackstonian outline of the law in the discourse of the profession.[172]

The classical scheme was based on an interlocking set of hierarchial distinctions, each of which served to focus lawyers' attention on what was thought primary and essential, and what merely peripheral, in the body of legal materials. Thus, the classical scientists

---

170. *See, e.g.*, Pound, *Classification of Law*, 37 HARV. L. REV. 933, 938-40 (1924).

171. *See, e.g.*, G. GILMORE, *supra* note 36, at 74-81. A leading expression of this contemporary viewpoint is Llewellyn's semi-mystical notion of "situation sense." K. LLEWELLYN, *supra* note 6, at 121-22.

172. The oddity, from our perspective, of the pre-classical scheme is the theme of Kennedy, *supra* note 28.

drew a basic line between substantive law on the one hand and procedure and remedies on the other, with the former treated as primary and the latter as merely instrumental.[173] Applying that distinction, they treated the distinction between law and equity, potentially an ideologically charged clash of governance by rule with judicial discretion, only as an aspect of the peripheral law of remedies.[174] Within substantive law, they distinguished public law from private, treating private law as the core and public law as the peripheral and anomalous hybrid of law and politics.[175] Within private law, their fundamental subcategories were contract and tort, which corresponded respectively, in the classical image of society, to a broad realm of freedom governed by the principle of the mutual consent of individuals and a narrow realm of collective control governed by a principle of liability for injury wrongly done. They extruded the "collectivist" principle of unjust enrichment from contract without receiving it into tort, and hence left it in a secondary doctrinal position. Finally, they isolated the law of property as the doctrinal dumping ground for the anomalous survivals of the pre-liberal family and land-based legal order.[176]

I have stated the classical categorical scheme in deliberately political terms in order to show that it implied value judgments that most modern lawyers would not accept—for instance, its assignment of peripheral roles to procedure and to public law. But the classical scientists never put these judgments forward as potentially controversial claims. They rather treated their conceptual scheme as a neutral system of categories within which all legal controversy would take place. Within this scheme, the classical scientists made

---

173. *See supra* note 50. For an analysis and effective ironical reversal of this classical ordering, see Arnold, *The Role of Substantive Law and Procedure in the Legal Process*, 45 HARV. L. REV. 617 (1932).

174. For a statement of the core of the Langdell-Ames theory of equity, see Ames, *Christopher Columbus Langdell*, *supra* note 102, at 476; for a summary statement of the theory see C. LANGDELL, SUMMARY OF EQUITY PLEADING, *supra* note 50, at 27-40. The implications of the traditional view of equity are drawn out in Hohfeld, *The Relations Between Equity and Law*, 11 MICH. L. REV. 537 (1913); Pound, *The Decadence of Equity*, 5 COLUM. L. REV. 20 (1905).

175. *See supra* notes 128-32 and 134 and accompanying text. I believe it was this ordering, rather than any attempted integration of public and private law, that was most characteristic of classical orthodoxy. *Compare* Kennedy, *Toward an Historical Understanding of Legal Consciousness: The Case of Classical Legal Thought in America, 1850-1940*, *supra* note 6, for the "integration" thesis.

176. I owe this overall picture of the classical private law ordering mostly to the pathbreaking analysis in Duncan Kennedy's unpublished manuscript on classical legal thought, D. Kennedy, The Rise and Fall of Classical Legal Thought, 1850-1940, *supra* note 6.

further and obviously controversial assumptions, the most general of which was that abstract legal concepts such as contract and tort had essences, in which scholars could discover principles that in turn could dictate determinate legal judgments.

It was this essentialist approach to legal argument that the post-classical critics assaulted and overthrew, along with much of the lower-level doctrine derived through it. These Realist writers focused their intellectual energy on the task of critique. Most of them, in their constructive moments, also pursued the enterprise of creating a legal policy science. Those Realist critics who did not believe in policy science tended to confine their constructive work to the problems of fact-finding, and to discern those highly particular bottom-level rules and practices that they believed directly affected legal decision. Their characteristic project was the replacement of general and abstract legal categories by narrow and concrete ones.[177]

Almost all modern theorists, after forcefully rejecting the classical belief that this or that legal rule is "inherent" in this or that legal concept, have gone on to suppose that if general conceptual schemes cannot supply decisive major premises for legal judgments, they can have no importance at all. The roles of such schemes in elementary pedagogy and in indexing legal materials seem relatively trivial. Thus, scholars generally no longer treat what Holmes called "the arrangement of the law," the architecture of its concepts, as worth their serious attention.[178]

But categorical schemes have a power that is greatest when it is

---

177. The "narrow-category" idea differentiated Legal Realist writers like Radin, Green, Arnold and Llewellyn from earlier critics of classical thought like Holmes and Pound. The earlier critics had continued to pursue the ordering of the law into "philosophical" abstract concepts, while abandoning the classical ideal of formal reasoning from these concepts to case-decisions. For characteristic statements of the "narrow category" idea, see Llewellyn, *Some Realism About Realism*, 44 HARV. L. REV. 1222, 1237 (1931); Radin, *The Theory of Judicial Decision, or: How Judges Think*, 11 A.B.A. J. 357 (1925). For applications, see K. LLEWELLYN, CASES AND MATERIALS ON SALES 561 (1931) (note on "title"); Arnold, *Criminal Attempts—The Rise and Fall of an Abstraction*, 40 YALE L.J. 53 (1930); Cook, *supra* note 169.

Apart from the "narrow category" approach to legal doctrine, the two other distinctive features of Legal Realism were the iconoclasm of most Realists and the serious interest some of them took in quantitative and behaviorist study of legal institutions. *See* Schlegel, *American Legal Realism and Empirical Social Science: From the Yale Experience*, 28 BUFFALO L. REV. 459 (1980).

178. There have been occasional moments of realization that the Langdellian structuring of the first-year legal curriculum decisively shapes the legal consciousness of students, with subsequent unsuccessful flurries of effort at designing the curriculum along "functional" lines; *see* R. Stevens, *supra* note 4, at 471-75, 511-15. The occasional direct challenges to the classic private law

least noticed. They channel the attention of those who use them, structuring experience into the focal and the peripheral. In so doing, they influence judgment much as the agenda for a meeting influences the results of its deliberations. Heedless of this power of categories, modern legal theorists have not supplanted the classical ordering but have left it to half-survive in the back of lawyers' minds and the front of the law school curriculum, where it can shape our thinking through its unspoken judgments—Langdell's secret triumph.

VII.

Many of the post-classical critics wished to replace the classical science of legal principles with a Benthamite policy science. In this, they followed Holmes' advice that "the true science of the law" lay not in "logical development as in mathematics" but rather in "the establishment of its postulates . . . upon accurately measured social desires."[179]

But it is striking how little progress (if progress is the right word) has been made toward basing law on the accurate measurement of desires. The main accomplishment of decades of earnest preachment on behalf of policy science seems to have been that in recent years lawyers and judges sometimes (law teachers and scholars more often) have come to invoke the comforting metaphor of "balancing" when they discuss choices that involve the conflict of incommensurable values—the choices that less comforting modernist discourses call "political" or "existential."[180]

---

ordering have left the placid hegemony of the classical ordering unshaken. *See, e.g.*, L. FRIEDMAN, CONTRACT LAW IN AMERICA (1965), G. GILMORE, *supra* note 36.

A more significant change in legal consciousness was represented by the Legal Process movement of the 1950's, as authoritatively expounded in H. Hart & A. Sacks, The Legal Process (1958) (unpublished). The Legal Process school integrated procedure, public law and administrative process into a general theoretic framework for the legal system based on the organizing concept of "institutional competence." But Legal Process theory did not challenge either the classical private law ordering based on tort and contract, or the ultimate primacy of private law and of judicial decision within the legal system ("private ordering," "principled adjudication").

179. HOLMES, COLLECTED PAPERS, *supra* note 3, 225-26.

180. For a critique of the use of "weighing" and "balancing" metaphors where agreed methods of measurement or ordering are patently lacking, see A. DONAGAN, *supra* note 26. Holmes often spoke of line-drawing along a continuum to express the judicial function in hard cases, a metaphor that does away with the implication that the judge has access to a set of scales that will do his work for him. His opinion in Pennsylvania Coal Co. v. Mahon, 260 U.S. 393 (1922), for example, points to the competing considerations thought relevant to decision without anywhere suggesting that they have pre-existing "weights."

Apart from the balancing idiom, legal discourse largely retains its orthodox form. On official occasions, lawyers and judges still mostly talk in terms of rules and principles, presupposing right answers even to hard questions of law and disfavoring explicit arguments of policy. The contemporary school of thought led by Ronald Dworkin argues that this orthodox discourse is too durable to be treated in legal realist fashion as mere myth and rhetoric, and has tried to formulate a legal theory that is consistent with orthodox premises and yet escapes the standard modern critique of classical orthodoxy.[181]

A movement in legal theory that has closer links to the Benthamite dream of policy science is the school of law and economics. But, on closer inspection, that school turns out to be neoorthodox too. Its leader, Richard Posner, says that economic analysis cannot supplant, but only predict and criticize, a course of legal decision carried on case-by-case according to orthodox methods. And Posner finds "efficiency," with all the connotation of approval that term carries in his theory, in the content as well as the methods of Langdellian private law.[182]

With all their differences, these neo-orthodoxies have in common their response to a current nostalgia for classical legal theory. To understand what is more than crudely political in this nostalgia, one must recall and try again to feel the pull of the simple tenets of Langdell's creed: law is a science; its materials are all in law books;

---

181. "The 'myth' that there is one right answer in a hard case is both recalcitrant and successful. Its recalcitrance and success count as arguments that it is no myth." TAKING RIGHTS SERIOUSLY, *supra* note 25, at 290. As noted, *supra* note 27, Dworkin has disparaged efforts at classical-style conceptual ordering, for reasons that are not clear given his general approach. Other contemporary writers in the same vein have enthusiastically revived the search for a structure of general principles behind the law. *See, e.g.*, C. FRIED, CONTRACT AS PROMISE (1981); R. EPSTEIN, A THEORY OF STRICT LIABILITY: TOWARD A REFORMULATION OF TORT LAW (1980); G. FLETCHER, RETHINKING CRIMINAL LAW (1977).

182. The efficiency of late nineteenth century private law is a pervasive theme of Posner's work; *see, e.g.*, Posner, *A Theory of Negligence*, 1 J. LEGAL STUD. 29 (1972). His preference for autonomous and traditional legal method over direct application of economic analysis by lawyers and judges emerges from Posner, *Some Uses and Abuses of Economics in Law*, 46 U. CHI. L. REV. 281, 284-87, 297-301 (1979); Posner, *The Present Situation in Legal Scholarship*, 90 YALE L.J. 1113, 1113-119 (1981). A quick look at the first published opinions of Posner, J., confirms the traditionalism of his method; they are classical in their austerity, brevity, absence of footnotes, and absence of interdisciplinary apparatus of any kind. Thus even an antitrust case evokes no economic analysis beyond the minimum required by precedent. *See* Products Liability Ins. v. Crum & Forster Ins., 682 F.2d 660 (7th Cir. 1982). The style aspires to the elegant directness of Holmes and Hand—aphorisms and all. *See* Muscare v. Quinn, 680 F.2d 42, 45 (7th Cir. 1982) ("Three appeals in a case about a goatee are enough.").

behind the mass of those materials are a few simple principles; and discovery of those principles will allow us to "master the ever-tangled skein of human affairs." These tenets may have the appeal they do to many legal scholars because, if classical orthodoxy was only a pseudo-science, at least it was an occasionally elegant one that allowed a certain ingenuity in its application, as compared to the pseudo-science of balancing and policy that succeeded it. Law students must be tired of hearing how Policy X balanced against Policy Y produces Legal Rule Z—the Papa Bear, Mama Bear, Baby Bear fable of our contemporary classrooms and more advanced upper courts.[183]

The neo-orthodoxies drawn from economics and moral philosophy resemble classical legal science in their capacity to promote structured puzzle-solving of a sometimes interesting kind. But, in contrast to the classical theory, they dilute the autonomy of law (and hence, potentially, the status of the profession) by shifting research outside the law library; this compromises their appeal to lawyers and confines them even within legal academia largely to the ghetto of courses designated as peripheral by titles beginning "Law and. . . ."[184] For this reason, they have little chance to succeed as our ruling legal ideology the still-dominant hybrid of Legal Process

---

183. Connoisseurs of this form of discourse will have their favorite examples. As a teacher of Constitutional Law, I am inclined to vote for the argot surrounding the "levels of scrutiny" in present-day equal protection jurisprudence. On the other hand, when I teach Torts, I am drawn to the California Supreme Court's often-repeated statement that in deciding what duty to impose in negligence cases it will consider: "the foreseeability of harm to the plaintiff, the degree of certainty that the plaintiff suffered injury, the closeness of the connection between the defendant's conduct and the injury suffered, the policy of preventing future harm, the extent of the burden to the defendant and consequences to the community of imposing a duty to exercise care with resulting liability for breach, and the availability, cost and prevalence of insurance for the risk involved." Rowland v. Christian, 69 Cal. 2d 108, 443 P.2d 561, 70 Cal. Rptr. 97 (1968). Here, the banal domesticity of Mama and Papa Bear is replaced by an ill-assorted menagerie in unseemly orgy. This is not the "Grand Style" reborn.

184. Charles Fried sees and attempts to forestall this threat in the essay cited *supra* note 99; Richard Epstein, *see supra* note 181, has always attempted to sustain a genuinely autonomous legal discourse in his doctrinal work, at the cost of an element of the arbitrary in his conclusions. Posner's judicial style, *supra* note 182, reflects his sense of the importance of legal autonomy. *Compare* Arnold, *Judge Jerome Frank*, 24 U. CHI. L. REV. 633, 633-34 (1957):

As a judge he had only one disqualification. He lacked that narrowness of purpose, that preoccupation with the law as a separate discipline, that exclusion of social and economic considerations, which removes the "Law" from the everyday world and thus makes it such an impressive and important symbol. . . . Certainly it is true that the idea of federal judges roaming the stormy fields of economics, sociology, psychiatry and anthropology, their black robes flapping in the winds of controversy, is a disquieting one, even to the writer.

theory and the remnants of classical orthodoxy. They will probably never supply a scheme of categories and concepts that actually shape legal argument and judgment, though they no doubt can play the humbler role of reducing the gap between legal scholarship and the rest of the intellectual world.

Apart from their conceptual ordering of the law, the classical scientists' main achievement was to articulate better than have any other Anglo-American lawyers the curious second-best utopia that animates the legalist mind. They left behind them a memorable and illuminating elaboration of the coolly seductive fantasy that, even in the absence of genuine communal solidarity, an industrial society might nonetheless be held together by a structure of legal doctrine that, conceived in the pure spirit of science and possessed of its elegant rigor, transcends the ugly partisan struggles of politics, and at the same time defines the boundaries of the sovereign self in a way sufficiently practical to resolve real human disputes.

A SEMIOTICS OF LEGAL ARGUMENT†

Duncan Kennedy‡

I. Introduction

My impression is that when people interested in legality appropriate the theory or philosophy of language, they tend to focus on the
rule form and the "facts" in the world to which the rules are applied.
For example, what does language theory tell us about the meaning of
a statement such as "you must be 35 years old to be eligible for elec-
tion to the Presidency?" In this paper, I pursue a different kind of
borrowing, focussing on what language theory might offer the as yet
rudimentary theory of legal argument.

By legal argument, I mean argument in favor of or against a particular resolution of a gap, conflict, or ambiguity in the system of legal
rules. In this form of argument, it is the practice to deploy stereotyped "argument-bites," such as, "my rule is good because it is highly
administrable." Argument-bites come in opposed pairs, so that the
above phrase is likely to be met with, "but your rule's administrability
comes from such rigidity that it will do serious injustice in many particular cases."

Starting with the argument-bite as a basic unit, I propose a set of
inquiries into legal argument, using language theory as a source of
analogies. First, there is the lexicographical or "mapping" enterprise
of trying to identify the most common bites. Second, there is an inquiry into the generation of pairs and their clustering into dialectical
sequences, rituals of parry and thrust. The response above might be
answered, "there will be few serious injustices in particular cases because my rule is knowable in advance (unlike your vague standard)
and parties will adjust their conduct accordingly." Third, there is the
second-order mapping task of identifying the major clusters (some
candidates: formalities as a precondition for legally effective expres-

---

† Copyright © 1989 by Duncan Kennedy. An earlier version of the main article
appeared in R. Kevelson, 3 Law and Semiotics (1989). The Appendix is original to
this issue.
‡ Professor of Law, Harvard Law School.

sions of intent, compulsory contract terms, existence and delimitation of legally protected interests, liability for unintended injury).

The fourth inquiry is into the consequences of the argument-bite idea for the phenomenology of legal argument. If arguments come in stereotypical bites, then it is at least plausible that (1) they get their meaning from one another, in the sense that words do, (2) that to be intelligible to a legal audience one must stretch one's thought on their Procrustean bed, so that there is always a gap or discontinuity between the subject and his or her argument, something at once constrained and strategic about the choice of distortions, and (3) that the course of the legal argument will be at least somewhat independent of the particular topic, that is the particular gap, conflict or ambiguity in the rule system to which it is apparently quite specifically addressed, so that argument is the play of argument-bites (as well as an evocation of the possibilities of a real situation of choice).

It is an interesting question whether legal argument is possible in its highly self-serious contemporary mode only because the participants are at least somewhat naive about its simultaneously structured and indeterminate (floating) character. The rest of this paper is mainly concerned with the first two tasks: that of developing a lexicon and that of attempting to identify some of the operations or transformations of argument-bites that legal arguers use to generate a meaningful exchange.

II. DICTIONARY ENTRIES

The following is a list of argument-bites in random order. It is of course not exhaustive, but rather fragmentary. The two principles of selection will become clear below.

legal protection of the fruits of labor gives an incentive to production

the proposed solution will be easy to administer

no liability without fault

only the legislature can obtain the information necessary to make this decision rationally

the defendant should have looked out for the plaintiff's interests (altruistic duty)

the law, not community expectations, should determine the outcome

the proposed solution lacks equitable flexibility

people have a right to freedom of (this kind of) action

immunity will discourage the plaintiff's desirable activity

judges make decisions every day with no more information than they have here

pacta sunt servanda (promises should be kept, period)

liability will discourage the plaintiff from looking out for himself (*i.e.*, from taking precautions)

the proposed rule defeats the defendant's expectation of freedom of action

as between two innocents he who caused the damage should pay

the plaintiff should have looked out for his own interests (been self-reliant)

the role of the judge is to apply the law, not make it

legal protection inhibits competition in markets for goods and ideas

the proposed rule corresponds to community expectations

no such right has ever been recognized at common law, so the judge has no power to intervene

there is prima facie liability for intentional harm absent an excuse

the proposed rule protects the plaintiff's reliance

the common law evolves to meet new social conditions

people have a right to be secure from (this kind of) injury

liability will discourage defendant's desirable activity

liability will encourage the defendant to take precautions

rebus sic stantibus (only as long as circumstances remain the same)

III.   ARGUMENT BY MAXIM AND COUNTERMAXIM

I selected this particular randomly ordered list because I can use its members to illustrate a basic structure of legal argument, namely the pairing of arguments as maxim and countermaxim. Another way to put this is to say that a competent legal arguer can, in many (most? all?) cases, generate for a given argument-bite at least one counter argument-bite that has an equal status as valid utterance within the discourse. While responding to an argument-bite with one of its stereotypical counter-bites may be wholly unpersuasive to the audience, it is never incorrect, at least not in the sense in which it would be incorrect to answer an argument-bite with an attack on the speaker's character or with a description of the weather.

This selection of argument-bites also allows me to propose a tentative typology, which I will use to order my pairs, but not further explain or justify here. The categories are substantive argument-bites, used to characterize party behavior in relation to the proposed rule, and systemic bites, used to characterize the rule in terms of the institutional values of the legal system. I subcategorize substantive arguments in terms of their sources in general political/ethical discourse as based on morality, rights, social welfare or community expectations. Among systemic bites, I distinguish those that have to do with administrability from those that refer to conflicting theories of the role of courts *vis-a-vis* legislatures (institutional competence arguments).

I have omitted the whole category of arguments about the correct interpretation of authorities (*e.g.*, arguments to the effect that a precedent does or does not "govern," that a statute does or does not "cover" the case). But it is worth noting that the "policy" arguments below are often deployed to support a particular interpretation of a case or statute, or to resolve a conflict of authority, as well as to deal with cases understood to be "of first impression."

A.   *A Typology of Argument-Bites in Pairs*

1.   *Substantive Arguments*

a.   *Moral Arguments*

the defendant should have looked out for the plaintiff's interests (altruistic duty)
vs.
the plaintiff should have looked out for his own interests (been self-reliant)

as between two innocents he who caused the damage should pay
vs.
no liability without fault

pacta sunt servanda (promises should be kept, period)
vs.
rebus sic stantibus (only as long as circumstances remain the same)

b. Rights Arguments

people have a right to be secure from (this kind of) injury
vs.
people have a right to freedom of (this kind of) action

c. Social Welfare Arguments

immunity will discourage the plaintiff's desirable activity
vs.
liability will discourage defendant's desirable activity

liability will encourage the defendant to take precautions
vs.
liability will discourage the plaintiff from looking out for himself
(*i.e.*, from taking precautions)

legal protection of the fruits of labor gives an incentive to
production
vs.
legal protection inhibits competition in markets for goods and
ideas

d. Expectations Arguments

the proposed rule corresponds to community expectations
vs.
the law, not community expectations, should determine the
outcome

the proposed rule protects the plaintiff's reliance
vs.
the proposed rule defeats the defendant's expectation of freedom
of action

2. Systemic Arguments

a. Administrability Arguments

the proposed solution will be easy to administer
vs.
the proposed solution lacks equitable flexibility

b. Institutional Competence Arguments

no such right has ever been recognized at common law, so the
judge has no power to intervene

vs.

there is prima facie liability for intentional harm absent an
excuse

the role of the judge is to apply the law, not make it

vs.

the common law evolves to meet new social conditions

only the legislature can obtain the information necessary to make
this decision rationally

vs.

judges make decisions every day with no more information than
they have here.

B. Remarks on Argument by Counter-Bite

The phenomenon of the countermaxim is complex. The following remarks are no more than suggestive. First, argument-bites are
conventional. What makes a particular sentence an argument-bite is
nothing more nor less than that people use it over and over again (or
use a phrase that is its equivalent in their understanding), with a sense
that they are making a move, or placing a counter in the game of
argument.

Second, each argument-bite is associated in the minds of arguers
not with one but with a variety of counter-bites. The list above illustrates only a few of the modes of opposition of bites. I will shortly
attempt a typology of oppositional moves, or operations.

Third, an extended argument for a particular resolution of a gap,
conflict or ambiguity in the rule system will be only relatively structured. In other words, only a part of the material will be recognizable
as the play of bites. Arguments occur in particular contexts, and
these contexts give them content that is arbitrary from the point of
view of structural analysis. It is rarely productive to take the structural point of view to the extreme of reducing everything in the argument to the mechanical reproduction of moves or operations.

Fourth, it is nonetheless true that every legal argument within a
legal culture is by definition relatively structured. Indeed, this is what
we mean when we situate the argument in our legal culture, rather
than in lay discourse or philosophical discourse or (to pick an example at random) French legal culture.

IV.   Operations in Legal Argument

By an operation I mean a "transformation" of an argument-bite by "doing something" to it that gives it a very different meaning, but one that is nonetheless connected to the starting bite. The prototype of an operation, as I am using the term here, is the simple procedure of adding "not" to a phrase, so as to indicate that it is untrue rather than true, as in "I am not French." This phrase is obviously closely related to "I am French," although it has an altogether different meaning [!?!].

The power of structuralist methodology is that it shows that what at first appears to be an infinitely various, essentially contextual mass of utterances (parole) is in fact less internally various and less contextual than that appearance. It does this by "reducing" many of the particular elements of the discourse to the status of operational derivatives of other elements.

When I say, "I am French," and you respond, "No, you are not French," there is less going on, less complexity to deal with, than if you responded, "I don't understand your agenda." The reason being that "you are not French" adds a new meaning to the conversation through a simple, familiar transformation of, an operation on, "I am French," rather than by adding what appears, at least at first, an altogether new thought.

A.   A Typology of Operations

1.   Denial of a (Factual or Normative) Premise

Argument by denial means accepting the relevance of your opponent's argument but denying one of its factual or normative premises. For example:

(morality)
no liability without fault
vs.
I agree that there should be no liability without fault, but you were at fault here, so you are liable.

(morality)
pacta sunt servanda (promises should be kept, period)
vs.
there was no promise

(morality)
pacta sunt servanda (promises should be kept, period)
vs.
True, but I kept my promise

(rights)
plaintiff has a right to security from (this kind of) injury
vs.
this kind of right exists, but defendant did not injure plaintiff

(rights)
plaintiff has a right to security from (this kind of) injury
vs.
no such right exists

(utility)
liability will discourage defendant's desirable activity
vs.
liability will not in fact discourage the activity

(utility)
liability will discourage defendant's desirable activity
vs.
defendant's activity is undesirable

(administrability)
the proposed solution will be easy to administer
vs.
the proposed rule is not in fact administrable

Denial of a factual premise will typically lead to a reframing of the facts presented by the other side so as to support the attack. Classic reframing techniques exploit the ambiguities of crucial concepts like fault, causation and free will to reverse an opponent's presentation.

2. Symmetrical Opposition

The most striking form of oppositional pairing is between two maxims appealing respectively to the plaintiff's and the defendant's points of view as it will always be possible to argue them within a particular cluster. Some examples:

(morality)
the defendant should have looked out for the plaintiff's interests (altruistic duty)
vs.
the plaintiff should have looked out for his own interests (been self-reliant)

(rights)

plaintiff has a right to be secure from (this kind of) injury

vs.

defendant has a right to freedom of (this kind of) action

(utility)

liability will discourage defendant's desirable activity

vs.

immunity will discourage plaintiff's desirable activity

(utility)

legal protection of the fruits of labor gives an incentive to production

vs.

legal protection inhibits competition in markets for goods and ideas

(expectations)

the proposed rule protects the plaintiff's reliance

vs.

the proposed rule defeats the defendant's expectation of freedom of action

(administrability)

the proposed solution will be easy to administer

vs.

the proposed solution lacks equitable flexibility

This operation might be called "Hohfeldian" rather than "symmetrical" opposition, since it was Hohfeld who first identified the ambiguity in our common legal usage of the word "right" that often masks it when we are speaking in the rights mode. Both arguments are, once both are on the table, patently partial or incomplete, just because each ignores its symmetrical pair.

It seems reasonable to describe the relationship as operational because once one has learned the "trick" of appealing to the defendant's right to freedom of action every time the plaintiff appeals to her right to be secure from this kind of injury, one no longer sees the two arguments as independent. Likewise with the defendant's protest that liability will chill his desirable activity, and the plaintiff's symmetrical claim that unless protected he will cut back on his highly beneficial pursuits. The appearance of X in close proximity to Y no longer seems a function of the irreducible particularity of context, but rather of the structure of legal argument itself.

Again, this is not to say that the arguments will always be equally convincing. Quite the contrary. Nor that as a matter of fact the appearance of X on the plaintiff's lips will automatically elicit Y on the lips of the defendant. Y may not occur to the defendant. Or it may seem tactically unwise to invoke a right to freedom of action (suppose the issue is civil liability, and the defendant's conduct is indisputably criminal). Yet when Y does occur in response to X, we experience, if we recognize the operation, the relative coherence or intelligibility, as opposed to the relative arbitrariness of legal discourse.

3. Counter-Theory

By a counter-theory, I mean a response which simply rejects the normative idea in the principal argument-bite. There is no quick shift from one point of view to another, as in symmetrical opposition, but direct confrontation.

(morality)
no liability without fault
vs.
innocent victims should be compensated

(morality)
pacta sunt servanda (promises should be kept, period)
vs.
rebus sic stantibus (only as long as circumstances remain the same)

(expectations)
the proposed rule corresponds to community practice
vs.
the law, not community practice, should determine the outcome

(institutional competence)
no such right has ever been recognized at common law, so the judge has no power to intervene
vs.
there is liability for intentional injury in the absence of an excuse

(institutional competence)
the role of the courts is to apply law, not make it
vs.
the common law evolves to meet new social conditions

4. Mediation

Mediation differs both from symmetrical (or Hohfeldian) opposition and from counter-theory because it acknowledges a conflict of claims and proposes a way to resolve it on the arguer's side. The mediator argues for a principle or a balancing test that will settle the matter, either in general or in this particular case. For example, the counter-theory to "no liability without fault" might be "innocent victims should be compensated." "As between two innocents . . .", on the other hand, acknowledges a claim on both sides, but proposes a principle of liability based on causation to resolve the conflict.

(principle)
no liability without fault
vs.
as between two innocents he who caused the damage should pay

(balancing)
innocent victims should be compensated
vs.
as between two innocents, it is cheapest to let the losses lie where they fall

(balancing)
rebus sic stantibus (only as long as circumstances remain the same)
vs.
the utility of promise keeping will be undermined if people see their obligations as merely contextual

(principle)
plaintiff has a right to security from (this kind of) injury
vs.
plaintiff's ordinary right must yield to defendant's fundamental right

(balancing)
plaintiff has a right to security from (this kind of) injury
vs.
defendant's right outweighs plaintiff's right

(balancing)
liability will discourage defendant's desirable activity
vs.
plaintiff's activity is more desirable than defendant's

(balancing)
your proposed solution lacks equitable flexibility
vs.
on balance, the gain in certainty outweighs the lack of flexibility in this case

Mediation requires the arguer to acknowledge the conflict between a pair of superficially powerful arguments that we produced above either by symmetrical opposition or by theory and counter-theory. It is therefore an operation performed on a pair, rather than on a single argument-bite. This should serve to emphasize the point that there is no natural or pre-given unit of analysis in the semiotics of legal argument. Sometimes the appropriate unit seems quite clearly to be the bite, sometimes it seems equally clearly to be a pair of bites, a cluster, or, as we will see, the bite with its support system.

5. *Refocussing on Opponent's Conduct (Proposing an Exception)*

Refocussing on your opponent's conduct means particularizing within the general context of your opponent's argument. You concede the premise, but point out that she has behaved in a way that makes the valid premise inapplicable in this case. Refocussing differs from denying that the facts support the argument, or denying the normative premise, because it proposes an exception rather than challenging the argument as a whole.

Because there is an almost infinite number of ways in which we can imagine refocussing, it is arguable that we are slipping here over the line between an operation and the multiplicity of arbitrary, contextual, opportunistic, strategic behavior. Yet there is a patterned quality to the responses below. They are quite abstract, and it is easy to apply them in dozens and dozens of contexts without submerging the abstraction in particularity. Refocussing seems at least to merit tentative status as an operation.

(morality)
no liability without fault
vs.
this injury was an anticipated cost of doing business (Pinto)

(morality)
innocent victims should be compensated
vs.
plaintiff could have gotten out of the way (LeRoy Fibre)

(rights)
plaintiff has a right to security from (this kind of) injury
vs.
plaintiff has forfeited his rights by his conduct in this case

(rights)
defendant has a right to freedom of (this kind of) action
vs.
defendant has forfeited his rights by his conduct in this case

(utility)
immunity will discourage plaintiff's desirable activity
vs.
but if there is liability, plaintiffs will behave strategically
(blackmail defendants)

(utility)
liability will discourage defendant's desirable activity
vs.
but if there is immunity, defendants will behave strategically
(blackmail plaintiffs)

(administrability)
the proposed solution lacks equitable flexibility
vs.
because the parties can adjust their behavior to the rule, its lack
of equitable flexibility is not important

(administrability)
the proposed solution will be easy to administer
vs.
the inability of some parties to master the formality will
accentuate inequality of bargaining power

There is an interesting and important set of stereotypical responses to refocussing, such as that "the exception would swallow the rule," and "the distinction is illusory" ("collapsing the distinction"). Not to mention "loopification." But for another time.

6. Flipping

Flipping is appropriating the central idea of your opponent's argument-bite and claiming that it leads to just the opposite result from the one she proposes:

reverse fault: when a person who innocently injures another innocent refuses to compensate, he is at fault

reverse competition: only the establishment of legal rights to economic advantage will prevent cut throat competition from leading to monopoly

reverse community expectations: following community expectations would be undemocratic because those expectations have been significantly formed by the prior course of judicial decision

reverse unequal bargaining power: interfering with freedom of contract will lead to pass-through of the cost and impoverish the people you are trying to help

reverse paternalism: to insist in the face of people's actual failings that they be self reliant is to impose your values on them

reverse administrability: the pursuit of rules in this area has spawned such complexity that a general equitable standard would increase rather than decreasing certainty

reverse institutional competence: leaving the decision to the legislature is a form of lawmaking because it establishes the defendant's legal right to injure the plaintiff

7. Level Shifting

It is permissible to answer an argument-bite for the plaintiff with a pro-defendant argument-bite from another pair. Indeed, this is one of the most common ways to argue. I say your rule lacks administrability. You respond that your rule tailors liability to fault. And so on. Level shifting is a highly "permissive" operation, meaning that there are lots of maxims to choose from when changing the subject. But there is an important restriction. For the shift to make sense, it must be to an argument-bite associated with the particular legal issue at hand. To use a phrase from the next section, it must be to another bite within the cluster.

B.   Concluding Remark on Operations

It is easy to fall into the error of believing that what I have been calling operations are a true "logic of legal discourse." We may be able to transform "plaintiff has a right to security from (this kind of) injury" into, "defendant has a right to freedom of (this kind of) action," by the operation of "symmetrical opposition." But it most certainly does not follow (a) that any other maxim can be so transformed, or (b) that any maxim that can be will, in fact, be so transformed by lawyers and judges in practice. Sometimes yes, and sometimes no, depending on . . . "the circumstances." I have little confidence that we will be able to establish the actual "scope" of operations in legal argument other than by trial and error.

I constructed my typology in a relatively empirical or pragmatic fashion, by first listing familiar arguments, then inventing a typology, then playing with items and abstractions until time ran out. There was a temptation, once I had defined a set of operations, to invent arguments that are not part of the vocabulary in use, but "ought to be." For example, symmetrical opposition seems a particularly important operation, and it would be satisfying if one could carry it out on every item in the dictionary. As I set out to list examples, I was often in doubt, and found myself trying hard to "come up with" an argument-bite that would show the generality of the operation. For example, is the following pair a "genuine" instance of symmetrical opposition?

> (institutional competence)
> a decision for the plaintiff would be law making, not law application
> vs.
> a decision for the defendant would be law making, not law application

I am not sure.

The answer would seem to require a more precise definition of "symmetrical opposition" than I gave above. A more precise definition might well throw into question some of the examples of the operation that at first seemed paradigmatic, and also lead to the generation of new examples. And so on.

The appeal of this activity, of working toward an exhaustive mechanics of transformation, is that it gives the illusion of mastery of a whole discourse. But, as I said before, every actual instance of an extended argument in favor of a particular resolution of a gap, conflict, or ambiguity in a rule system contains large quantities of contextual matter. The contextual matter influences the formulation of the argument-bites that are its grid.

The problem is deeper yet. The distinction between a bite and a merely contextual argument is so blurry, and so much in motion through time, that there is no hope of a definitive dictionary or of a definitive typology of operations (any more than there is with a living language). For example, the distinction between social welfare arguments about activity levels and about precautions was clearly formulated for the first time well after I began to work on this project.

Given the intractability of the discursive mass from which one must mine argument-bites, and the ease with which one can construct them once one has devised some operations, constructed bites threaten to force out their rougher but authentic counterparts. Furthermore, as I developed my typologies, I found myself repeatedly rewriting the one sentence bites in the dictionary, so that they would "fit" better.

Legal semiotic discourse seems (at every moment, and why not?) to replace its object of study with a pseudo-object more amenable to

its internal requirements. Why not: the more of legal argument and the less semiotic invention we include in the object of study, the more interesting the analysis will be, by which I mean the more political it will be—the more capable of disquieting power.
[And then there is the possibility that the academic study of operations might influence those very operations . . .]

V.   SUPPORT SYSTEMS AND CLUSTERS

In this section, I extend the notion that argument-bites get their meaning, and legal argument gets its intelligibility, from the system of connections between bites.

A.   *Support Systems*

An argument can be more or less developed. At one extreme, it may be one sentence long: "no liability without fault." At another, that one sentence is supported by pages of material. Some of this material will consist of reasons why we should accept the one sentence argument. These reasons may themselves be conventional, to the point that they are best understood as argument-bites, and as constituting a "support system" for the "lead" bite. Since the system of supporting bites is implicitly present in the mind of the arguer when she deploys the lead bite, it should be understood as one of the sources of that bite's meaning, just as the opposing bites everyone knows we can generate through operations are part of that bite's meaning.

I suggested above that we categorize arguments in four substantive modes (morality, rights, utility, and expectations), and two systemic modes (administrability and institutional competence). We often use substantive modes as "ultimates," or arguments that do not need further justification. By contrast, it is more common within legal discourse to see institutional competence and administrability arguments as in need of support from the substantive arguments.

But this is only a matter of convention. In our legal culture, people think of morality, rights, etc., as providing explanations for action that are satisfactory in themselves, but they also, from time to time, choose to "go behind" them. The distinction between substantive and systemic modes is one of degree only. In fact, bites in each mode can support bites in each of the other modes, producing a complex system.

We support institutional competence arguments with subarguments in each of the substantive modes. For example:

judges should be restricted to law application because it is
inefficient for them to engage in law making

vs.

judges should evolve the common law because this will be better
for the general welfare than always waiting for the legislature

private actors have a right to be free of liability except where
there is precedent

vs.

the community expects people who injure others without an
established privilege to be held liable

it would be unfair to the parties for the judge to resolve their
case without the kind of information that only the legislature
can obtain

vs.

it is immoral for the judges to decline jurisdiction on the
grounds that someone else might have been able to decide more
competently.

The above arguments are reversible ("it is immoral for the judge
to meddle with the parties without the kind of information only the
legislature can obtain," etc.).

We also support institutional competence arguments with administrability arguments: "judges should apply, not make the law,"
with, "otherwise there will be hopeless uncertainty." We support administrability arguments with subarguments in the four substantive
modes ("the certainty of rules — as opposed to the uncertainty of
standards — benefits everyone in the society by eliminating unneces-
sary disputes"), and also with institutional competence arguments
("only a regime of rules, and not a regime of standards, is consistent
with the judicial role of law application, as opposed to law making").
In other words, the two types of systemic argument are mutually
supporting.

The appeal to expectations can be used in an ultimate way: "the
proposed rule is bad because it would violate the expectations of the
parties, period." But expectations arguments are often supported in
the other three modes: "people have a right to have courts follow
their expectations," "it is socially beneficial for courts to follow expectations," "it would be immoral for courts to frustrate expectations."
Moreover, we can toss in systemic reasons for following expectations:
"following expectations will give law certainty, whereas courts following their own views would be hopelessly uncertain"; "the non-demo-
cratic nature of courts means they have to follow expectations or be

guilty of usurpation." And so on through the other substantive modes.

The ability to generate the support system for an argument-bite, picking and choosing among its elements to fit the context, is as important to the arguer as the ability to "counter-punch" an opponent's bites. Our ability to understand and assess the value of an argumentative sequence is heavily dependent on our imaginative ability to place each bite in its implicit support system, and understand the response to the bite as also a response to that system.

B. Clustering

Although this is not the place for a full discussion, at least a few preliminary thoughts on clustering seem necessary in order to fill out the ways in which argument-bites acquire meaning. A cluster is a set of arguments that are customarily invoked together, when the arguer identifies his raw facts as susceptible of posing a particular kind of legal issue. Argument-bites acquire meaning not only through their oppositional relationship to bites we generate through operations, and not only from their relationship to bites they support and are supported by, but also from the other members of the cluster.

From the great mass of facts, the lawyer selects those that he or she thinks can be cast as "relevant" to one of the preexisting rule formulae that together compose the *corpus juris*. Then the lawyer works to recast both facts and formula so that the desired outcome will appear compelled by mere rule application. The argumentative apparatus we have been discussing is, remember, deployed in order to resolve a gap, conflict or ambiguity in the rule system.

The problem is situated for the participants according to which rule or rules need interpretation. The rule, in turn, is situated in one of the conventional or intuitive arrangements of the *corpus juris*. But it is also situated on a map of "types of legal issues" that occur over and over again in different parts of the *corpus juris*. Some examples of these recurring problems are:

(1) Should judges grant any kind of legal protection to the interest asserted by plaintiff? If so, what degree of protection?

(2) Should judges impose liability for this type of unintended, non-negligent injury?

(3) Should judges require a formality before recognizing an expression of intent as legally binding? How should they deal with failure to comply?

(4) Should judges impose a non-disclaimable duty on anyone who enters a contract of this particular kind?

To my mind, one of the most urgent tasks of legal semiotics is to identify other clusters of this kind. A disproportionate number of the bites discussed above come from the particular "cluster" that arguers deploy in debates about the definition and delimitation (through defenses) of legally protected interests. There is a distinct intentional torts bias to the whole discussion. Nonetheless, we could begin to break the bites out into clusters as follows:

1. Formalities Cluster

(denial)
defendant induced plaintiff's pre-formality or extra-formality reliance, so should compensate plaintiff's loss
vs.
defendant did not induce, plaintiff did not rely, plaintiff was not injured

(symmetrical opposition)
defendant induced plaintiff's pre-formality or extra-formality reliance, so should compensate plaintiff's loss
vs.
protecting plaintiff's reliance would defeat defendant's expectation of freedom of action up to the moment of formality

(focussing on opponent's conduct)
defendant induced plaintiff's pre-formality or extra-formality reliance, so should compensate plaintiff's loss
vs.
plaintiff's reliance was the product of gullibility and wishful thinking
vs.
defendant was manipulating the formality with full knowledge of the plaintiff's ignorance and naivete

(symmetrical opposition)
the proposed formality will be easy to administer
vs.
the proposed formality lacks equitable flexibility

(reverse administrability)
the pursuit of rules in the area of formalities has spawned such complexity that a general equitable standard would increase rather than decreasing certainty

(refocussing on opponent's conduct)
the proposed formality lacks equitable flexibility
vs.
because the parties can adjust their behavior to the formality if
they want to, it is paternalistic to disregard it after the fact

(reverse paternalism)
to insist in the face of people's actual failings that they self reliantly
adjust their behavior to the formality is to impose your values on
them

(mediation)
the proposed formality will be easy to administer
vs.
the inability of weak parties to master the proposed formality will
unacceptably accentuate inequality of bargaining power

(reverse unequal bargaining power)
undermining the formality will lead to pass-through of the cost and
impoverish the people you are trying to help.

2. *Compulsory Terms Cluster*

(counter-theory)
the defendant should not be bound because his choice was
unwise
vs.
second guessing the defendant's choice is paternalistic unless he
is an infant or insane

(counter-theory)
the defendant should not be bound because the plaintiff had superior bargaining power
vs.
the law has no concern with unequal bargaining power

(flipping)
courts increase social welfare by refusing to enforce contracts
based on unequal bargaining power
vs.
interfering with freedom of contract will lead to pass-through of
the cost and impoverish the people you are trying to help

(counter-theory)
it's not the role of the courts to make contracts for the parties
vs.
since the equity of redemption, courts have always intervened
against overreaching

And so on.

I argued that the distinction between counter-argument by operation and mere contextual or opportunistic counter-argument is blurred. Likewise for support systems and clusters. The formalities cluster blurs into the compulsory terms cluster. In a given context, it will be hard to distinguish between formulaic argument-bites from a cluster and arguments more "authentically" emerging from the facts. A given argument-bite ("no liability without fault") may appear in many clusters, along with some but not all of its counter-bites.

It may well be impossible to establish an exhaustive list of operations, or to correctly delimit the clusters extant at a given moment in the history of legal argument. A given argument-bite's countermaxims, support system and cluster are three indefinite series of associated items. The point is that we listen to the bite, when an opponent deploys it in a particular doctrinal context, with the other members of the cluster already in mind. What we hear depends on those unspoken bites, just as it depends on each bite's support system and countermaxims.

The discussion of "nesting," below, is situated in the cluster that arguers invoke when they have identified the legal issue as involving the definition, through specifying defenses, of the contours of a legally protected interests.

C. Concluding Remark on the Interdependence of the Meanings of Argument Bites

The claim that words "get their meanings" not from the things or ideas they signify but from their relationships with other words is often presented in a way that is, to put it mildly, mystifying. I want here to make an analogous claim about argument-bites, but one that seems to me relatively straightforward.

When a practised legal arguer puts forward a proposition such as "there should be no liability without fault," he or she does so with a professionally heightened sense of those words as "rhetoric." The legal arguer is more aware than the lay arguer, either consciously or close to consciously, that there are counter-arguments derivable by operation, that "no liability without fault" can be supported by subarguments based on rights, social welfare, administrability, and so forth, and that this argument is associated with the other arguments in a doctrinal cluster.

To say that the "meaning" of "no liability without fault" depends on its existence in relationship to "as between two innocents, he who caused the damage should pay," is to say that if we imagine eliminating the latter phrase from the vocabulary of argument-bites, then "no liability without fault" would *ipso facto* become a different, and likely a more powerful or valuable argument than it is when it is counterable by "as between two innocents . . . ." Of course, there would still be other counters, such as "but you were at fault." And the situation might be one in which "no liability without fault" seemed a weak or obtuse moral position, even though there was available no stereotyped, familiar "as between two innocents . . . " counterbite.

It is even possible that working *ad hoc*, or opportunistically, the other side might develop the very words "as between two innocents . . . " as their considered response to the deployment of "no liability without fault" in a particular case. But then "as between two innocents . . . " would be a somewhat surprising, complex, hard to evaluate, hand-crafted utterance, without the resonance that comes from repetition in thousands of other cases. It might carry the day, but if it did so, it would be as an example of the power of invention tailored to context.

It may at first seem hard to reconcile this thought-experiment, in which we imaginatively eliminate a bite from the lexicon, with the idea that we "generate" "as between two innocents . . . " from "no liability without fault" by the "operation" of "mediation." If this is the case, how could "as between two innocents . . . " not be part of the vocabulary of bites?

The answer lies in the fundamental proposition that the possibility of generating a bite by counter-theory does not guarantee that such a bite has in fact been generated, or indeed that such a counterbite will ever be part of the vocabulary. The system of bites, counterbites, support systems and clusters that exists at a given moment is a product of the actual history of a particular legal discourse, at the same time that it is the product of the logic of operations. An existing system is always incomplete, looked at from the point of view of possible operations, and always changing as new bites enter the lexicon and others change their form or fall out of use altogether.

Each change of this kind alters the possibilities of legal discourse, because it changes what is available to the arguer as stereotyped argument to be deployed across the range of fact situations as they arise. But each change also changes the meaning and effectiveness of the other bites in the system, because it changes arguers' conscious or unconscious expectations about what will be said in response to those bites. To take a recent example, the phrase "defendant should be liable because she is the least cost avoider" is a new argument-bite. Its presence in the repertoire of numerous legal arguers has changed the meaning of (lessened the value of) "no liability without fault" and also of "as between two innocents . . . " because neither of them seems at all responsive to it, though both belong to the same cluster of arguments about liability for unintentional injury.

The emergence of "she is the least cost avoider" has also changed the two traditional bites in a more subtle way. "No liability without fault" has as part of its support system a "social welfare argument" to the effect that "there is no social interest in shifting the costs of blameless activity." On the other side, "as between two innocents . . . " is supported by "activities should be made to internalize their true social costs." It is still unclear to what extent, if any, these support-bites retain coherence after the emergence of "she is the least cost avoider." Even if it turns out that the support bites are still sensible, the primary bites will change their meaning because they will evoke, between them, only a part rather than the whole of the available stereotyped economic arguments for fault and strict liability.

I think it probable that "she is the least cost avoider" will disappear from the lexicon, rather than persisting until a new equilibrium is reached. But if the new bite does persist, it is not at all likely that it will do so without affecting the whole system. The analogy (present to the mind of Saussure when he developed this analysis at the turn of the century) is to the impact of the appearance of a new commodity on the prices of all other commodities in a Walrasian general equilibrium system.[1]

VI. NESTING

"Nesting" is my name for the reproduction, within a doctrinal solution to a problem, of the policy conflict the solution was supposed to settle. Take the case of killing in mistaken self defense. In *Courvoisier v. Raymond*,[2] a shopkeeper shot and injured a person he thought was a looter emerging from a crowd of rioters. The person was in fact a policeman coming to his aid. In this fact situation, the

---

1. F. DE SAUSSURE, COURSE IN GENERAL LINGUISTICS 112-14 (R. Harris trans. 1986).
2. 23 Colo. 113, 47 P. 284 (1896).

courts have initially to decide whether there should be a defense of mistake in self-defense situations. A court taking up the question for the first time has to decide it in the context of considerable doçtrinal conflict over when mistake is a defense to the commission of an intentional tort.

Some of the considerations commonly advanced in favor of and against the defense are:

the shopkeeper shouldn't have to pay because he was not at fault
vs.
the shopkeeper should pay because as between two innocents he who caused the damage should pay

people have a right to act in self-defense when they believe they are in danger
vs.
people have a right to security of the person as they go about their lawful business

imposing liability would discourage people from the desirable activity of self-defense
vs.
refusing to impose liability would discourage people from assisting others in trouble

people expect to be able to defend themselves when they feel they are in danger
vs.
people don't expect to be harmed arbitrarily

allowing mistake is an example of equitable flexibility in imposing liability
vs.
the vagueness of a mistake standard will lead to uncertainty avoided by a rigid rule of compensation for deliberate injury

there are many analogies for this defense
vs.
no court has recognized this defense before

deciding the precise contours of a mistake defense requires input that only the legislature can command
vs.
courts do this kind of thing every day

Please resist the impulse to assess the strength of these arguments as they appear in this context. What we are concerned with is "nesting," a formal attribute of legal argument. Nesting occurs as follows. Let us suppose that the court accepts the argument in favor of a defense of mistake. It looks as though the defendant has won. But now suppose the plaintiff argues that the defendant's mistake was "unreasonable," meaning that a person of ordinary intelligence and caution would not have shot, under the circumstances, without more indication that he was in danger. Suppose the plaintiff concedes that the defendant acted in the good faith belief that he was in danger. Suppose the defendant in turn concedes he was less intelligent and cautious than the average man in the community.

In deciding whether reasonableness should matter, a court that has accepted the argument cast in the form above will consider a new version of the inventory:

if the plaintiff acted in good faith, he was not at fault
vs.
as between two innocents, he who caused the damage should pay

people are entitled to be judged according to their actual capabilities
vs.
people have a right to protection from the unreasonable behavior of others

an objective standard will deter people from defending themselves
vs.
a subjective standard will deter people from going to the aid of others

a subjective standard will encourage people like the plaintiff to pay attention to the actual danger they face in helping out
vs.
a subjective standard will encourage carelessness by people contemplating self-defense

the community does not expect more of people in danger than that they act in good faith
vs.
the community expects people in danger to act reasonably

adjusting the standard to the actual character of the defendant allows equitable flexibility
vs.
a "subjective good faith" standard is hopelessly vague and manipulable

this is the first time the court has imposed a reasonableness limitation on the right of self-defense

vs.

reasonableness is the general rule in defining permissible conduct

"Nesting" is the reappearance of the inventory when we have to resolve gaps, conflicts or ambiguities that emerge when we try to put our initial solution to a doctrinal problem into practice. In this case, we first deploy the pro and con argument-bites in deciding whether or not to permit a defense of mistake. We then redeploy them in order to decide whether to require that the mistake be reasonable. In this case, the courts have in practice chosen to honor the pro-defendant arguments in creating the defense, but to honor the pro-plaintiff (reasonableness) arguments in defining its contours.

This situation can be represented visually as follows:

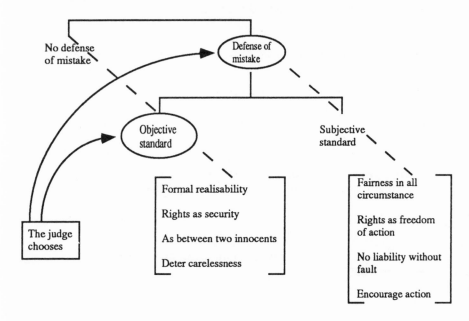

We might also represent the choice in terms of a continuum, as follows:

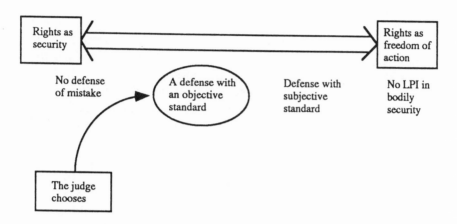

I would argue that this second representation in terms of a continuum conveys far less of the structure of legal argument than the nesting diagram, for two reasons.

First, practitioners of legal argument proceed, both within a given case and over a series of cases, from the more general choices to the more particular, arguing and then re-arguing, rather than debating the merits of a point on the continuum versus all the other points on the continuum. This, indeed, is one of the more powerful of all the conventions of legal argument.

Second, an equally powerful convention of legal argument is that argument and counter-argument are presented as simply "correct" as applied to the general question, without this presentation binding the arguer in any way on the nested subquestion. In other words, the judge can, without violating any norm of legal argument, state that "equitable flexibility is so important that it requires us to accept a defense of mistake here," and then turn around and state that "certainty is so important that we are obliged to reject a 'good faith' test in favor of reasonableness."

Of course, it may be true that what the judge is "really" doing is "balancing" the conflicting policy vectors to determine just that spot on the continuum where the benefit of certainty comes to outweigh the benefit of flexibility. Moreover, in some courts and in some doctrinal areas it is permissible for the judge to present the decision in this way. The nesting presentation is nonetheless privileged in argumentative practice.

My sense is that the reason for this is that the nesting presentation is associated with "objectivity." Judges prefer it because it harmonizes with the stereotypically judicial pole in the judge/legislator dichotomy. But that argument is for another place. For the moment, let me emphasize the general character of the nesting schema by offering another, much briefer example. In the case of *Vincent v. Lake Erie*,[3] a ship's captain chose to remain moored to a dock during a storm, and even reinforced his mooring lines, in spite of the fact that the ship's heaving against the dock was visibly damaging it. The question was whether the shipowner had to compensate the dock owner for the damage.

In this case, the nesting sequence begins with the question whether or not there should be a privilege of necessity. In other words, was the destruction of the dock a legal wrong? If so, then in most cases it would follow not only that the shipowner would have to compensate the dockowner for the damage, but also that the dockowner could, in self-defense, repel or unmoor the ship, and that the shipowner would be liable for an injunction against continuation, and potentially for punitive damages. In this case, the court would clearly have been unwilling to subject the ship owner to civil or criminal penalties, or to an injunction that would have forced his departure (had circumstances permitted), or to unmooring by the dock owner. But the court held that the shipowner had to pay the dock owner compensation, so that although the destruction of the dock was privileged, the privilege was conditional rather than absolute.

The arguments that courts and commentators advance in favor of a privilege of necessity are familiar from the previous exercise. They include ideas like "equitable flexibility," the absence of fault, the right to self preservation, the social desirability of preserving the more valuable piece of property, and so forth. These arguments prevail on the issue whether the ship owner has acted criminally, will be enjoined, or will be made to pay punitive damages.

When courts and commentators consider the question of simple money compensation for the destruction of the dock, they redeploy the inventory. This time, they come down on the side of compensation, explaining themselves by adopting the rhetoric of certainty, as between two innocents, the right of security, and so forth, the very

---

3. 109 Minn. 456, 124 N.W. 221 (1910).

arguments they rejected when deciding the prior question. This can be represented as "nesting" or in continuum terms:

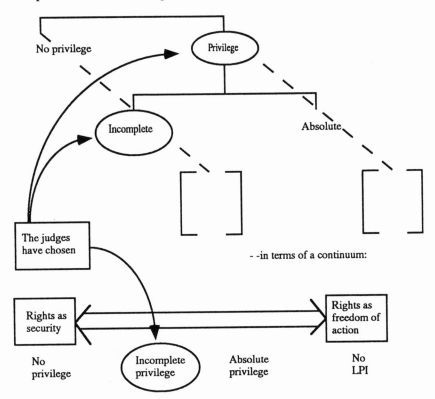

Nesting represents the conservation of argumentative energy. Within a given topic or cluster, there are far fewer arguments deployed than one would expect if one paid attention only to the seemingly endless variety of issues and subissues that arise. But nesting also represents the conservation of argument-bites. The play of bite and counter-bite settles nothing (except the case at hand). As between the bites themselves, every fight is a draw, and all combatants live to fight another day, neither discredited by association with the losing side nor established as correct by association with a winner. There are no killer arguments outside a particular context.

VII. CONCLUSION

Although the above is very tentative and obviously radically incomplete, I hope it is already apparent that it might be disquieting. In the introduction to this paper, I put this in the language of post-structuralism, for reasons that may be clearer at this point. The argument-bites I focussed on (how typical?) are defined by their counter-bites. Legal argument has a certain mechanical quality, once one begins to identify its characteristic operations. Language seems to be "speaking the subject," rather than the reverse. It is hard to imagine that argument so firmly channelled into bites could reflect the full complexity either of the fact situation or the decision-maker's ethical stance toward it. It is hard to imagine doing this kind of argument in utter good faith, that is, to imagine doing it without some cynical strategy in fitting foot to shoe. But I admit that these rather unconventional conclusions (unconventional within law, I mean) are only suggested by the above. The development of the linguistic analogy for legal argument may end up taking us in quite the opposite direction for all one can tell for sure at this point.

APPENDIX

There is now a small but substantial literature that adopts the general approach to legal argument described in this paper.[4] The more general post-modern approach to legal theory now has a literature too large to list fully.[5]

---

4. The contributions I am aware of are: DAVID KENNEDY, INTERNATIONAL LEGAL STRUCTURES (1987); Bakkan, *Constitutional Arguments: Interpretation and Legitimacy in Canadian Constitutional Thought*, 27 OSGOODE HALL L.J. 123 (1989); Boyle, *The Anatomy of a Torts Class*, 34 AM. U.L. REV. 1003 (1985); Frug, *The Ideology of Bureaucracy in American Law*, 97 HARV. L. REV. 1276 (1984); Gordon, *Unfreezing Legal Reality: Critical Approaches to Law*, 15 FLA. ST. U.L. REV. 195 (1987); Heidt, *Recasting Behavior: An Essay for Beginning Law Students*, 49 U. PITT. L. REV. 1065 (1988); Jaff, *Frame-shifting: An Empowering Methodology for Teaching and Learning Legal Reasoning*, 36 J. LEG. ED. 249 (1986); Kelman, *Interpretive Construction in the Criminal Law*, 33 STAN. L. REV. 591 (1981); Paul, *A Bedtime Story*, 74 VA. L. REV. 915 (1988); Schlag, *Cannibal Moves, An Essay on the Metamorphoses of the Legal Distinction*, 40 STAN. L. REV. 929 (1988); Schlag, *Rules and Standards*, 33 UCLA L. REV. 379 (1985). The most complete presentation of the basic ideas in the field, and of the canonical examples, is Balkin, *The Crystalline Structure of Legal Thought*, 39 RUTGERS L. REV. 1 (1986). *See also* Balkin, *Taking Ideology Seriously: Ronald Dworkin and the CLS Critique*, 55 UMKC L. REV. 392 (1987); Balkin, *Nested Oppositions*, 99 YALE L.J. 1669 (1990); Balkin, *The Hohfeldian Approach to Law and Semiotics*, in 3 LAW & SEMIOTICS 31 (Kevelson ed. 1989).

5. The works that I've read that are closest in inspiration to this essay are: M. KRAMER, LEGAL THEORY, POLITICAL THEORY, AND DECONSTRUCTION: AGAINST RHADAMANTHUS (1991); Ashe, *Zig-zag Stitching and the Seamless Web: Thoughts on Reproduction and the Law*, 13 NOVA L.J. 355 (1989); Balkin, *Deconstructive Practice and Legal Theory*, 96 YALE L.J. 743 (1987); Berman, *Sovereignty in Abeyance: Self-Determination and International Law*, 7 WISC. INT. L.J. 51 (1988); Boyle, *The Politics of Reason: Critical Legal Studies and Local Social Thought*, 133 U. PA. L. REV. 684 (1985); Crenshaw, *Demarginalizing the Intersection of Race and Sex: A Black Feminist Critique of Antidiscrimination Doctrine, Feminist Theory and Antiracist Politics*, 1989 Chicago Legal Forum 139; Dalton, *An Essay in the Deconstruction of Contract Doctrine*, 94 YALE L.J. 997 (1985); Frug, *Argument as Character*, 40 STAN. L. REV. 869 (1988); Frug, *Rereading Contracts: A Feminist Analysis of a Contracts Casebook*, 34 AM. U.L. REV. 1065 (1985); Heller, *Structuralism and Critique*, 36 STAN. L. REV. 127 (1984); David Kennedy, *Critical Theory, Structuralism and Contemporary Legal Scholarship*, 21 NEW ENG. L. REV. 209 (1986); David Kennedy, *The Turn to Interpretation*, 58 SO. CAL. L. REV. 1 (1985); David Kennedy, *Spring Break*, 63 TEXAS L. REV. 1277 (1985); Olsen, *The Sex of Law*, THE POLITICS OF LAW (2d ed., Kairys ed. 1990); Peller, *The Metaphysics of American Law*, 73 CALIF. L. REV. 1152 (1985); Schlag, *"Le Hors de Texte, C'est Moi": The Politics of Form and the Domestication of Deconstruction*, 11 CARDOZO L. REV. 1631 (1990); Torres & Milun, *Translating Yonnondio by Precedent and Evidence: The* Mashpee Indian *Case*, 1990 DUKE L.J. 624. *But see also Cardozo Law Review Symposium on Deconstruction and the Possibility of Justice* (1990); THE POLITICS OF INTERPRETATION (W. Mitchell ed. 1983); M. MINOW, MAKING ALL THE DIFFERENCE (1990). The longer this list got, the more arbitrary it began to seem. I am not suggesting a canon, and have only read a part of the literature.

According to Jack Balkin,[6] the idea of discussing legal discourse as deployed in dyadic choices between possible legal rules was "borrowed from various Structuralist thinkers." In a footnote, he cites C. Levi-Strauss, *The Raw and the Cooked* (1969) and 1 & 2 C. Levi-Strauss, *Structural Anthropology* (1963, 1976).[7] It is also a commonplace that critical legal studies approaches to legal reasoning are "just" a revival of legal realism.[8] Well, which is it?

It seems to me that the version of legal semiotics represented by this paper is a kind of jerry-built amalgam of elements from realism and structuralism, but not an "application" or "revival" of either. Though there is an element of fatheadedness in "tracing the origins of my thought," that is just what I'd like to do briefly in this appendix. My goal is not to settle the question of origins and influences (impossible to do in any case) but to contribute some raw material for the study of borrowing.

As I see it, there are three basic elements to the proposed semiotics of legal argument. These are: (1) the idea of reducing the "parole" of legal argument to a "langue" composed of argument-bites, (2) the idea of relating the bites to one another through "operations," and (3) the idea of "nesting," or the reproduction, in the application of a doctrinal formula, of the confrontation between argument-bites that the formula purported to resolve.

ARGUMENT BITES

The first idea, like the other two, was probably occurring to a lot of different people at more or less the same time. For me, it was a way to radicalize, for the purposes of a law school paper debunking "policy argument" in constitutional law, Llewellyn's famous article *Canons on Statutes*, which was reprinted as an appendix to *The Common Law Tradition: Deciding Appeals*.[9] Llewellyn had no interest in extending his critique of statutory interpretation to legal reasoning in general. The realists as a group were more preoccupied with the cri-

---

6. *The Crystalline Structure of Legal Thought*, 39 RUTGERS L. REV. 1, 5 n.9 (1986).

7. *See also* Balkin, *The Hohfeldian Approach to Legal Semiotics*, 3 LAW AND SEMIOTICS 31, 40-41 (R. Kevelson ed. 1989), *and* Balkin, *The Domestication of Law and Literature*, 14 LAW & SOC. INQUIRY 787, 806 n.24 (1989).

8. *E.g.*, Duxbury, *Robert Hale and the Economy of Legal Force*, 53 MOD. L. REV. 421 (1990).

9. K. LLEWELLYN, THE COMMON LAW TRADITION: DECIDING APPEALS 521-35 (1960).

tique of what they saw as formalist argumentative techniques than they were with reflection on their own beloved alternative of policy analysis.

The extension of the "bites" analysis from statutory interpretation to policy discourse meant rejecting the "reconstructive" impulse among the realists, which seemed (in 1970) to be an invasion of the more "irrationalist" or "existential" implications of their own work. Policy discourse at the time seemed deeply implicated in, indeed the major vehicle of the Cold War Liberalism against which the anti-war movement, the civil rights movement and the womens' movement were then aligning themselves.

The source in structuralism of the idea of reducing legal argument to bites was Levi-Strauss's discussion of "bricolage" in the first chapter of *The Savage Mind*.[10] Levi-Strauss's relativizes the distinction between rationality or technical reasoning and the activity of myth making. In spite of its pretensions to fit precisely whatever phenomenon it addresses, technical reasoning is inevitably the "jerry-building" (bricolage) of an edifice out of elements borrowed from here and there, elements initially meant for other purposes (and themselves therefore jerry-built of yet other, earlier bits and pieces). Legal argument, understood as the deployment of stereotyped pro and con argument fragments, seems a particularly good example of bricolage masquerading as hyper-rationality.

At first, this idea seemed useful mainly for classroom teaching. It was the basis for "mantras" of argument and counter-argument about contract formalities, for example. I used it, tentatively, in *Form and Substance in Private Law Adjudication*,[11] in developing the stereotyped pro-con exchange of arguments about the choice between rules and standards, and in a discussion of the problem of the conflict of rights in *The Structure of Blackstone's Commentaries*.[12] When I switched to teaching torts, I incorporated it into teaching materials, beginning with what then seemed the pair of pairs: no liability without fault vs. as between two innocents.

This article attempts a further incorporation of structuralist ideas by recasting the "canons" analysis of argument-bites in the terms of

---

10. C. LEVI-STRAUSS, THE SAVAGE MIND 16-22 (1966) (hot book in 1970).

11. Kennedy, *Form and Substance in Private Law Adjudication*, 89 HARV. L. REV. 1685 (1976).

12. Kennedy, *The Structure of Blackstone's Commentaries*, 28 BUFF. L. REV. 205, 355-60 (1979).

F. Saussure, *Course in General Linguistics*.[13] This represents a circuitous return to origins, since the idea of bricolage was itself an adaptation of the Saussurian theory of the sign.[14] I'm sure there are disadvantages to assimilating legal argument to the general analysis of signs. But the move seems to make available for legal semiotics many insights of the more general study that will advance the specifically legal enterprise.

It is a problem that discussions of Saussurian linguistics in the American intellectual community often make it sound as though signs "get their meaning from each other" in a way that utterly divorces them from their referents, indeed in a way that suggests that they "signify" nothing but their relations among themselves. In the "Concluding Remark on the Interdependence of the Meanings of Argument-Bites," in the text, I propose a much less metaphysical rendering of Saussure's insight.

OPERATIONS

The second element in the proposed semiotics of legal argument is the notion of an "operation." Jack Balkin is right in associating this idea with Hohfeld.[15] When Hohfeld pointed out the ambiguity in the common legal usage of the word "right", that it sometimes meant "privilege" and sometimes "claim," he suggested the possibility of answering every privilege-assertion with a claim-assertion.[16] This seems to me the prototypical operation.[17]

A second realist origin is in the early 20th century debate about the social utility of more or less extensive protection of intangible property rights. Holmes's dissent in the *Northern Securities* case,[18] along with his concurring opinion in *International News Service v. Associated Press*,[19] Learned Hand's opinion in *Cheney v. Doris Silk Co.*,[20]

---

13. F. SAUSSURE, COURSE IN GENERAL LINGUISTICS (1916, R. Harris trans. 1986) (hot book for me in the Spring of 1989).

14. *See* LEVI-STRAUSS, *supra* note 10, at 18.

15. *See* Balkin, *The Hohfeldian Approach to Law and Semiotics*, 3 LAW & SEMIOTICS 31, 32-35 (1989).

16. HOHFELD, FUNDAMENTAL CONCEPTIONS AS APPLIED IN LEGAL REASONING AND OTHER ESSAYS (1923).

17. *See* Kennedy & Michelman, *Are Property and Contract Efficient?*, 8 HOFSTRA L. REV. 711 (1980); Singer, *The Legal Rights Debate in Analytical Jurisprudence, from Bentham to Hohfeld*, 1982 WISC. L. REV. 975.

18. Northern Sec. v. United States, 193 U.S. 197 (1904) (Holmes, J., dissenting).

19. 248 U.S. 215 (Holmes, J., concurring).

and Chafee's article, *Unfair Competition*,[21] suggest a formal procedure for generating utilitarian "pro-property" and "pro-competition" arguments in any antitrust or unfair competition case.[22]

The structuralist element in the theory of operations was borrowed from J. Piaget, *Six Psychological Essays*.[23] Up to recently, it has seemed to me that the main value of Piaget's work for legal analysis lies in his theory of "accommodation" and "assimilation" in the development of "schemas."[24] A number of us have used these or roughly equivalent ideas from other sources in trying to work out a picture of the historical transformations of American legal "consciousness."[25] A second use of the Piagetian approach is in trying to

---

20. 35 F.2d 279 (2d Cir. 1929).

21. Chafee, *Unfair Competition*, 53 HARV. L. REV. 1289 (1940).

22. *See* Peritz, *The "Rule of Reason" in Antitrust: Property Logic in Restraint of Competition*, 40 HASTINGS L. REV. 285 (1989); Rogers, *The Right of Publicity: Resurgence of Legal Formalism and Judicial Disregard of Policy Issues*, 16 BEVERLY HILLS BAR ASSOC. J. 65 (1982).

23. J. PIAGET, SIX PSYCHOLOGICAL ESSAYS 130-31 (D. Elkind ed. 1967).

24. *See* J. PIAGET, PLAY, DREAMS AND IMITATION IN CHILDHOOD (C. Gattegno & F. Hodgson trans. 1962). *See also* J. PIAGET, THE CHILD AND REALITY 63-71 (1976).

25. *See* W. FORBATH, LAW AND THE SHAPING OF THE AMERICAN LABOR MOVEMENT (1991); H. HARTOG, THE PUBLIC PROPERTY AND PRIVATE POWER: THE CORPORATION OF THE CITY OF NEW YORK IN AMERICAN LAW, 1730-1870 (1983); M. HORWITZ, THE TRANSFORMATION OF AMERICAN LAW, 1780-1860 (1977); R. STEINFELD, THE DISAPPEARANCE OF INDENTURED SERVITUDE AND THE INVENTION OF FREE LABOR IN THE UNITED STATES (1991); M. TUSHNET, THE AMERICAN LAW OF SLAVERY, 1810-1860: CONSIDERATIONS OF HUMANITY AND INTEREST (1981); Alexander, *The Dead Hand and the Law of Trusts in the 19th Century*, 37 STAN. L. REV. 1189 (1985); Alexander, *The Transformation of Trusts as a Legal Category*, 1800-1914, 5 LAW & HIST. REV. 303 (1987); Casbeer, *Teaching an Old Dog Old Tricks: Coppage v. Kansas and At-Will Employment Revisited*, 6 CARDOZO L. REV. 765 (1985); Fineman & Gabel, *Contract Law as Ideology*, in THE POLITICS OF LAW: A PROGRESSIVE CRITIQUE (D. Kairys, ed. 2d ed. 1990); Fisher, *Ideology, Religion and the Constitutional Protection of Private Property*: 1760-1860, 39 EMORY L.J. 65 (1990); Freeman, *Legitimizing Racial Discrimination through Anti-Discrimination Law*, 62 MINN. L. REV. 1049 (1978); Frug, *The City as a Legal Concept*, 93 HARV. L. REV. 1057 (1980); Gordon, *Legal Thought and Legal Practice in the Age of American Enterprise, 1870-1920*, in PROFESSIONS AND PROFESSIONAL IDEOLOGIES IN AMERICA 70-110 (G. Geison ed. 1983); Gordon, *Critical Legal Histories*, 36 STAN. L. REV. 57 (1985); Hager, *Bodies Politic: The Progressive History of Organizational "Real Entity" Theory*, 50 U. PITT. L. REV. 575 (1989); Hurvitz, *American Labor Law and the Doctrine of Entrepreneurial Property Rights: Boycotts, Courts and the Juridical Reorientation Reorientation of 1886-1895*, 8 INDUS. REL. L.J. 307 (1986); Jacobson, *The Private Use of Public Authority: Sovereignty and Associations in the Common Law*, 29 BUFF. L. REV. 599 (1980); Kainen, *Nineteenth Century Interpretations of the Federal Contract Clause: The Transformation from Vested to Substantive Rights Against the State*, 31 BUFF L. REV. 381 (1982); Katz, *Studies in Boundary Theory: Three Essays in Adjudication and Politics*, 28 BUFF. L. REV. 383 (1979); Ellen Kelman,

understand how judges decide cases by "assimilating" or recasting the facts to fit the legal materials that exist at a given moment, while "accommodating" or recasting the materials to fit the irreducible particularity of the facts.[26]

This essay extends the Piagetian notion of a schema to legal argument about the choice between two possible rules or between two interpretations of a rule. Arguing about a choice is like sucking or shaking an object: it is an acquired cognitive procedure, a "praxis," a

---

American Labor Law and Legal Formalism: How "Legal Logic" Shaped and Vitiated the Rights of American Workers, 58 ST. JOHN'S L. REV. 1 (1983); David Kennedy, *Primitive Legal Scholarship*, 27 HARV. INT. L.J. 1 (1986); Kennedy, *Toward an Historical Understanding of Legal Consciousness: The Case of Classical Legal Thought, 1850-1940*, in 3 CURRENT RESEARCH IN THE SOCIOLOGY OF LAW (J. Spitzer ed. 1980); Kennedy, *The Structure of Blackstone's Commentaries*, 28 BUFF. L. REV. 205 (1979); Kennedy, *The Role of Law in Economic Thought: Essays on Fetishism of Commodities* 34 AM. U.L. REV. 939 (1985); Klare, *The Deradicalization of the Wagner Act and the Origins of Modern Legal Consciousness, 1937-1941*, 62 MINN. L. REV. 265 (1978); Krauss, *On the Distinction Between Real and Personal Property*, 14 SETON HALL L. REV. 485 (1984); May, *Antitrust in the Formative Era: Political and Economic Theory in Constitutional and Antitrust Analysis*, 50 OHIO ST. L.J. 257 (1989); Mensch, *The History of Mainstream Legal Thought*, THE POLITICS OF LAW (2d ed., Kairys ed. 1990); Mensch, *Freedom of Contract as Ideology*, 33 STAN. L. REV. 752 (1981); Mensch, *The Colonial Origins of Liberal Property Rights*, 31 BUFF. L. REV. 635 (1982); Minda, *The Common Law, Labor and Antitrust*, 11 INDUS. REL. L.J. 461 (1989); Nerkin, *A New Deal for the Protection of 14th Amendment Rights: Challenging the Doctrinal Bases of the Civil Rights Cases and State Action Theory*, 1 HARV. C.R.-C.L. L. REV. 297 (1977); Nockleby, *Tortious Interference with Contractual Relations in the Nineteenth Century: The Transformation of Property, Contract and Tort*, 93 HARV. L. REV. 1510 (1980); Olsen, *The Family and the Market: A Study of Ideology and Legal Reform*, 96 HARV. L. REV. 1497 (1983); Olsen, *The Sex of Law*, THE POLITICS OF LAW (2d ed., Kairys ed. 1990); Peller, *In Defense of Federal Habeas Corpus Relitigation*, 16 HARV. L. REV. 579 (1982); Peritz, *The "Rule of Reason" in Antitrust: Property Logic in Restraint of Competition*, 40 HASTINGS L. REV. 285 (1989); Rogers, *The Right of Publicity: Resurgence of Legal Formalism and Judicial Disregard of Policy Issues*, 16 BEVERLY HILLS BAR ASSOC. J. 65 (1982); Siegel, *Understanding the Lochner Era: Lessons from the Controversy Over Railroad and Utility Rate Regulation*, 70 VA. L. REV. 187, 250-59, 262 (1984); Simon, *The Invention and Reinvention of Welfare Rights*, 44 MD. L. REV. 1 (1984); Singer, *The Legal Rights Debate in Analytical Jurisprudence, from Bentham to Hohfeld*, 1982 WISC. L. REV. 975; Steinfeld, *Property and Suffrage in the Early American Republic*, 41 STAN. L. REV. 335 (1989); Stone, *The Postwar Paradigm in American Labor Law*, 90 YALE L.J. 1509 (1981); Sugarman & Rubin, *Towards A New History of Law and Material Society in England, 1750-1914*, in LAW, ECONOMY AND SOCIETY: ESSAYS IN THE HISTORY OF ENGLISH LAW 1750-1914 (G. Rubin & D. Sugarman, eds. Oxford 1984); Tarullo, *Law and Politics in Twentieth Century Tariff History*, 34 UCLA L. REV. 285 (1986); Vandevelde, *The New Property of the 19th Century*, 29 BUFF. L. REV. 325 (1980).

26. *See* Kennedy, *Freedom and Constraint in Adjudication: A Critical Phenomenology*, 36 J. LEGAL EDUC. 518 (1986); Kelman, *Interpretive Construction in the Criminal Law*, 33 STAN. L. REV. 591 (1981).

---

pre-structured "response" to a "stimulus." The stimulus is the demand for justification of an outcome. The structured response, in this model, is an argument for a rule, or for an interpretation of a rule, that will produce that outcome.

The goal is to catalogue the particular "operations" through which an arguer moves among argument-bites to construct the case for an outcome. The focus is on the identification of the very particular schemas linking one argument-bite with another. The crucial Piagetian concept here is that of "reversibility" of schemas.[27] When an arguer has attained the capacity to move from any bite to all others associated with it, *and back again*, he or she can, first, build an argument's initial rough draft simply by reaction to the opponent's formulation of his case, second, anticipate an opponent's argument simply by examining what she herself will say, and, third, carry on an internal version of the argument playing both parts.

On a quite different level, the experience of legal argument as operations defines the "tone" of modern legal consciousness, the loss of the sense of the organic or unmediated in legal thought.

As with the adoption of a Saussurian framework, reliance on Piaget has its dangers. It is common in the American intellectual community to think "Piaget is a structuralist," and that "therefore" he believes (1) that particular schemas and operations are innate, and (2) that "the structures determine what people think and do." First, the borrowing of Piagetian formalizations of the phenomena of reasoning (schema, accommodation, assimilation, operation, reversibility) does not at all imply borrowing whatever theory Piaget holds about their proper interpretation. While the biological status of "conservation of the object," is a tough question, it would be absurd to argue that either "no liability without fault" or "as between two innocents" is either innate or what "determines" an outcome.

Piaget's work on moral reasoning would appear to be the most relevant to legal reasoning, because Piaget there adapted his cognitive psychology to purposes not unlike ours here.[28] But his stage theory of moral development is about as far as one can get from the approach of this paper. The idea of "justice" toward which he sees children tending seems no more than a hodge-podge, an inadequately analyzed combination of cooperation, consent, autonomy, mutual respect and

---

27. *See* J. PIAGET, SIX PSYCHOLOGICAL ESSAYS 130-31 (D. Elkind ed. 1967).
28. *See* J. PIAGET, THE MORAL REASONING OF THE CHILD (Gabain, trans. 1965).

"reason."[29] He seems obtuse about the "operational" character of moral argument that his own work on cognition suggests. The adoption of the Saussurian framework represents for me the rejection of the notions that arguments determine outcomes by being correct (within the framework of a particular stage), and that there is a privileged or "highest" mode of argument.

Second, the common American understanding of Piaget's structuralism as a determinism analogous, say, to orthodox Marxism or socio-biology in social theory, or to orthodox Freudianism or behaviorism in psychology, is a misunderstanding. He seems most open to that charge when he is closest to discussing justice,[30] but this is where he is least useful to lawyers. As a cognitive psychologist, he seems closer to Levi-Strauss, for whom some structure is always given, but given as langue rather than as parole, and always changing.

NESTING

The third element in the proposed semiotics of legal argument is "nesting," or the reproduction of particular argumentative oppositions within the doctrinal structures that apparently resolve them. This idea owes a lot to the basic realist pedagogical technique of presenting the student with a series of hypotheticals that cause him or her to produce contradictory arguments over a sequence of cases. But I also borrowed it quite directly from C. Levi-Strauss, *The Savage Mind*,[31] in the ambiguous mode of bricolage.

There are three relevant notions, each with a nesting diagram, in *The Savage Mind*. The first[32] is that the elements of a system of plant classifications are arranged in oppositions that correspond to social divisions and practices. These oppositions are sometimes used and re-used according to a nesting pattern. His example is the use of *Chrysothamnus* as a signifier of maleness in opposition to *Artemisia* (sagebrush), signifying the feminine. The Navaho (according to Levi-Strauss) employ this general North American system, but also categorize *Chrysothamnus* as a feminine plant because it is used in assisting childbirth. He explains the "logic" of the system as follows:

---

29. *Id.* at 84-108.
30. *Id.*
31. C. LEVI-STRAUSS, *supra* note 10.
32. *Id.* at 48.

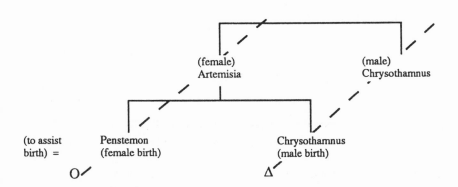

Chrysothamnus is male in the "main opposition," and plays the male role when it is reemployed *within* the female division. This synchronic presentation contrasts with a later exploration of the diachronics of structures.[33] Levi-Strauss discusses how the structure we see may be unintelligible without understanding its history. He imagines a tribe divided into three clans, with each name symbolizing an element:

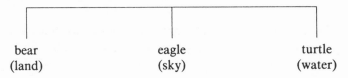

bear	eagle	turtle
(land)	(sky)	(water)

He continues: "Suppose further that demographic changes led to the extinction of the bear clan and an increase in the population of the turtle clan, and that as a result the turtle clan split into two sub-clans, each of which subsequently gained the status of clans. The old structure will disappear completely, and be replaced by a structure of this type:

---

33. *Id.* at 67-68.

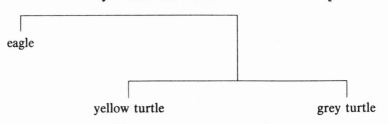

eagle

yellow turtle   grey turtle

Levi-Strauss speculates that "after this upheaval the three clan names might survive only as traditionally accepted titles with no cosmological significance." But it is also possible that the tribe will understand what has happened as a "logical" transformation of the original system. The new scheme might be intelligible because "there were originally three terms, and the number of terms is still the same at the end. The original three terms expressed an irreducible trichotomy while the final three terms are the result of two successive dichotomies; between sky and water and then between yellow and grey."[34]

Then comes what seemed to me the punch line: "It can be seen therefore that demographic evolution can shatter the structure but that if the structural orientation survives the shock it has, after each upheaval several means of re-establishing a system, which may not be identical with the earlier one but is at least formally of the same type."[35]

A third suggestive passage contrasts endogamy with exogamy. According to Levi-Strauss, exogamous systems practice either "restricted" or "generalized" exchange, with the former indicating that marriage partners for group A must be from group B, but not from groups C, D, etc. This leads to the following diagram:

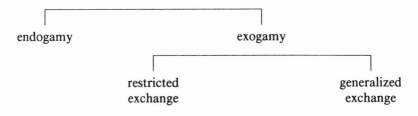

endogamy   exogamy

restricted   generalized
exchange   exchange

Levi-Strauss comments: "It will be seen that restricted exchange, the 'closed' form of exogamy is logically closer to endogamy

---

34. *Id.* at 68.
35. *Id.*

than the 'open' form, generalized exchange."[36]

Back to law. It seemed to me, as an amateur left wing jurisprude in 1970, that the Hart & Sacks *Legal Process* materials of 1958 represented the current liberal orthodoxy, and played a role in legitimating the passive response of academics and judges to the "crises of the time." In a paper critiquing those materials, I argued that they were but the latest in a succession of responses to attacks on the distinction between legislation and adjudication. Each attack had managed to discredit an earlier version of the distinction, but had lead to a new version of similar structure. My diagram was utterly contextual, but turned out (to my surprise and delight) to look very like the Levi-Strauss prototypes described above:

Transformation of Utopian Rationalist Thought

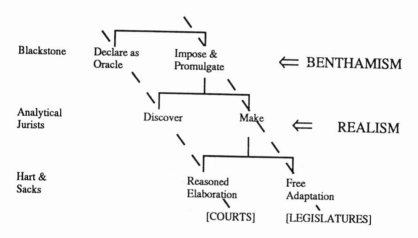

There are several steps between this and the classroom diagrams of *Courvoisier v. Raymond* and *Vincent v. Lake Erie*. I won't try to work them out here.[37] Nesting is first of all something that happens, a phenomenon. It is also quite mysterious, and needs further study and interpretation.[38] I admit to a prejudice in favor of trying to "discover" things like this, as opposed to elaborating internally the realist

---

36. C. LEVI-STRAUSS, *supra* note 10, at 123.
37. *See* Kennedy, *supra* note 11; Kennedy, *supra* note 12.
38. *See* Balkin, *Nested Oppositions*, 99 YALE L.J. 1669 (1990).

or structuralist (or whatever) paradigms on whose intermixing discovery seems to be dependent.

Freedom and Constraint in Adjudication: A Critical Phenomenology

Duncan Kennedy

This paper attempts to describe the process of legal reasoning as I imagine I might do it if I were a judge assigned a case that initially seemed to present a conflict between "the law" and "how-I-want-to-come-out." Such a description, if at all true to experience, may be helpful in assessing the various claims about and images of law that figure in jurisprudential, political, and social theoretical discussion. It may also be helpful in assessing what law teachers teach future lawyers about the nature of the materials they will use in their profession. But I will have little to say about these implications, aside from a polemical afterword.[1]

I am not sure what difference it makes to the phenomenology of adjudication whether I begin with this situation rather than another. The whole experience of law may be sufficiently the same thing through and through so that wherever you start, you end up with approximately the same picture. Or it may be that there is no experience of legality that's constant without regard to role and initial posture of the case. What I am convinced of is the need to start with *some* particularization. I don't find myself at all convinced when people start out claiming they can tell us about judging without some grounding in a specific imagined situation.

***

The judge is a federal district court judge in Boston. I am from Boston. I'm more a ruling class elite type than a local politician or notable type, which is why I choose the federal forum. But what's most important is that the judge

Duncan Kennedy is Professor of Law, Harvard Law School. A shorter version of this article will appear as a chapter in Alan Hutchinson & Patrick Monahan, The Rule of Law: Ideal of Ideology (Toronto, 1986).

1. Note on sources: I think of this exercise as an extension of the legal realist project, as exemplified in Felix Cohen, The Ethical Basis of Legal Criticism, 41 Yale L.J. 201 (1931), Karl N. Llewellyn, The Common Law Tradition: Deciding Appeals (1960), and Edward H. Levi, An Introduction to Legal Reasoning (1949). The description of legal materials as presenting a field open to manipulation owes much to Wolfgang Kohler, Gestalt Psychology: An Introduction to New Concepts in Modern Psychology (New York, 1947)., Kurt Lewin, The Conceptual Representation and the Measurement of Psychological Forces, 1 Contributions to Psychological Theory, 4 (1938), and Jean Piaget, Play, Dreams, and Imitation in Childhood, trans. C. Gattegno and F. Hodgson (New York, 1962). My emphasis on work derives from Karl Marx, Economic and Philosophical Manuscripts of 1844-1845, in Early Works, trans. Benton (New York, 1975). The overall conception and philosophical premises derive loosely from JeanPaul Sartre, Being and Nothingness, trans. Hazel Barnes (New York, 1956) and Jean-Paul Sartre, Critique of Dialectical Reason, trans. Alan Sheridan-Smith (London, 1976).

is responsible for deciding this case, rather than a party or an observer or an advocate. I am going to be looking at law as a person who will have to apply it, interpret it, change it, defy it, or whatever. I will do this in the context of the legal and lay community that follows what federal district court judges do, and with the possibility of appeal always present to my mind.

The more complex conditions of this inquiry have to do with the polarity between my initial impression of "the law" and my initial sense of how-I-want-to-come-out. How-I-want-to-come-out might be based on my having been bribed and wanting to keep my bargain, or on a sense of what decision would be popular with my community (legal or local), or on what I thought the appeals court would likely do in the case of an appeal. It might be based on a sense that the equities of this particular case are peculiar because they favor an outcome different from what the law requires, even though the law is basically a very good one, and even though it was on balance a good decision to frame it so inflexibly that it couldn't adjust to take account of these particular equities.

Or it might be that I disagree with the way the law here resolves the problem of exceptional situations, believing that it could have been crafted to be flexible to take care of this case. Or it could be that I see the law here as "unfair" in the sense that, taking the rest of the system at face value, it would be better to change this rule. This rule might be an anomaly. (Later I will take up the question of the rules about the judge changing the rules.)

Instead of any of these objections, imagine that I think the rule that seems to apply is bad because it strikes the wrong balance between two identifiable conflicting groups, and does so as part of a generally unjust overall arrangement that includes many similar rules, all of which ought in the name of justice to change. I mean to suggest a "political" objection to the law, and a how-I-want-to-come-out that is part of a general plan of opposition.

Again, the experience of legality may well be different according to the character of the "I want" that opposes "the law." All I insist on is this: it is useless to discuss the conflict of "personal preference vs. law" without specifying what kind of preference we are dealing with.

***

Here's what I mean by my initial impression that the law requires a particular outcome. Suppose there is a strike of union bus drivers going on in Boston. The company hires nonunion drivers and sets out to resume service. On the first day union members lie down in the street outside the bus station to prevent the buses from passing. They do not disturb the general flow of traffic, and they are nonviolent. The local police arrest them and cart them off, but this takes hours. They are charged with disturbing the peace and obstructing a public way (misdemeanors) and released on light bail. The next day other union members obstruct, with similar results. The buses run, but only late and amid a chaotic jumble. The company goes into federal court for an injunction against the union tactic.

When I first think about this case, not being a labor law expert, but having some general knowledge, I think, "There is no way they will be able to get away with this. The rule of law is going to be that workers cannot prevent the employer from making use of the buses during the strike. The company will get its injunction."

I disagree with this imagined rule. I don't think management should be allowed to operate the means of production [m.o.p.] with substitute labor during a strike. I think there should be a rule that until the dispute has been resolved, neither side can operate the m.o.p. without the permission of the other (barring various kinds of extraordinary circumstances). This view is part of a general preference for transforming the current modes of American economic life in a direction of greater worker self-activity, worker control and management of enterprise, in a decentralized setting that blurs the lines between "owner" and "worker," and "public" and "private" enterprise.

My feeling that the law is against me in this case is a quick intuition about the way things have to be. I haven't actually read any cases or articles that describe what the employer can and can't do with the m.o.p. during a strike. I vaguely remember *In Dubious Battle*, a Steinbeck classic I read when I was 16. But I would bet money that some such rule exists.

If there is a rule that the employer can do what he wants with the m.o.p., I think it will probably turn out to be true that there is relief in federal court (under the rubric of unfair labor practices?). If relief is available, I have a strong feeling that the workers threaten irreparable injury to the employer, so that he can show the various things usually required to justify an injunction. But I also vaguely remember that federal courts aren't supposed to issue injunctions in labor disputes.

There is lots of uncertainty here. I am not sure that a federal district court has jurisdiction under the labor law statutes to intervene on the employer's behalf when the local authorities are already enforcing the local general law about obstructing public ways. I am not sure that if there is a basis for federal intervention an injunction is appropriate. I will have to look into all these things before I'm at all sure how this case will or should come out.

On the other hand, I am quite sure the employer can use the m.o.p. as he pleases. And I am quite, quite sure that if there is such a rule, then the workers have violated it here. I am sure that what I mean by the rule is that the employer has both a privilege to act and a right to protection against interference, and that what the workers' did here *was* interference.

Since the supposed rule of law that I don't like won't get applied so as to lead to an injunction unless all the uncertainties are resolved, against the workers, I do not yet confront a direct conflict between the law and how-I-want-to-come-out. But I already have the feeling of "the law" as a constraint on me. It's time to ask what that means.

***

The initial apparent objectivity of the objectionable rule. I use the word objectivity here to indicate that from my point of view the *application of the rule to this case* feels like a nondiscretionary, necessary, compulsory procedure. I can no more deny that, if there is such a rule, the workers have violated it, than I can deny that I am at this minute in Cambridge, Massachusetts, sitting on a chair, using a machine called a typewriter. The rule just applies itself. What I *meant* by interfering with the owner's use of the m.o.p. was workers lying down in the street when the employer tries to drive the buses out to resume service during the strike. I'm sure from the description that the workers actually intended to do exactly what he rule says they have no right to do.

Note that this sense of objectivity is internal—it's what happens in my head. But the minute I begin to think about the potential conflict between the law and how-I-want-to-come-out a quite different question will arise. How will other people see this case, supposing that the preliminary hurdles are overcome?

Sometimes it will seem to me that everyone (within the relevant universe) will react to this case as one to which the rule applies. I imagine them going through the same process I did, and it is instantly obvious that they too will see the workers as having violated the rule. If this happens, the rule application acquires a double objectivity. The reaction of other people is an anticipated fact like my anticipation that the sun will rise tomorrow or that this glass will break if I drop it on the floor.

It is important not to mush these forms of objectivity together. It is possible for me to see the case as "not clearly governed by the rule" when I do my interior rule application, but to anticipate that the relevant others will see it as "open and shut." And it is possible for me to see it as clear but to anticipate that others will see it as complex and confusing.

***

The next thing that happens is that I set to work on the problem of this case. I already have, as part of my life as I've lived it up to this moment, a set of intentions, a life-project as a judge, that will orient me among the many possible attitudes I could take to this work.

It so happens that I see myself as a political activist, someone with the "vocation of social transformation," as Roberto Unger put it. I see the set of rules in force as chosen by the people who had the power to make the choices in accord with their views on morality and justice and their own self-interest. And I see the rules as remaining in force because victimized groups have not had the political vision and energy and raw power to change them. I see myself as a focus of political energy for change in an egalitarian, communitarian, decentralized, democratic socialist direction (which doesn't mean these slogans are any help in figuring out what the hell to do in any particular situation).

***

Given my general orientation, the work I am going to do in this case will have two objectives, which may or may not conflict. I want these specific workers to get away with obstructing the buses, and I want to move the law as much as possible in the direction of allowing workers a measure of legally legitimated control over the disposition of the m.o.p. during a strike.

If my only objective were to avoid an injunction against lying down in front of the buses during this strike, I would be tempted toward a strategy that would allow me to avoid altogether the apparent legal rule forbidding worker interference. I could just delay, in the hope that the workers will win the strike before I'm forced to rule. I could focus on developing a new version of the facts, and hope to deny the injunction on that basis, or I could look for a "technicality" having no apparent substantive relevance (e.g., the statute of frauds, a mistake in the caption of a pleading).

On a more substantive level, I could put my energy into researching the issues of federal jurisdiction and the appropriateness of an injunction. Here, if the effort paid off, I might be able to move the law in a way favorable to workers in general, even though the move wouldn't formally address worker control over the m.o.p. during a strike.

But the strategy I want to discuss here is that of frontal assault on the application of the rule that the workers can't obstruct the company's use of the m.o.p. If this strategy succeeds, the result will be both to get the workers off in this case *and* to accomplish my law reform objective. There will be a small reduction in employers' power to invoke the state apparatus will be somewhat reduced, a change that will be practically useful in future legal disputes over strikes. And the mantle of legal legitimacy will shift a little, from all out endorsement of management prerogatives to a posture that legitmates, to some degree, workers' claims to rights over the m.o.p.

***

What I see as interesting about the situation as I have portrayed it up to this point is that we are not dealing with a "case governed by a rule," but rather with a perception that a rule probably governs, and that applying the rule will very likely produce a particular (pro-employer) result. The judge is neither free nor bound. I don't see it that way from inside the situation. From inside the situation, the question is, Where am I going to deploy the resources I have available for this case? The issue is how should I direct my *work* to bring about an outcome that accords with my sense of justice. My situation as a judge (initial perceived conflict between "the law" and how-I-want-to-come-out) is thus quite like that of a lawyer who is brought a case by a client and on first run-through is afraid the client will lose. The question is, Will this first impression hold up as I set to work to develop the best possible case on the other side?

Having to work to achieve an outcome is in my view fundamental to the situation of the judge. It is neither a matter of being bound nor a matter of being free. Or, you could say that the judge is both free *and* bound—free to deploy work in any direction but limited by the pseudo-objectivity of the rule-as-applied, which he may or may not be able to overcome.

***

Isn't what I am doing illegitimate, from the standpoint of legality, right from the start? One could argue that since I think the law favors the company I have no business trying to develop the best possible case for the union. But this misunderstands the rules of the game of legality. All members of the community know that one's initial impression that a particular rule governs and that when applied to the facts it yields X result is *often* wrong. That's what makes law such a trip. What at first looked open and shut is ajar, and what looked vague and altogether indeterminate abruptly reveals itself to be quite firmly settled under the circumstances.

So it is an important part of the role of judges and lawyers to test whatever conclusions they have reached about "the correct legal outcome" by trying to develop the best possible argument on the other side. In my role as an activist judge I am simply doing what I'm supposed to when I test my first impression against the best pro-union argument I can develop.

If I manage to develop a legal argument against the injunction, the ideal of impartiality requires me to test that argument in turn against a newly worked-out best counterargument in favor of the company. Eventually, my time will run out, and I'll just have to decide.

What would betray legality would be to adopt the wrong attitude at the *end* of the reasoning process, when I've reached a conclusion about "what the law requires" and found it still conflicts with how-I-want-to-come-out.

For the moment, I'm free to play around.

***

The euphoric moment in which I conceive legal reasoning as "playing around with the rule" doesn't last long. What follows is panic as I rack my brain for *any* way around the overwhelming sense that if the rule is "workers can't interfere with the owner's use of the m.o.p. during a strike," then I cannot do anything for the union. I am ashamed of this panic. It's not just that I'm not coming up with anything; I also feel that I *should* be coming up with something. It's a disgrace—it shows I lack legal reasoning ability. I feel like a fool for trumpeting the indeterminacy of doctrine and claiming to be a manipulative whiz.

As my panic deepens, I begin to consider alternatives. If I can't mount an attack on the rule-as-applied, maybe I will have to research the earlier contract between the union and the bus company. I have a strong feeling that contracts are manipulable if one applies concepts like good faith, implication of terms, and the public interest, all relevant here. Maybe I'll have to try to "read something in." But this approach is clearly less good than going right for the rule itself.

Then I start thinking about the federal injunction aspect of the case, as opposed to the labor tort aspect. I'm sure that the combination of the 1930s anti-injunction statute with federal court injunctive enforcement of at least some terms in collective bargaining agreements (after *Lincoln Mills?* I can't quite remember) must have made a total hash of the question of when federal courts will grant injunctions. If only I could worry just about *that*, I bet I could easily come up with a good pro-worker argument. But that move is also less good than going for the rule.

Then there are the really third-rate solutions based on the hope that the facts will turn out to be at least arguably different than they seemed to be when I first heard about the case, and that the company's lawyers will make a stupid technical mistake.

***

All the while I'm desperately racking my brains. I think I have good, maxims for legal reasoning, but what are they? The rule represents a compromise between two conflicting policies, so there must be a gray area where the terms of the compromise are not clear. But this case seems clear. There are *always* exceptions to the rule. But I can't think of any here.

When an idea starts to come, it just comes, little by little getting clearer, as

I work to tease it out, flesh it out, add analogies. Here it is:

Of course (oh, how I love to feel that reassuring "of course" tripping off my tongue at the beginning of an argument), it is not *literally* true that the workers are forbidden from "interfering with the owners' use of the m.o.p. during a strike." They can picket and use all kinds of publicity measures to dissuade people from riding the company's buses.

Here I begin to lose my grip again. Lying down in the roadway is a far cry from picketing, which doesn't interfere at all *physically* with the company's use of the buses and is after all justified as an exercise of First Amendment rights. This exception won't do me any good.

After more false leads and panic (I try manipulating the concept of "owner" to get the workers a piece of the action, but that tactic just seems to push me into the inferior implied contract route) I come back to my exception. The workers did lie down in the street to block the buses, but they did not intend to and did not in fact use force to prevent them from rolling. After all, they submitted peacefully to arrest. And the press was everywhere. Obviously the worker on the ground *could not have* physically prevented the bus from rolling, because it could have rolled right over him.

Still, on those two days of lie-ins the company failed to resume service in the fashion it had planned. The workers did physically obstruct the owner's use of the m.o.p. and were delighted to do so. The disruption wasn't just a side effect.

On the other hand, maybe I can argue that the demonstration was a symbolic protest, an attempt to (a) exert moral suasion on the company by impressing it with the extreme feeling of the workers and their willingness to take risks, their sense that the company is theirs as much as management's, and (b) a gesture toward the public through the media.

I will emphasize the non-violent civil disobedience aspects: a physical tactic that *could not in fact* have prevented the use of the m.o.p. by the company, and submission to arrest.

I could hold that because of these factors there should be no federal labor law injunctive remedy beyond what is accorded under state law (narrow version). Or that this demonstration is the exercise of First Amendment rights, so that injunction of a nonviolent civil disobedient protest would be an unconstitutional restriction of expression, even though it is of course perfectly permissible for the state to arrest the demonstrators and subject them to its normal criminal process (broad version).

By this time, I'm getting high. I have no idea whether this line of argument will work. I have even lost track of exactly how this argument can be brought to bear in the employer's federal court action for an injunction. (This is probably because I've gotten into an argument on the merits before clarifying in my own mind what the basis of federal jurisdiction may be, and before getting into the anti-injunction Wagner Act issue.) But I am nonetheless delighted. My heart lifts because it seems that the work of legal reasoning within my pro-worker project is paying off.

***

What I've tried to do here is to turn this into a First Amendment prior restraint (or at least a "free speech policy") case. I relied on the idea that there had to be some limit to the employer's freedom from interference, came up with picketing by trying to imagine what the workers certainly *could* do to him, and then looked for an extension of the picketing idea to embrace the particular facts of this case.

Another way to put it is that I stopped imagining the rule of "no interference" as the only thing out there—as dominating an empty field and therefore grabbing up and incorporating any new fact-situation that had anything at all "sort of like interference" in it. I tried to find the other rules that set the limits of this one, so I could tuck my case under their wing. Once I identified those other affirmative rules (protecting picketing and other First-Amendment-based attacks on the employer's use of the m.o.p.), I restated the facts of the lie-in to emphasize those aspects that fit (nonviolence, submission to arrest, one prone body can't stop a Sceni cruiser bus unless the Sceni cruiser wants to be stopped).

***

The minute I get rolling, new wrinkles occur to me. Maybe we should see the lie-in as an appeal by union workers to the nonunion replacement bus drivers. It is they, not the union members, who actually stop the buses on the street and fail thereby to carry out the company's plan to resume service. It would be all right to try to persuade the nonunion replacements with flyers, to picket them, to threaten them with anger and nonassociation, to guilt trip them and swear at them. The lie-in is just a small extension of those tactics. It is a physical statement to them. Will this fly? I have no idea. It is part of the brainstorming process, rather than a deduction of the rule that covers the case. It is part of the work of producing lots of alternative ways at the problem, hoping that one of them will break through. I am already wondering whether it's even worth the time to pursue this approach further.

***

As I euphorically contemplate my "breakthrough" from panicked blankness into a swirling plethora of possible legal arguments, I come up against a disturbing thought. By redefining this as a First Amendment case, I have not *abolished* the old rule that once seemed to settle everything. I've just limited its scope. It is still true that (except in these cases I've been discussing) the workers can't interfere with the owner's use of the m.o.p. during a strike. For example, I think, looking now for a core case that will resist my First Amendment foray into the soft periphery of the rule, if the workers went into the company's garage and physically appropriated the buses, there would be clear interference of the type the rule was meant to prevent.

Three reactions to this thought: (a) I'm disappointed that, fantasy aside, my holding could do no more than chip away a little, though a little is not nothing, at the owner's power. (b) Then I worry that the hypothetical I've just constructed is the hypothetical I was afraid the lie-in might be—the hypothetical in which there is just nothing you can do, because if the rule is in force, it applies to the case in an objective, ineluctable way. (c) But then I think, maybe I could unsettle this one too. Let's hypothesize some more facts. And I have a crazy flash to the tort law doctrine of "recapture of chattels" which says that the owner of a chattel can't use force to recapture it from a person who seized it under a claim of right without using force. Suddenly I'm wondering whether that means the employer would have to sue in conversion and go through the whole trial before there would be an order for return of the chattel, supposing the union got hold of it in just the right way. And so on.

***

The question is not whether my initial off-the-wall legal intuitions turn out to be right. They *may* eventually generate at least superficially plausible legal arguments. But maybe it will turn out that the law is so well settled in another direction that I will have to abandon them and try something else the minute I get out *Gorman on Labor Law* and *Prosser on Torts.* Legal reasoning is a kind of work with a purpose, and here the purpose is to make the case come out the way my sense of justice tells me it ought to, in spite of what seems at first like the *resistance* or *opposition* of "the law."

***

Resistance or opposition is the characteristic of the law when I anticipate it as a constraint on how-I-want-to-come-out. But if my initial sense had been that the law was "on my side," it would be a resistance or opposition from the point of view of the company. I would experience it as a protective barrier I was building around my position, perhaps, or as armor I need to fit to my particular body so that the other side won't be able to strip it away or penetrate it. If I had no sense of "which way the law goes on this," so that each side had an equal opportunity to make a persuasive legal argument, I might experience the law as a body of raw material out of which to "build my case," or perhaps as a mass of wet clay that two opposing potters are each trying to shape before it hardens.

The image changes according to how the law initially presents itself in relation to how-I-want-to-come-out. But in each case I am suggesting that one of the ways in which we experience law (not the only way, as we'll see) is as a medium in which one pursues a project, rather than as something that tells us what we have to do. When we approach it this way, law constrains as a physical medium constrains—you can't do absolutely anything you want with a pile of bricks, and what you can do depends on how many you have, as well as on your other circumstances. In this sense, that you are building something out of a given set of bricks constrains you, controls you, deprives you of freedom.

On the other hand, the constraint a medium imposes is relative to your chosen project—to your choice of what you want to make. The medium doesn't tell you what to do with it—that you *must* make the bricks into a doghouse rather than into a garden wall. In the same sense, I am free to work in the legal medium to justify the workers' actions against the company. How my argument will look in the end will depend in a fundamental way on the legal materials—rules, cases, policies, social stereotypes, historical images—but this dependence is a far cry from the inevitable determination of the outcome in advance *by the legal materials themselves.*

***

The metaphor of a physical medium does not help us solve the problem of just how constraining the law is. All it does is suggest that we should understand both freedom and constraint as aspects of the experience of work—chosen project constrained by material properties of the medium—rather than thinking in the back of our mind of a transcendentally free subject who "could do anything," contrasted with a robot programmed by the law.

One might accept the notion that legal argument is manipulation of the legal materials understood as a medium and still believe that the medium constrains very tightly. An absolutely basic question is whether there are some outcomes that you just can't reach so long as you obey the internal rules of the game of legal reasoning. These would be "things you just can't make with bricks," or silk purses you can't make with this particular sow's ear.

For the moment, make any assumption you want as to how tightly the medium constrains the message. Perhaps there is only one correct legal result in most cases, or perhaps there are some results that you simply can't reach through correct legal reasoning, or perhaps there will be a legally plausible course of reasoning to justify any result that you might want to reach.

What I want to ask is how, rather than how tightly law constrains, when we understand it as a medium through which my liberal activist judge-self pursues social justice. When we are clearer about this it will be time to ask, first, whether it is ever (or sometimes, or always) possible in the last analysis to have a conflict between the law and how-I-want-to-come-out, and, if so, what the ethics of the conflict may be.

***

My model of constraint is that people (me as a judge) want to back up their statement of a preference for an outcome (the workers should not be enjoined) with an argument to the effect that to enjoin the workers would "violate the law." We can't understand how this desire to legalize my position constrains me without saying something about why I want to do it.

First, I see myself as having promised some diffuse public that I will "decide according to law," and it is clear to me that a minimum meaning of this pledge is that I won't do things for which I don't have a good legal argument. (This statement says nothing about just how tightly this promise constrains me as to the merits).

Second, various people in my community will sanction me severely if I do not offer a good legal argument for my action. It is not just that I may be reversed and will have broken my promise. It is also that both friends and enemies will see me as having violated a role constraint that they approve of (for the most part), and they will make me feel their disapproval.

Third, I want my position to stick. Although I am free to decide the case any way I want in the sense that no one will physically prevent me from entering a decree for either side, I am bound by the appellate court's reaction. By developing a strong legal argument I make it dramatically less likely that my outcome will be reversed.

Fourth, by engaging in legal argument I can shape the outcomes of future cases and influence popular consciousness about what kinds of action are legitimate—as here, for example, I can marginally influence what people think about worker interference with the m.o.p. during a strike.

Fifth, every case is part of my life-project of being a liberal activist judge. What I do in this case will affect my ability to do things in other cases, enhancing or diminishing my legal and political credibility as well as my technical reputation with the various constituencies that will notice.

Sixth, since I see legal argument as a branch of ethical argument, I would like to know for my own purposes how my position looks translated into this particular ethical medium.

I might be able to achieve some of these objectives at least some of the time without engaging in direct challenges to my initial intuition that the law is adverse. I don't want to be absolute about it, since I can conceive situations in which I think I would go quite unhesitatingly for a "nonlegal" approach. But there will be many, many situations in which it appears that, if I wish to achieve my goals, the only way or the obviously best way is to try legal argument.

***

Note that I would have to do *something* even if I wanted to grant the injunction. When I say that my first impression of the law is that it favors the employer's case, I mean that I don't anticipate any difficulty in working up a good argument for the injunction. I see that project as easy, as not much work.

By contrast, deciding *not* to enjoin involves not just the work of pushing pencil across paper to get down thoughts already well worked out before I even begin, but the work of creating something out of nothing. This is a cost of deciding for the workers, and it has at least two aspects. First, the work of creating a good legal argument is hard, scary, and time-consuming. I have limited resources in my life as a judge, and the workers are asking me to allocate them here, when I could put them into some other hard case or just spend all my time on easy cases. My limited store of time and energy for the hard work of creating legal arguments that go against my first impression of what the law is constrains me from doing all kinds of things I could do as judge if I weren't constrained.

I don't want this point to sound minor, because it isn't. There are lots and lots and lots of rules I would like to change or at least reform. If I could do it by fiat, perhaps I would do a lot of it, do it quite fast, and in a way that might be called holistic. But if I have to generate a legal argument for every change, there is no way I can do a lot, do it fast, or do it holistically.

***

The second way in which I experience the law as a constraint in my hypothetical is that it is one of the determinants of what we might call the "legitimacy cost" of deciding for the workers. Just as there are competitors for my time and creativity as a legal arguer, there are also competitors claiming shares of the *mana* or *charisma* or whatever that attends my position as a judge. I have leeways or, to put it another way, the mere fact that I decide something makes people think it was legally right to decide it that way. But there are limits to this legitimating power, and every case raises them.

In our case, assume that *everyone* has the same initial impression that the law favors the employer. If I decide for the employer, people who know that this decision goes against my personal views may grant my decision some increased legitimacy. They may see me as more able to indicate what the correct legal result is in the next case, because they believe I perceived and followed the law in this one, even when I didn't like it.

This factor aside, no one will be able to say much about "what kind of judge he is" from my decision to go along with the collective initial impression. Going along would be costless in terms of legitimacy. My legitimating power is depleted or augmented only when I try to do something out of the ordinary.

I imagine this effect to be a function of two aspects of the situation. The first is the degree of "stretch" from our initial impression of the law to the result I decree. The second is the impact on this distance—we might call it the obviousness gap—of my opinion defending my out-of-the-ordinary result.

The greater the initial perception of stretch, the more of my stock of legitimacy is at stake. Of course, the very notion of legitimating power is that I can reduce the perceived distance between what the law requires and what I decree just by decreeing it. That is the nature of my institutional *mana* or *charisma*. But nothing guarantees that my legitimating power will cause people to see this result as the one that was right all along. That outcome depends on how great the stretch was, and in my own case it is likely that the stretch will be much greater than I can overcome just because the president of the United States has put some black robes on me.

If my automatic legitimating power falls short of fully normalizing the outcome, I will lose legitimating power for the next case—my stock will be depleted—*unless* I devise an opinion (cast as a legal argument) that makes up the deficit, or even increases the stock. In order to make up the deficit I have to write an opinion that will convince the good faith observer struggling to understand what the law is that in fact my result was not out of the ordinary at all. Rather it was a correct perception, albeit a minority perception, of what the law really required all along.

In other words, I can build up my legitimating power through instances of persuading people through legal argument. If they have had the experience of my "being right" before, experiences of my changing their view of the law, then they will be susceptible in the future to believe what I tell them the law is, quite independently of the argument I can muster.

The greater the initial distance between my proposed result and what one would expect, the greater the positive value of persuading the observer through legal argument. You will attribute power to me just in the measure that you find yourself saying, "I never thought he could persuade me of *that!*" Even if I don't persuade you, I gain power if you say, "He didn't convince me, but I never thought he could get me to take the proposition seriously, and here I am arguing hard against it!" On the other hand, if the distance was small to begin with, persuading you that I was right in my initial impression will do no more than very marginally increase my store of legitimating power.

I also increase my power to the extent that my persuasive efforts spill over from this particular case and cause you to reassess other outcomes you had thought pre-eminently legally correct. This is my ability to make my case a "leading case" that will be cited over and over in increasingly distant reaches of law-space as the years go by. My name on that opinion is a help the next time I have an unconventional view on the merits, because it has increased my legitimating power even if in the next case I don't have much in the way of an argument.

***

In this very mechanical model of law as a constraint on the judge, I find myself in a *situation*, defined by my initial impressions of what the law is and of how-I-want-to-come-out. In this situation, I have to decide how I want to allocate my energy among "causes," and estimate the consequences for my project as an activist judge of deciding one way or another.

The constraint imposed by the law is that it defines the distance that I will have to work through in legal argument if I decide to come out the way I initially thought I wanted to. "The law" constrains in that it is an element of the situation as I initially experience it. It is the "field" of my action.

†††

In describing the work of legal reasoning, I have thus far kept to the drastically simplified situation in which there is a rule, a case that the rule appears to cover, and a counter-rule that is initially beyond the periphery of awareness. We need to complicate things.

In my previous examples I treated the rules as autonomous entities that were there in my consciousness independent of cases. I think this treatment corresponds to the way I experience legal rules in real life. It is not true that they are inductive derivations from cases or that they are predictions of what the courts will do. They are much less than either of these: they are verbal formulae I think I know to be "valid" (even though I am often not sure what that means and always aware that my knowledge may turn out to be superficial) that are present like so many random objects floating around in my mind.

One can get access to dozens or hundreds of them—such as "the workers can't interfere with the m.o.p. during a strike"—without having to justify them independently through any inductive or pragmatic process. They are just things we learned in law school or from the newspapers or from reading treatises or from reading cases. They are primary not derivative entities in legal consciousness.

We cite cases as authority for rules. But we also use cases to fill in the actual meaning of the rule when it is open to doubt. In other words, though the rules exist independently of the cases, it is also true that some cases are an essential part of our understanding of what the law of the field "is." This means that decided cases are part of the medium I have to shape if I want to make a persuasive legal argument that the workers shouldn't be enjoined from lying down in front of the buses.

The cases that are most obviously part of the meaning of a rule, rather than mere applications of it, are those we currently see as marking its boundary with a counter-rule. Suppose we have an earlier labor case in which the question was whether there was a First Amendment right to mass picketing, and the courts ruled that there was not, and that the activity should be enjoined as an unfair labor practice or as a tortious interference with the employer's right to use the m.o.p. during a strike. That case is "on the boundary" if it is the "furthest" the employer's right has been extended and the furthest the workers' right of expression has been cut back. If a mass picketing case were followed by a case holding that individual picketing is also tortious, then that case would be the one on the boundary, *if* I perceived individual picketing as at the same time less of an interference with the employer's property rights, and more plausibly a protected speech activity.

The process by which we arrange the cases into a pattern along the boundary, and also within the undisputed territory of one rule or the other, should be understood as a gestalt process. When someone describes the cases, I nonreflectively grasp them as arranging themselves into a particular constellation. For example, I might just instantly understand that mass picketing is more of an interference than individual picketing, and that a lie-in blocking the street is more of an interference than either.

But it does not always happen that the cases arrange themselves for me into neat constellations. For example, I might perceive mass picketing as more of an interference than individual picketing, but also think it more rather than less deserving of First Amendment protection. After all, mass picketing involves associational as well as speech rights. I might then find it hard to arrange these two types of cases along the boundary between expressive and property rights: maybe they occupy adjoining sectors of the boundary?

The point of this discussion is that our new case, *as it initially presents itself to consciousness*, is situated in a field that contains not only a rule that appears to cover it (no interference with the m.o.p. during a strike) but also many instantiating cases. These appear to establish the rule's meaning. For example, if a case has established that you can't mass picket, then you "obviously" can't obstruct the buses by lying down in the street.

In my initial example of legal reasoning, all I had to do in order to tuck this case under the wing of the counter-principle of free speech was restate both the free speech rule and the facts, until the first covered the second. But if there are decided cases along the boundary I am trying to "move" through restatement, I have to deal with them, unless my restatement of the rule leaves them "undisturbed." I have to "move" them by restating their facts and their holdings until they fit my new formulation of the general rule.

"Movement" is possible because these arrangements that seem so objective as they initially present themselves to consciousness are not in fact anywhere near as solid as chairs or tables. It is a common experience that the constellation shifts or dissolves as one contemplates it. It is also much more common with gestalts of this kind than with the dining room furniture arrangement that you can persuade me, by mustering images and moral arguments, that my initial perception was all wrong. Contrary to my first impression, you

argue, mass picketing is "really" more protectable than individual picketing. I hope to persuade you that, contrary to both our initial impressions,
the lie-in to block the buses was more worthy of protection than either mass
or individual picketing.

***

It may be useful, or at least amusing, to extend the metaphor of the field in
order to distinguish between manipulating the facts of a precedent and
manipulating the holding. I imagine the facts of the case (I learned them
from the opinion or from somewhere else, such as a classroom or a newspaper) as defining *the position of the case in the field of law*. We may grasp
that position as close to a boundary line, or on it, or as so far within the
boundary that these facts seem "easy" and the general rule just "applies
itself" to them. Legal argument with the facts of the case means restating
them so that the case appears in a different part of the field than it did
initially.

Remember that my objective is to make my lie-in look like a case plausibly
covered by the rule permitting speech-type interferences with the m.o.p.,
rather than like a case clearly governed by the rule of no interferences with
the m.o.p. Suppose that a mass picketing case has already gone against the
workers. My first impression is that the lie-in is "even worse" from an
interference point of view, and simultaneously "weaker" as a speech case. I
will try to restate the facts of the mass picketing case to make it reappear in
the field as more of an interference than the lie-in, and as less plausibly a case
of protected speech.

I will do this by emphasizing that, in the mass picketing case, the court
found that the workers were trying to physically prevent substitute workers
from entering the plant, and that the situation was always on the verge of
violence. I will de-emphasize the opinion's references to the signs and
shouted slogans of the mass picket. By contrast, I will argue that the workers
in the lie-in submitted peacefully to arrest, and could never have physically
prevented passage of the buses by lying in front of them.

My hope is that you will eventually perceive the two cases as located in just
the opposite position from that you saw them in initially, so that I can draw
the boundary between rather than around them. Mass picketing will then
fall on the side of interference, the lie-in on the side of speech.

***

Changing the position of a precedent in the field is, as I've been describing
it, analogous to changing the position of the case before us—the lie-in. But
the analogy is misleading to the extent that the precedent, unlike the lie-in,
comes already equipped with a holding. This complicates matters
considerably.

If the facts of the precedent are on the boundary, then its holding is *part of*
the boundary. The holding is a rule, or at least a little sub-rule, defining, in
the abstract manner of any rule, a range of cases beyond this particular
instance of mass picketing. These cases "in the vicinity" or "close to on
point," along with any future fact-situation that might be "on all fours"
with it, are "settled" by the precedent. In other words, the holding of a case

structures the field around the point represented by the fact situation of that case.

I must be able to restate the holding as well as the facts of the mass picketing case if I want to reposition my lie-in case with respect to the boundary. The work of restating the holding is closer to the work of restating the general rule than it is to that of repositioning a fact-situation. For example, after I've restated the facts of the mass picketing case to emphasize forcible interferences with passage of substitute workers into the plant, I may want to restate the holding too. I will play down the original opinion's claim that because this was "action" it can receive First Amendment protection only if it was "unequivocally symbolic." I will claim that what the court prohibited was coercion of substitute workers, rather than an attempt at persuasion. This statement of the holding will make it easier to restate the general rule to include nonviolent civil disobedient lie-ins under the rubric of protected expression.

***

We might think of the holding of the case as a line extending through the point represented by the facts. The line defines a set of cases that the holding has resolved one way or the other. When I redefine the holding, I inflect the line in some way, changing its direction so that it "covers" a different set of hypothetical situations. Thus, when the mass picketing case becomes a case about "coercion vs. persuasion," it helps define the boundary between forbidden and permitted union activity differently than it did when it was about how "action" is unprotected unless "unequivocally symbolic."

The inflection of the line is desirable because, once I have done it, I won't have to spend a lot of time explaining how the lie-in is "unequivocally symbolic." I can admit that it is "action." My (much easier) argument will be that it is clearly persuasive rather than coercive action. Further, my new holding for the mass picketing case makes a nice little piece of the new boundary I am drawing between First Amendment cases and interference-with-property-rights cases. Mass picketing is not closely analogous to nonviolent civil disobedience, now that we've identified it as problematic because "coercive." So there is no inconsistency in forbidding it while tolerating lie-ins.

***

Extending the field analogy yet a step further, we can use it to incorporate the "broadening" and "narrowing" of holdings into our analysis. Narrowing the holding, by restating it as a rule that depends for its application on many potentially idiosyncratic details of the particular case, is a shortening of the line that extends through the fact-situation in the field. It means that there will be fewer hypothetical fact-situations "covered" by the holding, and the case will therefore have less structuring effect on the field around it. Broadening is the opposite maneuver.

***

Policies as forces in the field. Policy arguments are reasons for adopting a particular holding or mini-rule. They are aimed more specifically than philosophical or social theoretical justifications of whole systems and more abstractly than appeals to the raw equities immanent in "the facts." Policy argument is "second order" in relation to rule application or argument from precedent. It presupposes conscious choice about how the structure of the field should look, as opposed to simple subsumption of the facts to a norm that I grasp nonreflectively as part of gestalt.

The arguer can pick and choose from a truly enormous repertoire of typical policy arguments and modify what he finds to fit the case at hand. The arguments come in matched contrary pairs, like certainty vs. flexibility, security vs. freedom of action, property as incentive to labor vs. property as incipient monopoly, no liability without fault vs. as between two innocents he who caused the damage should pay, the supremacy clause vs. local initiative, and so on.

A policy is not invalidated just because I ignore it in a case where it arguably applies. Our rough notion is that the two sides of the matched pair "differ in strength" from case to case. We might see the property-as-incentive-to-labor argument as very strong if the issue is whether there should be any private rights at all in mechanisms of interstate commerce, but as quite weak if the question is whether there should be a right to prevent peaceful individual picketing of an interstate bus company involved in a labor dispute.

The moment when I switch from one of the matched pairs to the other in response to a change in the fact-situation can be quite dramatic. In this case, I might firmly believe that the interests in security and peaceful access to public spaces strongly support state law criminal sanctions against the lie-in. I might then turn around and argue against a federal injunction of the lie-in, on the ground that people should have a right to nonviolent civil disobedient protest, even if it inconveniences the public and the employer, and that repressive measures will make violence more rather than less likely.

In a typical legal argument, policies are elaborated and strongly asserted without regard to their matched pairs. When I argue for state law criminal penalties, I don't have to explain, either as judge or as advocate, the rational basis of my endorsement of "nip it in the bud" here, and my contrary endorsement of "repression breeds violence" when we get to the injunction. In a sense, then, the practice of legal arguers (lawyers, judges, treatise writers) is endlessly contradictory. I assert my policy as "valid" and as "requiring" an outcome, and then blithely reject it and in the next case, endorse its exactly matching opposite without giving any meta-level explanation of what keys me into one side or the other.

From the inside, however, I know from the beginning that this is just "the way we do" legal argument. I don't take the surface claim that the policy is "valid" and "requires" the outcome seriously at all. I work with a model of the opposing policies as forces or vectors, each of which has some "pull" on any given fact-situation. They *seem* logically contradictory (how can I believe, at the same time, that "there should be no liability without fault," and that "as between two innocents he who caused the damage should pay") or so indeterminate that they can serve only as after-the-fact rationalizations of decisions reached on other grounds (who knows whether the injunction will "nip violence in the bud" or "just drive it underground and make it worse"?). But there is a sense in which both policies are valid at the same time, in every case. The question is which one turns out to be "stronger," or to weigh more in a "balancing test" applied to these particular facts, rather than which is correct in the abstract.

We can represent the process of arranging cases in a field, and the process of fixing a boundary between permitted and forbidden acts, in terms of this imagery of vectors and balancing. For example, the imaginary mass picketing and individual picketing cases discussed earlier had fact situations and holdings, but they also "involved" or "implicated" various policies. The mass picketing case implicated the general social policy in favor of political association and the general social policy against the use of force to resolve disputes. (Each case implicates as many policies as I can plausibly think up. Those mentioned here are illustrative, not exhaustive.)

Suppose we see the lie-in, in relation to mass picketing, as a "better" First Amendment case, and as a less serious interference with the employer's use of the m.o.p. during a strike. The "second order" interpretation of this intuitive ordering is that pro-speech policies apply more strongly, and pro-property policies less strongly, than in the mass picketing case. As we move from fact-situation to fact-situation across the field, the speech policy gets weaker, and the property policy stronger, until at the boundary they are in equilibrium. At this point a very small change in the relative forces of the policies produces a dramatic change in result. We "draw the line" and treat cases beyond the line repressively.

What this means is that we have to add to our model of the field of law the notion that, at every point in the field, contradictory policies exert different levels of force. Boundary lines in the field represent points of equilibrium of opposing forces. At points not on boundaries, one or another set of policies predominates. The policies are to be understood as gradients; they are strongest in the "core," where a given general rule seems utterly obvious in its application and also utterly "appropriate as a matter of social policy." The argument set supporting the general rule diminishes in force as we move from the core outward toward the periphery, and ultimately to a boundary with another general rule.

***

The boundary appears to me as "there" in three quite different ways. First, it is a line, a rule that was implicit in the statement of the general rule. For example, I may see the idea that there shall be no laws against "free speech" as implicitly including nonverbal expression. Second, the boundary is a line running through all the limiting cases. Suppose that individual but not mass picketing is all right; that threats of nonassociation with substitute workers but not threats to call demand notes are all right. The boundary "connects the dots." Third, as we have just seen, the boundary is like the line in a magnetic field formed by iron filings exactly balanced between two distant magnets. State law criminal penalties against a lie-in are desirable and don't violate the first amendment, but the addition of a federal injunction is undesirable and would be unconstitutional, say, because the injunction is just a little bit "too much."

We have already discussed legal argument as the restatement of general rules and the re-selection of facts so that a case that initially appeared "covered" by rule A turns out to be covered by rule B. And we have discussed the manipulation of the facts and holdings of precedents to redefine the boundary. My goal in policy argument is analogous. First, I develop a potential holding for my lie-in case, such as that there shall be no federal injunction of nonviolent civil disobedient protests in labor disputes. Then I develop some policy arguments as to why this rule is preferable to an alternative (usually a straw man) or to the rule proposed by the employer. For example, I argue that if the workers feel strongly enough to undergo arrest and criminal charges, they almost certainly feel strongly enough to do something violent if they are not permitted their symbolic protest. It follows that, far from "nipping violence in the bud," an injunction will likely lead to unorganized individual acts of violence, such as shooting out bus tires on the open highway.

But this argument is unlikely to be enough. Once I have taken the step into the "second order," forsaking the strategy of mere rule application, I evoke in the mind of my audience the whole force field of this area of law. I will now have to take steps to preserve the coherence of the overall policy "picture." This means restating policy arguments in other decided cases. For example, suppose that in the mass picketing case the court justified a prohibitory rule on the ground that unless you nip violence in the bud it develops until it is unstoppable.

My problem is that in the lie-in case I am arguing that worker anger makes it important to tolerate civil disobedience, and this position seems inconsistent with a "nipping in the bud" strategy against mass picketing. In order to restore order to the field, I will "distinguish" the mass picketing case as follows. Mass picketing is essentially uncontrollable and naturally tends to escalate toward violence. In the civil disobedience case, by contrast, the police exercise detailed and intense control. Though the initial emotion may be greater in the lie-in, the setting allows the release of emotion without escalation. Since the situation is already under control but still serving to release emotion, an injunction is likely to be counterproductive overkill.

[Let me remind the patient reader that I have no idea whether the preceding policy arguments and distinctions are "any good," that is, whether they would be persuasive to a person a little knowledgeable in the field. One begins the work of legal argument enveloped in ignorance of what the law "is" and with little sense of what may be the conventional wisdom about how the law works in practice. I will find out about these matters by doing research and by asking people. In consequence, I'll flatly abandon some arguments while I develop others. What I am trying to do here is describe what the work process in its initial stages feels like from the inside.]

***

The boundary can be cast either as a rule (a determinate outcome on easily determined facts) or as a standard (ad hoc judgment required) applying a value, like good faith or reasonableness, or an abstraction, like forseeability or promotion of competition. When the standard is a value, argument that a particular fact-situation meets the standard will often look a lot like policy argument—may indeed merge by degrees into it. There are "formal" arguments for rules and for standards, against rules and against standards. These are policy arguments about the appropriateness of using a rule or a standard in the particular case.

***

Social and historical stereotypes. These are part of the stock in trade of legal argument. By a social stereotype, I mean, for example, the raw image of "worker blocks bus"—an unshaven large burly white man without a tie or jacket aggressively obstructing innocent third-party passengers (us!) who have to sit passively until someone comes to their aid. I might reverse the stereotype by expanding the time frame of the story, a la Kelman, and adding lots of facts, until we get "bus monopoly's intransigence finally breaks patience of Job-like toilers." Historical stereotypes are ideas like "the nineteenth century was a time of agrarian individualism so it was natural for people then to accept the doctrine of *caveat emptor.*"

Overruling. If policy argument is second order in relation to mere rule application, overruling is third order. Without question that there are *some* circumstances in which, as a federal district court judge, I can redraw the boundary between permitted and forbidden conduct without restating the facts of cases, so that cases find themselves looking at a boundary where once they were looking at home, and looking at home across an open space where once there was a boundary.

There are maxims about overruling. The district court, a trial court, should be less quick to do it than an appeals court. It is more permissible to overrule a doctrine riddled with exceptions, and consequently more honored in the breach than in the observance, than to overrule a vital modern doctrine that dominates its field like a young Mars. And so forth. There are cases in which a course of law reform has become the norm, so that *not* to overrule a case would appear an abuse of discretion. (Suppose that the Supreme Court had upheld separate-but-equal public playgrounds facilities after desegregating schools, public accommodations, government offices.)

When I first began thinking about this subject, the possiblity of overruling seemed a dramatically important aspect of the judicial activist's situation. Indeed, it seemed to mean that there is no such thing as a conflict between "the law" and how-I-want-to-come-out, since I can change the law by overruling to make it correspond to my heart's desire. On further reflection, this has come to seem a shallow view.

First, though overruling is a third order practice, it is nonetheless subject to the calculus of legitimacy I have been describing. I can't overrule with impunity any more than I can disturb the field with impunity in any other way. The set of maxims by which the overruling decision will be judged are pretty vague, but if the decision isn't convincing, I will find myself less able to persuade the next time around and feeling guilty about violating role constraints.

Second, my power to overrule, seen as a kind of ultimate power to reorder the field, is counterbalanced by the notion of legislative supremacy. I can't "overrule" a statute. *But* the statute may be trumped by the state and federal constitutions, of which I am interpreter here. *But* though I can use the constitutions to overrule the statute, I have no power to overrule the constitutions themselves. *But* even this is not the end of the story, since the constitutions don't seem, a priori, to be any more conceivably self-applying than any other set of legal norms. Many great cases branch down from the sacred texts, and these I *can* overrule.

The upshot of these twists and turns is that I decide about overruling enmeshed in the field of law, subject to its typical constraint that I argue persuasively across some perceived obviousness gap, or forfeit my charismatic power and get reversed on appeal into the bargain. It is an added power; it enhances my freedom to make the law correspond to how-I-want-to-come-out beyond what it would be if I had always to work in the first order of rule application or the second order of policy argument. But it liberates me as a technological innovation might liberate a worker in a medium—as, say, the invention of new casting techniques changes the possibilities of sculpture. New techniques bring new constraints along with new possibilities. They change as well as reducing the experience of constraint. It becomes harder than it was before to say with authority what can and cannot be done in the medium. But the overruling option does not make the judge all-powerful.

***

Typical field configurations. As I initially apprehend it, a legal field is more than just a collection of general rules, boundaries, precedents, and vectors. I will almost certainly experience it as patterned, as a field with a particular configuration. Of course each field is different from every other one. But in the gestalt process by which we grasp it, we employ—albeit nonreflectively—what we might call "configuraiton-types." We get a cognitive grip on the particularity of a given field by relating it to one or more of these types, distorting it in the process.

We can loosely array configruation-types according to how impacted they are. By this I mean that some fields seem to offer more opportunities for one kind or another of legal argument than others. Here are my candidates, beginning with the type that seems to offer least opportunity for overcoming whatever the initial distance may have been between the law and how-I-want-to-come-out.

The impacted field. In the impacted field boundaries are long straight lines, meaning that there are general rules determining the limits of general rules. For example, we might have a rule that "protected speech," must be either speech or the dissemination of written texts. The "further we go" without making exceptions (e.g., we uphold censorship of a dance performance with obvious political content, or of a mime show) the longer the straight boundary line. In the impacted field, there are a substantial number of cases distributed in a regular pattern along the boundary, dispelling any doubt that the rule means what it says. The dance and mime cases have actually been decided.

Moreover, the courts deciding them did so with holdings that carefully incorporated the cases under the most general statement of the general rule, in the process reaffirming all the earlier cases along the line, while predicting that at points in between the decided cases the courts would adhere to the existing pattern. Behind the lines, there is a nice scatter pattern of easy cases, and they get easier and easier as you approach the core, all in accord with the gradient hypothesis about social policies. This pattern makes it hard to imagine "parachuting in," so to speak, with a surprise case permitting peacetime national security censorship of a newspaper editorial criticizing the government.

When I apprehend the field as impacted, I apprehend it as hard to manipulate. Those long straight boundaries, reenforced at regular intervals with precedents whose holdings exactly track the line, will defy the arts I have been describing. My initial sense will be that, unless I can do my work on the facts of the lie-in itself, I am going to be in trouble. But remember that we are not speaking of actual, objective properties of the field, but rather of my initial apprehension of it.

When I set to work, for example, at reading a lot of those cases I vaguely remember, everything may change. I haven't yet tried to restate the rules and cases and policies in a serious way. My initial impression, that the field is impacted, is as much a *product* of my initial fear that I won't be able to come up with a viable legal argument for the lie-in as it is a *cause* of that fear. If you wait a minute, the field may suddenly look a lot different, as happened above when I finally began to see a way to tuck the lie-in under the wing of the First Amendment.

***

The case of first impression. Sometimes the field presents itself as structured everywhere except in the vicinity of the case at hand. The boundary line is vague throughout the area of the lie-in; no precedents appear nearby; and, significantly, the policy vectors seem to be of about equal force, not just along a thin line of equilibrium, but throughout the border region. If the vectors are about equal and also relatively very strong, it is not just a case of first impression, but a "great" case. If the vectors are weak, then it is the routine case of penny-ante judicial creativity.

If the field has this structure, but the lie-in seems to fall outside the area of indeterminacy, a basic argumentative tactic is to restate the facts to put it there. This changes the situation from an adverse one, in which rule application seems to settle things against me, to a neutral one, in which everyone will concede that there are good legal arguments on both sides, and the whole proceeding has the air of a solemn sports event.

The impacted field and the case of first impression represent constraint and freedom as they are conceived within the legal tradition itself. The case of first impression does not threaten that tradition because the freedom involved is, first, exceptional, and, second, freedom constrained by its narrow context. The case is a kind of clearing of freedom in the endless forest of constraint. Because we exercise freedom where there is no constraint, it doesn't threaten constraint. Moreover, the judge's action fills in a part of the clearing, so that the freedom of cases of first impression can be understood as self-annihilating. The more times judges exercise this freedom the less of it there will be, as the boundaries get staked out with case by case.

The following configuration-types differ from both the impacted field and the case of first impression because of their ambiguity. Rather than presenting themselves either as hopeless (constraint) or as open (freedom), they present themselves as opportunities whose ultimate meaning we will fix through the work of argument.

***

The unrationalized field. Imagine that there are lots and lots of cases in the general vicinity of the boundary, some coming out for the workers and some for the employer. But they are decided "on their facts," with minimal argumentation and narrow or conclusory or obviously logically defective holdings. Just because there are so many cases clustered around the boundary, there are many, many occasions for rearrangement by restatement of facts. This will be especially true where there are lots of details available for each precedent (so the restater has free play in selection) or almost no details at all (so the restater can dismiss the case as ambiguous). A field of this kind invites an opinion proposing a new rule and showing how all the old cases, properly understood, are consistent with it. Because the earlier cases are unrationalized but numerous, the exercise may be particularly convincing as "order out of chaos," and a great relief to the audience. Or it may fail miserably, leaving things more disorderly than they were before.

***

The contradictory field. This is the situation in which there are lots of cases on both sides, but the company has won some that seriously impair free speech, and the workers have won some that seriously impair employer control of the m.o.p. during a strike. The courts have prohibited all picketing, say, but have permitted unlimited secondary boycott activity.

In a situation like this, connecting the dots so as to draw the boundary requires a zig-zag line that cuts deep first into one territory and then into the other. Each opinion fully restates the policy vectors so that it looks as though the outcome is "required." But the result is that a given policy appears to vary widely in force at points that are near each other in the field.

These rapid fluctuations along a contorted boundary suggest that "something is wrong." The boundary between strict liability and negligence in the law of unintentional tort has much this quality. Cases that openly impose strict liability are only part of the picture (though, as every law student knows, it is hard to decide what is an "ultrahazardous" activity, given the precedents and the ambiguous definition). There are also so-called "historical" instances, as with animals and nuisance. There are situations such as res ipsa loquitur and the manipulation of informed consent in which the courts impose de facto strict liability behind a screen of fault rhetoric. And courts interpret the reasonable person standard to permit liability without fault, right next to cases in which they "individualize" the standard to prevent that outcome.

There are lots of arguments for strict liability and lots of arguments for the fault standard in these cases. The problem is that if one took the arguments in any of the cases seriously, one ould have to overrule dozens and dozens of cases based on the opposed policy in the matching pair. Consequently, almost any case can appear to be of first impression, since virtually all cases seem to fall midway between cases decided for strict liability and cases decided for the fault standard. Instead of a field divided in half by a straight line that represents an equilibrium of forces, we have an extremely complex structure shot through with interstices. There really is no boundary. Every point not occupied by a recent precedent is contestable.

***

The collapsed field. A field collapses, in this lingo, when the policy arguments on one side of the boundary get restated so as to abolish the boundary. One of the contending general rules then appears correctly applicable across the field so as to obliterate the counter-rule.

Collapse is usually an event quickly recognized to threaten the whole enterprise, so the collapsing argument is not just "accepted." Rather it is there as a possible, plausibly legal, incontestably legitimate and sometimes highly persuasive argument *in every single case.* On the other side are ad hoc appeals to factual peculiarities, arguments harking back shamelessly to a more innocent time, mistakes, intuitionistic protests against collapse, but no coherent argument for a line that would hold against the collapsing argument.

In *Shelley v. Kraemer,* if enforcement of discriminatory covenants is state action, then the private sphere "disappears," since all private arrangements are dependent for their structure on enforcement of private law ground rules. In *Wickard v. Fillburn,* if wheat grown for your own consumption affects interstate commerce by reducing demand, then it is hard to see what activity can ever be "intrastate." In *Pennsylvania Coal v. Mahon,* Holmes points out that all police power regulations "take property" in the sense of impoverishing some, but proposes to solve the problem only an incoherent test of "how much taking." In *Hoffman v. Red Owl Stores* and *Drennan v. Star Paving,* the court allows a promissory estoppel recovery where there was no gratuitous promise and indeed no consideration problem of any kind. There was merely a failure to comply with the formalities that indicate intent to make the promise binding. If promissory estoppel applies in such cases, it potentially abolishes formalities in any case where there was reliance.

***

The loopified field. The notion of loopification makes people uptight, and since it's not that important here, I'll just mention it briefly. We apprehend the field as loopified when supposedly easy cases in the heartlands of the territories of the opposing rules seem closer together (around the back, so to speak) than cases that are opposite one another along the boundary.

For example, the intimate relations of family members are simultaneously those that seem most clearly private (e.g., as described in *Griswold v. Conn* or *Roe v. Wade*) and those that, because of their implications for the public weal, are subject to the most intense and intrusive state regulation (as in the standardless determination of child custody in the "best interests of the child"). Or take promissory estoppel, which now applies most typically to a business transaction in which there has been a failure to comply with formalities and in which the measure of damages may actually be the expectancy. This core promissory estoppel case is hard to distinguish from the core case in which, according to the traditional wisdom of, e.g., *Baird v. Gimbel*, the doctrine simply has no applicability at all.

***

I hope, as I begin research on the lie-in case, that the field will present itself in a somewhat disordered configuration—as unrationalized, for example—and I fear that I will confront an impacted field, with my case firmly planted behind "enemy lines." One goal of legal argument is to recast the field so that it will end up looking impacted, but with the lie-in case now securely where it ought to be.

If the field looked well ordered for me initially but at the end of the argument the field looks contradictory, I have lost ground, even if I am still quite plausibly presenting the lie-in case as one that has to be resolved for the workers. On the other hand, if I begin with an unfavorable impacted field and end up with a plausible case of first impression, or a plausible case in a loopified field, I have done quite well.

The reason you want to end up with an impacted field (with your case favorably placed) is that the impacted field's orderly boundaries, its neatly disposed precedents, with their congruent holdings and smooth policy gradients, is the very image of legal necessity. If you persuade your audience that the field is like this, the audience will see the decision-making process as a simple exercise in rule application. The case will "decide itself."

By contrast, a case in a contradictory field, no matter how plausibly presented, can't seem necessarily to come out your way. The chaotic configuration of the contradictory field—no matter where you are in the field there are cases all around that come out all different ways—is a symbolic representation of contingency dressed up to look like necessity. This may be a relief, given how bad things looked to start with, but it's never the ideal end of the argument about this case.

***

Remember, though, that this case is not the whole story. In my role as a liberal activist judge, I have long-term goals with respect to the configuration of the various fields I work in. For example, suppose that I can decide the lie-in case for the workers if I emphasize one aspect of the facts but in the process will reenforce a boundary in the field that I see as congealed injustice. My goal of law reform may be to collapse that boundary—say by establishing that there is no a priori distinction between worker rights in the m.o.p. and ownership rights—so that the concept of ownership cannot define a core of employer prerogative that must remain immune from worker meddling during a strike.

I may be willing to sacrifice something in the way of total convincingness in this particular lie-in case in order to disorder the field. Maybe I will emphasize the extent to which the holding of my lie-in case conflicts with holdings in the long string of picketing cases, so as to create a consciousness of discontinuity that will induce workers and their lawyers to expand the lie-in into a deep salient extending toward the core of the employer's property rights.

***

Just as I have multiple objectives in constructing my argument, I have multiple materials and a variety of different kinds of moves I can make with each element in the field. As I set about the task of argument, these possibilities generate a rough sense of an *economy of the field*. By this I mean that there are systems of trade-offs between desired objectives and between the different kinds of moves I can make with the materials available to me. For example, I just described a possible trade-off between making the most convincing possible argument against an injunction in this particular case and my long-term goal of destabilizing the rule that the workers can't interfere with the owner's use of the m.o.p. during a strike. Trade-offs at the level of goals are executed through decisions about which elements in the field to manipulate and how much. These are *strategies of execution* of a given field manipulation.

A strategy is a set of choices between, say, distinguishing a given case by restating its facts and distinguishing the same case by restating its holding. Or between distinguishing all picketing cases from the lie-in on the basis that the lie-in is civil disobedience, and distinguishing the lie-in from mass picketing on the ground that it's noncoercive, while emphasizing its similarity to individual picketing.

The notion is that there is a rough relationship of substitution between different manipulative moves. I have a choice between dramatically redrawing a boundary and dramatically restating the facts of cases so that they appear on the other side of an unmoved boundary. Moreover, choices between moves in one part of the field—or with respect to one element, say, precedents—influence and indeed constrain the choices that are available in other parts of the field.

I have been developing through the preceding discussion a particular strategy for arguing against an injunction of the lie-in. Some elements of the strategy are: the choice of a First Amendment general defense of the action; the choice not to attack state law civil and criminal penalties short of injunction; the choice to distinguish mass picketing cases as coercive rather than as "not speech," and so on. It seems obvious to me that there must be other possible strategies, though for the moment the only one that comes to mind is that of using the Wagner Anti-injunction Act.

One of the effects of adopting a strategy is a kind of tunnel vision: one is inside the strategy, sensitive to its internal economy, its history of trade-offs, attuned to developing it further but at least temporarily unable to imagine any other way to go.

But a strategy is also a *practical commitment*. Because it hangs together, the strategy imposes multiple constraints on how I respond to any new aspect of the case. It's not just a matter of logical consistency: the strategy has a tone and a style. For example, hard-nosed nip-it-in-the-bud rhetoric about mass picketing will be in tension with repression-just-makes-it-worse rhetoric in the lie-in, even though there is no logical problem. Moreover, a strategy is an investment of time. Once I've put in the work of developing its many interlocking parts, it will cost me plenty if I respond to a new question with an answer that would force revision of everything that's gone before.

***

In legal argument as in other production processes, practitioners have an intuitive idea of efficiency in the deployment of the available materials. Anyone who has done legal argument knows what it means to do it "neatly" or "elegantly," meaning at a minimum expenditure of . . . something. A part of this complex notion is that if you are mainly interested in who wins the particular case, you should persuade us that the lie-in is nonenjoinable with the least possible restatement of the facts and holdings of other cases, the least possible rearrangement of policy vectors, and the least possible movement of the boundary between free speech and interference with property. If, by contrast, you want to "make some law," you should do that, too, so as to accomplish the greatest possible movement of the boundary with the least possible disturbance of the other elements of the field.

A kind of quotient notion emerges. Success at the skill of legal argument can be measured by how little you disturb the field in order to persuasively achieve a given restructuring, whether it's a big restructuring through law making or a small one by making sure the good guys win this case. It's the ratio rather than the absolute amount of movement or of disturbance that counts.

††††

My uncertainty about whether I will succeed in making a convincing argument. Up to now I have presented the activity of argument as a kind of work, undertaken in a medium, with a purpose. The purpose was to convince the audience that, contrary to our initial impression, a decision denying an injunction in the lie-in is in accord with the law. I undertake this argumentative labor with a number of ulterior motives, such as avoiding reversal on appeal, fulfilling my obligation to the public, and so forth. I hope that by developing a convincing argument against the injunction I will avoid a loss of credibility as a judge (indeed, I hope to increase my credibility through a strong opinion).

There is an ideal scenario in which I am able to represent the legal field so that the law corresponds exactly to how-I-want-to-come-out. What was initially an impacted field with the lie-in unequivocally prohibited (an easy case) becomes, to the surprise of my public, an impacted field in which the lie-in is a case that is clearly permitted (or at least not enjoinable). I close a large obviousness gap by a field manipulation that is notably elegant—a dramatic change in outcome with surprisingly little disturbance of the elements of the field.

When my reasoning turns out this way, I feel euphoria, indeed a moment of dangerous omnipotence, delight at the plasticity of the natural/social field-medium, and narcissistic ecstasy at the favorable reaction of my public (not to speak of sober joy at all the good I will be able to do with my increased credibility). But before you put me down as an egotist, I want to add that some element of this pleasure is quite legitimate. I had an intuition about the justice of the situation—how-I-wanted-to-come-out in this case was in accord with an intuition that the law as I initially apprehend it was unfair to a particular group. If I have succeeded in making the law fairer to that group, my pleasure will be in part an altruistic emotion that seems to me no cause for shame: I will have helped out. Too bad it doesn't always turn out that way.

I will describe below some of the ways things don't turn out ideally. But first dwell for a bit on my uncertainty, as I begin my argument, about what will happen during its course. I have an initial estimate, a guess about how large the obviousness gap is, about the resources I will have to marshal in order to overcome it, and about the chances that I will fall short to one degree or another. But why can't I tell in advance the more or less precise dimensions of my problem, the means at my disposal, and the quality of my solution? I don't know *why*. But here is *how* I don't know in advance.

***

Projection. I may have misjudged the way the field will look to other people. I'm trying to persuade not only myself but also some hypothetical public. But I have to construct their way of seeing it on the basis of my own vision. It often happens that the field looks to me at first glance at least unrationalized and very possibly contradictory, while others see it as at least close to impacted. In other words, I know I have a bias, measured by the vision of others, toward seeing the field as undetermined, as unstructured, as open to all kinds of manipulation. Remember that my initial apprehension of the configuration of the field is a gestalt process, very firmly located in the eye of the beholder, yet dependent on stimuli that are external. Other people seem to me to see the field as always impacted, and adversely at that, until they have put an inordinate amount of pain into loosening it up.

Virtu. The skill of legal argument is to close a big obviousness gap with minimal disturbance of the elements of the field. It is the skill of combining the different moves—restating facts and holdings and rules and policies and stereotypes—in such a way as to achieve multiple goals at minimal cost.

There is no way to be sure you will be able to do this the next time you try. How much you can change the field through argument is a property of *yours*, that is, it is determined by your skill, as well as a property of the field, but the property of yours is unknowable in advance. There is such a thing as a good day and such a thing as a bad day. Internal psychic factors like adrenalin, panic, fatigue, but also internal factors that seem random, or psychoanalytically knowable after the fact, all impinge. Life is a gamble, here as everywhere else.

Hidden properties. My initial apprehension of the field doesn't tell me that much about it. An analogy is my initial apprehension of a body of water through which I am going to navigate a boat. I can see the surface of the water but usually not what lies beneath it. Yet lots and lots of signs on the surface indicate what is beneath. Some people are terrific at "reading" the surface; others not so good. But no matter how good you are at reading, there is lots that just isn't knowable in advance. In legal argument, I have no way of knowing with any precision what is contained in the hundreds of cases I haven't read that might be relevant to my problem, or in the thousands of other legal materials scattered across creation waiting to be put to use here.

***

The consequence of these different kinds of uncertainty is that I can never know in advance whether it will be possible to develop a legal argument for how-I-want-to-come-out that will persuade any part of my audience. Sometimes, the problems are obvious from the start. I never break through my initial panicked sense that this is a case the workers can't possibly win. It sometimes happens that my sense that they can't possibly win emerges slowly as I pursue what at first seemed like a promising course of argument.

Sometimes it's less dramatic than running up against the brick wall of the experienced objectivity of the rule. Maybe it turns out that I can make an argument that is "plausible" but won't actually convince many people; or that I can convince my audience that the law is a lot more favorable to the workers than they thought, but not so favorable as to prohibit an injunction of this particular illegal action. I may come up with a field-manipulation that strikes me as clumsy or just plain wrong—one that wouldn't convince me for a minute of anything—but which I think will appeal to this pubblic as highly plausible.

I experience the course of events as contingent. I don't have, and I know I don't have, a technique for predicting with a high degree of certainty what will happen to my first impression of conflict between the law and how-I-want-to-come-out. I can only find out the actual posture of the law by going through the work of argument. While it's happening, the situation seems to open toward a multiplicity of possible outcomes, none of which would violate any strongly held theoretical tenets.

***

When I've finished, I may be able to represent what happened as the necessary consequence of the "state of the law" when I began. But I won't really know why it turned out the way it did. In particular, if I fail to develop a plausible legal argument against an injunction of the lie-in, I won't know whether the reason was that I lacked skill in manipulating the field or that the "inherent properties of the field" were such that there was nothing I could have done. Did I screw up, or was I doomed from the start?

I am not in a condition of total ignorance about the failure. Next week another judge or lawyer may produce an argument against enjoining the lie-in that is highly plausible, and dissolves the felt objectivity of the rule, at least as applied to this case. If that happens, I will say to myself, with a lot of confidence, that my failure last week was a failure of skill rather than something preordained by the latent structure of the field. Or I may discover a whole series of earlier unsuccessful attempts to argue the case convincingly and conclude that my failure was not so shameful after all.

Knowledge of this kind is consistent with the sense of radical contingency I am asserting here. When someone else does what I couldn't do I learn that my failure was a failure of skill; and there is suggestive evidence in the failure of others that my failure was a consequence of the properties of the field. But it isn't possible to prove convincingly that there was just no way to make it fly. You can't prove it can't be done.

I have had many times the initial apprehension of the objective coverage of a case by a rule. I have many times started out thinking, "no way." And I have had many times the experience of apparent objectivity dissolving under the pressure of the work of legal argument. I have no theory that tells me in advance when that will happen and when it won't. I just have to try and see. When it doesn't work, sometimes someone else can do it. And sometimes I come back to the problem later and succeed where before I seemed to fail through no fault of my own. *From the inside*, what happens to my initial experience of the rule as objective is radically contingent.

I can imagine what it would be like to be able to tell in advance whether or not the rule's objective self-application will stand the test of time and effort. I can imagine having a technique, like the technique of a surveyor, say, that would tell me with great confidence that if I extend a bridge's span at a particular angle in a particular direction it will eventually hit the other side of the ravine at a predetermined spot. But that's just not the way it is in legal argument, at least for me. And in all honesty I have to say that people who think differently have, in my experience, turned out not to know what they are talking about.

***

[*The quantitative question*. It seems irresistible to ask at this point some such question as, "How often will the field be impacted or otherwise unbudgeable through legal argument?" If this is a question about the experience of a particular judge or group of judges, then it is at least intelligible. We could devise an empirical investigation into that experience, perhaps through interviews about past cases. We could even attempt an historical inquiry, based on more diffuse and suggestive data, into how the experience of judging has changed through time. Some of my own work is in this mode. I would venture the hypothesis that experiences of the manipulability of the field have become steadily more common in American history since 1776.

But I don't think the question is usually asked with this kind of answer in mind. It is a question about the *nature* of the field, about an objective property of the legal materials in use in a society at a particular moment in its history. That there can be no answer to the question posed in this way seems to me implicit in what I have already said.

The field is unknowable except through experience, and there is no "value neutral" perspective from which we can assess the "correctness" of a report of immovability. Whether judges have the experience may vary with how hard and how often they try to manipulate the field when it initially appears impacted. It may vary with the critical techniques available in their legal culture to dissolve the initial appearance of objectivity. It may change according to the quantity and the particular quality of the flow of cases they adjudicate, and according to whether they must habitually consider cases from many autonomous jurisdictions.

It is probably overdetermined by all of these things at once, and by many other aspects of judicial reality as well. One of these aspects is probably the extent to which judges learn in law school to anticipate that socially constructed systems of meaning, and particularly law fields, will be open to multiple interpretations. If we decided to "count" experiences of objectivity, we would have to decide what counts as an instance. But there just isn't any "natural" set of assumptions, any model of the "juge moyen sensuel" to use as a standard in determining what particular law fields are "really" like. The quantitative question is simply unanswerable.

What then can be said of the body of legal materials "itself," considered in isolation from the particular contexts within which particular judges experience it? Not much. We have no reason to believe that the field is *ever* unbudgeable otherwise than as a consequence of the failure of particular judges to find a way to budge it. But we cannot assert the contrary either: it *may* be true that a given field was experienced as immoveable because it *was* immovable, and that's all there was to it.]

†††

The normative power of the field. Throughout the discussion to this point, I have spoken as a judge who knows how he wants to come out and is vigorously trying to bring the law into accord. Sometimes I apprehend the law as plastic and cooperative, sometimes as resistant or even adamant, but me and my favored outcome are always the same. It is now time to critique the how-I-want-to-come-out pole of our duality. First, however, let's reify it with an acronym: HIWTCO.

HIWTCO is not a datum given externally, something that comes into the picture from outside. HIWTCO is *relative to the field.* This is true in the weak sense that I have decided HIWTCO in response to a question posed in terms of the existing social universe that includes law. I don't want these particular workers, living in our particular society under a particular set of legal rules to be enjoined from lying-in. I can't even formulate HIWTCO without referring to this legal context to give that result a meaning.

***

But HIWTCO is relative to the law field in a much more interesting and important way. I've been treating the law field as though it were a physical medium, clay or bricks, when what it is in fact is a set of declarations by other people (possibly including an earlier me) about how ethically serious people ought to respond to situations of conflict. As I manipulate the field, I am reading and rereading these declarations, apparently addressed to me, and trying to absorb their messages about what I ought to do. Indeed, before I ever heard of this case, I was already knowledgeable about hundreds of opinions by judges and lawyers and legislators about how to handle conflicts roughly analogous to this one.

As a preliminary matter this means that we are *not* dealing with a confrontation between "my gut feeling about the case" and the law, unless we understand my "gut" as an organ deeply conditioned by existence in our legalized universe. I simply don't have intuitions about social justice that are independent of my knowledge of what judges and legislators have done in the past about situations like the one before me. Other actors in the legal system have influenced, persuaded, outraged, puzzled, and instructed me, until I can never be sure in what sense an opinion I strongly hold is "really" mine rather than theirs. I don't even think such a question has an answer.

But the more important point is that my initial impression of conflict between the law and HIWTCO may disappear because HIWTCO changes, as well as because I manage to change the law.   Further, the very resistance of the law to change in the direction of HIWTCO may impel HIWTCO to change in the direction of the law. I may find myself persuaded by my study of the materials that my initial apprehension of HIWTCO was wrong. I may find that I now want to come out the way I initially perceived the law coming out. This is what I mean by the normative power of the field.

***

I try to move the law in the direction of HIWTCO, and to the extent the law is resistant, I find HIWTCO under pressure to move toward the law. But neither HIWTCO nor the law field are physical objects. If I experience "pressure" as I read through the legal materials, if the very fact of my initial apprehension that the law favors the employer exerts pressure, it is because the field is a message rather than a thing. It is a message of a kind I'm familiar with, a message of a kind I've dealt with before. Indeed, I am one of the authors of the message.

Precedents come to me as stories called fact situations that judges resolved in particular ways. What they did interests me in the way an earlier painter's work might interest a later painter. But interest is too weak a word. Especially when they are put together in patterns, precedents reveal possibilities that it would have taken me a long time to come up with, or that I might never have come up with at all. I look at six outcomes, and I say to myself, "Oh, they devised a strategy of banning all picketing, but allowing just about any kind of secondary boycott. Hmm. I wonder why. Oh, I get it, they had a rough distinction between physically confrontive and nonconfrontive tactics. Or maybe they were concerned with workers' freedom not to contract in the boycott cases, and worried about the implications for business combinations if they banned labor combinations."

Just studying these patterns may change my view because the study ill set my mind going in directions that it otherwise wouldn't have taken. But there is also the elemental normative power of any outcome reached by people I identify with. Because I think they were up to the same thing I am up to, *whatever* they came up with has in its favor my initial sense that it's probably what I would have come up with too.

I place my lie-in in the field among the various precedents, as more of an interference than, for example, individual picketing. Immediately, the analogical weight of the precedents pulls me toward wanting to come out as "the law" would have me come out. "Given what I know about what they were up to, by inference from the way they came out in those cases, I think they would have come out as follows in this case. If they would have come out that way, then I should come out that way too." This is the first order normative power of the field.

***

The second order normative power of the field comes from the fact that all these judges (and others) have left us more than just a record of fact-situations and outcomes. They wrote opinions full of overtly normative explanations of outcomes obtainable by reference to rules and policies. There are hundreds of particular statements about *why* we should come out in a particular way under particular circumstances, sometimes very particularly defined circumstances, but sometimes how we should come out in large classes of fact situations quite abstractly defined (e.g., the workers can't interfere with the owner's use of the m.o.p. during a strike).

Now the practice of recording outcomes for fact-situations, along with messages about why those outcomes are ethically and politically and legally correct, is no great mystery to me, since I do it all the time. I know first-hand what it means to try to indicate for the future how some future dispute should be resolved, and I have a good idea of what it is like to succeed. The person you've tried to influence says to you something like, "I had this problem, and I wondered what you would have to say about it, so I looked up your decision in the X case, where you gave your theory of what disruptive tactics labor should be permitted to use during a strike, and I found it very helpful. In fact, you might say what I did in the Y case was try to apply your theory. Of course, you may think I botched it completely."

I believe that it is possible to record messages about how to deal with future situations which will be intelligible to actors in the future, that it is possible for those actors to set out to "follow" the messages or directions, and that sometimes they do actually do something that is well described as "following the message." I sometimes feel that the people who set down all these messages that together make up the field had in mind something like the case before me and intended to instruct me to resolve it in a particular way. They are telling me not only that this is the rule they would apply, and here's how to apply it, but also that it is the *right* rule, that it is the way I ought to come out.

The second order normative power of the field comes from the fact that I identify with these ought-speakers. I respect them. I honor them. When they speak, I listen. I even tremble if I think I am going against their collective wisdom. They are members of the same community working on the same problems. They are *old*; they are *many*. They are steeped in a tradition of serious ethical inquiry whose power I have felt on countless occasions, a tradition that seems to me a partially valid great accomplishment of the often cruddy civilization of which I am a tiny part.

***

It is no good telling me that my reverence for the messages of these ancients is "irrational." It's not a question of rationality. When I read their words, it is as though I myself were talking. (Of course, when I'm reading my own earlier opinions, it *is* me in an earlier incarnation who's talking.) I am not able to treat their ethical pronouncements about how to decide cases like this one as though they were a set of randomly generated possible answers to a math problem. In that case, I test each answer "coldly," so to speak, without any investment at all in its correctness or incorrectness. But as I sit reading the messages of the ancients about cases like this one (or even, I may sometimes feel with horror, about this very case neatly anticipated), I can't remain neutral. I want them to agree with me. And I want to agree with them. I feel I *ought* to agree with them.

In this state of mind, I may find myself adopting the voice of the ancients, knowing what they are talking about when they extol the sacredness of owner's rights and feeling that what they are saying accurately expresses something that I think too. I set out to manipulate the field so that the law would favor the lie-in, but in order to do that I have to enter into the discourse of law. In the process, I have to undergo its intimate prestige. I discover that I know what they were talking about because I myself am capable of thinking just what they thought. At that point, the normative force of the field is just one side in an interior discussion between my divided selves about who really should win this case anyway.

***

Who is the field? The messages that constitute the field are on one level just a set of verbal formulae. On another, they are speech I imaginatively impute to the "ancients." On a third level, the resistance of the field is another name for my ambivalence about whether or not I should enjoin the lie-in. To the question "who is the field," the answer has ultimately to be that the field is me, resisting myself.

***

Conversion. It is possible that I will resolve my ambivalence by adopting the field as I initially apprehended it as a correct ethical statement as well as a correct perception of what the law is. In other words, I will find that I no longer want to come out against an injunction, but rather that my intuition of social justice is now that an injunction ought to issue, just as I initially thought the law required. But this is only one of many possible modes of interaction and ultimate equilibration of the law and HIWTCO. Here are some of the other possibilities.

I move the law and the law moves me. The outcome may be a modification of HIWTCO that brings it into accord with a new view of the field, one substantially different from my initial apprehension. Such a compromise might involve conceding that these workers went too far, though the law will not enjoin all lie-ins. Or it might involve not enjoining these workers but conceding that my initial pro lie-in position went much too far, so the workers better not take the next step they appear to be contemplating.

A compromise, like restatement of the law to correspond to HIWTCO, or conversion of HIWTCO to correspond to the law, has the peculiarity of *resolving* the initial perceived conflict. But this may not happen. The law may move me, and I may move the law, but the two may end up still in conflict, albeit less in conflict. It's also possible that the normative pull of the field will leave me confused or ambivalent, where I had earlier been quite clear about HIWTCO. Or the reverse might happen: a vague sense of HIWTCO ends up clarified through the imagined dialogue with the ancients. As always, from inside the practice of legal argument the outcome is radically indeterminate.

***

How it sometimes doesn't work. What I have just described might be called the counter-ideal to the scenario in which I manipulate the law-field to correspond to HIWTCO. Here, the law field manipulates HIWTCO, stimulating first ambivalence and then perhaps outright conversion to the other side. But the field is no more necessarily normatively powerful than I am necessarily manipulatively powerful.

To have normative power, the field must present itself as objectively favoring an outcome. Since normative power resides in the voice of the ancients, which is also just the voice of my ambivalent other half, I must be able to "read" the field in order to feel its power. The field must present itself as at least somewhat impacted, rather than as unrationalized, collapsed, contradictory, or loopified. What I mean by those configurations is just that I can't integrate the cacophony of ancient voices into a single voice with a message. The disordered fields may influence me in the sense that after exposure to them HIWTCO changes in one direction or another. But they are not exercising normative power, by which I mean the power to persuade me to a view you are trying to persuade me to.

***

But even supposing I have a sense of how the law comes out which I can contrast with HIWTCO, it does not follow that the field will exercise normative power. The message I apprehend as "the law" is at several removes from a conviction of my own about what I want to do. It is a message I have to decode, rather than a thought immediately accessible to me inside my own mind (without making too much of the mediate/immediate distinction). There will always be an element of mystery as to whose message it is, whether I have properly understood it, whether it is "applicable" here at all. Until I "make it my own" and begin to argue the side of the law against HIWTCO, the message hovers between the life I can give it and the status of dead formula.

The message is from the past, from people who put it together in the past (including my past self, if I was involved). Even if I can understand it and enter into it, it is yesterday's newspaper, queer-looking because so much has happened that it doesn't and couldn't take into account. The message that is the field was not developed by a clairvoyant as a message to the future; it is the product of judges deciding cases and writing opinions to deal with their problems, thought with an eye toward the shape of the field for future cases. The way we constructed the field dates it and thereby deprives it of the normative bite it would have if it spoke in the voice of someone looking over my shoulder as I study the facts of the lie-in.

***

The message was composed by other people, though I may have played a small part myself. I conceded that just about any message I can understand will have some normative power, if it is a normative message. That I can understand it at all means that there was another person out there thinking about this problem, with that degree of community with me that mere personhood alone is enough to establish. From that communal identification, however limited it may be, comes the power to move me just by saying "you ought to do thus and so." But there are others and there are others.

I will interepret the field as a message from particular others of a particular historical moment, and, as I particularize, I may find myself less and less convinced. The architects of the law of labor relations applicable here were turn-of-the-century conservative state court judges and New Deal reformers.

I have mixed feelings about both groups and about the legal structures of which these by-ways of labor law form a part. At least, my own evaluation of the message and its senders seems to have a great effect on how and how strongly I feel it. Moreover, there are other pulls beside the normative one that I know are there but whose individual contributions to the force field around me are indistinguishable, at least as I initially experience them.

***

Influences on the relation between HIWTCO and the law other than the normative power of the field. I have been describing how I ultimately want to come out as the product of an interaction between my evolving apprehension of the law field and my intuition of social justice. In my experience, this interaction is partly a series of events that is happening to me. It is also partly a series of events that I am making happen through my interpretive construction of the field, which powerfully affects its normative power. But it turns out that my initial intuition of justice under the circumstances is open to other influences than only the normative power of the field.

I consult my "gut" against the background of my situation as a judge. In that situation there are definite advantages and disadvantages to a rapprochement between HIWTCO and the law as it now appears to me. I have interests in agreeing with the law and interests in maintaining my disagreement. I worry that these are powerfully modifying what the outcome would have been in their absence—what it would have been had I dealt only with an intuition of justice and a law field capable of exercising normative power.

I also worry about their status: are these influences that should be resisted or that should be treated as legitimately normative in the same way the voice of the ancients is legitimately normative?

***

The principal influences against merging HIWTCO into whatever I think the law may be—the principal sources of non-normative resistance to the normative power of the field—are the psychological cost of conversion and terror of the disaster of false conversion. On the other side, the principal non-normative influence pushing HIWTCO in the direction of what I see as the law is fear that I won't be able to develop a plausible legal argument for my position, with attendant unpleasant consequences no matter what course of action I undertake.

I am going to discuss these various cost and benefits as influences on HIWTCO—that is, as constitutive of my experienced conviction about the proper outcome. This is odd. It might seem more appropriate to discuss costs and benefits as elements in my decision about what to do, when and if it appears there is an irreconcilable difference between the law and HIWTCO. Indeed, all these costs and benefits of divergence will again become relevant at the point when "I" have to choose a course of conduct. But I want to take them up here as elements constituting HIWTCO because I believe that they impinge first at this unconscious level—eliminating or exacerbating conflict, rather than setting the terms of its resolution.

These costs and benefits also influence my apprehension of the law. It is important, now that we are in the phase of relativizing HIWTCO, not to lose

247

track of the extent to which I constitute the field, both through my interpretation of its configuration and through the work of legal argument. The gestalt process of interpretation and the work of argument go on under the influence of my fear that, if I disagree with the law, I will be forced into an untenable corner of civil disobedience or craven surrender, or undergo false conversion. My choice to see the field as, say, contradictory rather than as impacted in an unfavorable way will be in part a product of my interest in seeing it that way, given my fear of a sharp conflict with HIWTCO.

***

The costs of conversion. I don't want to be converted to the view that I should enjoin the lie-in. My initial opinion that there should be no injunction is in character: as soon as it occurs to me I hold it dear as an emanation of my true self. Like a collection of knick-knacks, my opinions, along with my past, my work, my family, are a store of treasures I don't want to give up.

My social identity, moreover, is bound up with the ritual of agreeing, publicly, with others about issues like this. Other people see me as a person who holds particular kinds of views, and they like me or dislike me partly on that basis (however lamentable such superficiality on their part may be). I'm dependent on their good opinion. If I change my views, some will regard me as a turncoat, as weak-willed or stupid, a fluff-head or an opportunist.

Those who tend to favor management aren't likely to form favorable opinions that will make up for what I lose by conversion, since they won't know whether to trust me. Still worse, perhaps, is my sense that those who hold the view I might convert to—that the injunction should issue—are a bunch I'd hate, as of now, to join. When I think of myself as one of them, I shrink from my imagined turncoat self.

Legal argument, in which I take up and work with the message of the field, and maybe end up espousing it against my current correct and virtuous position, looks like working in a nuclear plant at the risk of radiation sickness. It looks like fooling around with heroin: you think you have it under control, and one morning you wake up already addicted. You've gone from one (good) state to another (bad) state without ever having a moment of choice about it.

I think this fear of being converted without choice, somehow forced from one's own view into another, is deep in almost everyone involved with law. It leads progressive-minded people to ask things like, "Will law school warp my mind?" Or to assert that they think something is legally right but totally morally wrong. Or that law is made-up noise that reinforces things as they are, so it's not worth the trouble to argue within its (even though it's manipulable) when the facts cry out for direct moral response.

Even if in contemplation I admit that the conversion might be to a "better view," I still don't want it to happen. Just because it's a better view doesn't mean that moving to it is painless. I don't want to be converted, but I do believe in the possibility of progress in my own views. I believe things now that I used to think were stupid, and I think I'm better off for having been through the process of enlightenment, however painful. So my fear of conversion is qualified by my longing for truth and for change and interesting conflict.

***

I may still be deeply influenced against the normative power of the law field by the fear of *false conversion*. Maybe what looks like a very compelling legal, moral, utilitarian, political argument against HIWTCO has a flaw a mile wide. Maybe the company's lawyers even know it does, and maybe I'll be suckered into believing it because I lack constructive as well as critical argumentative ability. (I might be great most of the time but have screwed up here, despite my previous record.) If this happens, I will experience a momentary pleasure of conversion (with attendant mild pains), followed by a subsequent devastating awakening to my own mistake, then humiliation if I change my mind back, and shame if I find myself unable to admit my error and forced to persist in pretending my new wrong position is right.

My sense that I'd better hold on tight to HIWTCO, insulate it against the power of the field, is strengthened by my knowledge that it's not only normative power that's in play here. There is something pure and cutely idealistic about listening to the ancients because one thinks what they have to say may be of value in one's search for the ethically correct result. But suppose that I'm drawn into a false conversion not by earnest openness to enlightenment but by my opportunistic interest in avoiding controversy? I resist the normative power of the field in part because I distrust my own construction of the field.

***

Reasons for changing HIWTCO to correspond to the law (other than the normative power of the field). It's not that a divergence between HIWTCO (no injunction) and the obvious legal solution ("of course the employer can get an injunction") has to produce trouble for me. Where I am out of line I may be able to persuade people that I have the better legal case; indeed, the divergence may be the occasion for me to increase my fund of credibility. But if there is a divergence, and I persist in my position rather than letting myself be persuaded that I was wrong and "the law" was right, I have to be ready for the possibility that I will be unable to produce a plausible legal argument for my position. If this happens, I will be in a corner. I may not be able to avoid a painful controversy.

Fear of this controversy will influence how I see both HIWTCO and the field, and influence them in such an intrinsic, automatic way that I won't be able to be "outside" the influence and neutralize it. Sometimes, in spite of the most intense vigilance on my part, fear has eroded my opposition to an outcome until without ever being aware of it I have "gone over to the other side."

***

The devil's compact. I want to discriminate between more and less crass, reasons for abandoning HIWTCO. The less crass is fear of finding myself in violation of the devil's compact: that I will either defend my position as plausibly in accord with law, or change it, or withdraw from the case.

I entered the devil's compact when I took my oath of office as a judge. The compact is between me and an imagined public, but it is also a rough way of describing what I think will be the practice of various real people I know, or who can communicate with me through newspapers, letters, popular magazines, law reviews, or bar journals.

Many people believe there is a sharp distinction between action according to law and lawless action. If it appears to them that I have no plausible legal argument for how I want to come out but, nonetheless persist rather than changing my view or withdrawing from the case, they will say I have violated the elementary meaning of the agreement under which I direct the use of state force.

There are people whose good opinion is important to me whose belief in the devil's compact is such that they will condemn me for violating it even if they think the outcome I favor is the just one. They see it as an aspect of the judge's job that she is supposed to bring about outcomes that are unjust when the law is unjust. If you don't like the job, you shouldn't take it. Once you take it, you either do it or refuse to do it (withdraw from the case).

I was aware when I took office that if I were to publicly reject the compact, I probably would not be allowed to become a judge. When I took the job without raising the issues I am about to raise here, I allowed some people to think that I agreed to the terms of the compact. The fact that many liberals and some conservatives understand it in a way that modifies it so much as to make it almost meaningless is irrelevant to my point. People who believe in the compact were necessary, I imagine, for me to become a judge, and it is with them that I entered the compact.

On the other hand, I think the popular conception of law is internally contradictory, embracing the notions that (a) "the law is the law," a determinate result-producing technique, and (b) the law is intrinsically an affair of justice, so that it is always "for the best," and lacking any theory at all of how conflicts between (a) and (b) are to be resolved. Lay people tend to be surprised when the law turns out to be plain unjust, and surprised also when it turns out to be indeterminate or patently determined by "external" factors such as controversial ethical or political views.

Furthermore, the devil's compact presupposes a view of the relation between the law and HIWTCO that initiates know is false. The manipulability of the field is much greater than the lay public realizes, even if we concede that there is no intelligible way to answer the quantitative question, "How manipulable?" And the point at which the field "sticks," presenting itself as an objective message there's no way to evade, is much more arbitrary than even the legal profession realizes.

This point, at which I am supposed to refuse to exercise my power in favor of the workers, is indeed one of perceived objectivity of the field. But I cannot affirm that it is a point at which the law was "just not on their side," because the problem may be that I was not sufficiently skillful, or didn't have enough time, to find their argument. Even if we *are* at a point of objective field adversity (I can't prove such points don't exist), it is not a point that is part of an intelligible pattern.

If the field constrains the judge only in this arbitrary manner, it doesn't make sense to claim that constraint is the workers' quid pro quo for accepting an unjust outcome in any particular case. The devil's compact, if I try to impute it to the litigants rather than to myself as the judge, is vitiated by a mistake as to fundamental terms, a mistake of which I had prior knowledge.

Suppose that I persist in HIWTCO even though it differs from the law as I perceive it after exhausting my resources of legal argument against it. I will then face a choice such that, whatever I do, I will feel terrible. I therefore have a strong motive to somehow reconceive HIWTCO so that it accords with the law and thereby prevent my painful dilemma from ever reaching the level of consciousness.

***

What determines the outcome of the interaction between the field and HIWTCO? From inside the practice of legal argument, the only possible answer to this question is that *I* determine the outcome. As I work to manipulate the law field in the direction of HIWTCO, I have a strong feeling that I am acting in the world, remaking it to fit my intentions. If I manage to restate the law so that it plausibly requires my preferred outcome, I will see this as my accomplishment.

As I develop the case against an injunction of the lie-in, I am restating the law about lie-ins. At some point, I may "get the message" of that law and find myself developing it in my own mind as an argument against the position I have been taking, against HIWTCO. Then at some point I may find that "I am changing my mind" and then that "I have changed my mind." In that case, I will feel that it was my own decision to bring HIWTCO into accord with the law.

It is a little hard to figure out what it means to have an "I" inside me who is capable of changing "my mind" that is both the same as that "I" and different enough so that "I" can determine it rather than just *being* it. But it is my experience that HIWTCO is undetermined right up to the moment when something has happened that moots the question. I can always change my mind about HIWTCO, and I have on occasion found myself changing my mind very late in the game.

But this way of putting it, though true to occasional experience, overstates my freedom by making it sound as though I were omnipotent. Remember that even in the first moment of confronting the problem I want to come out one way or another in the context of my life-project as a judge and of the law as I already know it. These contexts are givens that have shaped me before I begin to reshape them. I decide already positioned somewhere, having no choice about that somewhere, able to move only by work that takes time.

As soon as I set to work on the particular law field, I undergo its influence, an influence that is partly normative and partly the product of my fear of finding HIWTCO ultimately in conflict with the law. On the other side are all my good reasons for sticking to my initial conviction, reasons whose influence I can never fully neutralize.

As I work on the field, following a strategy that has its own internal economy and takes time to execute, the field and HIWTCO change and influence one another and change and influence one another some more. If I am lucky, this process appears to have an unforced inner tendency toward convergence, so that eventually the law and HIWTCO are the same, one way or another. But whether and how this consequence occurs is very much a function of aspects of the situation over which I have little control.

First, there is my initial apprehension of the law field, which I just "get" as impacted, contradictory, or whatever. Then there is my strategy, which takes me down a path I can't know in advance. Although I choose it, I don't control the consequences of my choice, since the field has hidden properties, and I have particular biases and only what skill I can muster for the occasion. Then there is the time factor, which means that sooner or later, if convergence does not occur, I will have to stop working on the field, unsure whether its current state is an irremediable aspect of its "true nature" or an artifact of my blundering.

I am now repositioned, so to speak. It's true that I can still change my mind about HIWTCO and that I am free to make one of a number of choices about how to play things, if HIWTCO and the law as I have reconstructed it are in conflict. But it is also true that I will make these choices constrained by where I started and by all my decisions about how to develop the field. What I have done is irreversible in the sense that I can't just "go back" to the way I used to see things. And I've run out of time to *work* the field backward (or forward). I'm stuck where I am and have to decide from here.

***

What to do in case of conflict between the law and HIWTCO. My answer to this question is unhelpful: it depends on the circumstances.

1. Go along with the law. In spite of my conviction that social justice requires me to deny the injunction, I issue it, along with an opinion denouncing the law and urging reform. I make the very convincing legal argument for an injunction that comes to mind in an impacted field such as this one. A crucial question is how I explain my obedience, that is, my willingness to act as the instrument of injustice.

2. Withdraw from the case. I neither issue the injunction nor deny it. I withdraw, explaining that I think the law is unjust and that my feelings against it make it inappropriate for me to preside and repugnant to me to be involved in administering this regime. A crucial question is how I justify begging off while insisting that someone else do the dirty work, if I intend to stick around for the more attractive assignments.

3. Decide against the injunction on the basis of what the law should be. I deny the injunction, honestly explaining my inability to come up with a plausible legal argument against it. Though I may be reversed on appeal (and quickly at that), I exercise what power I have to further HIWTCO. This may be decisive if the litigants are evenly matched out in the world. Accept what consequences my bureaucratic superiors and my colleagues and peers decide to inflict (highly indeterminate). I appeal to them to accept my outcome as the correct one in this and future cases, thereby changing the law. A crucial question is who authorized me to take the law into my own hands.

4. Decide against the injunction on the basis of an implausible legal argument. Maybe it will look good to others, even though I think it stinks; I can never be sure in advance. Maybe it will turn out in my own hindsight to be a better argument than I thought. But what about the dishonesty of bad faith argument?

5. Decide against the injunction on the basis of fact findings I know to be false. As the trial judge, I decide to pretend to believe an account of the facts of the lie-in that I know to be false, and deny the injunction on that basis. This is obviously an extreme measure.

Afterword

The rule of law. I can imagine hypothetical situations in which each of these courses of action in the face of conflict would be appropriate. I don't think any of them can be either endorsed or excluded a priori. But I am aware that it is often argued that the meaning of the rule of law is obedience to the devil's compact, and that the only permissible course of action for a judge confronting a conflict between the law and how he wants to come out is *always* to follow the law.

Given the practice of judging as I have just presented it, and especially given the apparently arbitrary character of eruptions of perceived objectivity in the course of manipulation, I find this argument unconvincing. But that is for another time. From within the perspective of my imagined judge, the story is over when she reaches the moment of decision. Whether she should *always* follow the law in cases of conflict is a question that we answer as best we can through reflection and argument about our political system, about the actual laws in force within that system, and about particular cases.

***

Social theory. The judge has to decide what to do from a position. That position depends on the givens of the judge's life-project, on the body of legal materials and the facts of the case as grasped at the beginning of the process, and on the work the judge has done on those materials and facts. In deciding, the judge risks but may also gain credibility, depending on the obviousness gap between the common perception of "the law" and HIWTCO.

On this basis, we might hypothesize that the probability that judge will move the law so as to achieve any given result is smaller in proportion as the work and the credibility risk involved are greater, and that the total quantity and quality of work available from the judicial labor force limit the total amount of legal movement we can expect in any direction.

For this hypothesis to be useful in studying the role of law in a given social formation, we would have to study both the legal materials and the culture of judges in order to determine, by an essentially imaginative rather than positive procedure, how they are likely to construct given fields, and how much work will appear to them to be involved in different kinds of field manipulations. We would also need to know how often divergences between their initial apprehension of the law and how-they-want to-come-out will motivate them to work hard at manipulation and risk credibility. On the basis of such knowledge, we might speak meaningfully of law as a general constraint on the exercise of state power in the society in question.

Note that without this "internal" information about how judges perceive law fields the notion of law as a constraint on state power is essentially meaningless. We have to know "constrained in what position from moving what distance" before we know anything at all. Note also that this hypothesis is merely "inertial." It says nothing about "inherent tendencies" of the legal materials to develop in particular directions. The total available labor time may be deployed in any way at all, but that it is limited means that movement is constrained.

Whether this description of judging could form the basis of a theory of "inherent tendencies" or directions of development of legal materials is a very difficult question. On the one hand, the judge experiences the normative power of the field as directed toward a particular outcome, and we might develop a social psychology of what this direction will be for a given body of materials. On the other, the field moves only because the judge moves it, and this he does in accord with how-he-wants to come-out, under the constraint of having to work at manipulation and to risk credibility.

A sufficiently complex social psychology might allow us to describe meaningfully the way in which a judiciary with a particular set of political commitments will interact with fields it experiences as having normative power in particular directions. But the notion that the normative power of law fields is directed toward particular patterns of substantive outcomes seems to me tenuous, at least at the moment.

Of course, most social theorists simply assume that "law" *is* one thing or another and can be treated as a kind of block contributing to a larger edifice. To the extent the experience of law is as I have described it, this approach makes little sense.

***

Jurisprudence. Imagine you are a professor of jurisprudence, in possession of professional knowledge of the nature of law. Suppose you approach me in my dark cloud of ignorance of whether or not I will be able to overcome the gap between the law and how-I-want-to-come-out. You argue that legal rules, like the rule that the workers can't interfere with the owner's use of the m.o.p. during a strike, *never* determine the outcome of a case. And since the legal rules are the only things that stand in the way of my coming out the way I want to come out, I have no problem. Legal theory indicates that I am home free, or at least that I ought to be home free. If I'm not, it's because I've failed at legal argument, not because of any properties inherent to the field I'm trying to manipulate.

You can expect me, in my role of humble law artificer, to ask you how you can be so sure. You might respond that since Wittgenstein we know that no rule can determine the scope of its own application. It follows more or less directly (unless you insist on a detour through semiotics, structuralism, and deconstruction) that the mere statement, "the workers can't interfere with the owner's use of the m.o.p. during a strike," tells us *nothing* about whether or not they can lie in to block substitute workers from driving the buses out of the garage onto the great American highway. There is a whole world of interpretation, inherently subjective and indeed perhaps even inherently arbitrary (from the standpoint of my humble artificer's idea of reason), that we have to go through to get from the rule to "the facts." And "of course" the facts aren't any more "just there" than the rule.

My experience with legal argument doesn't allow me to meet your jurisprudential position on its own ground. What I can say as a legal arguer is that sometimes I come up against the rule as a felt objectivity, and can't

254

budge it. This doesn't mean that I agree with it or that I think anyone would necessarily condemn me if I disregarded or changed it. All it means is that I say to myself, "Here's the rule that applies to this case;" "we all know that this is the rule;" and "here's how it applies;" and "Everyone is going to apply it that way."

I am perfectly aware that the rule is not a physical object and that deciding how to apply it involves a social, hence in some sense a subjective process. But there is this procedure I've performed many times in my mind, in many different contexts, of applying a rule to a fact-situation. I've many times had discussions with others in which we formulated rules together, seemed to agree about their terms, then engaged in a series of applications, and found that once we'd agreed on the formula we came up with the same answer to the question: how does the rule apply *here?*

I believe that it is possible to communicate with another person so that we both have roughly the same rule in mind. I believe that it is possible to communicate with another so we both have roughly the same fact-situation in mind. And I believe that when we both come up with the same answer to the question, "How does the rule apply to the facts?" it is sometimes meaningful to describe what has happened as "we applied the rule to the facts."

In the situation I most fear as a liberal law-reforming judge when I have studied the various rules that I think might apply to the lie-in, I conclude that everyone will agree that the employer has a right to an injunction under the rules as we all understand them to be as of now, and that to change this particular rule would be unconstitutional. This conviction might be based on an "identical" case decided by the Supreme Court yesterday, or it might be based on a rather long and abstract chain of reasoning by analogy. But it might happen. And if it happened I would face some pretty tough choices about what to do in the case.

As I said, this declaration of faith in the possibility of communication and in the at least occasional intelligibility of the procedure of rule application doesn't meet your fancy argument on its own ground. I have no idea *why* this stuff happens. As I see it, your fancy argument is that I can't show an "objective basis" or a rationale or an explanation of rule application that will prove that any particular application was "correct." Indeed, the notion of correctness, at least as we usually use the word in math or science or logic just isn't applicable.

From my position inside the practice of legal argument, I can't say anything one way or another about this fancy argument. I have no way of knowing, from inside the practice, why it is that sometimes the field gives way but sometimes refuses to budge at all. Maybe when it seems unbudgeable it's just because I didn't find the catch that releases the secret panel. Maybe my sense that we communicated the rule to one another and then each "applied" it and that that's where the result "came from" is a false sense, a hopeful or sentimental or, in this lie-in case, a paranoid interpretation of the random fact that we agreed on the outcome, rather than a reflection of a common experience. From inside the practice of argument, I just don't know.

***

I will be very irritated indeed if you turn around on me now and reveal that you were just using the fancy argument to make me concede the truth of some form of positivism or objectivism about law, or at least legal rules. It was a good trick, but I claim to have evaded it. I have been saying all along that legal argument is the process of creating the field of law through re-statement rather than rule application. Rule application is something that does happen, but I *never* experience it as something that *has* to happen. It is an outcome as contingent and arbitrary from the point of view of jurisprudence as that in which the field is gloriously manipulable.

I dealt here with a case in which my initial apprehension was that the law was clear against the workers, but I was able to undermine the perceived objectivity of the rule (at least in a preliminary way). That was an example among many possible of how an initial apprehension of ruledness can dissolve. Sometimes I approach the field in an agnostic frame of mind, and just can't figure out what the rule is supposed to be; sometimes I can't decide whether the facts are such that the outcome specified by the rule is triggered or not. Sometimes it seems there are several possible answers to the question and I don't have any feeling about which is correct. Sometimes I'm initially quite sure what the rule is and how to apply it but a conversation ·with another person who has reached a different set of conclusions leaves me feeling neither that I was "right" nor that she was "right," but rather that the rule was in fact hopelessly ambiguous or internally contradictory all along.

If you tell me that there is always a right answer to a legal problem, I will answer with these cases in which my experience was that the law was inde-terminate, or that I gave it its determinate shape as a matter of my free ethical or political choice. It is true that when we are unselfconsciously applying rules together, we have an unselfconscious experience of social objectivity. We know what is going to happen next by mentally applying the rule as others will, and then they apply the rule and it comes out the way we thought it would. But this is not in fact objectivity, and it is *always* vulner-able to different kinds of disruption—intentional and accidental—that suddenly disappoint our expectations of consensus and make people ques-tion their own sanity and that of others. This vulnerability of the field, its plasticity, its instability, are just as essential to it as we experience it as its sporadic quality of resistance.

The rule may at any given moment appear objective; but at the next moment it may appear manipulable. It is not, *as I apprehend it from within the practice of legal argument*, essentially one thing or the other.

If this is what it is like to ask the nature of law from within the practice of legal argument, then the answer to the question must come from outside that practice. All over the United States and indeed all over the world there are professors of jurisprudence who think they possess professional knowledge of the nature of law. Where are they getting it from? For my own part, I think their answers to questions like those I have been addressing are just made up out of whole cloth. Show me your ground before you pretend to be moving the earth.

LEGAL FORMALISM
AND INSTRUMENTALISM—
A PATHOLOGICAL STUDY

David Lyons†

Holmes and those who followed in his wake believed they were rejecting a rigid and impoverished conception of the law (often called "formalism") which had, in their view, adversely affected judicial practice. They spawned a collection of doctrines that Professor Summers dubs "pragmatic instrumentalism"[1]—fittingly so-called both because they viewed the law as an eminently practical instrument and because they were so strongly influenced by the philosophical pragmatists William James and John Dewey.

This essay has two parts. The first and longer part identifies and examines the basic doctrines of formalism and instrumentalism. The arguments offered by instrumentalists against formalism suggest that both schools generally agree on two fundamental points. First, the law is rooted in authoritative sources, such as legislative and judicial decisions (a "source-based" view of law). Second, legal judgments that are justifiable on the basis of existing law can be displayed as the conclusions of valid deductive syllogisms the major premises of which are tied very tightly to the authoritative texts (a "formalistic model" for legal justifications). The difference between the schools concerns the question of whether law is complete and univocal. Formalists are understood to argue that existing law provides a sufficient basis for deciding all cases that arise. This belief, in combination with the formalistic model for legal justifications, leads the formalists to conclude that the authoritative texts are logically sufficient to decide all cases. In denying this, instrumentalists appear to have the better of the argument. I shall go further, however, to argue that the formalistic model for legal justifications, which is shared by formalists and instrumentalists alike, is subject to serious question.

The second part of this essay examines criticisms by instrumentalists of "formalistic" judicial practice. I argue that these criticisms appear ill-founded and that the doctrines of formalism provide little, if

---

† Professor of Law and Philosophy, Cornell University. A.B. 1960, Brooklyn College; M.A., Ph. D. 1963, Harvard University.
[1] Summers, *Pragmatic-Instrumentalism in Twentieth Century American Legal Thought—A Synthesis and Critique of Our Dominant General Theory About Law and Its Use*, 66 CORNELL L. REV. 861 (1981). Professor Summers's Article is assumed here as a guide to these doctrines.

any, basis for the sort of practice to which instrumentalists have objected.

I

FORMALISM AND INSTRUMENTALISM COMPARED

A. *Legal Formalism*

Legal formalism is difficult to define because, so far as I can tell, no one ever developed and defended a systematic body of doctrines that would answer to that name. We have no clear notion of what underlying philosophical ideas might motivate its conception of the law. It is sometimes tempting to suppose that there has never been any such thing as a formalistic theory of law, but only pregnant pronouncements by some legal writers which lack any coherence or theoretical foundation, combined with judicial practices that are thought (soundly or unsoundly) to embody the attitudes of those writers. Although the instrumentalists were distressed by a variety of judicial and juristic errors, their reactions must be our principal guide to formalism.

Part of what is meant by formalism is this: The law provides sufficient basis for deciding any case that arises. There are no "gaps" within the law, and there is but one sound legal decision for each case. The law is complete and univocal. According to Summers, formalists hold that law is "traceable to an authoritative source."[2] This leads one to inquire, however, about what counts as an authoritative source. One must assume that authoritative sources include legislative and judicial decisions or authoritative records of them. But what else might they comprise?

The question is crucial because some of those who have been called formalists have also been understood to argue that law is determined not just by such mundane human actions and decisions, but also by what is sometimes called "natural law." Natural law has never been laid down as law in any ordinary way, so far as our ordinary legal records show. One jurist who suggests this view is William Blackstone, who, although sometimes called a formalist,[3] wrote in his *Commentaries* that "no human laws are of any validity, if contrary to [the law of nature that is dictated by God]; and such of

---

[2] *Id.* at 867 n.4, item 6.
[3] *See* Hart, *Positivism and the Separation of Law and Morals*, 71 HARV. L. REV. 593, 610 (1958).

them as are valid derive all their force and all their authority, mediately or immediately, from this original."[4]

Blackstone's position is usually understood as follows: Nothing counts as law unless it derives from, or at least accords with, God's dictates. If we assume that Blackstone was a formalist and that formalists believe law is complete, then we must understand him as arguing that human law is not only rectified by divine command but also completed by it. In other words, some of our law comes only from *extra*ordinary authoritative sources. This last point is important because it suggests the shape formalism might have to take in order to secure the formalists' claim that law is complete, without surrendering any of their other fundamental claims. Because formalism is assumed to tie law very closely to authoritative sources, the class of sources must be expanded into the supernatural realm in order to supply sufficient law to close all the gaps left by authoritative, mundane sources.

The idea of a "natural law that is dictated by God" functions in theories like Blackstone's as a specific conception of a more general concept which an atheist, for example, would interpret differently: that of "moral law." Blackstone thus suggested the more general view (which exposed him to biting comments from Bentham and others) that nothing counts as law unless it is morally acceptable, and there is as much law as morality requires. Law is not only thought to have moral sources but is regarded as morally infallible as well. The instrumentalists, however, knew better than that.

This reading of Blackstone stresses a kind of authority at the base of law and, hence, might be credited as formalism. Despite the possibility of such an interpretation, I think we should follow Summers, who I take it conceives of a "source-based" conception of law in narrower and more mundane terms, excluding the supernatural. This renders formalism more plausible and more deserving of serious critical attention. Straw men impede the progress of legal theory.

This understanding of formalism is compatible with Blackstone's remarks on another, more faithful reading. Blackstone can be understood to say not that morally objectionable law does not exist, but rather that there is no automatic moral obligation to obey it. "Natural law" is relevant to determine when ordinary human law "binds in conscience." This is not an uncommon view among natural lawyers. It was developed most clearly by Aquinas,[5] who argued that human

---

[4] 1 W. BLACKSTONE, COMMENTARIES ON THE LAWS OF ENGLAND 41 (8th ed. 1783).
[5] 2 T. AQUINAS, BASIC WRITINGS OF SAINT THOMAS AQUINAS 794-95 (A.C. Pegis ed. 1945).

laws are either just or unjust, and that one has an obligation to obey just laws, but not all unjust laws. Human laws are unjust when they fail to serve the common good, when they exceed the lawmaker's authority, when they distribute burdens unfairly, or when they show disrespect for God. One is morally bound to obey such an unjust law only when circumstances demand it, in order to prevent scandal or disturbance.

If we understand Blackstone (who was not so clear) along the lines suggested by Aquinas, then Blackstone may be interpreted as saying that "natural law" provides a standard for determining when human law merits our obedience. Under this sympathetic interpretation, Blackstone could be credited with an ordinary source-based view of law. Thus, he would qualify as a formalist—provided, of course, that he also espoused certain other doctrines, to which we now turn.

Our sketch of formalism amounts so far to this: First, the law is rooted in authoritative sources, like legislative and judicial decisions; second, it is complete and univocal. But what makes it "formalistic"? That label turns on a third doctrine—namely, that law decides cases in a logically "mechanical" manner. In other words, sound legal decisions can be justified as the conclusions of valid deductive syllogisms. Because law is believed to be complete and univocal, all cases that arise can in principle be decided in this way. This is the *formalistic model* for legal justifications. These three doctrines capture the essence of formalism when it is viewed as a type of legal theory.[6] They do not, however, explain what may be called the "formalistic method" in judicial *practice*, which will be discussed below.

B. *Instrumentalism*

Ironically, it is more difficult to pin down the doctrines of instrumentalism, because this school of legal thought is determined by the writings of a variety of jurists. They do not always agree and, indeed, are not always self-consistent. Consider, for example, the instrumentalists' attitudes towards what Summers calls "valid law."[7] One finds three views in unhappy aggregation. Summers claims that instrumentalists share with formalists a source-based conception of law, but that they also embrace the predictive theory. Some instrumentalists, however—the radical fringe on the edge of legal realism—are "rule skeptics." The rule skeptics claim that real law consists only of

---

[6] Moreover, they seem to cover all of Summers's twelve points. *See* Summers, *supra* note 1, at 867 n.4.

[7] *Id.* at 896.

past judicial decisions, which are understood as limited to their specific holdings, without any further binding implications. No two of these views are compatible.

What is a "source-based" view of law? Presumably, it means that courts are bound by certain authoritative texts or decisions. If the relevant texts or decisions are entirely neglected, judicial decisions or their justifications are that much in error. Authoritative sources establish legal limits or constraints upon judicial decisions. This is not to say they are sufficient to determine a uniquely correct decision in each case or that they must be applied syllogistically. Instead, they must be given their due weight, however that is to be understood.

Rule skepticism clearly does not square with a source-based view of law, for it implies not just that judges are liable to decide cases as they please, but that they are legally free to do so. Furthermore, the idea that laws are "predictions" of what courts will probably decide sits well with neither of these other instrumentalist notions of law. The prediction theory is advanced as a conception of law that goes beyond past decisions. It is meant to perform a task that rule skepticism avoids, but it cannot possibly do that job. A prediction of judicial decisions is not the sort of thing that can bind a court; it cannot serve as a normative standard with which a judge might or might not comply. If a decision accords with a prediction, it may confirm the prediction, but it does not demonstrate that the decision is legally sound. The fact that a decision falsifies a prediction is in no way indicative of judicial error.

Radical rule skepticism can be understood as a way of trying to cope with a puzzling legal phenomenon. If a court acts when existing law seems to provide insufficient guidance, its capacity to help shape the law may not be puzzling. A court's departure from the literal reading of a statute or from a binding precedent, however, may be puzzling if its decision effectively establishes new legal doctrine. It may seem as if one cannot account for the efficacy of such decisions except by holding that *all* law actually is made by courts. Courts themselves cannot be seen as laying down *general* standards, however, for this would only introduce the same problem all over again. Hence, the logical extension of this argument is rule skepticism, which claims that there never is any determinate law aside from specific holdings in past cases.

The question is whether it is more reasonable to conclude that (1) there are legally binding standards from which courts can sometimes effectively depart, even if they do so erroneously, or (2) there are no legally binding standards, which excludes the possibility of judicial error. The following observations may be useful. To acknowledge the possibility of judicial error is to assume neither that law provides a unique answer to every legal question nor that when law provides one, it does so with logical conclusiveness, excluding all argument to the contrary. Judicial error may be the failure to follow the *best* legal arguments or the *strongest* legal reasons, as is usually assumed when judicial decisions are criticized on one legal ground or another. Furthermore, one who believes that courts can err is not committed to the view that such cases have no effect on the law. One might believe that judicial decisions pronouncing new legal doctrines do not always succeed in entrenching those doctrines into the law. Such entrenchment occurs when subsequent courts follow the decision. A novel decision, however, is not always followed—not even by the same court. If a court fails to follow its own previous decision, then, according to the radical realist, it has nothing to explain. The court cannot be regarded as changing either the law or its interpretation of the law, because that would imply that there is law beyond specific holdings. The opposing view maintains that a court might fail to follow its own previous decision either by mistake or because it believes it made an error that it wishes to rectify. This seems to fit our usual ways of thinking when we are not spinning theories about the law, and it is incumbent on legal theories to account for any divergence from these legal phenomena. It may also be admitted, however, that it is incumbent on the opposing theorist to explain how and when judicial mistakes become entrenched within the law.

Despite the excesses of its skepticism, the theory of the radical realists represents a clearer and more consistent overall legal philosophy than its instrumentalist competitors. It can be understood as suggesting that a judicial decision is justified when, but only when, it serves (perhaps to the maximum degree possible) the interests of those who will be affected by the decision. Although many other instrumentalists endorse this normative theory, their views are inconsistent with it, because they believe that past legislative and judicial decisions serve as constraints upon the decisions that can be justified in a particular case. Thus, these nonradical instrumentalists are committed both to the view that courts are bound by past legislative and judicial decisions and that they are not so bound. Their official normative theory does not conform to their understanding that courts are bound by other authoritative decisions. One cannot consistently maintain that those past decisions must have some influence on the decision in the present case—that they provide authoritative standards to be followed—while arguing that the case at hand must be decided solely by consideration of the likely consequences.

To see what is wrong with the normative theory of radical realism, one must ask what would make it right. Two conditions must be satisfied. First, there must be no basis for supposing that past legislative and judicial decisions are properly regarded as binding. Second, the proper basis for judicial decisions must be simple, direct utilitarianism. Hence, we must ask why others assume that past legislative and judicial decisions properly guide judicial decisions.

One nonutilitarian explanation is that judges have morally committed themselves to being bound by such decisions and to deciding cases in light of whatever law there is. They have accepted this public trust, as everyone understands. This is not necessarily an absolute obligation; one can find examples in which deciding a case according to the law conflicts with a judge's more salient nonjudicial obligations. The judicial obligation of fidelity to law is limited in other ways as well. It is conditional upon being voluntarily undertaken; a judge coerced into serving on the bench under a brutally corrupt regime is, if bound at all, not bound in the way that judges are ordinarily bound by the public trust they willingly assume. Furthermore, there may be limits on the moral scope of such obligations. Just as it makes perfectly good sense to hold that soldiers in wartime are not legally or morally bound by certain orders—such as those clearly and openly intended to have the soldiers commit atrocities—so it makes perfectly good sense to hold that some law may be so morally corrupt as to lie outside the limits of a judge's obligation of fidelity to law.

For such reasons, we might infer that the law must satisfy some moral minimum if judges are to be regarded as bound by past legislative and judicial decisions. The procedures must satisfy minimal conditions of fairness, the outcomes must satisfy minimal constraints of justice, or both. Without such assumptions, the idea that judges are "bound" to follow the law or that judges are expected to render "justifiable" decisions is unintelligible. We merely play misleading and possibly pernicious games with serious and important ideas like obligation and justification unless we suppose that they are linked significantly to factors such as those we have just listed. The alternative is a mindless sort of authority-worship—the notion that mere "legal" authority (in the narrowest sense), which is compatible with the worst sorts of abominations the world has suffered under law, is somehow capable of creating a real "obligation" and is capable of "justifying" what it does to innocent victims. Legal positivists sometimes seem to employ such a desiccated conception of "legal" authority, obligation, right, and justification, though they truly have no need for it. The upshot is confusion about the relations between law and morals. Just as we need not suppose that law and morals are completely divorced in order to recognize that law is morally fallible, we need not suppose that law automatically possesses any genuine authority in order to analyze its structure, systematize its restrictions, or appreciate that it is something to contend with in practice.

It is reasonable to suppose that the more moderate instrumentalists make such relevant assumptions about the law they see themselves as bound by and that such considerations explain why past legislative and judicial decisions bind courts and limit the scope of their decision-making power. As Summers observes,[8] nonradical instrumentalists seem to accept a source-based view of law, as do all instrumentalist judges in practice, whatever they may say when writing about the law.

C. *Moderate Instrumentalism and Formalism Compared*

How do these moderate instrumentalists diverge from formalism? Surprisingly, not by very much. They too have a source-based view of law, which distinguishes them from the radical realists. They reject, however, the "formalistic" notion that law is complete and univocal. Unlike the radical realists, the moderate instrumentalists believe that there are laws between the gaps; unlike the formalists, they believe that there are gaps between the laws.

This does not address the third aspect of formalism—the formalistic model for legal justifications. It is tempting to suppose that instrumentalists reject this doctrine as well; after all, they attribute much less significance to the role of formal logic in the law than do the formalists. It is worth asking, however, what is meant by the instrumentalists' complaints about the formalists' excessive use of formal logic. One factor that complicates matters is that these issues are sometimes framed in terms of the logical character of "judicial reasoning." But "judicial reasoning" is ambiguous; it can refer to the logical relations between premises and conclusions, or it can refer to the thought processes of judges. The former is something logicians study, while the latter is a field for psychologists. Although psychologists concerned with the logical character of thought processes require training in logic, logicians need no training in psychology. Claims about the role, or lack thereof, of formal logic in judicial reasoning are correspondingly ambiguous. One who has a formalistic conception of logic, or of legal justifications in particular, assumes that all good arguments are deductive. One who has a formalistic conception of thought processes, or of judicial thinking in particular, assumes that

---

[8] *Id.* at 900.

our thoughts run along deductive lines. These ideas are quite independent. One might deny, for example, that judges' thought processes always proceed along straight deductive paths before they arrive at a tentative decision, yet believe that sound judicial decisions can be presented as the conclusions of valid deductive syllogisms with true legal propositions as the major premises and factual assumptions as the minor premises. Thus, an instrumentalist who maintains that formalists have exaggerated the role of logic in adjudication might simply mean that judicial *thoughts* do not run along syllogistic lines.

This point is innocent enough, but it is often misunderstood. It is sometimes suggested, for example, that if judicial thought processes are not syllogistic, then later presenting the corresponding judicial opinion in syllogistic form is hypocritical and involves some form of rationalization (in the pejorative sense). The recognition that judicial thought is not always shaped by syllogistic reasoning may lead to the conclusion that formal logic has no real role in "judicial reasoning." But this would be mistaken. Entertaining hypotheses in a variety of ways is compatible with the justification by rigorous argument of those that survive systematic criticism, and this combination is indispensable as well as routine in all spheres of inquiry and all respectable disciplines. Indeed, it is sometimes a virtue for judicial thought to be relatively unfettered, but the justified decision must take account of all relevant considerations, verify the premises adopted, and include only sound reasoning. If opinions generally did that, we should have no instrumentalist complaints of excess logic.

Another factor that complicates the instrumentalists' attitudes towards formal logic is their emphasis on factual considerations in judicial decisions. Their innocent and innocuous point is that law applies to cases only in relation to factual assumptions that are made. In other words, law's actual implications for cases depend on the facts, while its de facto applications depend on presumed facts. The determination of the facts, however, cannot be solely a matter of deductive reasoning. The basis for the latter claim is the familiar point that factual statements about what has happened or is likely to happen in the natural world are always established by evidence that is logically insufficient to entail those statements. This does not reflect badly on logic, but is merely a symptom of two phenomena. First, empirical conclusions logically outstrip the evidence that confirms them. Second, the confirmation of empirical conclusions is therefore necessarily *non*deductive. This is hardly central to legal theory, and formalists are without reason to deny it. Moreover, it concerns the preliminary arguments needed to establish factual premises used in the justifications of judicial decisions. It should be emphasized that formalists cannot be understood to deny that factual considerations play a decisive role in legal decisions. No one in his right mind believes that law dictates decisions in particular cases independently of the facts; one cannot even classify a case without making factual assumptions about what goes on in the world. Formalists assume that facts need to be established in order to justify judicial decisions. Their idea that legal justifications are deductive concerns the arguments for judicial conclusions only *after* factual premises have been established.

Even after consideration of these elementary points, something clearly remains of the instrumentalists' concern about formalism's dependence on logic. They seem to argue that formalists make a pretense of deducing decisions from the law when the law does not, in fact, support those deductions. Alternatively, formalists are deluded by their theory into thinking that they can rely solely on law, and they stretch the law in order to do so. But concepts are not so precise and legal norms are not so wide as to cover every case that does arise. According to instrumentalists, there are gaps within the law that formalists do not recognize.

This is not only a complaint about "formalistic" adjudication, but also a reflection of the differences in legal theory previously discussed. It is partly definitive of formalism that it regards law as complete and univocal, and partly definitive of instrumentalism that it regards the law as, at best, incomplete. This brings us back to the differences between formalism and instrumentalism, which first led us into this thicket of logical theory. Now that we have emerged from the undergrowth, what can we say about the third aspect of formalistic theory? Do instrumentalists reject the formalistic model of legal justification, as their complaints about formalism's excess use of logic might lead one to suspect?

The instrumentalists might be interpreted to maintain that deductive, syllogistic argument is fine, as far as it goes. Unfortunately, it won't take us far enough to reach the conclusion that formalists desire—namely, that law is complete and univocal. The law, instrumentalists would say, simply does not extend so far. If we are faithful to the texts provided by the authoritative sources, we find that they are vague and sometimes conflicting, subject to alternative interpretations, and therefore incapable of supporting logically adequate, conclusive arguments for judicial decisions in all cases.

There is some reason to interpret instrumentalist criticism in this way, even though it commits the instrumentalists to questionable philosophical assumptions. One reason is that these assumptions are quite commonly made, especially within "tough-minded" legal theory, such as instrumentalists claim to possess. This interpretation also makes moderate instrumentalism parallel to legal positivism, just as philosophical pragmatism, which seems to underlie instrumentalism, is parallel to the traditional empiricism that seems to underlie positivism.

The general picture of these two theories we then get may be stated as follows. Moderate instrumentalists and positivists alike embrace a source-based conception of the law as well as a formalistic model for legal justification; partly *because* of this combination, they reject the formalistic notion that law is complete and univocal. Instrumentalists, like positivists, emphasize that because the interpretation of authoritative legal texts and their application to cases are often controversial, reasonable arguments are often possible on both sides of a legal issue. Since there are no hard and fast rules for adjudicating such disputes, positivists conclude that law in such cases is indeterminate—not yet fully formed, needing judicial legislation. Instrumentalists most likely have a similar view of the law. They assume that law is determinate on an issue at a given time only if its identification and application are, roughly speaking, mechanical. Hence, law is gappy and incomplete, and judicial discretion must be exercised and law created in hard cases. Thus, rather than rejecting the formalistic model of legal justification, they merely insist on its limitations.

This sort of view is so widely accepted today that it is important to understand its presuppositions and limitations. The instrumentalists make the decisive assumption that law is not determinate if it is controversial, for law is thought to be gappy and indeterminate only when reasonable legal arguments are possible on both sides of a legal question. That occurs, however, just when the content of law is controversial—when competent lawyers can reasonably disagree about it. It relates to the formalistic model of legal justification in the following way: When law is controversial in the sense that reasonable legal arguments are possible on both sides of a point of law, then the law *cannot* be identified and interpreted mechanically by means of deductive, syllogistic arguments. Considerations must be weighed on both sides of the issue, and there is no rule fixing how that must be done. Hence, deductive logic cannot govern the justificatory arguments that are then made.

This reasoning exposes a more fundamental assumption of formalism, instrumentalism, and positivism: Nondeductive reasoning is incapable of adequately establishing any conclusion. Perhaps the assumption should instead be articulated as follows. If, in principle, it is impossible to prove a proposition by presenting it as the conclusion of a sound deductive argument—that is, where true premises absolutely entail the conclusion—then there is no such fact as the one ostensibly represented by the proposition. Taken as a general claim, this is either an idle philosophical prejudice or else represents very radical doubt about the possibility of knowledge. For, as we have already observed, the most respectable conclusions of the "hardest" of the sciences always logically outstrip the evidence and other considerations used to establish them. Such conclusions are never decisively proven in a logically water-tight manner. Therefore, when we claim to know what they assert, it is conceivable that we are mistaken. The view under consideration takes this to imply that in such cases there is no natural fact corresponding to the scientific conclusion. It is not that we are liable to be mistaken, but that there is nothing to be mistaken about.

This reading of instrumentalism is supported by the similarity between its underlying philosophical empiricism and the philosophical views that appear to underlie legal positivism. Empiricism can be understood to claim that what we can know about the world must be discovered by the use of our ordinary senses. But both British Empiricism, which is the dominant influence behind legal positivism, and American philosophical pragmatism generally assume a particular version of this theory that regards what goes on in the world as ultimately "reducible" to "hard" observable facts by means of rigorous entailments or deductive logical relations. Applied to physics, for example, this version of empiricism has led some philosophers to maintain that there "are" no sub-atomic particles such as electrons, at least not in the full-blooded sense in which there "are" particle accelerators such as synchrotrons. This is so because only the latter are perceived "directly." Therefore, sub-atomic particles have no more substance than the physical evidence for them, such as configurations on a photographic plate taken from a cloud chamber.

This version of empiricism is compatible with a source-based conception of law combined with a formalistic model for legal justifications. The "hard data" are the authoritative texts and their literal implications. The "four corners" of such texts, stretched only to include their most literal implications, represent the limits of real, determinate law. All the rest is mere "theory."

D. Does Law Go Beyond the Texts?

If the preceding discussion is accurate, formalism and instrumentalism share two out of three central doctrines, and we can account for the instrumentalists' contention that formalism stretches the law to create implications where no clear implications can honestly be found. Given their mutual assumptions, the instrumentalists seem to have the superior position. If we conceive of law as so thoroughly determined by authoritative texts, as both schools of legal thought appear to do, it seems implausible to suppose that law is complete and univocal, for the texts are not collectively univocal, and are often unclear.

We need not rest on the above assumptions, however; instead, we need to ask why we should conceive of law in such a way. Perhaps it is inescapable. After all, the texts are taken as authoritative, and the texts admittedly have somewhat uncertain implications. But we can move too quickly here. We cannot derive such significant conclusions about *law* from such innocent facts about *texts* unless we make certain assumptions about what law is. In other words, we can jump from the verbal limits of authoritative texts (such as statutes and records of judicial decisions) to the gappiness of law *only if we assume that law is fundamentally a linguistic entity,* that law is exhausted by the formulations of such texts and their literal implications.

This assumption may be questioned once it is identified. After all, the law is not just a collection of words. Why must we limit ourselves to thinking about the substantive content of the law in terms of its authoritative words and their literal implications? The obvious explanation is that law is a human artifact, fashioned with words like those in the authoritative texts. The words are not the beginning and end of the law—law is a social institution, too—but they represent its normative content. Whatever content the law has, it has because of what we have put into it.

It is important to recognize that this theory represents not just a source-based conception of the law, but one that is bound by the formalistic model for legal justification. Its general appeal rests to some extent on the tacit assumption that nondeductive arguments are somehow suspect, so that we cannot derive law from authoritative texts using anything but literal readings and strict implications. This opinion hardly comports with our most respected intellectual practices outside the law, but doubt about the theory need not rest entirely on such analogies.

The question we must face is whether it is reasonable to maintain that law goes beyond the authoritative texts and their strictly deduced implications. The following argument suggests that this position is tenable.[9] The point is not to establish an alternative conception of the law, but rather to show that alternative conceptions are feasible and that the doctrines we have found embedded in both formalism and instrumentalism are themselves just theories about the law which are neither self-evident nor self-certifying, but require substantial justification.

---

[9] This argument is adapted from R. Dworkin, Taking Rights Seriously 131-37 (1978).

One need not unqualifiedly endorse the following argument to recognize its point. It involves what are sometimes called "vague standards" in the law. The due process clause is an example. Calling it a "vague standard" suggests that the due process clause is mainly an empty vessel waiting to be filled with doctrines supplied by covertly legislative activities of courts. This is the view I wish to challenge. In so doing, I shall ignore the complication that decisions based on the clause today must take into account past judicial treatments of it. The point of ignoring such authoritative interpretations is that it provides the central reading around which other factors must be understood to turn. For example, it may be customary to read the due process clause in terms of the "intentions" of the Framers. This would have to be acknowledged in any final decision about how to interpret and apply the clause today. That particular approach, however, is to be considered here *only* as a direct reading of the clause itself. The due process clause is most naturally read to prohibit the government from doing certain things to a person in the absence of fair procedures. Once this is agreed, we can focus on the requirement of fair procedures.

Why should we think the due process clause vague? Perhaps because it does not tell us what is fair. The criteria of fairness are not to be found within the four corners of the text, nor can they be inferred from it. We must go beyond the text to determine what the clause prohibits, if indeed it can be understood to prohibit anything— if it is determinate enough to do that.

One thing is certain. The clause concerns fairness, not something else, such as economic efficiency. That it requires fair procedures is all but explicit—what else could "due process" mean? Only a wild theory could support the claim that the clause requires procedures to be economically efficient. Hence, the clause must have some meaning—at least enough to tell us what it is about, thus excluding some other possibilities.

Let us pursue the analogy with economic efficiency. Imagine a law that requires some activity to be "economically efficient" without defining economic efficiency. How could a court apply it? First, the text would have to be understood as assuming that there is such a thing as economic efficiency; that it makes sense to suppose that certain activities are economically efficient and that some are not; that some judgments about efficiency are true and others are false; and that criteria of efficiency are determinable in principle, at least in specific contexts. A court applying such a requirement must therefore identify appropriate criteria of economic efficiency. It will soon discover that there are alternative conceptions of efficiency; it must weigh the relative merits of those alternative conceptions as well as their relevance to the specific context at hand. It must then proceed on the assumption that in each context, some conception is most appropriate. But the court might find this assumption indefensible. It might find that there is absolutely no reason to prefer one specific conception of efficiency to another in the particular context. If so, assuming the two equally tenable conceptions are not practically equivalent, the court must make an arbitrary selection.

Suppose, however, that did not happen. Suppose the court concludes that some specific conception of economic efficiency is the most appropriate, at least for the specific context in question. It must then attach that conception to the law, providing the law with more content than it had originally, but not so that it would be legislating freely. That is, if there really are reasons for preferring one conception of economic efficiency to others in a given context, the assumption of the law in question would be true; if the court correctly identifies and applies that conception, it is simply carrying out its legal mandate. It would be faithful to the text, but it would not be limited to the four corners of the text and its literal implications.

To reach a preferred interpretation, the court must consider economic theory. If economic theory provides a correct answer to the court's question, it cannot be arrived at mechanically. Therefore, the court's justificatory argument for its interpretation cannot be mechanical. This leads us to the main point of the argument: A judicial decision need not be limited to the words of the authoritative texts and their literal implications in order to be based firmly on those sources.

Moreover, a court could make a mistake in such a case. If, in a given case, a single best criterion of economic efficiency exists, but the court instead adopts another, its reading of the law would be mistaken, for it would have incorrectly applied the economic efficiency requirement. There is, however, nothing problematic in the idea that even the highest court within a jurisdiction can make a legal mistake (or so we must agree if we do not swallow the most extreme rule skepticism of the radical realists).

Let us return to the due process clause example. Just as a court in the preceding hypothetical would have to defend a particular conception of economic efficiency, a court applying the due process clause must defend a particular conception of fairness suitable to the case in order to ensure fidelity to the clear meaning of the text at hand. No such conception, no principle of fairness, is implicit in the clause. But it does not follow that a court that goes beyond the four corners of the text and its literal implications is not doing precisely what the Constitution requires—no more, and no less.

If the due process clause requires that certain procedures be fair, courts cannot adhere to it if there is no such thing as a fair procedure.

It makes no sense to require that procedures be fair unless one believes that such procedures exist—that is a presupposition of the clause. The only plausible reading of the clause, judging from the text, is that this is what the Framers must have assumed. Anyone who takes seriously the task of applying that part of the law must share this assumption.

One could not follow the law literally if its presupposition were false—that is, if there were no such thing as a fair procedure. We are in no position, however, to assume that there is no such thing as a fair procedure. We seem quite capable of distinguishing clearly fair procedures from clearly unfair procedures. It may be difficult to articulate fully the criteria by which we make such judgments, but much has been written on the subject, and one could begin there for help.

Some theorists profess to believe that there is really no such thing as a fair procedure because moral judgments are inherently, inescapably, unavoidably, and irremediably arbitrary. It is not just that people can easily make mistakes in this area, or that people tend to "rationalize" their prejudices in the pejorative sense. Instead, the very distinction between sound and unsound moral judgments is untenable. Such thought represents the most radical kind of moral skepticism.

Some instrumentalists have flirted with this notion, though it hardly comports with their own notions of what judges ought or ought not to do, which they present as defensible. In any event, radical moral skepticism seems an unsuitable attitude for a judge, because it requires both cynicism and hypocrisy. It is questionable what significance a moral skeptic can attach to an undertaking of fidelity to law or to the idea that a judge must justify his judgments. Of course, most if not all of those who regard themselves as "tough-minded" moral skeptics limit this to abstract theoretical pronouncements, which are dissociated from their reasoned use of moral concepts in other contexts and their acceptance of responsibilities.

If we do not approach the due process clause encumbered by the burdens of moral skepticism, how must we understand it? The general approach is clear: One must defend a particular conception of fairness and apply it. One might get it right and then be faithful to the law, not only in aspiration but also in decision. Alternatively, a court might get it wrong because it has committed a significant error of moral theory. Assuming that there is a right answer to the moral question, there is a correct reading of the clause. This reading is faithful to the text even though it is not limited by the four corners of the document and the literal implications of the text. Because such an answer could not be arrived at by deducing it from fixed premises, a court's justificatory argument for its interpretation of the clause cannot be mechanical.

This method of understanding the due process clause and other "vague standards" may be contrasted with two others. One is to assume that the clause must be understood in terms of certain examples of fair and unfair procedures that the Framers accepted or would have been prepared to accept upon reflection. Another is to interpret it in terms of current popular conceptions of fair procedures. There may, of course, be good reasons for adopting such approaches to understanding legal provisions. One must recognize, however, that if the due process clause literally requires fair procedures, then these approaches are theory-laden in very significant ways. Adopting either approach involves either a departure from the text or a theory of what fair procedures are or how they can be determined.

Take the latter case. The due process clause requires that certain procedures be fair. To apply it by asking what procedures the Framers would have considered "fair" requires the assumption that fair procedures *are* whatever the Framers believed them to be. To apply it by asking what procedures would popularly be credited as fair amounts to the assumption that fair procedures *are* whatever popular opinion suggests they are. Such criteria of fairness are implausible. The due process clause assumes that there is such a thing as fairness; this is not the same as some particular individuals' conception of fairness, which might be mistaken. We therefore cannot use one of these approaches to such a clause without a powerful theory to support it.

The original approach suggested, which involves the application of an appropriate conception of justice, does not avoid theory. It proposes that courts must engage in theoretical deliberations in order to be faithful to the text and carry out its legal mandate. If that is right, then a source-based conception of the law does not commit one to the formalistic model of legal justification; it is, in fact, incompatible with that narrow view of legal reasoning. It follows that the formalistic model, which seems fundamental to both formalism and instrumentalism, is untenable. What the law has to say about a legal matter is not limited to the literal reading of and strict deductions from authoritative texts. Only a radical moral skeptic can avoid this conclusion, but such a skeptic would have no clear understanding of judicial responsibilities.

Finally, consider the issue of completeness—the one that seems most directly to divide this pair of legal theories. We have no clear idea why formalism regards law as complete, but we do have some idea about instrumentalism's opposite conclusion. So far as instrumentalism regards the law as gappy because it interprets legal sources by means of a formalistic model, its conclusion is unwarranted. If law is incomplete, it is not simply because we must go beyond the texts. For the law sometimes mandates, in effect, that we go beyond the text not only to find the facts, but also to unveil those further considerations that help make up the law on a particular subject.

II

INSTRUMENTALISM AND JUDICIAL PRACTICE

One of the preoccupations of instrumentalists has been judicial practice. According to Summers, "their critique of formalist legal method may be their most important single achievement."[10] I shall conclude with a brief review of this critique and its relations to theoretical doctrines like those we have discussed.

Summers mentions several charges of judicial malpractice that instrumentalists lay at the door of formalists. They abuse logic, overgeneralize case law, artificially distinguish cases, introduce legal fictions instead of facing up to the need for judicial legislation, and fail to decide cases in light of community policy.[11] These charges have varying connections with general theory—connections that the instrumentalists appear to have exaggerated. Several, but not all, seem related to differences of doctrine. If we are correct that formalists believe the law provides a complete decision procedure, while instrumentalists deny it, then this disagreement underlies some of the charges of judicial malpractice. For instrumentalists believe there is sometimes insufficient legal basis for decisions when judges they regard as formalists purport to find such bases in the law. Thus, it is natural to expect the instrumentalists' criticism that formalistic judges overgeneralize case law and otherwise overextend the law by introducing fictions and ignoring community policy.

The latter point reminds us that instrumentalists embrace a particular normative theory, which they do not always balance successfully against their acknowledgement of existing law. If instrumentalists believe that decisions unsupported by existing law should be made in light of community policy, then they have two bases for disagreement with judges who decide cases differently. First, others may believe that the law provides sufficient basis for deciding cases that instrumentalists believe require judicial legislation. Second, they may believe that grounds other than community policy legitimate decisions that the law does not adequately determine. Instrumentalists, with a naive utilitarian outlook, seem to assume that no other normative theory is rationally tenable—all other views reflect either a disguised

---

[10] Summers, *supra* note 1, at 909.
[11] *Id.* at 910-13.

consideration of the consequences of decisions on the interests of those affected, or some superstitious form of valuation. Such an attitude, however, leads inexorably to the extreme realism of the radical fringe of instrumentalism, because it leaves no room for the notion that past legislative and judicial decisions demand some measure of respect even if their guidance is not optimific. To insist on maximum promotion of satisfactions and on deference to past authoritative decisions only when that deference could reasonably be expected to have such optimific consequences is to deny that courts are bound in the slightest degree by statutes or precedent. One cannot have it both ways; one must either go with the radical realists or drop such naive utilitarianism. But if naive utilitarianism is surrendered, the charge of failure to decide cases in light of community policy is limited to cases in which the law provides insufficient basis for decision. "Community policy" thus becomes shorthand for "whatever standards are properly applied in such a case." Hence, the issue between formalists and instrumentalists reduces once again to that of completeness or incompleteness in the law. The question thus becomes whether and when the law provides no basis for decision, and what standards then properly apply.

Instrumentalistic criticism of "formalist legal method" sometimes does reflect theoretical disagreement, but not always very clearly. For example, consider, in light of Summers's imaginary example,[12] the criticism that formalistic judges "abuse logic." The majority of a court holds that a child cannot collect damages from negligent individuals as compensation for injuries received during its period in utero. The court's argument is elegant: (1) this child had no rights that could have been violated, because (2) the capacity to possess legal rights presupposes the capacity to have legal duties, and (3) an unborn child cannot have legal duties. The instrumentalist judge argues in dissent that (4) an unborn child can have legal rights without legal duties, because (5) "we as judges can alter these concepts as we desire to serve useful goals";[13] since there was a negligently caused injury, room can and must be made within the law for compensation through civil liability.

Before we examine the specific charge that logic is "abused" by the majority's decision, we should note that if we take these arguments at face value, they *agree* that the law speaks clearly about this particular case. The majority supports its decision with an argument that the dissenter does not dispute. Instead, *the dissenter advocates chang-*

---

[12] *Id.* at 910-11.
[13] *Id.* at 910.

ing the law. There is no need to "alter" the relevant legal concepts unless they lead to a decision that the dissenter believes should not be reached. Therefore, at least on the surface, the disagreement concerns whether to change the law by judicial legislation. Before addressing this issue, let us analyze these opinions more closely.

The majority claims that capacity for legal rights presupposes capacity for legal duties, which it characterizes as a kind of "symmetry." This is supposed to represent a "formalistic" attitude, because formalists are supposed to prize such aesthetic values and read the law as embodying them.[14] That sounds silly; perhaps we can make it seem a bit more plausible.

First, formalists are supposed to regard the law as complete. If, as we have argued, this means going beyond the authoritative texts and their literal implications, it must involve elaboration of the law on the basis of some theory of how to understand it. Constraints that any such theory would have to respect include precisely those that Summers mentions, namely "coherence, harmony, and consistency with existing law."[15] However law is read beyond the four corners of the texts, as an elementary matter of theory-construction it must respect those texts and develop systematically. In other words, these values are not vices but virtues once it is agreed that law extends beyond the four corners of the texts. Unfortunately, this way of working out the implications of the law does not adapt itself to the formalistic model for legal justifications. Formal logic alone will not generate such theory-based extensions of the texts. Therefore, logic must be abused if it is made to serve the illusion that the texts can be so stretched.

Second, the alleged symmetry exemplified in the majority's second claim is a familiar extension of a real symmetry embedded in normative systems. It is often asserted that rights and duties (or obligations) are "correlative," and there are cases in which this appears undeniable.[16] If Alex owes Basil five dollars, then (1) Basil has a right to payment of five dollars from or on behalf of Alex and (2) Alex has a duty (is under an obligation) to pay Basil five dollars. The corresponding right and duty are two sides of a single normative relation; they stand or fall together. Thus, it is plausible to claim that some pairs of rights and duties are logical or conceptual correlatives, and it would not be misleading to refer to this as a kind of "symmetry" in the law.

---

[14] *Id.*
[15] *Id.* at 867 n.4, item 5.
[16] This idea is discussed in Lyons, *The Correlativity of Rights and Duties,* 4 Nous 45 (1970).

But not all alleged relations between rights and duties are like that. It may be contended, for example, that Alex himself cannot have rights without duties, in the sense that one has no valid claim against others unless one respects others' claims on one. Alex cannot legitimately claim any rights unless he lives up to his obligations and responsibilities. This could be characterized as a kind of "symmetry," but it is significantly different from the one discussed above. This sort of claim represents a substantive proposition of fairness, not a mere logical or conceptual correlation. This proposition is distorted, however, in the opinion of the majority on the court. Those who are incapable of assuming obligations or responsibilities cannot be regarded as irresponsible and, thus, to have forfeited any claim to have their rights respected. Hence, mental incompetents and new-born infants, for example, presumably possess rights that we are bound to respect, despite their inability to reciprocate. The law apparently respects this moral proposition, because both mental incompetents and new-born infants presumably possess, for example, the right not to be deprived of life without due process of law, although they lack the capacity for legal duties. If that is correct, then the majority's decision is based on a false principle—an imaginary symmetry—and its conclusion cannot be sustained.

If the argument thus far is right, and the majority's "symmetry" proposition is mistaken, is the majority guilty of "an abuse of logic"? That charge seems misleading or confused. Given the court's assumptions, its conclusion follows by the strictest logic. The dissenter is in no position to claim it is an abuse of logic, because he accepts both the majority's assumptions and its reasoning and only wishes to circumvent the proceeding by changing the law. If the decision is wrong, it is wrong either because its premises are false, as suggested above, or, as the dissenter urges, the decision is so objectionable that a responsible court should take the law into its own hands and change it. Logic itself, however, is neutral with respect to all these issues. Of course, it might be imagined that the very quest for "symmetry" involves an abuse of logic. But that would be mistaken—logic argues only for such symmetries as logic guarantees. Because the sort of symmetry predicated by the majority involves a substantive point of fairness, which it overextends, logic is silent on the matter.

Moreover, formalism as we understand it cannot be blamed for the specific decision of the court in this case. Formalistic judges assume that the law is determinate in all cases, and if they are mistaken, they will read the law as determinate when in fact it is not. Formalists, therefore, may stretch the legal facts, but this leads in no particular direction. If one is going to discover illusory "symmetries" in the law, there is no telling what one might claim to find. The quest for symmetry is too vague a basis for fixing formalistic judges in any particular direction.

One might contend that the clash between formalist and instrumentalist judges is more social than theoretical. Formalism is often characterized as politically and economically "conservative." It has been associated with judicial decisions that secure the interests of the economically powerful against those who suffer at their hands. The trouble with this interpretation of formalism is that it has no causal connection with the type of theory we have described. Some aspects of our law tend to favor the powerful against those who would encroach on their established rights, but other aspects tend to favor those whose rights are violated by the rich and powerful. If formalism systematically favors one side over the other, that is not because it favors symmetries or imagines the law to be more complete than it actually is. Rather, it is because the individuals who compose that group are biased and possibly dishonest, though perhaps as dishonest with themselves as with the community at large. This is not to deny that legal battles reflect economic struggles, or that legal theory can be politically motivated. What the critics of formalism fail to demonstrate, however, is that formalism is especially related to one side of these battles, or that instrumentalism is especially related to the other side.

The instrumentalists' criticism of the imaginary decision discussed above is worth probing further, for such criticism appears faithful to the instrumentalist tradition and reveals some difficulties for its practitioners. The instrumentalist dissenter claims that "we as judges can alter these concepts as we desire to serve useful goals." If we take the dissenter at his word, his criticism has the following implications: The majority's premise that capacity for rights assumes capacity for duties is a true proposition of law; the court has the capacity to make it false by changing the law; and such modification is perfectly proper. Thus, on a literal level, the dissenter must be understood as arguing either that changing the law in order to serve useful goals is *authorized by law* or that the court *should act unlawfully*. Assuming that instrumentalists do not typically call on courts to act unlawfully, we should probably understand them as supposing that the law empowers courts to act as courts of equity. This is an interesting proposition, but it may not be what is really meant; its literal meaning readily can be doubted.

Recall our discussion of the formalistic model of legal justification, which, together with the source-based view of law, led to the idea that law consists of whatever can be read from authorized texts or is literally implied by them. I argued earlier that this cannot be assumed to exhaust "the law," because an adequate account of what the law requires and allows may take us beyond the four corners of its texts. Hence, we can understand the idea of *changing a legal concept* (*e.g.*, to effect equity), which the dissenter prefers, in two ways: as a matter of adjusting our understanding of the law by going beyond a doctrinaire or literal reading of it (which may be inadequate), or as a matter of changing law by neglecting some binding considerations or introducing others without adequate legal basis. If the latter is what the instrumentalist dissenter has in mind, he is calling on the court to act unlawfully. If he has the former notion in mind, however, then he desires not so much a change in the law as a change in our understanding of it.

I doubt that the latter is the appropriate interpretation of the dissenter's opinion; it would be more characteristic of an instrumentalist to maintain that the law on the subject is really indeterminate. In that case, we cannot read the dissenting opinion literally. The dissenter does not believe that the court should "alter these concepts as we desire to serve useful goals," but instead he believes that the law needs to be shaped because it is not yet capable of deciding the case at hand. Because he believes the court is engaged in a legislative activity (which is not just a matter of correcting an inadequate understanding of existing law), the dissenter urges the court to serve useful goals. If that is what the dissenter means to say, then his criticism of the majority opinion is poorly framed, at best.

In sum, if we take the instrumentalist at his word, he is urging the court to ignore existing law and illegally change it. If we take him in some other way suggested by his general position, then we find his comments at best hyperbolic and unilluminating. As I believe that Summers accurately captures the spirit and character of instrumentalist criticisms of formalistic legal practice, I must demur from his appraisal of those criticisms. Very little legal method can be traced to formalistic legal theory. Instrumentalist criticisms of judicial practices seem themselves to suffer from overgeneralization and logical confusion. Furthermore, instrumentalists appear to embrace a naively utilitarian normative theory, and their recommendations concerning judicial legislation are, accordingly, unreliable.

* * * *

If my original suspicions were sound, formalism is a nontheory, developed by instrumentalists who see themselves as battling theory-laden judicial practice that ignores human values. Instrumentalism is itself half-formed out of radical empiricism, developed on the verge of skepticism toward theory as well as substantive values, including those with which it wishes to be identified. Ambivalence about theory, values, and the law itself runs right through instrumentalism. This makes that body of legal doctrine an accurate reflection of a significant stream of American thought.

WHAT HAS PRAGMATISM
TO OFFER LAW?

RICHARD A. POSNER*

"[T]he great weakness of Pragmatism is that it ends by being of no use
to anybody."

—T. S. Eliot[1]

I.

The pragmatic movement gave legal realism such intellectual shape
and content as it had. Then pragmatism died (or merged into other philosophical movements and lost its separate identity), and legal realism
died (or was similarly absorbed and transcended). Lately pragmatism
has revived, and the question I address in this Article is whether this
revival has produced or is likely to produce a new jurisprudence that will
bear the same relation to the new pragmatism as legal realism bore to the
old. My answer is no on both counts. The new pragmatism, like the old,
is not a distinct philosophical movement but an umbrella term for diverse
tendencies in philosophical thought. What is more, it is a term for the
same tendencies; the new pragmatism is not new. Some of the tendencies
that go to make up the pragmatic tradition were fruitfully absorbed into
legal realism, particularly in the forms articulated by Holmes and Cardozo; others led, and still lead, nowhere. The tendencies that many years
ago were fruitfully absorbed into legal realism can indeed help in the
formulation of a new jurisprudence, but it will be new largely in jettison-
ing the naive politics and other immaturities and excesses of legal realism.[2] This refurbished, modernized realism will owe little or nothing,

* Judge, United States Court of Appeals for the Seventh Circuit; Senior Lecturer, University
of Chicago Law School. This is the revised text of a paper presented at the Symposium on the
Renaissance of Pragmatism in American Legal Thought, held at the University of Southern California Law Center on February 23 and 24, 1990. I thank Cass Sunstein for helpful comments on a
previous draft.

1. T.S. Eliot, *Francis Herbert Bradley*, in SELECTED PROSE OF T.S. ELIOT 196, 204 (F.
Kermode ed. 1975) (essay first published in 1927).

2. I present my full argument for this new jurisprudence in my book, THE PROBLEMS OF
JURISPRUDENCE © 1990.

however, to the new pragmatism—if indeed there is such a thing, as I doubt.

Histories of pragmatism[3] usually begin with Charles Sanders Peirce, although he himself gave credit for the idea to a lawyer friend, Nicholas St. John Green, and anticipations can be found much earlier—in Epicurus, for example.[4] From Peirce the baton is (in conventional accounts) handed to William James, then to John Dewey, George Mead, and (in England) F.S.C. Schiller. Parallel to and influenced by the pragmatists, legal realism comes on the scene, inspired by the work of Oliver Wendell Holmes, John Chipman Grey, and Benjamin Cardozo and realized in the work of the self-described realists, such as Jerome Frank, William Douglas, Karl Llewellyn, Felix Cohen, and Max Radin. Pragmatism and legal realism join in Dewey's essays on law.[5] But by the end of World War II both philosophical pragmatism and legal realism have expired, the first superseded by logical positivism and other "hard" analytic philosophy, the other absorbed into the legal mainstream and particularly into the "legal process" school that reaches its apogee in 1958 with Hart and Sacks's The Legal Process. Then, beginning in the 1960s with the waning of logical positivism, pragmatism comes charging back in the person of Richard Rorty, followed in the 1970s by critical legal studies—the radical son of legal realism—and in the 1980s by a school of legal neopragmatists that includes Martha Minow, Thomas Grey, Daniel Farber, Philip Frickey, and others. The others include myself, and perhaps also, as suggested by Professor Rorty in his comment on this paper, Ronald Dworkin—despite Dworkin's overt hostility to pragmatism[6]—and even Roberto Unger. The ideological diversity of this group is noteworthy.

In the account I am offering (not endorsing), pragmatism, whether of the paleo or neo varieties, stands for a progressively more emphatic rejection of Enlightenment dualisms such as subject and object, mind and body, perception and reality, form and substance; these dualisms being regarded as the props of a conservative social, political, and legal order.

---

3. Illustrated by D. HOLLINGER, IN THE AMERICAN PROVINCE: STUDIES IN THE HISTORY AND HISTORIOGRAPHY OF IDEAS 23-32 (1985); J. SMITH, PURPOSE AND THOUGHT: THE MEANING OF PRAGMATISM (1978); H.S. THAYER, MEANING AND ACTION: A CRITICAL HISTORY OF PRAGMATISM (1968).

4. See Nussbaum, Therapeutic Arguments: Epicurus and Aristotle, in THE NORMS OF NATURE 31 (M. Schofield & G. Striker eds. 1986); see also id. at 41, 71-72.

5. Notably his essay Logical Method and Law, 10 CORNELL L.Q. 17 (1924).

6. See infra note 23.

This picture is too simple. The triumphs of science, particularly Newtonian physics, in the seventeenth and eighteenth centuries persuaded most thinking people that the physical universe had a uniform structure accessible to human reason. It began to seem that human nature and human social systems might have a similarly mechanical structure. This emerging world view cast humankind in an observing mold. Through perception, measurement, and mathematics, the human mind would uncover the secrets of nature (including those of the mind itself, a part of nature) and the laws (natural, not positive) of social interaction—including laws decreeing balanced government, economic behavior in accordance with the principles of supply and demand, and moral and legal principles based on immutable principles of psychology and human behavior. The mind was a camera, recording activities both natural and social and alike determined by natural laws, and an adding machine.

This view, broadly scientific but flavored with a Platonic sense of a world of order behind the chaos of sense impressions, was challenged by the Romantic poets (such as Blake and Wordsworth) and Romantic philosophers. They emphasized the plasticity of the world and especially the esemplastic power of the human imagination. Institutional constraints they despised along with all other limits on human aspiration, as merely contingent; science they found dreary; they celebrated potency and the sense of community—the sense of unlimited potential and of oneness with humankind and with nature—that an infant feels. They were Prometheans. The principal American representative of this school was Emerson, and he left traces of his thought on Peirce and Holmes alike. Emerson's European counterpart (and admirer) was Nietzsche. It is not that Peirce or Holmes or Nietzsche was a "Romantic" in a precise sense, if there is such a sense. It is that they wished to shift attention from a passive, contemplative relation between an observing subject and an objective reality, whether natural or social, to an active, creative relation between striving human beings and the problems that beset them and that they seek to overcome. For these thinkers, thought was an exertion of will instrumental to some human desire (and we see here the link between pragmatism and utilitarianism). Social institutions—whether science, law, or religion—were the product of shifting human desires rather than of a reality external to those desires. Human beings had not only eyes but hands as well.

Without going any further, we can see that "truth" is going to be a problematic concept for the pragmatist. The essential meaning of the word is observer independence, which is just what the pragmatist is inclined to deny. It is no surprise, therefore, that the pragmatists' stabs at defining truth—truth is what is fated to be believed in the long run (Peirce), truth is what is good to believe (James), or truth is what survives in the competition among ideas (Holmes)—are riven by paradox. The pragmatist's real interest is not in truth at all, but in belief justified by social need.

This change in direction does not necessarily make the pragmatist unfriendly to science (there is a deep division within pragmatism over what attitude to take toward science).[7] But it shifts the emphasis in philosophy of science from the discovery of nature's laws by observation to the formulation of theories about nature that are motivated by the desire of human beings to predict and control their environment. The implication, later made explicit by Thomas Kuhn, is that scientific theories are a function of human need and desire rather than of the way things are in nature, so that the succession of theories on a given topic need not bring us closer to "ultimate reality" (which is not to deny that scientific *knowledge* may be growing steadily). But this is to get ahead of the story, because I want to pause in 1921 and examine the formulation of legal pragmatism that Benjamin Cardozo offered in his book published that year, *The Nature of the Judicial Process.*[8] Most of what Cardozo has to say in this book (and elsewhere) is latent in Holmes's voluminous but scattered and often cryptic academic, judicial, and occasional writings. But the book is worthwhile and important as a clear, concise, and sensible manifesto of legal pragmatism and harbinger of the realist movement.

"The final cause of law," writes Cardozo, "is the welfare of society."[9] So much for the formalist idea, whose scientistic provenance and pretensions are evident, of law as a body of immutable principles. Cardozo does not mean, however, that judges "are free to substitute their own ideas of reason and justice for those of the men and women whom they serve. Their standard must be an objective one"—but objective in a pragmatic sense, which is not the sense of correspondence with an external reality. "In such matters, the thing that counts is not what I believe to be right. It is what I may reasonably believe that some other man of normal intellect and conscience might reasonably look upon as right."[10]

---

7. *See, e.g.,* Levi, *Escape From Boredom: Edification According to Rorty,* 11 CAN. J. PHIL. 589 (1981).

8. B. CARDOZO, THE NATURE OF THE JUDICIAL PROCESS (1921).

9. *Id.* at 66.

10. *Id.* at 88-89.

The thing that counts the most is that legal rules be understood in instrumental terms, implying contestability, revisability, and mutability. Few rules in our time are so well established that they may not be called upon any day to justify their existence as means adapted to an end. If they do not function, they are diseased. If they are diseased, they need not propagate their kind. Sometimes they are cut out and extirpated altogether. Sometimes they are left with the shadow of continued life, but sterilized, truncated, impotent for harm.[11]

A related point is that law is forward-looking. This point is implicit in an instrumental concept of law—which is the pragmatic concept of law, law as the servant of human needs, and is in sharp contrast to Aristotle's influential theory of corrective justice. That theory is quintessentially backward-looking. The function of law as corrective justice is to restore a preexisting equilibrium of rights, while in Cardozo's account "[n]ot the origin, but the goal, is the main thing. There can be no wisdom in the choice of a path unless we know where it will lead. . . . The rule that functions well produces a title deed to recognition. . . . [T]he final principle of selection for judges . . . is one of fitness to an end."[12] The "title deed" sentence is particularly noteworthy; it is a rebuke to formalist theories that require that for a law to be valid it must be "pedigreed" by being shown to derive from some authoritative source.

Where does the judge turn for the knowledge that is needed to weigh the social interests that shape the law? "I can only answer that he must get his knowledge . . . from experience and study and reflection; in brief, from life itself."[13] The judge is not a finder, but a maker, of law. John Marshall "gave to the constitution of the United States the impress of his own mind; and the form of our constitutional law is what it is, because he moulded it while it was still plastic and malleable in the fire of his own intense convictions."[14]

The focus of *The Nature of the Judicial Process* is on the common law, but in the last quoted passage we can see that Cardozo did not think the creative powers of the judicial imagination bound to wither when confronted by the challenge of textual interpretation. Although the self-described legal realists (from whom Cardozo, conscious of their excesses,

---

11. *Id.* at 98-99.
12. *Id.* at 102-03.
13. *Id.* at 113.
14. *Id.* at 169-70.

carefully distanced himself)[15] added little to what had been said by Cardozo and before him by Holmes, a notable essay by Max Radin[16] clarifies and in so doing emphasizes the parity of statutes and the common law. Judges, it is true, are not to revise a statute, as they are free to do with a common law doctrine. But interpretation is a creative rather than contemplative task—indeed judges have as much freedom in deciding difficult statutory (and of course constitutional) cases as they have in deciding difficult common law cases.

Yet, despite Radin's notable essay and the realists' salutary effort to refocus legal scholarship from the common law to the emergent world of statute-dominated law, legislation proved a challenge to which the realist tradition, from Holmes to the petering out of legal realism in the 1940s and its replacement by the legal process school in the 1950s, was unable to rise. The trouble started with Holmes's well-known description of the judge as an interstitial legislator, a description that Cardozo echoes in *The Nature of the Judicial Process*. The implication is that judges and legislators are officials of the same stripe—guided and controlled by the same goals, values, incentives, and constraints. If this were true, the judicial role would be greatly simplified; it would be primarily a matter of helping the legislature forge sound policy. It is not true. The legislative process is buffeted by interest-group pressures to an extent rare in the judicial process. The result is a body of laws far less informed by sound policy judgments than the realists in the heyday and aftermath of the New Deal believed. It is no longer possible to imagine the good pragmatist judge as one who acts merely as the faithful agent of the legislature. Indeed, the faithful-agent conception has become a hallmark of modern formalism—judges as faithful agents *despite* the perversity of so many of the statutes that they are interpreting.

A closely related failing of legal realism was its naive enthusiasm for government, an enthusiasm that marked legal realism as a "liberal" movement (in the modern, not nineteenth-century, sense) and is part of the legacy of legal realism to today's neopragmatism. As strikingly shown by the other papers and the comments and floor discussion at the Symposium for which this Article was prepared, today's legal pragmatism is so dominated by persons of liberal or radical persuasion as to make the movement itself seem (not least in their eyes) a school of left-wing thought. Yet not only has pragmatism no inherent political

---

15. *See* B. CARDOZO, *Jurisprudence*, in SELECTED WRITINGS OF BENJAMIN NATHAN CARDOZO: THE CHOICE OF TYCHO BRAHE 7 (M. Hall ed. 1947).

16. *See* Radin, *Statutory Interpretation*, 43 HARV. L. REV. 863, 884 (1930).

valence, but those pragmatists who attack the pieties of the Right while exhibiting a wholly uncritical devotion to the pieties of the Left (such as racial and sexual equality, the desirability of a more equal distribution of income and wealth, and the pervasiveness of oppression and injustice in modern Western society) are not genuine pragmatists; they are dogmatists in pragmatists' clothing.

Another great weakness of legal realism was the lack of method. The realists knew what to do—think things not words, trace the actual consequences of legal doctrines, balance competing policies—but they didn't have a clue as to how to do any of these things. It was not their fault. The tools of economics, statistics, and other pertinent sciences were insufficiently developed to enable a social-engineering approach to be taken to law.

I want to go back and pick up the thread of philosophical pragmatism. When *The Nature of the Judicial Process* appeared, John Dewey was the leading philosopher of pragmatism, and it is his version of pragmatism that is most in evidence in Cardozo's book and other extrajudicial writings.[17] Dewey continued to be productive for many years, but until the 1960s there was little that was new in pragmatism. Yet much that was happening in philosophy during this interval supported the pragmatic outlook. Logical positivism itself, with its emphasis on verifiability and its consequent hostility to metaphysics, is pragmatic in demanding that theory make a difference in the world of fact, the empirical world. Popper's falsificationist philosophy of science is close to Peirce's philosophy of science; in both, doubt is the engine of progress and truth an ever-receding goal, rather than an attainment. The antifoundationalism, anti-metaphysicality, and rejection of certitude that are leitmotifs of the later Wittgenstein and of Quine can be thought of as extensions of the ideas of James and Dewey. By the 1970s and 1980s, the streams have merged and we have a mature pragmatism represented by such figures as Davidson, Putnam, and Rorty in analytical philosophy, Habermas in political philosophy, Geertz in anthropology, Fish in literary criticism, and the academic lawyers whom I mentioned at the outset.[18]

---

17. I discuss the matter of Cardozo's pragmatism at greater length in my Cooley Lectures, CARDOZO: A STUDY IN REPUTATION, to be published in the fall of 1990 by the University of Chicago Press.

18. For good recent discussions of pragmatism from a variety of perspectives, see ANTI-FOUNDATIONALISM AND PRACTICAL REASONING: CONVERSATIONS BETWEEN HERMENEUTICS AND ANALYSIS (E. Simpson ed. 1987); J. MARGOLIS, PRAGMATISM WITHOUT FOUNDATIONS: RECONCILING REALISM AND RELATIVISM, in 1 THE PERSISTENCE OF REALITY (1961); R. RORTY,

There is little to be gained, however, from calling this recrudescence of pragmatism the "new" pragmatism. That would imply that there were (at least) two schools of pragmatism, each of which could be described and then compared. Neither the old nor the new pragmatism is a school. The differences between a Peirce and a James, or between a James and a Dewey, are profound. The differences among current advocates of pragmatism are even more profound, making it possible to find greater affinities across than within the "schools"—Peirce has more in common with Putnam than Putnam with Rorty, and I have more in common (I think) with Peirce, James, and Dewey than I have with Cornel West or Stanley Fish. What is more useful than to attempt to descry and compare old and new schools of pragmatism is to observe simply that the strengths of pragmatism are better appreciated today than they were thirty years ago and that this is due in part to the apparent failure of alternative philosophies such as logical positivism, but more to a growing recognition that the strengths of such alternatives lie in features shared with pragmatism, such as hostility to metaphysics and sympathy with the *methods* of science as distinct from faith in the power of science to deliver final truths.

If both the old and the new pragmatisms are as heterogeneous as I have suggested, the question arises whether pragmatism has any common core, and, if not, what use the term is. To speak in nonpragmatic terms, pragmatism has three "essential" elements. (To speak in pragmatic, nonessentialist terms, there is nothing practical to be gained from attaching the pragmatist label to any philosophy that does not have all three elements.) The first is a distrust of metaphysical entities ("reality," "truth," "nature," etc.) viewed as warrants for certitude whether in epistemology, ethics, or politics. The second is an insistence that propositions be tested by their consequences, by the difference they make—and if they make none, set aside. The third is an insistence on judging our projects, whether scientific, ethical, political, or legal, by their conformity to social or other human needs rather than to "objective," "impersonal"

CONTINGENCY, IRONY, AND SOLIDARITY (1989); C. WEST, THE AMERICAN EVASION OF PHILOSOPHY: A GENEALOGY OF PRAGMATISM (1989); Levi, *supra* note 7; PRAGMATISM: ITS SOURCES AND PROSPECTS (R. Mulvaney & P. Zeltner eds. 1981); Putnam & Putnam, *William James's Ideas*, 8 RARITAN 27 (Winter 1989); RORTY, CONSEQUENCES OF PRAGMATISM (ESSAYS 1972-1980) 160-66 (1982); Rorty, *The Priority of Democracy*, in THE VIRGINIA STATUTE FOR RELIGIOUS FREEDOM: ITS EVOLUTION AND CONSEQUENCES IN AMERICAN HISTORY 257 (M. Peterson & R. Vaughan eds. 1988). The work of the new legal pragmatists is illustrated by Farber, *Legal Pragmatism and the Constitution*, 72 MINN. L. REV. 1331 (1988); Grey, *Holmes and Legal Pragmatism*, 41 STAN. L. REV. 787 (1989); Minow, *The Supreme Court 1986 Term—Foreword: Justice Engendered*, 101 HARV. L. REV. 10 (1987).

criteria. These elements in turn imply an outlook that is progressive (in the sense of forward-looking), secular, and experimental, and that is commonsensical without making a fetish of common sense—for common sense is a repository of prejudice and ignorance as well as a fount of wisdom. R.W. Sleeper has helpfully summarized the pragmatic outlook in describing Dewey's philosophy as "a philosophy rooted in common sense and dedicated to the transformation of culture, to the resolution of the conflicts that divide us."[19] Also apt is Cornel West's description of the "common denominator" of pragmatism as "a future-oriented instrumentalism that tries to deploy thought as a weapon to enable more effective action."[20]

II.

It should be apparent that what I am calling the core of pragmatism or the pragmatic temper or outlook is vague enough to embrace a multitude of philosophies that are profoundly inconsistent at the operating level (anyone who still doubts this after the examples I gave earlier would do well to recall that Sidney Hook and Jürgen Habermas are both distinguished figures in pragmatic philosophy), including a multitude of inconsistent jurisprudences. Indeed there is a serious question—the question raised by the quotation from T.S. Eliot that is the epigraph of this Article—whether pragmatism is specific enough to have any use, specifically in law. To that question I devote the balance of the Article. I shall be brief and summary; the reader is referred to my forthcoming book[21] for elucidation of the points that follow and for necessary references.

1. There is at least one specific legal question to which pragmatism is directly applicable and that is the question of the basis and extent of the legal protection of free speech. If pragmatists are right and objective truth is just not in the cards, this may seem to weaken the case for providing special legal protections for free inquiry, viewed as the only dependable path to truth. Actually the case is strengthened. If truth is unattainable, the censor cannot appeal to a higher truth as the ground for foreclosing further inquiry on a subject; but the libertarian, in resisting censorship, can appeal to the demonstrated efficacy of free inquiry in enlarging knowledge. One can doubt that we shall ever attain "truth," but not that our knowledge is growing steadily. Even if every scientific

---

19. R. SLEEPER, THE NECESSITY OF PRAGMATISM: JOHN DEWEY'S CONCEPTION OF PHILOSOPHY 8-9 (1986).
20. C. WEST, *supra* note 18, at 5.
21. *See supra* note 2.

truth that we accept today is destined someday to be overthrown, our ability to cure tuberculosis and generate electrical power and build airplanes that fly will be unimpaired. The succession of scientific theories not only coexists with, but in fact contributes greatly to, the growth of scientific knowledge.

The pragmatist is apt also to be sympathetic to the argument that art and other nondiscursive modes of communication, and the "hot" rhetoric of the demagogue, and even of the flag or draft-card burner, ought to be protected. The pragmatist doubts that there are ascertainable, "objective" standards for establishing the proprieties of expression and therefore prefers to allow the market to be the arbiter. It is a plausible extension of Holmes's marketplace-of-ideas approach—an approach that rests on a pragmatist rejection of the proposition that there are objective criteria of truth.

2. The pragmatic outlook can help us maintain a properly critical stance toward mysterious entities that seem to play a large role in many areas of law, particularly tort and criminal law. Such entities as mind, intent, free will, and causation are constantly invoked in debates over civil and criminal liability. Tested by the pragmatic criterion of practical consequence, these entities are remarkably elusive. Even if they exist, law has no practical means of locating them and in fact ignores them on any but the most superficial verbal level. Judges and juries do not, as a precondition to finding that a killing was intentional, peer into the defendant's mind in quest of the required intent. They look at the evidence of what the defendant did and try to infer from it whether the deed involved advance planning or other indicia of high probability of success, whether there was concealment of evidence or other indicia of likely escape, and whether the circumstances of the crime argue a likelihood of repetition—all considerations that go to dangerousness rather than to intent or free will. The legal factfinder follows this approach because the social concern behind criminal punishment is a concern with dangerousness rather than with mental states (evil or otherwise), and because the methods of litigation do not enable the factfinder to probe beneath dangerousness into mental or spiritual strata so elusive they may not even exist.

Similarly, while interested in consequences and therefore implicitly in causality, the law does not make a fetish of "causation." It does not commit itself to any side of the age-old philosophical controversy over causation, but instead elides the issue by basing judgments of liability on social, rather than philosophical, considerations. People who have caused no harm at all because their plans were interrupted are regularly punished for attempt and conspiracy; persons may be held liable in tort law when their acts were neither a necessary nor a sufficient condition of the harm that ensued (as where two defendants, acting independently, simultaneously inflict the harm, and only one is sued); and persons whose acts "caused" injury in an uncontroversial sense may be excused from liability because the harm was an unforeseeable consequence of the act. The principle of legal liability can be redescribed without reference to metaphysical entities such as mind and causation. This redescription is an important part of the project of a pragmatic jurisprudence, although it will not please those for whom law's semantic level is its most interesting and important.

There is nothing new about endeavoring to puncture the law's metaphysical balloons. It was a favorite pursuit of the legal realists. But they did it with a left-wing slant. They were derisive of the proposition that a corporation had natural rights, since a corporation is just the name of a set of contracts. But they were not derisive of the idea of corporate taxation, though, since the corporation is not a person, it cannot bear the burden of taxation. The ultimate payors of the corporate income tax are flesh-and-blood persons, by no means all wealthy, for among them are employees as well as shareholders.

3. Pragmatism remains a powerful antidote to formalism, which is enjoying a resurgence in the Supreme Court. Legal formalism is the idea that legal questions can be answered by inquiry into the relation between concepts and hence without need for more than a superficial examination of their relation to the world of fact. It is, therefore, anti-pragmatic as well as anti-empirical. It asks not, What works?, but instead, What rules and outcomes have a proper pedigree in the form of a chain of logical links to an indisputably authoritative source of law, such as the text of the United States Constitution? Those rules and outcomes are correct and the rest incorrect. Formalism is the domain of the logician, the casuist, the Thomist, the Talmudist.

The desire to sever knowledge from observation is persistent and, to some extent, fruitful. Armed with the rules of arithmetic, one can drop a succession of balls into an urn and, if one has counted carefully, one will *know* how many balls there are in the urn without looking into it. Similarly, if the rule of the common law that there are no nonpossessory rights in wild animals can be thought somehow to generalize automatically to the rule that there are no such rights in *any* fugitive natural resource, then we can obtain the "correct" rule for property rights in oil and gas without having to delve into the economics of developing these resources. The pragmatic approach reverses the sequence. It asks, What is the right rule—the sensible, the socially apt, the efficient, the fair rule—for oil and gas? In the course of investigating this question, the pragmatist will consult the wild animal law for what (little) light it may throw on the question, but the emphasis will be empirical from the start. There will be no inclination to allow existing rules to expand to their semantic limits, engrossing ever greater areas of experience by a process of analogy or of verbal similitude. The tendency of formalism is to force the practices of business and lay persons into the mold of existing legal concepts, viewed as immutable, such as "contract." The pragmatist thinks that concepts should be subservient to human need and therefore wants law to adjust its categories to fit the practices of the nonlegal community.

4. The current bulwark of legal formalism, however, is not the common law, but statutory and constitutional interpretation. It is here that we find the most influential modern attempts to derive legal outcomes by methods superficially akin to deduction. The attempts are unlikely to succeed. The interpretation of texts is not a logical exercise and the bounds of "interpretation" are so expansive (when we consider that among the verbal and other objects that are interpreted are dreams, texts in foreign languages, and musical compositions) as to cast the utility of the concept into doubt. Pragmatists will emphasize the role of consequences in "interpretation," viewed humbly as the use of a text in aid of an outcome. They will point out, for example, that one reason we interpret the sentence "I'll eat my hat" as facetious is that the consequences of attempting to eat one's hat are so untoward.

In approaching an issue that has been posed as one of statutory "interpretation," pragmatists will ask which of the possible resolutions has the best consequences, all things (that lawyers are or should be interested in) considered, including the importance of preserving language as a medium of effective communication and of preserving the separation of powers. Except as may be implied by the last clause, pragmatists are not interested in the authenticity of a suggested interpretation as an expression of the intent of legislators or of the framers of constitutions. They are interested in using the legislative or constitutional text as a resource in the fashioning of a pragmatically attractive result. They agree with Cardozo that what works carries with it the best of title deeds; they prefer the sturdy mongrel to the sickly pedigreed purebred.

Take the old jurisprudential chestnut, discussed briefly in *The Nature of the Judicial Process*,[22] whether a "murdering heir" shall be allowed to inherit. The wills statute allows testators who comply with certain formalities to leave their property to whomever they please. There is no exception for the eventuality in which the beneficiary named in the will murders the testator. Should such an exception be interpolated by the courts? The answer, to the pragmatist, depends on the consequences. On the one hand, it can be objected that by interpolating an exception the courts will relax the pressure on legislators to draft statutes carefully and will violate the principle that legislatures rather than courts prescribe the penalties for criminal behavior. On the other hand, there is a natural concern that allowing the murderer to inherit will encourage murder; a reluctance to pile more work on already overburdened legislatures; and recognition that disinheriting the murderer is apt to fulfill, rather than to defeat, the testator's intentions, which is the ultimate purpose of the wills statute. A testator who foresaw the murder would not have made the murderer a beneficiary under the will; so if no exception to the wills statute is recognized, farseeing testators may decide to insert express provisions in their wills disinheriting murdering beneficiaries. The courts can save them the trouble by interpolating such a provision by interpretation. All these consequences have somehow to be analyzed and compared if the courts are to interpret the wills statute pragmatically.

Further complicating the interpretive picture in general is our current understanding of the legislative process, a more critical understanding than reigned when Cardozo, the legal realists, and the realists' successors in the legal process school wrote. We no longer think of statutes as typically, let alone invariably, the product of well-meaning efforts to maximize the public interest by legislators who are devoted to the public interest and who are the faithful representatives of constituents who share the same devotion. The wills statute can probably be viewed in faithful-agent terms, but many other statutes cannot be. The theory of social choice has instructed us about the difficulties of aggregating preferences by the method of voting, while the interest-group theory of politics in the version revived by economists has taught us that the legislative process often caters to the redistributive desires of narrow coalitions and, in so doing, disserves the public interest, plausibly construed. Under pressure of the insights of both theories it becomes unclear where to

---

22. The case is Riggs v. Palmer, 115 N.Y. 506, 22 N.E. 188 (1889), and the discussion is in B. CARDOZO, *supra* note 8, at 41-43.

locate statutory meaning, problematic to speak of judges discerning legislative intent, and uncertain why judges should seek to perfect through interpretation the decrees of the special-interest state. The main choices in "interpretive" theory that the new learning allows are either some version of strict construction or a pragmatic approach in which, recognizing the difficult and problematic nature of statutory interpretation, judges use consequences to guide their decisions, always bearing in mind that the relevant consequences include systemic ones such as debasing the currency of statutory language by straying too far from it.

Mention of systemic concerns should help demolish the canard that legal pragmatism implies the suppression of such concerns in favor of doing shortsighted substantive justice between the parties to the particular case.[23] The relevant consequences to the pragmatist are long run as well as short run, systemic as well as individual, the importance of stability and predictability as well as the importance of justice to the individual parties, and the importance of maintaining language as a reliable method of communication as well as the importance of interpreting statutes and constitutional provisions freely in order to make them speak intelligently to circumstances not envisaged by their drafters.

5. Pragmatism has implications, some already sketched under the rubrics of formalism and interpretation, for the theory of adjudication—of what judges do and should do. Although professional discourse has always been predominantly formalist, most American judges have been practicing pragmatists, in part because the materials for decision in American law have always been so various and conflicting that formalism was an unworkable ideal.[24] But after a bout of conspicuous judicial

---

23. An implication readers might draw from Dworkin's statement in *Law's Empire* that "the pragmatist thinks judges should always do the best they can for the future, in the circumstances, unchecked by any need to respect or secure consistency in principle with what other officials have done or will do." R. DWORKIN, LAW'S EMPIRE 161 (1986). This is an impoverished conception of pragmatism, one that merges pragmatism with act utilitarianism.

24. Against the suggestion that "pragmatism provides the best explanations of how judges actually decide cases," Dworkin argues that it "leaves unexplained one prominent feature of judicial practice—the attitude judges take toward statutes and precedents in hard cases—except on the awkward hypothesis that this practice is designed to deceive the public, in which case the public has not consented to it." *Id.* Dworkin is inferring judges' attitude from the rhetoric of judicial opinions, and this is perilous, because judges are not always candid and also because they often are not self-aware. Even if judges are consistently and deliberately deceptive, this would not impair the soundness of the pragmatic *explanation* of judicial behavior. Similarly, a lack of public consent would have nothing to do with the explanatory power of the pragmatic explanation. The issue of consent is in any event artificial, since judicial opinions are with rare exceptions written to be read by lawyers, not by lay people, and have in fact virtually no lay readership. Since Dworkin knows all these things as well as I do, I infer that his discussion of judicial behavior and legitimacy, like so much discussion in law, is itself highly rhetorical.

activism that lasted several decades, there is renewed interest in approaches that favor continuity with the past over social engineering of the future—approaches embraced by many quondam judicial activists eager to conserve the work of the past decades against inroads by conservative judges, and by many conservatives who believe that the judiciary remains committed to liberal policies. There is renewed talk of tradition, of embodied but inarticulate wisdom (embodied in precedent, in professional training, in law's customary language), of the limitedness of individual reason and the danger of precipitate social change. The cautionary stance implicit in these approaches is congenial to the pragmatist, for whom the historical record of reform efforts is full of sobering lessons. But pragmatists are not content with a vague neotraditionalism. They know it will not do to tell judges to resolve all doubts against change and freeze law as it is, let alone to return to some past epoch in legal revolution (1950? 1850?). As society changes, judges, within the broad limits set by the legislators and by the makers of the Constitution, must adapt the law to its altered environment. No version of traditionalism will tell them how to do this. For this they need ends and an awareness of how social change affects the appropriate means—how, for example, the coming of the telegraph and the telephone altered the conditions for regulating contracts. They need, in short, the instrumental sense that is basic to pragmatism.

6. This brings me to the question of the relation between pragmatism and our most highly developed instrumental concept of law, the economic. Among the recurrent criticisms of efforts to defend the economic approach as a worthwhile guide for legal reform is that the defenders have failed to ground the approach securely in one of the great traditions of ethical insight, such as the Kantian or the utilitarian. The criticism is sound as observation, but not as criticism. The economic approach to law that I defend—the idea that law should strive to support competitive markets and to simulate their results in situations in which market-transaction costs are prohibitive—has affinities with both Kantian and utilitarian ethics: with the former, because the approach protects the autonomy of people who are productive or at least potentially so (granted, this isn't everyone); with the latter, because of the empirical relation between free markets and human welfare. Although it is easily shown that the economic approach is neither deducible from nor completely consistent with either system of ethics, this is not a decisive objection from a pragmatic standpoint. Pragmatists are unperturbed by a lack of foundations. We ask not whether the economic approach to law is adequately grounded in the ethics of Kant or Rawls or Bentham or Mill

or Hayek or Nozick—and not whether any of those ethics is adequately grounded—but whether it is the best approach for the contemporary American legal system to follow, given what we know about markets (and we are learning more about them every day from the economic and political changes in Communist and Third World countries), about American legislatures, about American judges, and about the values of the American people.

The economic approach cannot be the whole content of legal pragmatism. Because it works well only where there is at least moderate agreement on ends, it cannot answer the question whether abortion should be restricted, although it can tell us something, maybe much, about the efficacy and consequences of the restrictions. One value of pragmatism is its recognition that there are areas of discourse where lack of common ends precludes rational resolution; and here the pragmatic counsel (or one pragmatic counsel) to the legal system is to muddle through, preserve avenues of change, do not roil needlessly the political waters. On a pragmatic view, the error of *Roe v. Wade*[25] is not that it read the Constitution wrong—for there are plenty of well-regarded decisions that reflect an equally freewheeling approach to constitutional interpretation—but that it prematurely nationalized an issue best left to simmer longer at the state and local level until a consensus based on experience with a variety of approaches to abortion emerged.

7. To those who equate economics with scientism and who consider pragmatism the rejection of the scientistic approach to philosophy,[26] my attempt to relate the economic approach to pragmatism will seem perverse. But scientistic philosophy—the attempt to construct a metaphysics, a theory of action, an ethical theory, a political theory or what have you that has the rigor and generality that we associate with the natural sciences—is not at all the same thing as social science, which is the application of scientific method to social behavior. Most pragmatists have not disbelieved in the utility of scientific method. Quite the contrary, pragmatism in the style of Peirce and Dewey can be viewed as a generalization of the ethic of scientific inquiry—open-minded, forward-looking, respectful of fact, willing to experiment, disrespectful of sacred cows, anti-metaphysical. And this is an ethic of which law needs more. I am not saying that the economic approach to law is rooted in or inspired by

---

25.   410 U.S. 113 (1973).

26.   For a clear statement of this rejection, see Rorty, *Philosophy as Science, as Metaphor, and as Politics,* in THE INSTITUTION OF PHILOSOPHY: A DISCIPLINE IN CRISIS? 13 (A. Cohen & M. Dascal eds. 1989).

pragmatism, for in truth it is rooted in and inspired by a belief in the intellectual power and pertinence of economics. But economic analysis and pragmatism are thoroughly, and I think fruitfully, compatible.

8. There is renewed interest in the rhetoric of law.[27] This may appear to have nothing to do with pragmatism, but the appearance is misleading. By making the concept of "objective truth" problematic, the pragmatic distrust of foundations expands the range in which metaphor and other forms of emotive argument may legitimately upset belief. In Holmes's pragmatic metaphor of the marketplace of ideas, competing theorists, ideologues, and reformers hawk their intellectual wares. Knowing how important persuasion is in the market for goods and services, we should not be surprised to find it playing a big role in the market in ideas as well. We should expect change in law to be related not only to politics and economics and not only to the correction of error, but also to new slogans, metaphors, imagery, and other means of bringing about changes in perspective.

III.

With muddling through offered as one method of pragmatic jurisprudence (see point 6), one may wonder whether that jurisprudence has progressed an inch beyond *The Nature of the Judicial Process*. Certainly the essence of that jurisprudence is in Cardozo's book and indeed can be found much earlier, though in a more elliptical form, in Holmes's writings, especially "The Path of the Law."[28] But there has been some progress since 1921. Reviewing my eight items, we can see that Cardozo had a solid pragmatic grasp of the weakness of formalism (point 3) and a good pragmatic theory of adjudication (point 6), but free speech was not an issue about which he was much concerned (point 1); the critique of intention and causation (point 2) was less developed than it is today and certainly less salient in Cardozo's thinking; he was uninterested in interpretation and unrealistic about the legislative process (point 3); and he was innocent of the economic approach to law as a self-conscious methodology (point 6)—it did not exist in 1921, or indeed until half a century later—but like most good common law judges he had intuitions of it.[29] A closely related point is that the application of scientific method to law

---

27. *See* R. POSNER, LAW AND LITERATURE: A MISUNDERSTOOD RELATION 269-316 (1988), and references therein.

28. Holmes, *The Path of the Law*, 10 HARV. L. REV. 457 (1897).

29. Professor Landes and I discuss an example—Cardozo's decision in Adams v. Bullock, 227 N.Y. 208, 125 N.E. 93 (1919)—in W. LANDES & R. POSNER, THE ECONOMIC STRUCTURE OF TORT LAW 97-98 (1987).

lay in the future (point 7). Cardozo in his judicial opinions was very much the rhetorician (point 8), but his essay on judicial rhetoric[30] is a disappointment—cute, civilized, but unanalytic.

Although pragmatic jurisprudence embraces a richer set of ideas than can be found in *The Nature of the Judicial Process* or "The Path of the Law," one can hardly say that there has been much progress, and perhaps in the nature of pragmatism there cannot be. All that a pragmatic jurisprudence really connotes—and it connoted it in 1897 or 1921 as much as it does today—is a rejection of a concept of law as grounded in permanent principles and realized in logical manipulations of those principles, and a determination to use law as an instrument for social ends. It signals an attitude, an orientation, at times a change in direction. It clears the underbrush; it does not plant the forest.

---

30. B. CARDOZO, *Law and Literature*, in SELECTED WRITINGS OF BENJAMIN NATHAN CARDOZO: THE CHOICE OF TYCHO BRAHE 339 (M. Hall ed. 1947).

THE PRAGMATIST AND THE FEMINIST

MARGARET JANE RADIN*

I want to discuss pragmatism and feminism. I undertake this project not because I have read everything considered feminist or pragmatist by its writers or readers, although I wish I had, but rather because I have discovered that in my own work I am speaking both of pragmatism and feminism. I desire to explore how pragmatism and feminism cohere, if they do, in my own thought, and I write with the hope that what I find useful will be useful for others as well.

I offer four interlinked short essays in which I think I am "doing" both pragmatism and feminism. Actually writing pragmatist-feminist analysis is one way to explore the question I pose, and perhaps it is the way most in the pragmatic spirit, or at least closest to the practice side of pragmatism. There is a theory side of pragmatism too, however, and I am interested in suggesting a broader theoretical connection between feminism and pragmatism as well.

I. THE DOUBLE BIND

I begin at the point it became clear to me that I was combining pragmatism and feminism. That point was in my thinking about the transition problem of the double bind in the context of contested commodification of sexuality and reproductive capacity.[1] If the social regime permits buying and selling of sexual and reproductive activities, thereby treating them as fungible market commodities given the current capitalistic understandings of monetary exchange, there is a threat to the personhood of women, who are the "owners" of these "commodities." The threat to personhood from commodification arises because essential

---

* Professor of Law, Stanford University; formerly Carolyn Craig Franklin Professor of Law, University of Southern California Law Center. A.B. 1963, Stanford University; M.F.A. 1965, Brandeis University; J.D. 1976, University of Southern California.

1. *See* Radin, *Market-Inalienability*, 100 HARV. L. REV. 1849, 1915-36 (1987) [hereinafter Radin, *Market-Inalienability*]; Radin, *Justice and the Market Domain*, in MARKETS AND JUSTICE 165, 185-88 (J. Chapman & J. Pennock eds. 1989) (NOMOS XXXI) [hereinafter Radin, *Justice and the Market Domain*].

attributes are treated as severable fungible objects, and this denies the integrity and uniqueness of the self. But if the social regime prohibits this kind of commodification, it denies women the choice to market their sexual or reproductive services, and given the current feminization of poverty and lack of avenues for free choice for women, this also poses a threat to the personhood of women. The threat from enforced noncommodification arises because narrowing women's choices is a threat to liberation, and because their choices to market sexual or reproductive services, even if nonideal, may represent the best alternatives available to those who would choose them.

Thus the double bind: both commodification and noncommodification may be harmful. Harmful, that is, under our current social conditions. Neither one need be harmful in an ideal world. The fact that money changes hands need not necessarily contaminate human interactions of sharing,[2] nor must the fact that a social order makes nonmonetary sharing its norm necessarily deprive or subordinate anyone. That commodification now tends toward fungibility of women and noncommodification now tends toward their domination and continued subordination are artifacts of the current social hierarchy. In other words, the fact of oppression is what gives rise to the double bind.

Thus, it appears that the solution to the double bind is not to solve but to dissolve it: remove the oppressive circumstances. But in the meantime, if we are practically limited to those two choices, which are we to choose? I think that the answer must be pragmatic. We must look carefully at the nonideal circumstances in each case and decide which horn of the dilemma is better (or less bad), and we must keep re-deciding as time goes on.

To generalize a bit, it seems that there are two ways to think about justice. One is to think about justice in an ideal world, the best world that we can now conceive. The other is to think about nonideal justice: given where we now find ourselves, what is the better decision? In making this decision, we think about what actions can bring us closer to ideal justice. For example, if we allow commodification, we may push further away any ideal of a less commodified future. But if we enforce noncommodification, we may push further away any ideal of a less dominated future. In making our decisions of nonideal justice, we must also realize that these decisions will help to reconstitute our ideals. For example, if we commodify all attributes of personhood, the ideal of personhood we

2. *See* Radin, *Justice and the Market Domain, supra* note 1, at 175-86.

now know will evolve into another one that does not conceive fungibility as bad. The double bind, then, is a problem involving nonideal justice, and I think its only solution can be pragmatic. There is no general solution; there are only piecemeal, temporary solutions.

I also think of the double bind as a problem of transition, because I think of nonideal justice as the process by which we try to make progress (effect a transition) toward our vision of the good world.[3] I think we should recognize that all decisions about justice, as opposed to theories about it, are pragmatic decisions in the transition. At the same time we should also recognize that ideal theory is also necessary, because we need to know what we are trying to achieve. In other words, our visions and nonideal decisions, our theory and practice, paradoxically constitute each other.

Having discovered the double bind in true pragmatic fashion, by working on a specific problem, I now see it everywhere. The double bind is pervasive in the issues we have thought of as "women's issues." The reason it is pervasive is to be sought in the perspective of oppression. For a group subject to structures of domination, all roads thought to be progressive can pack a backlash. I shall mention here a few other examples of the double bind: the special treatment/equal treatment debate, affirmative action, the understanding of rape, and the idea of marriage as a contract.

When we single out pregnancy, for example, for "special treatment," we fear that employers will not hire women. But if we do not accord special treatment to pregnancy, women will lose their jobs. If we grant special treatment, we bring back the bad old conception of women as weaker creatures; if we do not, we prevent women from becoming stronger in the practical world.[4] Feminist theory that tends toward the ideal, the visionary side of our thought about justice, has grasped the point that the dilemma must be dissolved because its framework is the conceptual framework of the oppressors (who define what is "special" and what is "equal"). But feminist theory that tends toward the nonideal practical side of our thought about justice has also realized that if the dominant conceptions are too deeply held at this time, trying to implement an alternative vision could be counterproductive. My personal

---

3. See Radin, *Market-Inalienability*, *supra* note 1, at 1875-76; Radin, *Reconsidering the Rule of Law*, 69 B.U.L. REV. 781, 816-17 (1989).

4. For an overview of the special treatment/equal treatment debate, see H. KAY, *Text Note: Ensuring Non-Discrimination*, in TEXT, CASES AND MATERIALS ON SEX-BASED DISCRIMINATION 566-72 (3d ed. 1988).

view is that in the case of pregnancy, the time has come to convince everyone that both men and women should have the opportunity to be parents in a fulfilling sense, and that the old conceptions of the workplace now can begin to give way. But I think that each women's issue situation, such as pregnancy, workplace regulation to protect fetuses, and height and weight restrictions, will have to be evaluated separately, and continually re-evaluated.

If there is a social commitment to affirmative action, in this nonideal time and place, then a woman or person of color who holds a job formerly closed to women and people of color is likely to be presumed to be underqualified.[5] More women and people of color will hold jobs, but few will be allowed to feel good about it. The dominant group will probably be able to make women and people of color meet higher standards than those applicable to white males, and yet at the same time convince everyone, including, often, the beneficiaries of affirmative action themselves, that as beneficiaries they are inferior. But what is our alternative? If there is no affirmative action commitment in place, far fewer women and people of color will hold these jobs; yet those who do, whatever vicissitudes they endure, will not endure this particular backlash. The pragmatic answer in most cases, I believe, is that backlash is better than complete exclusion, as long as the backlash is temporary. But if backlash can keep alive the bad old conceptions of women and people of color, how will we evolve toward better conceptions of the abilities of those who have been excluded?

Our struggle with how to understand rape seems to be another instance of the double bind. MacKinnon's view—or perhaps an oversimplified version of her view—is that under current conditions of gender hierarchy there is no clear dividing line between the sort of heterosexual intercourse that is genuinely desired by women and the sort that is unwelcome.[6] There can be no clear line because our very conception of sexuality is so deeply intertwined with male dominance that our desires as we experience them are problematic. Our own desires are socially constituted to reinforce patterns of male dominance against our own interest.[7] "Just say no" as the standard for determining whether rape has occurred is both under- and overinclusive. It is underinclusive because women who haven't found their voices mean "no" and are unable to say

---

5. *See* Radin, *Affirmative Action Rhetoric*, PHIL. & SOC. POL.'Y (forthcoming 1990).
6. *See* C. MACKINNON, FEMINISM UNMODIFIED 85-92 (1987); MacKinnon, *Feminism, Marxism, Method, and the State: An Agenda for Theory*, 7 SIGNS: J. WOMEN CULTURE & SOC. 515, 532 (1982).
7. MacKinnon, *supra* note 6, at 533-42; C. MACKINNON, *supra* note 6, at 85-92.

it; and it is overinclusive because, like it or not, the way sexuality has been constituted in a culture of male dominance, the male understanding that "no" means "yes" was often, and may still sometimes be, correct.[8] MacKinnon's view is painful. If there is no space for women to experience heterosexuality that is not suspect, what does that do to our self esteem and personhood in a social setting in which sex is important to selfhood?

The other prong of the double bind—roughly represented by the views of Robin West—is that we should greet all of women's subjective experience with acceptance and respect.[9] That view is less threatening to personhood in one way but more so in another. How can we progress toward a social conception of sexuality that is less male-dominated if we do not regard with critical suspicion some of the male-dominated experiences we now take pleasure in?[10]

The last example of the double bind I want to mention is the conceptualization of marriage. Is marriage to be considered a contract in which certain distributions of goods are agreed to between autonomous bargaining agents?[11] Upon divorce, such a conception of marriage makes it difficult for oppressed women who have not bargained effectively to obtain much. Or is marriage to be considered a noncontractual sharing status in which the partners' contributions are not to be monetized?[12] Upon divorce, such a conception makes it difficult for oppressed women who have contributed unmonetized services to their husbands' advantage to obtain much. The idea of contractual autonomy may be more attractive in our nonideal world if the alternative is to be submerged in a status that gives all power to men. Yet the autonomy may be illusory because oppression makes equal bargaining power impossible. At the same time,

---

8. Nevertheless, in our current nonideal circumstances, "just say no" may be the best legal standard to adopt. *See* S. ESTRICH, REAL RAPE 29, 38, 101 (1987).

9. *See* West, *The Difference in Women's Hedonic Lives*, 3 WIS. WOMEN'S L.J. 81 (1987).

10. A related instance of the double bind is our attitude toward battered women. Are they weak-willed victims of false consciousness? If so, we view them as degraded selves, so how will they find the self-esteem to free themselves? Or (the other side of the double bind) do we view their situation as one that they are choosing? If so, do we risk trying to bring about empowerment by pretending it already is present? *See* Littleton, *Women's Experience and the Problem of Transition: Perspectives on Male Battering of Women*, 1989 U. CHI. LEGAL F. 23.

11. *See, e.g.*, Shultz, *Contractual Ordering of Marriage*, 70 COLUM. L. REV. 207 (1982).

12. *See, e.g.*, Prager, *Sharing Principles and the Future of Marital Property Law*, 25 UCLA L. REV. 1 (1977).

the reinforcement of individualist bargaining models of human interaction is contrary to our vision of a better world and may alter that vision in a way we do not wish.[13]

Perhaps it is obvious that the reason the double bind recurs throughout feminist struggles is that it is an artifact of the dominant social conception of the meaning of gender. The double bind is a series of two-pronged dilemmas in which both prongs are, or can be, losers for the oppressed. Once we realize this, we may say it is equally obvious that the way out of the double bind is to dissolve these dilemmas by changing the framework that creates them. That is, we must dissolve the prevalent conception of gender.

Calling for dissolution of the prevalent conception of gender is the visionary half of the problem: we must create a new vision of the meaning of male and female in order to change the dominant social conception of gender and change the double bind. In order to do that, however, we need the social empowerment that the dominant social conception of gender keeps us from achieving.

Then how can we make progress? The other half of the problem is the nonideal problem of transition from the present situation toward our ideal. Here is where the pragmatist feminist comes into her own. The pragmatist solution is to confront each dilemma separately and choose the alternative that will hinder empowerment the least and further it the most. The pragmatist feminist need not seek a general solution that will dictate how to resolve all double bind issues. Appropriate solutions may all differ, depending on the current stage of women's empowerment, and how the proposed solution might move the current social conception of gender and our vision of how gender should be reconceived for the future. Indeed, the "same" double bind may demand a different solution tomorrow from the one we find best today.

---

13. *See* Radin, *Justice and the Market Domain, supra* note 1, at 244. Clare Dalton has expressed well the "Heads the man wins, tails the woman loses" irony of the double bind. Dalton relates how patriarchal judges can deny the claims of women in palimony suits either by deciding that no contractual relationship exists because the state presumes that these kinds of relationships are too intimate to be touched by contract, or else by deciding that no contractual relationship exists because the state presumes that these kinds of relationships are too distant to be included in the contractual model. *See* Dalton, *An Essay in the Deconstruction of Contract Doctrine,* 94 YALE L.J. 997, 1106-13 (1985).

II. THE PERSPECTIVE OF DOMINATION AND THE PROBLEM OF BAD COHERENCE

Women's standpoint is not an ossified truth that some feminist academicians have chiseled in stone for all women to worship; rather, it is a kaleidoscope of truths, continually shaping and reshaping each other, as more and different women begin to work and think together.

Rosemarie Tong[14]

It was when I said,
"There is no such thing as the truth,"
That the grapes seemed fatter.
The fox ran out of his hole.

You . . . You said,
"There are many truths,
But they are not parts of a truth."
Then the tree, at night, began to change,
Smoking through green and smoking blue.

Wallace Stevens[15]

Over the past few years I have been continually struck with some points of resonance between the methodology and commitments of many who call themselves feminists and those of certain important figures in the new wave of pragmatism.[16] It now seems to me that the points of resonance between feminism and pragmatism are worthy of some exploration.

I begin with an awareness that there is something problematic about my ambition to talk theoretically about pragmatism and feminism together. I want to avoid the type of exercise that tries to define two "isms" and then compare and contrast them. Insomuch as they are lively, these "isms" resist definition. There are a number of pragmatisms. At least there are distinctive strains stemming from Peirce, James, and Dewey, and the new wave may be considered a fourth pragmatism. There are also a number of feminisms. One recent survey of feminist

---

14. R. TONG, FEMINIST THOUGHT: A COMPREHENSIVE INTRODUCTION 193 (1989).

15. W. STEVENS, *On the Road Home*, in THE COLLECTED POEMS OF WALLACE STEVENS 203 (1954).

16. Joseph Singer and I gave a dialogue presentation entitled "The Feminist Turn in Moral Philosophy" at the Critical Legal Studies Feminist Conference in 1985. The title was intended to be provocative: we were discussing Hilary Putnam and Richard Rorty.

thought lists them as liberal, Marxist, radical, socialist, psychoanalytic, existentialist, and postmodern.[17]

One way to frame the investigation I have in mind would be to start with the question, Is feminism "really" pragmatism? (Or, is pragmatism "really" feminism?) If this is the question, one way to respond to it—a way I think would be both unpragmatic and unfeminist—is to ask what commitments or characteristics are common to all the pragmatisms we are certain are pragmatisms, and ask what commitments or characteristics are common to all the feminisms we are certain are feminisms. We would then see whether the feminist list includes both the necessary criteria for being pragmatist and enough or important enough criteria to be sufficient for being pragmatist, or whether the pragmatist list includes the necessary and sufficient criteria for being feminist. This definitional response is a blueprint of conceptualist methodology, an abstract exercise in reification that promises little of interest to a pragmatist or a feminist.

In a more pragmatic and feminist spirit of inquiry, we might ask instead another question. Of what use might it be to think of feminism and pragmatism as allied, as interpenetrating each other? In this and the next essay I will pursue this question in various ways. In order to do so I still have to engage in some problematic cataloguing, but at least it will be easier to deal with the inescapable incompleteness of that way of seeing matters. I can explore how in some ways it might be useful to consider pragmatism and feminism together, without having to have a definite answer to the (to a pragmatist inapposite) question of what pragmatism and feminism "really are." Feminism and pragmatism are not things; they are ways of proceeding.

The pragmatists were famous for their theory of truth without the capital T—their theory that truth is inevitably plural, concrete, and provisional. John Dewey wrote, "Truth is a collection of truths; and these constituent truths are in the keeping of the best available methods of inquiry and testing as to matters-of-fact . . ."[18] Similarly, William James wrote:

> Truth for us is simply a collective name for verification processes, just as health, wealth, strength, etc., are names for other processes connected with life, and also pursued because it pays to pursue them.

---

17. R. TONG, *supra* note 14, at 1. *Cf.* A. JAGGAR, FEMINIST POLITICS AND HUMAN NATURE 8, 10 (1983) (categorizing feminisms as liberal, Marxist, radical, and socialist).

18. J. DEWEY, EXPERIENCE AND NATURE 410 (2d ed. 1929).

Truth is *made*, just as health, wealth and strength are made, in the course of experience.[19]

Pragmatism and feminism largely share, I think, the commitment to finding knowledge in the particulars of experience.[20] It is a commitment against abstract idealism, transcendence, foundationalism, and atemporal universality; and in favor of immanence, historicity, concreteness, situatedness, contextuality, embeddedness, narrativity of meaning.

If feminists largely share the pragmatist commitment that truth is hammered out piecemeal in the crucible of life and our situatedness, they also share the pragmatist understanding that truth is provisional and ever-changing. Too, they also share the pragmatist commitment to concrete particulars. Since the details of our life are connected with what we know, those details matter. Thus, the pragmatist and the feminist both arrive at an embodied perspectivist view of knowledge.

It is not surprising that pragmatists have stressed embodiment more than other philosophers,[21] nor that feminists have stressed it even more. Once we understand that the details of our embodiment matter for what the world is for us (which in some pragmatist views is all the world is), then it must indeed be important that only one half of humans directly experience menstruation, pregnancy, birth, and lactation. So it is no wonder that feminists write about prostitution, contract motherhood, rape, child care, and the PMS defense. It is not just the fact that these are women's issues that makes these writings feminist—they are after all human issues—but specifically the instantiation of the perspective of female embodiment.

Another pragmatist commitment that is largely shared by feminists is the dissolution of traditional dichotomies.[22] Pragmatists and feminists have rejected the dichotomy between thought and action, or between theory and practice. John Dewey especially made this his theme; and he also rejected the dichotomies of reason and feeling, mind and body,

---

19. W. JAMES, PRAGMATISM 104 (1975).
20. There is a strain of essentialist feminism that might be an exception. Some feminists, often labeled as "radical," tend to think there is a real nature of women, linked to female biology, that has been obscured but not shaped by the patriarchy. *See, e.g.*, A. JAGGAR, *supra* note 17, at 93-98. I believe Robin West's writing tends in this essentialist direction, especially her apparent claim that morality rests on some kind of primeval Womanhood that is pre-linguistic. West, *Feminism, Critical Social Theory and Law*, 1989 U. CHI. LEGAL F. 59, 80-82.
21. *See, e.g.*, J. DEWEY, *supra* note 18, at 248-97 (chapter 7, entitled "Nature, Life and Body-Mind").
22. Some feminists have sought instead to elevate the "feminine" and downgrade the "masculine" side of the traditional dichotomies. As I shall say later, I find the pragmatist dissolution preferable. *See infra* text accompanying notes 47-52.

nature and nurture, connection and separation, and means and ends.[23] In a commitment that is not, at least not yet, shared by modern pragmatists, feminists have also largely rejected the traditional dichotomy of public (man) and private (woman). For these feminists, the personal is political.[24]

One more strong resonance between the pragmatist and the feminist is in concrete methodology. The feminist commitment to learning through consciousness raising in groups can be regarded as the culmination of the pragmatist understanding that, for consciousness to exist at all, there must be shared meaning arising out of shared interactions with the world. A particularly clear statement of this pragmatist position is found in Dewey's *Experience and Nature*. Dewey's treatment is suffused with the interrelationship of communication, meaning, and shared group experience. In one representative passage, Dewey says:

> The heart of language is not "expression" of something antecedent, much less expression of antecedent thought. It is communication; the establishment of cooperation in an activity in which there are partners, and in which the activity of each is modified and regulated by that partnership.[25]

The modern pragmatists' stress on conversation or dialogue stems from the same kind of understanding.

The special contribution of the methodology of consciousness raising is that it makes new meaning out of a specific type of experience, the experience of domination and oppression. In order to do so, it must make communication possible where before there was silence. In general, rootedness in the experiences of oppression makes possible the distinctive critical contribution that feminism can make to pragmatism. Feminist methodology and perspective make it possible to confront the problem of bad coherence, as I will now try to explain.

Pragmatists have tended toward coherence theories of truth and goodness.[26] Coherence theories tend toward conservativism, in the sense

---

23. As Dewey says in the preface to the second edition of *Experience and Nature*, "The chief obstacle to a more effective criticism of current values lies in the traditional separation of nature and experience, which it is the purpose of this volume to replace by the idea of continuity." J. DEWEY, *supra* note 18, at ix.

24. *See, e.g.*, C. MACKINNON, TOWARD A FEMINIST THEORY OF THE STATE 191 (1989).

25. J. DEWEY, *supra* note 18, at 179. The entire chapter is a remarkably eloquent expression of the view that mind itself depends upon discourse, the collective possession and use of language. *See id.* at 170, 173, 183-85.

26. This statement is subject to dispute. Hilary Putnam, for example, espouses "internal realism" or "pragmatic realism." *See* H. PUTNAM, THE MANY FACES OF REALISM 17 (1987). Putnam takes this view to be both characteristically pragmatic and a rejection of coherence theory. Others

that when we are faced with new experiences and new beliefs, we fit them into our web with as little alteration of what is already there as possible. James said that "in this matter of belief we are all extreme conservatives."[27] According to James, we will count a new idea as true if we can use it to assimilate a new experience to our old beliefs without disturbing them too much.

> That new idea is truest which performs most felicitously its function of satisfying our double urgency. It makes itself true, gets itself classed as true, by the way it works; grafting itself then upon the ancient body of truth, which thus grows much as a tree grows by the activity of a new layer of cambium.[28]

James also said that truth is what is good in the way of belief,[29] meaning that we should, and do, believe those things that work best in our lives.

---

take the pragmatic test of truth to be coherence, often referring to W.V.O. Quine's famous assertion that "our statements about the external world face the tribunal of sense experience not individually but only as a corporate body." Quine, *Two Dogmas of Empiricism*, in FROM A LOGICAL POINT OF VIEW 20, 42 (2d ed. 1980). In repudiating the boundary between the analytic and synthetic, Quine espoused a "more thorough pragmatism" than those who retained such a distinction. *Id.* at 46.

Perhaps the controversy over whether pragmatism espouses coherence theory is fueled by a loose use of the term coherence. If coherence refers just to the totality of existing practices and institutions, then a sophisticated pragmatist would not want to use it as the measure of truth, because on this view coherence becomes mere conventionalism: it does not take into account the ideals and critical visions that also properly belong to the totality of our circumstances. On the other hand, if coherence does include all of our ideals and critical visions, all of our possible meanings, then perhaps a sophisticated pragmatist would espouse it as amounting to the broadest form of immanent holistic understanding.

In this expansive understanding of coherence, it would perhaps be problematic to speak of bad coherence, as I do in the text, because the field over which coherence is supposed to organize understanding already includes whatever ideals and critical visions we would use for judging a situation bad. I use the term, however, to point out that some pragmatists at least implicitly adopt the narrow view that collapses coherence into conventionalism, and hence tend to find truth or goodness in the status quo. These complacent pragmatists are indeed vulnerable to the criticism that there is no room in their scheme to find the status quo on the whole bad or unjust. *See infra* text accompanying notes 30-31 and 54-66.

27. W. JAMES, *supra* note 19, at 35.

28. *Id.* at 36. James elaborated on how we choose what theories to class as true:

> Yet in the choice of these man-made formulas we cannot be capricious with impunity any more than we can be capricious on the common-sense practical level. We must find a theory that will *work*; and that means something extremely difficult; for our theory must mediate between all previous truths and certain new experiences. It must derange common sense and previous belief as little as possible, and it must lead to some sensible terminus or other that can be verified exactly. To "work" means both these things; and the squeeze is so tight that there is little loose play for any hypothesis. Our theories are wedged and controlled as nothing else is. Yet sometimes alternative theoretic formulas are equally compatible with all the truths we know, and then we choose between them for subjective reasons. We choose the kind of theory to which we are already partial; we follow "elegance" or "economy."

Id. at 104.

29. *Id.* at 42.

To those whose standpoint or perspective—whose embodied contextuality—is the narrative of domination and oppression, these coherence theories raise a question that is very hard for the pragmatist to answer. Is it possible to have a coherent system of belief, and have that system be coherently bad?[30] Those who have lived under sexism and racism know from experience that the answer must be yes. We know we cannot argue that any given sexist decision is wrong simply because it does not fit well with all our history and institutions, for the problem is more likely that it fits only too well. Bad coherence creates the double bind. Everywhere we look we find a dominant conception of gender undermining us.

But how can the pragmatist find a standpoint from which to argue that a system is coherent but bad, if pragmatism defines truth and good as coherence? Inattention to this problem is what makes pragmatism seem complacent, when it does. One answer to the problem of bad coherence, which the pragmatist will reject, is to bring back transcendence, natural law, or abstract idealism. Another answer, which the pragmatist can accept, is to take the commitment to embodied perspective very seriously indeed, and especially the commitment to the perspective of those who directly experience domination and oppression.

What this leads to, first, is either an expansive view of coherence that leaves room for broad critique of the dominant understandings and the status quo, or else, perhaps, to denial that pragmatism espouses coherence theory.[31] Its other consequences need exploring. It seems that a primary concomitant of the commitment to perspectivism might be a serious pluralism. "We" are looking for coherence in "our" commitments, but the most important question might be, Who is "we"? A serious pluralism might begin by understanding that there can be more than one "we." One "we" can have very different conceptions of the world, selves, communities, than another. Perhaps, at least practically speaking, each "we" can have its own coherence. Dominant groups have tended to understand themselves without question as the only "we," whereas oppressed groups, simply by virtue of recognizing themselves as an

---

30. If the notion of coherent badness causes philosophical difficulties, see *supra* note 26, then we could speak here of integrity in badness or merely consistency in badness. The point is that we can experience a situation in which almost everything about the status quo—our language, our social priorities, our law—reflects and expresses racism or sexism. We need a way to recognize that this situation is bad or unjust, indeed worse or more unjust than a situation that is on the whole just and has only small pockets of injustice that can be seen to lack coherence (or integrity, or consistency) with the whole.

31. *See supra* note 26.

oppressed group, have understood that there can be plural "we's." Perhaps, then, we should understand the perspective of the oppressed as making possible an understanding that coherence can be plural.

A serious pluralism must also find a way to understand the problem of transition, as the "we" of an oppressed group seeks to change dominant conceptions in order to make possible its own empowerment.[32] One important problem of transition is false consciousness. If the perspective of the oppressed includes significant portions of the dominant conception of the world, and of the role of the oppressed group in it, then the oppressed perspective may well be incoherent, rather than a separate coherence to be recognized as a separate "reality." If this is a useful way to view the matter, then we can say that the perspective of the oppressed struggles to make itself coherent in order to make itself real.

What leads some pragmatists into complacency and over-respect for the status quo is partly the failure to ask, Who is "we"? And what are "our" material interests? Why does it "work" for "us" to believe this? It is not necessary for pragmatists to make this mistake. Dewey, especially, understood the connection between truth, goodness, and liberation.[33] He argued cogently that many of philosophy's earlier errors, such as belief in eternal abstract forms, were expressions of the social position of philosophers as an elite leisure class.[34] But the mistake is tempting for a pragmatist whose perspective is that of a member of the dominant group, because from that perspective it seems that one has "the" perspective. I suggest that feminism, in its pragmatic aspect, can correct this complacent tendency. The perspective of domination, and the critical ramifications it must produce once it is taken seriously, seem to be feminism's important contribution to pragmatism.

---

32. Indeed, there is a transition problem in the very commitment to take seriously the perspective of oppressed groups, because attention to the group *qua* group risks reinforcing the old categories of subordination. *See* Brewer, *Pragmatism, Oppression, and the Flight to Substance*, 63 S. CAL. L. REV. 1753 (1990); *Afterword*, 63 S. CAL. L. REV. 1911, 1922-24 (1990).

33. *See, e.g.*, Putnam, *A Reconsideration of Deweyan Democracy*, 63 S. CAL. L. REV. 1671, 1681-83 (1990).

34. *See* J. DEWEY, *supra* note 18, at 119-20. "The conception that contemplative thought is *the* end in itself was at once a compensation for inability to make reason effective in practice, and a means for perpetuating a division of social classes. A local and temporal polity of historical nature became a metaphysics of everlasting being." *Id.* at 119.

III. A MEDIATING WAY OF THINKING?

In *Pragmatism: A New Name for Some Old Ways of Thinking*,[35] William James asked us to recognize a distinction between two opposing philosophical temperaments or ways of construing the world. He labeled these characteristic habits of thought as "tender-minded" and "tough-minded." In *In a Different Voice: Psychological Theory and Women's Development*,[36] Carol Gilligan asks us to recognize a distinction between two opposing conceptions of morality or paths of moral development. She labels these characteristic moral personalities as ethics (or ideologies) of "care" and of "justice." Gilligan associates the ethic of care with the moral development of mature women, and the ethic of justice with the moral development of mature men. The ethic of care is the "different voice" of women.

For those who are struck with the parallels between pragmatist and feminist thought, it is tempting to associate feminism with the tender-minded prong of James's dichotomy. It is also tempting, in view of Gilligan's striking findings and our subsequent reflection upon women's culture, to associate feminism with the ethic of care prong of Gilligan's dichotomy. Both of these tempting assimilations are mistaken. Moreover, there is a great deal to be learned from understanding the way in which they are mistaken.

In order to see why it is tempting to think of feminist thought as tender-minded, consider how we might schematically understand the characteristics of the moral conceptions labeled caring and justice. The following list probably summarizes the way we think of the distinction:

Ethic of Care	Ethic of Justice
nonviolence	equality
needs, interests	fairness, rights
contextual	universal
responsibility, nurture	desert, rights
attachment, connection,	separation, autonomy,
community	individualism
interdependence	independence
cooperation	competition
concrete, embedded,	abstract, universal,
perspectival	principled
narrative	systematic

---

35. W. James, *supra* note 19, at 13.
36. C. Gilligan, In a Different Voice: Psychological Theory and Women's Development (1982).

intuitive	logical
emotional	rational
web	hierarchy

Concentrate for a moment on the part of the justice list that characterizes this conception as abstract, universal, principled, systematic, logical. In contemporary intellectual culture we are inclined to regard logic as cold and hard, and to regard universal, systematic, all-encompassing structures as intellectually rigorous and appropriately rational. Those who associate the justice list with men would say that this inclination reflects the fact that contemporary intellectual culture is masculine. On the other hand, important aspects of the care list—feeling, responsiveness to needs and interests, nurturing, interconnectedness, intuition—are regarded as soft, mushy, unrigorous, and sentimental in contemporary intellectual culture. Cold, hard, rigorous: in other words, tough. Soft, sentimental, nurturing: in other words, tender.

If this is what James meant by tough-minded and tender-minded, Kant and Rawls would be the quintessential examples of tough-minded thinkers. Perhaps G.E. Moore, or perhaps Kierkegaard or Sartre, would be tender-minded. If this is what James meant, it is easy to see the correlation between tough-mindedness and the conventionally masculine, and tender-mindedness and the conventionally feminine. We would be tempted to add other ways of thought to the tough, masculine list, such as market rhetoric, cost-benefit analysis, rigid entitlements, and going by rules rather than situated judgment. Richard Posner would be tough because he can countenance baby selling if it enhances efficiency,[37] and Richard Epstein would be tough because he can countenance abject poverty and homelessness for the same reasons.[38] Robert Nozick would be tough because he can countenance one person dying of thirst if water rights are owned by another.[39]

But this is not at all what James meant. In the intellectual culture in which he drew up his lists, he meant to contrast idealist rationalism with skeptical empiricism. Here are the opposing traits as James presented them:

THE TENDER-MINDED	THE TOUGH-MINDED
Rationalistic (going by 'principles'),	Empiricist (going by 'facts'),
Intellectualistic,	Sensationalistic,
Idealistic,	Materialistic,

---

37. See, e.g., Posner, The Regulation of the Market in Adoptions, 67 B.U.L. REV. 59 (1987).
38. See R. EPSTEIN, TAKINGS 315-23 (1985).
39. See R. NOZICK, ANARCHY, STATE AND UTOPIA 180-81 (1972).

Optimistic,	Pessimistic,
Religious,	Irreligious,
Free-willist,	Fatalistic,
Monistic,	Pluralistic,
Dogmatical.	Skeptical.[40]

For James, the tender-minded are those who need the reassurance of a systematic, all-encompassing ideal structure. They need the security of believing that the world is one; that it is, and must necessarily be, good; that there is a perfect, absolute reality behind the imperfect appearances in which we live; and that all things necessarily tend toward perfection and the salvation of the world. The tender-minded need formal systems, principles, a priori reality, and complete rationality. The tough-minded, on the other hand, do not need to postulate a better and more unified world above, beyond, or beneath the messy and conflicting particulars in which we live—the facts as we know them. The tough-minded have the temperamental wherewithal to live with incompleteness, openness, uncertainty, skepticism, and the nonideal. For us today, universal logic and systematicity are cold, hard, and crystalline. But for James, they— that is, the need for them—evidenced vulnerability and tenderness.

It is evident that the quintessential tender-minded thinker to which James opposed his radical empiricism must be Hegel. Indeed, he mentioned two contemporary turn-of-the-century strands of tender-minded philosophy, the more important of which is "the so-called transcendental idealism of the Anglo-Hegelian school."[41] Among its exponents he included T.H. Green, Edward and John Caird, Bernard Bosanquet, and Joseph Royce.

If we try to be true to James, perhaps the foremost tender-minded thinker of today would be Roberto Unger. His work is thoroughly systematic, and it is neo-Hegelian. Even though John Rawls is not a transcendental idealist and is neo-Kantian rather than neo-Hegelian, we would probably also have to think of Rawls as tender-minded rather than tough-minded, because neo-Kantianism, no less than neo-Hegelianism, tries to find all-encompassing first principles and to build ideal theories systematically upon them. Perhaps indeed James's distinction would lead us to consider tender-minded all theorists who need universal, ideal, abstract, algorithmic structure.

---

40. W. JAMES, *supra* note 19, at 13.
41. *Id.* at 16.

What we have seen so far is that our current philosophical culture, perhaps including a conventionally accepted complex of traits divided into the masculine and feminine, tempts us to misunderstand what James meant by his distinction between tough-minded and tender-minded theories and temperaments. Although it is important to understand this, it is more important to understand that James introduced the distinction not to embrace one of its prongs, but rather to try to dissolve it or bridge it.

James offered pragmatism as a "mediating way of thinking."[42] Pragmatism is a way of understanding our simultaneous commitments to optimism *and* pluralism, to concrete empiricism *and* principles, to an incomplete and dynamic universe *and* to the possibility of perfection that our ideals impel us unceasingly to hope for and work for. It was important for James that pragmatism allow us to retain a religious commitment, though not the kind of religion characteristic of the tender-minded. Indeed, although James's sympathies are in many ways with the tough-minded—he is interested foremost in the pluralistic and incomplete nature of the world, the never-ending variety and criss-crossing conflict and interconnectedness of facts—he tells us that pragmatism must include all ideas that prove best for people to hold (the most useful, the ones that work the best). This means that pragmatism includes some of the commitments of tender-mindedness:

> One misunderstanding of pragmatism is to identify it with positivistic tough-mindedness, to suppose that it scorns every rationalistic notion as so much jabber and gesticulation, that it loves intellectual anarchy as such and prefers a sort of wolf-world absolutely unpent and wild and without a master or a collar to any philosophic class-room product, whatsoever. I have said so much in these lectures against the over-tender forms of rationalism, that I am prepared for some misunderstanding here, [but] I have simultaneously defended rationalistic hypotheses so far as these re-direct you fruitfully into experience.[43]

Pragmatism does not prefer a wolf-world because that is not a world that would be good for human beings. That is not a human world, not a conception of the world that works for us, and not one that makes us flourish as best we can. For James pragmatism is capacious:

> On pragmatic principles we cannot reject any hypothesis if consequences useful to life flow from it. Universal conceptions, as things to take account of, may be as real for pragmatism as particular sensations are. They have indeed no meaning and no reality if they have no use.

---

42. *Id.* at 26.
43. *Id.* at 128.

But if they have any use they have that amount of meaning. And the meaning will be true if the use squares well with life's other uses.

Well, the use of the Absolute is proved by the whole course of men's religious history. The eternal arms are then beneath.[44]

So James finds that we have used the idea of the absolute because we need to fall back and float upon the eternal arms.

James's own solution does not favor any such floating. His religion of pragmatism is neither optimistic (tender-minded: the world's salvation is inevitable and we need do nothing about it) nor pessimistic (tough-minded: there is no salvation and we cannot do anything about it). Instead, it is "melioristic"—the world's salvation is possible, and *it depends upon what we do about it*. Whether or not we follow James and choose to think of it as religious, this is one of the deepest commitments of pragmatism, its commitment to the interconnection, indeed the inseparability, of theory (vision) and action (practice). "In the beginning was the Act,"[45] wrote Goethe at the dawn of the romantic era, and perhaps this commitment of pragmatism to the significance of our actions is what it retains of romanticism. It seems so in passages such as this:

> Does our act then *create* the world's salvation . . .? Here I take the bull by the horns, and in spite of the whole crew of rationalists and monists, of whatever brand they be, I ask *why not?* Our acts, our turning-places, where we seem to ourselves to make ourselves and grow, are the parts of the world to which we are closest, the parts of which our knowledge is the most intimate and complete. Why should we not take them at their face-value? Why may they not be the actual turning-places and growing-places which they seem to be, of the world—why not the workshop of being, where we catch fact in the making, so that nowhere may the world grow in any other kind of way than this?[46]

The optimism of pragmatism is not the static and secure optimism of the world in which everything is already fixed, could we but know or understand it, but rather the dynamic and risky optimism of a "workshop of being" in which reality is always incomplete and always dependent upon our practice.

---

44. *Id.* at 131.

45. *"Im Anfang war die Tat."* GOETHE, FAUST PT. I ln. 1237 (C. Thomas ed. 1892). This is to be understood, of course, as countervailing the Gospel of St. John, "In the beginning was the Word." Pragmatists traditionally are wary of emphasis on words without action or without commitment to actual results in the world. Perhaps Richard Rorty's stress on conversation or dialogue can prove uncomfortable for pragmatism, if conversation becomes a category apart from practical action.

46. W. JAMES, *supra* note 19, at 138.

James did not argue that we should accept pragmatism because it is a more rational system. Rather, he argued pragmatically that we should be pragmatists because when we look at our various commitments and practices we should recognize that pragmatism fits them best, that pragmatism will work best for us. If we accept everything on either the tender-minded or the tough-minded list, we are forced to deny, for the sake of supposed philosophical consistency, things on the other list that are very real and important to us.

When we see feminism in its pragmatic aspect, I think it will be easy to conclude that feminists should not easily relinquish what are important attributes of the ethic of justice because of the present conventional association with a version of masculinity that needs to be transcended. When we see feminism pragmatically, we may be impelled, rather, to affirm both lists, suitably metamorphosed. Perhaps feminism, as well as earlier pragmatism, can be a middle way.

In the wake of Gilligan's work, many feminists did affirm that there is something essentially female about the moral structure characterized in the care list. These feminists also affirmed that this female morality is good, indeed that women's "different voice" is not just different from, but better than, male morality, and should be the guide to moral and political progress.[47] It did not take long for other feminists to point out, however, that this simple identification with the care list might be a bad mistake.[48]

Rather than a window into an essentially female form of character and development or female kind of knowing and acting, the ethic of care in our current world might be an artifact of coping with oppression. It might be the expression of what is most useful for a group that exists in bondage, in victimhood.[49] If so, it is the expression of "femininism,"[50] not feminism, and its moral significance is complex. Its traits will be a mixture of cooptation with defiance, and sycophantism with subtle subversion. It will not be something either to affirm wholeheartedly or to reject out of hand.

Certainly, it seems that male ideology invented the polarities of rationality and just deserts versus emotions and nurturing, and then

---

47. *See, e.g.*, Ruddick, *Preservative Love and Military Destruction: Some Reflections on Mothering and Peace*, in J. TREBILCOT, MOTHERING: ESSAYS IN FEMINIST THEORY 231 (1983).

48. *See, e.g.*, Williams, *Deconstructing Gender*, 87 MICH. L. REV. 797 (1989).

49. *See, e.g.*, Hantzis, *Is Gender Justice a Completed Agenda?* (Book Review), 100 HARV. L. REV. 690, 700-03 (1987).

50. I learned this word from Kathleen M. Sullivan. "Femininism" connotes the misunderstanding of today's conventional femininity as some kind of real woman's nature.

found the rational pole to be dominant, suitable for the market and the public world, and the emotional pole to be subordinate, suitable for the family and the private world. Much of the eighteenth- and nineteenth-century rhetoric about the nature of womanhood makes this clear. To exalt the ethic of care leaves the polarities intact. It just reverses their signs. As others have pointed out, a group that seeks liberation from a dominating system of thought should be very suspicious of adopting its categories.[51]

What would a feminist middle way look like? It might recommend that all of us, women and men, are morally inclined toward both care and justice, and that neither women nor men should impoverish themselves with the conventional categories of femininity and masculinity. The feminist middle way would not want to relinquish the concrete knowledge that women have gained through living, working, creating, and surviving under male domination. This is a perspective that is unique and important for humanity. The actions and commitments of those who struggle to find room for themselves, and ultimately to free themselves, in a world whose formulating conceptions are not of their making, are indeed indispensable in the pragmatic "workshop of being." As I argued earlier, this perspective is the best way for pragmatism to confront the complacent tendency to be satisfied with coherence with the past. But neither would the feminist middle way want to deny women the right or the ability to engage in the theoretical joys of cold, hard logic and of rational system building, nor to deny women the practical power of standing at the top of a hierarchy, in a position of authority, and meting out just deserts.

The feminist middle way cannot be understood, however, as some kind of synthesis between the two lists. It would be unpragmatic, and perhaps incoherent, to seek some overarching universal conception or set of principles that could harmonize "attachment, connection, community" with "separation, autonomy, individualism," or "cooperation" with "competition," or the concrete with the abstract, or the intuitive with the logical, or the narrative with the systematic. Instead, the pragmatist middle way recommends two things for feminism: (1) We should recognize that sometimes one of the opposing modes of thought is appropriate, and sometimes the other, and no theory—only situated judgment—will tell us which one to adopt and when; (2) we should recognize that the traditional conceptions of the modes of thought on each list are

---

51. A. LORDE, *The Master's Tools Will Never Dismantle the Master's House*, in SISTER OUTSIDER 112 (1984).

inadequate insofar as they are part of a universal world view that denies the modes on the other list.

It could be that both the ethic of care and the ethic of justice are caricatures of morality. These caricatures have seemed plausible because to some extent they fit with contemporary conventions of femininity and masculinity. It could be that human beings, whether male or female, need both ethics to function morally. If we are pragmatists, we will reject static, timeless conceptions of reality. We will prefer contextuality, expressed in the commitment of Dewey and James to facts and their meaning in human life, and narrative, expressed in James's unfolding "epic" universe and Dewey's historicism. If we are pragmatists, we will recognize the inescapability of perspective and the indissolubility of thought and action. Indeed, as I have said, these pragmatist commitments are shared by many feminists, and they make it useful to think of many forms of feminism as sharing a great deal with pragmatism.

These pragmatic commitments nevertheless do not compel us to affirm the ethic of care and deny the ethic of justice, even if the realities of the narrative epic as it has so far unfolded have produced these contrasting ethics as the salient conventions of our day. James thought that if we reflected hard and honestly about our experiences and ideals, and our hopes and commitments, we would be neither tender-minded nor tough-minded, but would find a middle way that is truer to ourselves. So too today, it may be that we need not exalt either the characteristics of conventional femininity or conventional masculinity, but rather that we can define a middle way that is truer to ourselves, including what we hope to become.

IV. THE STRUGGLE OVER DESCRIPTIONS OF REALITY AND ITS CONSEQUENCES FOR LEGAL DISCOURSE

One useful consequence of putting pragmatism and feminism together is that we need not deny that certain philosophical commitments are distinctively feminist just because they seem to be pragmatist too. Joan Williams writes that "the attempt to claim the new epistemology for women is unconvincing simply because the new epistemology has been developed largely by men."[52] By "the new epistemology," Williams means the "view of truths as necessarily partial and contextual," which she associates with "philosophers from Frederick [sic] Nietzsche and the

---

52. Williams, *supra* note 48, at 806.

American pragmatists to Martin Heidegger and Ludwig Wittgenstein."[53] I think Williams moves too quickly here. Of course, it is correct that pragmatism, with its commitment to perspectivism, is not the exclusive province of females. But I have argued that the commitment to perspectivism finds its concrete payoff in the perspective of feminism and in the perspectives of oppressed people generally. Rather than affirming that there is no specific feminist perspective because men have espoused perspectivism, it is pragmatically better, as I have argued above, to affirm that the standpoint of people who have themselves been dominated and oppressed makes it possible to see and confront the problem of bad coherence. Their standpoint therefore assumes a crucial importance.

For the legal actor who accepts the significance of the perspective of the oppressed, the important issues must be, (1) How can we recognize bad coherence in our legal institutions? and (2) How can we use this recognition to change those institutions? In order to approach these issues for pragmatist-feminist legal theory, I suggest we can start with a distinction between two kinds of coherence. Like all pragmatic distinctions, I do not mean this one to be hard and fast.

There seem to be two ways to construe coherence, which I will call conceptual and institutional. If traditional pragmatism is best understood as expressing a coherence theory, its thrust is primarily conceptual. James's conservatism about belief was connected with what conceptions we should hold to be true,[54] especially in light of recalcitrant experience (to use Quine's later phrase).[55] On the other hand, complacent pragmatists are tempted to focus on existing institutions and not just conceptions. These different ways of construing coherence have ramifications for the problem of bad coherence. As I shall explain, dominant forms of legal pragmatism have been especially conservative because they have embraced institutional—not just conceptual—coherence.

If our world view exhibits bad coherence at the conceptual level, then we are unable to formulate and think about any opposing views. Indeed, it does not make any sense to speak of bad coherence at the time, for we can only see it in retrospect, if we change our conceptions and come to see our past understandings as bad. This might have been the situation with slavery in the ancient world. It might have been unthinkable to conceive of human beings in such a way that there could be any plausible argument that all people are equal and that slavery is wrong.

---

53. *Id.*
54. *See supra* text accompanying notes 27-29.
55. *See* Quine, *supra* note 26.

Some pragmatists might say that in this situation we have no standpoint from which to say that slavery is bad, and hence that it is meaningless, except in retrospect, to think of this situation as "bad" coherence. Pragmatists who adopt conceptual coherence as the test of truth need not be conservative about all institutions.[56] Nor need the conceptual meaninglessness be static. The methodology of consciousness raising is one way people can emerge from the unthinkable (silence) to an alternative conception of the world (voice). Perhaps that is the point at which it becomes meaningful to speak of bad coherence.

With institutional bad coherence the situation may be different. If our social world exhibits bad coherence at the institutional level but not at the conceptual level, then our institutions uniformly exhibit the bad conception of things, but it is possible for at least some of us to conceive that things might be otherwise. This might have been the situation in the last days of coverture. All our legal institutions treated women as subordinate to their husbands, yet it was possible for some women to think of themselves otherwise, and to envision a legal regime that would recognize their changed self-conception. If bad coherence exists only at the institutional level, then the possibility of transition opens up. How can a newly conceivable alternative conception find the power to make inroads into the coherent legal order held in place by the dominant conception of the world?

The problem of institutional bad coherence is the point where the enlightened pragmatist, the pragmatist-feminist, can make the most significant contribution to legal theory. The unenlightened, complacent pragmatist tends to argue that since "truth" about the world is found in conceptual coherence, legal "truth" should be discerned by reference to institutional coherence. The enlightened pragmatist must counter this conservative non sequitur by finding a way to transform alternative conceptual possibilities into legal realities. She must find a way that "the law" can be understood to include the conceptions of the oppressed as they are coming to be, even if the weight of legal institutions coherently excludes them. In other words, the transition problem in this guise is how to make thinkable alternatives into institutional commitments.

---

56. Conceptual coherence may be an expansive view of coherence in the sense discussed above. *See supra* note 26. When coherence includes all our ideals and critical visions, many existing institutions may be found wanting.

Dworkin's Hercules can be understood as a complacent pragmatist judge.[57] This reading of Dworkin might not represent his real views, if we were to ask him. Yet I think it is a fair picture of how a reader might understand his work, taken as a whole. Although Dworkin confusingly, and I think irresponsibly, gerrymanders the word "pragmatism" to mean crass instrumentalism,[58] it is clear that he is a pragmatist of sorts. Pragmatism is reflected in his commitment to the ubiquity of interpretation, and his concomitant commitment to finding meaning in assembling concrete events (institutional coherence and fit), rather than to measuring correspondence with abstract truth or justice.

Hercules is conservative because Dworkin accepts the flawed analogy between truth as conceptual coherence and legal truth as institutional coherence. Hercules, the ideal interpreter, must find the interpretation that coheres best with all that has gone before in the legal system. He is not allowed to say that the web of previous precedent is coherently wrong,[59] or, in his chain novel analogy, that the narrative to which he must add is a bad story so far.[60]

Of course, Hercules is allowed to find that some of our institutional history, as embodied in concrete decisions, is mistaken. Any adherent of coherence theory must allow some of the old commitments to be given up when confronted with a new problem. Dworkin argues conservatively that the proper theory of mistake is to give up as little as possible. He does not even provide any serious discussion about how every once in awhile a paradigm shift must come about, to parallel the avenue pursued by conceptual pragmatists in science.

For the oppressed this means the status quo must change very slowly, if at all. For example, how would Hercules deal with *Plessy v.*

---

57. Ronald Dworkin introduces Hercules, "a lawyer of superhuman skill, learning, patience and acumen," to represent the ideal judge. R. DWORKIN, TAKING RIGHTS SERIOUSLY 81, 104-05 (1978). Hercules plays the same role in *Law's Empire*, described there as "an imaginary judge of superhuman intellectual power and patience who accepts law as integrity." R. DWORKIN, LAW'S EMPIRE 239 (1986).

58. *See* R. DWORKIN, LAW'S EMPIRE, *supra* note 57, at 95, 151-64.

59. R. DWORKIN, TAKING RIGHTS SERIOUSLY, *supra* note 57, at 115-18. In speaking of the gravitational force of precedent, Dworkin argues that Hercules must treat the law as a seamless web of principles embedded in prior decisions.

60. R. DWORKIN, LAW'S EMPIRE, *supra* note 57, at 228-32. Dworkin compares judging to writing a chain novel, each writer interpreting the previous chapters in order to write a new chapter that fits with what has gone before.

Ferguson?[61] Dworkin argues that at the time of *Brown v. Board of Education*,[62] *Plessy* should not have been treated as compelling precedent, but he stops short of arguing that *Plessy* was wrong at the time it was decided.[63] Nor could he do so, it seems, since he admits that *Plessy* cohered well with its contemporary institutional legal, moral, and political universe. Toward the end of *Law's Empire*, Dworkin makes a distinction between the integrity required by justice and the integrity required by all of the virtues that the legal system must balance.[64] Perhaps he might argue that the integrity of justice would have recommended that *Plessy* was wrong at the time, even though institutionally coherent with its surroundings. Since Dworkin appears in the end to measure justice by the same kind of institutional coherence, it seems to me that such an argument would fail.

Of course, Dworkin does argue that things have changed and that it was coherently right by 1954 to ignore *Plessy*. But how did things change? Not, it appears, with any help from the legal system. In Dworkin's conservative theory the legal system was required to hold fast to the old description of the world,[65] composed by the dominant order and expressed in its institutions, until extra-legal forces dislodged it. Moreover, if Dworkin cannot argue that *Plessy* was wrong at the time it was decided because in his theory there is no foothold from which to argue that the system was institutionally coherently bad, then he has no room to admit the possibility that in some ways our system is coherently bad today. All he can say is that some of the coherent things we are doing today will probably seem wrong in retrospect, not that they are wrong now. That is small consolation to the oppressed.

In contrast to complacent legal pragmatists are the legal writers who have stressed the crucial importance of the perspective of the oppressed and its consequences for a serious pluralism. These writers, such as Robert Cover, Frank Michelman, and Martha Minow,[66] are essentially at

---

61. 163 U.S. 537 (1896).

62. 73 U.S. 1 (1952).

63. R. DWORKIN, LAW'S EMPIRE, *supra* note 57, at 379-89.

64. *Id.* at 404-07.

65. *See* W. STEVENS, *The Latest Freed Man*, in THE COLLECTED POEMS OF WALLACE STEVENS 204 (1954) ("Tired of the old descriptions of the world/The latest freed man rose at six and sat/On the edge of his bed."). On the affinity of Stevens and pragmatism, see Grey, *Hear the Other Side: Wallace Stevens and Pragmatist Legal Theory*, 63 S. CAL. L. REV. 1569 (1990). *See also* Radin, *"After The Final No There Comes A Yes": A Law Teacher's Report*, 2 YALE J. OF L. & HUMANITIES 253 (1990).

66. I think of these writers because of my own situatedness in the discourse of legal theory. It is equally important to think in this context of "critical race theory." *See* Bell, *Foreword: The Civil Rights Chronicles*, 99 HARV. L. REV. 4 (1985); Delgado, *When a Story is Just a Story: Does Voice*

work on the particular transition problem posed by institutional bad coherence—that is, the problem of institutional bad coherence in the context of excluded but conceivable alternatives.

In his resolutely anti-statist view of law, Cover wanted to make us aware of how in our commitments we create and inhabit a *nomos*. He wanted to make us concretely aware of the way meaning, including legal meaning, is inseparable from commitment and action. Reversing the old positivist slogan that judges should apply, not make, the law, Cover argued that the role of judges, like the roles of all who interpret authoritative texts for those who are committed to them, is rightly "jurisgenerative."[67] Cover drew attention in particular to the "hermeneutic of resistance,"[68] because he wanted us to see the deep and all-encompassing significance of the standpoint of those who are dominated and oppressed.

In many ways consonant with the work of Cover, both Minow and Michelman plead with us to drop the prevalent conception of the judicial role as one in which our hands are tied by abstract rules laid down.[69] Minow and Michelman urge that the best role for the judge in our legal system is to try to grasp the world from the perspective of the dominated, to hear the outsiders who have been silent and are now trying to speak, and to make concrete our deepest ideals of inclusion when the conventions of our day—"our" dominant perspective—run counter to them. In other words, Minow and Michelman ask us to allow the transitional possibilities opened up by the developing perspectives of the oppressed to infiltrate the dominant institutional coherence.

Minow "links problems of difference to questions of vantage point."[70] In "urg[ing] struggles over descriptions of reality,"[71] Minow echoes James's call for a workshop of being, but adds the perspective that only concrete participation in struggle can give. Michelman argues that pluralism is necessary for the evolutionary self-reflection appropriate to

---

Really Matter?, 76 VA. L. REV. 95 (1990); Matsuda, *Looking to the Bottom*, 22 HARV. C.R.-C.L. L. REV. 323 (1987); Matsuda, *Public Response to Racist Speech: Considering the Victim's Story*, 87 MICH. L. REV. 2320 (1989). We should also look to the emerging perspective of gay and lesbian writers. *See, e.g.*, Cain, *Feminist Jurisprudence*, 1989 BERKELEY WOMEN'S L.J. 191 (arguing that feminist jurisprudence ignores the lesbian perspective).

67. Cover, *Foreword: Nomos and Narrative*, 97 HARV. L. REV. 4 (1983).

68. *Id.* at 48-53.

69. Michelman, *Foreword: Traces of Self-Government*, 100 HARV. L. REV. 4, 32-33 (1986) [hereinafter Michelman, *Traces*]; Michelman, *Law's Republic*, 97 YALE L.J. 1493, 1532-37 (1988) [hereinafter Michelman, *Law's Republic*]; Minow, *Foreword: Justice Engendered*, 101 HARV. L. REV. 10, 70-95 (1987).

70. Minow, *supra* note 69, at 13-14.

71. *Id.* at 16.

our best self-development, and that pluralism depends upon listening to the perspectives of the oppressed. He also argues that "judges perhaps enjoy a situational advantage over the people at large in listening for voices from the margins."[72] If they are willing to be sympathetic, judges, with their concrete knowledge of legal history and institutions and of their malleable character

> are perhaps better situated to conduct a sympathetic inquiry into how, if at all, the readings of history upon which those voices base their complaint can count as interpretations of that history which, however re-collective or even transformative, remain true to that history's informing commitment to the pursuit of political freedom through jurisgenerative politics.[73]

Minow and Michelman embrace pluralism through taking seriously the perspective of the oppressed. This allows them to find, unlike Dworkin, that courts can take the lead sometimes in the search for better justice. Dworkin's Hercules does not admit the perspective of the oppressed. He cannot, because his task is to find coherence with existing institutions, and the oppressed have not made those institutions. They are outsiders. Perhaps through consciousness raising, or through struggle over descriptions of reality, they have created a thinkable perspective, but their perspective is not represented in the institutional artifacts of the power structure.

Even without the search for the excluded perspectives, Hercules would be truer to the critical spirit of pragmatism if Dworkin were attentive to the ways pluralism is built into our system of legal interpretation. Hercules has no colleagues in making his decisions, and this picture is quite untrue to our practice. After all, as Michelman points out, there is a reason why appellate courts decide things in groups, why they deliberate and why they issue plural opinions even when their deliberation is done.[74] The reason is that conversation and dialogue in appellate decisionmaking represent judges' interaction in the context of commitment, for the decisions of courts matter to people's lives, and no judge is unaware of this. This judicial interaction is crucial to our idea of what might be the best result.

A serious pluralism makes possible an understanding of the deep role of discourse in the way conceptions and practices are made and re-

---

72. Michelman, *Law's Republic, supra* note 69, at 1537.

73. *Id.*

74. Michelman, *Traces, supra* note 69, at 16-17.

made, and thus makes possible a commitment to dialogue among alternative conceptions. Even the occasional conceptual paradigm shift can only find the old dominant description of the world to be wrong in retrospect. It cannot help us find that today's dominant description is wrong. For that, we must realize that another perspective is always possible. The best critical spirit of pragmatism recommends that we take our present descriptions with humility and openness, and accept their institutional embodiments as provisional and incompletely entrenched. Pragmatism recommends this openness in the only way pragmatism can—because it seems to work best for human beings. It is time for the openness and critical spirit of pragmatism to infiltrate pragmatist legal theory. Feminism can lead the way.

LAW, MUSIC, AND OTHER PERFORMING ARTS

SANFORD LEVINSON AND J. M. BALKIN†

"[I]nterpretation" is a chameleon. When a performing musician "interprets" a work of music, is he expressing the composer's, or even the composition's, "meaning," or is he not rather expressing *himself* within the interstices of the score?

—Richard Posner[1]

Today the conductor, more than any one musical figure, shapes our musical life and thought. That may not be how things *should* be, but it is the way they are. In a future, fully automated age, it may be that the conductor, along with all performing musicians, will be obsolete. Musical creators are working toward that day, assembling electronic scores that, once put on tape, never vary. . . . But until that unfortunate day is here, let us be thankful that there still remain interpretive musicians to synthesize the product of the composer. For without the interplay between the minds of the creator and interpreter, music is not only stale, flat and unprofitable. It is meaningless. . . . Musical notation is an inexact art, no matter how composers sweat and strive to perfect it. Symbols and instructions on the printed page are subject to various interpretations, not to one interpretation.

—Harold Schonberg[2]

The legislature is like a composer. It cannot help itself: It must leave interpretation to others, principally to the courts.

—Jerome Frank[3]

---

† Levinson is St. John Garwood Chair in Law, University of Texas School of Law. Balkin is Charles Tilford McCormick Professor of Law, University of Texas School of Law. The authors wish to thank Joseph Dodge, Doug Laycock, Dennis Patterson, Richard Posner, Robert Post, Tom Seung, Allan Stein, Carol Weisbrod, and Jay Westbrook for their comments on previous drafts, as well as the participants in faculty workshops at Rutgers-Camden School of Law and the University of Texas School of Law, where earlier versions of this essay were presented.

[1] R. POSNER, THE PROBLEMS OF JURISPRUDENCE 271 (1990).
[2] H. SCHONBERG, THE GREAT CONDUCTORS 23-24 (1967).
[3] Frank, *Words and Music: Some Remarks on Statutory Interpretation,* 47 COLUM. L. REV. 1259, 1264 (1947).

I. PROBLEMS FOR THE PERFORMING ARTIST: BEETHOVEN'S F-NATURAL, SCHUBERT'S REPEATS, AND THE FEDERAL LAND POLICY AND MANAGEMENT ACT OF 1976

The eminent pianist and writer Charles Rosen has noted that "[t]here is an irritating or piquant wrong note in the [score of the] first movement of Beethoven's first piano concerto, a high F-natural where the melody obviously calls for an F-sharp."[4] What accounts for an "obvious" error by this giant of classical music? The answer, says Rosen, lies in the developmental state of the piano when Beethoven composed the concerto: the piano keyboard stopped at F-natural, which therefore established the limit of what was physically possible for a performer to play. To be sure, Beethoven might have written "aspirationally" and composed what, though impossible under current conditions, could nonetheless be aspired to under some future imagined state. Thus Rosen writes of a piano sonata in which Beethoven "asks for a successive *crescendo* and *diminuendo* on a single sustained note," even though "the instrument that can realize this has not yet been invented."[5] But at least this suggests that Beethoven was capable of envisioning the possibility of radical transformation regarding piano design and wanted to signify an intention should those possibilities ever be realized. What, then, does the performer do with the F-natural, where Beethoven appears instead to have acquiesced to the limits of the instrument?

Though the piano that can simultaneously heighten and reduce the sound level of the same note apparently still awaits its development, the piano has indeed been transformed beyond the instrument known to Beethoven in Vienna. Indeed, the expansion of the keyboard happened only shortly after the composition of the first concerto; high F-sharps soon were available to both composers and performers, as exemplified by Beethoven's own use of this note in a number of subsequent compositions, including, interestingly enough, a cadenza meant to be performed as part of the first concerto.[6] He did not, however, return to the initial composition and physically change the notation of the earlier F-natural, in spite of an announced intention, in Rosen's words, "of revising his early

---

[4] Rosen, *The Shock of the Old* (Book Review), N.Y. REV. BOOKS, July 19, 1990, at 46, 48.

[5] *Id.* at 48.

[6] *See id.*

works in order to make use of the extended range."[7] What, then, is a performer to do when she comes to the measure in question? Should she feel bound by the "plain meaning" of the written score, which displays the F-natural, or ignore it and play what Rosen, a gifted pianist, calls the "obviously" preferable F-sharp?

What note should be played is only the first question. Just as important is another. Should we expect the performer, along with playing whatever note she thinks preferable, to offer a "theory" of musical performance that explicitly offers a justification for the note played? Such a theory, for example, would recognize the presence of such contending factors as the standard meaning of musical notation (to those trained in reading music), the composer's presumed intent, the likely sound heard by the initial audiences of the piece, the expectations of the modern audience, or purely aesthetic desirability—i.e. (or is it e.g.?) the production of beautiful and satisfying sequences of sound. Consider also our reactions if the performer gave as a response to our question, "Why did you play that note?" something like, "I just perform and play the note that feels right to me. If you want a theory of performance, go ask someone else. I can't imagine why you would expect one from me, or why you would feel that being given a theory would be of any use."[8]

If we expect the performer to be able to defend her choice to F-sharp or not to F-sharp, would we (however that "we" is defined) advise the performer to look not only at traditional musical materials, but also at what lawyers have done when deciding the meaning of legal notation? It should already be obvious that a lawyer (including, paradigmatically, an adjudicator) engaged in the performance of legal practice—for example, by being asked to construe a statute or a Constitution—can easily be presented with what appear to be equally "obvious" mistakes and be confronted by similar dilemmas of interpretation. Consider, for example, a provision of the Federal Land Policy and Management Act of 1976 that requires firms with unpatented mining claims on federal lands annually to reregister those claims "prior to December 31."[9] What is the status of a claim filed *on* December 31?[10] What do we

---

[7] *Id.*

[8] *Cf.* Fish, *Dennis Martinez and the Uses of Theory*, 96 YALE L.J. 1773 (1987) (asserting a lack of a relationship between theory and practice).

[9] Federal Land Policy and Management Act of 1976 § 314, 43 U.S.C. § 1744(a) (1988).

[10] *See* United States v. Locke, 471 U.S. 84 (1985). This case is discussed by Judge

expect from the legal performer faced with giving meaning to the ink on the page, and how, beyond the obvious difference in subject matter, would those expectations differ from those directed at the musical performer?

Before answering that question, we ask our readers to consider one more musical example, this time from the piano sonatas of Franz Schubert. The great pianist Alfred Brendel has indicated that he feels no duty to follow the repeat signs that appear at the end of the first sections (the so-called "expositions") of Schubert's last piano sonatas.[11] It has, apparently, been believed since at least the late nineteenth century that "these repeats were vestigial manifestations of an archaic mentality and therefore merely pro forma."[12] One reason offered for skipping the repeats is that most members of a modern audience have in fact heard, perhaps repeatedly, the pieces in question (and, of course, they can, by purchasing a record, repeatedly hear the piece, even if previously unknown to them, in the future); they therefore do not benefit from the repeats being played in the same way as did earlier audiences who only rarely could hear any given piece of music.

A second reason deals with contemporary concert practices. Most modern audiences expect three sonatas in the course of a concert, to be played within a two-hour period. Taking all of the repeats would require violating one of these expectations. People would either feel "cheated" by being presented with a meager program or imposed upon by the demand that they remain in the concert hall for two-and-a-half hours in order to get their full allotment of three sonatas.

Brendel's advice to skip the repeats has not met with universal enthusiasm. Neal Zaslaw, a professor of music at Cornell University, believes that "there is no evidence that the repeats . . . were not meant at face value," and he goes on to add that "[r]epeats are repeats, not question marks. They are there because the composers intended them."[13] To be sure, Professor Zaslaw is no fanatic. He

---

Posner in R. POSNER, *supra* note 1, at 267-69, in which he criticizes the majority of the Court for barring claims filed on December 31 because they are not "prior" to that date.

[11] *See* Brendel, *Schubert's Last Sonatas: An Exchange* (Book Review), N.Y. REV. BOOKS, Mar. 16, 1989, at 42, 42-43; *see also* Zaslaw, *Repeat Performance* (Book Review), N.Y. REV. BOOKS, Apr. 27, 1989, at 58-59 for a lengthy letter to the editor responding to Brendel's argument.

[12] Zaslaw, *supra* note 11, at 59.

[13] *Id.*

"see[s] nothing wrong with omitting them if time is short, the evening growing late, the performer or the audience seeming tired."[14] He laconically notes that even the greatest composers, "who made their livings by composing and performing frequently and to order, understood and accepted the realities of adapting the music to the occasion."[15] Still, he seems to suggest, one ought at least both have a good reason for ignoring the repeats and have the decency to admit that one is rejecting the composer's intentions on the matter. Again, one wonders, what is a performer to do, with what rationale, and might a conversation with one's counterparts in the law be at all helpful?

This essay is a review of *Authenticity and Early Music*,[16] a collection of essays that exemplify the heated debates now occurring over what is variously called the Early Music Movement or the Authentic Performance Movement. The movement itself has diverse features, including the rediscovery of forgotten music, especially that of the pre-Baroque period, and the careful reconstruction and renovation of period instruments.[17] But the more controversial aspect of the Early Music Movement is the claim of its followers that music should be played according to the "authentic" performance practices of the era in which it was composed.[18] The phrase "early music" has thus become somewhat of a misnomer. The study and application of performance practices of the Renaissance has paved the way in the past twenty years for authentic performances of the Baroque period—Vivaldi, Bach, and Handel, and then on to the music of the classical period—Beethoven, Haydn and Mozart. Nor have the devotees of authentic performance been content to rest with the close of the eighteenth century. For example, one of the most controversial early music conductors of Beethoven, Roger Norrington, has begun issuing "authentic" renditions of Berlioz, Mendelssohn, and Schumann symphonies. If Schumann's *Spring Symphony* is made authentic, can Brahms be far behind?

As Will Crutchfield explains in his essay, these developments have created considerable anxiety in "traditional musicians," an anxiety, Crutchfield argues, that is well justified:

---

[14] *Id.*

[15] *Id.*

[16] AUTHENTICITY AND EARLY MUSIC (N. Kenyon ed. 1988).

[17] *See* Kenyon, *Authenticity and Early Music: Some Issues and Questions,* in AUTHENTICITY AND EARLY MUSIC, *supra* note 16, at 1.

[18] *See id.* at 4-5.

They know it will not stop with Beethoven any more than it stopped with Bach ten years ago. The movement not only hits them in the pocketbook, but questions the very basis of their art. It is as though we told a generation of scientists that their Ph.Ds were based on a now discredited body of theory—say Ptolemaic astronomy—and now, sorry, the degrees are no good. Worse: it is as though we had been told that Ptolemy was right after all.[19]

As Crutchfield suggests, great sums of money—in recording contracts and record sales—and great professional power and prestige are at stake in the debates over authentic performance. It is no accident that Raymond Leppard, one of the foremost interpreters of Baroque music in an earlier generation, looks askance at the claims made by disciples of authenticity, some of whose recordings inevitably compete with his own.[20] The monetary interest alone, a cynic might suggest, is enough to attract the attention of lawyers. Of course, that is not quite the reason we became interested in these matters. Our interest is in the theory of interpreting commands. We are legal academics writing primarily, we presume, for other legal academics, who are either legal performers in their own right or, with at least some regularity, critics (in the sense of evaluators) of the legal performances of others.

There are two obvious questions raised by our writing this review, even prior to the specific points we will be making below. The first concerns competence. Are we reviewing the book as "experts" who can claim some special training in the areas being discussed by the book's contributors and offer critical assessments of and contributions to the scholarly literature of musicology? The answer, in the case of one of us (Levinson), is unequivocally no; though he listens to music a great deal, his critical acumen is limited almost entirely to "knowing what he likes." The case for the other (Balkin) is a bit more complicated,[21] but he would also make no claims to being a member of the musicological scholarly community to which one ordinarily looks for "authoritative" pronouncements about the quality of scholarly work. But so what? Why would one believe that one must be an "expert" in an area in order to have

---

[19] Crutchfield, *Fashion, Conviction, and Performance Style in an Age of Revivals*, in AUTHENTICITY AND EARLY MUSIC, *supra* note 16, at 19, 20.

[20] *See* Kenyon, *supra* note 17, at 7-8.

[21] Balkin, unlike Levinson, studied composition and orchestration in his youth, and has published an article on Puccini's opera *Turandot. See* Balkin, *Turandot's Victory*, 2 YALE J. OF L. & HUM. 299 (1990).

interesting things to say about a given book? And this question, it should be noted, is as true for books about law (about which we *are* suitably certified experts) as for books about early music. One of us (Levinson) has written a book explicitly attacking the notion that conversation about constitutional law should be restricted to those who have been properly credentialed.[22] Thus, if we are so bold to review a book on early music, we should not be afraid to see books on law reviewed in *Early Music*, the leading journal in that field. On the contrary, we would welcome such reviews, at least if musicians think there are any useful comparisons to be made.

This last point leads to a second, equally obvious, question: Why should any lawyer care in the slightest about the debates occurring in the alien field of music (or musicologists about the debates played out in the legal academy)? Richard Posner, the author of one of the quotations opening this essay, devoted much of his book *Law and Literature: A Misunderstood Relation*[23] to attacking the premise that legal analysts really have anything to learn, at least professionally, from the interpretive dilemmas faced by their colleagues in departments of literature. "[T]here are," wrote Posner, "too many differences between works of literature and enactments of legislatures [or of constitutional conventions] to permit much fruitful analogizing of legislative to literary interpretation."[24] One of us (Levinson) had written that "[t]here are as many plausible readings of the United States Constitution as there are versions of *Hamlet*."[25] Though agreeing that *Hamlet* and the Constitution both present many genuine interpretive puzzles, Posner insists that they are "so different from each other that it is unlikely that a *Hamlet* scholar will have anything useful to say about the Constitution or a constitutional scholar anything useful to say about *Hamlet*."[26] Posner's allusion to musical performance in the

---

[22] *See* S. LEVINSON, CONSTITUTIONAL FAITH 49-50 (1988) (defending a "protestant" approach that minimalizes institutional authority and invites all citizens to participate as equals in constitutional dialogue).

[23] R. POSNER, LAW AND LITERATURE: A MISUNDERSTOOD RELATION (1988).

[24] *Id.* at 218.

[25] Levinson, *Law as Literature*, 60 TEX. L. REV. 373, 391 (1982). Interestingly, most readers have read this passage as asserting the infinite malleability of the Constitution rather than, say, the limited number of plausible versions of *Hamlet*. This probably says more about the layman's views about plausible artistic interpretation than it does about Levinson's views of the Constitution. *See infra* note 64. Here Posner attacks the utility of discussing *Hamlet* and the Constitution together rather than the view that either has a particular set of plausible meanings.

[26] R. POSNER, *supra* note 23, at 263.

opening quotation notwithstanding, it is unclear whether his skepticism about insights from literary scholars would dissipate if they were replaced by insights from musicologists.

We think that Posner is wrong in dismissing the potential benefits of communication between literary and legal analysts, but we also think that the question is not truly a theoretical one, as suggested by Posner's use of the word "unlikely" rather than, say, "inherently impossible." The ultimate test in regard to the interplay of law and literature, music, or any other field is the practical aid given the analyst, the felt sense of illumination provided by thinking about Beethoven's F-natural or *Hamlet* while wrestling with the possible meanings of a statute, regulation, or the Constitution of the United States.

Posner's dismissal of the potential interaction between legal analysts and disciplinary outsiders (or vice versa) begs a number of important questions. One is the assumption that there would have to be a transdisciplinary theory of interpretation-in-general that could be applied to all texts in order for different disciplines to have important things to say to each other. In fact, many modern students of hermeneutics have rejected the plausibility of a "science" of "interpretation in general."[27] As a tradition now identified with Wittgenstein and his successors insists, there are only "practices," each constituted by inchoate and unformalizable standards that establish one's statements or, indeed, pianistic performances, as "legitimately assertable"[28] by persons within the interpretive community[29] that constitutes the practice in question.

At the same time, an increasingly common practice in the contemporary academy is precisely to look outside the narrowest disciplinary boundaries for potential insight in solving the puzzles presented by one's own disciplinary materials. To adopt Claude Lévi-Strauss's famous notion, the essence of the post-modernist, post-structuralist interpreter is to be a *bricoleur*, who resourcefully and opportunistically borrows whatever tools might be available to solve particular problems at hand.[30] There are obvious similarities

---

[27] *Cf.* R. RORTY, PHILOSOPHY AND THE MIRROR OF NATURE 8-11 (1979) (arguing that standards of correct judgment differ among various disciplines and that neither philosophy nor any other master discipline can impose its own external standards on them).

[28] S. KRIPKE, WITTGENSTEIN ON RULES AND PRIVATE LANGUAGE 78 (1982).

[29] *See* S. FISH, IS THERE A TEXT IN THIS CLASS? 303-71 (1980).

[30] *See* C. LÉVI-STRAUSS, THE SAVAGE MIND 16-36 (1966); G. GARVEY, CONSTITUTIONAL *BRICOLAGE* 15 (1971).

between bricolage and contemporary pragmatism. The *bricoleur* is not a self-conscious theorist. What justifies using any given tool is its usefulness. There is no theoretically *a priori* way of deciding what tools are either "essential" or "absolutely inappropriate." Thus the pragmatist temperament, which is most likely to reject the notion of a transcendental science of interpretation, is also the most likely to look to other disciplines for analogies and comparisons that might be useful in the pragmatist's own work. Ironically, it is only after one gives up the dream of a single tool useful on every occasion that one begins to see the merits of the diverse tools available for construction, whether of buildings or of theories.

Indeed, Judge Posner, who has recently announced himself a pragmatist in his book, *The Problems of Jurisprudence*,[31] has hardly practiced what he preached in *Law and Literature: A Misunderstood Relationship*;[32] and his later writing suggests he may now be somewhat more latitudinarian. He has, for example, recently published a devastating review of Robert Bork's originalist jurisprudence under the title *Bork and Beethoven*.[33] Posner raises, but does not consider at any real length, some of the questions elaborated in the present review. He notes particularly, and valuably, that conservative intellectuals associated with the magazine *Commentary* seem both to embrace Bork's originalism—the view that "original intent" should control constitutional interpretation—and to be hostile to what on the surface seems to be a very similar view, identified with partisans of "authentic" performance—that a musical performer should try, as much as possible, to recreate the original sounds of a musical composition.[34] He is certainly correct in noticing that explanation of this apparent inconsistency requires some analysis of the cultural moment in which both make their respective appearances. Indeed, it is precisely the insight displayed by juxtaposing Bork and Beethoven (or, more accurately, Bork and *Commentary*'s music critic Samuel Lipman) that seems to disconfirm the rigid disciplinary separations advocated in *Law and Literature: A Misunderstood Relation.*

---

[31] R. POSNER, *supra* note 1.
[32] R. POSNER, *supra* note 23.
[33] Posner, *Bork and Beethoven* (Book Review), 42 STAN. L. REV. 1365 (1990) (reviewing R. BORK, THE TEMPTING OF AMERICA: THE POLITICAL SEDUCTION OF LAW (1990)).
[34] *See id.*

Given that we, too, consider ourselves pragmatists, we certainly have no desire to criticize Posner's argument by positing another equally aprioristic notion that reading literary theory or musicology will *necessarily* be helpful. Nor, certainly, do we wish to argue that law, literature, and music are identical enterprises operating under similar rules of practice. They are not. But to concede that law and music are importantly different does not necessarily imply that they do not also share enough similarities to make comparison useful (and, once more, we emphasize that pragmatic usefulness is the primary criterion we are employing).

Rudyard Kipling put the matter succinctly: "[W]hat should they know of England who only England know?"[35] Presumably one can paraphrase (though not parody) Kipling by asking "what should they know of Texas tort law who only Texas tort law know" (the justification, presumably, for teaching in our classes *de facto* comparative tort law rather than concentrating on the law of a single jurisdiction); "what should they know of tort law who only tort law know" (the justification, presumably, for asking our students to compare the notion of warranty as developed in contract law against developments in the products liability branch of tort law); or "what should they know of American tort law who only American tort law know" (the justification, presumably, for offering to our students courses on other societies' responses to the problems treated by American tort law). So the question ultimately becomes, "What should they know of law who only law know"? Obviously one can know a great deal about England without leaving its shores, and one can make the same claim about the other examples. But is Kipling really "refuted" by that recognition? Would we not, instead, say that few people cannot learn more about their own society by experiencing another? Is this not why most of us refer to travel as "broadening"? Surely this term implies more than simply amassing information about a different society. Rather, it suggests that a realization of how they do things in Tanzania will provide insights into how we behave here in the States. This has certainly been our own experience, and, we are confident, the experience of most of our readers.

Why does Posner, who is notably catholic in his own intellectual interests and well aware of the importance of looking outside

---

[35] Kipling, "The English Flag," *quoted in* OXFORD DICTIONARY OF QUOTATIONS 298 (3d ed. 1979).

traditional legal materials for insight into the law, reject the utility of a lawyer's reading literary theory? The primary reason seems to lie in Posner's insistence that law and literature are fundamentally different enterprises, with fundamentally different points. "A poet tries to create a work of art, a thing of beauty and pleasure."[36] This is, for Posner, presumably true of literary writers in general, even if their genre is the novel or short story rather than the poem. The legislature (or the constitutional convention), on the other hand, "is trying to give commands to its subordinates in our government system."[37] The notion of "command" is central to Posner's theory. "A command," he says, "is designed to set up a direct channel between the issuer's mind and the recipient's; it is a communication, to be decoded in accordance with the sender's intentions."[38] Nor is Posner alone in this view. Robin West, normally no great ally of Posnerian thought, concurs: "legal interpretation is the attempt to ascertain the meaning behind a command; literary interpretation is the attempt to ascertain the meaning behind an artistic expression."[39]

In their differentiation of law and literature, both Posner and West take the poem and the novel as the model of artistic expression. This is a fortunate example for both scholars, since the poem and the novel seem to have little to do with the phenomenon of command. Although Shelley might have claimed that poets were the unacknowledged legislators of mankind,[40] that designation is clearly metaphorical in a way that is not true of the senator or representative anguishing about a vote or the military commander ordering troops into action. Posner thus argues that "[l]aw is coercion rather than persuasion,"[41] and he offers the interpretation of military orders as a good analogue to statutory interpreta-

---

[36] R. POSNER, *supra* note 23, at 240.

[37] *Id.*

[38] *Id.*

[39] West, *Adjudication is not Interpretation: Some Reservations about the Law-as-Literature Movement,* 54 TENN. L. REV. 203, 277 (1987).

[40] *See* M. SHELLEY, A DEFENCE OF POETRY (1821), *quoted in* OXFORD DICTIONARY OF QUOTATIONS, *supra* note 35, at 505. See also Samuel Johnson's quite similar statement, "[The poet] must write as . . . the legislator of mankind, and consider himself as presiding over the thoughts and manners of future generations; as a being superior to time and place." S. JOHNSON, RASSELAS (1759), *quoted in* OXFORD DICTIONARY OF QUOTATIONS, *supra* note 35, at 282.

[41] R. POSNER, *supra* note 23, at 249. *See also* R. POSNER, *supra* note 1, at 296 (1990) ("Agreement on the meaning of legal texts may in many cases depend ultimately on force—law's ultimate backing.").

tion in general.[42]   For her part, West asserts that "[l]aw is a product of power," and that legal interpretation is criticism of power.[43]

It is not the purpose of this review to question Posner's or West's reliance on law-as-command or law-as-emanation-of-power, although both of us believe that undue emphasis on this theory produces an impoverished account of law.[44] Indeed, for purposes of this review, we will gladly accept their view that law does indeed often command in a way that a poem or a novel does not. We will also acknowledge that there has been too much insistence that techniques of poetic interpretation could prove useful to the legal analyst, and that law-and-literature scholars have overemphasized the similarities between law and literature and underemphasized the differences. But note that what is interesting about the examples that lead off this review—Beethoven's F-natural and Schubert's repeats—is that they appear to be law-like commands. Consider in this context the comments of early music apostle Christopher Hogwood regarding the discovery of new material relevant to a composer's presumed intentions: "That's the wonderful thing, I think, about coming across new versions of pieces or new evidence. Suddenly that gives you this extra energy: 'Ah, a new set of instructions for embellishment . . . ah, wonderful!'"[45] If this is not a command theory of language, we do not know what would be.

Indeed, when one looks at any musical score, one is faced predominantly not with expression, but command. For what is a musical score but a series of *directions* concerning tempo, meter, pitch, rhythm, attack, and orchestration that are to be carried out over time by a group of performers? To be sure, the skilled musician can read a score like the ordinary person can read a novel, but this is not normally the way either enjoys music. Rather, one listens to the result of the commands brought to life by the performers so instructed. We can therefore imagine a continuum of artistic genres, some of which are more command oriented, like the musical score, and others which are less so, like the poem and

---

[42] *See* R. POSNER, *supra* note 1, at 272-73.

[43] West, *supra* note 39, at 277.

[44] At the same time, we believe that an account of law which focuses only on community-enhancing or permissive aspects is equally impoverished. *See, e.g.,* Levinson, *Conversing about Justice,* 100 YALE L. J. 1855 (1991).

[45] Taruskin, *The Pastness of the Present and the Presence of the Past,* in AUTHENTICITY AND EARLY MUSIC, *supra* note 16, at 150 (ellipsis in original) (quoting Christopher Hogwood).

the novel. The differences are, like those in all continua, a matter of degree. Even a poem may contain instructions (whether explicit or implicit) on how it is to be read—for example, through punctuation and accent marks. Far closer to the musical score is the play, which includes both the lines to be spoken by actors and the relevant stage directions. To be sure, plays can be read silently without performing them, and studied and appreciated like poems and novels. But most people would agree that the artistic expression in a play is not fully realized except through its performance on the stage. Dramatic genres thus undermine the distinction between interpretation of artistic expression and interpretation of command, for a play's artistic interpretation requires interpretation and observance of commands.

At first glance it might seem odd to speak of the lawyer or the judge as a "performer" of law. But in fact, the comparison, first noted by Jerome Frank, is quite apt.[46] As John Chipman Gray, one of the precursors of realism, pointed out at the turn of the century, the texts we call law are not law-in-action but only sources of law—they require the interpretation and application of lawyers, judges, and other legal officials to become law in the sense of a practice of social regulation.[47] Just as the music of the *Eroica* is not identical with its score, but needs a performer to realize it, so too the social practice of law is not fully identical with its written texts, but needs the activity of those entrusted with its performance to be realized.[48]

Another reason often given to doubt the relevance of artistic interpretation to legal interpretation is the differences in consequences that flow from the interpretive act. Legal interpretation affects people's lives and fortunes, whereas nothing of consequence flows from what literary interpreters do. A second, related claim is that unlike artistic interpretation, adjudication is distinctively an act of power.[49] Thus, Professor West argues that adjudication, although in form an interpretive act, is actually an "imperative act"—"an exercise of power in a way in which truly interpretive acts, such as literary interpretation, are not."[50]

---

[46] *See* Frank, *supra* note 3, at 1264.

[47] J. GRAY, THE NATURE AND SOURCES OF LAW 170 (2d ed. 1921).

[48] *See* Frank, *supra* note 3, at 1270-71. For a similar argument, see D. KORNSTEIN, THE MUSIC OF THE LAWS 108 (1982). The foreword to this book of essays, interestingly, was written by Robert Bork. *Id.* at 9-12.

[49] West, *supra* note 39, at 277.

[50] *Id.* at 207.

As to the first point, it seems clear that more rides on whether a young lieutenant obeys what she believes to be a mistaken order of her commander than if Alfred Brendel takes a repeat in a Schubert sonata. But that is true only because of the particular examples offered. In fact, much more may turn on certain directorial decisions in mounting productions of plays or operas than the adjudicated result of the average fender-bender. As noted above, the authentic performance movement is controversial not merely because of its hermeneutic claims, but because it threatens to throw a large number of traditional performers out of a job. If Maestro Norrington is correct, the New York Philharmonic would be best advised to keep its nose out of Schubert, Dvořák and the Romantics—the backbone of the modern symphony orchestra's repertory—to say nothing of Beethoven and Mozart. It had best stick to music it can play authentically—Shostakovich and perhaps Walter Piston. No doubt this will have a significant impact on its subscriptions. It will have an even greater effect on recording contracts, whose royalties often make up a sizeable chunk of a first-class orchestra's revenues. The authentic performance movement is controversial because it has thrown down the gauntlet—play Beethoven with extra woodwinds and an extremely astringent string tone or do not play him at all.

To be sure, Roger Norrington does not have the same power that the Supreme Court does. He cannot enjoin the New York Philharmonic from playing music "incorrectly," and those who disagree with him can offer competing readings of the music, unlike lower courts who are presumably bound by Supreme Court interpretations of federal law.[51] But even if Norrington has less power to enforce conformity with his views than an appellate court, it is a mistake to view him as having no power at all, especially to the extent that his devotees gain control and influence over institutions that shape our musical tastes and preferences.

One need only look at changes in the *Penguin Stereo Record Guide*[52]—a record collector's bible authored by contributors to *Gramophone Magazine*—to see what is at stake in the debates over authenticity in terms of economic power, status, and artistic prestige. In the second edition, published in 1975, the authors speak paternalistically but often approvingly of the very small

---

[51] We are indebted to Richard Posner for this point.

[52] E. GREENFIELD, R. LAYTON & I. MARCH, THE PENGUIN STEREO RECORD GUIDE (2d ed. 1975).

number of authentic performances of Baroque music then recorded; in their view, it's quite all right if you like that sort of thing.[53] But traditional performances constitute virtually all recommended albums of Baroque music. As the Eighties progressed, more and more authentic performances, first of Baroque, and then of Classical music appeared. In the 1984 successor volume, *The Complete Penguin Stereo Record and Cassette Guide*,[54] the authors express their approval of many individual "authentic" performances, tempered with occasional distress at the new fundamentalism that appears to inform them.[55] "Traditional," rather than "authentic," performances, however, constitute the lion's share of recommendations.[56] In the work's latest incarnation, *The Penguin Guide to Compact Discs*,[57] published this past year, the field of Baroque music has been largely ceded to authentic performers. It is assumed that most listeners will want such performances, although recommendations are still offered for those who insist on more traditional

---

[53] Discussing Nikolas Harnoncourt's and Gustav Leonhardt's cycle of Bach cantatas for Telefunken records, which at that time was virtually the only example of authentic performance committed to record, the authors note that the use of boys instead of female sopranos "will undoubtedly deter some collectors." *Id.* at 45. Although generally supportive of the project, the authors complain of "a certain want of rhythmic freedom" and too much "expressive caution" in the performances, so that "the grandeur of Bach's inspiration is at times lost to view." *Id.* The tendency to accent all main beats heavily, they note, is "a constant source of irritation throughout the series." *Id.* at 47.

[54] E. GREENFIELD, R. LAYTON & I. MARCH, THE COMPLETE PENGUIN STEREO AND CASSETTE RECORD GUIDE (1984).

[55] For example, in the middle of a highly positive review of Herman Bauman's recording of the Mozart Horn Concertos on a valveless horn, the authors note:

> We are not convinced that the playing of 'original instruments' always demonstrates their full expressive potential and in the case of the french horn it would seem perverse to use a valveless instrument, when a narrow bore modern horn . . . can sound the same, yet produce uniformity of timbre and stay in tune throughout its compass.

Id. at 682. Similarly, in the book's introduction, the authors argue:

> While it is undoubtedly valuable to have an educated opinion of what the music sounded like in the composer's own time, sometimes considerations of scholarship—however dedicated—seem to inhibit the spirit of the music-making. Advocates of the 'authentic' school often seem to regard any kind of expressive licence as reactionary . . . .

Id. at vii.

[56] *See, e.g., id.* at 21-24 (offering recommendations for Bach's *Brandenburg Concertos*); *id.* at 65-67 (Bach's *St. Matthew Passion*); *id.* at 1165-69 (Vivaldi's *Four Seasons*).

[57] E. GREENFIELD, R. LAYTON & I. MARCH, THE PENGUIN GUIDE TO COMPACT DISCS (1990) [hereinafter GUIDE TO DISCS].

versions.[58] With millions of classical music discs sold each year on the recommendations of *Gramophone* and similar magazines, it is clear that interpretive debates are hardly exclusively about matters of expression.[59]

As for Professor West's second point—that legal interpretation is an act of power, while artistic interpretation is not—we think this borders on the naive. One does not have to be a Nietzschean to recognize the struggles for power and prestige involved in debates over artistic interpretation. Indeed, the essays in *Authenticity and Early Music* speak of nothing so much as the battle for authority between early music acolytes and their traditional opponents.[60] Richard Taruskin complains loudly of the "authoritarian" appropriation of the word "authenticity" by early music advocates,[61] while

---

[58] *See, e.g., id.* at 22 (recommending Trevor Pinnock's performance of Bach's *Brandenburg Concertos* while suggesting alternatives "[f]or those who still cannot quite attune their ears to the style of string playing favoured by the authentic school").

[59] And, as Nicholas Kenyon reports in his introduction to *Authenticity and Early Music,* record companies have indeed found that authenticity sells:

> [I]t quickly became clear to the record companies that the legend 'Performed on Authentic Instruments' was regarded as some sort of seal of Good Musical Housekeeping, and the implication of much of their activity was that the use of such instruments guaranteed or at least went some considerable way to ensuring 'authentic' performance. Eventually we reached the absurd situation where the American company releasing the Academy of Ancient Music's recording of the Pachelbel Canon affixed a sticker to the disc proclaiming: 'Authentic Edition. The famous Kanon as Pachelbel heard it.' Those of us who had difficulty knowing what Pachelbel looked like, never mind what he heard like, had some problems with this.

Kenyon, *supra* note 17, at 6.

[60] *See, e.g.,* Taruskin, *supra* note 46, at 139 (noting that the classical music scene "has lately taken on the appearance of a 'battlefield,' . . . [and] we are fighting it out, in this book and elsewhere.") (quoting Crutchfield, *A Report From the Battlefield,* N.Y. Times, July 28, 1985, at 1.).

[61] Taruskin, supra note 45, at 138-39 ("One is hardly free to say, 'I prefer inauthenticity to authenticity,' or, 'I prefer inappropriateness to appropriateness,'—at least if one is interested in maintaining respectability with the crowd that swears by the *Harvard Dictionary [of Music]*."). Interestingly enough, Judge Posner has also criticized the "authoritarianism" of those who look to "tradition" for privileged insight into the law. *See* R. POSNER, *supra* note 1, at 448.

Will Crutchfield begins his essay by noting that the authentic performance movement "has come to resemble a juggernaut, a steamroller, a conquering army."[62]

Like Professor West, we also may have too easily accepted that the paradigm of interpretive debate was a solitary scholar lecturing on Keats' *Ode to a Nightingale* from a lectern. Yet it has become increasingly clear that many acts of interpretation are performative utterances which simultaneously constitute acts of power.[63] Rather than seeing the legal act of interpretation as exceptional in its complicity with power, we would suggest that it is quite the other way around. The legal act of interpretation, which clothes power through an act of cognition, is the normal, paradigmatic act of interpretation, while an imagined quiet "powerless" lecture on Keats is the exception.

Moreover, we think that West's and Posner's arguments about legal power confuse the effects of interpretive difficulties with their causes. It may well be true that because the meaning of the Constitution is debatable, people's lives will be affected by what interpreters do. Thus, significant consequences turn on the existence of interpretive difficulties. But this fact is not the *cause* of interpretive difficulty. The cause is the semiotic nature of the command—the fact that the Constitution contains commands encoded in signs requiring interpretation in the light of existing conditions. It is because both the text of the Constitution and the score of Beethoven's *Pastorale* Symphony are commands inscribed in signs that must be interpreted by performers that difficulties of interpretation arise. Once again, we do not deny that the consequences of the exercise of interpretive power should be in the mind of the interpreter as she interprets, and that they might serve as reasons for interpreting one way rather than another. But the interpreter's power does not create her interpretive difficulties—

---

[62] Crutchfield, *supra* note 19, at 19. Crutchfield reports that the opera director Frank Corsaro has even coined a phrase for the increasingly common experience of being frustrated in one's artistic attempts by the new musicological fundamentalism: he calls it being "gesellschafted." *Id.* at 20.

[63] *See* S. FISH, DOING WHAT COMES NATURALLY: CHANGE, RHETORIC AND THE PRACTICE OF THEORY IN LITERARY AND LEGAL STUDIES 135-36, 306, 309 (1990).

rather it is the interpretive difficulties which give rise to her power over others.[64]

---

[64] In discussing the relationship of law to music with colleagues, we have also witnessed again and again the unquestioned assumption that, unlike legal interpretation, there are really no standards for judging artistic interpretation, and that, in contrast to legal interpretation and legal scholarship, there is really no good way to say that one performance or interpretation is better, richer, or more faithful than another. We suspect that lawyers and legal scholars who speak in this way have never attended a piano competition. Indeed, the entire system of education and training for musicians is premised on the assumption that some performances are better than others. The same assumption underlies record reviews, critical reviews of concerts, and a host of other institutions that are devoted largely to sorting, judging, and evaluating musical performance and musical talent. This is not to say that people do not disagree heatedly over these matters, or that views about interpretation do not change historically; we would only point out that the same is true of legal interpretation and of legal judgments of quality in scholarship or in judicial reasoning.

We think that the exaggerated emphasis on artistic subjectivity by lawyers and legal scholars forced to confront the analogies between law and music is a projection of what are thought to be undesirable characteristics of the self onto the Other. By opposing law to art in this manner, one is able to suppress the emotional and subjective elements of legal judgment by projecting them onto the opposite, art, while simultaneously downplaying the possibility of reasonableness and impartiality in artistic judgment. *See* Balkin, *The Domestication of Law and Literature,* 14 LAW & SOC. INQUIRY 787, 794 (1989); *cf.* Torres and Brewster, *Judges and Juries: Separate Moments in the Same Phenomenon,* 4 LAW & INEQUALITY 171, 181-85 (1986) (Ideological construction of juries as "emotional" allows judges to suppress recognition of their own biases and unreasonableness.).

As this essay went to press, we came across a fascinating case that yokes legal and artistic interpretation together, and thus actually requires a legal judgment about the plasticity of artistic standards. The Tams-Witmark Music Library, which licenses the rights to the Cole Porter musical "Anything Goes," has denied director Martin Teitel the right to stage the musical with a man in the lead role of Reno Sweeney (created on Broadway by Ethel Merman). *See* Shewey, *Anything Goes . . . Well Almost,* Village Voice, Apr. 23, 1991, at S2, col. 4. Previous productions on Fire Island and in Dallas were such a success that Teitel's unusual casting was reported in the trade press, at which point Tams-Witmark objected. (Teitel has met Tams-Witmark's action with a sex discrimination suit of his own.) *Id.* The standard Tams-Witmark licensing contract states that there will be "no additions, transpositions, or interpolations of any kind," although the musical is regularly performed in a modified, edited, and reconstituted fashion without complaint. *Id.* Thus in practice, at least, the question may boil down to whether the proposed innovations go too far. Shewey argues that "[i]t's patently clear that Tams-Witmark's objections stem from homophobia, especially dismaying considering Porter's own homosexuality." *Id.* Perhaps Teitel's alteration is no more a breach of the agreement than setting the musical in the present rather than in the 1930's. Nevertheless, in interpreting the contract, we would think it highly irresponsible for a court to find in the director's favor solely on the grounds that no one can tell whether or not a production is faithful to the musical's score and book. No matter how this particular case should be decided, there must be some point at which outraged theatergoers could demand their money back on the grounds that the play promised to them had not, in fact, been performed. We thus maintain once again that legal and musical interpretation are not as different as they first appear; for in musical, as well as in legal interpretation, not anything goes.

II. HOW TO PERFORM MUSIC AUTHENTICALLY—*A LA RECHERCHE DU TEMPS PERDU*[65]

To take up Kipling's metaphor again, perhaps the best way to understand what other countries and cultures contribute to our understanding of England is to begin the journey itself. One quickly discovers that examples like Beethoven's F-natural or Schubert's repeats do not even begin to exhaust the many different kinds of controversies that may arise over performing the music of the (relatively distant) past. We begin, then, with the interpretation of commands in Beethoven's Symphony No. 6 in F, the *Pastorale*. Consider the following exegesis, given in a booklet accompanying the compact disc recording of Beethoven's Sixth Symphony by The Hanover Band, an English group fully committed to the task of performing music "in a form which [the composer] would recognise."[66] There is a certain irony in the Hanover Band's aspiration, given that Beethoven went deaf well before the composition of the *Pastorale* Symphony. It becomes a zen-like question (as in "what is the sound of one hand clapping?") to ask how one would have the slightest idea what Beethoven might "recognise" as the sound of a symphony that in fact he never heard or could hear fully, save in his own mind.

But of course the Hanover Band probably intended to produce the sonic effects experienced by Beethoven's non-hearing-impaired contemporaries. Even if one grants the plausibility of the Hanover Band's ambitions, their achievement is a daunting task, as illustrated by some of the issues discussed in the booklet. They include, but are not limited to, such aspects of musical performance as trying to recreate "the original orchestral sound" (which means in effect offering "an intimate, chamber music approach"), assigning to notes

---

[65] We allude here not only to the title of Proust's epic example of twentieth century modernism, but to the implications of the different English translations offered in its stead. The standard translation is *In Remembrance of Things Past*. Vladimir Nabokov, among others, has preferred the more "literal" *In Search of Lost Time*. *See* V. NABOKOV, LECTURES ON LITERATURE 208 (F. Bowers ed. 1980). The two titles have quite different implications. We believe that the debates over "authentic" musical performance turn on whether one can truly recover the past or whether one must realize that those times are irredeemably lost, and the concomitant necessity of recognizing that we live exclusively in our own time, separated and alien from the past.

[66] C. BROWN, THE HANOVER BAND (1988) (pamphlet accompanying compact disc version of *Beethoven's Symphony No. 6 'Pastoral'* (Nimbus Records 1988)).

the pitch assigned to them in the eighteenth century, mimicking "a late 18th-century feeling for tempo," and presenting "the dramatic address to rhythmic accent and dynamic colour which eyewitnesses [earwitnesses?] describe in Beethoven's own performances."[67] Also characteristic of "authentic" performance is the Hanover Band's emphasis on the use of "original" instruments, which can mean physical objects either originally produced at the time of composition and performance or built more recently in conformity to what is known about the instruments available at the relevant time. This means, among other things, that horns will have no valves, that pianos will produce sounds quite different from a modern Steinway, and that violins will use catgut instead of contemporary metallic strings.

The sonic effects produced by early music enthusiasts like Hogwood, Norrington, and the members of the Hanover Band are clearly different from what many listeners will be used to. For example, modern string players move their fingers slightly on sustained notes to produce a warmer tone, an effect called vibrato.[68] Early music players eschew vibrato, producing a string tone that has variously been described as sour, astringent, or vinegary.[69] Woodwinds and horns often sound out of tune, despite the best of intentions and the most skilled players. In the classical piano concerto, the pianoforte is replaced by the earlier fortepiano, which despite its name produces sounds that are more often piano than forte. Hogwood's tempi are usually much faster than even the fastest traditional performances and display a certain rigidity, while the Hanover Band apparently believe that authenticity requires more flexible changes in tempo than those often heard in traditional performances. Above all, authentic performance produces lighter and more transparent textures in Baroque and Classical music, with

---

[67] *Id.*

[68] THE NEW HARVARD DICTIONARY OF MUSIC 910 (D. Randel ed. 1986) [hereinafter THE NEW HARVARD DICTIONARY].

[69] One of the most amusing aspects of the reviews in *The Penguin Guide to Compact Discs* is their constant assurances to readers that the strings in their recommended authentic performances do not sound half as bad as one would expect. *See, e.g.*, GUIDE TO DISCS, *supra* note 57, at 299 ("Collectors fearful of the vinegary tone often produced by period violins will find their ears beguiled by sounds of great beauty."); *id.* at 29 ("Kuijken . . . shows that authentic performance need not be acidly over-abrasive."); *id.* at 23 (describing Pinnock's performances as "not too abrasive"); *id.* at 35 ("[T]hese accounts [of Bach solo violin music] are as little painful or scratchy as you are likely to get in the authentic field.").

a corresponding loss of weight and, some would say, grandeur.[70] The more expressive utterances—for example those in the slow movements of Mozart symphonies—tend to be downplayed,[71] and the general feeling is one of buoyancy and even lack of seriousness, or in Richard Taruskin's words, of music that "seems ready virtually to blow away."[72]

Do these innovations bring us closer to authentic performance, whatever that might mean? Let us begin with the insistence on using original instruments. Malcolm Bilson, an early music specialist who has recently recorded a cycle of Mozart's piano concerti using a fortepiano, has argued not only that Mozart's sonatas sound significantly different when played on a late-eighteenth century piano, but that a performance played on such a piano was importantly better, because more authentic, than one played on a modern Steinway. Charles Rosen disagreed, and he used Bilson's protest as an example of the ideological nature of the "authentic" performance movement in early music.[73] Professor Zaslaw, whom we have earlier seen in a debate over repeats with Alfred Brendel, tried to mediate between Rosen and Bilson. Zaslaw argued that the eighteenth-century Stein or Walter pianos used by Mozart and the twentieth-century Steinway or Bösendorfer pianos available to Rosen "are extraordinarily sophisticated instruments, each perfect in its own way. The two types are quite different, having been consciously designed to satisfy two very different aesthetics. Each can do things that the other, with all the good will, musicianship, and brilliant pianistic techniques in the world, cannot do."[74]

Rosen responded, however, that Zaslaw's attempted reconciliation still subscribed to the "erroneous and anachronistic assumption that the conception of an eighteenth-century work was identical with the sound we think the composer expected to hear."[75] He particularly took exception to Zaslaw's statement that both the Stein and

---

[70] *See, e.g., id.* at 447 (reviewing Trevor Pinnock's performance of Handel's *12 Concerti grossi*, Op. 6).

[71] *See, e.g., id.* at 682-83 (reviewing Hogwood's performances of the late Mozart symphonies).

[72] Taruskin, *The Pastness of the Present and the Presence of the Past,* in AUTHENTICITY AND EARLY MUSIC, *supra* note 16, at 188.

[73] *See* Rosen, N.Y. REV. BOOKS, Nov. 8, 1990, at 60 (replying to letter by Malcolm Bilson).

[74] Zaslaw, N.Y. REV. BOOKS, Feb. 14, 1991, at 50 (letter to the editor).

[75] Rosen, N.Y. REV. BOOKS, Feb. 14, 1991, at 50 (responding to Zaslaw's letter in the same issue).

Steinways are "each perfect in their own way," responding that "there are aspects of the music of Stravinsky, Bartok, Boulez, and Carter that can only be imperfectly realized on a Steinway. I see no reason to accept a claim of perfection on behalf of the Stein."[76] To the extent that anyone believes that a Stein is "perfect" for the performance of Mozart, Rosen argued, "that is only and tautologically because Mozart *is* to them what he sounds like on a Stein."[77] To believe that the Stein was "really so 'perfect' for Mozart" would presumably require that one believe as well that "the greater sustaining and singing power of the new pianos made soon after Mozart's death would be a falling-off from this absolute state."[78] Rosen freely concedes that "the 'improvements' in construction entailed a loss of certain tonal qualities as well as a gain of others. Zaslaw's position, however, implies that all the changes be seen as nothing but a loss and a degeneration from the ideal sound."[79] Zaslaw's assertion that Stein pianos were "'consciously (and successfully) designed to satisfy' an aesthetic" is dismissed as "a naive claim that ignores conflicting aesthetic ideals and all manner of mechanical problems that stand in the way of constructing pianos."[80] Rosen thus accuses Zaslaw (and Bilson) of being committed to a notion that there is one best way of presenting Mozart, and he writes a sentence that certainly should strike a familiar chord in anyone familiar with equally acrimonious disputes in the world of legal interpretation: "Multiple possibilities of realizing a musical text are a basic tradition of Western music . . . ."[81]

But deciding on what kinds of instruments to play is only the beginning. One must also decide on the numbers of instruments, which can obviously make a significant difference in terms of volume, tonal balance, and the like. Yet Harold Schonberg notes that "[o]ften Bach, like most other composers of the time, did not specify instrumentation, and he would use whatever was at hand."[82] What explains this? The answer is that, "[u]ntil Haydn and Mozart came along—and, indeed, for many years later outside of the big European cities—the orchestra was altogether a flexible

---

[76] *Id.*
[77] *Id.* (emphasis in original).
[78] *Id.*
[79] *Id.*
[80] *Id.*
[81] *Id.*
[82] H. SCHONBERG, *supra* note 2, at 29.

affair" in terms of the numbers of particular instruments represented and, of course, the quality of the particular players.[83] Thus a specific "composer's orchestration depended upon the groups involved," and, indeed, "[o]rchestration would be adapted to fit the needs of individual players."[84] There is no proof that previous composers expected that later generations would confine themselves to the same size orchestras they were forced to accept. Roger Norrington's attempt to achieve an authentically sized orchestra for his performance of Berlioz's *Symphonie Fantastique* based on 1830 Paris models is particularly troublesome in this respect; if there is one thing we know about Berlioz, it was that no orchestra was too large for his tastes.[85]

The Hanover Band is considerably smaller than most contemporary orchestras, with a far greater emphasis on the woodwinds. The reason, of course, is that this reflects the orchestras found in Vienna at the end of the eighteenth century. The members of the Band are directed not by a conductor standing on a podium, as is contemporary practice, but rather "either from the violin or from the keyboard as is in keeping with the period and according to the repertoire."[86] We are told, no doubt accurately, that "Beethoven directed many performances from the fortepiano added by propulsive internal direction given by the first violin."[87] What was good enough for Beethoven should, presumably, be good enough for Bernstein, at least if one's goal is fidelity to the former. It does not appear, though, that any early-music enthusiasts adopt the practice of early conductors who kept time by loudly beating a stick on the floor so as to be heard by the members of the orchestra.[88]

"The matter of pitch," we are told, "is crucial to a faithful reconstruction."[89] Today's "standard pitch" sets the A above

---

[83] *Id.* at 28.
[84] *Id.*
[85] *See id.* at 113-14 (describing Berlioz's ideal orchestra of 465 instruments and a 360 person chorus).
[86] C. BROWN, *supra* note 66.
[87] *Id.*
[88] *See* H. SCHONBERG, *supra* note 2, at 26, 28.
[89] C. BROWN, *supra* note 66. On pitch, see Fantel, *Equipment That Plays in the Key of Flexibility*, N.Y. Times, Aug. 26, 1990, at 26, col. 1. Fantel, who writes about "sound" for the *New York Times*, notes that "Beethoven's notion of C differs from ours," and goes on to observe not only that "[t]oday's performances, adhering to the modern convention of 'standard pitch,' take no account of this," but also the fact that compact disk players generally do not allow the listener to adjust the pitch of a recording. *Id.* The market has recognized this defect, though, and it is now possible to buy CD players that "are capable of tuning the music up or down by as much as

middle C at 440 cycles per second. The Hanover Band, after much research, adopts "an A sounding at 430 cycles per second."[90] Not surprisingly, such differences in pitch produce somewhat different sounds. It is worth mentioning in this context what is perhaps the *reductio ad absurdum* of this striving for historically-informed reproduction of sound. In Christopher Hogwood's recording of Beethoven's Third Symphony, the *Eroica*, he purports to recreate the initial performance of the music by "a very powerful company (consisting almost entirely of amateurs)."[91] Thus the performance features, among other things, the "uncomplicated, rhythmical" approach found in amateur performances even in the present.[92] If the first performance of the *Eroica* was mediocre, Hogwood seems to be arguing, well then, that is the price one pays for authenticity.

If the aural picture historically experienced by the work's first audience is the true test of authenticity, it is difficult to know whether Hogwood's suggestion is to be dismissed out of hand or fervently embraced. Indeed, one might go even further in the reconstruction of the exact sounds produced at the premieres of the Beethoven symphonies. Instruments used during the late eighteenth century were often out of tune, especially as the performance progressed, because of the limitations of the stings used at the time, for example. Presumably, then, it would violate the "rule of recognition," as adopted by the Hanover Band or by Hogwood, to play the music consistently in tune, as that is a distinctly "modern" expectation, based on subsequent developments in the technology of musical instruments.[93] Emphasis on recreating the actual

---

a whole note." *Id.* Fantel somewhat naively suggests, however, that the listening public might "leave the matter of pitch strictly in the hands of the performers." *Id.* The members of the Hanover Band would respond, though, that most performers cannot be trusted, that only *they* are presenting the *authentic* Beethoven experience.

[90] C. BROWN, *supra* note 66.

[91] Hogwood, *Hogwood's Beethoven*, THE GRAMOPHONE, Mar. 1986, at 1136, *quoted in* Taruskin, *supra* note 45, at 140.

[92] *See* Taruskin, *supra* note 45, at 141 (quoting Clive Brown, notes to Oiseau-Lyre 414338).

[93] This is by no means a fanciful concern. We normally expect top-flight modern symphony orchestras to play in tune, but our expectations about what "in tune" performance consists in depends upon several factors, including the invention of horns with valves and the universal adoption of the even tempered scale in the nineteenth century. To preserve acoustically pure intervals in one key necessitates that some intervals in other keys will deviate from acoustic perfection, and the more harmonically distant the key, the greater the disadvantage. *See* THE NEW HARVARD DICTIONARY, *supra* note 68, at 422, 837-38. Different methods of "tempering" or slight adjustment of the scale to compensate for this problem were devised and

conditions of performance, finally, leads one to ask whether recordings proclaiming such "authenticity" should not include coughs, wheezing, and other sounds that were undoubtedly heard in Viennese drawing rooms and concert halls during the playing of the music.   At some point one crosses the line that separates scrupulousness from absurdity, but unfortunately one's confidence in the ability to locate that line has been seriously undermined by Hogwood's and the Hanover Band's pronunciamentos.

Of course, not everyone agrees with the Hanover Band's approach to correct interpretation.   And indeed, the authors of *Authenticity and Early Music* are united primarily by their skepticism, if not outright hostility, to the ideology revealed in the Hanover Band booklet.   For these writers, Proust's title[94] should undoubtedly be translated to emphasize the "lostness" of the past and, consequently, the inability to present a performance today that could meaningfully replicate earlier performances.   All of them would agree with Robert P. Morgan's observation that "we cannot re-create the 'aura' of the original (to borrow Walter Benjamin's useful term), no matter how hard we try."[95]   Difficulties concerning the maintenance or manufacture of "original" instruments or the "proper" pitch of C are only the beginning.   Thus, writes Morgan, "[p]erhaps even more critical . . . than original performance inflections is the deeper context in which the works were originally experienced—their status as integral components of a larger cultural environment that has disappeared and is fundamentally irrecoverable."[96]   Morgan offers as "only the most obvious" example that much "early music was not intended to be performed in concert."[97]   To take another example, Bach composed his

---

employed during the 1600s and 1700s. The title of Bach's *Well-Tempered Clavier* refers to one such method, no longer used today. *See id.* at 838. Eventually, the equal temperament approach gained dominance, but this temperament is not necessarily the same one originally used when early music was first performed. *See id.* at 624, 838. Valveless horns of the type used in Beethoven's era play notes that do not precisely match an even tempered scale, *see id.* at 364, 380, and thus performers must use various devices (such as partially closing off the bell of the horn with the right hand) to approximate the correct pitch. *See id.* at 381. Some out of tune performance on original instruments is also due to the performer's inability to control various aspects of the instrument, for example the gradual loosening of the sounding strings on early stringed instruments or pianos.

[94] *See supra* note 65.

[95] Morgan, *Tradition, Anxiety, and the Current Musical Scene*, in AUTHENTICITY AND EARLY MUSIC, *supra* note 16, at 71.

[96] *Id.*

[97] *Id.* In the classical and Romantic periods, chamber and solo instrumental music

masses and his religious cantatas to be performed in church as part of the devotional exercises of committed Lutherans.[98]

Perhaps the best way of understanding the problem is by pondering a recent promotional advertisement offered by an Austin, Texas public radio station promising a performance of a Bach mass "just as Bach would have heard it." This advertisement was presumably directed to people eating dinner in their homes, to others working at their places of business, and to still others driving in their cars. The idea that if we wish to recapture the "authentic" experience of Bach or Beethoven all that is necessary is to pop a tape of Hogwood into our car stereo as we speed down interstate 35 seems increasingly preposterous the more that one thinks about it. Moreover, the very idea of *recorded* music that can be purchased as a commodity in stores (the *St. Matthew Passion*—on sale now for only $3.99!)—and can be played over and over again at our whim—is completely foreign to the phenomenology of musical performance in Bach's time, and indeed, of all musical culture until well into the twentieth century.[99]

As Morgan writes, "if we take the notion of context at all seriously, we are left with the painful realization that *any* concert performance of this music constitutes a basic perversion of its original intentions."[100] What he terms "[t]he authentic function of the music," an interesting term for him to adopt, "is lost to us and cannot be reconstituted. As soon as we place these works in a museum, we wrench them out of their own frame and utterly transform their original meaning."[101] Morgan concludes his essay by accusing the authenticity movement of "plac[ing] older music in a museum," which, he goes on to note, is an essentially "modern invention,"[102] created precisely at the moment in our culture when we recognized the ineluctable pastness of the past and thus felt the necessity to preserve what was no longer part of our living

---

would usually be performed in the home or at small social gatherings. *See* Rosen, *supra* note 4, 75, at 50; Holland, *Heard the One About the Madcap Trill?*, N.Y. Times, Apr. 7, 1991, at 25, col. 1 ("[A] lot of music we now listen to silently was written for noisy dinner parties.") (interview with Alfred Brendel).

[98] *See* Taruskin, *Facing Up, Finally, to Bach's Dark Vision*, N.Y. Times, Jan. 27, 1991, at 25, col. 1.

[99] *See* W. BENJAMIN, *The Work of Art in the Age of Mechanical Reproduction*, in ILLUMINATIONS 217-251 (H. Zohn trans. 1969).

[100] Morgan, *supra* note 95, at 71.

[101] *Id.*

[102] *Id.* at 81.

experience in an antiseptic environment suitable for distanced observation.

Morgan draws a contrast between placing early music in the equivalent of a museum and treating it as part of an ongoing tradition. Ironically enough, a *living* tradition involves participants who feel (and this word is used advisedly) comfortable engaging in their own interpretations, their own transformations of the materials that constitute their identity. What allows one, for example, to consider him or herself a "traditional" Jew is surely not some fantasy that one is doing exactly what was done 3000 years ago in ancient Israel, but rather a felt confidence that one is participating as the latest member of a recognizable way of life whose transhistorical identity has endured whatever the surface changes. Few traditions assume stasis as the operative condition of life.

As Will Crutchfield writes, "[o]ne of the unthought-of things the great composers assumed, wanted, and needed was the conviction and passion of great performers,"[103] who would offer their own emendations of the composer's score. Exemplifying Crutchfield's point is the distinguished theater and opera director Jonathan Miller, who writes of his hope "that by the first night a performance has emerged that has the possibilities of an enormous amount of spontaneous growth and amplification" generated by the performers themselves.[104] He mentions his delight, upon seeing a particular performance of *Rigoletto* that he had directed for the English National Opera, in discovering a host of "things that I had never seen before and never asked them to do." Indeed, "Whenever I have gone back to watch *Rigoletto* I have been delighted to find that it is a truly emergent production,"[105] a collaborative relationship among composer or playwright (who may, of course, be long dead), director, actors and singers, and audience.

For most of us, this notion of living tradition is most obvious in popular music. What makes Thelonious Monk's *Round Midnight* a true "classic" of jazz is most certainly *not* its ability to be endlessly re-presented in a single canonical note-for-note form, but rather its ability to serve as the basic setting for creations by other great musicians. Even if one exempts jazz from the discussion due to its deliberately improvisatory form, one can find much the same idea of a living tradition in performances of pop, soul, and rock music.

---

[103] Crutchfield, *supra* note 19, at 25.
[104] J. MILLER, SUBSEQUENT PERFORMANCES 117 (1986).
[105] *Id.* at 118.

One might also adopt, as Jonathan Miller does in his discussions of the interpretation of plays, Noam Chomsky's distinction between the deep and surface structures of grammar. In Miller's words, "there are an infinite series of sentences, all of whose *surface structures* are different but that can nevertheless express the same *deep structure.*"[106] It is therefore altogether possible (and legitimate) that "an enormous variety of actual performances" can be faithful to the underlying deep structure of the particular piece that is being interpreted.[107]

Nevertheless, (and, we might add, alas), there are popular musicians who themselves are increasingly indicating disdain for those who ostensibly "'distort[popular music] in all kinds of insidious ways that are losing track of [the composer's] original authentic sound.'"[108]   Morgan is quoting a "bright young star" of the New York cabaret scene, Michael Feinstein, who has produced an album which "attempts a re-creation of Gershwin's popular songs in their original form," using original orchestrations and texts.[109] Morgan fumes: "This from, of all things, a cabaret singer—a type *traditionally* committed to extremely personal, even blatantly idiosyncratic stylizations."[110]   Feinstein's album is entitled, as might be expected, *Pure Gershwin.* The work of cultural anthropolo-

---

[106] *Id.*

[107] J. MILLER, *supra* note 104, at 118. Having introduced Chomsky into the discussion, we hasten to distance ourselves from any commitment to the general structuralist program that Chomsky is famous for (and that Miller is adopting). Post-structuralist critiques, after all, have argued forcefully against the notion of unique and identifiable deep structures that provide the kind of baseline that Miller strongly endorses to constrain interpretive license. One might respond to Miller's distinction by wondering whether continuous changes in surface over time might lead to what everyone would admit were really profound changes in structure. If the evolution of *Rigoletto* continued apace for ten years in his absence, Miller might well discover, upon his return, that the cumulation of so-called "surface alterations" had made his original artistic conception virtually unrecognizable.   *Cf.* Balkin, *Constitutional Interpretation and the Problem of History* (Book Review), 63 N.Y.U. L. REV. 911 (1988) (discussing cumulative effects of commerce clause decisions). Similarly, the history of jazz music has demonstrated that the original notion of variations in melody, while preserving "deep" harmonic structure, eventually led to substituted harmonies in the be-bop era, the adoption of improvisation on modal scales in lieu of harmonic structure in the work of Miles Davis' first quintet, and finally to Ornette Coleman's "free jazz." M. GRIDLEY, JAZZ STYLES 40, 44, 51, 120-22, 177-78, 195-201 (1978). For a general discussion, see J. COLLIER, THE MAKING OF JAZZ: A COMPREHENSIVE HISTORY (1978).

[108] Morgan, *supra* note 95, at 78 (quoting Holden, *Cabaret's Bright Young Star,* N.Y. Times, June 29, 1986, § 6 (Magazine), at 33, col. 2).

[109] *Id.*

[110] *Id.*

gists may be particularly helpful in understanding what lies behind the use of the "pure" in such settings.[111] To label those whose interpretations differ from one's own "impure" is no small rhetorical feat. Indeed, it is structurally similar to describing one's opponents as "heretics."[112] Such language suggests the smell of the *auto-de-fe* rather than a willingness to acknowledge the legitimacy of competing perspectives. As Morgan observes with regard to Feinstein's ambitions, "[a]pparently it is no longer Mabel Mercer's or Bobby Short's Gershwin we want [or will even tolerate as an acceptable possibility], it is some sort of reincarnation of Gershwin himself."[113] To switch back to "classical" music, it is no longer Leonard Bernstein's or the New York Philharmonic's Beethoven we should want, but rather the Hanover Band's reincarnation. Such an approach, ironically enough, seems not only to embalm a tradition, but to be unfaithful to what is historically known about "original" performance practice, which allowed, indeed celebrated, improvisation.[114]

Richard Taruskin is perhaps the most polemical (and entertaining) of the opponents of the authentic performance school, which he rechristens "authenticistic."[115] His essay, "The Pastness of the Present and the Presence of the Past," casts scorn upon almost all of the claims suggested or implied by the proponents of "authenticity" in early music. Thus, as against the comment by one writer that "an ideal performance is one that perfectly realizes the composer's intentions,"[116] Taruskin responds that "[w]e cannot know intentions, for many reasons—or rather, we cannot know we know them."[117] In Taruskin's view, "'once the piece is finished, the composer regards it and relates to it either as a performer if he is one, or else simply as a listener.'"[118] As for fidelity to text, he

---

[111] *See, e.g.,* M. Douglas, Purity and Danger: An Analysis of Concepts of Pollution and Taboo (1978) (describing the cultural construction of "impurities" that must be suppressed).

[112] *See* R. Bork, *supra* note 33, at 4, 11 for just such a denunciation of opponents.

[113] Morgan, *supra* note 95, at 78.

[114] *See* Brett, *Text, Context, and the Early Music Editor,* in Authenticity in Early Music, *supra* note 16, at 106-07.

[115] Taruskin, *supra* note 45, at 148.

[116] *Id.* at 138 n.8 (quoting Grant, *On Historical Authenticity in the Performance of Old Music,* in Essays on Music in Honor of Archibald Thompson Davison 341 (1957)).

[117] *Id.* at 145.

[118] *Id.* at 147 (quoting Taruskin, *On Letting the Music Speak for Itself: Some Reflections on Musicology and Performance,* 1 J. Musicology 340 (1982)).

quotes the composer George Perle's view that "[t]he greatest single source of bad performance . . . is literalism . . . 'It's what you expect nowadays.'"[119]

Taruskin also joins most of his fellow essayists in criticizing the historical tendentiousness of many of the "authentic performance" devotees. He argues that many early music performers are simply imposing their own aesthetic preferences under the guise of "authentic" performance practices. He gives the example of David Wulstan's performances of Renaissance choral music, which attempted to "'obtain as nearly as possible the sound of the great English Sixteenth Century Choirs.'"[120] After some experimentation with the traditional men-boy choirs, Wulstan switched from boy trebles to women, arguing that "'[b]ecause boys' voices now break early, they tend to find the high vocal parts . . . overtaxing: with proper training, however, girls' voices can produce exactly the right sound.'"[121] This seems a perfectly plausible accommodation until Taruskin points out that Wulstan (like everyone else alive today) had never heard the sound of a "great English Sixteenth Century Choir."[122] Authentic performance, Taruskin argues, is really the imposition of a post-Stravinskian modernist aesthetic to the music of the past. It is a creation of our own times, satisfying modern aesthetic preferences which are nevertheless justified and even sanctified by claims of historical accuracy.

Interestingly, Taruskin does not condemn *per se* the practice of making Mozart and Beethoven sound like Stravinsky; he objects, rather, to the claim that this modernization of sound is in fact authentic, and the related claim that this "authentic" practice is the only permissible way to perform early music. Taruskin at last reveals himself to be both a pluralist and a pragmatist in matters of musical performance. The test of an artistic interpretation for him, presumably, is whether it "works" aesthetically—whether it produces a pleasing and satisfying experience to the persons of our own era.[123]

We have purposely forborne from pointing to all of the obvious affinities between the arguments made (and attacked) by those interested in the performance of early music and those made by

---

[119] *Id.*
[120] *Id.* at 144 (quoting Chislett, notes to Seraphim LP 60256 (works of Tallis)).
[121] *Id.* (quoting Chislett, notes to Seraphim LP 60256 (works of Tallis)).
[122] *Id.*
[123] *See id.* at 204-07.

legal analysts concerned with how one should engage in legal performance. A statute or a constitution is, indeed, *not* a poem; it *is* designed to structure other people's behavior in certain important ways. But, then, so is the score of a symphony or the text of a play. And the word "structure" is purposely elusive, leaving open the possibility that the particular passions (and, dare we say, political commitments) of the gifted performer might have as much to do with the performance possibilities she chooses as some impossible fidelity to purportedly timeless and acontextual commands contained in the texts. *Authenticity and Early Music* should thus be of interest to anyone interested in problems of legal interpretation.

But that is only one of the reasons for suggesting that a law-and-music scholarship can complement the already flourishing genre of law-and-literature. Perhaps more important than recognition of the affinities of interpretive dilemmas generated by having to work with texts, as important as that recognition may be, is the insight provided into more general issues of cultural development.

III. Interpretation and Modernist Anxiety

It is our thesis that the early-music movement is best understood as attempting what the English historian Eric Hobsbawm calls the "invention of tradition."[124] Hobsbawm defines "'invented' traditions" as "responses to novel situations which take the form of reference to old situations, or which establish their own past by quasi-obligatory repetition."[125] Faced with "the constant change and innovation of the modern world," one engages in an "attempt to structure at least some parts of social life within it as unchanging and invariant."[126]

Hobsbawm contrasts this pseudo-traditionalism to participation in a living and developing tradition, and, interestingly, one example he gives is the English common law, which he argues is characterized by a remarkable combination of "flexibility in substance and formal adherence to precedent."[127] In Hobsbawm's view, the common law could never "afford to be invariant, because even in 'traditional' societies life is not so."[128] Variance means change,

---

[124] *See* Hobsbawm, *Introduction: Inventing Traditions*, in THE INVENTION OF TRADITION 1-14 (E. Hobsbawm & T. Ranger eds. 1983).

[125] *Id.* at 2.

[126] *Id.*

[127] *Id.*

[128] *Id.*

which means history and the realization of "break[s] in continuity."[129]   Paradoxically, to the extent that one feels firmly rooted in a culture, such changes may be easily assimilated and treated, as we saw earlier, merely as surface manifestations of deeper unchanging continuities that legitimate the enterprise. Thus, it is crucial to note that Charles Rosen, after arguing that "[m]ultiple possibilities of realizing a musical text are a basic tradition of Western music," immediately follows with the clause, "a tradition which no longer apparently has any reality"[130] for "authentic" performance devotees.   As "breaks" increasingly become defined as "ruptures" separating the past and the present, the stage is set for those who, dismayed by present practice, preach return to the purity of the past.   Such revivalist movements, "common among intellectuals since the Romantics, can never develop or even preserve a living past (except conceivably by setting up human natural sanctuaries for isolated corners of archaic life), but must become 'invented tradition,'"[131] committed to stasis and condemning as impurity, heresy, and defilement what a truly living tradition might see simply as admirable "adaptability."[132]

Many of the essays in *Authenticity and Early Music* are not centrally concerned with "proper" standards of interpretation at all. They ask a much deeper question: What explains the development at this juncture of our culture of a movement organized around the notion of authenticity in musical performance?   This question has implications reaching far beyond the particularity of music; it touches on central aspects of the experience of modernity in Western culture as a whole, including, most certainly, its legal aspects.   Thus the study of music, on the surface so different from law, enables us to see things in our own discipline that were there all along but hidden by our very familiarity with it.   By studying what the crisis of modernity has meant in music, we can better understand its impact on the law.   To handle this crucial topic adequately would require a book of its own.   This essay can do nothing more than sketch some points of comparison and suggest further questions for investigation.

There are many ways of describing the phenomenon of modernity and its relation to what has come to be called the

---

[129] *Id.* at 7.
[130] Rosen, *supra* note 75, at 50.
[131] Hobsbawn, *supra* note 124, at 8.
[132] *Id.*

postmodern condition. We might view modernity as the increasing recognition, especially since the Enlightenment, of the conflict between reason and tradition, including revealed religion, as modes of understanding the world.[133] We might understand it as the increasing victory of secular or worldly conceptions of life over the religious and transcendent.[134] We might view it as the increasing replacement of traditional modes of social organization by the bureaucratization and rationalization of society,[135] or as the eventual collapse of the concept of reason into a barren instrumentalism.[136]

We emphasize that modernity is a contested theoretical concept, which might be extended to much of Western culture since the Renaissance or restricted to the particular cultural issues of the late nineteenth and twentieth centuries, which is our particular focus.[137] Moreover, the features often ascribed to modernity are not always peculiar to the "modern" age, however it is defined. For example, the tension between reason and tradition characteristic of the modern age scarcely begins with the twentieth century, or even with the Enlightenment. One can find anti-traditionalism in the rationalism of Descartes and the skepticism of Hobbes, and still further back in debates in ancient Greek thought. Although we see the conflict between reason and tradition, and the concomitant sense of the disintegration and collapse of tradition as an integral part of what we call "modernity," we do not claim that it is unique to the modern era. Indeed, it is more likely that history is full of what might be called "modernist crises" in many different lands and

---

[133] *See* I. KANT, *What is Enlightenment?*, in FOUNDATIONS OF THE METAPHYSICS OF MORALS AND WHAT IS ENLIGHTENMENT? 85 (L. Beck trans. 1959); D. HARVEY, THE CONDITION OF POSTMODERNITY: AN ENQUIRY INTO THE ORIGINS OF CULTURAL CHANGE 12 (1989).

[134] *See* T. SEUNG, CULTURAL THEMATICS 246-59 (1976); G. HEGEL, PHILOSOPHY OF HISTORY 442 (1902).

[135] *See* 2 M. WEBER, ECONOMY AND SOCIETY, AN OUTLINE OF INTERPRETIVE SOCIOLOGY 1381-1462 (G.Roth & C. Wiltich eds. 1968); M. WEBER, THE PROTESTANT ETHIC AND THE SPIRIT OF CAPITALISM 182 (T. Parsons trans. 1958).

[136] This theme is probably most associated with the Frankfurt School of critical theory. *See* J. HABERMAS, LEGITIMATION CRISIS (1975); M. HORKHEIMER, ECLIPSE OF REASON (1947); M. HORKHEIMER & T. ADORNO, THE DIALECTIC OF ENLIGHTENMENT (1972).

[137] *Compare, e.g.,* T. SEUNG, *supra* note 134 (describing the creation of a modern "Faustian ethos" which separates the Middle Ages from the Renaissance) *with* M. BERMAN, ALL THAT IS SOLID MELTS INTO AIR: THE EXPERIENCE OF MODERNITY 16-17 (1982) (suggesting that the first phase of modernity begins in sixteenth century, but emphasizing modernity as a creature of the nineteenth and twentieth centuries).

times. To speak of modernity, thus, is to speak of one particular cultural moment in Western thought, when the conflict between reason and tradition not only becomes central, but is commingled with other elements that are more peculiarly of our age, such as mass industrialization, and the increasing rationalization and bureaucratization of society.

In this essay we focus on a single strand of the experience of modernity—our relation to the past and, in particular, to the cultural traditions that constitute it. From this perspective, the experience of modernity is the increasing sense of isolation and estrangement from the past and from tradition, spurred on by constantly accelerating changes in culture, economy, and technology.[138] Viewed solely as the collapse of tradition and separation from the past, "modernity" is surely nothing new. Each generation throughout history has probably spoken of the "good old days" that are long past.[139] One can find jeremiads bewailing the loss of past tradition to change and cosmopolitanism throughout human history, and to the this extent the present era has more in common with previous ones than theorists of modernity often admit.[140] What distinguishes our own particular "modern" period is an accelerating spiral of technology and bureaucracy unlike any other in human history; as a result, the sense of distance and fragmentation from the past appears to have become a central, pervasive, and seemingly permanent element of the experience of culture.[141]

---

[138] *See, e.g.,* L. SCAFF, FLEEING THE IRON CAGE: CULTURE, POLITICS, AND MODERNITY IN THE THOUGHT OF MAX WEBER 18 (1989) (describing progenitors of modernism as sharing a "consciousness of a dynamic and wrenching destabilization of transmitted cultural traditions"); C. SCHORSKE, FIN-DE-SIÈCLE VIENNA: POLITICS AND CULTURE xix (1980) (describing the modern sense of demise of tradition in "a whirl of infinite innovation"); M. BERMAN, *supra* note 137, at 15, 13 (describing the modern period as "a maelstrom of perpetual disintegration and renewal, of struggle and contradiction, of ambiguity and anguish[,]" which generates in people both "a will to change—to transform both themselves and their world—and . . . a terror of disorientation and disintegration, of life falling apart").

[139] *See* Luban, *Legal Traditionalism,* (forthcoming 43 STAN. L. REV. (1991)).

[140] *See id.*

[141] As Marshall Berman argues, nineteenth and twentieth century modernism is distinguished by a

dynamic new landscape . . . . [of] steam engines, automatic factories, railroads, vast new industrial zones; of teeming cities that have grown overnight, often with dreadful consequences; of daily newspapers, telegraphs, telephones and other mass media, communicating on an ever wider scale; of increasingly strong national states and multinational aggregations of capital; of mass social movements fighting these modernizations from above with their own modes of modernization from below; of

Moreover, "modernity," as suggested by Hobsbawm's essay, is linked to the development of a specifically historical sensibility that focuses on the cultural segmentation of time rather than its continuity. An increased attention to the historicist elements of culture brings with it an understanding of the profound differences between the perceptions of times past (and irrevocably lost) and those of our own. It is just such an understanding that leads us to develop periodizations of time—e.g., "ancient times," the "middle ages," and the like—that serve not only to divide the calendar but also to mark significant changes of consciousness that separate the inhabitants of one culture from those of another.   Some may applaud such changes as have occurred, as is true of those who see history as a progressive liberation from the cultural blinders dominating past epochs. Others may instead bewail these changes and see them instead as symptoms of decline from some presumably better state of things in the past.[142]   But perhaps now more common is the rejection either of applause or of dejection, which are themselves recognized as the products of specific cultural moments, in favor of a somewhat more detached acceptance of the inevitability of change and our inability to place such changes as occur within any master narrative.   Our awareness of the breaks between the past and our present situation is joined with a confidence (if that is the right word) that the future will bring equal ruptures that will lead to our own epoch being understood as merely one specific cultural moment.   As one of the greatest living historians, David Brion Davis, reminds us, "in the future our own mixtures of insight and blindness will be interpreted from that then-present perspective from which one tries to understand the past. *We will then be perceived in ways that we cannot perceive ourselves.*"[143] It is precisely this awareness of perceptual gaps, of commitments to such fundamentally different paradigms of understanding that characterizes much of modernist sensibility.

---

an ever-expanding world market embracing all, capable of the most spectacular growth, capable of appalling waste and devastation, capable of everything except solidity and stability.

M. BERMAN, *supra* note 137, at 18-19.

[142] *See, e.g.,* A. BLOOM, THE CLOSING OF THE AMERICAN MIND 85 (1987) ("Country, religion, family, ideas of civilization, all the sentimental and historical forces that stood between cosmic infinity and the individual, providing some notion of a place within the whole, have been rationalized and have lost their compelling force.").

[143] D. DAVIS, THE PROBLEM OF SLAVERY IN THE AGE OF REVOLUTION, 1770-1823, at 15 (1975) (emphasis added).

The literary scholar Paul Fussell, writing about the impact of World War I on Anglo-American culture, argues that "the most pervasive contribution of modern war to modernist culture is irony, widely perceived to be . . . the 'normative mentality' of modern art."[144] Just as Roland Barthes is said to have noted that one can unabashedly say "I will love you forever" only once in one's life, so does an awareness of historical situatedness cause us to stand at a suitable distance from our own most deeply held convictions. To put it mildly, questions about the meaning of authenticity, whether of one's beliefs or practices, go to the heart of modernist culture.[145]

As Will Crutchfield notes in his essay "Fashion, Conviction, and Performance Style," the word *authenticity* has many meanings. It may refer to fidelity to the composer's intentions, or to the composer's text.[146]   Yet, Crutchfield insists, there is a more appropriate meaning of authenticity of performance: "This authenticity is what the standee at the opera means when he says he has heard 'the real thing,' 'the genuine article.'"[147]   When a performance is authentic in the sense of genuineness, "we feel the music and musician are one . . . . The Irish theologian William Fitzgerald supplied . . . the right citation for this: 'That is called Authentic, which is sufficient unto itself, which commends, sustains, proves itself, and hath credit and authority from itself.'"[148]

The notion of authenticity as genuineness is deeply tied to the concept of tradition and one's relation to the past. The authentic performance is immersed in a tradition, so that the tradition springs from within it unself-consciously; it is the living embodiment of tradition, of the past. That is why it is sufficient to itself, and needs authority from no outside source. Hence another meaning of "authentic" is idiomatic, sincere, and unaffected. Nevertheless, this conception of authenticity leads to what we might call the "paradox of authenticity." The more one self-consciously tries to be authentic to a tradition, the less authentic one's practice becomes; conversely, true authenticity always emerges where one least expects it, and indeed, it emerges virtually without any effort on the part of the actors who are enmeshed in authentic practice.

---

[144] Fussell, *Introduction* to THE NORTON BOOK OF MODERN WAR 24 (1991).

[145] *See* L. TRILLING, SINCERITY AND AUTHENTICITY 97-98 (1972).

[146] Crutchfield, *supra* note 19, at 24.

[147] *Id.*

[148] *Id.* at 24-25.

At the risk of frivolity, we might offer a gustatory example drawn from our mutual experiences in the Southwestern United States. We refer, of course, to Tex-Mex cuisine. For those who have not been introduced to this contribution of the great state of Texas, Tex-Mex is an adaptation (some purists would say adulteration) of traditional Mexican dishes by both Chicanos and Anglos living in Texas. Tex-Mex cuisine has by now become quite popular around the United States. Indeed, from Seattle to New York City one can see signs advertising "Authentic Tex-Mex Cuisine." As one might suspect, those of us from Texas have only contempt for such assertions of authenticity, similar, we suspect, to the response of a French visitor to being taken to the "Paris Restaurant, featuring authentic French cuisine." Yet at the same time, there is something quite bizarre about the notion of *authentic* Tex-Mex food. This is, after all, a cuisine whose delicate flavors are produced by prodigious quantities of canned Ro-Tel tomatoes and great slabs of Kraft Velveeta. From the standpoint of "authentic" Mexican food, Tex-Mex is itself an abomination, a veritable monument to inauthenticity.

And yet, at the same time, there is no doubt that Texans can always spot an authentic Tex-Mex institution.[149] The streets of East Austin are full of them, and people are quite vocal about their favorites. Indeed, some people even prefer Tex-Mex to other types of Mexican food. The inauthentic has become the standard of authenticity. The alteration of old habits, the addition of new ingredients, the catch-as-catch-can recombination of elements has produced a new cuisine in its own right that can be authentically or inauthentically reproduced. And the moment that we realize that there can be "authentic" Tex-Mex cuisine—itself the product of a previous inauthenticity—at that moment the possibility of "inauthentic" Tex-Mex cuisine arises.

It is perhaps only a slight exaggeration to say that many of the problems of modernity and its relation to tradition are summed up in the sign that promises us "Authentic Tex-Mex Cuisine." Each tradition is the result of previous adulteration and abomination. Each tradition by becoming a tradition nevertheless asserts its own authenticity. The self-conscious search to regain and recapture that

---

[149] Of course this statement simply raises the issue of authenticity in the form of another question: Who, after all, counts as a "Texan?" For example, both Levinson and Balkin live in Texas but hail originally from North Carolina and Missouri, respectively.

authenticity nevertheless produces inauthentic performance. And the very unself-conscious activity involved in adulteration nevertheless produces ever new examples of the authentic, the authentic that is not yet recognized as such.

We can understand an important aspect of modernity through the concept of authenticity, by which we mean the idea of an organic connection to tradition. Modernity might be described as the experience of feeling self-conscious about one's relationship to the past and to tradition, isolated and alienated—in a word, inauthentic. The paradox of authenticity promises us that the modernist will both invariably fail at regaining this lost authenticity and invariably succeed in epitomizing an authentic experience—the authentic experience of separation from the past, which is the authentic experience of modernity.[150]

All of which brings us back to the early music movement. A question that fascinates several of the authors in *Authenticity and Early Music* is why the concept of authenticity has taken center stage, whether as hero or villain, in our own lifetimes. The idea of "authentic" performance practices would have seemed bizarre to earlier ages. A composer of early music, wrote the music historian Donald Grout, would be "astonish[ed] at our interest in such matters. Have we no living tradition of music, that we must be seeking to revive a dead one?"[151] Will Crutchfield notes:

> [I]f you were an Italian singer in 1888, you did not think of singing Rossini style for Rossini and Mozart style for Mozart and Verdi style for Verdi. You just *sang*. The way you sang—how you felt a crescendo, where you would instinctively accelerate, where you would feel the need to make an ornament, what a good pianissimo note sounded like to you—would have been in the style of the cultural situation of 1888, a style that developed in symbiosis with the middle and late operas of Verdi, along with the secondary composers such as Ponchielli who were active at the

---

[150] Because people usually desire what they feel they most lack, often the more self-conscious a person is, the more avidly she will seek authentic experience. Thus, it was no accident that the Romantic era was both an era of extreme self-consciousness and an age which stressed the importance of authenticity. *See* M. BERMAN, THE POLITICS OF AUTHENTICITY: RADICAL INDIVIDUALISM AND THE EMERGENCE OF MODERN SOCIETY 312-15 (1970) (emphasizing the importance of Montesquieu and Rousseau to the development of the romantic concern for authenticity, and showing the roots of the modern concern for authenticity in romantic self-consciousness).

[151] Taruskin, *supra* note 45, at 141 (quoting Grout, *On Historical Authenticity in the Performance of Old Music*, in ESSAYS ON MUSIC IN HONOR OF ARCHIBALD THOMPSON DAVISON 346 (1957)).

time. . . . The concept did not yet exist of different style-complexes that could be stuck into the heads of performers like a floppy disc into a word processor depending on what program was desired that evening.[152]

There are several reasons for the previous lack of concern with authentic performance. During the nineteenth century there was still a continuous outpouring of what we *now* label "classical" music. Thus performers focused more on performing the new music of the 1800s, and less upon preserving a repertory of old classics, as is the case today. One played Mozart and Beethoven as one would play other music. There was no division of classical versus early romantic versus late romantic music. There was simply music, and it was performed according to the best stylistic practices of the day.[153] These stylistic practices colored the music of the past in terms of the tastes of the present. But this coloration was not noticed, because the cultural subject saw herself as at one with the past, not even conscious of following a tradition of performance.

To modern ears, the difference between Mozart and Mahler, or between Rossini and Puccini, is so great that it is difficult to comprehend this mindset. Perhaps the best analogy is to the popular music of today—rock and roll. When Bruce Springsteen plays a cover of "Twist and Shout" during a 1990's rock and roll concert, he simply plays the music as a rock and roll song. He does not engage in self-conscious inquiry into early 1960's performance practices. Nor does the audience find this at all unseemly. Nevertheless, rock and roll performance has changed greatly since the 1950s and 60s, due in part to developments in electronic instrument and recording technology, the increased importance of

---

[152] Crutchfield, *supra* note 19, at 22-23.

[153] In understanding this point, it is important to distinguish compositional from performance styles. The music of Liszt and Wagner, for example, shocked their nineteenth century contemporaries because of its harmonic audacity, and was often seen as a betrayal of sound compositional principles and traditions. But these qualms about new harmonic practices did not lead nineteenth century critics to think that earlier music should be *performed* differently than contemporary music. We emphasize, however, that the gradual breakdown of the tonal system of harmony by the beginning of the twentieth century, and the development of a musical avant-garde divorced from popular tastes, did eventually contribute to the modern experience of separation between performers and composers of "classical" music, as discussed *infra* text accompanying notes 155-57. We simply note here that these effects had not yet fully been felt in the nineteenth century.

the large stadium or arena as a venue for concerts, and even the development of the music video.[154]

Interestingly, no one *yet* thinks it very important to duplicate the earlier sound exactly. That is because, to paraphrase the song, it's still rock and roll to us. One can easily predict, however, that future Michael Feinsteins will make it their mission to present purportedly pure Buddy Holly or Little Richard songs and to denigrate as illegitimate and contemptible the versions played by performers like Springsteen and others whom we now benightedly identify as great rock-and-rollers in their own right.

There is an important connection between being unself-consciously within a cultural tradition that is still growing and developing, and a similar unself-consciousness about authenticity in performance. It is precisely because we don't think about authenticity very much when it comes to rock music that we can be quite sure that rock and roll is still a living tradition of popular culture, in a way that (for example) ragtime is not. As Will Crutchfield puts it:

> The great benefit of this close, narrow correspondence between contemporary composition and performing style—as we can still observe it in popular music, on historic recordings, in a very few elder statesmen among today's artists, and in specialists centering their work in the music of today—is that the performer can be so confident in the basic grammar and syntax of his stylistic language that true improvisation, true spontaneity of utterance, becomes possible within it. If the thriving triangular relationship between composers, performers, and the public had not broken down, historically informed performance would be neither likely nor desirable today.[155]

This triangular relationship between new music, audience, and performer began to deteriorate for what is now called "classical" music around the turn of the century. Although contemporary "classical" music continues to be written and performed, it has lost much of its audience, partly because of its deliberate embrace of atonality and partly because of its avant-gardist tendencies. A new generation of performers has sprung up who see their basic task not as the performance of contemporary music but the preservation of a classical repertory which extends roughly from the Baroque period to the beginning of the twentieth century. The classical performer becomes less and less the advocate of new music and more and

---

[154] *Watch, e.g.,* MTV.
[155] Crutchfield, *supra* note 19, at 23.

more the curator of museum pieces. But the very notion of the museum, which suggests preservation of the past, also suggests separation from it as well.[156] This distancing and alienation of the performer from the cultural tradition that spawned the music she regularly performs occurs in stages, and it appears differently in different subjects. The process is gradual; the performances of the 1950s seem more distanced than the performances of the 1920s, even if the former in turn seem terribly old-fashioned by today's standards.

The recognition of one's separation from a cultural tradition triggers two characteristic reactions. The first is to cling ever more tenaciously to the tradition as it is perceived to exist. The fear that the center will not hold, and that one must therefore reassert its centrality all the more urgently, creates a feeling of uncertainty and apprehension. This is the experience of modernist anxiety. The unease of modernism, where "all that is solid melts into air,"[157] produces the emotional search for resonance, tranquility, solidity, and stability.

And yet the problem of modernity is precisely the self-consciousness that we have become partly alienated from the past. For the past, once the process of alienation has begun, can never fully be recaptured. The further removed in time one is from tradition, the less one can regain the sense of organic unity with it. Because one cannot recapture the spirit of what has been lost, one attempts to recapture the letter—that is, the concrete historical manifestations of the tradition. The result in classical music is what Crutchfield calls the "museum model" of authenticity—"the precise reconstruction of sounds as near as possible to those heard by the composer."[158] This attempt is doomed to failure, if its goal is to recapture authenticity in the sense of organic connection to tradition. The mere imitation of a tradition does not really bring the tradition back to life. A crucial difference separates improvisation within the tradition and careful imitation of previous examples. The improvisor extends and alters the tradition by unself-consciously living

---

[156] For an illuminating discussion of the problem, see Donath, *The Gene Autry Western Heritage Museum: The Problem of an Authentic Western Mystique,* 43 AM. Q. 82 (Mar. 1991) (criticizing the Autry museum for displacing historical meaning in favor of an unreflective worship of the western mystique).

[157] M. BERMAN, *supra* note 137, at 15. The original phrase, of course, comes from Marx. *See* K. MARK & F. ENGELS, *Manifesto of the Communist Party,* in THE MARX-ENGELS READER 338 (1972).

[158] Crutchfield, *supra* note 19, at 25.

within it, while alteration is precisely what the imitator fears most. It is precisely this fear of alteration, Crutchfield argues, that the Early Music Movement must overcome if it is to avoid becoming a sterile and lifeless project:

> If we resurrect historical information on performing style simply to settle on 'correct' ways of playing, to promulgate and refine rules, to settle questions . . . if we seek nothing more than to write dozens more programs for the floppy discs we insert in students' brains—then it would be better if we had never started. If instead we seek an immersion in the disciplines of the past . . . because we aspire to the freedom and the power that can be gained through purposeful accomplishment—then historically informed performance may enable some of our performers to create anew for themselves the life-giving musical culture that swarmed around musicians in healthier times without their having to think about it. . . . The crucial challenge is to keep that aliveness in mind as the goal; though it can be approached only indirectly, it is more important than the correctness.[159]

The deliberate search for authenticity thus inevitably fails but, paradoxically, also inevitably succeeds. The experience of this search to regain authenticity is itself authentic to our time—it is the authentic experience of modernity. Thus, as Richard Taruskin suggests, the "authentic" performance movement is really the imposition of the aesthetic of modernism on the music of the past.[160] Despite the claims of its advocates, "authentic" performance of music does not present music as it really was, whatever that mysterious phrase might mean. Rather, "authentic" performance presents music how we really like it (or at least how contemporary musicians like it)—dressed in modernist garb to suit the tastes of our era, not Bach's or Mozart's.[161] The advocate of authenticity is quite right that her goal is to make Mozart sound fresh and new to our ears. But this goal has not been achieved by producing what Mozart really sounded like. Rather, it has been achieved by making him sound modern—with lighter textures, faster tempi, and austere and astringent string tone.[162] We have adapted Mozart to our age just as the romantics adapted him to theirs, only we have done it under the banner of "authenticity." However,

---

[159] *Id.* at 25-26.

[160] *See* Taruskin, *supra* note 45, at 152, 155, 167-69.

[161] *See id.* at 197-98, 203-04.

[162] *See id.* at 187-88, 190-91 (tracing stylistic changes in performances of Bach's Fifth Brandenburg Concerto).

the felt need to make performance "authentic," even when the result is really quite modern, is wholly authentic to the modern era.

The second characteristic reaction produced by modernity is the recognition that the past cannot be regained. It is to embrace, or at least to accept, the alienation of the spirit from its historical moorings. It is to comprehend our relation to the past as artificial and instrumental—to see the past as separate from us, but nevertheless something we can use for our own purposes. This reaction to modernity leads to the eclectic use of the past, to the juxtaposition of different elements of different traditions, in short, to pastiche. It is the type of modernist response that eventually leads towards what is now called post-modernism. When tradition becomes instrumental, we embrace it with a wink and a nod. Everyone, including the interpreter, knows that the performance is, in some sense, inauthentic, and that the interpreter is playing a role. But this does not raise concern, as long as it serves the purposes (aesthetic or otherwise) of the interpreter. By forsaking modernist anxiety, the interpreter moves closer and closer towards post-modern irony.[163]

The post-modern response to the crisis of modernity in art creates a artistic discourse that closes in upon itself and becomes increasingly self-referential. Postmodernism shares this feature with some earlier forms of artistic modernism. The subject of culture increasingly becomes culture itself. This tendency meshes with the postmodernist practice of pastiche, as previous cultural artifacts are juxtaposed and referred to in order to call up their various cultural associations in the mind. It meshes as well with the postmodernist attitude of irony and detachment—the previous work of art is referred to not to reassert what it means or conveys, but to comment on it or even undermine it. A good example of post-modern pastiche, irony, and self-reference is the recent film, *The Freshman*,[164] in which the actor Marlon Brando deliberately parodies his earlier role as the mafia chieftain Don Corleone in *The*

---

[163] Because of the similarities between postmodernism and modernism, there is considerable debate among philosophers and historians of culture over whether postmodernism is truly a different and separate stage of culture, or is instead merely a later stage of modernism. *See* D. HARVEY, *supra* note 133, at 113-18. This should hardly be surprising, as both concepts are heavily contested in theoretical discussion. In this essay, we view postmodernism as furthering some but not other features present in modernism—for example, modernist irony as opposed to modernist anxiety.

[164] *The Freshman* (Tristar Pictures 1990).

Godfather.[165] The creators of the film make the young hero a film student who attends classes on cinematic history and technique, so that lectures about and scenes from *The Godfather* can be liberally interspersed throughout the movie. The hero is taken under the wing of Marlon Brando's character, who reminds the student eerily of the Godfather in the film he is studying in class. In turn, Brando does not play a mafia don; rather, he plays Marlon Brando playing a mafia don. Brando's performance is a continual reminder to the audience that he is playing a role, that he knows he is playing a role and that he knows that the audience knows he knows he is playing a role, and so on indefinitely.[166]

Robert Morgan's essay identifies these two reactions to the modernist predicament—anxiety and detachment—with the different compositional approaches of Arnold Schoenberg and Igor Stravinsky.[167] Schoenberg, the founder of atonal composition, represents the earlier stage of modernist anxiety. Already fully self-conscious of the tradition of western classical music from Bach and Beethoven to the present day, Schoenberg feels the weight of

---

[165] *The Godfather* (Paramount Studios 1972).

[166] It is worth mentioning in this context the movie's remarkable final scene, which involves Bert Parks serenading a group of very rich gourmets who have gathered to feast on the meat of freshly killed endangered species. As the latest victim-to-be is paraded before them, Parks proudly sings "[t]here she goes, your komodo dragon." A few moments later, he is offering a spirited rendition of Bob Dylan's "I Ain't Gonna Work on Maggie's Farm No More." Parks' presence in the movie is left completely unexplained. What is the meaning of juxtaposing Parks—a longtime symbol of the Miss America Pageant (itself a symbol of American values of an earlier era)—with the selfish excesses and insatiable appetites of 1980's materialism represented by the slaying of the hapless reptile? Is the reference to the soon-to-be devoured dragon a sly accusation that the Miss America Pageant is nothing more than a ritualized "meat market"? What is meant by the juxtaposition of Parks with the music of Bob Dylan, a symbol of the rebellious 1960s, which began to put the values characterized by the Miss America Pageant into question? Is Parks' refusal "to work on Maggie's farm" a reference to his firing by ungrateful pageant directors who (it is rumored) felt that because he had so visibly aged, he no longer presented the right image? Is Parks, like Brando, a knowing participant in the ironies of the movie, or is he, as his performance suggests, blissfully unaware of the subtexts and subsubtexts of his performance? Finally, are the creators of the movie really making a statement through this pastiche of cultural icons, or are they simply having fun and perhaps even laughing at us for noticing the inexhaustible possibilities of cross reference? The mind boggles—and of course, that is precisely the way the postmodern artist would have it. To take the movie seriously is not to take what it says seriously. To be engaged with it is simultaneously to become detached from the cultural symbols that it invokes.

[167] *See* Morgan, *supra* note 95, at 60.

tradition heavily on his back.[168] He routinely describes his artistic goals in terms of progress—of moving forward with the project of the western musical tradition. Schoenberg sees himself as one who must carry on the traditions that burden him in the best way he knows how.[169] He thus views atonal composition as an inevitable development of western musical practices:

> Schoenberg . . . holds the traditional view, but in a form whose very extremity shows that it is reaching a critical, and perhaps even terminal stage. He understood his own development as a logical and necessary continuation of the dominant compositional tendencies that had (in his view) consistently shaped the mainstream of serious western music. This explains Schoenberg's discomfort at being considered a revolutionary—a composer in some way fundamentally separated from the past. In his own eyes, the course he followed offered the only possible realization of the musical implications inherent in the work of his greatest predecessors. Schoenberg believed his music to be progressive, certainly, but not in its basic aesthetic (or even technical) assumptions, fundamentally different from the music of the past.[170]

In contrast, Stravinsky shows much more of the ironic detachment of a later stage of modernism. Although he is not himself a postmodernist, he displays several modernist attitudes that in the hands of later artists will eventually blossom into what we now call the postmodern temperament. He picks and chooses different stylistic features from different eras, melding them in compositions by the force of his personality.[171] Unlike Schoenberg, Stravinsky sees himself as fully separated from the past, studying it not to continue it but to borrow from it piecemeal for his own purposes. The result is a compositional eclecticism characteristic of Stravinsky's style. As Morgan argues, Stravinsky's modernism presaged the compositional attitudes of the present day, in which "[c]omposers adopt and discard musical styles at will, not only from work to work but within single compositions."[172] In their search for musical styles to adopt for their own purposes, contemporary composers are considerably more eclectic even than Stravinsky, for "[t]hey do not limit themselves to the repertory of western concert music, but extend their grasp to music of other cultures, popular music, folk

---

[168] *See id.* at 60-61.
[169] *See id.* at 61-62.
[170] *Id.* at 60-61 (footnotes omitted).
[171] *See id.* at 65-66.
[172] *Id.* at 66.

music, jazz, etc., moving freely back and forth across cultural boundaries as well as temporal ones."[173]

Yet this eclecticism of the modern composer itself betrays a fact about the culture of the present—the felt absence of a cultural center, of a tradition of one's own. There is, Morgan says, "no well-defined sense of the musical present."[174] The loss of a cultural center, he argues, is simply the flip side of the Stravinskian attitude towards history. "Only when the current moment loses an essential character and personality of its own, and thus loses its ability to cast its own peculiar coloration on the past, is one able to look upon the past with such detachment and objectivity."[175] According to Morgan, one who recognizes, even embraces, such a notion of our situation, must also recognize that "the concept of culture, at least as previously understood, becomes extremely shaky."[176] More important, perhaps, is the recognition that "[o]ur sense of the musical present, and thereby of our own musical selves, is fatally threatened, dissolving into a patchwork of disconnected fragments snatched from here, there, and everywhere."[177] Few have better described the postmodernist sensibility.

It is interesting in this light to compare Stravinsky's compositional practices with his attitudes about musical performance. Stravinsky demanded strict adherence to the musical text.[178] Indeed, he pronounced that "[t]o interpret a piece [of music] is to realize its portrait, and what I demand is the realization of the piece itself and not of its portrait."[179] Elsewhere he invidiously contrasted, against loathsome "interpretation," what he termed objective "execution"—"the strict putting into effect of an explicit will that contains nothing beyond what it specifically commands."[180] As Taruskin argues, the essence of performance for

---

[173] *Id.*

[174] *Id.*

[175] *Id.* at 67.

[176] *Id.*

[177] *Id.*

[178] *See* Taruskin, *supra* note 45, at 181.

[179] I. STRAVINSKY, PROGRAM, STRAVINSKY FESTIVAL, LONDON SYMPHONY ORCHESTRA 41 (1979), *quoted in* Levinson, *On Interpretation: The Adultery Clause of the Ten Commandments,* 58 S. CAL. L. REV. 719, 724 (1985).

[180] I. STRAVINSKY, THE POETICS OF MUSIC 163 (A. Knodel and I. Dahl trans. 1956). Of course Stravinsky's demand for objectivity does not avoid interpretive difficulties, even of his own works. In the 1920's, desperate for money, Stravinsky arranged his orchestral compositions for player piano. On these pianola rolls, the dance at the end of his famous ballet *Rite of Spring* "is much faster than on any recordings, including his own 'final' versions of 1960 and 1961." *A Dance to the Death,* THE

Stravinsky was "scrupulous fidelity to the letter of the text, and an ascetic avoidance of unspecified nuance in the name of expression."[181]   As we should already have come to expect, Stravinsky denounced those whose interpretations differed from his own not only as mistaken, but also, far more significantly, as perpetrators of "criminal assaults" and "betrayals."[182]   In fact, Stravinsky's eclecticism and his demands for "objectivity" in performance are two sides of the same coin.   It is precisely because one has become so detached from the past and thus from a living tradition encompassing earlier music that one must make reference to "objective" indicia—for example, the written text, the actual size of the musical forces at the first performance, and so on.

Indeed, not only are detachment and objectivity two sides of the same modernist coin, but, more surprisingly, so are the desires for authenticity and novelty.[183]   Morgan points to the deep connection between the search for novelty in musical culture—whether it be new techniques of composition or the desire to make Bach and Mozart sound fresh and new to our ears—and the search for performance practices of the past.   Both searches are a means of expressing dissatisfaction with the present.[184]   One can escape the present either by catapulting to the future, or by attempting to recapture the past and make it one's own.   The modernist always runs, even if she cannot hide.

If modernity has so thoroughly dominated musical culture in this century, it would be surprising if we did not see similar effects in legal culture as well.   Obvious examples abound, the most obvious, ironically, being the insistence on the unique legitimacy of original intention as a guide to constitutional meaning.[185]   With

---

ECONOMIST, Apr. 6, 1991, at 89. Ben Zander, the conductor of the semi-amateur Boston Philharmonic, has studied the piano rolls and concluded that they reflect Stravinsky's original intentions, but that Stravinsky compromised later because the first orchestras that tackled the piece simply could not perform his complex music at the speed he desired. *Id.* Is a conductor who performs the *Rite* at the faster speed engaging in objective "execution" or loathsome "interpretation"? Did Stravinsky, who performed and recorded the *Rite of Spring* in more than one way, engage in fraudulent "interpretations" of his own music?

[181] Taruskin, *supra* note 45, at 181.

[182] *Id.*

[183] *See* Morgan, *supra* note 95, at 75.

[184] *Id.* at 75-76.

[185] *See* R. BORK, *supra* note 33, at 6-8. We are grateful to Robert Post for pointing out that Thomas Hobbes (whose pessimism, skepticism about values, and statism have much in common with Judge Bork's philosophy) also developed a highly originalist theory of interpretation. *See* D. HERZOG, HAPPY SLAVES: A CRITIQUE OF CONSENT

modernity comes historicism—the understanding that the past has become alien to us and the desire to recapture what is slipping away. With detachment comes anxiety, and, as Hobsbawm suggests, the desperate attempt to deny the meaningfulness of history even as one denounces one's contemporaries for having deviated so far from purported models of the past.[186] Those who disagree are, as Stravinsky asserted, not merely mistaken, but criminal assailants on the uniquely legitimate way of performing constitutional analysis.

Our thesis is that we will find evidence of modernist anxiety and detachment, with a concomitant quest to regain "objective" indicia of performance and the invention of sacralized "traditions," in many different areas of culture, including, most certainly, both the general legal culture and its bastion of self-consciousness, the legal academy. By focusing on Robert Bork's jurisprudence of original intention as a quintessentially modernist response, we suggest an important difference between our perspective and that presented by David Luban in his interesting and important article, *Legal Modernism*.[187] Luban argues that the Critical Legal Studies movement represents the best analogy of modernist art to law.[188] The work of CLS scholars, in Luban's view, shares with modernist art a penchant for provocation, a feeling of homelessness in the world, and a tendency towards self-consciousness and self-commentary about its own production.[189] Although Luban takes as his model of inquiry modern art rather than musical performance, and although he assigns to the modern what some might now call postmodern, his discussion of the characteristic features of modernity is largely consistent with our own. For example, Luban's emphasis on "homelessness" as a recurring motif in modernist art[190] describes from another perspective the sense of separation

---

THEORY 145 (1989). Thus the turn to "originalism" is not unique to our current (twentieth century) brand of modernism; it also shows how twentieth century modernism has many antecedents. Moreover, Post's example is an excellent demonstration of how heavily contextual judgments of modernism are. Hobbes is certainly not "modern" in contrast to twentieth century thinkers, but in another sense he is a veritable architect of modernism in his demolition of Aristotelian traditionalism. *Cf.* Balkin, *Nested Oppositions* (Book Review), 99 YALE L.J. 1669, 1678-82 (1990) (depending on context, cultural concepts are always both exemplified by and in opposition to their concrete historical manifestations).

[186] *See supra* text accompanying notes 125-32.

[187] *See* Luban, *Legal Modernism*, 84 MICH. L. REV. 1656 (1986).

[188] *See id.* at 1656-59.

[189] *See id.* at 1657-59.

[190] *See id.* at 1660.

from tradition and from the past we have seen as characteristic of modernity.

There is much insight in Professor Luban's article. Nevertheless, we disagree with its thesis that legal modernism manifests itself most clearly in the work of CLS scholars or others on the left side of the political spectrum. It is worth noting that, as a historical matter, many leading cultural modernists were scarcely left-wing. As Daniel Bell has written, "[i]n discussing modernism, the categories of 'left' and 'right' make little sense. . . . Nietzsche, Yeats, Pound, and Wyndham Lewis were politically to the right."[191] Although Picasso's radical political sympathies were well known,[192] so were Ezra Pound's proclivities towards fascism.[193] Lionel Trilling has noted the irony of contemporary liberal intellectuals' embrace of modernists as heroes, noting that Proust, James Joyce and Andre Gide were "indifferent to, or even hostile to, the tradition of democratic liberalism as we know it," and "do not seem to confirm us in the social and political ideals which we [liberals] hold."[194]

Yet modern culture—and the response to modernity—comprises far more than those who are selectively identified as "modernists." A culture embraces *all* who live within it. Jerry Falwell is just as much a part of the contemporary American culture produced by the experience of modernity as is Cher, even though each is almost totally uncomprehending of the other (and even though each is in some way a reaction to the other). Modernity is an experience felt by all persons in a culture, even if in different degrees, and even if the reactions to it may be different in different quarters. Two billiard balls may move in opposite directions because of the same cause, a third billiard ball which has struck each object differently. Thus, to adopt Robert Morgan's example, Schoenberg's self-conscious attempt to follow tradition is just as modernist in its own

---

[191] D. BELL, THE CULTURAL CONTRADICTIONS OF CAPITALISM 51 (1976).

[192] *See* A. HUFFINGTON, PICASSO: CREATOR AND DESTROYER 282-311 (1988).

[193] On Pound, see J. DIGGINS, MUSSOLINI AND FASCISM: THE VIEW FROM AMERICA 246-47, 437-39 (1972). Even Wallace Stevens, the newly found darling of contemporary legal pragmatists, was not immune from the allure of facism. *See id.* at 245 (describing Stevens' support of Mussolini and his belief that fascism would merely be "'a transitional phase' of a state which hopefully would, like [Stevens'] poetry, wrest order from chaos and thereby lessen the 'disillusionment' and 'misery' in the modern world" (quoting W. STEVENS, LETTERS OF WALLACE STEVENS 289-90, 295 (H. Stevens ed. 1966))).

[194] L. TRILLING, THE LIBERAL IMAGINATION: ESSAYS ON LITERATURE AND SOCIETY 286 (1954).

way as Stravinsky's embrace of eclecticism. And Stravinsky's detachment led to both his instrumental use of the past for novelty's sake and his moralistic pursuit of the past via "objective" indicia of performance. In legal terms, modernity has brought us both Critical Legal Studies *and* Robert Bork.[195]

Luban's account of legal modernism, we think, overemphasizes the avant-gardist response to modernity at the expense of those trying to come to terms with tradition and the past either through an anxiously self-conscious adherence to tradition (Schoenberg) or through objectifying the past in concrete terms (Stravinsky). And here the modernist tendencies of the early music movement can provide a useful corrective. The fear that the past is slipping away and the redoubled search to regain tradition is not a *retreat* from modernism—it *is* one manifestation of the modernist experience, one version of modernist anxiety. The difference between the modernist and the premodernist is precisely that the modernist feels that there is something that has been lost. The conserving (but not necessarily conservative) response to modernism that is represented by Schoenberg is precisely the desire to cling to a receding tradition in order to relieve this sense of anxiety. While the modernist complains of anxiety, the premodernist asks "what anxiety?"[196]

For this reason, an inquiry into legal modernity must consider both the Schoenbergian as well as the Stravinskian attitudes towards tradition and the past.[197] It follows that we are likely to see the effects of legal modernity not only in the structural equivalent of the avant-garde in law, but in more mainstream reactions as well. If there are undoubted modernist themes in the work of CLS scholars, they are no less present in the work of the political right or the political center. Throughout the political spectrum one will find analogies both to Stravinsky's dual detachment and objectivity and Schoenbergian anxiety. No single view is uniquely "modernist"; all join in trying to make sense of our particular cultural moment, which features an ever-growing sense of disorder and fragmentation.[198]

---

[195] *See* Schlag, *Missing Pieces: A Cognitive Approach to Law,* 67 TEX. L. REV. 1195, 1216, 1228 (1989).

[196] And, we should add, the postmodernist also asks, "what anxiety?"

[197] This is not, of course, to say that Schoenberg and Stravinsky represent the only two possibilities. We agree with Morgan, however, that these two examples throw considerable light on the experience of modernity in music, as well as in culture generally.

[198] For a discussion emphasizing the presence of fragmentation in American law

IV. LEGAL MODERNISM AND THE PURSUIT OF "AUTHENTICITY"

What we have called legal modernity, like so much else in American law, can already be seen in the thought of Oliver Wendell Holmes, and in particular in his most iconoclastic work, *The Path of the Law*,[199] an essay which, almost 100 years after its presentation, still contains the power to startle.[200] Although *The Path of the Law* has many themes, one of its most striking is its author's attitude towards history and tradition. "[I]f we want to know why a rule of law has taken its particular shape, and more or less if we want to know why it exists at all," argues Holmes, "we go to tradition."[201] But one does not study history and historical doctrine for the purpose of veneration. Quite the opposite, for the understanding that a rule is historical "is the first step toward an enlightened scepticism, that is, towards a deliberate reconsideration of the worth of those rules."[202] In a truly remarkable metaphor, Holmes tells us that "[w]hen you get the dragon out of his cave on to the plain and in the daylight, you can count his teeth and claws and see just what is his strength."[203] Perhaps reflecting the origins of Holmes's own modernist thought in the maelstrom of the Civil War,[204] he makes clear that examining the "dragon" of historically-rooted rules "is only the first step. The next is either to kill him, or to tame him

---

and jurisprudence, see R. POSNER, *supra* note 1, at 203, 296. For a postmodern explanation of legal fragmentation and a delightful romp through the categories of modernism and postmodernism, see Schlag, *supra* note 195. While Schlag emphasizes the epistemological aspects of modernity and postmodernity, we emphasize their broader cultural manifestations.

[199] O.W. HOLMES, *The Path of the Law*, in COLLECTED LEGAL PAPERS 167 (1920).

[200] One is tempted to say that legal modernity begins with Holmes, but in fact the history of legal modernity is considerably more complicated. Moreover, Holmes's thought did not arise out of a vacuum. One of us (Levinson) has devoted considerable effort to showing the influence of a much earlier stream of thought—Emersonianism—on Holmes. S. Levinson, Skepticism, Democracy, and Judicial Restraint: An Essay on the Thought of Oliver Wendell Holmes and Felix Frankfurter, ch. 1 (Ph.D dissertation, Harvard University 1969). Thus, Holmes's thought combines both older and more foreword-looking elements, which is part of its endless fascination for historians and other scholars. In beginning our discussion of legal modernism with Holmes, we use Holmes as many others have—as less a progenitor than as a symbol of trends that have become central to American legal thought.

[201] O.W. HOLMES, *supra* note 199, at 186.

[202] *Id.* at 186-87.

[203] *Id.* at 187.

[204] *See* S. NOVICK, HONORABLE JUSTICE: THE LIFE OF OLIVER WENDELL HOLMES 43-52, 65-68, 71-73 (1989) (discussing profound impact of war on Holmes and describing the three times he was wounded in battle—at Ball's Bluff, Antietam, and Fredricksburg).

and make him a useful animal."[205]   This stunning imagery precedes the well-known Holmesian injunction that "[i]t is revolting to have no better reason for a rule of law than that so it was laid down in the time of Henry IV."[206]   And for Holmes "[i]t is still more revolting if the grounds upon which it was laid down have vanished long since, and the rule simply persists from blind imitation of the past."[207]   The liberating cure is to reject "antiquarianism" and instead to become the student of economics and statistics. Thus, in a famous phrase, Holmes asks us to wash our traditional beliefs about law and legal traditions in "cynical acid."[208]

The modernism of Holmes is not the modernist anxiety of Schoenberg, who feels the past slipping away and must strive to regain it and follow its commands. It is rather the modernism of Stravinsky, for whom the past is an alien thing, to be used instrumentally in future compositions. The very comparison of history to a monster suggests that the past has already become strange to us, that we have already begun the process of detachment and separation. Another great modernist, James Joyce, speaking through the character of Stephen Daedelus, wrote of history as a nightmare from which he was trying to awake.[209]   Whether Holmes would have gone quite that far, there can be no doubt that he had only disdain for those who put their faith in history and its "teachings" without reflection about the value and cogency of those purported lessons. The purpose of studying history is not to revere it, but to analyze it—to show it "in the daylight" and "count [its] teeth and claws."[210] And this analysis can only proceed, as Morgan points out, "when the current moment . . . loses its ability to cast its own peculiar colouration on the past [so that one] is able to look upon the past with such detachment and objectivity."[211]   In *The Path of the Law,* the legacy of the past is now described as "dogma," itself a word richly redolent of Protestant reformers' critique of the encrusted traditions of the Church they sought to overthrow.[212]

---

[205] O.W. HOLMES, *supra* note 199, at 187.

[206] *Id.*

[207] *Id.*

[208] *Id.* at 174.

[209] *See* J. JOYCE, THE PORTABLE JAMES JOYCE 674 (H. Levin ed. 1966) (excerpts from *Ulysses*).

[210] O.W. HOLMES, *supra* note 199, at 187.

[211] Morgan, *supra* note 95, at 67.

[212] O.W. HOLMES, *supra* note 199, at 169.

378

The theme of detachment from the legal tradition is also clear in Holmes's call for a social scientific approach. If the legal tradition is a dragon, we are no longer its subjects. Rather, we are to become zoologists, whose purpose is to study and even dissect the creature. The "man of the future" is a social scientist because the goal of legal study has moved from exposition and interpretation of legal texts and doctrines to the study of law as a social phenomenon. "It is perfectly proper," as Holmes pointed out in his essay *Law in Science and Science in Law,* "to regard and study the law simply as a great anthropological document."[213] An anthropologist, unlike the native, observes the culture from a psychic distance rather than participating in its beliefs and performing its rituals unself-consciously.

Finally, Holmes's iconoclasm is consistent with another way of looking at the experience of modernism—as a perceived conflict between reason and tradition, a tension which manifests itself, for example, in the conflict between the search for truth through rational inquiry and the need for faith in the teachings of revealed religion.[214] Holmes makes quite clear that he reconciles this conflict in favor of what he perceives to be reason—in this case the instrumental reason of fitting means to ends—and against received dogmatic tradition. The future of the law is as the servant of reason, which for Holmes is nothing more than rational calculations designed to achieve most effectively what the community wants.[215] The inefficacious dogmas of the past, on the other hand, are to be eliminated as much as possible.

To be sure, the modernity we find in Holmes is not yet full-fledged. There is an undercurrent of optimism in these remarks that bears neither traces of anxiety about what is slipping away nor doubts about the efficacy of the scientific approach. One could well write an article on "Holmes's last paragraphs," the conclusions to his otherwise pessimistic and sometimes even savage remarks that suddenly transform the occasion into one of hope and (relative) optimism about one's place in the world. Thus *The Path of the Law* concludes by Holmes telling his audience that through the analysis

---

[213] O.W. HOLMES, *Law in Science and Science in Law,* in COLLECTED LEGAL PAPERS, *supra* note 199, at 210, 212.

[214] We emphasize here that this characteristic feature of modernity by no means originates with Holmes, or even with modernity itself. *See supra* notes 136-41 and accompanying text.

[215] *See* O.W. HOLMES, *supra* note 213, at 225.

of the "remoter and more general aspects of the law you not only become a great master in your calling, but connect your subject with the universe and catch an echo of the infinite, a glimpse of its unfathomable process, a hint of the universal law."[216] Whether a remnant of his grandfather's Calvinist sensibility or a continuing reflection of the influence of Ralph Waldo Emerson's transcendentalist faith in the ultimate resolution of all apparent tensions and contradictions,[217] there is little of the more contemporary sense of intellectual anxiety about the lack of even a "hint" of some unified perspective of the world. Nor is there any sense of irony about the situation that Holmes finds himself in; it does not occur to him that historicizing the work of previous judges calls into question whether his own work is simply another form of "dogma," to be treated as such by a later generation capable of placing *him* in a discrete historical setting and recognizing his own blindness and lack of insight.[218]

Nevertheless, the seeds of legal modernity are clear enough in *The Path of the Law*. It was therefore entirely fitting that Jerome Frank would see Holmes as a model in his appropriately titled book *Law and the Modern Mind*.[219] Frank's veneration of Holmes is characteristic of the further development of legal modernity we find in the work of the Realists. The Realists are commonly thought to have launched an attack on the autonomy of law and legal reasoning. But the autonomy of law is of at least two types. The first is the autonomy of law from politics or social beliefs. The second, and equally important sense of autonomy is the autonomy of law from other disciplines, which generates a faith that discrete "legal" methods of analysis will be sufficient to solve legal problems.[220] Because legal decisions might be better explained by the study of social forces than by the results of doctrinal argument, and because legal issues need the expertise of the economist or sociologist, "the

---

[216] *Id.* at 202. And those familiar with Holmes's famous dissent in *Lochner v. New York* are likely to overlook his argument that the test of legislative reasonableness is whether a statute would "infringe fundamental principles as they have been understood by the traditions of our people and our law." Lochner v. New York, 198 U.S. 45, 76 (1905) (Holmes, J., dissenting).

[217] For an extended comparison of Holmes and Emerson, see S. Levinson, *supra* note 200.

[218] Still less is Holmes's attitude post-modern in his desire to fashion a grand, all-encompassing theory of law.

[219] J. FRANK, LAW AND THE MODERN MIND (1930).

[220] *See* Balkin, *supra* note 64, at 795; Posner, *The Decline of Law as an Autonomous Discipline: 1962-1987*, 100 HARV. L. REV. 761, 762-66 (1987).

man of the future," as Holmes puts it, must be acquainted with social science.[221]

With the rise of legal realism, new forms of legal scholarship emerge. Previously, the goal of much legal scholarship had been to explicate or interpret existing law, to offer the best interpretation of legal materials through traditional forms of doctrinal argument. The rise of realism brings with it an additional goal—to suggest policy based reasons for development of legal doctrine in one direction rather than another, even if these policy based reasons are not suggested or implicated by the language of existing legal materials. The realist approach begins to separate the goals of scholarship from those of the bar, although eventually the practicing bar would assimilate the approach of "going beyond the cases," at least in part.[222]

A second and more significant development is the attempt to study law as a social artifact, as Holmes's "great anthropological document." The result is a scholarship where one studies the behavior of lawyers and judges, not to further or contribute to their interpretive enterprise, but rather to study the enterprise itself. The most extreme example of this approach is Herman Oliphant's suggestion that scholars might dispense with the study of doctrine altogether and investigate instead the effects that certain "stimuli" (i.e., facts) had on the "responses" (i.e., opinions) produced by judges.[223] Oliphant's behaviorist approach to legal scholarship, while not universally adopted by the realists, is nevertheless characteristic of a new sense of detachment from the practice of law. The legal scholar has, to a large degree, left the tribe and become an anthropologist. We normally think of realism as the study of "law in action" and thus a movement closer towards what the law "really is." Yet this very goal ironically produces a separation or estrangement between the student and the thing being studied. "Objectivity" requires that the member of the tribe no longer take at face value the natives' explanations for what they are doing. Dispassion requires distance. One cannot pour cynical acid on one's *own* skin.[224]

---

[221] O.W. HOLMES, *supra* note 199, at 187.

[222] *See* Rubin, *The Practice and Discourse of Legal Scholarship,* 86 MICH. L. REV. 1835 (1988).

[223] Oliphant, *A Return to Stare Decisis,* 14 A.B.A. L.J. 73 (1928).

[224] As Professor Schlegel reminds us, the realist study of law as a social artifact had at least two versions. One might engage in social scientific research with an eye to eventual suggestions for reform, a position that Schlegel associates with William

Modernity has had a lasting legacy on the forms of legal scholarship in at least three respects. The first is the self-consciously interdisciplinary character of legal scholarship. This essay is no exception. A second is the increasing amount of scholarship, especially in the elite journals, that is about other legal scholarship, rather than about primary legal materials like statutes and cases. Legal scholarship becomes an increasingly self-contained, self-referential discipline, which is "about itself" as much as it is about the legal world outside, either law on the books or law in action. As interdisciplinary movements like law and economics or law and literature spring up, they begin to focus not on their relationship to the work of lawyers and judges, but to their own internal coherence and justification. Legal interpretation is replaced by legal theory, which is replaced by meta-theory, which is replaced by meta-meta theory, and so on.

The third feature is the fragmentation of legal scholarship into new genres such as feminist scholarship, critical legal scholarship, or law and economics. As a result of this fragmentation, it is increasingly difficult for lawyers and legal academics to agree on what good legal scholarship is and how to evaluate it. To some extent, this was always true, as soon as legal scholarship specialized into different subject matters like pleading, property, trusts, and so on. Yet there was a feeling that good legal reasoning transcended doctrinal boundaries, and that the reasonably intelligent contracts professor could recognize it in the work of a colleague who wrote about equity or the law of agency and partnership. The creation of "genres" of scholarship, like law and economics or feminist jurisprudence, which cut across traditional legal departments and categories, undermines such confidence today. Both fields are highly specialized with separate canons; they have very different intellectual approaches and scholarly goals which may, in some instances, be mutually critical of each other. Giving a piece written in one genre to a person who specializes in another may produce consternation, and perhaps even outright rejection.

O. Douglas and Charles Clark. Or one might engage in the scientific study of legal institutions for its own sake, a position Schlegel finds most clearly in the work of Underhill Moore. *See* Schlegel, *American Legal Realism and Empirical Social Science: From the Yale Experience*, 28 BUFFALO L. REV. 459, 517-19, 539-45, 567-69, 578-85 (1979); Schlegel, *American Legal Realism and Empirical Social Science: The Singular Case of Underhill Moore*, 29 BUFFALO L. REV. 195, 293-95 (1980).

The idea of a common language and a common vocabulary among legal academics, and indeed, a common canon of legal materials, has increasingly become a fiction. There is now an identifiable group of scholars who have read *A Jury of Her Peers*[225] or *The Critical Legal Studies Movement*[226] and consider them canonical texts. Other scholars may not have heard of either of these works, much less consulted them. Still others, having heard of them, may view them as, at the least, "outside" the law or, indeed, dangerous to the enterprise of law. Robert Morgan's fear that today "we no longer have a [musical] culture of our own," and that such culture as we do have has become "a patchwork of disconnected fragments snatched from here, there, and everywhere,"[227] is easily translatable to legal culture. Faced with this Heraclitian whirl of flux and discontinuity in the legal academy, some may be tempted to form authentic performance-of-legal-scholarship movements with a concomitant attempt to delegitimize those they now perceive as contributing to the flux.

As these comments suggest, there is much work to be done in exploring what modernity means for American legal culture. But it also seems clear that the study of the effects of modernity on legal culture requires us to have a point of comparison in other aspects of culture with which our self-identity is not so bound up. The anthropological study of law, in Holmes's time as in our own, requires a form of distancing. One reason to study the effects of modernity in music is precisely because of its distance from law and from our own everyday experiences as lawyers and legal scholars. It is that very distance which allows us to see comparisons within our own discipline that might otherwise go unnoticed or underemphasized. For the student of legal modernity, then, a trip beyond our own cultural moorings may well be not only a helpful but even a necessary tool of research.

---

[225] Glaspell, *A Jury of Her Peers,* in THE BEST SHORT STORIES OF 1917, 256-82 (E. O'Brien ed. 1918).

[226] Unger, *The Critical Legal Studies Movement,* 96 HARV. L. REV. 563 (1983).

[227] Morgan, *supra* note 95, at 67.

V. CONCLUSION: LAW, MUSIC, AND OTHER PERFORMING ARTS

Felix Frankfurter described as "the single most important utterance in the literature of constitutional law"[228] John Marshall's admonition that "it is a *constitution* we are expounding."[229] Equally important is Marshall's insistence that the Constitution be interpreted so as to "endure for ages to come, and consequently, to be adapted to the various *crises* of human affairs."[230]   It has always been feared, though, that too much "adaptation" would mean not the endurance, but rather the death of the Constitution. Yet how is one to tell the difference? Only half in jest do we announce that the subtext of this review is the question whether the performance of constitutional interpretation is better analogized to the Hanover Band's version of the *Pastoral Symphony* or to a jazz improvisation on Thelonious Monk's *Round Midnight*.[231] We do not mean to suggest that the choice must be exclusively between these two alternatives. Many other musical analogies might be suggested as well. We do mean to suggest that asking such questions—and wrestling over the answers—helps to illuminate the enterprise of constitutional analysis, including the particular problems posed by this enterprise for those who must confront the profound impact modernity has had on our political and legal culture.[232]

---

[228] F. FRANKFURTER, *John Marshall and the Judicial Function*, in FELIX FRANKFURTER ON THE SUPREME COURT: EXTRAJUDICIAL ESSAYS ON THE COURT AND THE CONSTITUTION 534 (P. Kurland ed. 1970).

[229] McCulloch v. Maryland, 17 U.S. (4 Wheat.) 316, 407 (1819).

[230] *Id.* at 415. Not the least of Marshall's rhetorically brilliant gestures is italicizing "crises" instead of "adapt" and "Constitution" instead of "we." *See* Schlag, *The Problem of the Subject*, 69 TEX. L. REV. (forthcoming 1991).

[231] For a recent musing on the similarities between the Constitution and jazz, see Ely, *Another Such Victory: Constitutional Theory and Practice in a World Where Courts are No Different From Legislatures*, 77 VA. L. REV. 833, 837 n.10 (1991) ("On the Constitution as a Lead Sheet.") (italics omitted).

[232] *Cf.* D. KORNSTEIN, *supra* note 48, at 110 ("For all we know, one night this week Zubin Mehta . . . will stand at his podium and whisper to the New York Philharmonic: 'We must never forget that it is a *symphony* we are expounding.'").

Professor Ely suggests that "those who assert the possibility of differentiating valid from invalid constitutional interpretation on the basis of 'craft limits' of a sort they assert are recognized in the arts are likely to be badly disappointed when they get around to a close examination of the analogues." Ely, *supra* note 231, at 837 n.10. The reason is, apparently, that "every time there develops what appears to be a consensus among musicians (and their listeners), to the effect that a certain interval is unacceptable noise, someone who can't be dismissed on any principled basis as 'not a real musician' starts using it, and others often follow." *Id.* Of course, this does not demonstrate that the analogy is useless, only that it cannot serve to legitimate particular limits on the practice of constitutional interpretation by appeal to existing

It is often our proudest boast that we in the United States live within the embrace of a constitutional tradition whose origins we can locate and whose continuity we can celebrate even two centuries later. Yet, as we have seen, explaining what it means to adhere to a tradition, particularly in an age of modernist self-consciousness, is itself an extraordinarily difficult assignment. Although tradition seems to imply stasis as much as modernity implies change, in fact, as Roxana Waterston points out, "'tradition' really describes a process of handing down, and as such is just as dynamic and as historical as any other social process."[233] Yet the abstract ideals of fixed tradition and mutable modernity are simultaneously motivating factors in this dynamic of change. Thus "[t]radition, like history, is something that is continually being recreated and remodelled in the present, even as it is represented as fixed and unchangeable."[234]

"craft values." And that fact is itself quite interesting.

However, because Ely sees that the analogy to jazz is not much use in legitimating the sort of limits on constitutional interpretation he would like to exist, he conludes that it is not clear what we can learn from the analogy of jazz to constitutional law. *See id.* But for someone who is less interested than Ely in legitimating judicial review by distinguishing it from legislation, and is more interested in asking questions about how legitimation actually occurs, one learns a great deal from the analogy about how seemingly "objective" standards or craft values are constantly altering themselves. Thus, Ely sees his analogy as "not much use" precisely because it does not serve his particular project—because he does not want to conclude that the craft of judicial interpretation, like that of musical interpretation, is always altering itself historically. On the other hand, a person with a quite different project (understanding the phenomenon of constitutional interpretation and how elites justify it to themselves and to others) might find the analogy useful for precisely the reasons that Ely rejects it.

We think this example demonstrates something quite important about the pragmatic enterprise we are engaged in. First, for different projects (legitimation vs. anthropology) different tools may be more or less useful to the task, and thus different analogies will be more or less useful. Second, it does not follow from Ely's discussion that analogies between law and the arts are not possible, or that they will not stimulate thought, but rather that one's ability to use analogies to convince others with very different agendas will be limited because they will tend to reject analogies which move in directions they do not like, and the more unusual the analogy appears, the easier it will be for them to reject it out of hand. This should come as no surprise to anyone who has ever had a discussion with someone with a very different agenda. Thus while asserting that analogies can be helpful, the pragmatist always understands that analogies become more or less useful tools of discussion and persuasion depending upon the audience they are directed to.

[233] R. WATERSON, THE LIVING HOUSE: AN ANTHROPOLOGY OF ARCHITECTURE IN SOUTH-EAST ASIA 232 (1990).

[234] *Id. See also* Balkin, *Tradition, Betrayal, and the Politics of Deconstruction,* 11 CARDOZO L. REV. 1619 (1990) (discussing conceptual affinities between tradition and betrayal in constitutional law).

Perhaps the best illustration of the belief that we are participating in a living tradition is found in Justice John Marshall Harlan's well-known analysis of the meaning of "substantive due process" in *Poe v. Ullman*.[235] Harlan looked to the "balance [between the liberty of the individual and the demands of organized society] struck by this country, having regard to what history teaches are the traditions from which it developed as well as the traditions from which it broke. That tradition is a living thing."[236] Interestingly, Harlan's description of a "living" tradition explicitly involved both continuity with and alterations of previous tradition.[237] It is perhaps no coincidence that Robert Bork, the self-styled apostle of "original intent," describes Harlan's arguments as "entirely legislative" and denounces the opinion as simply a way station toward the "intellectual catastrophe" of *Griswold v. Connecticut*.[238]

We believe that in *Poe*, as elsewhere, Harlan showed himself to be a quintessential *performer* of constitutional law. Another major theme of this review is the importance of grasping the performative aspect of engagement with the law. This is obvious in the case of a judge, but it is present as well in the acts of a vigorous public critic of judges, such as Robert Bork.[239] Insofar as law is a performative art, insight can be gained from looking at performance practices (and theory) in other arts.

Thus, we believe that legal scholars have something to learn from Jonathan Miller's views on the challenges facing anyone called upon to direct a play, and in particular his attack on the notion "of the primary status of the text . . . as a literary work."[240] Those who hold such a view, he suggests, believe

> that in some peculiar way the play is at its very best when read quietly by the informed reader, who somehow manages to dramatize in his or her imagination a performance that is more congruent with the intentions of the author than *any* particular performance could ever be, and *all* performances then represent a lapse from this ideal state.[241]

---

[235] 367 U.S. 497 (1961).

[236] *Id.* at 542.

[237] *See* Balkin, *supra* note 234, at 1617-18.

[238] R. BORK, *supra* note 33, at 234.

[239] *See* S. LEVINSON, *supra* note 22, at 18-53; Balkin, *supra* note 107, at 937 n.116 (discussing role of non-judicial interpretations of the Constitution).

[240] J. MILLER, *supra* note 104, at 22.

[241] *Id.*

Though there may be an important sense in which "great plays can be said to exist without being theatrically performed,"[242] one would wonder "why a writer had chosen to cast his ideas in the form of a play at all"[243] inasmuch as the conventional meaning assigned the genre "play" includes performance.[244] "I cannot deny the fact that each time a play is staged the production is inevitably a limited version of the range of possible interpretations," but, nonetheless, "the destiny of a great play is to undergo a series of performances each of which is incomplete, and in some cases may prove misleading and perverse." Still, "[b]y submitting itself to the possibility of successive re-creation, . . . the play passes through the development that is its birthright."[245] Miller's analysis applies to music as well. Although it is surely possible to read a music score and to construct an "ideal" performance in one's mind, this is surely not the conventional practice of experiencing music. Enacted performance, for most of us, is inextricably linked with notes on a page.

Is this not also true of law, especially as conceptualized by those realists, influenced by Holmes, who emphasized "law in action"? Did they not ask us to focus on the *performances* of actual people—ordinary citizens, lawyers, police, public officials, and judges—rather than to concentrate on mere "law on the books," i.e., the text independent of its performance? To be sure, one can read the texts of the law as collected in statute books and the like, but in that guise they are only in a state of limbo. They await their performance by legal actors and actresses or, to shift the metaphor, by virtuosos of the law who can interpret melodic lines in the law in ways overlooked by previous players.

---

[242] *Id.* at 23.

[243] *Id.*

[244] Indeed, Miller points out, "[t]here is a tendency to forget that for a playwright like Shakespeare the written script was not intended for publication but as an aid to performance without any view to a distant posterity." *Id.* Miller would also presumably endorse recent suggestions by Shakespeare scholars that what we refer to today as the "texts" of the plays, deviation from which presumably is questionable, are themselves creations of a decidedly post-Shakespearean moment that overlooks the fact that his own actors felt altogether comfortable engaging in their own "contributions" to the manuscripts handed them. Thus Stephen Orgel notes that Shakespeare wrote his plays for performance rather than as publications to be read outside the theater. "Shakespeare habitually began with more than he needed," so that "his scripts offered the company a range of possibilities, and . . . the process of production was a collaborative one of selection as well as of realization and interpretation." *See* Brett, *supra* note 114, at 106 (quoting Orgel, *The Authentic Shakespeare*, 21 REPRESENTATIONS 1, 7 (Winter 1988)).

[245] J. MILLER, *supra* note 104, at 23.

It should now be clear why a review that began by considering how to perform Beethoven's first piano concerto should have gone on to address how those designated to engage in legal performance, like judges, interpret statutes or the Constitution. We believe that there is indeed a relation between law and music, derived in part from their common textuality and necessity for subsequent performance. And it should also by now be clear why studying this relationship of common textuality draws us more and more into the study of culture as a whole. For performance, whether legal or musical, is always situated in a culture and reflects the distinctive problematics of that culture. Thus, if ours is a modern culture, our interpretations, our subsequent performances of law and of music, must be understood in the light of the tangled and complicated experience of modernity and its gradual transformation into what is now called the postmodern. Although we have only begun to explore the complexities of the subject in this essay, we firmly believe that any deep understanding of legal thought in the twentieth century requires legal scholars to confront the meaning of modernity for law and legal culture. To the extent that the study of other aspects of culture, including music, must also confront questions of interpretation and subsequent performance under the shadow of modernity, we believe that comparative study can aid us in our more parochial task of understanding the law itself. We think we understand our own "England" better by having visited other shores, and we are confident that others can benefit from the same experience.

We are not suggesting that one best understands England by emigrating from it and establishing one's permanent life elsewhere; similarly, we doubt that one can best understand law by spending all of one's time on what follows the "and" in various "law and . . ." movements. But there are few people left who do not believe that at least some of one's time should be spent looking on what follows the "and," and the question is whether musical performance should become a suitable candidate for such study. We think that it should. We should have no trouble recognizing Richard Taruskin, Charles Rosen, Neal Zaslaw, and Christopher Hogwood as our own colleagues engaged in a common enterprise of trying to figure out how one meaningfully inhabits a practice of performance after innocence has been lost. They are all writing interesting, provocative, infuriating, and, most importantly, illuminating work that should interest any of us who daily wrestle with our own performance practices as lawyers, judges, or teachers of the law.

Acknowledgments

Balkin, J.M. "Deconstructive Practice and Legal Theory." *Yale Law Journal* 96 (1987): 743–86. Reprinted by permission of the Yale Law Journal Company and Fred B. Rothman and Company.

Bartlett, Katharine T. "Feminist Legal Methods." *Harvard Law Review* 103 (1990): 829–88. Copyright 1990 by the Harvard Law Review Association.

Brewer, Scott. "Pragmatism, Oppression, and the Flight to Substance." *Southern California Law Review* 63 (1990): 1753–62. Reprinted with the permission of the *Southern California Law Review*.

Grey, Thomas C. "Langdell's Orthodoxy." *University of Pittsburgh Law Review* 45 (1983): 1–53. Reprinted with the permission of the University of Pittsburgh Law School.

Kennedy, Duncan. "A Semiotics of Legal Argument." *Syracuse Law Review* 42 (1991): 75–116. Reprinted with the permission of the *Syracuse Law Review*.

Kennedy, Duncan. "Freedom and Constraint in Adjudication: A Critical Phenomenology." *Journal of Legal Education* 36 (1986): 518–62. Reprinted with the permission of the Association of American Law Schools.

Lyons, David. "Legal Formalism and Instrumentalism—A Pathological Study." *Cornell Law Review* 66 (1981): 949–72. Reprinted with the permission of *Cornell Law Review*. Copyright 1981 by Cornell University. All Rights Reserved.

Posner, Richard A. "What Has Pragmatism to Offer Law?" *Southern California Law Review* 63 (1990): 1653–70. Reprinted with the permission of the *Southern California Law Review*.

Radin, Margaret Jane. "The Pragmatist and the Feminist." *Southern California Law Review* 63 (1990): 1699–1726. Reprinted with the permission of the *Southern California Law Review*.

Levinson, Sanford and J.M. Balkin. "Law, Music, and Other Performing Arts." *University of Pennsylvania Law Review* 139 (1991): 1597–1658. Reprinted with the permission of the *University of Pennsylvania Law Review* and Fred B. Rothman and Company. Copyright 1991 University of Pennsylvania.